Differential Diagnosis and Treatment in Social Work

Differential Diagnosis and Treatment in Social Work

EDITED BY *Francis J. Turner*

WITH A FOREWORD BY *Florence Hollis*

The Free Press, *New York*   Collier-Macmillan Limited, *London*

HV
43
.T8

To Bert, brother and colleague

JUNE 17, 1935—JUNE 22, 1957

Foreword

HOW STRANGE it is that not until a half century after the publication of *Social Diagnosis* does a book appear in the social work field addressing itself specifically to the relationship between differential diagnosis and treatment! Over fifty years ago—in 1917—Mary Richmond wrote *Social Diagnosis*, a book dedicated to the then new idea that the social worker, like the physician, must think diagnostically, endeavouring to understand the nature of the disorder with which he is dealing in order to know how to alleviate it. This book so impressed practitioners that for many years it was a text, as if the subject of diagnosis were now understood and social casework could move on to concentrate on problems of treatment methodology. Even in the thirties, when psychoanalytic knowledge was permeating social casework, attention was directed not to diagnostic groupings, but rather to general principles of treatment on the one hand and the specifics of individualization of treatment on the other. It was not until the mid-forties that attention again turned to diagnosis, and the work started by Miss Richmond moved forward with concentration on the psychological component of diagnosis, often designated the "clinical diagnosis." Diagnosis had not been lost sight of during these intervening years, but the principles of social study and diagnosis presented by Miss Richmond seemed to provide sufficient guidelines for the type of diagnostic thinking upon which treatment was based until the mid-forties. This was a highly individualized approach with emphasis on ideosyncratic life happenings that could account for the problem under treatment.

With the emergence of the clinical diagnosis, attention began to turn to elements in personality which characterize some people to a greater extent than others, thus distinguishing a group of individuals who might respond in common ways to certain forms of treatment. It began to be recognized that knowledge of such groupings—of types of disorders, that is—could increase the ability of workers to fashion treatment more appropriately to the differentiated need of the individual. Furthermore, once such commonness was seen, knowledge could become cumulative and what was learned from the treatment of one individual could be put to the service of another suffering from a similar disability.

Dr. Turner's compilation is the first book to bring the results of this development to general attention and to provide the social worker a key to the diagnostically oriented articles of the past ten years. Not only is his selection of articles excellent, but the fact that he read virtually everything available in our English literature before making his selection means that this collection provides a reliable guide to the state of our current knowledge of work with differing diagnostic entities. Inevitably any other author would have made a somewhat different selection. I will leave it to the reviewers to comment on the merits of this or that inclusion or exclusion; Dr. Turner's choices seem excellent to me. His organization of the selections into the stages of human development, psychosocial pathology, physical handicaps, and sociocultural factors is logical and should enable the reader to locate easily material that will throw light on the difficulty about which he is seeking information. If no article is included which deals with the specific subject of concern, much may be learned from an article covering treatment of a related disorder.

In addition to Dr. Turner's contribution in making this material available, his Preface and the introductions to all of the major sections add greatly to the value of the book. I am strongly tempted to underscore some of his excellent points about diagnosis and about the education of the profession, but will content myself with urging you to read the Preface and the Part introductions with care. They contain many astute observations.

In the Part introductions Dr. Turner orients the reader to the writings in the area under consideration, briefly brings out important commonalities, and points to uncovered, or scantily covered, diagnostic areas. In the main, however, he allows the selections to speak for themselves. The coverage of the book is not meant to be exhaustive. The bibliographies within the individual selections will lead the reader to further references.

It is an important sign of the times that this book is addressed to group workers as well as to caseworkers and that in many categories material on group treatment is available. The extent to which these two social work methods supplement each other in treatment and the growing tendency for many workers to want to acquire some competence in both methods is one of the very interesting developments of the sixties. This book should contribute to the common knowledge of the two specialties.

A final contribution of the book upon which I should like to comment is its usefulness as a guide to further compilation of knowledge and to publication. As Dr. Turner notes, there is valuable information dealing with many diagnostic categories in agency records and reports which could be brought to light and published. This book can serve as a guide to prospective writers and to editors as to the gaps in our diagnostic literature. It can also provide points of comparison against which the practitioner reader's experiences can be studied. Articles based on either similar or different experiences should be written. While controlled experimentation and replication is the ultimate task of knowledge building, practical replication occurs constantly in our day-by-day work. Small groups of similar cases can be studied and reported upon, thus providing cumulative information about different diagnostic groupings.

It is altogether appropriate that *Differential Diagnosis and Treatment in Social Work* should appear so soon after the fiftieth anniversary year of *Social Diagnosis*. Dr. Turner is indeed making a substantial contribution to the teaching and practice of social work.

SCHOOL OF SOCIAL WORK
COLUMBIA UNIVERSITY, NEW YORK

Florence Hollis

Preface

THE PRIMARY GOAL of this book is to help social work practitioners provide more effective treatment to their clients. Obviously such a goal cannot be attained in a total manner; it requires that one segment of the therapeutic process be selected as a substructure. I have chosen to utilize the diagnostic process as a focal point. This segment was chosen because, on the one hand, it is so crucial to effective treatment and, on the other, it has been a weak point in our practice. The method I have chosen is to bring together in four parts a series of articles from the professional literature, each of which deals with a specific diagnostic variable and the resultant treatment implications.

To say that we are living in an age where quantities of available knowledge are rapidly expanding is already a cliché. Such knowledge expansion, with the accompanying proliferation of writings, creates serious problems for practitioners in all disciplines. Social workers in agencies are well aware that much has been written and is being written of import to their day-to-day practice activities. They are also most aware of the difficulty in maintaining anything more than a fleeting contact or haphazard sampling of what is available. Such sampling is often more anxiety provoking than satisfying, as the little reading and formal studying that is possible clearly alerts them to the quantities of material which perforce are left untouched. Concomitant with the awareness of quantity is the realization that all that is written is not necessarily gold; much valuable time can be wasted in locating and reading material which in fact is not as useful as some other might have been.

Someday in the not too distant future, an agency social worker wishing to know quickly and succinctly what has been written about the treatment of a particular kind of client will turn to the agency data-retrieval unit. This in turn will be electronically connected with a national centralized programed library. In a few minutes he will receive a "print-out" of the requested data. As yet such resources, while theoretically possible, are beyond the scope, structure, and resources of our agencies. For the present, agency practitioners wishing to obtain such data must turn to the literature. This is not an easy task. Rarely is there time available to undertake the required search, presuming there are library resources upon which to call. In the meantime books such as this are required.

Most social work practitioners are well acquainted with the major textbooks in individual and group treatment. These have tended to be treatises on treatment in general rather than the specific. Discussions of treatment of specific kinds of problems or diagnostic entities have largely been carried out in individual articles scattered through some 20 to 25 journals and going back 30 to 35 years. Thus, at best, a practitioner can only have a superficial knowledge of the precise type of practice-oriented literature available to him. Because of this, the tendency has been to teach and practice from general rather than specific knowledge and understanding about people and how to treat them. This has been effective, and I believe the majority of our clients have been helped to achieve improved psycho-social functioning as a result of the treatment they have received. When practitioners tend to operate from an intuitive and an *ad hoc* framework, it is clear that diagnosis in anything more than a diffuse manner is unnecessary. Effective as is such a general treatment style, a higher level of competence can be achieved when treatment is consciously and selectively based on a detailed diagnosis of the client. It is my conviction that many social workers would greatly improve the quality of their treatment if experience-based observations and discussions of the treatment implications of diagnostic entities found in the literature of the last few years were readily available to them.

The danger of bringing together articles dealing with specific diagnostic entities or variables is that this collection could be misused. There is the possibility of its being seen as a shortcut, as a "How to do it" book. The prospect of having a resource which will lay out a formula of therapy or a prescription of technique for each diagnostic entity is an attractive one. Unfortunately this is not such a book; anyone who tried to use it in this way would only be disappointed. What it does aspire to achieve is to give therapists some anchoring concepts, some experience-based bench marks, some specific analyses of points of theory which will give direction and basic structure to the treatment of clients. The test of the therapist's skill is a dual one: first, to understand how much his client is like other clients of the same type and thus utilize what the profession has said about them; second, to understand how he is different from all other clients thus necessitating a peculiar combination of therapeutic skills most appropriate to him in his individuality. To follow slavishly a prescribed formulation of treatment because the literature suggests it makes the therapist a technician (and a poor one at that) rather than a professional. Whether this latter is a more serious detriment to treatment than working from no diagnosis is a moot point.

The book is designed to serve as a resource to be used in combination with the "practice wisdom" of the practitioner. It is primarily seen as important for the person in the multifunctioned agency who is called upon to serve a wide range of presenting problems and client types; the practitioner in the small agency and the private practitioner, who does not have a well-endowed agency library and readily available colleague consultation; the student and the teacher. It perhaps won't be as useful to persons in more specialized settings. It is presumed that in such settings there would be a concentration of literature appropriate to the field, for example, the treatment of marital problems. The articles chosen for the book on this former topic or on any topic can only be seen as an overview or a viewpoint rather than an exhaustive treatment or the final word. To aid in a broader coverage than one or two articles could give, bibliographies, wherever present, have been included. Thus a person interested in searching for additional information on a particular syndrome or diagnostic variable is given some leads for further reading.

This book contains a predominance of articles on individual treatment. Originally I had hoped to locate an article dealing with the individual treatment of each topic and another dealing with group treatment. This was not always possible. In the literature there have been more individual treatment-based articles than group-based articles. It is hoped that in the future, there will be more written accounts of appropriate group treatment with other client-types. In seeking group articles for each topic there is a presumed implication that every diagnostic variable lends itself to some form of group treatment. This may be incorrect.

Throughout the articles there can be seen a recurring theme. The social work practitioner of today must be a multiskilled person, comfortable in individual, joint, and group treatment, as well as a person skilled in educative and collaborative activities. This does not imply a generic method in the profession, but the necessity of multiskills, and these at a high degree of competence. Truly, this is a formidable challenge.

One of the unfortunate results of the gap between the professional literature and the mainstream of practice has been a tendency to devalue traditional knowledge. It seems fashionable in some segments of current thinking to suggest that much of our traditional theoretical orientation be scrapped and replaced by newer concepts and practice approaches. It is said that our psychodynamic approaches have failed and are unnecessary in understanding clients. Such presumptive thinking is only as valid as the evidence upon which it is based, and laudatory tributes to new approaches do not establish their validity. If the newer approaches to therapy are more effective than those presently used, then we must adopt them. Responsible professional behavior demands this. To make this comparison requires a full understanding and utilization of the old and the new. I raise this point because of a conviction that much of the disappointment in the results of treatment stems not from a fault in our theory and its applications but from a failure to utilize fully the rich amounts of data, knowledge, and skill accumulated over the years. One of the causes of this failure to tap effectively the rich resources of accumulated professional expertise in our profession has been our reliance on oral tradition and the reluctance to set out in an organized useful way what we know, what we do not know, what has been effective, and what has not.

A further purpose in planning this collection was to highlight the necessity of improved diagnostic habits among practitioners. Is not urging the importance of diagnosis to practitioners but a further example of preaching to the converted? In school and agency recent generations of social workers have been assailed with the triad of study, diagnosis, and treatment. Now every student learns early in his professional training that the unity of the therapeutic process is made up of these three elements. Why then emphasize diagnosis? It is because of a growing awareness of the divergence between our value commitment to the importance of diagnosis and the reality of our practice. Time and time again, records of social workers are examined without being able to locate within them a place where a diagnosis was formulated and set out, which the social worker then used to formulate treatment objectives and goals. That some form of diagnosis is made is indisputable; otherwise there could be no way to account for the large numbers of clients whose psychosocial functioning is markedly improved as the result of the therapist's activities and skills. The process of diagnosis evidently is operating, but the fact of diagnosis is lacking. Why should this be of concern? It is because without the availability of a concrete diagnosis there is no way to assess the effectiveness of our treatment except in a globular way. There is no way of correlating the various forms of social work intervention in relation to particular presenting diagnostic variables and assessing their outcome. There is no way of planfully and carefully improving our effectiveness with our clients. Until we can be more precise in declaring how we assess people and what therefore we choose to do with them and for them, our practice efficiency will remain static.

Why this divergence between fact and process? The answers to this are elusive and uncertain. It is easy to utilize the accustomed mutual recriminatory reflex and attribute this omission to a lack of desired professional behavior. This is too simple and obviously incorrect.

Part of the reason seems to be tied up in our strong commitment to the necessity of individualizing the client and maintaining nonjudgmental attitudes towards him. The process of working towards and from a precise, although flexible and evolving, diagnosis seems to evoke in some an emotional response that in some way the client is depersonalized through categorization and judged through opinion. There is also a fear that diagnosis somehow excludes the client. The thinking is as follows: Treatment in social work requires full involvement of the client; diagnosis is a professional assessment made by us not the client; therefore if we emphasize diagnosis we overlook the client. Obviously this is a misunderstanding of the process.

A lack of experience or perhaps of training also seems to be involved in this underemphasis of diagnosis. If there is a value-based reluctance to diagnosis among practitioners, then it is to be expected that this is a skill which will not be given first-order priority. It is clear that if this skill is not acquired early in a professional career, it is increasingly difficult later to reorient oneself to it. I want to avoid overgeneralizing here; evidently many practitioners are highly skilled diagnosticians. The selections presented here demonstrate this.

Perhaps the most important explanation of this apparent gap in social work practice stems from the complex conceptual base from which we operate. The number of variables requiring assessment and the multitude of frameworks in which these can be assessed presents a formidable and, at times, seemingly overwhelming task for the practitioner.

Because there is not a single theory of psychosocial behavior which can serve as a unifying principle of practice, it is clear that the process of diagnosis must of necessity be a multifaceted one. Since in the diagnostic phase of treatment the therapist is bringing his professional judgment to bear on the information he has about the client, it is presumed that he has a framework in which he can order the data he has about the client and norms against which he can compare his client. In the complexity of our efforts to study our client in a biopsychosocial context, the process of synthesizing, interrelating, and then formulating a professional judgment about the client is indeed a monumental one. This should not deter us from attempting to do so even though we will never reach a point of complete satisfaction with our assessment of the situations with which we are confronted.

It has been implied at times that there is a danger in forming detailed diagnoses and then operating from them. Such a process, it is said, serves to make treatment too rigid by forming a "mind-set" towards the client. It is therefore better to keep our diagnosis flexible and open and permit the utilization of new understanding and perception of clients. It is true that a diagnosis must not become "locked in" so that we operate from it in an inflexible manner. To do this, of course, is a misuse of the diagnostic concept. Obviously, we are going to shift and clarify and make more precise and enrich our understanding of clients; this in turn will affect the goals and methods of treatment we set for and with them. In no way should this deter us from constantly striving to set out clearly our assessments of them. More treatment efforts are ineffective and more client and therapist time is used uneconomically when a diagnosis is not made than there are gains resulting from nondiagnosing in order to remain "flexible and open."

No doubt part of the reluctance to diagnose has resulted from misuse to which nominal diagnoses have been put. I am referring especially to the unidimensional type in which a one-word or a one-expression classification is used. Such terms are used to explain the entire client and by implication dictate the format of treatment. For example, Miss R is a defective, Mr. J is schizophrenic, the B's are a multiproblem family.

On the one hand, if a diagnosis consists of only such labels it deserves to be discredited; on the other, these labels or classifications have their place in spite of the current tendency to disparage them. It is one of the principal assumptions of this collection of articles that we have not used them sufficiently, nor appreciated the extent to which they could help us consciously and deliberately to plan our treatment of clients. That they must be used in consort with many other classifications or labels is also a prior assumption. For effective treatment it is essential to understand the significance of the individual variables designated by the "labels" as well as the peculiar and unique combination of them as presented in the life and person of each client.

Classification in any professional activity must not become an end in itself. Whatever other purposes are served, the process should and must be a pragmatic conceptual tool to assist us in applying the rich and extensive body of knowledge accumulated over the years. Viewing classificatory thinking about clients as a useful tool rather than an absolute helps us achieve some perspective about the classification systems presently available to us. It is clear that we do not have the last word in typologies of clients and the significant variables which must be assessed for effective treatment. Similarly, systems we presently use are far from perfect and complete. It is inevitable that most of them will be replaced as better understanding is achieved and as we become more skilled in integrating the multiple bodies of knowledge from which we draw our understanding of clients.

Our profession does not have a closed body of knowledge. Hence the concepts from which we operate are in constant flux. Theory is formulated in order to be replaced by better theory, better in the sense of helping us more effectively to achieve the treatment goals deemed desirable by the values of the profession. True as this is, we are not thereby excused from utilizing today what we already know.

A further reason for preparing this collection stemmed from a research interest. I was curious to explore the actual situation of the literature. I was aware that articles existed on some categories of clients; for example, we know that there has been a wealth of data on the character-disordered clients in recent years. I did not know how extensive the coverage might be. Have we clearly addressed in our literature the entire range of diagnostic variables customarily considered as being essential to effective treatment? Thus, beyond the wish to produce a book useful to practitioners, I was also interested in locating possible gaps in the literature, to point out strategic areas in which well-thought-out and carefully written articles are required. Some of the gaps which were located will be discussed in the introduction to each Part.

It was further hoped that by bringing together writings which set out our practice, concepts, and thinking in an easily accessible way, practitioners would be given an opportunity to test their "practice wisdom" against the opinions of their colleagues. In this way, we can assess what of our present thinking is still valid, what needs to be replaced with new insights, what can be refined by imaginative experimentation, and lastly, how our traditional understanding of clients can be enriched with new combinations of skills.

There was a further reason underlying this project. From time to time serious concerns have been exhibited as to the extent and diversity of our knowledge. It is hoped that the breadth of areas addressed in the literature and contained here will help to give a better appreciation of the richness of our practice knowledge. On the basis of this idea, I tended to select articles written by social workers over those written by our colleagues in other disciplines. This was not done exclusively, of course, but presuming the articles were judged to be comparable and relevant to the design of the book, authorship by a social worker was used as a criterion of selection. I realize that this can contribute to professional insularity of which we have suffered more than enough. My own conviction is that we are growing to even greater interprofessional collaboration at all levels. To do this effectively and responsibly necessitates that we know our own field well. It is to aid in this latter task that I have kept the book more social work oriented. I do hope, though, that the collection of readings will be of interest and use to members of other disciplines. Of course, some articles written by members of other disciplines were included. Such articles were selected in which the treatment methods discussed were clearly appropriate for social workers. Thus, for example, an article dealing with the pharmacological treatment of depression would not be considered here, although one discussing some form of treatment utilizing relationship therapy would be. In the same way, it is also hoped that some increased appreciation will be gained as to the complexity of client functioning and responsible therapy. Recent conferences and writings have devoted some attention to the possibility of a generic method of practice to be taught to all aspirants to the profession. Much has been said about the necessity for others without comparable training to be able to do some of the direct work with clients presently assigned to social workers. Obviously there is some merit in examining these ideas. It is known that some understanding of treatment principles can be learned by others. It is also obvious to those directly in contact with clients that *more* rather than *less* specialized knowledge and skill is required to understand, involve, and treat many of the persons who come or are referred to us for treatment. There is a growing need for practitioners of a very high level of competence, who have clear and demonstrated diagnostic and treatment skills.

In searching for articles and in selecting them an effort was made to cover all the professional journals which include articles of import to social work practitioners, as well as standard social work journals. I am aware that a considerable amount of data was missed. For example, frequently papers are given at conferences, speeches given to meetings, and reports made to agencies which do not find their way into the mainstream of professional reading. Many of these are of high calibre and should be more widely available. It is hoped that this book will serve to draw out some of these and to encourage people to make their views more broadly known.

Selecting a framework useful for organizing the wide range of topics located in the literature was difficult. The goal was to utilize articles dealing with a specific diagnostic variable or entity rather than a type of service or problem. Thus adoption, unmarried mothers, deserted wives, separated couples, or other problem or service classifications were not employed. It is not always easy to distinguish between a diagnostic variable with specific treatment implications and a problem classification with a multitude of causes so that little or nothing can be said about generic treatment implications. There are some types of situations which are both a problem for treatment and a variable in diagnosis affecting the method of treatment selected. For example, although treatment of unmarried mothers was not included I did include delinquent youth.

I was particularly interested in finding articles which discussed the therapeutic considerations which result from a precise part of our total assessment of the client. It is assumed that all treatment must be geared to the whole person and not to particular parts of that person. It is also understood that there are dangers in categorizing a segment of a client's total psychosocial functioning and selecting our treatment approach specific to that segment. The danger is the well-known one of stereotyping. It is the extent to which the individual person can be partialized and yet treated as a whole that determines the effectiveness of our treatment methods. It is clear that selective treatment skills are necessary with schizophrenic clients, yet there are no schizophrenic clients as such. There are young, recently married, working class, rural-oriented, dull normal, Irish Catholic schizophrenic clients. Our treatment will be most effective when we can begin to understand the significance of each of these variables and whatever others are important and the peculiar combination of treatment methods most appropriate for different constellations of variables.

The variables which were finally chosen were divided into the traditional biophyschosocial triad based on a framework of human growth and development stages. Obviously it would be much easier for all if a unitary theory of psychosocial functioning could be devised so that clients would only have to be assessed along one dimension. Unfortunately, we are a long way from this and for a long time to come we have to live with the problems arising from the fact that societal man is a most complex creature. To try to understand and explain him in a manner that will permit us to aid him effectively to achieve improved psychosocial functioning will demand a complex conceptual framework. Complex as is our present conceptual basis of human behavior, undoubtedly there are other dimensions whose significance we probably do not realize, such as some genetic, cosmotic or time-space factors.

No apologies are made for utilizing traditional psychodynamic headings. It is true that there has been recent serious questioning of the utility of classical dynamic interpretations of behavior. No one denies these present difficulties. They require constant critical re-examination in the light of current practice. This doesn't mean that they are to be ignored; for they have supplied and will continue to supply a framework in which people can be understood and, even more importantly, effectively treated. When they are replaced, as is the lot of all theory, it must be done by validated reliable concepts.

In selecting the headings under which topics were gathered there was an additional difficulty that must always be considered in diagnosis. This is the different levels of precision which exist between and among the various diagnostic variables. The presence or the lack of precision affects the degree of exactness with which we can discuss the treatment implications of each variable. For example, our division of clients by socioeconomic classes is a much less precise variable than the distinction between the types of neuroses or between character-disordered and border-line clients.

As our knowledge about these variables grows and more specificity is developed, our precision in formulating treatment goals and methods will grow also. It is hoped that much of what has been written in these pages will be replaced with further experiences, new concepts, and generalizations. It is hoped that the ideas presented in the various articles will be subjected to the keen scrutiny of our colleagues who are secure in their practice and rich in experience. It is hoped that imaginative, responsible experimentation will provide us with new insights and suggest new therapeutic approaches for consideration. In such instances the most useful form of replacement would be by means of scholarly articles building on the past and adding the new. I would hope most seriously that this book would have to be re-edited in a few years, on the basis of new insights, further writing, and an increased acceptance of our responsibility to translate our knowledge into a form readily accessible to our colleagues.

Much remains to be done in improving our diagnostic categories, in clarifying their definitions and descriptions, in specifying commonly accepted indicators, and in developing optimum treatment approaches. In the meantime the practitioner must use the knowledge presently available to him, fully aware of its inherent limitations. It is the purpose of this book to make one segment of this knowledge more accessible to him.

GRADUATE SCHOOL OF SOCIAL WORK   *Francis J. Turner*
WATERLOO LUTHERAN UNIVERSITY
WATERLOO, ONTARIO, CANADA

Acknowledgments

IN RETROSPECT I am amazed at the number of persons with whom I have been involved and upon whom I have relied for assistance in preparing this book. This awareness evokes a sense of gratitude as well as a deepened insight into the interdependence of man in our society.

Of the many typists who have worked on various sections, Mrs. M. Morrissey of Ottawa and Mrs. J. McEvoy of Waterloo have been particularly efficient. The excellent periodical library of the School of Social Welfare of the University of Ottawa at St. Patrick's College was indispensable in the preliminary search and selection of the articles. The staffs of this library and of Waterloo Lutheran University were especially accommodating. Mrs. Helen O'Grady, M.S.W., and several Ottawa social work students contributed greatly in the location and assessment of the articles. The support and consultative help of The Free Press were excellent.

One of the most gratifying aspects of this work was the myriad of friendly and encouraging letters received from the various authors whom I contacted in regard to locating articles and obtaining permission to use them. In a similar way, the cooperation of the various editors of the journals involved is noted with appreciation. Especially I would like to mention Mrs. Elinor P. Zaki of Family Service Association of America and Mrs. Beatrice Saunders of the National Association of Social Workers. I am particularly thankful to Florence Hollis for her foreword.

Throughout the project the patience, encouragement, and assistance of my wife Joanne and the curiosity of Francis and Sarah were indispensable in a multitude of ways.

To all, my deepest gratitude!

F.J.T.

Contents

FOREWORD   *by Florence Hollis*

PREFACE

ACKNOWLEDGMENTS

The Delinquent Adolescent

The Young Adult

Marriage

Old Age

Death

Part 2 Psychosocial Pathology   155

Neurosis

Character Neurosis

Character Disorders

Addictions—Alcohol

Addictions—Narcotics

Dependency

Sociopathy

Sexual Deviations

Borderline States

Depression

Psychosis—Schizophrenia

Part 3 Physical Handicaps 353

The Brain-Injured Child

Cerebral Palsy

Epilepsy

Mental Retardation

Organic Psychiatric Disorders

Arthritis

Asthma

Blindness

Cancer

Cardiac Disorders

Deafness

Diabetes

Hemophilia

Quadriplegia

Tuberculosis

Part 4   Sociocultural Factors

Ethnicity

Part 1

Stages of Human Development

The articles in this section were selected to give an overview of the literature dealing with the diagnostic and treatment implications of various stages of human development. An important factor among the many continua on which the client must be located to understand him and thus effectively to treat him is his stage of development. This variable is a basic dimension in understanding clients in that it gives an underlying orientation to the method and direction of treatment.

This dimension of diagnosis has always been an important one for the profession. Considerable attention has been given to it. For example, for many years services and specialities in practice have been formulated around divisions of developmental stages such as services to children, school social work, youth services, marital counseling and services to the aged. To a great extent the framework of our agencies' structure still tends to divide practice, and thus clients, by some dimension of age or status. This appears to be changing. There are clear indications that today's practitioners and agencies are called upon to demonstrate competence with a wide range of clients and client problems. Because of the importance of this approach to understanding clients it was anticipated that there would be an abundance of material considering various facets of this continuum. This in fact was the case.

A large number of articles dealing with treatment of children were located. The group of four articles selected covers a variety of approaches. These include direct work with the child; work with the mother; work with the father; work with groups of children; and one with a program of treatment for children with a particular type of problem. Articles in the literature principally deal with children living in their own homes. Because many social workers do work directly with institutionalized children, Selma Fraiberg's article is important. In all these articles on children a common theme is observable; that is that treatment with children is necessarily long term.

Generally the articles dealing with treatment of children tend to focus on children from about the age of six upward. It is interesting that more hasn't been written about the social worker's role with disturbances in very young children. Obviously treatment in these situations would be principally directed to parents or parent substitutes. With increased collaboration between social workers and pediatricians (a recent journal advertisement sought a "pediatric" social worker to practice with a group of pediatricians), it is to be hoped further articles will be forthcoming.

In the direct treatment of children, mention is frequently made of the importance of some form of play therapy. No article was found which dealt directly with the indicators, methods, and materials of play therapy. This topic has of course been addressed by writers in other disciplines. In view of the amount of play therapy of various forms conducted by social workers, there is need for considerably more formal discussion of this therapeutic technique. In many instances practitioners embark on this with little formal training and only a general understanding of its dimensions and utility.

The subject of adolescence and its related topic delinquency are well covered in the literature. In the selection of articles these were considered as separate topics although not distinct, the latter being a subdivision of the former. Several of the authors emphasized that in working with adolescents it was imperative that the therapist's ideas and attitudes about this period of development be kept clear and objective. Reference is made to the importance of understanding the period of adolescence in our culture both in sociological and in psychological terms to avoid developing an overly pathological viewpoint.

The Rabichow article on learning difficulties in adolescence is important. Many adolescents with whom social workers come in contact do have school problems as part of their difficulties. Much has been written about school and learning problems in younger children and an insufficient amount about similar problems in adolescents. With the latter group there is the differential factor of the prospect of leaving school immediately or in the near future, a choice not available to younger children.

Few articles dealing with adolescence fail to mention difficulties and conflicts in sexual maturation; at the same time little direct reference was made in the articles, nor were entire articles found devoted to the direct treatment implications of these. Because such problems, for example, masturbation, are considered to be so prevalent and to create considerable anxiety, it was expected more reference would be made to these areas in the treatment of adolescents.

The articles dealing with delinquent adolescents present three different approaches to this type of client. All emphasize the necessity of patience and timing with the delinquent client. The first focuses primarily on individual treatment of delinquents, where a particular dynamic "defensiveness" is predominant. The Lerman article identifies and emphasizes the necessity of utilizing a range of social science concepts as well as the personality dynamics of the client to intervene effectively with them. The capability of the social worker for comfortably utilizing both individual and group skills is stressed. The third article addresses the institutionalized delinquent. Although specifically focussed on female delinquents, Dr. Hersko's discussion is relevant for male and female delinquents. Important emphasis is put on the necessity for self-awareness and control in the therapists, since countertransference is easily aroused by this type of client.

Many excellent articles were located in the literature which addressed various disturbances in the marital relationship. There are interesting similarities in the four articles which are included. All emphasize the prevalence of transference and countertransference phenomena in these cases and the necessity of understanding and dealing with them. There is frequent reference to a similar length of treatment; it is six to nine months. All make mention of the use of individual and joint interviews with the recommendation that these techniques are usually concurrently not as an either/or approach. Although it is acknowledged that two workers are sometimes necessary, generally one therapist is preferable. The final article examines the particular technique of joint interviewing and discusses both the indicators and the specific dimensions of the technique. This is particularly useful for persons who have been more accustomed to individual interviews and who are interested in developing this treatment method as one of their skills.

In examining the literature for this section, no material was located which dealt with the single adult. It is clear that many social workers are called upon to treat persons in this category. It is presumed that there would be some commonalities of diagnosis and treatment which could be brought together into a paper. It would be interesting to obtain the accumulated experience of skilled practitioners with this type of client.

In recent years it has been frequently suggested that as a group social workers have ignored the aged client. If this is so, the literature certainly does not indicate it. Several excellent articles were located which examine many facets of the nature of the problems of the aged and suggestions for their treatment. The two articles in this section emphasize the necessity of clarifying our own attitudes to the aged and understanding commonalities of this group of clients, in order to individualize them and formulate suitable objectives and plans for treatment.

In the final article in this section, dying, the ultimate stage in human earthly existence is addressed. The author stresses the necessity of seeing this situation, emotionally laden as it is for all, as a professional responsibility, to be met and dealt with in the same manner as any other and not to be avoided out of our own discomfort.

In conclusion, using the stages of human development as a diagnostic variable requiring specific therapeutic considerations can serve only as one part of the assessment process. It is clear that extended practice experience has demonstrated that there are commonalities in behavior and problems requiring specific and predictable treatment approaches in the various ages and roles of human life. It is also clear, and each author reminds us, that the client must be diagnosed from a variety of other variables before a treatment plan can be properly devised.

It is expected that subsequent professional writing will further clarify the implications of this dimension.

The Treatment of a Type of Chronically Rejected Child

Annette Jacobsohn

Families Requiring Long-Term Treatment

The interest in writing this paper arose in the course of a study in our agency concerning the nature of our long-term cases, i.e., cases that have been or are anticipated to be active for more than two years. The paper does not, however, intend to survey all of these cases but rather to focus on a particular type of long-term case, the treatment of which has been found to be alternatingly frustrating and rewarding.

The type of case I wish to discuss is the one where the child with whom the family and the agency are concerned suffers from chronic maternal rejection, a rejection which is actively aggressive and punitive.

In general, the element of maternal rejection is to a considerable extent accountable for the long-term nature of the treatment required. However, this element is often not discovered or fully taken into account, and, therefore, tends to bedevil the treatment process. This bedevilment takes two forms: apparent improvement takes place after a period of treatment, only to collapse again; secondly, when the contact is then resumed and continued with little further movement one begins to question the usefulness of continued treatment and grows anxious about what seems to be a waste of time.

It is, of course, true that in all cases treatment should be based on a thorough understanding of the intrapsychic and interpersonal dynamics. However, I think that the element of rejection is often overlooked because other factors are also observable, seemingly accessible to treatment and appear to be sufficient cause for the presenting problem. (The presenting problems may actually be of any variety—behavior disorders, neurotic traits, borderline functioning, and so on.)

A brief word about literature on the problem: We have of course become quite familiar with the concept of rejection in the guise of over-protection. Dr. David Levy's book on *Maternal Overprotection* published in 1943 and papers written by him and others dating back to about 1929,

Reprinted with permission of the author and the *Journal of Jewish Communal Service;* from XXXIX (Spring, 1963), pp. 293–299.

have defined and elucidated this concept. We have also a number of papers on the individual treatment of rejected children. At the same time we find frequent comments on the difficulty of treating rejected children because their mothers will sabotage treatment.

About the latter type, some comments should be made regarding the concept of rejection. The one word actually covers a rather intricate process and may in a sense be a misnomer except where applied to a situation where the mother has lost all interest in the child. We do use the term *rejection* when we mean the opposite of acceptance. When the mother feels "I can't stand this child; I'd like to get rid of him; he feels like a stranger," we call it rejection. The interesting point is, of course, that she never does what she wishes to do; the rejection never becomes a *fait accompli*. Psychically, the mother needs to have things just as they are, wishing to rid herself of the child and keeping him. From the point of view of the child's psyche this experience of being unloved yet kept also becomes of central importance.

There are a variety of needs in the mother which lead to the wish to reject the child. The particular mother type I am planning to deal with here is the one who unconsciously is using the child as a whipping boy for wrongs she feels have been perpetrated upon her. She might be called the punitive mother, and in the course of being punitive she may also become neglectful, let alone depriving.

I mean to discuss here the treatment only of those cases where a specific child is rejected and other siblings are essentially accepted although they may have various emotional difficulties too. I am excluding the mother who is borderline and whose general ego fragility requires a special kind of treatment approach.

Further, I am referring to rejection which began in early infancy, where we have a history of the mother never being able to feel that she could adequately meet her child's needs. However, in telling us about this the mother will typically speak of the child being "difficult from the start," not that she herself was having difficulties.

It is this very blaming of the child for the difficulties that makes the treatment task so complicated. Sophisticated mothers of our day may of course say that "it must be my fault," but essentially the mothers I have in mind genuinely feel that it is the child who is difficult and provokes their wrath. They will admit their reactive rejection of the child, but not the basic rejection. Their guilt also will be both conscious and unconscious—their conscious guilt brings them for treatment, makes them superficially co-operative often to the point of achieving superficial improvement. Unconsciously, however, their rejection of the child continues and both this and their ensuing unconscious guilt prevents their being related to the child's needs. The child, on his part is of course truly deprived and truly afraid. In addition, however, his behavior becomes geared toward maintaining himself by being especially controlling and toward revenging himself on the rejecting mother. The fact that he is constantly confronted with his mother's greater acceptance of his siblings adds to the fire. The vicious cycle is thus firmly established.

When we try to understand the punitive mother's need to reject the child we find that this is in response to a sense of herself having been deserted, deep down by her own mother, although consciously she may speak of desertion by mother substitutes which may include sisters, mothers-in-law, even husbands. The resulting rage is expressed toward the child because its actual source cannot be faced. What is referred to here is, of course, the re-awakening of old unresolved dependency problems, not the transitory sense of heightened dependency experienced appropriately by the pregnant woman, or the mother of a newborn infant. If she is left in the lurch during this period for reality reasons she may develop intrapsychic problems, but these are more accessible to consciousness and more easily resolved; she is better able to "forgive and forget" and allow herself the joys of motherhood.

Interestingly enough we find that where rejection of a child takes place there are usually not the overt troubles with families of origin that we find in other situations. It is as if the dependence-independence struggle, the struggle over control and submission, had been suppressed only to re-emerge between mother and child with redoubled force. We find further that there are often no overt marital difficulties but more often that the parents superficially form an alliance against the rejected child. Thus, in a sense treatment of these cases can mean that in order to help the child a lot more people have to become upset than were so originally. The difficulty is, however, that we are often dealing with people whose overall adjustment and functioning in other areas are only "fair" and their ego strengths are not such that one can sanguinely trust that they will survive satisfactorily a challenging of their present adjustment.

Mother's Treatment Needs

In considering treatment approaches in these cases I think we must be really prepared to meet the clients where they are—the reasons why they come and what they expect from us runs mostly counter to why we see them and what we expect to do for them. There is usually a request for the child to be "corrected, straightened out, made to realize . . . ," the mother, herself seeks "guidance and advice . . ." which, if given she subverts and if withheld she will seek elsewhere. All attempts at confrontation or even at being related to her feelings will be strongly resisted with denial, cancellations, excuses, etc. It is therefore quite difficult to establish a "therapeutic alliance." I think that actually the first year needs to be devoted to establishing a relationship of some sort which permits a therapeutic focus to be found. The mother will often continue contact purely in order to assuage her guilt and rather than fight with this, we are best advised to use this time to assess her personality and her needs from stray remarks, behavior, and all available forces, and from a diagnosis more or less "in spite of her," as her direct statements will usually all be geared to how impossible the child is and every-thing else will be denied. I have found in a particular case that I have been treating, that this groundwork was laid while mother and child had separate workers and that during this time they each felt cared for. The case was then assigned to me for work with both mother and child and interestingly enough I felt that both now benefitted from my knowing the other and my being able to appreciate what they were talking about when they complained. I have also found, with some surprise that my interest in her child and my observations have cheered the mother. It is as if this had given her some hope of yet climbing out of the abyss of guilt and despair. We must remember that the need actually to bring the child for treatment is a shock to the mother because it means that the dangerous game she has been playing has actually had bad results.

It is only when the child has made some progress and the presenting problem is somewhat ameliorated; when the mother herself has felt fed by our interest in the problem she brings—I am putting it this way rather than our interest in her because she cannot usually stand too direct a relatedness to her feelings—that we can begin to ask the question "Suppose your problem with your child were quite resolved, how would you feel?" The particular mother I have in mind replied jokingly "Oh, I guess I'd have to find someone else to beat up." Never had she admitted directly that she beats the child out of her own need. Then she added with seriousness "I do so wish, though, that I would not do it to a living thing." It was relatively soon after this that she casually began to ask for help with her being generally so aggressive with all her children and for the first time we began to talk directly about her feelings. However I carefully avoid questioning her behavior with her children but I rather use opportunities to express concern about how hard she is on herself. I similarly avoid reference to any negative feelings she might have towards her own mother but note silently that there are more frequent references to the spirit in which her mother raised her.

As this type of mother is in a treatment situation only because of her child and is easily frightened off by anything that suggests her own need for treatment, I use opportunities to comment on her feelings towards her child which are so painful to her. Surprisingly enough when I ask her "What do you think your child really needs?" she replies "If he were treated with kindness and patience he would prosper." What now becomes revealed is that essentially it is masochism that prevents her from allowing herself to be a good mother. She, the punitive mother, is essentially self-punishing. She deprives herself of the enjoyment of meeting her child's needs, she burdens herself with guilt. She punishes herself for her resentment of her own mother.

If at this point we bring her mother in by asking "What would be your mother's attitude on this or that question?" we begin to get a feeling response: "Oh my mother . . . with her there was no such thing as 'I don't want to,' " and so on.

Treatment Needs of the Child

Children who suffer from maternal rejection, I often think, are comparable to children who have been severely physically malnourished or undernourished. Their presenting problems are not necessarily directly attributable to maternal mistreatment or deprivation. However, just as in the case of physical illness the patient will recover more or less successfully in accordance with the relative strength and sturdiness of his body, so the child with a specific psychological disorder will respond more or less successfully in accordance with the relative sturdiness of his ego.

The child who is subjected to maternal rejection, as well as suffering from specific problems in functioning or adjustment, needs to be fed as well as helped to correct his ideas. As in the case of physical undernourishment this process is complicated. The digestive system having adjusted itself to a starvation diet can only absorb small quantities of nourishment and if tempted to take in too much will respond with upset. In psychological terms this is equivalent to the psychic system being threatened by the offer of too much love. In fantasy the affection starved child will long for the good mother, similarly as the person suffering from hunger will dream of the banquet. The disturbed child will have fantasies of being adopted by the worker, fantasies which will occur in response to anyone who is related to the child in an interested, unambivalent manner as long as the child is still capable of affect hunger. These fantasies are accompanied by guilt towards the parents in defense against their jealous retribution. Awareness of this on the part of the worker is of the greatest importance. The child must be given to in order to be strengthened and yet care must be taken that not more tension is created than is bearable. Around this issue runs the debate pro and con actual physical feeding and giving. Essentially one wants to create an atmosphere and offer a relationship that will be conducive to growth and the correction of misconceptions. This, in itself, is the true gift to the child (or any client or patient). Essentially whatever therapist and child client do together must be justifiable in these terms, the relationship must remain a distinct and special one, not play into the fantasies of the child but be conducive to their revelation. This is, of course, in a sense a professional platitude and true of all therapeutic relationships. I am, however, stressing it here because the emotionally rejected child presents a special appeal to the sympathetic adult. As mentioned initially several papers have been written describing in detail the treatment of individual children suffering from rejection and it is not my plan to do this here but rather to point out how some of the difficulties can be coped with. For the sake of accuracy, however, I want to qualify the above by saying that in actuality the rejected child, of course, often presents himself in a manipulative, controlling and often suspicious and highly guarded manner distrusting the very offer of a good relationship.

Theoretically the child could be helped by being transferred to a different, loving environment. In reality we still think that the trauma is too great and recommend placement only in those cases where the active pathogenic factors in the home environment outweigh the trauma of forced separation. The cases which we are discussing here are those where there is enough parental interest in the child that can be positively mobilized.

Why does the treatment of these children take so long? As described above, the child has to take in the therapeutic experience little by little if he is not to get into unbearable conflict with himself and his environment. The contact may therefore continue over several years with the frequency of interviews adjusted to current needs. On the whole, interviews held once a week are more advisable than more intensive contact, in order to avoid over-stimulation.

What the therapist provides apart from a different emotional experience is a means of strengthening the child's evaluation of reality. In a sense the development of seemingly unhealthy defenses were necessary for the child. Protected by guardedness, suspiciousness, manipulativeness, control, he can lead his own life, restricted, deprived but with relative equanimity. Therapy is an interference with these defenses, a demand is made on the child to exercise his critical faculties and keep alive his desires to gain gratification from his environment. This, however, must be done with such caution as to prevent depression or inappropriate acting-out.

Another reason for the long term treatment needs of these children is the fact that the more the child is biologically dependent on the parent the more will he be oriented towards the parent. He can, therefore, only tackle certain problems in his relationship with them as he gains relative independence. From this one might plan to provide contact according to the needs of the developmental period: periods where work with parents is more intensive than with the child and periods where one would encourage the provision of other resources (group work centers, camps, big sisters or brothers) in order to provide special nurture. Then there can be times when only the child is seen weekly and contact with the parents is less frequent.

Treatment Approach with Fathers

In discussing the treatment needs of the fathers of maternally rejected children, I am limiting myself to highlighting what I think are some of the characteristics of their position. We distinguish them here from those fathers who themselves reject their child in primary fashion because the child is experienced as a rival for the fulfillment of their own dependency needs. As in the case of the mothers, I am excluding here too, borderline individuals who need a special treatment approach.

In the cases under discussion our assessment of the family as a whole suggests that the essential treatment considerations need to be given to mother and child. However, we find that the father often has potentially many positives to offer and in involving him it is our intent to help him find areas where he can use himself constructively in furthering the growth of the child without threatening the mother.

Initially, however, he is likely to be in a state of anger, guilt and helplessness. No rational behavior on his part appears to be of any use vis-à-vis the unconsciously determined attitude of his wife. Of course being himself subject to unconscious needs, he will identify with either the aggressor or the victim or punish them both by withdrawing emotionally.

As mentioned initially, we frequently find such a father in superficial alliance with his wife. Having often been somewhat removed from the situation during the child's infancy, having relied either on his wife's apparent "strength" in managing or on the help she received from others, he does not become involved in the problem between mother and child until it has clearly developed to the point where the child has become "the problem" and he feels called upon to exercise his authority to enforce respect for the mother.

As also mentioned above, marital problems are frequently denied in these cases, although their existence is evident from indirect remarks. Just as the child is not enjoyed and is experienced as a burden, so the marriage is not enjoyed actively, there are trivial complaints and the absence of open friction is mistaken for happiness. I think that frequently the husband and wife have met with some defeats in the course of their marriage which have re-aroused old feelings of inadequacy. They feel guilty and in the ensuing mild depression they withdraw from each other and retreat to a somewhat more immature level than they are potentially capable of.

We frequently find that when we first suggest to such a father that he become involved in the treatment process he is quite unproductive. He comes because his wife wants him to, feels that it would be sufficient to work with her as she and he are in agreement one with the other, or that the problem lies between mother and child and he has nothing to do with it. He often disengages himself after a brief contact in the beginning but his interest in what is happening can become aroused at a later point.

When we discover at a later stage that these fathers are capable of making a contribution to the resolution of the problem, we frequently chide ourselves for not succeeding in involving them earlier. However, I think, it may well be true that mother and child have first had to feel the need for treatment and have derived some benefit from it before the father is willing to contribute.

The father will of course have his own personality problems which we would want to understand, however, as long as we are clear that the problem is chiefly between mother and child we may have to let father be out of it until he himself is ready to come. In the particular case I have in mind, the father has been reinvolved through monthly joint interviews with his wife (in the meantime he has regularly brought his daughter for her interviews). I involve him in this way when his wife reported some casually expressed interest by him in the child's treatment and at the same time some wish for his wife to withdraw from treatment herself as she became more acutely upset with herself.

The Integration Process

I should now like to discuss briefly the possibilities of helping the parents and the child to accept each other. This, I think, essentially depends on the degree of movement that the mother can make and in the case I have alluded to above I think this might be possible. As with the mother, with the child, too, we find considerable masochism. She is enjoying the relationship with the worker, has gotten a good deal of negative feelings towards her mother off her chest, but she refuses to talk in response to direct questions, she maintains that "you cannot make me talk" and that she will keep her "secrets." This opportunity for opposition to the worker is welcome as she can live it out safely. Gradually of course the secret begins to emerge—it is her power of being able to make her mother punish her by being very bad and then making her forgive her by being very good. Why should she give up these powerful secret weapons unless she can really be sure that her mother would love her voluntarily? Both mother and daughter can now be shown how they interact and they begin to have a sense of choice about it. The father has been helped to find a place for himself which is neither "away from it all" nor "right in the middle" so that now he is available to do some rescue work when mother and child have gotten themselves into an impasse, and at this point of treatment they will permit him to do this. I think with this we should be able to envisage the maintenance of improvement. Depending then on the age of the child and his growing strength to face up to his own problems some further more individually geared and insightful therapy might be considered.

A Therapeutic Approach to Reactive Ego Disturbances in Children in Placement

Selma Fraiberg

Among the gravest consequences of placement is the child's inability to form new object relationships following loss. A very large number of children in institutions and foster home care are permanently damaged and may never recover the capacity for making meaningful human ties. Frequently

Reprinted from the *American Journal of Orthopsychiatry*, XXXII (January, 1962), pp. 18–31. Copyright, the American Orthopsychiatric Association, Inc. Reproduced by permission of the author and the Association.

the casework treatment of such children is blocked by the characteristic defenses against affect which these children display and by their inability to make an attachment to the caseworker—the indispensable condition for treatment.

This paper describes and illustrates a casework approach that was developed in the course of working with a small group of latency-age boys in institutional placement. The treatment employed a specialized adaptation of an analytic technique that should be entirely within the competence of a caseworker and within the defined limits of casework treatment. It consisted mainly of working through the defenses against affects and of reviving the affects around the initial trauma of placement. Concurrent group treatment was employed for continuing diagnosis, to test the movement in object relationships, and to provide a milieu in which readiness for new ties might be gratified.

This work was part of a program jointly sponsored by the Tulane School of Social Work, the Children's Bureau of New Orleans, and the Protestant Children's Home. In this report I shall confine myself to the casework treatment and illustrate with selected cases.[1] I wish to mention, however, that our experience in the use of concurrent group treatment demonstrated not only the value of the group as an adjunct to casework treatment but opened up the possibility in our minds that for selected cases, group treatment might operate independently to bring about favorable therapeutic results.

The setting in which this work was carried out is in many ways typical of institutions that provide care for the dependent and neglected child in our country. The Protestant Children's Home was built nearly 100 years ago as an orphanage. There is a high iron fence surrounding the grounds and the children are still housed in dormitories according to age groups. The house-parents are mainly middle-aged men and women with limited education and, of course, they have no special educational preparation for work with children. Many of the children are severely disturbed and have been placed in the institution because of earlier failures in foster homes. There are no clinically trained staff members. At the time of our study casework services were provided for the children and their families by the Children's Bureau and other agencies in the community.

We chose the Junior Boys Division for our study. The ten boys in this group ranged in age from eight to eleven. The housemother, Mrs. Lindstrom, was a woman in her middle sixties, who somehow managed the difficult job of caring for a group of gravely disturbed children who would have taxed the best gifts of a clinically trained worker. She was strict in her discipline, and some of her demands for good behavior were undoubtedly excessive. But she also had sympathy and affection for her children, and as we worked together she learned to become more lenient and more tolerant in certain important areas.

[1] All cases reported here were seen in casework treatment on a once-a-week basis.

II

I will begin this report with a description of the treatment of George. George was 11 years old when we began treatment. He was the oldest of five children, all of whom had been placed by the parents two years earlier. At the time of placement the parents were considering divorce. The mother planned to return to work, and the children had become such an emotional and financial burden to her that she appeared dangerously close to a severe depression. The plan was for temporary placement, but as two years passed by it became clear that the mother might never bring herself to reunite her family. The father had disappeared after the divorce.

In preplacement interviews the mother described George as the chief problem among her children. He was described as very stubborn and aggressive and subject to stormy outbursts of temper. In the early months of placement at the institution George presented the full battery of his behavior problems. Both the institution and the school reported belligerence and bullying of other children, much fighting, and provocative behavior. But gradually, the record shows, George gave up his fighting and his bullying and became a rather passive and tractable child. The complaints now were of another order. He had become whiny and fearful of bigger boys in the institution. He brought constant complaints of being beaten up by the bigger boys and of having his toys destroyed by them. About the second complaint the boys in his group seemed genuinely baffled and claimed that George himself had been seen destroying toys that his mother had sent him and would then accuse other children of having broken them.

Along with this shift from active to passive came two new developments. George had begun to gain weight rapidly, and at the end of the first year in placement he had gained 30 pounds. During the second year he continued to eat voraciously and to gain weight. He was about 40 pounds overweight when I first met him. He had wet the bed occasionally prior to placement. By the time internalization of his conflicts had been completed, at the end of the first year, George had become a constant bed-wetter. Often he wet two and three times a night.

When I first saw George he was an obese, sluggish youngster with a round pink face. He never smiled. His nails were bitten to the quick. His speech was mushy, indistinct—devoid of affect.

In the early interviews with George I was impressed by certain characteristics of his relationship with me. He was affable, superficially friendly, garrulous, and yet he was completely uninterested in the new caseworker. One had the impression that caseworkers were interchangeable, that one would do as well as another. He was sorry that he had to give up his previous worker. He had even expressed some regret to her when he learned of the transfer, but none of this feeling could be recovered when I invited him to talk about his feelings about the transfer. I began to understand that his relationship to me, to previous workers, and to members of the institutional staff derived from his feeling of helplessness. We were protectors against the danger of hunger, abandonment, and a variety of physical dangers. And because these relationships were important only for providing need satisfaction and protection, any one member of the staff could substitute for another. During the first months of treatment he almost never mentioned his housemother, Mrs. Lindstrom, unless I initiated discussion through questions. This, I learned, was not to be taken as a deficiency in the capacities of the housemother; it was a result of George's absence of interest in or involvement with the adults who cared for him. During the same period he never showed any interest in me or curiosity about me.

Like most children in placement George clung to a fantasy about his parents and the reasons for his placement. His mother, in the fantasy, wanted all of her children at home but she didn't have enough money to keep them. When she saved enough money she would bring the children back home. There was no criticism of his mother and there were no reproaches. On many occasions the mother neglected to visit the children when she had promised. George, if he discussed these occasions at all, reported them factually and without affect.

Our earliest work, then, began to deal with the defenses against affects. I used every good opportunity to give George permission to feel and to show him omissions of justifiable feelings of anger or disappointment and displacements of affect. Very early in treatment we began to understand why the defenses against aggression were so strong. On one occasion when George got into a fight with one of the boys in his school (and it was indeed nothing more than a mild fight in which they pushed each other around), George spent the better part of his hour alternating between restrained fury at his enemy and fear that he would be sent away to a correctional institution for delinquent boys.

There were two components in this exaggerated fear of consequences for aggression. One, of course, was the expectation that any aggression, no matter how mild, would result in his being sent away. The other clearly was that the exaggerated punishment was equal to the strength of the undischarged aggression; he was afraid of the destructive power of his rage. Through a number of examples of such exaggerated fear of punishment I began to help George see that he was really afraid of his own feelings, that the anger inside was so strong at times that he feared that if it came out he might really hurt someone. I helped him to understand that the more he talked about his feelings in the interview the less need he would have to fear these feelings.

Gradually we began to understand various forms of displacement of anger. George's fear of attack by other boys, his constant complaints of being picked on, began to diminish when he understood how these fears were to a certain measure tied up with his fear of his own anger. Sometimes I could draw his attention to his savage nail-biting as he talked about anger, and he was impressed to see how feelings could be connected with such a symptom.

We went further and began to establish some links between bed-wetting and the feelings of anger and fear that he kept inside him.

Yet he was only able to experience anger and resentment toward other children. He could in no way acknowledge feelings of anger toward the adults in the institution, toward teachers, or toward me. Once when I felt he was struggling with hostile feelings toward me I asked him what he thought would happen if he should feel angry toward me and tell me. And he said, without a moment's hesitation, "Why you would go away!" He said this with such conviction that I could tell him now that I thought that this fear was connected with a real happening in his life, that this must have been the way he felt when mother placed him in the home. I said that all children are afraid that if they are naughty or have any angry thoughts mother or daddy might go away and leave them, and I said that when children are placed away from home they can't help but feel deep inside that maybe it was because of something they had done or because they had been naughty.

From this point on in the interview George seemed to be struggling with all kinds of feelings. Several times he was in tears or close to tears. I encouraged him to talk more about mother and father and his feelings about placement. When he began attacking his nails again I tried to get him to tell me what he was feeling. Was it possible, I asked, that even when a child loved his parents he might feel some anger toward them, too, for disappointing him? With this George turned away so that I might not see his tears, and in a voice full of fury he said, "Sometimes I think I'm gonna be in this place for four more years and that I'm never going to go back to my own home."

As more and more feeling welled up within him he began to talk for the first time about the beginning period of placement. He remembered when his mother first told the children they were going to a Home. He didn't know what it would be like and he even thought it would be fun to live in a place with many other kids and have swings and slides. "And then I remember the first night and everything was so strange and I woke up in the middle of the night and it was dark and I didn't know where I was and my bed was all wet. . . . And then the next day when I woke up I looked out of the window and I saw all the bars around the place and the gates were locked." (The "bars" were the high iron fences around the 100-year-old institution.) I said, "I think it must have made you feel as if you were in jail. It must have made you feel that being here was like a punishment." He nodded in silence.

In this session we established the first connections between George's fear of his aggressive impulses and his feeling that placement was a punishment for being bad. This hour initiated many new developments. George, who had been the scapegoat of his group and who exhausted the adults of the Home with his whining and constant complaints of persecution, now began to fight back. George was as astonished as his former tormentors were. There was tremendous relief in him when he found that he could fight back and hold his own even with the older and more powerful boys. For a while it was difficult to keep the fighting under control. I got him to exercise some judgment in the fighting and to get a good measure of his rage and hostility back into the therapeutic hours where it might do some good. At the same time I was in close communication with George's housemother and with the director of the institution. Their understanding of the meaning of this behavior enabled them to handle a number of difficult situations with a firm and non-punitive approach. After a few weeks the aggressive behavior subsided to something close to normal for a boy of this age. Now we saw that George was no longer afraid of his own aggression or afraid of monstrous punishments for having aggressive feelings.

From this we could understand that one of the decisive factors in the transformation of aggression had been the experience of separation. To be aggressive was to invite abandonment, and when our work established the connection between these two factors and the separation experience George could experience anger once again. With even this much work there was some symptomatic relief. George's nails, which had been bitten to the quick, were now beginning to grow. The bed-wetting improved temporarily. Also there was now considerable improvement in schoolwork, with George boasting that he was getting a better report card than he had ever had in his life.

Yet the whole area of his ambivalence toward his parents remained barely touched at this point. Now, however, there was a new theme in George's communications. He worried about people dying. He worried about his father. He didn't know where he was. He could be dead for all anyone knew. He missed his Dad. Sometimes he worried that his mother might die. From his fantasies it was very clear to me that his fears were closely connected with destructive wishes toward his parents. I now understood, too, another reason why it was so difficult for George to express even mild hostility toward his parents. For the child who is separated from his own parents the hostile and destructive wishes are necessarily more dangerous than for the child who still has his parents. For all children the physical presence of the parents is a reassurance against the danger that the loved persons may be harmed or destroyed by the child's own bad wishes. In the absence of his parents George could not tolerate his own dangerous fantasies, for he could not have reassurance against the omnipotence of his thoughts.

"Is it really true," George wanted to know, "that you could put a curse on someone and make them die?" He didn't think so but he had seen a story on television once. In one session he brought forth a number of such stories having to do with fictional events in which evil wishes brought about the illness or death of "someone." When I began to relate these fears to his own fears that bad wishes might harm someone he quickly denied that he ever had such thoughts. Then, very tentatively, he began to explore this dangerous territory with me through offering stories about a fictional boy who did have such thoughts. In the course of this hour we talked about his fears that bad wishes could come true and I again linked these fears with the experience of placement and the feelings that angry thoughts could cause someone to go away. At the end of this session George, for the first time since I had met him, looked relaxed and happy.

In the play-group meeting the following week George did something unprecedented. He got angry toward his group leader for allowing someone to use his materials and he announced that he was quitting the group. But when he told me about this experience in his next session he assured me that he didn't really intend to quit the club. He liked his group leader a lot; he just got good and mad at her that day. Sally, he reported marveling, had not been mad at him; she was "real nice about it." He seemed tremendously uplifted by this experience. It was one of the first occasions offered us in which George could allow himself to show hostility toward an adult whom he liked and to do so without fear that he would lose the love of that person.

During the same week George's housemother reported a most interesting set of observations. For several days George had been playing baby, in a clowning act in the dormitory. The big 150-pound baby crawled from one end of the room to the other, under beds and under furniture, emerging to be petted like an infant by Mrs. Lindstrom, who went along with the game with some amusement. At the same time Mrs. Lindstrom reported that George had become very affectionate toward her, telling her how swell she was and how he loved her. He even made a written declaration of love in the form of a mock certificate of honor with her name on it.

These events marked another turning point in George's treatment. Now we began to see the beginnings of a strong positive attachment to Mrs. Lindstrom and qualitatively richer relationships with both the director of the institution and his play-group leader. And at just this point we were suddenly confronted with some new behavior that baffled all of us. With all the gains on the side of relationships with adults and with all the new satisfactions that he seemed to be receiving, George was now involved in conflict in another sphere. Both the group leader and the housemother reported that George was in constant battle with Jimmy, one of the scapegoats in his group. George had appointed himself chief tormentor of Jimmy and constantly provoked fights with him. From various pieces of material in treatment I was certain that George's hatred of Jimmy was based upon an identification with him but I could not clearly establish the basis of this identification.

Then in one interview when George had spent most of his hour reciting a litany of hate against Jimmy I asked him what he thought was the trouble with Jimmy, what made Jimmy behave this way. "I'll tell you!" George said promptly. "He's full of hate. That's what his trouble is. Just full of hate. That's why he steals, too. Just full of hate." I replied, "Well, you may be right. But why do you think he is full of hate?" The answer was, "I don't know and I don't care." I said, "I think he is full of hate because he feels that nobody loves him." And then to my surprise George said, "Then I guess me and him is in the same boat, 'cause I ain't got nobody to love me either." He began to cry. "I'm just as bad off as he is. I ain't got no Daddy and my

Mama, I don't think she's ever gonna take us home and I think the only way I'm gonna get out of this place is when I'm big enough to work."

Now I asked if this made George wonder if his mother loved him, too? He nodded, choked up. I asked if this made George "full of hate" at times, too, because he could not understand why his mother had done this? He hesitated, then said painfully, "Sometimes." Now for the first time George could express his bitterness toward his mother and his longing for her. In this interview he talked about how fat he had grown; he remembered that he had not been overweight before coming to the Home. I helped him see how miserable and lonely he must have been and how eating was a way of easing the hurt then and now.

From this point on in treatment George's ambivalence toward mother became accessible to us with the full strength of the powerful feelings involved. He no longer consoled himself with the fantasy that his mother was going to take the children back, and he made the heartbreaking observation that mother herself no longer talked about making a home for the children again.

On one occasion when two of the boys in his group were preparing to return home, several of the other boys circulated stories that they, too, were going home—stories that were really painful fictions. George was overwhelmed with jealousy and spent hours in bitter tirades against his mother. During this time he became involved in open conflict with his mother and there was one episode in which the strong feelings of George and his mother initiated a Sunday afternoon drama. The mother had taken the children home for a Sunday visit. George was apparently short-tempered and volatile for most of the day, quarreling with his mother and each of his siblings in turn. At one point when George and his brother Martin were bickering, the mother lost her temper and sent both children out of the house and locked the door. The two boys pounded on the door and screamed to come in but the mother would not open the door. George was in a fury as he told me this story.

When we sorted out all the complicated feelings in this episode I was able to show George two aspects of his reactions. On the one hand were the real and justifiable reactions to being locked out of the house. In another way, I suggested, the whole episode hurt him so deeply because it made him feel that mother didn't want him in her home, that she was "sending him away" and that being closed out of his house was just exactly the way he felt living away from home. With this George's rage began to subside and he began to struggle with tears.

As we worked through the ambivalent feelings toward mother during these months George showed considerable growth in all areas of his life. That summer after the first eight months of treatment we all observed that George had actually become a happy child. His relationships to his housemother and the director of the home were warm and spontaneous and he could even afford now to express negative feelings toward them at times. At one period during the summer, when George's mother began to speak about the possibility of bringing her children back home, George's reactions were very interesting. He was genuinely happy at the prospect but, he told me soberly, he would miss Mrs. Lindstrom and the director very much. He said that if he went back to his mother he would ask the director if he could come back to the Home to visit "maybe three times a week." However, his mother changed her mind again, and even this George was able to manage, with understandably strong feelings but without regression.

In summarizing the casework achievements in the fall after ten months, we saw that George had demonstrated his capacity to make new love attachments and that his relationship to his own mother had grown freer. There was less overt conflict with mother now, and with increased satisfactions in other areas of his life he seemed able to accept the pain of separation and mother's own limitations. He was able to handle his relationships with other boys within the institution with confidence and without undue aggressiveness. But he could fight when he needed to. There was now real pleasure in school and in learning—an unexpected and welcome bonus for treatment. Arithmetic was still a rough spot, mainly because of academic deficiencies brought about by three years of daydreaming in class, but George was energetically applying himself to mastery of tables and other fundamentals neglected since the third grade and his teachers reported favorably on his progress. There was some modification of the symptom picture that came about very clearly through the therapeutic work on the defenses against affects. Nail-biting, for example, disappeared completely. The voracious eating was curbed. There were no further weight gains and even some slight weight reduction. (I made no effort to deal with eating as a symptom except to occasionally connect eating with longing and aggression.)

But the enuresis remained. Clearly the casework treatment that had centered on affects and their transformations would not bring about symptomatic relief in this area. I knew that the enuresis was intimately connected with fears concerning masturbation and sex play, and until this material could be worked through there was no possibility of cure. In the second year of treatment it was necessary to modify the therapeutic approach in order to deal successfully with the sexual conflicts associated with the enuresis. This part of the treatment does not concern us here, of course, since we are primarily concerned with the method employed in the first year for bringing about the restoration of object ties.

In summary, those conflict areas and transformations of affect that were clearly reactive to the separation from parents were accessible to the casework treatment approach I have described, and the morbid process proved to be reversible.

It was undoubtedly an advantage to the therapy that George was already in latency at the time that separation from his parents took place. And yet we were most interested to see that in another of our cases, ten-year-old Brian, who was placed in the institution at the age of four, we had a therapeutic achievement that surpassed our expectations. I shall only briefly mention this case for illustrative purposes. . . .

Brian, when I first saw him, was one of the most severely depressed children I had ever seen. He was completely passive and withdrawn, a sad little gnome who sat on his bed looking into space, and who had no connections to any other human being. No one within the institution could say at this point that he had a relationship to Brian. I realized from reading his record that periods of severe depression had recurred throughout his stay at the institution dating from age four. There were other periods when he seemed less depressed, but characteristically he was withdrawn, and the picture of a grave, unsmiling, silent little boy remained little changed during the six years of placement. Brian's mother was described as mentally ill (diagnosis not available) and four of the six children were placed after mother demonstrated her inability to give even physical care to the children. Brian, the youngest, was mother's favorite. Throughout placement she has maintained contact with him through visits. The ties to father and his common-law wife were also maintained on an irregular basis.

My private estimate of the possibilities of reaching Brian through casework treatment was a pessimistic one. Brian had no conscious memory of a time before placement and the remaining ties to the parents were very thin. His capacity for object ties could not be judged. Ego functioning had broken down in vital areas. He had failed his last grade in school in spite of good intelligence.

Almost as soon as the caseworker began to touch upon "feelings" with Brian she found herself the object of transference reactions that were so dense and complex that at first we had great difficulty in understanding the events of treatment. At the beginning there was no evidence of a strong positive transference in the treatment sessions and yet the passive and lethargic little boy began to come alive and began to communicate with adults and other children at the Home. There was no question that the tie to the caseworker had meaning and value to him, yet many hours were spent in almost complete silence. Previous caseworkers had also reported such silent hours with Brian.

As the caseworker repeatedly encouraged expressions of feeling, and gave permission to feel, Brian became visibly afraid. And when feeling first emerged in these sessions it came through in the form of terrible inarticulate grief and rage. He would kick savagely at the chair while he sat mute and helpless. He would cry hopelessly and inarticulately. It was as if the grief and rage were so elemental that there were no words that could express them. As more and more affect emerged the caseworker found herself in the center of a strange, wordless drama, the object of passionate hate and longing yet walled off from understanding by the child's silence.

There were no words, we thought, because there were no conscious memories to which these feelings could attach themselves.

But as the pressure of these painful affects grew stronger we began to see elements of the past revived in the present. During a period when the caseworker saw many reactions in Brian that showed that he was jealous of other boys who came to see her, Brian characteristically closed her out. Then on one occasion at the close of the interview Brian refused to leave and finally buried his head in his arms and burst into tears. He could not speak of his grief, but the next hour he entered in a hostile mood and for the first time put his rage into words. He didn't want to see the caseworker, he said. He wished she weren't his caseworker. He wanted to be left alone. Then, in a passionate outburst he accused the caseworker of liking other boys who were her clients better than she liked him, and he burst into tears. When the caseworker attempted to talk with him he ran out of the room. In the next sessions he renewed his fury with the caseworker, and finally in one climactic hour he screamed, "I hate you! I hate you!" and then, sobbing, said, "Go see Roger. Go see Jimmy. Not me." At one point he jumped on a chair to reach a storage cupboard and pleaded with the caseworker to give him everything that he saw, crayons, glue, and color books. Finally he desperately demanded that she give him a model airplane that belonged to another child. When the caseworker explained that these things must remain in the office he began to cry and shouted, "You won't give me *anything!*" He ran out of the room sobbing.

Only after Brian could express grief and rage and longing in transference to the caseworker was he able to express his positive feelings for her and enter into a relationship that showed affection and trust. It is important to note that during this whole stormy period in transference, there was very little affect outside of treatment; all these strong feelings centered on the caseworker. In every other area—in the institution, in the play group, and in school—all of our reports showed Brian reaching out to people and finding pleasure in play and in schoolwork. He had become spontaneously affectionate toward his housemother; he had a strong attachment to his play-group leader, and as we followed his development in the play group we discovered skills and qualities of leadership that surprised all of us. Group treatment made a substantial contribution to the therapy by providing opportunities for growth and a favorable milieu for Brian's growing capacity for object relationships. It is also important to note that Brian, who had been failing in school the year before treatment, completed this academic year with an excellent report card.

In Brian's case, then, the affects associated with loss of the love object in the preoedipal phase were revived in transference, and the casework treatment permitted a reliving in the transference of grief and rage, with recovery of the capacity for object ties and excellent gains in ego functioning.

The therapeutic results in Brian's case surpassed our expectations. From an analytic point of view there is much in this case that I wish we understood better. The specific connections between events in transference and events in the past could not be established through a casework treatment; these could only be known through employing an analytic method. And we do not understand how a depression of such severity should have responded in favorably to a casework treatment. We cannot be certain, of course, that so a child with such severe depressive tendencies the tendency will not reassert itself. But this recovery through casework treatment is still a substantial gain, and the child in latency who can make attachments once again and who can feel again may be less vulnerable in adolescence and later life.

III

In such cases as these, a child who has once experienced ties to the original object—however ambivalent these may have been—can recover the possibility of making new attachments through a therapy directed toward reviving affects and working through the experience of loss. As we should expect, the method will not have any usefulness in those cases where a child's inability to attach himself derives from failure to establish meaningful human ties in the earlier stages of ego development. In one of our cases, for example, our earliest superficial observations led us to expect a favorable outcome in treatment. Pete seemed less damaged than any other child in our group. While his relationships were qualitatively poor there were no signs of serious withdrawal and no symptoms. But as we worked with Pete in casework and in the group we discovered that we had erred gravely in our original assessment. After eight months we found that none of us felt he really knew this child. Pete was charming, ingratiating, and somehow unconnected with any other person in his environment. We began to see that here there was real impoverishment in the ego, a deficiency and an incapacity in forming human ties that was not reactive to object loss but that derived from failures in human connections in the earliest phases of personality development.

In those cases where the child's inability to form new object ties is a reaction to loss with consequent transformations of affects we have, I believe, a generally favorable condition for recovery through therapy. One of the strongest therapeutic assets we have in working with such children in placement is the readiness to form a transference neurosis. As Anna Freud pointed out many years ago in her remarks on transference in child analysis, when a child is separated from his original love objects and moved to a new environment he may be expected to transfer to the new environment libidinal and aggressive impulses that originated in the relationships to the original objects. The condition of placement, of separation from the original objects, makes possible the development of a true transference neurosis.

If we observe closely during the early weeks and months of placement we can often find a variety of behaviors directed toward foster parents, cottage mothers, and caseworkers that are clearly repetitions of earlier experiences with the original objects. In a treatment home or institution with clinically trained personnel we can actually make use of these transference reactions in therapy and help the child achieve insight into his behavior. Or it may happen that reliving the past in the present with the corrective afforded by a benevolent institution and its personnel may, in itself, bring about the resolution of old conflicts. The transference neurosis and its handling should provide the key to the therapeutic effects of milieu therapy.

Now in the institution in which our work was carried out and most other institutions that provide custodial care for neglected and dependent children we have no clinical facilities and the houseparents ordinarily have little training to equip them to understand the complexities of child behavior following placement. The child's grief or withdrawal in the initial stages of placement is experienced by the cottage parents as a reproach or a criticism, as if they had failed to make the child happy. Mourning, then, is seen as something that must be gotten over quickly, and the cottage parent may exert himself in making the child happy and making him forget.

After an initial period of emotional neutrality toward the substitute parents we can usually expect some transference reactions to manifest themselves; old conflicts are revived in the new setting. Many children struggling with the crushing burden of their ambivalence toward the parents who deserted or surrendered them will transfer the hostile and negative feelings toward the new objects and preserve an unambivalent love for the absent parents. In the absence of clinical training, the cottage parent can hardly be blamed for reacting with injury and perhaps with anger to the child's repudiation of him and to the negative and provocative behavior that the child produces. The behavior from the cottage parents' point of view is bad behavior, "sassiness," impudence, and ingratitude—an indication to the cottage parents that this child needs to learn who is boss. There may be a period of conflict for a while and then we may learn that the child is much improved, that he is settling down in the institution and making a better adjustment. It sometimes happens, as in the case of George, that these achievements, which make the child far easier to live with, were made at the expense of symptoms, ego restrictions, and loss of the capacity to form new ties. The whole process is invisible to the cottage parents and no blame should be attached to their failure to understand this most complex sequence of behavior.

This brings us to examine the prophylactic measures that grow out of such studies of children in placement. The morbid process that eventually brings about a transformation of affects will only be visible to clinically trained eyes. This means that the caseworker of the child in placement must regard the first months following placement as the critical period, the time when the morbid process can be halted and reversed because the affects associated with separation are still available. Direct work with the child during this period and educational work with the cottage parents and other institutional personnel could make this a period of working through the reactions to placement. When grief and longing and reproaches to the parents are regarded as permissible feelings by the cottage parents and such feelings can be communicated to the caseworker by the child, the child may not have to resort to pathological defense. When hostility is transferred to the new objects and to the caseworker himself, cottage parents may be helped to understand the irrational feelings of the child, to see these feelings as displacements, and to deal with them without defensiveness and counter-aggression.

The caseworker, himself, is often the object of the child's hostile feelings —realistically as the person who took the child away from his parents, in fantasy as the kidnapper of helpless children, and as a convenient transference object for hostile feelings toward the parents. If the caseworker makes use of the feelings that have attached themselves to his person and his role and if he makes use of transference reactions to cottage parents and institutional personnel, he can help the child to examine these feelings and to see them also as part of the ambivalence toward the original parents. It should then be possible to work through the ambivalent feelings toward the parents and to help the child find new solutions in his new environment. Only then is the child free to make new attachments in the institution.

Acknowledgments

The writer wishes to express appreciation to these colleagues who collaborated in the program: Miss Ethel van Dyck of the New Orleans Children's Bureau carried major responsibility for the casework treatment in consultation with the writer. Miss Rita Comarda of Tulane University School of Social Work was supervisor of group treatment. Miss Sally Matlock, at that time a student in the Tulane School of Social Work, was leader of the treatment group. Miss Miriam Gaertner, director of the New Orleans Children's Bureau, Miss Adele Eisler, assistant director of the Children's Bureau, and Mrs. Carol Hamrick, director of the Protestant Children's Home, gave generously of their time and counsel throughout our study.

The writer served as coordinator and consultant for the project and carried one child in casework treatment.

Discussion

CATHARINE D. BERWALD: It is a pleasure to hear and discuss a paper which is so interesting and so lucid. The subject is one of tremendous importance for all persons concerned in any way with children who must be placed away from their own homes, whether in institutions or foster homes. The damaging effect of the separation on the child, if the separation is not worked through, is all too familiar. But so often the agencies and workers responsible for these children do not know what to do, and they compound the damage by putting the child through placement after placement without recognizing what the difficulty is. Lack of staff, inadequate facilities, etc., are often given as excuses. The work described in this paper was done, not in a treatment institution nor a psychiatric clinic, but in a custodial institution with no clinically trained staff. This excellent work was done under the direction of one consultant who had the knowledge and experience necessary to define the treatment aims and teach the various people involved what they needed to know to accomplish the aims.

A positive aspect of this work was the deliberate limitation of the therapeutic goal, namely, the working through of the trauma of separation to free the child for new relationships. The case material presented makes clear exactly how the procedures used brought about their results, and those results ought to encourage other agencies to try to do likewise. However, the work described emphasizes the ability of the therapist to know what to say, how and when to say it, and above all, what not to say. This ability is the hallmark of the experienced therapist. It indicates a high degree of training, or an excellence of supervision which is often not available in agencies. There can be a danger in expecting performance beyond the real ability of caseworkers; this is a danger of which Mrs. Fraiberg is well aware, and she has dealt with it in her excellent paper on professional responsibility. Perhaps the answer would be for child placement agencies and institutions to make sure that there is on the staff someone with the necessary training and experience to give the kind of leadership described in this paper.

I was especially happy that Mrs. Fraiberg included a description of the work with the cottage parents and emphasized the importance of teaching them to understand the child and his behavior so that they could support the child's therapy. Her emphasis on the importance of their understanding transference manifestations was of interest. In my own experience such training of cottage parents has been of the greatest importance in enabling them to support individual treatment as well as to handle the children in a way consistent with the therapeutic goals. This kind of training of cottage parents has implications for work with foster parents as well. This is exactly the kind of help foster parents so often need.

The particular use of the group work sessions in conjunction with the individual treatment was intriguing. Our institution has used them in a similar way and I was curious to know more of the details of the coordination of the two in this situation. I would like to know the nature of the contacts with the parents of the children, the handling of visits, and the differences encountered in working through the trauma of separation with children whose parents were no longer in the picture. Of course, this is not at all fair. Mrs. Fraiberg gave us exactly what she said she would, an effective measure to deal with a problem which is so important, and so often neglected. I hope she will write more about this project, but, in the meantime, this paper can be an important influence in the whole field of child welfare because it proves what really can be done to correct the damaging experience of separation in children and to prepare them for the new relationships they so badly need.

A Group Work Approach to the Isolated Child

Ralph L. Kolodny

Physical illnesses or injuries have an emotional impact, whatever their genesis and time of onset. It may be said that, irrespective of a child's emotional adjustment prior to the advent of an incapacitating illness or accident, it is virtually inevitable that emotional difficulties will follow in its wake.

Social group workers must be particularly concerned with the child's problems of social adaptation, which frequently reflect these difficulties and often compound them. Aside from his own hypersensitivity regarding his physical disability, it is more than likely that the physically handicapped child will be confronted in his neighborhood with a group of normal children who at best show but limited tolerance for his inability to participate adequately in play. This may deprive the handicapped child of those intimate associations with peers through which youngsters normally dilute the intensity of their attachment to parents and work out a more realistic and effective relationship with the world outside the home. It also places a heavy burden upon the child's family, who must provide the major resources for his recreational life.

One way to meet the problems inherent in this situation is to provide services for groups of handicapped children who meet in centrally located agencies under various auspices. Here the handicapped child may be able to reach out safely to others his own age, learn to feel more at ease with his condition, and find opportunities as he matures to take action with other handicapped people on matters of common concern. Groups of this kind perform a vital function and their growth has been heartening. They cannot, however, readily be used for homebound children, nor do they directly affect the handicapped child's relationships with his normal peers, the majority group among whom he must make his life. In fact, such groups may serve unwittingly to "ghetto-ize" the handicapped child and inhibit his entry into other relationships and experiences from which he could derive stimulation and gratification, given the proper opportunities and support.

Recognition of these facts has stimulated some organizations and agencies to involve handicapped children in substantial social contacts beyond those they have with their handicapped fellows, and to bring

---

Reprinted with permission of the author and the National Association of Social Workers, from *Social Work*, Vol. 6, No. 3 (July, 1961), pp. 76–85.

handicapped and normal children together in various types of groups.[1] The Department of Neighborhood Clubs of the Boston Children's Service Association has been extremely active in this effort for the past twenty years. Hopefully, our experiences will offer guidelines to others interested in this particular group of children and this important segment of group work practice.

Throughout its existence the department has primarily concerned itself with the socially isolated child.[2] Because of this it has been called upon to provide service to boys and girls with a wide variety of physical handicaps, including a number who are homebound. These children are referred by hospital social service departments, specialized agencies for the handicapped, and—occasionally—parents. In most instances the department does not place these children in groups made up of others who are similarly handicapped. Its usual procedure is, instead, to form a club around each of the referred children in his own neighborhood, the other members of the club being drawn from among his physically normal peers. This provides the handicapped child with an opportunity to participate in the kind of group experience that would ordinarily be inaccessible to him because of his physical limitations, the reluctance of his peers to reach out to him, or his own reticence.

There are many questions to be considered in any undertaking of this kind. The issues range from those of a medical, psychodynamic, or group dynamic nature to those which relate to staff development, interagency relationships, and costs.[3] Of central importance are questions pertaining to intake, group formation, and programing. The following material focuses on these three aspects of the department's work and illustrates the procedures and problems involved in each. It also suggests the type of contribution this approach can make to the over-all rehabilitation of the handicapped child.

Intake Policies and Group Formation

The department has consciously avoided formulating a detailed and fixed set of policies regarding the kinds of children whom we will accept for service. Our feeling is that with our present knowledge it would be premature for group work agencies to establish neatly defined criteria in this regard. It

---

[1] Among such agencies have been the Community Council of Greater New York, through its demonstration project on group work with the handicapped; the Girl Scouts and Boy Scouts of America, and the New York Herald Tribune Fresh Air Fund.

[2] For a general description of the department's service see Ralph Kolodny, "Research Planning and Group Work Practice," *Mental Hygiene,* Vol. 42, No. 1 (January 1958).

[3] Some of these issues have been discussed in other presentations or articles. See Marjory Warren, "Meeting the Specialized Needs of Handicapped Children Through Group Work," *Proceedings of the Tenth Governors' Conference on Exceptional Children* (Chicago: State of Illinois, Commission for Handicapped Children, 1953); and Ralph Kolodny, "Therapeutic Group Work with Handicapped Children," *Children,* Vol. 4, No. 3 (May-June 1957).

is important that considerable latitude be permitted a department such as this if it is to explore the boundaries of group work with the handicapped and is not to exclude children whose situations appear on the surface to be untreatable, but who might actually be reached by this service. We do have criteria upon which the disposition of referrals is based, but these are broadly conceived rather than sharply defined.

In order to be accepted for service the child must be socially isolated or likely to become so after hospitalization. He cannot be so intellectually retarded that he will have obvious and continuous difficulty in understanding children his own age. He may be emotionally disturbed, but not to the extent that he will be unlikely to tolerate relationships with others in a group or have any interest in program activities.[4] The child need not be ambulatory, but if he is not, he must be able to engage in a substantial range of sedentary activities. If these requirements are not met and a case cannot be accepted, the department helps the referring agency to find other resources for helping the child.

The department's acceptance of a referral does not, of course, bind the child referred and his parents to accept the service. Preliminary interpretation of the service is made to them by the referring medical social worker, but it remains for the group worker, through one or more home interviews, to make the final interpretation. If during these interviews the child and his parents decide they wish the service (in a substantial majority they do), the worker then begins the process of forming a group.[5]

Suggestions for potential group members are usually first obtained from the youngster and his mother. If they are not in a position to suggest members, the worker, with their permission, then uses neighborhood schools or agencies as resources for this purpose. As he discusses suggested members with parents or with school or agency personnel, he keeps the following requirements in mind in assessing their suitability for the group: *1]* the member should be about the same age as the referred child;   *2]* he should be able to accept a limited and sometimes sedentary type of program;   *3]* he must be able to control impulses to act out physically;   *4]* he should not be so competitive that he will be unable to tolerate the demands for attention which the referred child may make upon the leader;   *5]* he should not have displayed excessive fear of the referred child's condition if he has had previous contacts with him; and   *6]* there should be some likelihood of his being enthusiastic about the idea of a club as something he himself might enjoy.

Following these discussions the worker makes home visits to suggested

---

[4] The existence of an emotional disorder in a case referred for service becomes one more factor to be assessed. Evaluation of its implications for group work can be made by the worker, who has the benefit of the suggestions of the child's therapist, if there is such, and the advice of the department's psychiatric consultant. It is not considered by itself a sufficient reason for nonacceptance of a referral.

[5] In 1956, for example, in 9 of the 12 cases referred the parents and the child decided that they wanted the service.

members and their parents in order to interpret and enlist their interest in the group. Unless he is patently unsuited for the group, if a suggested member indicates a desire to join, he is allowed to do so. While this policy sometimes leads to difficulties, a rigid screening system for membership would be most difficult to operate. The use of diagnostic testing in order to evaluate suitability for membership, for example, would give rise to many complications. Even were parents to permit such testing, which is unlikely, the procedure would lead to serious problems arising from the exclusion of some of the children tested. Moreover, the selection of members according to narrowly specific criteria is often made unfeasible by the limitations of the peer population in the neighborhood.

The groups the department forms are kept purposely small—usually from five to eight members. Most begin by meeting in the handicapped child's home. As soon as it is feasible, however, meeting places are rotated so that the homes of other members are used as well. If a youth-serving agency exists in the neighborhood, meetings may be held there, occasionally at first and later regularly. The choice of meeting place and the process of movement to other meeting places depend upon a combination of factors: medical restrictions on the handicapped child's movement, his emotional readiness to leave his own home for meetings, the physical suitability of the home for meetings, the availability of neighborhood resources, and the age of group members.

Problems During Referral and Formation Periods

The problems that develop during the referral and formation period are equal in importance to those that arise once the group is under way and must be given equally close attention. We have found it necessary to disabuse ourselves of the notion that parents, in their gratitude for an opportunity to move the handicapped child out of isolation, will welcome this service without reservation. Most parents, of course, want their children to lead less constricted lives. At the same time, it is only natural for them, because of the various pressures to which they have been subjected in the course of their children's illnesses, to display some ambivalence when presented with the offer of this service. Isolation of the child may be bad, but exposure also has its drawbacks and parents have strong feelings about it. Under these circumstances close contact between the referring agency and the department becomes particularly necessary during the referral and formation period. Both the referring caseworker and the group worker must be prepared to be quite active at this time. Through accepting parental anxieties and hostilities, searching with parents for contributions they can make to the group, and showing an interest in parents as individuals, they can support them to a point where they will be able with some security to share the child with a new outsider.

Parental ambivalence is not always severe or immediately obvious, but its existence is inevitable. The group worker, therefore, must be alert to its presence and, when it is extreme, willing to understand and move with the parent as he or she hesitates, vacillates, and behaves in what may appear to be an immature way. Mrs. L, mother of a 7-year-old girl with nephritis, offers a case in point. She displayed some interest in a club for her daughter when the caseworker at the hospital spoke to her about it. The department worker who telephoned her later discovered, however, that she had some reservations. The worker suggested that she could visit Mrs. L at home to discuss them, but Mrs. L thought she would rather come to the office. An appointment was made for the next week. On the morning for which it was scheduled Mrs. L called to ask for a new time. This was set. Shortly afterward the department worker called the caseworker at the hospital and was surprised to learn the following:

> Mrs. L had come to the hospital social service office that morning and it was from here that she had called to cancel the appointment. She had made no appointment with Miss N (the caseworker) but had "just dropped in." Mrs. L had expressed much concern about the club to Miss N. She was afraid Alice (her daughter) wouldn't know how to play with other children. Miss N explained that this would be the purpose of the group, to help Alice learn to play with children her own age. Mrs. L wanted to know specifically what the group would do and Miss N mentioned that the group worker would help the members to carry out their own ideas. When Mrs. L expressed some concern that Alice wouldn't have any ideas, Miss N reassured her that the group worker would also have ideas and suggestions. Miss N reported that by the time she left Mrs. L seemed interested in the group again. Miss N believed that Mrs. L is feeling guilty about having someone else come in and do what she thinks should be her job. It became apparent, she said, that actually Alice doesn't have any friends. When Mrs. L wondered where the group members would come from, Miss N was able to reassure her by pointing out that they could come from the immediate neighborhood or nearby school.

The department worker sent a letter or reminder to Mrs. L about the next appointment, but she again canceled. She did, however, respond favorably to the renewed offer of a home visit. She and her daughter were at home when the worker came and a thorough exploration of their questions took place. The group began to meet a month later. Shortly afterward Mrs. L had another interview with the caseworker, who called the department worker and advised her that Mrs. L "seemed much more relieved about the group and was very pleased."

It is necessary also to recognize what this new experience means to the handicapped child himself and to realize that, along with the promised pleasure, it poses a threat of sorts. The group worker needs to try to reduce the child's anxiety over participation in a club by seeing him several times before the group begins to meet and building a relationship through which the child can begin to perceive him as a source of support. During these contacts he can also help the child by relating this experience to other experiences with which the child is familiar and to skills and interests he has already developed.

Objectives

Once a group begins to meet, the leader's basic objective in his work with the handicapped child is to help him to function within the limits imposed by his handicap, but also to learn through experience the range of activities and relationships available to him despite his physical condition. Care is exercised not to deny the child's incapacities or force him to compensate for a lack of ability by becoming hyperactive. The aim is to help him discover, through testing in a protected situation, alternatives to social withdrawal or overcompensation.

Within the context of this objective various goals are developed, not only on the basis of the child's physical handicap, but also in relation to his feelings toward himself and his conception of the attitudes of others toward him. For example, in cases where the handicapped child is a homebound boy, one of the department's objectives is to provide reinforcement, through a male leader and peer group, for the child's sense of his own masculine identity. His exclusive association with his mother for long periods makes this important.

Helping the child to develop and begin to follow through on realistic vocational goals is an important objective in work with the severely handicapped youngster, who may keep this matter on the level of fantasy unless the worker, through programing and marginal interviews, enables him to take concrete steps in this direction. This attention to vocational goals, expressing the worker's confidence in the child's adequacy, can also increase the child's faith in his own capabilities.

Although the worker does not focus directly on helping the child to gain insight into, and resolve, the basic feelings associated with his handicap through the group experience, he is concerned with helping him to face and handle more adequately the problems in social relationships that accompany it. He is therefore interested in reducing whatever need the child may have to deny the reality of his handicap. At the same time, especially with the homebound child, one of the worker's objectives is frankly, through activities, sometimes to divert the child from preoccupation with his condition. Excitement and change in the life of such a child are too often confined to negative experiences such as a reinjury or recurrence of symptoms. The club gives him an opportunity to anticipate a potentially pleasurable event each week and to develop relationships with others which may afford him emotional gratification between meetings. This can help to relieve some of the depression associated with his condition.

In speaking of goals it should also be made clear at this point that, although by design this paper is focused exclusively on the handicapped child himself, this is not the case in the leader's actual work with the group. On the contrary, he is concerned with and attentive to the feelings and interests of all the members. Department workers pay close attention to the developmental needs of each group member and are also prepared to help with crises in the lives of members both within and outside the club whenever these occur. Adolescent members of a department club, for example, use this type of group as they would any other, for ventilation, information, and support around heterosexual matters, educational and vocational aspirations, and the problems of growing independence from the family. They are encouraged to do so by the worker, who uses his understanding of individual and group dynamics and his program skills to provide guidance and outlets in these areas to all the members. In addition, department workers from the very outset make themselves available as social workers to the families of all members of their groups and are frequently called upon to counsel parents or help them to use appropriate social, psychological, or medical resources. The department does not regard the normal children as figures to be exploited for the benefit of the handicapped child. While the latter may have a markedly greater need for relationships than other members, our aim is to make his association with them *mutually* advantageous.

There are five major aspects of the approach used by the worker in helping the handicapped child to move toward the goals described. These are:

1.   Accepting the handicapped child's maladaptive behavior, such as overdependence, denial, and overcompensation or withdrawal.

2.   As trust develops, helping him to become more aware of the effects of this behavior on his relationships with others, and of alternatives to it.

3.   Enabling other members to react without undue deference or serious antagonism to his demands on the worker by giving them consistent individual attention, which includes the provision of opportunities for the ventilating of feeling about this experience.

4.   Beginning with program activities well within his ability and even sometimes giving him special preparation for them.

5.   Later, challenging his tendency to cling to the familiar through exposing him to carefully planned activities which are not beyond him, but which do clearly call upon him to extend himself.

In implementing these steps the worker must give careful attention to the conditions governing group interaction which are created by the presence of a youngster who is in some ways severely limited in his physical movement and whose feelings are profoundly affected by this limitation. The kinds of considerations to which the worker must pay heed might best be illustrated by a discussion of some of the issues involved in the use of program activities in a group of this type.

Programing

In groups composed of physically normal children, shoving, pulling, hugging, and wrestling are often prominent features of social interaction. The handicapped child and the members of his group, however, must exercise considerable restraint in regard to the direct expression of feeling through physical activity. The handicapped child may be fearful of his own aggressive impulses—active physical contact with another youngster may be actually dangerous for him. The other members must in some cases curb their tendency to grab or push, even in a mild way, and the usual opportunities for aggressive play of a direct sort may be denied them in this setting. Under these conditions it is important that the group's program include activities through which the generalized aggression that members may feel can be expressed and sublimated. In groups in which the handicapped child has very limited ambulation and there can be only minimal physical activity, the worker can still provide experiences through which aggressive impulses may be expressed in a controlled and enjoyable manner. The effect of the activities the worker introduces in order to provide those experiences depends, in large part, upon his relationship with the members. If he is unable to accept even verbal expressions of hostility among members or toward himself, no activity he uses is likely to provide appropriate channels for aggression. If, however, the worker feels some hostility to be inevitable, is prepared to accept it, and believes that aggression can be utilized for constructive ends, he can create a climate in which sublimation can take place.

In devising activities for this purpose he may rely on a variety of media. Wide use can be made of materials that can be struck and pounded. Clay modeling and woodworking are, of course, quite useful in this connection. Balloons may be substituted for balls in games which require throwing and hitting. Other media are also available. In round-robin story-telling, for example, in which one member begins and the others continue a story, an opportunity is afforded members to ventilate hostility if they wish and to exercise their creative urge at the same time. Some sedentary games provide youngsters with a chance to "attack" without hurting or being hurt and to "fight" without destroying. The game of "battleship" is of this type. In this game through plotting ship locations on a sheet of graphed paper, youngsters can figuratively sink each other's vessels until one team's fleet is "destroyed." Anticipation and excitement are built into this kind of game, and for the handicapped child especially, but for other members as well, there is an opportunity to release aggression that is potentially beneficial to all concerned. For, under these circumstances, youngsters may be helped to understand that, although giving vent to aggressive impulses through physical movement against another person cannot be countenanced in this type of club, the expression of aggression in some forms is natural, permissible, and constructive.

Although a well-structured and stimulating program is essential to the development of this type of group, it is important not to overemphasize this aspect of club life. Since the range of physical activity of members is limited by the presence of the handicapped child, a worker may feel under some compulsion continually to encourage the use of program activities which will create a "lively" atmosphere in the group. Implicit in this is the assumption that the handicapped child and his fellow members can only be happy when they are intensely involved in specific projects that engage all their attention. Unless he is careful, the worker may reinforce the handicapped child's tendency to rely excessively on organized projects and games as a basis for relating to others. Often such a child feels uncomfortable or even threatened if he has to relate without such props; though they bring him in contact with others, they enable him at the same time to maintain his psychological distance. While in the initial stages of the group these external supports may be essential, as the group develops the worker should encourage the attempts of members to discover spontaneous ways of relating to one another. It should also be recognized that the handicapped child in particular needs opportunities to disengage himself from activities without feeling disapproval by the worker or the other members of the group. It is important that he be given latitude to *be* with others without continually having to *do* something.

One of the persistent themes that runs through the program of a group is that of "movement." The worker is interested in helping the handicapped child to mobilize whatever capacities he has to move physically and to move out to others emotionally. It is expected that the personal investment of the worker in the child's emotional growth will be great. It should also be recognized, however, that he may likewise come to have a substantial stake in the expansion of the child's physical movement. This may stem from his concern that the child improve in every respect, but it may also be related to his own inability to face the child's realistic physical limitations. Consequently, there is always the possibility that a worker will overestimate a youngster's physical capabilities and program accordingly. This may not cause irreparable damage, but it does create unnecessary difficulties and reinforces whatever inability the child has to function within the bounds of his handicap.

To be sure, a worker will want actively to help a child make maximum use of his physical abilities. When increased physical activity can be of benefit to the child, a worker does well to devote substantial efforts to seeking out and using outside resources as well as the club program itself for promoting this.

Even as he looks for opportunities to help the child in this way, however, the worker has to avoid an exaggerated emphasis on increasing his physical activity, and to be wary lest—rationalizing his approach by saying he does not want to repeat in the group the inhibiting overprotection a youngster is receiving at home—he subtly pressure him to move beyond his physical limits. Naturally the worker wishes to avoid being overprotective. Perhaps the most direct way to accomplish this, however, is to make sure that any activity which clearly has an element of danger in it for the handicapped child is kept out of the program of the group; in this way the leader will not be forced to be unnecessarily protective.

Effects of the Service

Questions of formation and programing are interesting, of course, but what of results? Have we seen improvement in the attitudes or behavior of handicapped children in our groups? We have seen constructive changes. We are fully aware of the complexity of this matter and the need for caution in making judgments. We have had our share of difficulties and failures. Our experiences do lead us to believe, however, that a service such as that offered by the department can be of substantial psychological benefit to many physically handicapped children.

In the case of Steve, a 12-year-old double amputee, one sees this in the contrast between the youngster's frightened response to his club's first cookout and his reaction to this same activity a year later. The first time, despite his expression of interest and intensive preparation by the worker, Steve could not bring himself to go. He did not come to the assembly point, and when the worker stopped by his house he found Steve had suffered an anxiety attack and had been left exhausted by a severe siege of vomiting. Steve and his mother were distraught at this point and expected rejection by the worker, who had to go to considerable lengths to reassure them before going off with the group.

Some months later, however, after intensive work with Steve in the group and with his mother and Steve outside it, the youngster was able to consider going on another cook-out when this was proposed at a club meeting. This time he was ready at the appointed hour, and although at first fearful that he would be in some way overwhelmed, he soon entered into the activity with great spirit, helping to set the fire, volunteering for clean-up, and even participating in a baseball game after arrangements were made so that he could play. Throughout the afternoon he kept telling the worker what a pleasant surprise everything was.

For Linda, an 11-year-old-girl with *spina bifida*, the benefits of the service became apparent after many months when she was able finally to relate, first to the worker and then to her fellow members, without anxiously concealing some of the more unpleasant aspects of her physical condition. Having come to trust in her acceptance by others, she could treat such things as her use of a catheter quite openly rather than as a dark secret. This, in turn, made it possible for her to share happily in important new areas of activity with the other members. These developments were recorded by the worker, who first began to notice a change in the youngster on one occasion when she met her at school before a trip. Linda's catheter had become caught in the upper part of her brace, causing her some discomfort. When the worker offered to help, Linda reacted with embarrassment. Their ensuing conversation is described by the worker as follows:

I asked her if she felt funny talking to me about things like the catheter. Linda said she didn't like to think about it. I said that it was certainly easy to understand that she might be sensitive about being different from most people in this respect, adding, "But you know, Linda, I can still like you and want you to like me." Linda grinned broadly and commented that she thought I was the best club leader she had ever had.

Several weeks later when some of the members suggested an "overnight" at camp the worker was struck by Linda's ready assent and her subsequent eagerness to go. All Linda asked was that she have "some privacy." When the group planned for the trip at a later meeting Linda spoke quite openly of the medical supplies and apparatus she would have to take along. On the "overnight" itself her growing assurance and comfort with the physical aspects of her handicap became clearly apparent. At bedtime Linda permitted the worker to accompany her to the bathroom while she emptied her catheter bag, and then indicated that she wouldn't mind if the girls stayed in the room while she changed her clothing, as long as they kept looking at the fire and toasting marshmallows. The worker describes her behavior as follows:

> Linda spoke throughout in a normal tone of voice about these more personal things and the other girls could hear very easily what was being said. She apparently feels very much at home with them. They, in turn, evinced little interest in what she was doing, whatever their underlying curiosity. After everyone had changed into her pajamas, they went to bed and, after talking a bit, fell asleep. When we visited town the next day Linda declined offers of being pushed, and wheeled herself around the shops. She was showing a noticeable amount of independence by this time and I was not asked to push the chair or lift and carry as much as before.

In some instances there occurs a substantial alteration in the handicapped youngster's capacity to respond positively to the demands of approaching adulthood. This is seen in the following abstract from a summary report of Tim, who was referred to the department by a medical social worker when he was 13.

> Tim suffered from a rare congenital disease of the skeleton characterized by brittle bones, and had sustained 25 fractures during the first 13 years of his life. He was referred to the department because he was profoundly isolated from his peers. An extremely intelligent youngster, Tim had many scientific interests. He rarely followed through on these interests, however, but confined himself to fantasies about becoming a scientist. We attempted to help him give concrete expression to his vocational aspirations and learn ways of fulfilling them realistically. During the three years his group was in existence Tim and his fellow members were introduced through various program activities to a variety of scientific projects and procedures. He developed hobbies around electronics and radio. The department worked closely with Tim's home teacher in encouraging these hobbies. At the age of 16, having had no fractures for three years, Tim began to attend high school. He did extremely well there, displaying a genuine talent in technical subjects and a striking ability to make friends with his classmates. Tim is now a college sophomore and on the way to a scientific career.

There are, of course, many problems and questions connected with our approach which will continue to concern us and which demand intensive study. We need, for example, to extend and deepen our knowledge of the impact of this type of group experience on the normal as well as the handicapped children who participate in it. We need better understanding of how to handle the tensions that sometimes arise between the handicapped child and his parents as a result of the increased independence the child has acquired through the group experience. As we help the child to relate to his normal peers we also have to learn more about how to help him, at the same time, to feel comfortable with and a part of his own minority group, the physically handicapped. Finally, we not only need to increase our understanding of the meaning of the behavior of group members but must also constantly examine our own feelings as workers in this kind of situation.

The investigation of problems such as these presents all group workers with a continuous and arduous task. If, however, we are persistent in carrying it out; we can with greater assurance help handicapped children in increasing numbers to participate in and draw emotional nourishment from group experiences with their peers.

Social Casework with Elementary School Children Who Do Not Talk in School

Erma Blethen Parker, Trunette F. Olsen, and Margaret C. Throckmorton

To be quiet and to say nothing in a new, strange, and frightening situation is an understood and familiar ego defense. Beginning school involves leaving the mother's support and entering into new relationships. Most children show some transitory difficulties either at home or at school or in both settings, as they move into greater independence and the beginning of the learning process at school. Entrance into school is a critical point at which the socialization of the child is assessed in terms of the expectations of the kindergarten teacher and the intrinsic demands of the school situation itself. One of these expectations is the use of speech. Absence of verbal interaction is not only frustrating to the teacher but interferes with the entire educational process.

Since the inception of the school social work program in the Tacoma Public Schools in 1947, children who do not talk at school but speak elsewhere have continued to come to the attention of the staff. A study of this

Reprinted with permission of the authors and the National Association of Social Workers, from *Social Work*, Vol. 5, No. 2 (April, 1960), pp. 64–70.

problem was begun two years ago as a staff project. A survey of the literature in the field revealed a paucity of relevant papers and it is hoped that this preliminary study will stimulate others to publish their findings and case material.

Frame of Reference

The school social work program in Tacoma, which is part of the Division of Guidance and Special Services, was established after careful study of programs in other cities by a Guidance Committee composed of teachers, speech correctionists, and principals. The committee recommended that the service be headed by a psychiatric social worker and that staff members hold the M.S.W. degree. This recommended standard has been maintained.

Each social worker is responsible for consultation and casework services in three or four elementary schools, or for a population of approximately 1,700 pupils in kindergarten through the sixth grade. During 1958–59 the twelve school social workers served over 10 percent of the 19,000 elementary school children in Tacoma Public Schools either through consultation alone (6 percent) to teachers and principals, or additionally (4 percent) through direct casework services.

Referral for direct casework service is ordinarily initiated jointly by teachers and principals, often in informal conferences with the school social worker. Such referrals are accompanied by a written request. A study period of three to four weeks is begun by the school social worker, who may observe the child in the classroom, and who ordinarily has a diagnostic interview with the child as well as several interviews with his parents. The teacher is encouraged to keep anecdotal records of the child's behavior. This information is supplemented by reports from the principal and other teachers and often from the school nurse, the speech correctionist, and community agencies. The child's school record is studied. Additional psychological evaluations, including intelligence tests and projective studies, may be requested.

Psychiatric examination and consultation are available through a close working relationship with the community child guidance clinic and the community clinic for the study of mental retardation. For the past several years school-supported psychiatric consultation has been provided from special state funds. Private and clinic pediatric and neurological services are also utilized.

Scope of the Study

A review of case files from September 1947 through January 1959 revealed that there were 27 children referred for casework service who did not talk at school although they talked at home, and whose intellectual and physical development appeared to be within normal limits at the time of referral. Since more than 3,600 children received casework service during this period, the 13 girls and 14 boys under study comprised only about .7 percent of this number. Overall caseload ratio has been two boys to one girl. No significant difference in incidence of this symptom from year to year was found.

This is one symptom which has caused early referrals. Nineteen were referred during kindergarten, six during the first three months of first grade, and the remaining two children almost immediately after they entered the Tacoma school system in grades two and four.

Some use of speech in the classroom was reported in all cases prior to closing although this was minimal for one boy who moved to another city after four months. Two cases were closed in less than three months; 16, in from three to nine months; eight, in one and one-half to two years. Only one case remained open over two years. At the time of statistical review five cases were currently active.

Review of the 27 case records indicated that despite the unique constellation of each case, certain common problem patterns were discernible. Five children appeared to be reacting to stress because of environmental or cultural changes.[1] These cases included a boy whose father had died and whose timid mother moved the family from an isolated farm to Tacoma; two children who had experienced the loss of their mothers because of mental illness and hospitalization; and two Chinese brothers, twelve months apart in age, who started kindergarten at the same time. Brief casework services alleviated the symptom in these cases. These five children have been excluded from the discussion of dynamics which follows, as well as four children who were referred as having normal ability but were assessed by later psychological study as moderately retarded.[2] In the remaining 18 cases under discussion, the symptom was seen as based upon neurotic factors within the family structure. The discussion of dynamics in these cases must be viewed as a preliminary report awaiting further intensive studies of a larger number of cases.

In school, nonspeaking may be described as a passively hostile way of

[1] In a number of additional situations, not included in the study because there were no direct casework services, staff members have been consulted by teachers about children whose muteness in school followed severe environmental changes. One first-grade girl was adopted from a German orphanage by an army couple who shortly thereafter came to Tacoma. A first-grade boy, the youngest of a large family, was born in the Deep South and reared by grandparents in an isolated rural area. At five he was brought to live with his mother in a crowded urban district in Tacoma. With support and reassurance from the teacher and the family, these and other children who had experienced severe environmental changes began talking in school.

[2] Difficulty was encountered in psychological assessment of these children because of their speech inhibitions or refusal to speak at all in the testing situation. For example, one child, initially reported as having an I.Q. of 76, in a later study after casework treatment, attained an I.Q. of 99, which still was thought to represent less than his true ability. This child is now achieving academically at a superior level in junior high school despite a residual expressive handicap. Psychological studies assessed four other children as moderately retarded, one because of brain damage.

controlling the environment. This passive behavior frustrated the classroom teacher's basic function of education and aroused reactions of anxiety, concern, and irritation. In many nonverbal ways these children expressed defiance and resistance to authority. One teacher reported that a first-grade boy while drawing or painting consistently reversed colors, *e.g.*, using black when others used white. During a psychiatric examination, one child displayed indications of her hostility by letting things roll off the table and crash and letting them stay where they fell, breaking the crayons and splintering the pounding board.

Characteristics of Children and Parents

The dependency needs of these children were seen as excessive. Eleven of these 18 children were reported as not participating in any classroom activities at the time of referral. Several kindergarten children refused to remove their coats or hats and would not enter the classroom without being led. A teacher described one of these children as "frozen the first month of school—stood where left by older brother." Typically, other children in the classroom assumed a protective attitude, answering for the nonspeaking child, interpreting him to the teacher, and carrying out errands for him. The child's unspoken request for services in school might be viewed as both a passively hostile way of controlling the environment and an expression of the child's excessive dependency needs.

Fear and anxiety were considered to be components in these cases. Repeatedly it appeared that the child had been instilled with parental fears and anxieties. In some instances the child's fears appeared to be due to mouth injury and/or mouth punishment, such as slapping. In one case a kindergarten boy had a mouth injury superimposed upon an infantile heart condition (paroxysmal tachycardia) which had required the mother's twenty-four hour vigilance for the first eighteen months of his life. The removal of two abscessed teeth at three and a half, after the dentist had sent the mother out of the room, was seen as a traumatic incident for this child, occurring as it did in a relationship already suffused with anxiety. In another case the mother would slap the child across the mouth if the little girl said displeasing things. In both instances it was felt that the mouth became associated with pain and anxiety and that this influenced the choice of the symptom. The child's unspoken formulation might have been "It's dangerous to open your mouth." In confirmation of this the caseworker of the boy noted that he covered his mouth with his hand, as if to protect it the first time he laughed aloud in a play therapy session. Another child covered his mouth while answering questions during a psychological examination. The psychiatrist suggested that these children would be more apt to reply to questions if the social worker turned his back.

A number of these children had suffered severe or prolonged illnesses which involved separation from the mother, as in the three early hospitalizations of the boy whose infantile heart condition has been described. A girl had been hospitalized every winter with severe bronchial asthma. Another girl had severe allergies and a traumatic hospitalization at one year of age. Another child was a premature infant. Several of these children developed temper tantrums and refused to permit the mothers to leave them.

Intense jealousy of the younger children was found frequently. This appeared to occur when resentment was chiefly focused upon the mother and mother figures. The overstrong and infantile character of these children's attachment to the mother made displacement by a new baby especially difficult.

Frequently it seemed that no real separation from the mother had occurred. There was often a clinging quality to the child's relationship with the mother. Four of these children had a history of a reluctance to come to school, which was attributed to the mother's inability to relinquish the child to the school. Since the relationship with the mother had not permitted the emergence of the normal, independent self expected at this point of development, these children were not able to function in school away from the mother.

Children studied who used nonspeaking as their chief mode of defense in school seemed both very dependent upon their parents and at the same time angry with them, the hostility being directed more often toward the mother. As supporting evidence it might be cited that in several instances these children were reported to talk more freely with men than with women at home and elsewhere. Overt expressions of hostility were seldom reported among these children at the time of referral.

Parents of the children studied seemed as a group to be anxious and fearful, especially the mothers. Typically mothers of these children were described in case records as "timid," "shy," "nervous and upset," "overprotective," and "overpossessive." Some parents reported that they had always been afraid of new situations. Some fathers had been slow to talk in school and one father had stuttered as a boy. In a number of cases illnesses of these children had made unusually heavy emotional and physical demands upon parents. A strong ambivalent tie to the child frequently appeared to exist. There were often indications of an overprotective relationship with the child. Some parents were reported to be overcontrolling and others were reported to be unable to set limits with their children. As a group these parents appeared outwardly passive and relatively inactive socially. Several parents themselves were reported as resorting to nonspeaking when angry. In general, parental relationships lacked the relaxed ease of healthy parent-child relationships in which the child is helped to move appropriately toward independence.

The following dynamic factors were viewed as significant in the choice of the symptom of withheld speech in these eighteen children.

1.   Mouth injury or mouth trauma at the time a child was learning speech or severe or prolonged illness at this time especially in conjunction with separation from the mother.

2. Family patterns of nonspeaking—either on the part of parents when they themselves were young, or current patterns of nonspeaking as a retaliatory expression of hostility on the part of adults within the family.

3. Unsatisfactory nature of the mother-child relationship. The symbiotic relationship had not been resolved and deep feelings of frustration, with resultant anger, were experienced by both mother and child. The mouth remained cathected since normal infancy gratification had not been achieved.

Treatment

Treatment of the child in whom this symptom is diagnosed as neurotically based customarily operates on three fronts simultaneously. It involves working closely with teacher, parents, and child.

Teacher-Worker Conferences

The school social worker and teacher need to communicate freely as they plan together how they may help the child resolve his problems. Recognition of some of the stresses involved for the teacher is important. When a child's silence does not yield either to time or friendly effort the teacher may feel that this is due to something she has done or has failed to do. She feels at a loss to know what she should expect from the child or from herself. Frequently she does not know that there are other nonspeaking children in the school system. Letting her know that this does happen to other children and that this symptom when persistent is part of a tenacious syndrome may reduce her anxiety.

Classroom management is an area the teacher is immediately interested in discussing. The teacher needs to understand the significance of the passive role which the child has established in relation to other children. An early objective is to reduce as quickly as possible these secondary gains arising from the protective attitude of other children. Their activities, although seemingly helpful, obscure the one-to-one relationship between teacher and child. The teacher has to realize that she is the one who should be helping the child in the minimal necessary ways. Some dependency gratifications cannot be avoided since the teacher provides some gains by acting as the child's liaison with the group. However, an important shift in balance is achieved which brings the child and teacher closer together as he looks to her for help. This strengthens the teacher's feeling of control of the situation.

The worker can help the teacher understand that each small step toward independence represents real progress for the child. As the teacher feels more confident in her relationship with him she can communicate in nonverbal ways, as well as directly, her assurance that he can do many things for himself. Her relaxed manner can imply that he will respond when he is ready, thus preventing mounting tension. When the child's class participation increases, he wins respect from his classmates as they see him become more self-directed. As treatment progresses the teacher is often able to suggest classroom activities which, while holding general values for all, have specific therapeutic value for the nonspeaking child.

Work with Parents

Full participation of the parents, especially the mother, is of crucial importance. The information that her child does not talk at school when he is verbal at home may come as a surprise to the mother, although more frequently she has been aware of the child's shyness with strangers, including children. Nevertheless, she may feel that responsibility for the situation lies with the school. The mother needs the worker's sensitive understanding of her feelings of bewilderment, frustration, and worry as she tries to comprehend her child's situation.

Understanding begins with the discussion of the child's significant life experiences. Sometimes the events or conjunction of events which became traumatic for this particular child are not easy to identify, for the parents may not consider early experiences around a health problem, a family move from one location to another, or the birth of a sibling as having any causal connection. A careful exploration is necessary because so often traumatic events have occurred within the first two years of life. The task of remembering occurrences, dates, and sequences uses the parents' concern in a constructive manner and allays the possible threat to their adequacy in the parental role.

The adequacy of the parents must be supported by the school social worker as he and they examine not only the objective facts of the child's early experiences, but also the nature of the bond which grew up between them, fashioned as it was of external events and internal perception of these events by both child and parents. Whatever these events, their emotional equivalents have resulted in a disturbance of normal parent-child relationships, crippling the child's ability to differentiate and to attain wholesome levels of independence. As the parents' frustrations are accepted and their feelings put into words, their burden of guilt is reduced and they can be freed for deeper understanding of the situation in which they and the child are caught. The separation and individuation of parent and child thereby begins to evolve.

The worker anticipates with the parents the expected expressions at home of hostility as the child becomes less constricted in his expression of feelings. Overt expressions of anger toward the parents are usually difficult for them to accept since such behavior on the part of the child is ordinarily new. They need to understand and tolerate regressive expressions also, and to see them as evidence of movement. The parents need help in appreciating the child's need to move toward independence, as well as his fear of it. As the child's fear of his feelings diminishes he is helped to learn acceptable ways of expressing himself. The worker remains alert and responsive to the parents' own adaptive difficulties as growth and change occur in the child.

Treatment of the Child

Casework with the child is directed toward the development of a more stable and differentiated ego. This is undertaken in direct work with the child, although sometimes the child is initially unable to accept the worker without the presence and participation of the mother. The school is an appropriate setting for work toward release of the child's immobilizing fear and anger, since these emotions, basic to the difficulty, are exacerbated by the physical removal from the mother's presence. The child, aware that his behavior differs, is told in the beginning the reasons for his interviews with the caseworker. He is confronted with the expectation that he can change. The following case excerpt illustrates the beginning of treatment with a first-grade child.

> Deena was prepared for help from the caseworker by the teacher and the mother. Although she had become acquainted with me in the classroom, it was necessary to lead her by the hand from the classroom to the play therapy room for many weeks. At first Deena simply stood by the table upon which I had placed a variety of materials. She touched nothing, said nothing, just stood. There were long periods of silence which were broken by me. In a quiet tone I verbalized such feelings as "Sometimes it is hard to choose;" "Sometimes one is afraid to do things;" "Sometimes we want to do things but can't;" and "We don't like it when people tell us what to do." At times I would say, "This is your chance to choose and do what you want to." After another long silence, "Maybe you're afraid of me and wonder what I am going to say." Then I would reassure her that with me nothing was expected of her and that she could do as she pleased, but that she was going to see me once a week for an hour. She was told that she might be very mad at me for making her come, but because it was hard for her to talk to kids and do the things that other kids did in school she would be coming to see me. Maybe after awhile it would be easier for her to do the things she wanted to do herself.
>
> The first session Deena stood the whole time, but in the second hour after about twenty minutes she touched some of the toys in a gingerly way but did not play with them. In the third session she picked up some of the dolls and put them back in the box. During this time she was telling the mother that she liked to come to see me because there were so many things to play with. By the fourth session Deena manipulated the toys as soon as she came into the room, moving some of the toy cars one after another.

As the school social worker assesses the resistance of the child he can formulate definite goals. These children commonly need assistance in utilizing play materials, and the worker is often directive through his choice of materials and activities. It is easier to use the darts or the baby bottle if they are out in plain sight. Often it is well to verbalize what the child obviously feels. The worker represents both school and adult world to the child, including parents. Both become less threatening as the child's fears are diluted and drained by the worker's attitude, especially the child's fears of his aggressive impulses. As repression is relaxed by the child, energy may at first be expressed in primitive forms. A useful technique for assisting the child to cope with instinctual drives is the traditional, "Let's pretend." By use of this technique children can often master their fear through identification with the aggressor as they act out the aggressor's role in play. This is illustrated in the case of a kindergarten child where the diagnosis of severe early mouth traumata associated with dental work was confirmed by the psychiatric consultant.[3]

> The psychiatrist recommended that work be done with Martin involving orifices, with objects put into them and taken out, such as a ball into a basket. This was well tolerated by Martin, and I moved on to the use of clay. With the comment that I had to go to the dentist to get my teeth fixed, I made a shallow bowl of clay which, with bits of clay affixed to the rims for teeth, might pass for the mouth cavity. Martin copied my activity. In response to my comment that I hoped the dentist would not hurt me, Martin picked up a small mallet and began to pound on the clay mouth he had made. I put my hand to my jaw and made moaning sounds and complained that my teeth were really getting hurt. Martin made no sound but smiled broadly and increased the fervor of his attacks on the clay mouth. Aggressive play with clay mouths continued during the four succeeding sessions. In the fifth session, rather than destroying the clay mouth, Martin fed it a pretend piece of candy. After this he showed no further interest in playing with the clay mouth. In the second session of mouth play he began to speak to the worker, at first behind her back. There were three months of weekly sessions with Martin before school closed. In the late spring Martin began talking with his teacher. On a visit with his mother to the new school in another school district which he was to attend in the fall, he talked freely with the principal.

For the child who desperately needs some basic infantile dependency gratification the technique of "playing baby" is often useful as is seen in the following case illustration of a third-grade girl.

> Trudy went into a rather quick and close relationship with me and acted and played like a six-month-old baby or a year-old child most of the time. She liked to cuddle up against me and have me roll her all around the room on a cart. She wrote on the board "I love you" and later "I hate you." She would talk over the phone to anyone and she tried to control me by having me telephone her at home; this I refused to do.
>
> Concurrently my weekly interviews with the mother helped her gain a better understanding of her own feelings of anger about returning to work when Trudy was three months old. The mother discovered that her own shyness in school was related to anger she never realized she had felt toward her mother who went to work when she was eight years old. Trudy's feelings of resentment began to emerge at home as the mother realized that her employment had seemed like desertion to Trudy. The mother had not understood before why Trudy had never expressed affection toward her, even as a baby. At my suggestion the mother brought out baby pictures, discussed how she felt at having to go to work and leave Trudy, and how she herself had felt when her mother went to work. Trudy, a quiet, lady-like, silent child, now became sassy, defiant, and demanding of affection at home.
>
> During the summer the family moved and in the new school Trudy spoke freely with no evidence of any prior difficulty in communication. The mother reported that at home Trudy now made only normal demands for affection and appeared to have stabilized her behavior.

---

[3] It should be noted that casework focus on this level is not common in school social work as most school social workers do not have equal access to psychiatric resources.—SSW ED.

Speech is an ego function. When the time comes that the child uses sounds and words, significant ego growth has been achieved. The first sound may well be laughter, or a whisper, or a word repeated after the teacher or social worker. When this has been successfully ventured the child feels his strengthening capacity, and responds increasingly in class and on the playground. From this point the child can be expected to assume more initiative and responsibility in the play therapy sessions. For example, the child might be required to ask for what he wants. As he succeeds in this, the most difficult phase of treatment is over. Gradually the child learns to express his feelings appropriately, in ways acceptable for his age group. Resolution of the problem enables the child not only to speak but to take his rightful place as an individual free to learn, grow, and participate in the important experience of school.

The Adolescent

Counseling with Emotionally Disturbed Adolescents

Arthur K. Young

Adolescence, though fundamentally a physiological and psychological stage in the individual's development, has a huge social and cultural overlay. A great deal has been written about its prolongation but without awareness of how recent this phenomenon is. Dr. Luella Cole points out, in the foreword to her admirable book, that little more than half a century ago there was not one free public high school in the Borough of Manhattan.[1] The vast majority of children left school at 14, served some kind of apprenticeship for a couple of years, and were usually self-supporting by the age of 17.

Comparing this with the experience of adolescents today, particularly those of the middle classes, we can appreciate, first, that we are in the midst of a social change of sizable proportions and, further, that our society has barely begun to evolve the new attitudes and structures with which to contain this transition. Here and there the young people themselves devise ways of dealing with it. It is becoming a commonplace on the campus, for example, for a young couple to marry and for the husband to pursue his graduate work while the wife temporarily becomes the breadwinner. In this way they bridge the gap between dependence on the parents and establishment of the independent family our culture approves and needs. Even parents are coming to accept it as a reasonable response to the increasing disparity between sexual and economic maturity.

In general, however, adolescents are in a confusing position which cannot be attributed to developmental factors alone. In the area of sex, they are made sex-conscious at an early age by the world around them; in the economic sphere, material acquisitions are emphasized; but fulfillment must be postponed. Despite the many opportunities for creative activity which our culture offers, the adolescent is almost powerless to affect this "betwixt-and-between" state. If we can see that much of what we observe in adolescents is specific to today's urbanized, middle-class society and that our society

[1] Luella Cole, *Psychology of Adolescence* (New York: Rinehart & Company, Inc., 1953).

Reprinted with permission of the author and the National Association of Social Workers, from *Social Work*, Vol. 3, No. 1 (January, 1958).

makes for divided adolescents, as social workers we may be able to give our young clients the benefit of our increased capacity to distinguish between the individual and the social.

If we think of emotional maturity as a continuing process of establishing individual identity, then even under normal circumstances the adolescent faces a unique dilemma. In order to leave the dependency of childhood, he must become more like the adults around him, only to find that this, too, is a threat to individuality—and at a time when the ego is still relatively fluid and amorphous. His way of solving this dilemma is perfectly natural: he seeks allies and joins a kind of subculture of those who face similar problems. For a time he relinquishes part of his individuality to the group, but is amply compensated by the sense of self which he gains. His manner of dress, his interests, even his language are dictated and also sanctioned by this group identification.

With this in mind, the so-called "adolescent rebellion" may be seen in a different light. It is not a need to rebel as such, but a need to protect and to incubate the new self until it is strong enough to be on its own. Movement toward differentiation takes place in every adolescent, and adults cannot check it completely, no matter how hard they try. Adults can, however, influence the manner in which this movement is expressed, that is, whether it will assert itself constructively and creatively, or whether, if the adolescent is to become an individual at all, it will have to come out negatively and destructively.

Clearly, this is not the whole story, since adolescence cannot be separated from innate capacities and total life experience. But while we certainly want to understand the adolescent's development over the years, we need to be sensitive to influences that are being exerted at the moment, especially those which, by disturbing the normal process of differentiation and establishment of a worth-while self-image, nullify the real meaning of adolescence.

A high proportion of the adolescents who come to an agency are disturbed adolescents who were once disturbed children and will almost certainly become disturbed adults unless they are helped. They have been traumatized by unwholesome, neurotic relationships with their parents and might validly have been brought for help at almost any time in their young lives. They have been reared in a consistent state of emotional impoverishment or extreme tension and have been subjected to so much neglect or pressure to conform that they are unable to define themselves as individuals. They struggle in the vain and irrational hope that struggle itself will solve their problems by forcing either the self or the world to conform.

If one thinks in terms of broad patterns of pathology, such a description could also apply to younger children or adults. The facts of adolescence, however, make for a significant difference in the way the pathology is expressed and, therefore, in the orientation of the helping person. In the case of young children who need a great deal of parental support, one necessarily works intensively with the parents and the prognosis is scaled to the latter's ability to provide an environment conducive to growth. In dealing with adults, as in marital counseling, the goals apply not only to the individual client, but also to the spouse. The adolescent, however, requires less from his environment than the younger child and is required to give less to it than the adult. The corollary is that, even in a family agency, work with adolescents can focus more on individual needs than work with either young children or married adults.

This observation is further substantiated by a striking pattern one soon notices in working with seriously disturbed adolescents. Whereas they themselves are usually most rewarding clients, the opposite is frequently true of their parents. This is likely to be so regardless of one's approach; that is, whether help is directed toward the total personality of the parent or toward the problems caused by the disturbed behavior of the child.

Treatment without Parents

At Jewish Community Services of Long Island in the past three years there have been many instances in which the psychiatrist or social worker, in evaluating treatment and projecting future possibilities for some 200 adolescents and their parents, was forced to conclude that further treatment would not bring appreciable results until such time as the adolescent could live apart from his parents. Often the helping person may count himself and his young client lucky if he can cause even a temporary moderation of the grosser distortions in the parental attitudes.

The reason for this has already been implied. By and large, the really disturbed adolescent needed help years before it was made available to him, which certainly says something of importance about the nature of the parent-child relationship and about the chances of successfully treating such an adolescent by focusing on improving the relationship with his parents. When the latter is feasible, as it sometimes is, the task is relatively easy. But since it is not feasible in many cases, the helping person must give serious thought to separating the adolescent from his family—psychologically, if possible, but physically, if necessary.

Fortunately, there is another side to the picture. If we agree that the adolescent is now in a position to establish his own self-concept, we are in possession of a tool that is not available with younger children and the task becomes clearer. Our job is to support and even to affirm the adolescent's need to behave like an adolescent, to grope and fumble, to have plans and whims which differ from those of his parents, and to arrive at a sense of his own capacities apart from the destructive evaluation he has derived from them. Sometimes this involves an upward revision of the self-image, sometimes downward, sometimes it involves both at the same time. Whatever the actual process, the point is that it *can* have a fruitful outcome because, in contrast with younger children, the adolescent generally knows he is in conflict, either in an inner sense or with respect to social institutions, such as family and school.

The direction this suggests sounds easy on the face of it, but it is not.

Social workers, as well as parents, find it a problem to live with the doubtful and the unsettled and work with adolescents often brings out our own unresolved biases and conflicts. Unconsciously, workers often tend to over-identify with the disturbed adolescent, who has suffered greatly and is certainly in need of sympathy, or, more often, to represent cultural expectations with which he cannot cope.

There is also the tendency to assume that our own class values—usually middle class—are the only ones worth striving for. The result is often a strong but subtle pressure on the adolescent to internalize goals which reflect our own ideas, not his. After all, we feel, there is so much to do and so little time left in which to do it. But yielding to this kind of feeling can only defeat our purpose by creating in the worker-client relationship precisely the kind of pressure that made for emotional disturbance in the first place.

Let us turn now to the case of a disturbed adolescent which illustrates these generalizations.

A Divided Adolescent

Alvin Cohen was just past 15 when his mother, Mrs. Gold, applied to the agency. He was extremely difficult to live with, an argumentative, moody boy who had practically no friends, had failed every term at school, could not get along with his teachers or classmates, and spent almost all his free time either day-dreaming or working on scientific experiments which were his hobby. Mrs. Gold herself was an extremely disturbed woman who had for years been subject to periods of severe agitation and depression, and was now barely holding herself together. After 20 years of a marriage beset by economic hardship and marital disharmony, she had divorced Alvin's father. This occurred about five years before they came to the agency. Two years after the divorce, she had remarried, only to become a widow a year later.

Mr. Cohen, who was in frequent contact with Alvin and his former wife, was a man with minimal resources. Though well-meaning and friendly, he was weak, ineffectual, and almost entirely without intellectual interests. Whatever his capacities might once have been, he had obviously given them up years before. Now he was utterly bewildered by Alvin's demand for something more than tired tolerance.

Inevitably, Alvin's life reflected the disintegration of his family. He had had hardly two years of consecutive living with both parents. During his mother's frequent illnesses, he had been farmed out to relatives for varying periods, even as an infant. A report from a psychiatric clinic to which Mrs. Gold had taken him when he was five indicated only too well that he was practically predestined to emotional disturbance. Despite his low level of functioning, the clinic considered him basically an alert, friendly child, whose disturbance was "easily explained by his 'nervous' environment." Recommendations of placement for Alvin and treatment for Mrs. Gold were flatly rejected by her, and their stormy relationship continued, punctuated by periods in which she was quite unable to function.

When I first saw him, Alvin was a chubby, baby-faced lad, quite good-looking except for his deadpan expression. After an initial period of reticence, he spoke freely and with good choice of words, but with noticeable infantilisms. In the early interviews the minutest scrutiny failed to reveal a single area of life that gave him satisfaction. Even his scientific interests were pursued with such desperation and so much overinvestment that they often resulted in frustration and self-depreciation.

Alvin came to the first interview willingly and opened it by handing me the following letter:

> Dear Mr. Young,
>
>   I really can't say this to you directly so I am writing this letter. I have no friends except for one, Arthur B. Since my father is not living with me, I have to depend on my mother to answer all my problems. But now I feel I have a problem which my mother is not fit to answer. I feel free to talk only to my friend and he recommended seeing you.
>
>   Having no friends, I have resulted [sic] to immoral tactics. I haven't had any association with a girl, nor have I petted any girl. But I have had to satisfy my moral needs by practicing on myself an immoral habit. The sensation received was a perfect substitute for the loss of friends so I thought.
>
>   Now this habit has gone beyond my control and I cannot stop. My school work has suffered and I feel down in the dumps. I would rather that you wouldn't mention this to my parents, for I fear they would not understand. Is there something that you can recommend to help me? Turning the matter into your hands and hoping for a quick solution, I remain,
>
>   Sincerely yours,
>   Alvin Cohen

Beginning with what he had said in the letter I hastened to reassure him about his masturbation. Somewhat to my surprise, he got the "quick solution" he had asked for, and hardly a month later told me rather casually that he was no longer worried about it and that it was no longer beyond his control.

During this early period I encouraged him to let me know him from *his* point of view. He had never had a relationship with an adequate male and looked on his father with contempt. His mother left him utterly confused— he felt powerfully obligated to her, but simply could not cope with her perplexing pattern of alternately pushing him away and binding him to her. He himself vacillated between grandiose ideas of becoming the Super Scientist and feelings of utter worthlessness and incapacity. He attributed his sense of difference from other boys to his parents' divorce, made much of the fact that he and his mother had different surnames, and thought that if only his parents would remarry each other, his problems would be solved. Characteristically, his idea of achieving a better future was to recreate the very situation that was so bound up with his illness.

Recognizing after a few interviews with her that Mrs. Gold was neither interested in nor accessible to help, I put my emphasis on efforts to clarify with Alvin what he was seeking and to differentiate myself from his father and mother, who represented, respectively, abject submission and aimless struggle. His eagerness to work with me without his parents' participation was in itself a positive indication. He concentrated at first on his difficulties in school and in his social relationships, both of which led naturally to my suggesting psychological evaluation.

The testing resulted in a diagnosis of an incipient "chronic, undifferentiated schizophrenic condition" in a boy of excellent native capacity, manifested by bizarre ideation, impairment of thinking ability, disturbance of concentration, and impulsive disregard of the facts of everyday life—in short, a fragmented boy who needed, above all else, to achieve a sense of wholeness.

My activity during the ensuing weeks was based on the following evaluation: *1]* He needed help on an immediate level with his problems in school, in choosing a career, and in understanding his own capacities; *2]* he needed to get from me what he could not get from his parents—a relationship combining warmth and comfort with strength and interest; and *3]* as a deeply split human being, he needed someone who would take on the role of "assistant ego" and would represent, for the time being, the part of his personality that was all but missing—the ability to organize and integrate.

With this kind of approach, which met him as a confused adolescent, a deprived child, and a split human being, Alvin intuitively recognized my offer of something completely new in his experience. Soon after, when the agency helped his mother to commit herself to a mental hospital, he had someone on whom he could depend and was able to spend the months she was away to "come out from under," so to speak, to find friends, to make overtures to girls, to decide on a definite curriculum in school, and to translate into action his realization that his thoughts, feelings, and behavior had always been destructively influenced by his mother's confusing demands.

When she returned from the hospital, and he once more experienced her domination, he figuratively thirsted for independence, and, buoyed up by the success he had achieved during her absence, spent the summer away from her working at a resort. Once again, albeit with periods of discouragement and struggle, he found the wherewithal to measure up socially and on a job.

Up to now, I had largely avoided an interpretive or probing approach. The few times I had put out feelers in these directions, he had disregarded them, and he was right in doing so, for he needed a process of synthesis, of bringing together, rather than one which, by separating out his motives and feelings, could only have served to divide him further. But upon his return to the city, he was concerned with two related trends—understanding his mother and differentiating himself from her.

The content of the interviews changed. He turned to me to support him as he tested both inner and outer reality, used our relationship to break away from total dependence on his mother, and in doing so, began to assert his own self-appraisal and self-expectation. The cultural pressure to achieve, formerly felt as such a crushing force, was no longer so heavy. As he put it: "Thing are beginning to add up now, and I can see that there are other ways out." By this he meant that, understanding the connection between his past and his present, he was in a position to choose among realistic alternatives. Until now, he had been the creature of grandiose expectations to surmount the incredible indignities that had been his lot.

His failure to do so, he had interpreted as intrinsic inadequacy. Now, as he experienced release from feelings of guilt and obligation which had defied explanation, he was able to resist his mother's efforts to take up where she had left off. This, it seemed to both of us, was the crucial test—knowing that he could live with her under the same roof and still hold to his own self was ample proof that it had become an integral part of him.

Case of Lewis

It is readily apparent that the impact of cultural forces is felt most strongly—and, unfortunately, most negatively—by those who are in the least advantageous position within the culture. In our society, this is true of the Negro, and in working with Negroes we do, indeed, find that they face such an extremely complicated configuration of cultural influence as to tax the capacity of the most adequate.

Thus, the normal difficulties are further compounded for the Negro adolescent, who must find some way of achieving wholeness within two exceedingly divisive contexts—the conflictual demands of both the total culture and his own subculture. The structure of the Negro family, like that of other families, takes myriad forms, but almost invariably one sees evidence of struggle to harmonize two opposing demands: on the one hand, to measure up to white standards; on the other, to exemplify the white stereotype of the Negro as intrinsically inadequate.

The struggle usually takes either of the following forms: *1]* The parents have given up and seek to impose their defeatist attitudes on a child who has the endowment and the will to fulfill himself more creatively; or *2]* the parents, seeking to overcome the bitter fruits of discrimination, find their ambitions thwarted by the influence on their children of the neighborhood and the peer group.

This may be illustrated in the case of Lewis Hall who was referred to the agency at the age of 12 by the New York City Youth Board. The accompanying summary described him as a youngster who was alternately withdrawn and aggressive, who got along poorly with parents and siblings, associated with unsavory companions, was failing and a disruptive influence in school, had no apparent sense of guilt, and complained always that he was being "picked on" by everyone.

Lewis' parents symbolized his dilemma. His mother was a bright, capable woman whose bountiful resources enabled her to run a business and a home, give active leadership to her community, and derive enjoyment from her artistic talents. Mr. Hall, though intelligent and hard working, seemed satisfied with an unskilled job that was utterly lacking in opportunity for advancement. Though outwardly accepting of his wife's position of dominance in the family, he would from time to time show his real feelings by excessive drinking and by deriding her hopes and efforts.

When Lewis first came to the agency—confused, suspicious, angry, and obviously under duress—he looked on me as only the latest in a series of adults who had tried to do something *to* him, rather than *for* him. During the first few months of our long contact, he spent much of his time ignoring me and reading comic books, occasionally deigning to recognize my presence by playing dominoes with me.

That Lewis had worth-while capacities was demonstrated not only by my own impressions of him, but also by psychological testing. From the standpoint of individual pathology, he was certainly an emotionally disturbed child, almost devoid of the capacity to relate positively to adults, who had internalized the opposing attitudes of his parents. It seemed at least equally important, however, to recognize that he was responding—as, indeed, his parents were—to the cultural milieu and that while the psychologist's evaluation of him as "exhibiting psychopathic tendencies" and "functioning below capacity" was certainly valid, it was itself a judgment that had cultural origins. In Lewis' context, such a concept had little meaning, for he performed well up to capacity in the kind of functioning he chose to engage in.

Until he was almost 14, there was little indication that Lewis was making any use of our relationship, aside from keeping most of his appointments and even this was largely attributable to his mother's insistence. With the onset of puberty and with the gradual recognition of my difference from the other adults he had known, he began to take more personal responsibility both for breaking and keeping his appointments and for spontaneous expression of his resentment and confusion. The latter was epitomized in his statement to his mother: "The trouble is you're trying to bring me up like a white child."

Though I was never able to help the parents improve their own relationship, and succeeded only in promoting a more "neutral," less manipulative attitude toward Lewis, this was enough to free him to use what I offered: basically, a relationship with an adult around whom he could reorganize himself apart from the pressures of parents, school, and neighborhood, and with whom he could arrive at values arising from his own desires and capacities. Recognizing that his sense of inadequacy had its source in the taken-for-granted biases of his environment, he became less impulsive and more realistic in his choices. This was exemplified by his improvement in school and by his considered decision that, since he could not be a college man and would not be an errand boy, he would work toward becoming a skilled mechanic.

Conclusion

In the cases of Alvin and Lewis we find emotional disturbance in which both the divisive influences of our culture and the unifying forces, biologically based, of adolescence are important facts. While we cannot say in either case that a process has been completed, we can perhaps agree that the danger of schizophrenic adjustment in the one case and of psychopathic adjustment in the other has been lessened, and that something therapeutically valuable occurred which stemmed in large measure from the counselor's recognition of the influence of cultural expectations.

With both boys, the adolescent "tone" of their situations was indicated in the struggle with sexuality, the awareness of conflict with external forces, the wish to separate from the parents, the striving for independent relationships, and the confused response to divisive cultural elements.

Even disturbed adolescents with deficient capacity for reality-testing are well aware of cultural expectations to "amount to something." At best, therefore, there is little point in bringing such factors home to them; at worst, it puts the counselor on the side of the very forces in their lives which have been most oppressive. While we certainly want to help them live in the real world, we achieve our purpose, not by hammering away at what the world demands, but by recognizing their individuality and their right to find their own relation to social forces.

We see, too, the sense of dividedness, of conflict between acceptance of the parental image and the struggle to achieve identity. Though the real self was all but buried by unwholesome life experience and the immediate reality of distorted parental attitudes, each of these boys clung with awesome tenacity to his right to create a self of his own.

Supported by a relationship with an adult who can respect this right, their struggle to separate need not take the form of rebellion in either a destructive or self-destructive sense. But separation there must be in our individualistic culture and our ability to help the disturbed adolescent move away from his disturbing family psychologically and view his parents in sounder perspective is the key to the process. In that way, we further the dual purpose of supporting his movement toward maturation and preparing him for his place in today's world.

Casework Treatment of Adolescents with Learning Inhibitions

Helen Rabichow

As social workers and as citizens in a democratic society we have a firm philosophical conviction that every human being is entitled to the maximum opportunities that will stimulate and develop the emotional, intellectual, and social potentialities essential for personal growth, gratification, and

Reprinted with permission of the author and the National Association of Social Workers, from *Social Work*, Vol. 8, No. 4 (October, 1963), pp. 55–62.

adaptation. We believe that in turn this accrues to the enhancement and enrichment of the democratic process. Although the reality falls short of this ideal, we in the helping professions are nonetheless committed to deal with those factors that interfere with and threaten to disrupt the fullest development of capacities in each individual in our society. This is a many-splendored commitment and, at times, a seemingly overwhelming task. But it is better to light one candle than curse the darkness, and in casework our candle is the implementation of a therapeutic process directed toward coping with those psychosocial factors causing individual failure in adaptation. As we bring our specific understanding and skills to bear within this area of our special professional competence and, hopefully, as we achieve some measure of success thereby, we also bring a ray of illumination.

This paper will examine the relationship between certain emotional problems in adolescence and their manifestation in learning inhibitions. Two cases, referred specifically because of school underachievement and treated within the broader context of emotional disturbance, will be presented for illustrative purposes.

Adolescence is the "Age of Anxiety"

Freud described, as the most significant and most painful psychic achievement of the adolescent, his detachment from parental authority.[1] The strong conscious drives for independence, and at the same time the unconscious need to maintain dependence on the parents, result in various degrees of confusion. The adolescent is simultaneously experiencing biological as well as psychological changes, and he must cope with issues related to sexuality, competition, aggression, and hostility.

The expanding young ego is thus pressured from many different sides. The adolescent is not ready to adapt to the overwhelming pressure and demands of reality adjustment. Confused by such demands, he becomes impatient and impulsive; he attempts to run away and regress, afraid of the problems and consequences of growing up. Confusion and anxiety caused by these tensions lead to various defenses. When attempts to satisfy reality demands meet with failure, other defenses are developed against progress and growth. It is quite understandable in the light of this why adolescence has been called the "Age of Anxiety," not only for adolescents but also for their parents.

Emotional disturbance in adolescence manifests itself in a multitude of ways, and certainly not all emotionally disturbed youngsters use school and education as the arenas for enactment of emotional conflict. Indeed, some use intellectual achievement as a means of channeling conflictual issues. But far too many inhibit and obstruct the natural and innate desire for learning and, despite good intelligence, underachieve in the service of emotional conflict.

[1] Sigmund Freud, *Three Essays on the Theory of Sexuality* (London: Hogarth Press, 1953).

Learning is a highly complex process about which there is much still to be understood. It is known, however, that every human being has the basic impulse to survive, and that learning is a means to survival.[2] Learning is an organic process through which the individual strives toward intactness and self-preservation. If the individual survives, he must change, and growth brings change in the person himself. The complex environment in which the human being develops exerts different demands at different ages and changes from generation to generation. Individual growth and learning is the process whereby a human being continually adapts to the changing self and the changing environment, and strives to master both. The factor of change from within and from without threatens the survival of the individual as a whole. Thus, change causes discomfort and more anxiety, until by incorporation it becomes useful and gratifying. Not all change, however, implies growth. Change may induce regression rather than development, which, when transitory, is sometimes essential for integration and subsequent growth.

As the individual proceeds gradually from infancy through early childhood to adolescence and adulthood, his progress, theoretically, would be smooth and uninterrupted by phases of regression if the demands of his external world were always appropriately timed to his physical, intellectual, and psychological readiness to master the changed situation. But in fact this is not so, and adolescence in particular is a period of great upheaval, physically and psychologically. There are many stresses that cannot easily be mastered, the intactness of the personality is threatened, and there is a tendency to return to earlier, more satisfactory life periods. But regression, generally, is never complete, for it is met by the urge toward growth. Normally regression causes discomfort that reinforces learning in the interest of comfortable survival.

When a child's dependency has been gratified through constructive relationships with parents and teachers, learning occurs naturally, gradually, with a minimum of pain and disorganization. As the child moves from one developmental period to another there is repetitive reorganization and integration of the learning process, rather than disorganization. Insofar as his relationships have permitted resolution of normal conflicts as he has matured, he will have been positively conditioned to the pleasures of learning. Knowledge of eventual gratification will ease the momentary discomfort of learning.

Deterrents to Learning

But for many school learning, like living, is an anxious, precarious process. Strong deterrents to learning may be derived from many sources. Sexual conflicts and fantasies can interfere with the adolescent's ability to

[2] For discussion of basic learning principles and personality development see Charlotte Towle, *The Learner in Education for the Professions* (Chicago: University of Chicago Press, 1954), pp. 23–85.

study.[3] An adolescent whose childhood curiosity was mishandled may develop learning difficulties in special subjects; for example, science and biology can be threatening to the youngster who is struggling against allowing the emergence of repressed childhood curiosity about the creation of life and bodily functions. Children whose narcissism has been overly fed in childhood and those who were reared in overly permissive environments may, in adolescence, be unable to tolerate the tensions of competition with peers, striving toward mastery of knowledge, and postponement of immediate gratification, and withdrawal from learning may occur. Some children are proficient only under teachers who show a special liking for and interest in them, doing poorly under indifferent teachers.

It is, of course, obvious that a child can be so disturbed by traumatic occurrences at home as to be unable to concentrate. A child attempting to understand the anguished relationships between himself and his parents expends his energy in coping with emotions aroused by tragic home situations and has no motivation for study. In fact, he attempts to avoid unbearable pain by trying not to know what is going on. The need *not to know* is a fundamental difficulty in many learning disabilities. To learn means to learn painful facts, therefore all learning is feared and avoided.

In discussing pathological aggressiveness in children from broken homes, institutions, and orphanages, Anna Freud states:

> The pathological factor in these cases is not to be found in the aggressive tendencies themselves, but in a lack of fusion between them and libidinal (erotic) urges. . . . Emotional development . . . has been held up through adverse external or internal conditions, such as absence of love objects, lack of emotional response from the adult environment, breaking of emotional ties as soon as they are formed. . . . Owing to the defects on the emotional side, the aggressive urges are not brought into fusion and thereby bound and partially neutralized, but remain free and seek expression in life in the form of pure, unadulterated, independent destructiveness.[4]

Under such circumstances there are no drive derivatives that can be sublimated into academic work, and learning difficulties result.

Charles—Frustrated Needs

Charles, $15\frac{1}{2}$ at the time of his referral for treatment in August 1961 by the Institute for Juvenile Research, was failing in school despite superior intelligence. He also exhibited certain behavioral problems such as stealing and setting off firecrackers. The latter incident resulted in his expulsion from the private high school he was attending at the time. It was this school that suggested examination at IJR. Charles, in turn, was sent to a public high school.

[3] Sandor Lorand, MD, and Henry I. Schneer, MD, *Adolescents: Psychoanalytic Approach to Problems and Therapy* (New York: Paul B. Hoeber, 1962), pp. 251–271.

[4] "Aggression in Relation to Emotional Development: Normal and Pathological," in *Psychoanalytic Study of the Child*, Vol. 3 (New York: International Universities Press, 1949), pp. 41–42.

The psychological examination at IJR revealed that Charles was in the bright normal to superior range of intelligence, which was in striking contrast to his constricted, dull performance in school and on the projectives. It was concluded that the sparsity of responses on the projective tests was indicative of suppression of material that might well emerge with a lowering of defenses. Nevertheless, Charles was considered to be a good treatment risk.

Charles's background revealed a number of significant factors important to an understanding of his current problems in school functioning. His parents reported he was a desired and happy baby who sat up at 4 months, walked at a year, talked early and clearly, and was reading when he entered kindergarten. He was bottle-fed and weaned easily at one year. His mother was strenuous in toilet training and reported he was completely trained at 10 months, with no problems in this area.

At 2 Charles was hospitalized for eight days with a bronchitis infection. During this time parental visiting was limited because it was necessary to keep the room heavily humidified. Two weeks after Charles's return home, his mother went to the hospital to deliver his only sibling, Richard. About a month later a maternal uncle who favored Charles and was adored by him died. Thus, within a short period of time, Charles suffered three traumas, which resulted in a marked change in his behavior. His earlier bounce and spontaneity subsided, and he became more subdued.

In the second grade Charles began evidencing school difficulties. His attention wandered, he showed boredom, and he refused to do his homework, all of which provoked his teachers. It appeared he was not sufficiently stimulated, and his parents requested the school to move him ahead half a grade. This was done, and for a while he seemed more content, but this soon wore off. As the eighth grade approached, his parents enrolled him in a private school, where, perhaps because of smaller classes, he showed greater interest. Upon graduation he was enrolled in private high school, where the acting-out recurred, culminating in the expulsion mentioned previously.

At the time of Charles's beginning difficulties in school, he was already an excellent accordion player. But because of his problems, his parents felt the accordion lessons were too much of a strain, and when the family doctor agreed, the lessons were discontinued, over the boy's strenuous objections.

When Charles came to the agency he was working twenty hours a week delivering newspapers. He had never been given an allowance, and had been taking care of certain financial needs for a long time.

Charles's mother was a rigid, demanding woman, emotionally frustrated herself, with great anxiety about his underachievement in school. She pushed him hard in this area, at the same time withholding affection, attention, and gratification. She lacked real empathy for Charles and had little awareness of how her reactions and behavior toward him over the years were related to his problems. His failures represented a blow to her own narcissism, and she could provide little for him in terms of his needs. The father was a passive, angry man, reacting to his own unmet needs and able to give little to his wife and children. He had withdrawn considerably from family interaction, was concerned with his own health, and wanted only peace and quiet. He was unable to provide Charles with an adequate paternal figure for identification or gratification. The agency was able to involve the mother in therapy to some extent, on the basis of her own hopes for narcissistic gratification, but the father could not be engaged.

As the Danish philosopher Kierkegaard observed, although life has to be lived forward it can only be understood backward; in looking backward on Charles, we see a youngster who early suffered three traumas, which, coming so close together, is quite a load for a 2-year-old. Even more traumatic was the limited ability of his parents to provide emotional security and gratification at the same time that they were demanding achievement, specifically academic achievement.

Establishment of interest in school takes place in one of two ways: 1] The subject matter itself may touch on the needs of the child, firing his interest and involvement. Under such circumstances the subject matter becomes a source of gratification. 2] There is also the child on whom the subject matter is imposed, but who will learn because he is deriving gratification from satisfying parent and/or teacher relationships. In this case it is the relationship that is the stimulus for learning.

Charles was receiving gratification in neither way. Reacting with depression over lack of gratification, he got revenge by engaging in irritating antics designed to arouse attention, but which only resulted in further deprivation of love by adults. For example, the discontinuance of the accordion lessons could only verify his expectations from the world—mother makes you give up what you want. Since his longings to be satisfied were counteracted by the attitude that he never would be, his efforts became directed toward getting even with the depriver. A goal with a boy like Charles is to help him arrive at other than pathological ways of gratifying longings and needs. But before such a boy can achieve, he must receive emotional nourishment from another human being.

Nurture the Ego

Charles began treatment in October 1961 and is still being seen. In appearance he was childlike, thin, and looked forlorn and depressed, like a boy who figuratively and literally needed to be fed. He aroused sympathy immediately. He was rather uncommunicative and denied problems even when it was quite obvious he was in trouble. Initially, the main topics of conversation were his interests in automobile, airplane, and railroad models, and in chemistry. He was passive about school and, in fact, failed every subject the first semester he was in therapy. He did, however, begin to improve the second semester, and by June 1962 passed all his courses.

The caseworker was active with the school during this entire period and interceded in Charles's behalf time and again. The school personnel agreed to direct all complaints about Charles to the worker instead of the parents, and the worker interceded with the mother, encouraging her to ignore Charles's provocative behavior as much as possible. His school violations consisted of smoking, cutting classes, drawing obscene pictures in books, using the wrong exits, lighting matches in the physics lab (to impress a girl), and so on. Because Charles was in treatment, the school adjustment teacher, fortunately, was favorably disposed toward him, and Charles experienced some warmth from this relationship.

For months the worker continued to show interest in him on his own terms—discussing his models, going on excursions with him to look at others, praising those he made himself—and finally Charles began moving a little closer. He began to *take* more; for example, at first he refused even the offer of a coke, later he accepted a coke and then a hamburger, still later he ordered two hamburgers and french fries. The nature of the relationship offered by the worker in this period may be characterized as low in demand and high in gratification.

Early in June a marked change occurred. Charles became more verbal and animated and engaged in more direct discussion of problems. Whereas he had previously avoided the subject of school, he now volunteered the statement that if a teacher was interested in him, he was willing to do his homework and accept discipline, limits, and responsibilities. Under such circumstances, he maintained, he did not resent work. In other words, Charles was saying that when he is getting gratification in a relationship, he can meet demands and is willing to conform and please. He began expressing a desire to complete high school, indicating that this was important to him. He also began to manifest some capacity for making insightful observations and connections between his feelings and behavior. He admitted that he misbehaved in science class because of his resentment of his parents and teachers. It was following this discussion that Charles completed all his class assignments for this course and, in the teacher's words, "forced me to pass him."

Peer relationships began to improve. He brought a boy friend to meet the worker and the three engaged in a friendly interchange. Charles began attending boy-girl dancing parties, which he enjoyed, and he verbalized some interest in girls. These discussions and activities were quite appropriately adolescent. The worker noticed a change in Charles's appearance. He now combed his hair, carried himself erect, and looked more grown-up, less like a waif.

When Charles initially had spoken about his brother he manifested old resentments and negative feelings. He felt Richard was favored and that he, Charles, was always the culprit. As his hostility was released and accepted, he became more sympathetic toward Richard and began engaging in more activities with him. He later reported that his parents were beginning to realize that Richard was not always an innocent bystander, and this further diluted Charles's hostility. He then began reporting that his parents were changing somewhat; he was pleased when they permitted him to take driving lessons and when his father took him boating. Now when his mother insisted he do his homework he could more readily comply. Charles demonstrated a greater comfort in talking about his family and his feelings toward them and there was some subsidence of tension. As he was able to come a little closer toward meeting some of his parents' expectations, he received some gratification, which was a spur toward growth and less self-destructive behavior.

Of significance was the fact that Charles was able, through the relationship with the worker, to experience a feeling of hope and a measure of self-esteem. He became less depressed and responded in a more alive, eager manner. He spoke of the future with some hopefulness, indicating a wish to join the navy after high school graduation, and on one occasion added, "I can go to college later."

The plan is to continue with Charles, nurturing his ego and encouraging maturation. Because he has some capacity for psychological awareness, appropriate connections will be made to help him see how, out of his anger over frustrated ·needs, he has used school and learning in a negative, self-destructive, retaliatory fashion. Work will continue with the mother and the school to help solidify progress made and, hopefully, to resolve problems that will inevitably arise from time to time.

Carol—Fear of Growing Up

Carol was referred in November 1961 by her school because of deteriorating performance and behavior. She was 15½, already a senior, a very bright, potentially good student, who for the past two years had been cutting classes and periodically failing. It was also noted that she was withdrawn and participated in few school social activities, but volunteered regularly to help out in the attendance or program offices, which might permit her to remain out of classes. Her parents described her as a precocious child: by 2 she was doing simple pencil and paper tasks and by 3 she was beginning to read words. In grammar school she was double-promoted three times and her grades averaged "E" ("Excellent"). Her father said, "We have always known that she was an unusual child, but it has never been a problem until now."

Psychological testing in September 1961 revealed unusual ability in all areas. CA was 15–6, MA 20–11 (at least), IQ 138 (at least). Even these high test scores were considered a low estimate of her mental ability. Her vocabulary was excellent, comprehension keen, responses clear, and she was at ease with the language of the tests. On several TAT projective pictures she told long stories about the idealist who tries to do something unusual, to conquer the world, but ends up in mediocrity, wondering why he ever tried at all.

School reports and the agency's intake with the parents revealed an essentially benign and nonpathological history; problems seemed related to onset of pubescence. The parents appeared warm, genuinely concerned about Carol, and willing to be helpful in any way indicated.

Work with Carol was initiated in December 1961. She looked and dressed more like a sophomore than a senior, talked easily, although in a highly organized manner, her voice breathless with tension, and was sometimes close to tears. The initial content revolved around books, mostly philosophic and idealistic. She discussed Nietzsche, Emerson, Shaw, and Orwell. Within a few weeks she added Freud to her reading list. She felt strongly that all personal individuality was being stamped out in contemporary society and that conformity was threatening the individual, and she expounded views on communism, capitalism, and world affairs with great conviction.

She also engaged in tirades against the school system and the teachers, who, according to her, were idiotic, stupid, and lacking in inspiration. Nor was her family spared from heavy criticism. She attacked her father in particular, accusing him of being critical, old-fashioned, and talking too loudly on the phone. She granted that he was intelligent, although uneducated. She was annoyed with family criticism of her friends, an older, out-of-school group, even though she herself felt they did not have goals and were not her intellectual equals.

The caseworker listened sympathetically to Carol's defensive verbalizations, which included provocativeness, intellectualization, negativism, belittling of adult authority, projection of failures, and global philosophizing. Clues about her underlying fears and confusions emerged early, and her caustic verbalizations were seen as efforts, albeit frantic ones, to cope with the anxieties of relinquishing infantile gratifications and moving on in life with all its unknown but well-fantasied terrors. While on the one hand she stated with sureness her opinions about life and the affairs of the world, she began describing certain ghost stories, science fiction, and works of Poe as "powerful," and once commented, "I sometimes wonder if ghosts don't actually exist." She also began confessing worries about the June graduation, unhappiness about her high school record, and anxiety about being admitted to college. A theme she had written for her English class, entitled "The Lost Individual," lent itself to further exploration of her fears, which revolved more and more around growing up. She made comments such as "What's the use of growing up?" and "Sometimes I wish I could go back to the crib." She accepted the worker's interpretation of a phrase in her theme, "What's to become of us?" as meaning "What's to become of me?"

Accept Regressive Yearnings

When an adolescent is faced with a task beyond his immediate capacity to cope he may need to regress temporarily, and instead of being pushed ahead should be allowed to tread water or float for awhile, to catch his breath before he undertakes the long swim ahead. The adolescent, faced with the physical changes of puberty and its concomitant psychological and emotional changes, derives satisfaction from going back in memory to earlier periods and reliving them in a way that restores a measure of the infantile sense of omnipotence.[5] He can spin romantic fantasies and derive satisfactions that real life at the moment denies. Within reasonable limits this brings relief. There is a line in a play by James Barrie to the effect that God gave us our memories so that we might have roses in December; adolescence is the December of childhood.

Thus, the worker permitted Carol's regressive yearnings and took the position that her worries were not uncommon, that she was younger than her classmates and growing up might well be frightening to her, that she was fearful of what college represented, that she relied on thinking her way through to answers but this did not always work because feelings got in the way. Carol was reassured that June was still a long way off, that there was time to work out the problems confronting her, and that as she understood her fears she would be better able to master them. Shortly thereafter, Freud gave way to comic books and TV cartoons, and Carol reminisced about the good old kindergarten days when life was simple and comfortable and the summers when her greatest problem was to find the ice cream man. For a little while she indulged in baby talk.

At the same time that the worker accepted Carol's regressions and longings, she also interjected reassurance and confidence that current and future realities were not so frightening or overwhelming, that Carol had the capacity to cope with life, and that, in fact, there would be even greater gratification eventually in taking on the more demanding tasks of life as an adult.

This approach resulted in a subsidence of Carol's anxiety and a moving ahead. She became more positive toward school and more interested in her work. While she still expounded her views, it was with lessened intensity. She took a number of examinations for college entrance and did quite well. While she was still anxious about the prospect of college, she could discuss plans more realistically. With the worker's support and help, she applied for and obtained a summer job at the university she hoped to attend in the fall. This worked out well and she continued to hold the position during school term.

There was a waning of the hostility toward both her parents and adults in general. She moved closer to her mother, and her parents reported her greater involvement in everyday family activities. In the treatment interviews Carol was more relaxed, lighthearted, and spontaneous, less abstract, critical, and pushed. She also began moving away from the old group of friends and shifting to peers at school. On one occasion a friend of hers, already in college, arranged a double date with a college man, and while this frightened Carol a little, she was also pleased. She began testing out the worker on her growing interest in boys, albeit in a somewhat coy and childish way.

For Carol's birthday the worker purchased a makeup kit for teen-agers, and while Carol was startled as well as pleased by this symbol of increased

[5] Lorand and Schneer, *op. cit.*, pp. 217–236.

maturity, she immediately involved her mother in helping her use the kit, and from that point began wearing makeup regularly.

Thus, as Carol became increasingly secure within the relationship, had tested the worker in a variety of ways and found her consistently giving, understanding, supportive, and gratifying, she could unburden and admit that life was confusing and that she did not have all the answers. She could lean on the worker for guidance and direction and accept her reassurance. The worker provided Carol with a model for becoming an adult, and by identification Carol grew in the hope that she too could make the grade. By accepting and emulating an admired adult, the adolescent is provided with form and structure in an otherwise formless, diffuse, and chaotic world, and he can begin to discover his own self-identity.

What is seen in Carol is an intellectually precocious youngster with a good background, now reacting to a major developmental task of adolescence, namely, the issue of independence. Carol had advanced in the intellectual area and in school, on which her parents placed great value. But underneath was still a little girl, now frightened by the increased demands of growing up, facing college, boys, and more adult responsibilities. Emotionally she was unable to tolerate the anxiety this produced, and nonachievement in the school situation was one way of demonstrating nonreadiness. It must be remembered that the emotional IQ is as important as the intellectual one. Carol's behavior was her way of saying, "I am not big enough yet to face these things. I'm still a child, don't push." The goal in treatment was then, through the medium of a good therapeutic relationship, to dilute the anxiety that obstructed normal growth and to stimulate and release the natural strivings for development and maturation.

The educational process is most effective when the child is sufficiently problem-free to be able to direct his energy into learning.[6] Too many are struggling with emotional and social problems that interfere with personality development and school functioning. Learning disabilities are symptoms and reflections of the many conflictual issues that confront the adolescent. These he must be helped to resolve in order for him to arrive at adulthood with a reasonable degree of maturity and inner security so that he may take his place as a responsible citizen in a society of free men.

[6] Solomon O. Lichter *et al.*, *The Drop-Outs* (New York: The Free Press of Glencoe, 1962), pp. 245–269.

The Delinquent Adolescent

Casework Treatment of Delinquents Who Use the Primary Defense of Denial

Alice H. Collins and James R. Mackay

It is accepted today that casework is an essential tool in the treatment of clients in the correctional field and increasingly, caseworkers are finding that practice in this field is rewarding and challenging, calling on the skills they bring from a broad background of training and experience. Conversely, caseworkers with experience in corrections find their understanding of the client who is labeled "delinquent" illuminates their practice in regard to the client who has not been legally delinquent, but whose personality patterns are similar to those seen in the field of corrections.

This paper is based on casework experience with several hundred boys seen at intake, reviewed during their stay at four facilities and seen again at parole and on return for violation of parole. Emerging from this came the belief that there was a group of boys which could be identified, at least in part, by their unwillingness to admit the need for help. Many techniques were tried in an effort to reach these seriously delinquent boys who did not appear to be able to benefit from the program that met the needs of other boys. They were seen as belonging to the group who used the defense of denial in so massive a manner that it appeared to control their entire personality structure.

Forms of Denial

In general, such children are felt to be brazen liars when they are interrogated by the police or appear in court, and are so seen by the general public when their remarks are publicized. The denial of guilt may range from a flat "I wasn't there. . . . I wasn't driving, I was at home when it happened. . . . I didn't do nothing. . . ." to a denial of responsibility, an admission that the act might have occurred but that he was not a willing participant and therefore, not guilty. "He made me do it. . . . I just seem to pick the wrong kids to hang around with. . . . He said it was his car. . . . How should I know it was stolen? I was drunk. . . ."

Such statements may be what the public believes them to be—lies to

Reprinted with permission of the authors and the National Association of Social Workers, from *Social Work*, Vol. 4, No. 1 (January, 1959), pp. 34–43.

avoid punishment—yet to the professional eye and ear there is a difference between them, although it is not an easy difference to delineate. It rests, perhaps, in the voice and expression of the child making the statement in that he does not show the avoidance of glance, change in color, involuntary physical movements of the person suppressing or distorting the truth. He is wide-eyed and inappropriately calm and open in manner. He shows a different picture from the child who is lying because, actually, he is not lying—he is telling the truth as it appears to his conscious mind.

In his thinking, it follows logically that if he did not commit any offense, he needs no help now toward avoiding trouble in the future. Sometimes he makes it clear that he will not accept help because he should not be under the care of the agency in the first place, and, in fact, has no problems but the false ones of which he is accused. The more the offense is discussed in an attempt to establish a base for the need for help, the firmer becomes his denial of such need.

The child may use more subtle means to ward off help by agreeing that the offense was serious, that he should not have been involved but that he does not need to discuss it further because the whole experience "has been a lesson to him" and he will never again be guilty. He may use phrases gleaned from previous contacts with social workers and relatives to point out that he recognizes that no one can help him—he must help himself and he intends to do so. There is nothing really wrong with him now, he made a mistake in the past. He knows that and he will make no more in the future. Sometimes he may go on to describe his new-found conscience, his clear understanding of right and wrong, and his appreciation of the offer for help which he has demonstrated he does not need. It is not unusual for such conversations to take place even as the authorities are investigating a repetition of the first offense.

Even if the offense is not discussed by the caseworker and help is offered without reference to the authoritative setting which brings the child to the attention of the worker, the same tactics are met, though perhaps differently used. In the face of the most rejecting and demoralizing home situations that the child knows are known to the caseworker, he may assert that he does not need help from an "outsider" because his parents have been so good to him "they gave me everything" and conditions will be entirely satisfactory to him once he is free of the present restraints. Some of this applies to school where he did well, and to his relationship with his friends, who all liked him. Why, then, should he need the help the caseworker offers?

One other form that denial takes is seen more recently among the older children who are intelligent and who have been seen earlier in childhood by mental health agencies or have had access to books or television and movies concerning mental illness. Such children may acknowledge the act they have committed as being wrong and ask for a "psychiatrist," pointing out that since they are clearly mentally ill, they are not responsible. If treatment is then attempted in response to the request for help, it rapidly develops that the child wants to be cured from "outside", by a kind of psychological magic while his defense against his real feelings remains intact.

As has been reported by other investigators,[1] these are children who have known early experiences with rejecting, variable parents who have been unable to give them the consistent gratification that would have served to relieve their primary anxiety; at the same time their external environment has been threatening through the actual deprivation of essential physical care. The majority of such children have experienced loss of even such poor parental figures as they had—either through desertion, death or social action—and have experienced such loss more than once.[2]

The unrelieved anxiety so generated would overwhelm the weak ego if it permitted itself to feel it fully so that the ego has resorted to denial in order to defend itself and survive. Such denial may take one of two forms—fantasy and word and act.[3]

Most children give up this defense as the ego grows more able to cope with the anxiety aroused by internal and external stimuli, but children for whom the rewards of parental love are withheld and for whom the demands of reality are too harsh may cling to this defense or regress to it. The children under discussion here, because of the nature of the internal and external climate in which they grew up, were not able to develop to as high a level of ego functioning as is normal. They have continued to use denial as a defense so that it has become increasingly impregnable as the anxieties of their reality increased with the years.

Method of Treatment

While often the defense has served so well that there appear to be no signs of it, it must be constantly borne in mind that the anxiety is still there. Thus, in treatment, when anxiety is aroused, it is to be expected that the defense of denial will be mobilized, since this is the chief way which the ego has perfected for protecting itself. For casework success, an approach must be made to the problem of lowering anxiety if the defense is to be modified or abandoned for one which does not restrict the personality to a primitive level of development. Such an approach is made when the caseworker, as a result of the diagnostic appraisal, attempts to meet the child in the

---

[1] Beatrice R. Simcox and Irving Kaufman, M.D., "Treatment of Character Disorders in Parents of Delinquents," *Social Casework,* Vol. 37, No. 8 (October 1956), pp. 388–395.

——, "Handling of Early Contacts with Parents of Delinquents," *Social Casework,* Vol. 37, No. 9 (November 1956), pp. 443–450.

Also see Fritz Redl and David Wineman, *The Aggressive Child* (New York: The Free Press, 1957); August Aichorn, *Wayward Youth* (New York: Meridian Books, 1953).

[2] Irving Kaufman, "Three Basic Sources for Predelinquent Character," *The Nervous Child,* Vol. 11, No. 1 (October 1955), pp. 12–15.

[3] Anna Freud, *The Ego and the Mechanisms of Defense* (New York: International Universities Press, 1946), p. 89.

area that is of the greatest concern to him—in the difficulties he is having in maintaining his homeostasis. If this appears to overemphasize the importance of the defense, it is because this is precisely what the child himself is doing.

The method of treatment described below as having some measure of success with such children consists in the modification of the external reality and the restoration of loss to the point where anxiety is reduced. This is accomplished through the relationship of the child and the caseworker who presents himself as a kind, accepting, and consistently controlling parent figure. The relationship is dependent on the quality of the reality experience the child is having at the same time. The caseworker must see to it that, simultaneously with the development of the relationship, the reality is manipulated to contribute to the conditions of gratification which are necessary to these children. The duration of the treatment varies with the degree of ego damage but it is rarely accomplished in a short time.

As in every casework situation, a dynamic diagnosis is essential to successful treatment. If interviewing and testing reveal denial to be a major defense, the caseworker must consider in what ways it is used and how far it has restricted the ego, so that he may estimate the anxiety and depression that he knows are present and gauge the likelihood of the modification of such behavior. It must be borne in mind that if the defense of denial in fantasy persists too long, serious mental illness may result.

Whether the caseworker arrives at the diagnosis alone or with the help of other professional disciplines, he must now make a treatment plan that will take into account how best to help the child who refuses to admit his need. Nor is it sufficient to make plans for casework treatment alone. It is also necessary that the reality conditions of his life be made to contribute to his treatment. It is important for the caseworker who sees him in the institutional setting to make sure that the daily program of the child is interesting to him and offers some immediate rewards for good behavior, limitations upon loss of control, and an opportunity to succeed.

As casework proceeds, the worker needs to maintain a warm, accepting attitude but avoids agreeing with the denial. He accepts it as real to the client and may also, without contradiction or being punitive or insistent, state the attitude of society as personified by the judge, the police, and the probation officer. He does not try to "prove anything" but makes his position on the side of adult authority plain.[4] This is most difficult in the frequent cases where the caseworker recognizes that because of family background, cultural prejudices, and other handicaps, the child "never had a chance." His empathy for the child may lead him into resentment against the authority figures involved and the expression of this.[5]

---

[4] Martin Falsberg, "Setting Limits with the Juvenile Delinquent," *Social Casework*, Vol. 38, No. 3 (March 1957), pp. 138–142.

[5] Elliot Studt, "The Contribution of Correctional Practice to Social Work Theory and Education," *Social Casework*, Vol. 37, No. 6 (June 1956), pp. 263–269.

Three Cases

Jack was an illegitimate child, his mother having been committed to a school for the feebleminded immediately following his birth and not released until he was 12 years old. He lived in a succession of foster homes, none for more than two years, up to the time of his commitment to a training school at 13. Although he was found to have average intelligence, he had been in special classes most of his school life.

At 13, he came to the attention of the court, shortly after his return to his mother on her release. He was committed on the second offense and had spent some time in two training schools with brief paroles home. Repetition of the offense and one long and one short runaway during which he was involved in homosexual offenses with an older man led to his commitment to a closed training school. He was seen weekly by a caseworker over a period of fifteen months, at which time he was paroled.

Jack maintained that he was "sent away for nothing" for most of the first interviews. He minimized every offense, characterizing the pocket-book snatch from an old woman and the destruction of property as boyish pranks done with his friends. When the caseworker continued to point out the reality of his appearances in court, especially as a partner in frequent homosexual acts with the same man, he indignantly exclaimed, "Somebody committed an unnatural act on me . . . I didn't commit an unnatural act on him!"

During these early weeks, Jack was unable to conform to the rules of the training school. He wandered about where he knew he would be caught. While his infractions of the rules were punished, an effort was also made to find something in the program to interest him. This was difficult since he expressed no preferences and would participate in any placement only as far as he had to. He finally showed some interest in music and was accepted by the music teacher as a drum student, a placement he enjoyed and worked at.

Bob was committed when he was 12 for participating in a series of breaks into stores and gas stations. He was 15 when he was seen and on his second stay at the training school, having been returned for a second series of breaks, the last one involving $1,200. He was the only child of his mother's second marriage; he had an older brother who was married and in another city, and an older sister in a state mental hospital. His parents were divorced when he was 9 years old because of his father's drinking and extramarital affairs, the same reason for which his mother had divorced her first husband. His mother was a waitress in a nightclub and was said to drink to excess and to have a boyfriend of poor reputation.

In the early interviews, Bob did not minimize his guilt; in fact, he added details not known to the police. He pointed out repeatedly that while on his first parole he had been "mixed up," now he was all straightened out and there was no reason why he should not go home and "keep out of trouble." He maintained that the only problem he had was "how soon I can get out of here and go home"; he knew he could get and keep a job where his mother worked, everything would be all right, and there was nothing he wanted or needed to discuss with the caseworker.

In the institution he was involved in two violent fights with another boy and then he virtually isolated himself for some time, not talking or playing with other boys, volunteering for extra work with the avowed intention of "keeping out of trouble and getting home."

Tony was committed at 16 for an assault on a woman, for staying away from home nights and for being a "stubborn child," having been unknown to the courts until he was 14. His mother died when he was 3 years old and after some time in the homes of relatives, his father remarried and took him to live with him, the stepmother, an older brother, and younger stepbrother. At the time of Tony's commitment, the brother had married and left the home. Tony's father was interested in him but could not withstand the force of the stepmother's dislike of the boy and her insistence that he or she must leave the home. Tony had above-average intelligence, did quite well in school, and had musical talents. He impressed people as a most attractive boy.

He admitted his offenses and his trouble with his stepmother without apparent affect, but insisted that in the future he could and would return home and avoid difficulty. "If somebody starts getting on my neck or something, now I just walk away." He professed to like all the staff of the training school, and indicated that he understood himself very well and needed no casework help.

In the institution he was pleasant, compliant, and was given privileged placements as well as a leading part in the school play.

As in every casework relationship, as the interviews continue the worker accepts the material the client now begins to bring in and evaluates it in terms of its use to the client. It is likely now that the client will test out the caseworker in small, unobtrusive ways concerning the keeping of appointments, his attitude toward other members of the staff and other boys, the confidentiality of the interview (which the client will test out over and over again), and his willingness to be too acquiescent about the client's negative expressions toward others. The extreme ambivalence of the boy toward authority and the concomitant elements of control in the authority relationship are clearly seen at this time. It might be said that in a sense the child is trying to prove to himself that it would be foolish and unsafe to lower his defenses, to trust this person, and that he can only continue to survive as long as he denies his own ability to grow up and relate to reality as more than a very young child. Thus, the client presents himself on the one hand as a dependent child, passively wishing help, and then as an independent, aggressive individual not in need of help and questioning the motivation of the social worker who wants to help him.

In effect, the client at this time is in a very painful situation. He desperately fears to discover that this relationship, like all others he has known, will lead to loss, pain, and the renewal of the feelings of helplessness and loss against which he initially defended. At the same time, his testing behavior on the surface implies the converse—that he does not wish help and has little interest whether treatment continues or stops. However, within the relationship, he has found what he has wanted in a parent figure. If he lowers his defenses and lets himself become really involved with this person, he is vulnerable again to the pain of loss and the depression it engendered.

It is at this point in the treatment process that little progress is apparent. There is repetition of earlier material and the client appears to be unwilling or unable to move into new areas. The interviews are marked by a bored attitude on the part of the client, who makes it clear that he is there only under duress. There is a constant fencing on the part of the client, or at best, admissions and insights which prove on examination to be superficial—merely new angles of a well-tried defensive system.

In the face of this apparent impasse, the social worker may feel that nothing of importance has been accomplished except, perhaps, the perfection of the defensive system of the client. If the case is terminated at this point, there is almost the assurance that the delinquency, or a similar one, will be repeated. The child will appear to be the type of offender whom one sees categorized as bad, unteachable, not willing or able to profit from treatment, and consequently only to be reached through punishment. In actuality, it may be said that the child is fearful of moving deeper into a relationship that would expose him to a repetition of an earlier experience against which he is highly defended. The child must be allowed to continue to test the relationship, with the caseworker helping by remaining a constant figure and pointing out the reality of the relationship to the client.

Same Defense but Subtle Change

The caseworker will soon note that a subtle change has come into the client's behavior. While he uses the same defenses as heretofore, there is a new quality in this phase of the treatment process that is difficult to define or describe. For a period of time, there has been defiance in the denial—anger, rigidity in voice and manner. What is now apparent is perhaps analogous to that moment in the blind, raging temper tantrum of the young child when the alert parent senses that the fear and anger have blown themselves out and the continuing uproar means "Help me to stop!"

This same indescribable change seems to come into the relationship between the worker and the child. While the child maintains the same outward attitude of rejecting help, he comes to the interview with more enthusiasm, he smiles more often, he may "kid" with the worker, get angry or "fresh" with him, use more obscenity, and be more truly communicative. It is as though he were trying out the new relationship, but he is quick to retreat to the earlier position behind his defenses if any pressure is applied.

Excerpts from an interview with Jack after thirteen months of weekly meetings, are given here. His progress in the institution had been very stormy although the administration had tried to recognize even small gains.

CASEWORKER: What have you been doing this week?
JACK: Nothing.
CW: What?
JACK: You heard me. Nothing. . . .
CW: Were there some things you didn't want to talk about?
JACK: Not necessarily.
CW: *Are* there some things?
JACK: You asked the same question twice and you'll get the same answer twice—not necessarily!
CW: I was hoping the second time I'd get a different answer! (*Both laugh.*)
JACK: I wouldn't say there were some things I don't want to talk about . . . it doesn't bother me. . . . I just don't care. . . . (*yawns*). . . . I didn't sleep much

last night. (*Here follows an involved story about listening to a friend's borrowed radio.*) I wish I could get one from somewhere of my own. I ain't writing to my cousin no more.

cw: Why not?

JACK: Huh

cw: Why not?

JACK: Ah, she's full of s———, always feeding me that stuff . . . what do I care? . . . don't make no difference to me.

cw: What does she say?

JACK: She's always telling me "You can't go home." What is she telling me that for? I don't care. . . .

cw: Why?

JACK: I don't know. She says my mother's still sick over the last time. (*weak laugh*) . . .

cw: Did you ask her if you could go there?

JACK: (*softly, yawning*) Yeah. About a thousand times. I'm sick of it. When I get out . . . I'm not going to live there. I wouldn't live there.

For several interviews, Bob began by saying everything was "peaches and cream," but when the caseworker pointed out to him that he was spending most of his energy *not* thinking about the things that troubled him, he was able to talk about his early memories of his father whose early life, he had heard, was "just like me," shifting quickly again to statements about his boredom with the interviews. In the institutional program, his behavior was well under control and he was given some cottage responsibilities and played on a cottage basketball team.

Tony came to the interviews pleasantly and on time. He discussed what he professed to have heard his cottage master say—that "They are getting rid of this school soon," and that if he wished, he could ask the court to transfer him to an adult prison which he thought would be a much better place to "serve his time." He was still convinced that he would get into no more difficulties when he returned home because now his stepmother understood him better and wanted him. He mentioned talking all this over with his cottage master who agreed that he had "learned his lesson." He continued to have excellent behavior reports although he made no special friends among the boys.

Relaxation of Defenses

The caseworker is now at a crucial point in the treatment process and one most difficult for him. As the client gradually feels able to move deeper into the relationship in the direction in which he has been slowly moving over the past several months, there is a relaxation of the defenses. Within the safety of the treatment situation, the client is able to recognize that there is a pattern in his previous behavior and that this defensive structure has meaning for him. As the child is now faced with material that previously was inaccessible, he becomes highly anxious and the depressive feelings that have been buried are now felt directly. This is a stormy time in the relationship— the client often refuses to talk to the caseworker, accuses him of all kinds of deceptions, sets traps to demonstrate his unreliability, or refuses to come to interviews at all. He appears to be using every possible way of provoking the caseworker to reject him and terminate this painful period of beginning growth. He is almost in the position of a man, very painfully hurt in an accident, who begs his rescuers not to touch him because he cannot face the pain of healing.

At this interview Jack had flagrantly violated rules and had to be restricted to his room. He expressed disgust at seeing the caseworker and maintained that there was nothing to talk about, nothing was bothering him. When the caseworker refused to accept this, Jack countered by telling him of some of his homosexual activity in the training school which was not known to the administration, talking about it in a tone calculated to show how little he cared to conform to the standards he knew were acceptable and clearly provoking the caseworker to anger and rejection. The caseworker expressed his displeasure with such behavior, said he hoped it was thing of the past now and left, reminding Jack that he would see him next week.

For six interviews Bob's responses were monosyllabic—he had no problems, he found the interviews boring. In answer to any question he said, "I don't know." He said he saw no sense in coming to the interviews and wondered if "somebody" was working to prevent his parole, going on to accuse the caseworker directly of telling his cottage master about some drinking Bob had confided in the caseworker. To a question about what he wanted to talk about at one of these interviews, the reply was "Nothing."

At this time, he was refused parole home because of his mother's drinking, and when the caseworker tried to talk to him about that, he replied, "If she drinks, she drinks. It's got nothing to do with me."

He was having many arguments with the cottage personnel.

Tony continued to talk of his wish to go home and said, "My father says it'd be different if I come home now." The caseworker asked, "What does he mean?" Tony replied: "He said he was going to talk to her" (*stepmother*). Tony had a weekend at home and reported it as "perfect." While he insisted that he had no worries other than whether and when he would be permitted to return home, he was always polite and changed the subject frequently rather than refusing to answer the caseworker's questions.

The caseworker told Tony that he was going to be away on army training for two weeks. Tony appeared hardly to hear this but a moment later exploded into a long diatribe about the people at the training school who "leave you alone and don't talk to you," ostensibly centering on the administration's withholding final information about his return home. That night he made an unprovoked attack on a boy so hard that the boy had to be hospitalized. Since this was completely out of keeping with his usual behavior, the administration was inclined to believe his story that it was accidental and he was not punished.

Beginning of Emotional Growth

If the worker is strong enough to weather the final period of testing out described above and perseveres through it, he encounters the depression that the lowered defenses now allow to break through, flooding the ego with the threat of potential loss, of helplessness and pain. The client blames the caseworker for his unhappiness and at the same time clings to him in an acute dependent relationship. It is often difficult for the caseworker to deal with his own feelings of guilt at this point since he may feel that he has brought about too much suffering. He may also be concerned that the client may be permanently fixed in his dependence on him.

If, however, he can accept the client's feelings as a sign of positive growth, he will find that this stage does rapidly move over into that of growth in a more emotionally mature fashion. It is, indeed, rewarding after months of sparring and constant gains and losses, to see the client begin at last to show insight, to make appropriate sexual identifications, and to demonstrate the beginning of a useful superego development.

It is vital at this time in treatment that the external reality also prove rewarding to the client, since it is against the reality that the defense was erected in the first place. In the institution, it is important that progress be rewarded with tangible evidences of the pleasure of the staff in the boy's increasing maturity. Exception to institutional routines should, if possible, be made for the boy at this time and should be explained as resulting from a recognition of him as a more responsible individual. If possible, the reality of the community to which he will return should be made attractive to him, and if this is not possible, he should be helped to find resources there which are ready to help him as he needs them. Tangible rewards, letters, and visits will be more meaningful than words or a passive willingness to accept his application for help.

> *In the final interviews, Jack talked of his feelings when he had been confined to his room.*
> JACK: I don't like to be in my room.
> CW: You'd rather be in the program?
> JACK: I don't like to be in my room, period. . . .
> CW: What happens when you are?
> JACK: Nothing happens—I just get restless and bored. . . . When I got at this point anywhere else, I ran away.
> *He discussed the fact that he was trying to keep himself free of homosexual involvements and the manner in which he had found the staff, formerly seen as implacable enemies, as able to help him.*
> CW: You mean you are afraid you will get involved with him? (*a homosexual boy whom Jack has described as "a jerk" whom he hates*)
> JACK: That's right, you hit it on the nose. . . . I just pay no attention. . . .
> CW: Because if you did, you're afraid—
> JACK: I'm not afraid to get into trouble. I just don't want to have anything to do with him, period. If I get into trouble or not . . . He's got a lot of kids into trouble.
> CW: The masters know?
> JACK: They know, don't worry. They ain't stupid either. . . . One day he was in his room and I was trading funny books with him and I had a whole stack of funny books and Mr. C came over and he said, "Jack, I know you was having nothing to do with him—just trading books—I know," he says, "just pay no attention to him and you won't get into trouble!" I says, "I was just getting books" and he says, "I know!" He wasn't telling me like—you know—me and Mr. C get along good.
> CW: So you're trying to keep away from D?
> JACK: That's what I'm trying to do *most*.

Bob started the interview by saying that he wouldn't mind going to live with his brother if his mother would come too, because in his home town there was "nobody to hang around with but kids that have been in trouble, just hang around with a couple of them and before you know it, you're in trouble again." From this, he went into an angry account of the cottage relief matron he could not adjust to, and the caseworker accepted his angry feelings. At the next interview, he talked of his decision to go to his brother's house although his mother would not join them now, and went on to talk about his mother's drinking, saying that she always drank some, "like everybody else" except when he got in trouble and then it got worse. And he went on to say that she told him his father had taught her to drink—repeating his belief that he was just like his father. In the last interview, before he left for his brother's home, he discussed realistic plans for work and school, expressed some fears about the trip, and about making new, nondelinquent friends, and accepted reassurance in a mature manner. He followed out his plans and continued to do well.

When the caseworker came back from his trip, Tony hastened to tell him about the assault "accident" although he mentioned he had not told his father. He admitted to some worries about how things were going to go when he reached home and said he thought he would like to have "someone to talk to" when he left.

Because of his excellent institutional record, he was permitted to go to a work placement where he did so well he was "rewarded" by being allowed to go home at his urgent request and without consultation with the caseworker. Two months later he was returned for violation of parole because of two "unarmed assaults."

As with other such personality disorders, it is inevitable that regressions will occur when the conditions which caused the original difficulty are reactivated, as they often are in the difficult reality situations in which most of these clients must live. Loss of a friendly employer, a change in caseworker, the removal of a friend, all may bring a recurrence of the depression and a remobilization of the early defense against it. For this reason, such clients should be continued in some contact with their caseworkers for as long a time as possible after active treatment is terminated. If this is done, or if the worker to whom the case is assigned in a new agency understands the long road the client has traveled before, such regression can frequently be used for additional insights as the client comes to realize that he has not really "lost everything." No claims are made that such clients will be able to function as freely and with as great a degree of maturity as those whose early lives were not so severely traumatized. But they can function adequately, with a degree of happiness to themselves and safety to the community.

Summary

Clients who use the primitive defense of denial are frequently seen on correctional caseloads where they are placed by authoritative agencies.

To work successfully with such clients, the caseworker needs to recognize that this defense is held against the pervading depression felt by the client who has known early loss and rejection and who controls the resulting anxiety created by his reality situation by denying it and resisting any relationship which may cause a repetition of the early experience. Because the client is reacting against reality, it is essential that during treatment the environment be made as consistent and rewarding as possible.

The cases studied were institutionalized boys in training schools for delinquents. In treatment, the caseworker presented himself as a warm, accepting, consistent adult, identified with authority but not involved with institutional management. Treatment was carried on this basis for a long period of testing out on the part of the client who appeared to need to fend off the relationship he actually longed for, for fear of the loss which relationship had brought him in his earlier experiences. When treatment was continued in spite of his denial of need, and the environment was used positively, a period of depression followed the lowering of the defense any the beginning of emotional growth. Such growth was rapid and with the development of a more mature defensive system, the depression was greatly alleviated so that the client was enabled to live comfortably and safely in the community.

Group Work with Youth in Conflict

Paul Lerman

Previous writings and comments by practitioners serving adolescent groups that are in conflict with acceptable standards of behavior have begun to carve out a systematization of the assumptions underlying such a service. McCarthy and Barbaro,[1] writing from the experiences of the New York City Youth Board, identified some of the goals, principles, and procedures of working with hostile street gangs. Austin, in a recent issue of SOCIAL WORK, carefully outlined the goals and objectives of reaching-out efforts with groups, the stages of the worker-group relationship, and indicated the probable results to be expected from such an approach.[2] Richards, in a recent speech, spelled out a theoretical framework for understanding group-based deviant behavior in a dynamic fashion, and sharpened our focus in working with varied antisocial constellations—or forms—of youth groups.[3]

[1] James E. McCarthy and Joseph S. Barbaro, "Re-Directing Teen-Age Gangs," in Sylvan S. Furman, ed., *Reaching the Unreached* (New York: New York City Youth Board, 1952), pp. 98–126.

[2] David M. Austin, "Goals for Gang Workers," *Social Work,* Vol. 2, No. 4 (October 1957), pp. 43–50.

[3] Catharine V. Richards, "Finding a Focus for Work with Hostile Youth Groups," in *Social Work with Groups,* Selected Papers of the 1958 National Conference on Social Welfare (New York: National Association of Social Workers, 1958).

Reprinted with permission of the author and the National Association of Social Workers, from *Social Work,* Vol. 3, No. 4 (October, 1958), pp. 71–77.

These efforts have been extremely helpful to the field, but a need for translating some of the more generalized concepts into specific implications for practice still exists. The purpose of this paper is to focus on some of these implications, and perhaps add more "food for thought." In the main, extensive use of a single case will be used to suggest explicitly—and implicitly—the thinking, role, and methods of a trained worker servicing such a group. While the material that follows is based on the experiences at one settlement-type agency, it is felt that the practice implications can have wider applicability.

For practitioners working with youth groups in conflict, it is assumed that the antisocial acts of individuals cannot be understood—or coped with—unless we deal with factors other than just personality dynamics. Some of these factors are:

1. The internal relationships and the evolved roles, status, structure, norms, and persistency of interaction of the individual's immediate peer group.

2. The pressures toward conformity, and the interstimulating effects of group participation.

3. Predominant values of the significant people and institutions within the neighborhood life-space affecting the individual and his primary reference group.

4. The mode and style of personal controls of behavior prescribed, permitted, preferred, and proscribed by outside sources, *e.g.*, family, peer groups, police, precinct captain, etc.[4]

5. The reality aspects of the specific problem situation with which the individual is confronted, and the way, under subcultural influences, he perceives this "slice of life."

By pinpointing these factors, we are really restating—perhaps with different emphases—traditional group work concepts. However, the manner in which we perform the day-to-day job, and the techniques we may employ to work with the reality impact of conflict situations, may differ sharply from traditional agency practice. For example, recreation-type *Program*—traditionally a key tool in group work practice—may play only a minimal role in the ongoing work with such youth groups. But *Relationship* (that mutual feeling of liking, empathy, and trust), formerly the twin brother of Program, becomes the favored sibling of our practice.

[4] Robert K. Merton, "The Social-Cultural Environment and *Anomie*," in Helen L. Witmer and Ruth Kotinsky, eds., *New Perspectives for Research on Juvenile Delinquency* (Washington, D.C.: Children's Bureau Publication No. 356, 1956), pp. 32–33.

The foregoing comments are not meant to imply that this type of service involves a total reshuffling of group work principles. Rather, it is in the area of *what* we emphasize, and at *what* time we do this. Some of the areas of emphasis are as follows: *1]* active communication that we care—care an awful lot—about their problems; *2]* active demonstration that we are as nonjudgmental as we say—or imply; *3]* alert willingness to sympathize with their weaknesses, and support their strengths; *4]* overt expectation that they can participate in coping with their problems; *5]* flexibility, openness, and imagination in the role of the helpful adult; and *6]* coming to grips with our systems of values and class biases, as well as personality components.

To illustrate these ideas and to depict actual practice implications, the following case may prove helpful. The actual conflict situation involved stealing by three members of a group. The mode of referral, the pressures to perform the act, and the roles of the workers can be better understood by reviewing past work with the total group of which the three were members.

The group called themselves, colorfully enough, the "Wildcats." The *esprit de corps* is best described by repeating their cheer-like yells. One fellow would say, "Are we good?"—and the others would reply in unison, "We are good—we're the Wildcats!" They are 14 to 18 years of age, have an informal membership size that fluctuates around ten, and are mainly of third-generation Polish and Italian ethnic origin. The majority attend a public high school, and a few work as their fathers do—in manual-type occupations. Skill in sports, owning and/or driving a car, and ease in dealing with girls are high-status factors.

Individually, the majority are capable of exhibiting friendliness, courtesy, and consideration for adults. Collectively they are provocative, teasing, and often downright hostile toward adults and their institutions. They are quite proud of this masculine aggressive behavior, and even have a colorful slang phrase to depict their diluted sex play: "ball-busting."

When Scotty, the street worker, first made contact with the Wildcats, they were the object of much agency concern. The group was stealing agency property, defying staff, and disrupting other club meetings. The agency decided that they could no longer be served in the traditional manner.

In preparing to work with the group, Scotty learned that the group was interested in baseball and was toying with the idea of obtaining a clubhouse. He also learned that in the past the group had followed through on plans, provided they were really interested in doing so. His first formal contact with the group, originally to deal with their joining a softball league, coincided with their learning of the loss of the building worker. Seizing upon the reality of the situation, Scotty asked the group why they had not taken up an offer to use a basement for a clubhouse. After going through excuses for their inaction, a quick decision was made by the boys to have a try at it. The softball league had become secondary to their newly released interest. Hostility was expressed about the agency and its staff, but Scotty was dissociated from this frame of reference.

In the weeks that followed, the Wildcats proved wonderfully resourceful in cleaning, furnishing, and decorating their clubhouse. Approbation from Scotty was directly requested, and he warmly verbalized his admiration of their efforts. As he began to spend more time with them, he began to raise the realistic caution that if they could not control each other's behavior, the clubhouse might be lost. Neighbors would react to swearing, noise, and provocation in the same way that the agency had done—by removing them from the scene. He remained nonjudgmental, but continued to pose the problems caused by their behavior, and verbalized an expectation that they could act otherwise.

The Wildcats were finally forced to leave. Scotty used this reality situation to suggest they draw up a set of rules and internal group punishment for swearing, noise, wrestling, and so on, if they were to approach neighbors to get their club back. Scotty, together with high-status members, made house visits, but neighbors and the landlord balked at giving them another chance. The boys were angry, but quite capable of sizing up their own responsibility for the expulsion. Scotty supported this accounting for past deeds.

During this time and through the summer, Scotty and the boys (either in individual contacts, two's and three's, or larger constellations) discussed school, job outlook, the Army, marriage, their antisocial behavior on the corner, cars, batting averages, and the like. In most cases these were just bull sessions, but sometimes meaningful things happened. For example, one boy, with Scotty's support, and the approbation of a few other Wildcats, went to summer school to make up deficient credits. While antisocial behavior on the corner continued, a few of the boys with more impulse control were beginning to "bawl out" obstreperous members for swearing and acting up. Scotty supported these efforts.

In the fall the group was transferred back to the building-centered program, since it was thought they might be better able to accept more responsibility for their behavior. Agency staff also felt that they could act more consistently in limiting Wildcat members. The new worker was oriented to "antiseptically bounce" (in the words of Fritz Redl) the boys when they got out of hand. But in doing so, he was to leave the building with them and continue to be their worker for the night. Scotty, aside from occasional passing contacts, disengaged completely to allow Larry, the new part-time worker, to become the focal point of agency concern for their individual and group problems. This worked successfully until the stealing incident when both workers merged efforts.

John, a Wildcat of long standing and important status, came to Larry late one evening and told him he was in a "jam," having stolen goods at a local department store where he worked part time after school. Larry suggested he come in the next day to discuss it further. The same evening, Scotty learned about the incident from the agency executive, and it was decided that Scotty and Larry would work together because of the latter's lack of training and experience in handling such situations.

The next day, however, John approached Scotty directly at a high-school hangout. John did this at the suggestion of a teen-age boy of another clique whom Scotty had helped with a school problem. This boy was Scotty's referral agent.

In an interview at the agency, Scotty learned of the full extent of John's thefts, and the others who had stolen goods. Three Wildcats and two strange boys were involved. John claimed he had not taken anything when he first started the job, but after seeing Bob, heretofore a stranger, stealing and getting away with it, he told other Wildcats. Wildcat members asked him to steal for them, and one boy particularly, "Little Boy," encouraged him to make a business of it, promising to pay John for his efforts. Normally a boy who would not steal because of a strong sense of values, plus an ego appraisal mechanism that could look to the future consequences of getting caught, John succumbed to the pressure. He was given added impulse support by the presence at work of two newer additions to the Wildcats, Bill and Jim, who were eager to gain status in the group. All three were certainly "egged on" by the group.

Beside the weight of group pressures from the outside, John was also a member of the group that worked in the store. These group loyalties, with concomitant pressures for supporting impulses and acting out a norm of masculine behavior, were quite strong. But added to these pressures was the seductive example of watching someone else—a non-Wildcat—initiate the act and get away with the goods. Given this set of circumstances, it would have taken an unusual control system to prevent John from beginning his period of crime.

The store, at this point, only knew of Bob, the non-Wildcat member, and his escapades. He was out on bond, and his lawyer was trying to get the police to go after another boy (who had been fired weeks earlier for incompetency) as the major culprit. The police knew of John but had not told the store. It was apparent that the juvenile officer had not been involved, but that the regular police officers were handling a juvenile case. Knowing the reputation of the local police station for accepting bribes, Scotty surmised that this was the reason for the juvenile officer's not having been called in on the case, and no contact having been made with John's parents.

Frightened and confused, John asked what he should do. When Scotty reflected back the question, John answered, "The right thing." It became apparent that this meant excluding involvement of his parents, particularly his father. Because of the crisis element, and John's inability to come up with alternatives, Scotty posed alternatives that he might consider. The alternatives were geared to reality consequences that might follow, and not to any morality factor. Scotty felt that the case did not warrant consideration of a referral at that point. The alternatives were as follows:

1. *Don't do anything*—and continue to sweat it out in the hope that you will squeeze out of it.

2. *Tell your parents*—and ask them for help, even though they might be ashamed and angry.

3.   *Make restitution directly*—and get some of the stuff from the guys, pay the balance, and hope that parents and police won't be notified.

John, of course, balked most at the second and was apprehensive about the third alternative. The untrained worker, Larry who was also present but had remained silent, began to react, and started to push his own feelings. Larry began to argue for a course of action most consistent with his middle-class values, namely, tell all to Mom and Pop, and they will come through all the time. Without attacking Larry directly, Scotty pointed out that John had to live with the decision, and it would be better if he didn't feel he was being "pushed." Fortunately, because of the status feelings towards Scotty, Larry was able to catch the point and resume his listening role.

As discussion continued, John began to lean toward the third possibility, but was dubious about admitting any more to the store than he had told the police, namely, one-half of what he had stolen. Scotty pointed out the dangers of this approach if the store took a total inventory, and couldn't account for the goods in sales. Somebody would get caught "holding the bag," so realistically, if the third course were followed, it paid to tell the truth. Besides, this would be the "right thing."

As John seemed to become more comfortable with making restitution directly, Scotty suggested that the other two Wildcats, Bill and Jim, be called into the discussion. This was done to get a group decision now, for an act that would have to be done collectively, to make sense to the local store owner, and perhaps retrieve some of the goods without paying cash. The alternatives were reviewed with the boys, and concern expressed that the workers wanted to help them with the problem. Jim responded quickly, indicating he was glad they had been found out at last. New to the group and to the neighborhood, he seemed quite eager to please and be readily accepted by adults and peers.

Bill was extremely fearful of his father's finding out about his delinquent activities, and seemed resentful of John's "pulling" him into this confession, since his part was really so small. Scotty reminded him that he had tried to sell Larry some stolen socks a while ago, so he had "spilled the beans" himself. He sheepishly said, "Oh, yeah." These attempts on the part of John and Bill to minimize their responsibility in the stealing highlight the degree to which defenses can be manipulated to prevent shame and a sense of guilt from becoming overpowering. For John, the rationale that Bob did it first was offered to excuse the thefts. For Bill, the idea that he hadn't taken "much" was used as an alibi and a defense.

Without dealing with these defenses directly, Scotty dealt with the amount taken by each, writing it down on paper for all to see. John had stolen over $70 in goods, Jim about $60, and Bill "only" $15. In a nonverbal manner this procedure appeared to indicate that each boy was responsible for the definite amount, per individual confession. This approach seemed to make sense, and a sense of consensus was apparent. Just as group processes had furthered the loss of impulse control via mutual identification and the contagious thrill of stealing, so were the same dynamics coming into operation in support of the restitution idea. These responses to group pressures were as unconscious to them as their use of the workers as parental substitutes.

After Scotty suggested that they try and recover the goods, as this might save them money, it developed that most of the articles had been channeled through Little Boy for sale. Little Boy was sent for, and soon appeared in a swaggering, braggadocio manner. On learning of the boys' decision, he quickly made known what goods he had left. He also indicated that he had a number of automobile hubcaps in his possession, since he had also engaged in direct stealing. He spoke of these acts like a "big shot." Scotty knew from past work with the group that Little Boy was low in status because of poor sports skill, size, and lack of ease in dealing with girls.

Scotty told Little Boy that he was fond of him, and would like to help him stay out of the State Training School. If he could return the hubcaps as well as the store goods, he could get them off his hands and perhaps make a fresh start in keeping away from this type of activity. Scotty also suggested that there were other ways to prove that he was becoming a young man, and told him that he would not be turned in to the police, since workers at the agency acted in a confidential way. He said that he would bring the store goods, but not the hubcaps; they would be gotten rid of in his own way, and then he would cease his activity. Scotty said this was up to him to decide, but that we would like to help him now. Little Boy said he would being all that he had, but not the hubcaps. This was accepted.

While Little Boy and Bill left to get the goods, Scotty told the others he hoped that they would use their friendship and loyalty to Little Boy to help him stay away from trouble via stealing. As a club they could help each other stay out of "jams," as well as do just the opposite. They silently mulled over the idea.

After Little Boy returned with the goods, he told the workers that his father wanted his name kept out of it, since he had purchased some of the stolen goods from his son. Scotty said he would hold to this, just like other things the boys had told him and Larry. Little Boy commented that Scotty must know of thousands of things that kids did that were wrong, and tried to help them. Scotty affirmed this, and said he was still interested in helping Little Boy with the hubcap problem. The latter again said he would get rid of them and cease the activity.

The returned goods were then totaled and matched against the list of stolen goods for each boy. This procedure again highlighted each boy's share of responsibility for the stealing.

The next day all three boys arrived promptly at an agreed meeting-place, and together with Larry and Scotty made restitution at the store. Prior to this action, John had been slipped some money by Little Boy, who said that the boys had taken up a collection on his behalf. John paid $40, Jim $20, and Bill $7. The store executives accepted this display of "guts" in coming clean, and the boys rewarded them by showing the "easy" places where goods could be pushed out of the building.

After the incident, Scotty again disengaged, and Larry continued further work with the group around their responsibilities toward each other, as well as further attention to Little Boy.

Implications for Practice

1. There exists a peer subculture for each neighborhood, with a dominant code of keeping information from adults. Many teen-agers, outside the Wildcats, knew of the escapades, but none "ratted." However, a friendly adult can enter this world as a participant observer. From this vantage point he can offer concrete help to individuals and groups, redirect activities, and pose alternatives to antisocial values and acts. He can do this without violating this dominant code, as confidentiality is highly valued on a reality basis by these youthful clients. This lends support to the ethics of our profession in this area of work.

2. By becoming readily available and accessible in times of crises, a worker can build significant relationships and be of concrete, easily perceived help. Adults are judged more by actions than words. The status of a helping person must be an *achieved* one, and not merely ascribed from the outside, or implied by words. This status may or may not rub off on the agency he represents.

3. The values of significant adults, institutions, and groups in a neighborhood life-space must be taken into account. They may not be consistently on the side of socially approved behavior. The actions of the police and the father are key examples of society's ambivalence in this area.

4. Our strategic use of sources of individual controls must be reassessed. Besides an individual's sense of values—or superego structure—there are other sources of controls. The peer group and the teen subculture are potent ones to be considered. These social controls operate in face-to-face situations, and as a strong "push from the rear" in acting as a reference group for standards of behavior. Individuals differ in their susceptibility to witness the seductions of an initiator who acts out suppressed impulses and still control their own behavior. They also differ in their willingness to gain status via conformity, and in their need for a collective guilt sense to assuage their individual anxieties.

5. These youths are ambivalent in regard to wanting—or not wanting—controls imposed from the outside. Exuberant, and yet fearful of their impulses in acting masculine, they want adults to *tell* them what to do, yet they also want to revolt. While workers must be wary of falling into the trap of becoming a control source by their physical presence, they can aid internal controls by helping youth to assess consequences on a reality basis. This role in helping the youthful ego to look to the future—on a reality basis—can be a really helpful educational service.

6. The necessity for social group workers to engage in the practice of interviewing is sharply indicated in working with youth groups in conflict. Not only marginal interviews, but other types are necessary. Prolonged interviews over a period of time, as will be necessary with Little Boy, are certainly indicated. We also engage in interviews of individuals in a sub-group setting, but are not always as conscious of the dynamics involved. Sometimes, pairs might be seen, as this is the level on which they feel most comfortable in revealing fears, doubts, and hopes. Working with individual members can be helpful in giving emotional support in time of need, pointing up alternatives, reflecting consequences of thoughts or actions, and in continually building meaningful relationships with a friendly adult.

7. Our service to youth groups in conflict—as in all group work service—is geared to two levels of help, *i.e.*, groups and individuals. We are desirous of helping the total constellation achieve status-producing and satisfying products that are socially acceptable, because only a group entity can accomplish many of these worthwhile goals. These goals often go beyond agency walls, and the worker, to be helpful, should recognize and gear actions towards this larger life-space. Help to individuals in crisis situations and in terms of group-engendered problems are also valid services offered by group workers. Referrals are necessary, but are difficult and not always indicated.

8. The workload of the workers assigned to such groups must be arranged with great care. Such groups need more time to use the workers, although this should not be limitless, and there should be availability in time of crisis. Time must be made for bull sessions, interviews, and "hanging around."

9. The worker must be assigned to the group with the goal that he will serve it wherever the setting proves most conducive to using his assistance. If the group cannot use the building effectively, then the worker should reach out to the group. If the group is asked to leave the building for the night, then the worker should also leave with the group. They are his clients, and if the service cannot be offered in the building there should be no qualms about being of service outside; nor should their problems be "kicked" outside.

10. The use of trained and untrained personnel needs more consideration in this area of work, as well as in traditional settings. The concept of the team approach, as particularly utilized in hospitals, could certainly be used to good advantage. While we want untrained people to learn on the job, and not become overly dependent for answers or solutions from the trained group workers, there is room for flexibility in the handling of crisis situations, and problems of particular difficulty. The trained worker can directly use his professional skills, while the untrained worker can observe, much as an intern-in-training. The roles of Scotty and Larry are examples of this.

11. The impact of physical settings, and the kind of structures we build into our settings must be more consciously considered. Stealing in the store was made easier by the gaps in the back window. Controls can often be helped by the size of rooms, the distribution of furniture, the "status" of the meeting room, and by other seemingly, but important, mundane considerations.

12. The relationship of the worker to the group and the worker to the individual is our key potential for helping. Program and other environmental manipulations directed toward helping the ego immediately can be helpful but are usually secondary. Only if we truly "reach" these youth can they be helped to achieve more satisfying ways of handling the age-old conflict between the demands of culture and the imperious strivings of individual impulses. Hopefully, we can help them to become more socialized, without suppressing their desire to change the rules, and thereby change the world.

Group Psychotherapy with Delinquent Adolescent Girls

Marvin Hersko

This paper is based upon three years of experience in carrying out group psychotherapy with delinquent adolescent girls in a training school setting. However, I feel that the problems encountered in the treatment of these girls are essentially those inherent in the treatment of any adolescent group—male or female, delinquent or nondelinquent. Erikson has described adolescence as a developmental stage in which individuals are involved in a process of personal redefinition.[1] Every adolescent is faced with the problem of achieving a stable sense of identity which not only satisfies his inner needs but is also acceptable in his social environment. The delinquent has merely developed a particular solution to the identity crisis which all adolescents undergo. Therefore, I hope the reader will find most of the following observations relevant to his own work with adolescents.

One might reasonably ask whether it is possible to treat the adolescent patient. Certainly the adolescent lacks the reliable ego which is considered by many to be a prerequisite for successful psychotherapy. Furthermore,

[1] E. H. Erikson, "The Problem of Ego Identity," *J. Am. Psychoanal. Assoc.*, 4:56-121, 1956.

Reprinted from the *American Journal of Orthopsychiatry*, XXXII (January, 1962), pp. 169–175. Copyright, the American Orthopsychiatric Association, Inc. Reproduced by permission of the author and the Association.

adolescents are usually not motivated for psychotherapy, but are referred by others who are concerned about their welfare. The symptomatology, moreover, frequently consists of behavioral difficulties rather than of the inner distress which motivates most patients. The first problem, then, in the therapy of adolescents is to develop a genuine motivation for and involvement in the therapeutic process. The adolescent is extremely reluctant to ask for help, since this is usually experienced as a frightening confession of weakness. However, if the therapist reaches out to adolescents, expressing a warm interest in understanding and helping them, most adolescents will respond and begin to relate cautiously to him. Therapeutic goals should be set up in terms of the immediate concerns of the patients. These might include better control of impulses and better relationships with adults or peers, as well as relief from inner distress.

What kind of therapy shall we attempt with adolescents? Their emotional immaturity and their difficulty in verbalizing might suggest activity or play therapy. However, adolescents find such treatment difficult to accept because of their contempt for childish pursuits. Yet approaching them as adults with the usual techniques of intensive, uncovering psychotherapy is likely to prove equally frustrating and ineffectual. The adolescent typically responds to a deep, analytic approach with intense anxiety, with increased acting out, and frequently by withdrawal from therapy.

The usual group therapeutic approach must be modified because of the incomplete ego development of adolescent patients. Because of her weak ego the adolescent girl is self-centered, has poor control of her impulses, and has difficulty in benefiting from past experiences or in planning for the future. The greatest handicap to successful psychotherapy, however, lies in the adolescent's low tolerance for anxiety. The therapist must select techniques which maintain anxiety at a relatively low level. This automatically limits the depth and goals of the therapeutic process. Ego defenses should be supported and integrated rather than weakened by the therapist. Free association should not be used, nor should there be other efforts, such as dream interpretation, to uncover unconscious material. The task of the therapist is to encourage ego development and the synthesis of conflicting identifications rather than to foster insight into unconscious conflicts. Toward these ends, he will use a primarily supportive, educative approach and encourage identification with suitable adults[2].

Group involvement is habitual for adolescents so that the idea of receiving help in a group is usually not too threatening. It is comforting for them to know that others have problems and feelings similar to their own. It is also comforting for the adolescent girl to know that she will not have to cope with an unknown adult by herself, but will have allies in dealing with the therapist.

Yet, strangely enough, it is difficult to develop a sense of group unity with adolescents. The group members fear that the fact that they are receiving

[2] I. Schulman, "Transference, Resistance, and Communication Problems in Adolescent Psychotherapy Groups," *Int. J. Group Psychother.*, 9: 496–503, 1959.

psychotherapy means they are crazy. Hence, they are dubious about their own participation in the group and reluctant to identify with other members. Also, adolescents are always afraid of losing status with their peer group. They fear that others will interpret their involvement in therapy as weakness and dependency upon an adult, both of which are contrary to adolescent values and particularly to delinquent values.

Another obstacle to group solidarity is the deep distrust the members have for the therapist and for each other. They continually anticipate criticism and punishment from the therapist. The typical member tests both the therapist and the group—over and over again. For example, a girl may state that she is planning to run away in order to find out whether or not the therapist will violate the confidentiality of their relationship.

However, the greatest obstacle to the development of group unity is the lack of empathy on the part of the individual members for one another. This may be particularly true of delinquents, who are notoriously self-centered. They form groups not out of friendship but for mutual security against an adult world which is perceived as hostile. The delinquent adolescent girl feels incompetent to solve her problems. Furthermore, she does not believe that her peers really care for her or that they are capable of helping her. This difficulty in object relations probably reflects the traumatic nature of the early maternal relationship.

Another requisite for effective group therapy is the understanding and support of the current parental figures. If the adolescents are in an institution, mutual confidence and two-way communication between therapist and houseparents are essential. The therapist finds it helpful to know how the group members adjust to their living situation. Similarly, the houseparent can do a better job if she knows in general what the girls' problems are and what progress they are making in therapy. Such information can be reported by the therapist without revealing the specific experiences or feelings that the group members have expressed.

The first concern of the group members is to reassure themselves that they have not lost status by becoming patients. Secondly, they try to ascertain whether their free expression will lead to self-incrimination and to criticism or punishment by the therapist or by other authorities. When the group members have reassured themselves on these two points, they test to find out what advantages they can derive from the therapy situation. For example, they may try to manipulate the therapist into granting special privileges or making a favorable recommendation. Also, they will use the opportunity for free expression to abuse authority figures at great length and with much pleasure.

The therapist must be accepting of the feelings expressed, but he must not permit himself to be manipulated by the group members or seduced into agreeing with their complaints. Instead, the therapist must actively direct the group into discussing the group members' symptoms and their reality problems. The therapist should begin with feelings and behavior which are experienced as ego-alien by the group. The symptoms related, however, are more often characterological than neurotic. For example, group members are more likely to complain of uncontrolled stealing than of feeling depressed.

The common emotions underlying the symptoms of the different members should be pointed out frequently. This facilitates the group members' identifying with and supporting one another. The therapist must display an attitude of understanding but not condoning the antisocial feelings and behavior related by the group. Interpretation of symptoms should stress immediate causes rather than their roots in the unconscious, infantile needs of the group members. For example, stealing can be interpreted as the result of present anger or deprivation rather than as the result of feeling unloved as a child.

The therapist should focus the group discussion, as much as possible, upon the group members' currently important interpersonal relationships. A girl's present hostility toward a matron or parole officer is both more meaningful and less threatening to her than her hostility toward her mother. One can be sure that the neurotic pattern experienced in the original family constellation will be repeated with the significant individuals in the present environment. In fact the more undeveloped the ego is, the more exact will be the re-enactment. This is not to say that the group members cannot discuss with profit current difficulties in their parental relationships. For example, feelings of being distrusted or of resenting the controls imposed by the parents are fruitful subjects of discussion. However, any insight into deeper feelings such as her incestuous wishes toward the father or her death wishes toward the mother arouses unbearable anxiety and guilt in the adolescent girl.

In discussion of their interpersonal relationships, the conflicted self concepts of the group members will gradually become more apparent and of more concern to them. The members can be expected to show extreme sensitivity in this area so that a great deal of tact, support, and patience will be demanded of the therapist. Free discussion of the diffuse and conflicting self concepts of the group members is essential. Some of the important subjective dimensions within which the adolescent must locate herself are: dependency vs. self-sufficiency, good vs. bad, masculinity vs. femininity, and lower class vs. middle class. It is reassuring to the group for the therapist to point out that these are a universal problem of adolescence. Also, for the adolescent who characteristically sees either black or white, it is helpful for the therapist to indicate that shades of gray do exist, and that he is optimistic about the possibility of integrating conflicting, tentative identifications[3].

Because of the anxiety evoked, it is sometimes necessary to discuss problems in this area indirectly or by means of analogy. For example, one week all of my groups savagely tore into a girl whom they called a "mess." They complained that she was dirty and unkempt, that she engaged in sordid sexual activities, and that—worst of all—she "stunk." It was not possible at that time for most of the group members to accept their own

---

[3] M. Gitelson, "Character Synthesis: The Psychotherapeutic Problem of Adolescence," *Am. J. Orthopsychiatry*, 18: 422–431, 1948.

unconscious feelings of being "messes." However, the groups were able to discuss profitably why that particular girl became such a mess, how she must feel, and what she could do to help herself.

Traditionally, psychotherapy centers about the axis connecting past and present. With adolescents, however, therapy should center on the axis connecting present and future. The adolescent girl often feels helpless to control her fate. For example, our girls frequently expect to end up in prison no matter what they do. No doubt this feeling of futility originated in the repeated frustration of childhood wishes and endeavors. However, a more fruitful interpretation for present purposes would be that group members use their feelings of helplessness to justify maintaining an antisocial but gratifying way of life. Actually, the delinquent girl is afraid to give up the certainty of excitement for what to her seems like a slim possibility of finding love. The therapist must be able to sympathize with the loss of immediate gratification that conformity would entail. But he must convey that, in the long run, the adolescent will secure more gratification by accepting society than by rebelling against it. The therapist should use every opportunity to point out the socially acceptable ways of achieving status and of winning affection that are available to the group members.

The role of the therapist in the group treatment of adolescents is necessarily more authoritarian and less permissive than in the treatment of adults. It is essential that the members respect the therapist and know that he is in control of the group. The therapist has to be more active in beginning and maintaining the therapeutic process than he would be with adults. He must demonstrate the fact that there are underlying causes for all of the behavior and feelings of the group members. The therapist should stress that the group members are not helpless but are indeed responsible for their behavior—that they are capable, at least potentially, of self-control. The group members must realize that they can choose between alternative courses of action and that they can control, in large part, their own futures.

The therapist will, of course, use all of the customary techniques of group psychotherapy. However, he will be much more supportive and reassuring than he would be with adults. The therapist must also rely much more heavily than usual on educative techniques. For example, the group may need information on body functioning, or the members may need advice on how to apply for jobs. Most of all, adolescent delinquents need help in reality testing. Their perception is stereotyped and they see others as objects rather than as individuals. For example, they tend to see adults either as dangerous or as "suckers." They see their peers and themselves as tough or as weak. The therapist should offer alternative views to their distorted perceptions and encourage empathy with others. It has been my experience that a girl's antisocial orientation becomes untenable for her once she perceives that a person in authority really cares for her.

In short, with adolescents the therapist must be both more giving and more controlling than with most patients. In the process he discards his traditional "incognito" and reveals his own personality and, to some extent, his own values. This again is because the adolescent needs a helpful, reality-oriented relationship rather than a vehicle for the expression of unconscious, infantile needs.

A constant concern of the therapist is the maintenance of an optimal level of anxiety. If the anxiety level of the group drops too low, the session develops into a bull session. While this is frequently enjoyable, it is seldom therapeutic. On the other hand, if the anxiety level rises too high, acting out begins and withdrawal from the group is likely to occur. The therapist can lower anxiety by offering support or by directing the discussion away from a subject that is too threatening. Conversely, the therapist can raise anxiety by confronting the group members with a subject they have been resisting, and asking them to express their feelings.

With adolescent delinquents, the acting out of sexual and aggressive impulses is the chief resistance to the therapeutic process. Acting out signifies that the anxiety of the group has risen to a disruptive level. The acting out serves both to lessen awareness of painful emotions and to defend against getting close to the therapist. The relatively unstructured nature of therapy arouses anxiety about the adolescents' ability to control themselves and concern about whether the therapist is strong enough to control them. Acting out is also used by the group to test the therapist's affection and dependability. Its most common use, however, is that of diverting the group discussion from a subject that is too threatening.

If acting-out behavior is not stopped by the therapist, the entire course of treatment may be endangered. With delinquents, therapy fails more often because the therapist is overly passive than because he is overly controlling. It should be made clear that the group members' freedom applies only to verbal and not to behavioral expression. When acting out occurs, the therapist should encourage the group to discuss the behavior and particularly the underlying motivation. If acting out continues, the therapist should interpret this behavior and demand verbal rather than behavioral expression. Any group members who continue to act out should be requested to leave the session. Any girl who has been thus ejected should later be seen individually to gain a better understanding of her behavior and to assure her that the therapist still wants her in the group.

Adolescent delinquents will, of course, regard the group therapist with the distrust and hostility that they display toward all adults. Therefore, defiance can be expected as soon as the group members realize that the therapist will not retaliate. Paradoxically, the group members can also be expected to display a great deal of charm and apparent warmth, particularly when attempting to manipulate the therapist into granting them special privileges. However, these feelings can scarcely be considered transference since they are fully conscious, are typical of the group members' relationships with adults, and perhaps are realistic in light of their previous experiences.

The term transference should be confined to the displacement onto the therapist of the group members' unconscious, infantile emotions. The negative aspect of the transference feelings is most readily apparent. A great deal of irrational anger is directed toward the therapist because he is perceived as being punitive, depriving, and rejecting. The group members also frequently endow the therapist with magical power and moral superiority. These feelings motivate attempts to destroy the therapist's authority or to corrupt him.

At a deeper level, the therapist is perceived as potentially protective, nurturing, and loving. The intense oral-dependent cravings of the group members are released. These cravings are often expressed in fantasies of being children of the therapist. Thus there is a great deal of competition for the therapist's attention. Because dependency needs are most frightening to the group members, these needs are resisted most strenuously. Any dependency is experienced as putting them in an extremely vulnerable position. Rejection by the therapist would then become a severe blow to their already shaky self-esteem and would be construed as proof that they are indeed worthless and unlovable.

There are also, of course, erotic feelings directed toward the therapist. However, these are but thinly veiled incestuous wishes and are accompanied by tremendous guilt. Since the ego development of the group members is inadequate, they cannot tolerate intense feelings of guilt or anxiety. For this reason, it is best to discourage expression or analysis of the erotic aspect of the transference.

Countertransference difficulties are more pronounced with adolescent delinquents than with most patients. However, under this rubric I would not include annoyance with the group members because of their provocative behavior. Such annoyance is usually realistic, justified, and worth expressing. The term countertransference should be limited to the therapist's unconscious infantile needs which are aroused by the therapeutic process and directed toward the group members. Anger toward the group members because they frustrate the therapist's need to be controlling would come under this heading. There is also the danger of responding in an erotic manner to the group members. The seductiveness and physical attractiveness of the girls tend to arouse the repressed sexual needs of the therapist. There is also the danger of identifying with group members and thereby vicariously enjoying the antisocial exploits or feelings they relate. Such identification serves to reward and reinforce the group's delinquent tendencies.

Probably the most common countertransference problem is that of injury to the therapist's narcissism. First of all, the patients lack the usual faith in therapy and respect for the therapist. Secondly, because of the insatiability of their oral-dependent needs, many group members keep complaining that they are not being helped. Also, gratifying improvements in the group members usually take longer and are of lesser extent than with other patients. Finally, delinquent adolescents make it clear that they have no admiration or affection for the therapist, particularly if they sense that he needs these narcissistic supplies.

These countertransference problems require that the therapist understand his own adolescent conflicts and that his own delinquent tendencies are adequately controlled. He must, of course, still maintain the capacity for empathizing with adolescent delinquents. Also, the therapist should have a satisfying personal life so that he does not seek gratification of his own needs from his groups. Finally, the therapist should have a good under- standing of the dynamics of adolescent delinquents so that he can be realistic in setting treatment goals and selecting appropriate therapeutic techniques.

The Young Adult

Casework Treatment of Young Married Couples

Miriam Jolesch

During the early years of marriage, a young couple is likely to be exposed to a number of sources of potential conflict. Each partner must effect an emotional separation from his own family; each must achieve a sense of personal identity; each must learn to accept the role of husband or wife. Together the partners must gain a sense of identity as a family unit, over and above their identity as separate individuals. Accomplishing these developmental tasks may be so difficult for one, or both, of the partners that the marriage becomes threatened. Often, however, young couples having such difficulty can master the conflicts and crises typical of early married life if they are given casework treatment. This article is based on the author's experience in working with twelve young couples; in every instance, both marital partners were engaged in treatment.

In each of the twelve cases the request for help was based on the problem of unsatisfactory marital interaction. In eleven cases the wife was more concerned about the couple's failure to achieve gratifying interdependence in the marriage than was the husband. Most of the marital partners were in their mid-twenties; all of them were high school graduates, and some had had further education. The majority of the couples had been married from three to six years. They were economically secure, and the men had made a satisfactory vocational adjustment.

The Initial Period

The chief complaint verbalized by each of these young wives had to do with her feeling that her husband wanted to maintain his separateness from her and her distress at the emotional distance between them. In some instances the wife was troubled because her husband seemed to have so little time to spend with her and their children, although he managed to do many things outside the home. In other instances the complaint was not about outside interests but about the time and attention the husband

---

Reprinted with permission from *Social Casework*, XLIII (May, 1962), pp. 245–251.

devoted to his possessions, either at home or at work. Invariably the wife was lonely and felt disappointed and hurt by her husband's lack of attention. She saw the basic problem as one of the husband's failure to show interest in her in return for her efforts to build a give-and-take relationship with him. She was insistent that her husband as well as she would have to have help if the marriage were to be maintained.

The young husbands, however, were relatively unaware of the interaction problems that so disturbed their wives. They did not believe that there was a serious problem in the marriage, and they resisted applying for marital counseling. Most of them came to the agency in anger, often under the wife's threat of getting a divorce or after the couple had been separated for a short period. The reciprocal processes operating in their marriages were obviously provocative and depreciating to both partners, and neither partner was receiving the gratification he needed.

In ten of the twelve cases studied, the worker noted during the intake process that the wife had greater perceptiveness and sensitivity than the husband, and that she had also achieved a more advanced state of emotional maturity. She was miserably unhappy and freely expressed her anxiety. She seemed to be struggling to re-create the gratifying aspects of the family life she had experienced in the past, but her husband, who was well defended against anxiety, was unprepared to help her. Typically, the husband was threatened by the wife's desire for closeness, while the wife was threatened by the husband's need to isolate himself and put distance between them. Often the wife behaved in such a way that the interpersonal tension derived from the husband's avoidance of closeness was increased. For example, one young wife always managed to be talking on the telephone when her weary, uncommunicative husband returned from work. She never had the dinner ready; the children's clothing was always strewn around the room where her possession-centered husband would stumble over it and have to pick it up.

The central therapeutic problem with these couples was to engage and sustain the husband's motivation to use casework treatment, since he was the partner who evinced little concern about those aspects of the marital relationship that created so much anxiety and dissatisfaction in the wife. The same worker treated both partners in the twelve cases; treatment was considered successful in ten of the cases. In large measure the favorable outcome can be attributed to three factors: *1]* use of a combination of joint and individual interviews for the purpose of identifying individual reactive patterns basic to the conflict in marital interaction; *2]* timing of the joint interviews so that they were held only after each partner had made a positive transference to the caseworker and had become engaged in an examination of his own role performance; and *3]* focusing of treatment efforts on the interactional conflict. A couple was considered to have been treated successfully when the partners discovered that they could handle their problems to their own satisfaction and when it was clear to the worker that they had achieved a degree of interdependence that was gratifying to both of them.

The Intake Phase

The M case illustrates the typical interpersonal problems experienced by these young couples and the casework techniques used during the intake, exploratory, and treatment phases of the cases.

Mr. and Mrs. M—26 years of age and the parents of two boys, age 3½ years and 1 year—reminded the worker of a plump, ruffled robin redbreast and a dismal little wren as Mr. M plowed into the office ahead of his wife for their intake appointment. Mrs. M repeatedly accused her husband of resenting marriage and of being power- and success-hungry. She threatened to divorce him unless he would agree to having marital counseling. Mr. M, sitting at some distance from his wife, did not deign to glance at her; he was flushed, angry, and impatient with her complaints. He kept glancing at his watch as he stressed his fear that he would be late for an important business engagement. Speaking rapidly, he insisted that they did not have a marital problem: Their only trouble was lack of time to be together. When they did talk, his wife said silly things or asked silly questions that he had no time to answer—as she was doing now. He was convinced that the answer to her unhappiness was for her to join organizations, as his mother had done. He wanted the worker to know that he did not believe in marital counseling or any kind of therapy. He had come to the agency this time just to please his wife; he was too busy to stay for any lengthy discussion, and he did not expect to return.

When an applicant requests help in solving a marital problem, the intake interview is a joint one unless a serious objection is expressed by one of the marital partners. This type of interview affords the worker an excellent opportunity for perceiving both the verbal and nonverbal aspects of the marital interaction. In the case under discussion nothing that either Mr. or Mrs. M might have said in individual interviews could have conveyed so vividly Mr. M's feelings of puzzlement and anger, and Mrs. M's feelings of utter defeat, disappointment, and disparagement as did their unverbalized responses to each other. The very fact that Mr. M had come for an interview, and the puzzled quality of his negative reactions, gave the worker the impression that Mr. M, as well as his wife, did have some investment in the marriage. Emotional factors were blocking these people from functioning appropriately in their marital roles to such an extent that they seemed to be obtaining little real gratification from their marriage. Mr. M was getting satisfaction from his work and studies, and from indulging in an adolescent type of recreational activity with other young men. Mrs. M was extremely unhappy and maintained a passively hostile, hopeless attitude. She felt completely frustrated in her efforts to create a new and more congenial pattern of living.

As did many of the husbands in the cases studied, Mr. M tried in the joint intake interview to prove that his wife was wrong and that there was no marital problem. He insisted that he worked hard, provided well for his family, loved his children, and respected his wife, and that a man could not be expected to do more. He was angry. At first he insisted that he would be wasting his time if he kept appointments in the future because he was sure he could put his wife "on cloud nine" if only he had the time. However, as the interview progressed Mr. M began to recognize his wife's feeling of loneliness, hopelessness, and disappointment as a wife. He then agreed that he could manage to find the time to come in for a few more interviews. The worker did not mention his feelings of anger, but stressed the importance of finding time in which to attain the couple's mutual goals.

Mrs. M brought out little material other than her reiterated charge that her husband was eager for power and success, and that he was thoughtless, selfish, and disinterested in her and the children. It was the worker's impression that old conflicts had been revived in this marriage, as so frequently happens in early married life. The key problem was one of engaging the resistant partner, Mr. M, in order to determine whether treatment could be effective in helping the couple make new or better adaptations so that they could sustain the marriage.

It quickly became apparent to the worker that cases such as the ones considered here might easily be lost at the point of intake. Although most of these couples did not reveal markedly serious pathology, they seemed to be in danger of divorce unless both partners became engaged in improving their ways of interacting. The relative emotional health of the wife was the primary factor that operated to bring the husband to the agency. It also proved to be an important factor in the wife's decision to get a divorce in the two situations in which the husband could not be engaged in the treatment process. Casework experience has shown that it is often the deeply self-punishing wife who chooses to remain in an ungratifying marriage.

The joint intake interview is an important medium for engaging the resistant partner because in this interview the presenting problem can be observed and focused by the caseworker in terms of its interacting effects on the marital relationship. At intake, the worker must focus on the form rather than on the content of the interview. The content is made up of the complaints—the charges and the countercharges one partner makes against the other—and the resultant emotions expressed. The form is constitudet from the interplay of roles and the patterning of interaction resulting from this interplay. As the discussion in the joint intake interview is focused by the caseworker on the form of interaction—what is said, what is shown, what happens, and what all of this means in the marital situation—the two partners usually begin to be engaged in viewing their marital conflicts. As they do so, one partner's denial of marital conflict is weakened, as is the attacking posture of the other. This joint intake interview also enables the partners to confront their own feelings in a more unified manner. Each partner derives some measures of awareness that each must assume a degree of responsibility for attaining their mutual goal of sustaining the marriage.

The Exploratory Phase

In the intake process the worker should clarify the next steps to be taken and should design at least a tentative therapeutic plan in which both clients will have the motivation to participate. The important point to decide in the M case was whether joint or individual interviews would be better during the exploratory phase. The worker chose individual interviews on the basis of her initial diagnostic impression that Mr. M was reluctant to develop the close interdependent, or give-and-take, relationship his wife sought, and therefore was not ready for further joint interviews. Individual interviews were selected as the best means for obtaining a clearer grasp of the origin and severity of this problem for Mr. M, as well as for testing his capacity to mature within a therapeutic relationship. The worker's clinical impression of Mrs. M, who demonstrated anxiety combined with both a sensitivity in relation to her husband's needs and a real desire to give as well as to be given to, was that of a person with neurotic character traits and certain self-defeating tendencies.[1] The worker believed that in individual interviews with Mrs. M it would be possible to elicit quickly personal data needed as background for determining whether clarification of certain areas of her neurotic conflict which contributed to the marital problem would strengthen the marriage.

The young couples studied repeatedly transferred to their marital situations the fantasies and expectations they had had in relation to their parents. In working with the couples, the worker always found it important to explore the key relationships of each partner with his own parents. During the exploratory phase, individual interviews were chiefly used *1]* to obtain more quickly and economically personal and historical data needed to clarify certain aspects of individual behavior that seemed to be contributing to the interactional disturbance; *2]* to meet the need for an individual relationship with the worker, especially for the purpose of quickening individual maturation; *3]* to give the client an opportunity to talk to the worker in private, without his having to expose his feelings and attitudes to the partner and thereby build up resistance to treatment; and *4]* to relieve excessive anxiety.

The worker's tentative diagnostic impression in the M case was that Mr. and Mrs. M had not been able to achieve a satisfying degree of interdependence even after five years of marriage and the birth of two children, both of whom were planned. Mr. M, whose anxieties about his capacity to be a husband were well defended, was hectically pursuing his own goals. He perceived his wife as an object of gratification, just as he had perceived his father's relationship to his mother in that light. Direct interaction between the M's was minimal. Mrs. M was intensely frustrated, and she

---

[1] For a discussion of character neurosis, see Otto Pollak, Hazel M. Young, and Helen Leach, "Differential Diagnosis and Treatment of Character Disturbances," *Social Casework*, Vol. XLI, No. 10 (1960), pp. 512–17.

had a very poor self-image. Mr. M worked long hours in his father's business, in which he had a small part interest. Three nights a week he rushed home for a quick bite of supper before hurrying away to teach business classes in an extension course. His wife served him his meal. Then, while he ate and listened to news reports on the radio, she went next door for a cup of tea with her mother. Mr. M was very proud to have been asked to teach; he could not understand why his wife seemed so disinterested in his teaching. Usually he was so keyed up after his classes that he felt the need to unwind by going with some of his men students to listen to progressive jazz. Thus he stayed out until one or two in the morning three nights a week. Another two nights were devoted to studying at home. On one of these two evenings Mrs. M went out to play mah-jongg with some of her women friends. Sunday was the only day the family was together as a unit. Mrs. M, however, could not enjoy being with her husband this one day in the week because she could not recover sufficiently from her feelings of being deprived and depreciated—feelings that had become intensified because of her isolation from her husband during the other days of the week. They had established few gratifying patterns of marital interaction. Each partner wanted the other to sense his feelings intuitively and to meet his needs without being asked to do so.

Mr. and Mrs. M indicated clearly that they were both struggling to achieve maturity but were still clinging to the fantasy of the all-wise or omnipotent parent. Each one was following the identical pattern of his own parents. Each—but Mr. M in particular—was incompletely identified with his own sex role. Mrs. M had moved haltingly and uncertainly into the role of wife. She had exercised some of her mature, feminine impulses to give and to share, but her husband was unable to meet her countervailing need to be given to and nurtured. The worker decide to offer Mrs. M individual treatment as a means of restoring her self-confidence. The aim of individual treatment for Mr. M was to help him examine his role performance as a husband and father and to test his capacity to mature emotionally. It was considered important for them to be treated by the same caseworker so that, in both individual and joint interviews, the focus could be kept on their shared, long-term goal of finding their new identity as marriage partners. Although each of them seemed to have the desire to love and to be loved, they were not certain how they could achieve this goal together.

The Treatment Phase

The M's were treated over a period of five months. There were twelve individual interviews with Mr. M, nine individual interviews with Mrs. M, and seven joint interviews. Following the exploratory phase, treatment was based on the fact that the M's had enjoyed a brief period of mutual satisfaction prior to the birth of their second child. The first child had been conceived during the first year of marriage. Subsequently, the M's were separated for a year while Mr. M was in the Army. The second child was conceived soon after his return. Fathering this boy may have reactivated an unresolved childhood conflict against which Mr. M defended himself through his overdetermined, aggressive drive for success. His keeping himself emotionally distant from his wife was a defense against his deep feelings of inadequacy, or perhaps his oedipal guilt. His functioning as a husband was impaired. He was not particularly uncomfortable in the relationship except for his resentment of what seemed to him to be the unrealistic and undeserved nagging of his wife. He felt that she should be understanding and supportive of his goals. Always a few minutes early for his interviews, he came armed with books on accounting and business psychology, which he studied assiduously in the waiting room. In the first four interviews he talked at length about his interests, his studies, his accomplishments, and his pursuit of ambitious but reasonable goals for himself and his family. He felt that it was unrealistic for him to use precious time in keeping appointments with the worker when he had no problems. He was startled when the worker asked why he came early, but he quickly explained his need to keep ahead of schedule if he were to get through all of his daily activities.

Since Mr. M's narcissistic defenses seemed well integrated into his personality structure, the worker questioned whether Mr. M could accept a self-image that was less than strong, powerful, and successful in every way. Did he really need a wife's love and companionship? Repeatedly he emphasized that he saw no value for himself in having interviews with the worker. Eventually he admitted reluctantly that he liked to come: He enjoyed talking to the caseworker; he felt understood and respected; he wished he had more time. Later, when Mr. M began to think about his own sense of always being pressed for time, the worker believed that he was becoming involved in trying to work out new goals in his marriage. In his individual interviews he then began to examine his self-image, particularly the aggressive posture that he had developed in order to please his father. As he dealt with key areas of experience in his childhood, he began to reveal his feelings in relation to certain aspects of his behavior.

During this period Mrs. M was also having individual appointments. She was quickly able to face her own self-defeating patterns. After spending some time in discussing her interaction with her husband, she began to talk about her fear of asserting herself or of expressing anger. She made a connection between these fears and her childhood feelings as the older of two sisters. She had felt that her sister, who had developed a chronic cardiac condition at the age of six years, had pushed her away from the love and protection of her parents. Mrs. M began to understand her earlier pattern of suppressing anger toward her sister, whom she envied, and of passively waiting and hoping for attention and consideration. She learned to see that she had transferred this pattern into the marriage, and that she was behaving in a similar fashion toward Mr. M.

The Joint Interviews

The worker began to use joint interviews, in addition to individual interviews, at the mid-point in treatment, when each partner was showing some capacity for examining his own self-image and role performance. Joint interviews can be used productively when each partner has become able to attach the appropriate feeling to his own attitudes or behavior. Such interviews should bring into focus whatever is occurring in the present experiential or interactional situation. When the defensive behavior of each partner has diminished, the couple can begin to examine their interactional patterns. Joint interviews with the M's were held in the same week as the individual interviews to facilitate a more mature type of communication. Each of them grew not only in capacity to examine his own and the other's negative attitudes and patterns but also in ability to discover positive reactions he had previously denied. Reality distortions were corrected as the joint interviews progressed. Each partner became increasingly aware of his own unrealistic expectations of the other.

When an impasse was occasionally reached in a joint interview, or when their old reactions flared up, each partner was motivated to explore his immature pattern in the individual interview. This use of both individual and joint interviews tended to discourage regression. It was through the joint interviewing process that Mr. and Mrs. M first realized the faith they had in each other. After the long period of mutual frustration, each had become doubtful that this was so. The irrational fears each one had had were now removed. The process had begun in individual therapy, when Mr. and Mrs. M each had resolved some of their difficulty in expressing aggression. Their discussions in joint interviews hastened the process of neutralizing their fear of loving and hating the same person.

Treatment was terminated by mutual consent when both Mr. and Mrs. M felt that they no longer were withdrawing from each other. Both found that they were now having more gratification in their married life than they had believed possible. Mr. M had given up staying out late after his evening classes. Mrs. M noticed that her husband had been able to stand up to his father on a few occasions. She had stopped asking foolish questions. Mr. M proudly stated that his wife was even able to suppress her dislike of "blood and thunder" stories and was permitting him to tell her about a few of his experiences in the Army. Mr. M summed up his concept of what had been the major gain from their marital counseling experience in the simple statement, "I have matured."

In the 12 cases studied, it was found that joint interviews were used most effectively at the point where each partner is beginning the process of self-examination in the individual interviews. One caseworker shared by the marital partners seemed to represent to each of them a parent who was interested but neutral. Through the corrective emotional experience provided by the worker, the sense of personal worth of each partner was enhanced, and he became more tolerant toward the other. Usually the more highly motivated and relatively more mature partner had become less anxious by the time the joint interviews were instituted. As his anxiety lessened, his capacity to be more tolerant and to express himself verbally increased. This improvement in the healthier partner helped to sustain the motivation of the less motivated partner. In joint treatment interviews the caseworker must repeatedly communicate to the couple the way in which each partner's actions and reactions cause or exacerbate their mutual problems. As the worker repeatedly points out the various manifestations of the partners' behavior, the partners can begin to tolerate each other's individual ways of reacting. Each can begin to identify with the other as they face, and work together on, their contradictory feelings. Essential to this process is the caseworker who, they have both come to believe, knows, understands, and supports their mutual aim of finding security and gratification in the marriage. In this transference situation the caseworker represents a parent figure who supports their mature aims and who strengthens them in their separation from their parents. Changes in their perceptions occur. The adolescent fantasies they have carried into marriage fade away and are replaced by genuine object relationships.

Conclusion

These young married people had a deep wish to make a success of their marriages, but they were uncertain about how their aims could be achieved. In a majority of these cases the period following the birth of the second child was one of particular stress and crisis. After they were engaged in treatment, these partners wanted the family caseworker to help them achieve a new identity as marriage partners. In most instances delayed maturation was the fundamental cause of the marital problem. The wives, on the whole, seemed more ready to fulfill a marital role than did the husbands. The average time required to treat the younger couples in this group was from five to seven months. Similar methods were used successfully in two cases in which the partners were in their mid-thirties, but the time required was one year in one case, and twenty-two months in the other. The findings in the cases studied support the conclusions of Howard Parad and Gerald Caplan that stress reactivates earlier conflict and that help given at a time of stress can promote growth and maturation.[2]

[2] Howard J. Parad and Gerald Caplan, "A Framework for Studying Families in Crisis," *Social Work*, Vol. 5, No. 3 (1960), pp. 3–15.

The Management of Marital Counseling Cases

Helen S. Sholtis

The approach to the management of marital counseling cases presented in this article is aimed at reducing transference and countertransference reactions and increasing the ability of the marital partners to cope with family problems. Case management takes into account both strategy and tactics. Strategy is concerned with the structure of the interview and with timing, frequency, location, and type of interview, either individual or multiple-client. Tactics are concerned with the worker's interviewing techniques.

The stimulus for developing the case-management approach described here has been the recognition that unresolved transference and counter-transference reactions are among the chief causes of failure in marital cases.

The terms *transference* and *countertransference* are not used in accordance with their established psychoanalytic meanings. As used here the terms include both current reactions based on the interaction between worker and client and fixed characterological reactions inappropriately transferred to elements of the treatment situation.

The case-management approach discussed in this article grew out of an informal four-year study of the management of marital cases in one of the district offices of a large, nonsectarian family service agency. The aim of the project was to develop bases for determining whether one or two workers should be assigned to a marital case. Caseworkers and supervisors in the district seemed to prefer the assignment of only one worker to a case for the following reasons: administrative and supervisory demands are minimized; the caseworker's time and energy are conserved because collaborative conferences are unnecessary; mutuality of experience is afforded the clients; flexibility of treatment is increased because joint interviews can be scheduled as indicated; the threat of competition between the workers assigned to a case is eliminated. Furthermore, this approach enables the partners to maintain a consistent focus on partialized problems, to recognize distortions in

Reprinted from *Social Casework*, XLV (February, 1964), pp. 71–78, by permission of the author and the Journal.

motivation and behavior quickly, and to improve their verbal communication with each other.

Most of the marital cases carried in the district office were one-worker cases. In some instances the client-worker relationship had been complicated by this type of assignment. Therefore the question was asked: "In what combinations of motivation, capacity, and opportunity is one worker *unable* to handle the transference and countertransference reactions in a marital case?" One result of the project was the development of criteria for the assignment of two workers in a few special cases, but a more important gain was the evolution of concepts for differential case management that took into account the hazards of transference and countertransference intrinsic to marital counseling cases that are treated by one worker.

The Diagnostic Phase

In the district office the usual practice is to assign one worker to a marital case during the social study period, which usually requires from five to eight interviews. The caseworker informs the client that after the social study is completed a proposal will be made regarding such matters as the frequency of interviews, who is to be seen by whom, and the treatment goals. After the diagnosis is formulated, the plan for the management of the ongoing treatment is determined.

Although special circumstances are taken into account, the social study usually includes one or two individual interviews with each partner, a joint interview, and a home visit before the joint interview in which treatment recommendations are made. In the individual interviews the caseworker elicits the personal histories of the partners, their views of their courtship and marriage, and their feelings and thoughts about their current marital difficulties. He uses the joint interview to define areas of agreement and disagreement between the husband and wife about the nature and scope of their marital difficulties. Success in defining problems for which each partner agrees he has some responsibility is an important aspect of the treatment plan. Also important is an estimate of the partners' potential ability to discuss their difficulties without becoming overwhelmed by hostility.

The home visit and the interview in which the treatment recommendations are presented are given special attention in this article not only because of their importance for diagnosis and treatment but also because of the situational stresses experienced by clients and caseworkers at these points. If these stresses are denied, the result may be a superficial, rather than dynamic, implementation of the treatment plan.

The Home Visit

When the couple have minor children, the home visit is essential to the diagnostic evaluation of the marriage. Children, and any other members of the household, necessarily participate in some measure in the difficulties between the marriage partners. Lines of authority, means of communication, and shifting alignments among family members are universal elements of family life. Most couples mention other members of the household in the course of enumerating their complaints against each other, but a few avoid discussing other members of the household and try to avoid involving their children in quarrels that are supposedly contained by silence or midnight whisperings. In either instance, the home visit serves to clarify essential facets of the problem that might otherwise remain hidden, vague, or contradictory.

Despite the use of the home visit by the family service worker, the child welfare worker, and the public assistance worker, workers in marital counseling cases become anxious at the prospect of a home visit. In such a primarily psychological service a new dimension is added to home visiting because it is used for the explicit purpose of viewing family interaction. Although the caseworker knows that he is expected to interact on a friendly level with all family members and make detailed observations, he is faced with recurrent questions about explaining the purpose of his visit to the clients. He may himself wonder whether his visit is an unwarranted intrusion. Furthermore, he may question the basis of his authority for insisting on making the visit. In addition, he may be uncertain about his role in the clients' home, which is different from his role in his office, and about his ability to handle himself appropriately vis-à-vis three, four, or even five or more people instead of one or two. Many difficulties can be avoided, however, if certain general procedures and principles are followed.

Although the intake worker should lay the groundwork for the home visit, the ongoing worker should himself outline his entire plan for the social study in the first interview so that the clients' resistances can be brought to the surface and handled. It is important that both partners accept the home visit and participate in planning it. The visit should be scheduled when all family members can be present, usually before or after a family meal.[1]

The home visit is neither a social call nor an occasion for intervention in complex family interrelationships, however therapeutically intended. The flavor of the visit is more social than that of the office interview, and the caseworker should remember that he is a guest in the clients' home. In performing the guest-professional role, he should show respect for his host and hostess—graciously accept an offer of a cup of coffee, comment appropriately on the accomplishments or hobbies of family members, and ask permission of the parents before accepting the children's invitation to see the puppies in the basement, for example.

Most couples can accept the home visit as an appropriate procedure, but they may be concerned about its effect on their children and about how they should explain it to them. The thoughtful working over of ideas and feelings connected with the home visit in advance is also a means of clearly defining the caseworker's role so that the clients, in turn, may interpret the

---

[1] See Otto Pollak and Donald Brieland, "The Midwest Seminar on Family Diagnosis and Treatment," *Social Casework*, Vol. XLII, July 1961, p. 322.

visit appropriately to other family members. Obviously, the caseworker must understand his role and function so that he may be secure in setting conditions and in refusing to deal in subterfuges that the clients may claim will benefit the children. Careful preparation of the parents is always worth the time and effort and is usually repaid by a child's making such a remark as "You're from Family Service, the place where they help people get along together better." On the other hand, the caseworker can be disconcerted by such a remark as was made by one inadequately prepared client: "Okay, kids! Let's get the interaction going!"

In a few cases the clients' deeply entrenched resistances continue to operate despite the caseworker's best efforts. Before waiving the home visit as a condition for marital counseling, the caseworker should be certain that he knows the meaning of the resistances. By and large, he can feel secure in the truism that he is not allowed to treat what he is not allowed to diagnose.

The clients and the caseworker are richly rewarded by a well-planned, well-executed home visit. The clients know that the caseworker has gained a wider view of the family, that their failures are seen in the context of their achievements, and that their limitations are compared with the weight of their burdens. The caseworker has had an opportunity to correct his impressions of other members of the household and to balance the clients' projected images of their relationships and styles of life against their actual relationships and their inanimate, but telling, possessions. He has firsthand data for making a diagnosis, and he can also use these data in subsequent confrontations to document his view of the scope and nature of the clients' interactional problems.

The Recommendation Interview

From the start the caseworker has been preparing the clients for the short hiatus between the last social study interview and the interview in which treatment recommendations are made. This period should be as brief as possible, though time is needed for serious thought about the treatment plan and time must be allowed for thoughtful supervisory discussion of the diagnoses, individual and interactional, and the determination of a management plan.

The differential management plan should specify not only the ongoing interview scheme but also the problem areas, and those that seem to be workable should be earmarked. The worker is responsible for determining the problem areas; he must be able to focus interviews and to help the clients to translate masses of negative feelings into understandable complaints. Most such problem areas as money management, child care, household chores, in-laws, and recreation are everyday affairs, open to scrutiny on a behavioral and emotional level. Some clients prefer to maintain the treatment on a "who doesn't love whom" basis, and the worker may conspire with them by deciding that increased verbal communication between the partners will restore their happiness. The emphasis on verbal communication has positive results, however, only insofar as it helps to resolve clearly defined areas of faulty interaction in essential facets of family living. In other words, for *treatment* purposes, improved communication should be viewed as a means and not an end—which is not to disparage its value.

The recommendation interview is a bridge between the period devoted to the social study and that devoted to problem-focused treatment. It marks the end of the structured diagnostic phase, but not the end of diagnosis. It is the beginning of structured treatment, although all contacts should have had some therapeutic value. The caseworker's promise to present a diagnosis and a treatment plan and the clients' task of rejecting or accepting a trial period of treatment are responsibilities that arouse anxiety on both sides.

At this point the clients' anxieties are situational and reflect their ambivalence and fear about being faced with unpleasant truths and difficult alternatives. Some common fantasies of clients are that they are totally at fault, that they are mentally ill, that they should bring suit for divorce, or that they should have their children placed. A common defense is to seek to delay the "moment of truth." If the caseworker is also experiencing stress, he may resort to the same defense with the result that the interview develops around tangential material that is introduced by the clients and then seized upon by the caseworker. To the extent that anxieties remain untapped, hostility is increased on both sides and issues are likely to become befogged; it may result that the caseworker is defensive when he finally presents the diagnosis and the treatment recommendations and that the clients are annoyed by the time they receive them.

Social workers have long been in the position of sharing diagnostic thinking and of making treatment recommendations to clients, but the primarily psychological nature of marital counseling is, again, the differentiating element that creates stress for the caseworker. In psychiatric clinics practice has always been more explicitly structured in regard to diagnosis and treatment recommendations than it has in most social work agencies. Clinics, however, are team-oriented, and usually no one clinician carries the full responsibility for formulating a diagnosis and planning treatment.

The caseworker can deal better with his own and his clients' anxieties if he follows certain procedures. Making careful preparations for the interview is one of the most important. Furthermore, the caseworker should try to translate his professional formulations into language understandable to his clients. For example, he should explain character diagnoses in terms of difficulties in functioning that are understandable in the light of the past. He should explain a marital diagnosis in terms of the tenor of the marital relationship, showing the significance of the past for present functioning. He should expand initial complaints into defined problems in family interaction, and his treatment plan should be so designed as to deter clients from attempting to blame each other for their difficulties. He should be prepared to tap the strengths of the individuals and the family. It is helpful in the interview to make use of notes that list the important points to be covered.

In general, clients view the notes as evidence that careful thought has been given to their problems.

The caseworker should deal firmly with delaying maneuvers during the interview. He may begin by generalizing about the discomfort of the situation, but he should then present his findings and recommendations in capsule form. Once the situational anxieties are reduced, the caseworker should encourage full discussion of the points made and hold both partners responsible for their participation in the decision-making process.

In the beginning, the clients' motivation to complete the social study is usually enhanced by the fact that the initial commitment of time is limited, they are promised direct answers to questions about which they are curious and anxious, and they are free, when the treatment recommendations are made, to decide whether or not to continue. Later, their motivation to undertake a trial period of treatment is enhanced by their respect for the caseworker's honesty and competence and by their relief that the marital difficulties have been identified and partialized and seem to be workable. The climate and pace of treatment will be significantly affected by the caseworker's ability to use this opportunity to relate sensitively to the past and current reasons for the existence of the marital conflict, to delineate the problem areas, and to encourage the clients to begin by making immediate choices.

The Problem of Transference and Countertransference

The procedures and techniques that have been described are intended to provide a framework for discussing the concepts of differential case management that evolved from the study. It should be noted, further, that the criteria of case management were developed mainly in relation to the practice of women caseworkers. The district office staff believe that the sex of the caseworker is the most important single stimulus to the development of transference and countertransference reactions. Although skill, age, and race may influence the assignment of a worker to a specific case, it is the sex of the caseworker that often proves to be the major hazard or the most important help.

Sex is so integral a part of any marriage, so basic to the marriage contract, that caseworkers tend to be unaware of the triangle formed when they enter the life of a quarreling couple. Social workers talk about the parental role of the caseworker and the sibling rivalry of clients, about dependency needs and narcissistic wishes, all neatly desexualized. They are quick to recognize oedipal strivings in the four- and five-year-old, they carefully document the adolescent competition of a wife with her mother, but somehow they pass lightly over the same sexual ingredients in the treatment situation. This may be so because most of the clients in family service agencies are pregenitally fixated characters, leading the workers to be attuned to the childish nature of their behavior and strivings. The attendant mistake would be to assume that fixation at the oral or anal level means that the client has not experienced the impact of incestuous wishes, fears of castration, the quandary of sexual identity, and competition with members of both sexes. The primitive dependency needs of the person with an infantile character press for gratification, but sexual conflicts are also ready at hand, needing only slight stimulation or frustration to seek discharge in acting-out behavior.

The treatment triangle in marital counseling cases must, of necessity, be composed either of two women and one man or of two men and one woman. The first is more frequent, because of the preponderance of women caseworkers. The S case reflects elements of transference and countertransference that occur repeatedly in such a treatment triangle, however different the individual case patterns may be.

> Mrs. S applied to the agency feeling "put upon" and deprived by her husband. Her complaints were that he lacked interest in her and the children and in making home repairs. She alternated between expressing certainty that her husband would refuse to talk to the caseworker and insisting that he participate on an equal basis to prove his culpability and his interest in her. Mr. S admitted there were problems in the marriage and agreed to co-operate.
>
> The woman caseworker arranged a schedule of joint and individual interviews in which equal time was allotted to the two partners. She reported good progress during the early weeks of treatment, especially by Mr. S. Then a change occurred. The worker became aware of the fact that Mrs. S was provoking her husband, although she had agreed not to; she was accusing the worker of not understanding the situation; and she was canceling her appointments. Meanwhile, Mr. S basked in the caseworker's approval. The worker became more frustrated and angry at Mrs. S, who was sabotaging her treatment efforts, and more sympathetic toward the victimized husband. Soon Mrs. S telephoned to say that counseling had not helped her situation and that she did not intend to continue. In his termination interview, Mr. S shook his head ruefully, saying that the caseworker's effort had been a good one, but futile because his wife would never change. He acknowledged that he need not have been afraid that the two women would team up against him. And in this respect he was quite right: there is seldom that danger.

When Mrs. S had come to the agency she had been feeling deprived and undervalued by her husband as a wife, a mother, and a woman. She wanted to punish him, and, beyond that, she expected the caseworker to side with her and make him value her as a woman. Her feeling of injury was, of course, not lessened by her husband's sweet reasonableness with the caseworker or by the rapidity with which he acted on the caseworker's suggestions: he *did* agree to umpire the Little League games; he *did* repair the basement light. Bereft of specific complaints, Mrs. S felt more inadequate than she had before; she felt angrier, with less apparent basis for her anger. In essence, the caseworker was proving to be the better woman instead of helping *her* to be a better wife to her husband. Though the struggle with the caseworker was reminiscent of those Mrs. S had engaged in with her mother, Mr. S was, in reality, *her* husband. She was not obliged to tolerate the caseworker's competition, and, indeed, she did not.

The caseworker wrote this closing entry in the record:

> My judgment that Mrs. S was more motivated for help than her husband has not held up under the test of treatment. Though he is infantile, with strong dependent needs, he does respond to benign controls. Mrs. S, however, is so provocative that she appears to need her husband to remain inadequate in order to justify her rage. She appears unmotivated to change the status quo.

The caseworker was aware of her positive and negative countertransference reactions to the S's and put these in the context of their responses to her well-intentioned, not unskilled efforts. What she did not understand so well was the transferences they were acting out with her and the deeper wellsprings of her own countertransferences that were related to her competition with females. Since such competition in a treatment context is generally ego-alien and unconscious to caseworkers, the worker cannot be expected to be aware of her reactions without an intellectual structure, perhaps a supervisory one, that enables her to identify the problem and correct it.

Differential Case Management

There are two basic approaches to the management of marital counseling cases. Either one worker or two workers can be assigned to a case. If one worker is assigned, three variations are possible: the primary client may be the husband, or it may be the wife, or neither husband nor wife may be considered the primary client. When neither is considered the primary client, equal interviewing time is scheduled for each partner and joint interviews are an important component of the treatment. When one of the partners is the primary client, more interviews are scheduled for that person and joint interviews may or may not be included in the treatment plan.

The use of two workers and the selection of the husband as the primary client are alternative means for treating the small number of cases in which the husband initiates contact with the agency and demonstrates greater motivation for marital counseling than his wife. If a woman caseworker treats both partners, she usually finds herself in competition with the wife. When the wife experiences so much conflict about becoming dependent on a rival that she cannot use help, she may sabotage the efforts of her husband and the worker. Under these circumstances the wife should be assigned another worker, with whom she does not need to compete for her husband; thus allowance is made for appropriate dependence, and hostile aggression is reduced. As a result of the gratification of her dependency needs the wife's energy can be channeled constructively toward improving her behavior. It is preferable, however, to assign one male worker to the case if the husband is the primary client. This approach avoids this kind of transference problem—granted, of course, that the assignment is warranted by other considerations, such as age, level of skill, and so forth. If the case cannot be assigned to a male worker, then the proper management of the case indicates the assignment of two women workers, one for each partner.

Differential means of treating the large majority of cases in which the wife initiates contact are to consider neither spouse the primary client or to consider the wife the primary client. In some instances, the former choice has many positive features. Experience has shown, however, that its success is limited to cases lasting six to nine months, a shorter period of contact than is usual in the district in which the project took place. Even so, four conditions must be met before this approach is used: 1] There must be sufficient positive interchange between the marital partners to make the regular use of joint interviews constructive; 2] there must be a number of defined problem areas related to family management for which each partner carries some responsibility; 3] there must be sufficient motivation for problem-solving by the husband; 4] there must be in each of the partners a capacity to respond to education and direction without developing strong resistances.

The capacity to discuss intimate matters and to accept reasonable compromises without developing strong transference reactions appears to be a quality of young couples who are not defensive about acknowledging their ignorance of family responsibility. It is also a quality associated with some clients with restricted character formation who are habitually noninvolved. When untoward transference and countertransference developments do not prevent reasonable compromises by the partners, termination goals should be set early and the case closed when gains are apparent. The limitations of this approach, in which neither partner is the primary client, do not decrease its value for the relatively small number of cases in which it constitutes the full treatment or for the large group of cases in which it constitutes the initial phase of treatment.

Because of the fourth factor, the number of cases in which this approach is used throughout the period of treatment is small. Length of treatment bears a reciprocal relationship to transference and countertransference; that is to say, both time and investment are required to deal with resistances, and time and investment deepen transference and countertransference reactions that lead to the further development of resistances. Thus, as treatment continues, the case in which neither spouse is the primary client may become unworkable, and it may be necessary to make the wife the primary client. In the S case the early gains that were achieved through compromises over such issues as chores could have been consolidated if the woman worker had reduced the number of interviews with the compliant husband and increased the number with the rebellious wife. Just because the wife usually has a greater investment than her husband in the day-to-day functioning of the family, she should not be expected to change more rapidly than he. Mrs. S's capacity for change was hampered by her strong emotional investment in her family roles and failures, and her motivation for change was decreased as she witnessed her husband's rapid change, a change she thought was easily achieved and hostile toward her and seductive toward the woman worker. These facets of the wife's capacity and motivation for problem-solving can be understood and dealt with constructively. Cases meeting the first three conditions are better begun by considering neither partner the primary client because the husband's immediate co-operation is an important dynamic in the early phase of the case while issues are being defined and a general structure of communication and compromise is being developed.

The fourth condition, the capacity to respond to education and direction without developing strong resistances, affects the continuation of this approach rather than its initiation. Prognosis in this regard, however, is helpful in making case assignments. If the partners can make use of an approach by which neither is considered the primary client, it is appropriate to assign either a man or a woman as the caseworker. If it seems likely that before treatment is completed the worker will need to shift to an approach in which the wife is the primary client, assignment should be made to a woman. Signs calling for a shift in strategy vary: the hostile interaction between the partners may increase perceptibly; their complaints may become repetitious without any discernible positive movement despite reasonable joint planning; one of the partners may make either overt or covert complaints about the worker's expectations or helpfulness. If the transference difficulties are not anticipated, the clients may engage in destructive acting-out behavior, they may suddenly terminate treatment, or they may settle down to a nonproductive transference battle for control.

In some cases it is possible to decide on the approach in which the wife is the primary client by the end of the social study—for example, when the wife has applied to the agency but the case does not meet the conditions necessary for treating neither partner as the primary client. The wife is also made the primary client when her reaction to such special life stresses as childbirth, the death of a parent, or menopause has upset what had been a satisfying marital balance, the expectation being that primary work with her will restore the previous balance. Developments that may indicate a need for a change in strategy should be watched for carefully; work with the wife may lead to improvement in her functioning and to reciprocal changes in the husband that make it possible and advisable to involve both partners equally as a means of solidifying gains and initiating termination.

Summary

Most treatment failures in marital cases are thought to result from unresolved difficulties in transference and countertransference, stimulated by the formation of the oedipal triangle between the worker and the husband and wife. Problems of sexual competition and erotization may be avoided by assigning a worker whose sex is the same as that of the more motivated partner. The use of two workers is the best alternative approach when a qualified male staff member is not available to treat the husband as the primary client. A woman worker, however, should be assigned to cases in which the wife is the primary client from the outset, or in which it is suspected that the case will develop in that direction. The use of one worker is more flexible and economical than the use of two. However, if one worker is used, careful attention must be paid to signs of negative transference that may indicate the need for a shift in the case management. Treating neither partner as the primary client is an approach well suited to young couples who meet certain conditions. The caseworker's sex can then be disregarded.

Management planning begins with the assignment of a worker to conduct the social study. Various procedures and techniques that are discussed in this article help to accomplish the dual purpose of the social study: to engage the clients in a working relationship and to diagnose the clients and their problems. At the completion of the diagnostic phase, the recommendations of a clearly delineated treatment plan should be communicated to the clients in a structured interview.

The avoidance of oedipal rivalries is presented as a means of reducing transference and countertransference reactions in marital counseling; it is not a panacea for resolving resistances that result from pathological character formations. The latter, however, can be better understood and more effectively handled if they are not beclouded by reactions to oedipal elements in the treatment situation.

Regardless of the approach used, treatment is focused on defined areas of faulty interaction in family living. The over-all goals are to increase cooperation among family members and to improve patterns of family living within the limits of the clients' character structures, marital relationship, and social and cultural environment.

Acknowledgments

Grateful acknowledgment is made to Mrs. Betty French, formerly Assistant District Secretary, for her collaboration on the district marital study from which concepts for this presentation have been drawn.

Joint Interviewing: A Treatment Technique with Marital Partners

Joanne Geist and Norman M. Gerber

Joint interviewing is a valuable technique in the treatment of certain marital partners, especially when they have a mutual interest in a particular problem or problems within the marriage. For the purposes of this paper, joint interviewing is defined as one or a number of planned casework

Reprinted with permission from *Social Casework*, XLI (February, 1960), pp. 76–83.

interviews of an hour's duration of husband and wife together by one case-worker.[1]

In the Family Service of Cincinnati and Hamilton County, married clients are usually interviewed separately at intake by a worker in a central-ized intake department. An attempt is made to have the same intake worker interview both marital partners, but usually at different times. Usually, the partners are then assigned to the same caseworker for ongoing treatment. This worker may decide to see both partners in separate interviews, to have one partner treated by another worker, or to refer one partner to another social agency or to a psychiatric treatment resource. He may decide to work with only one partner or, in certain cases, he may see the partners in joint interviews. Whatever decision he makes is based on a treatment plan that is indicated by the psychosocial diagnosis.

The intake worker attempts to gain as much understanding of marital interaction as possible. The knowledge gained may lead the continuing worker to select joint interviewing as a primary technique to be used in the treatment process. He may also arrange joint interviews at other points in treatment if it appears that joint interviews would be of greater benefit than individual interviews to the marital partners involved. As the St. Paul study indicates, "Our choice of interviewing plan must depend upon what we see is needed and upon our skills in the process of planning and conducting interviews."[2]

"Marital diagnosis," the term used in this paper, refers to a clear understanding of the individual diagnosis of each partner and additional understanding of the marital interaction between them. The twelve cases used as the basis of this discussion included nine couples that continued in treatment, and three that did not continue. All the clients involved had character disorders; some of them were quite disturbed while others were relatively healthy.

In considering the use of joint interviews, the caseworker sees the following factors as diagnostically important: marital interaction, the degree of involvement of each partner, and the degree of concern of each partner. Of greatest single importance is the ability of each partner to maintain an

---

[1] For discussion of joint interviewing, see particularly: Sanford N. Sherman, "Joint Interviews in Casework Practice," *Social Work*, Vol. IV, No. 2 (1959); Max Siporin, "Family-Centered Casework in a Psychiatric Setting," *Social Casework*, Vol. XXXVII, No. 4 (1956), p. 167; M. Robert Gomberg, "Family Diagnosis—Trends in Theory and Practice," *Social Casework*, Vol. XXXIX, Nos. 2–3 (1958); Victor W. Eisenstein, M.D., *Neurotic Interaction in Marriage*, Basic Books, Inc., New York, 1956; M. Robert Gomberg, "Family Oriented Treatment of Marital Problems," *Social Casework*, Vol. XXXVII, No. 1 (1956); David Hallowitz, Robert A. Clement, and Albert V. Cutter, M.D., "The Treatment Process with Both Patients Together," *American Journal of Orthopsychiatry*, Vol. XXVII, No. 3 (1957); Rex A. Skidmore, "The Joint Interview in Marriage Counseling," *Marriage and Family Living*, Vol. XVII, No. 4 (1955), p. 349.

[2] *Casework Notebook*, Family Centered Project, Greater St. Paul Community Chest and Council, Inc., St. Paul, Minn., 1957. See Chapter 13 on family interviewing.

interest in and to use his concern about mutual interests. It has been found that a concern about mutual interests, expressed by both marital partners, becomes the basis for establishing the focus of treatment and for maintaining a treatment relationship. "In treatment, joint interviewing has merit only if the participants can feel some togetherness in their desire to focus upon a common problem. Lacking this, individual interviews become necessary until this condition can be met."[3] One cannot stress too strongly the fact that the partners must have an interest that is mutually shared and to which they both relate in coming to the agency. Also it is diagnostically important to discover the factors that have led to upsetting the marital balance, since this knowledge will clarify the quality of the interaction and will lead to a further understanding of the dynamics of the marital relationship. When joint interviews are used, understanding the marital interaction takes on even greater meaning in relation to the worker's helping these persons find more satisfactions from each other in the marriage, as well as in restoring the equilibrium in the marriage and thereby benefiting the children.

Diagnostic Indications for Joint Interviewing

In casework with marital problems, certain situations occur that seem to indicate the desirability of planning joint interviews. The caseworker's use of these situations as diagnostic clues to the need for interviewing marital partners together has grown out of an increased understanding of marital interaction and a growing awareness that a variety of techniques is needed in helping to restore marital balance.

1.   *When there is a breakdown in verbal communication between marital partners.* At intake each partner may speak of not being able to discuss his concerns with his spouse. Restoration of communication between them sometimes is extremely difficult when individual interviews are continued. Each partner is expressing the same worries and concerns as the spouse but neither can share them with the other in a way that leads to a solution of the difficulty. The joint interview can help to create an atmosphere in which the partners attempt to re-establish communication with the help of the caseworker.

> Prior to joint interviews, Mr. and Mrs. A each expressed the feeling of being "left out" by the other. In individual interviews they made some of the following remarks: "My husband doesn't take me anywhere. He only wants to work or stick his nose in a book. He married me to have a housekeeper. I want to feel close to him but he won't let me." "My wife never gets up to fix my breakfast. She wants a handyman around but not a husband. She gets all upset about meeting people. I'd like my friends to meet her but she doesn't want to." Despite the worker's encouraging them to discuss these complaints with each other, they did not do so. In joint interviews each of the clients did discuss these complaints and the caseworker was able to help them explore their feelings and increase their ability to talk with each other without constant distortion.

[3] *Casework Notebook, loc. cit.*

2.   *When there is distrust of the other partner's actions.* Marital partners may misinterpret feelings and facial expressions, as well as words. Because of this distrust, the nonjudgmental role of the caseworker, in separate interviews, can be misinterpreted as taking the partner's side, particularly when the caseworker raises questions about the behavior of the partner who is being interviewed. In a joint interview each has a chance to see that the caseworker raises questions about the other in order to help them as a couple to find their own solutions. Thus they are able to see the caseworker and themselves more realistically.

> Individual interviews with Mr. and Mrs. B led to the following situation. When Mr. B was seen alone he frequently voiced his suspiciousness about his wife's sexual role with the male worker. Alone, Mrs. B consistently provoked situations that would add to her husband's suspiciousness and then condemned his lack of faith in her ability to be a loyal wife. When the worker tried to help each of them by raising questions about the other, his effort was misinterpreted to mean that he disbelieved the statements made. When the worker was able to bring them together in a joint interview and then raised questions about their suspicions, they were able to handle the matter and to solve part of the conflict.

3.   *When the degree of security of one or both marital partners is too slight for them to work individually with the same worker.* Some clients seem unable to permit the spouse to see the worker individually; but when they are seen as a couple they are able to work productively on their problem. This kind of competition for the caseworker's attention can be put to constructive use. Unresolved sibling rivalry may be the reason for a client's inability to feel secure in separate interviews. If so, separate interviews may arouse the feeling that he needs to compete for a parent's love and attention and that he is inadequate. These feelings can sometimes be dispelled by participating in joint interviews and being reassured that the worker is as interested in him as in his partner.

> After joint interviews were begun in the C case, it became apparent that Mrs. C was suspicious of her husband's relationship with his female caseworker and that he derived pleasure from fostering the suspiciousness. Mrs. C had not been able to reveal this in individual interviews, but could bring it up in joint interviews when she could observe that her fantasies were without a basis in reality. Mr. C could express his anger toward the caseworker for not favoring him and could recognize that his provocativeness was delaying the restoration of marital balance which he actually desired as strongly as his wife did.

4.   *When there is a lack of focus in individual interviews.* Sometimes the material presented and discussed in individual interviews, although apparently meaningful, results in little or no change in the marital situation. The caseworker needs to be aware of the client's current living situation and his expressed desire for some change. Often individual interviews are used to drain off complaints about the partner, and the area of mutual concern is not given enough attention.

5.   *When the client himself asks for joint interviews and the caseworker senses the client's intuitive knowledge that this is the best method of solving a particular problem.* The caseworker should examine the client's motivations when he requests joint interviews. Often the worker will interpret this request as the client's effort to control the situation when this may not be the meaning of the behavior.

> The C's mentioned above asked for joint interviews after a long period of individual interviews. The caseworker, although dubious about the wisdom of this procedure, was willing to try it because treatment progress had come to a standstill. In retrospect it appeared that the clients had sensed the best method of help for them. Marital balance was fairly quickly restored. Although the case has now been closed a year, the caseworker has been in touch with the couple and they have continued to feel able to solve their problems together without disruption of the marital balance.

6.   *When the caseworker senses intuitively that the use of joint interviews would be the treatment method of choice.* The caseworker may be unable to give explicit diagnostic reasons for his method because less is currently known about this method of interviewing than about individual interviews, and, hence, he is less familiar with it.

> Mr. and Mrs. D had been known to the agency since 1954. In their first contact with the agency they were both seen by the worker in individual interviews. They failed to return after one contact. When they returned to the agency in 1956, each partner was assigned to a different worker. Again, after one interview each, they discontinued. In 1958 they again applied to the agency for service. The worker felt that joint interviews ought to be tried because no other treatment method had worked. When the marital partners were seen in joint interviews they were able to express their mutual concern about their 5-year-old child who was quite destructive in his acting-out behavior toward his peers. In joint interviews the worker was able to help Mrs. D with her fears about losing control over her child and at the same time was able to relate to Mr. D and help to reduce his sense of exclusion from his wife's concern.

Treatment Techniques

We have found certain treatment techniques to be particularly successful in joint interviewing. Before initiating joint interviews with a couple, the worker should clarify with each marital partner the fact that they will be talking together to work toward a solution of their problems because of their mutual concerns.

1.   *Limit setting.* It is extremely important for the worker to set limits as a means of enabling the marital partners to tolerate their anxiety in a more comfortable manner. Setting limits is an aid in focusing the interviews as well as in helping the marital partners channel their energies toward constructive and appropriate handling of their mutual concerns. The caseworker sets limits by not allowing one marital partner to be overcontrolling in the verbal

communication during the joint interview. By suggesting to the more passive, nonverbal partner that his opinion is needed, or that it is important for him to raise questions about what the marital partner is saying, the worker enables both partners to reach some balance in solving the problem through communication.

It is important to stress that doing this does not mean permitting the couple to have a free-for-all in the office. Instead, it provides an opportunity for carrying on the interview within a structured atmosphere in which the caseworker is the leader. When both partners become too vociferous in their comments, the worker attempts to maintain control by diluting the emotional charge that is taking place between them. He tries to retrace the first steps of the argument by seeking the facts, thus enabling the marital partners to develop ideas about how their own behavior and distortions have led to the argument. At the same time the marital partners are able to gain some control of their impulses for more profitable use in the future. The worker's presence offers a protective atmosphere which enables the clients to accept the limits he has placed on them. Thus he can provide a healthy ego ideal to which they can relate themselves as treatment progresses.

> In the beginning of treatment Mrs. B monopolized the joint interviews. She clearly indicated that she was a hysterical, masochistic personality. Mr. B, a suspicious, hostile personality, only evoked tears from Mrs. B when he talked to her. Consequently, he tried to avoid saying anything. However, Mrs. B would manipulate him into a position where he would lose control and yell loudly at his wife. Mrs. B, becoming hysterical, would depreciate her efforts as a wife and mother. The worker commented that they had not come to the office to yell and fight with each other, since this would not solve the problems they faced as parents. The worker added that, since they were paying a fee, he thought they should try to use the hour to their best advantage. Although this helped to calm them down somewhat, Mrs. B continued to bait Mr. B. The worker suggested directly that she get hold of herself and try to tell him what had happened, step by step, that had led to this argument. Mr. B just sat in the chair, daring the worker to ask him his side of the argument, which by plan he wasn't going to give. When the worker asked for his opinion about what his wife was saying and he refused to give any, the worker suggested to Mr. B that he, the worker, would not allow any outbursts by the wife while Mr. B was speaking, since Mr. B had not interrupted when she had spoken. Only then were they able together to discuss the situation with the worker.

2. *Clarifying the distortions and lack of trust in each marital partner.* It is our opinion that either partner's distortions are essentially a defense, masking his own uncertainties in handling his feelings, and that they result in perpetuating an unhealthy marital interaction. When these distortions are clarified, a balance in the three-way therapeutic relationship can be maintained.

> In one joint interview Mr. B stated that he wished they could save money; he'd like to invest in stocks. Mrs. B turned to the caseworker and said, "You see he doesn't want me to have a new vacuum cleaner." She then told her husband that they would save more if he'd help her to go over the budget. He then told the caseworker, "My wife never wants me to have anything. I want

a new electric drill but I just have to give all my money to her." Their distortions, so obvious to the caseworker, had to be painstakingly pointed out to each client. An entire interview was focused on the above remarks and it took genuine effort on the part of each client to think through these angry reactions and try to understand how they had come to feel this way.

3.   *Universalizing and educational techniques.* We have found that using the technique of universalization helps marital partners such as these through giving them an idea of what other people do and why they do it. The use of educational techniques also can serve as a demonstration, in a general way, of how certain situations can be handled. Thus, the worker can help the marital partners by relieving some of their anxieties and by presenting to them a healthy ego ideal to which they can relate. Quite frequently, marital partners try to place the caseworker in the position of a referee on a specific point which, on the surface, is so isolated from the main problem that its discussion does not help in reaching a solution. Thus, through the caseworker's helping the marital partners to focus on the general rather than the specific by referring to what other people do and think, facts are elicited that enable both marital partners to move toward a specific solution of their problem. Moreover, the caseworker avoids being put in a position of being a referee and can place the responsibility for solving the problem with the marital partners.

> Mr. and Mrs. D were upset about the acting-out behavior of their 5-year-old child. What was clearly indicated in the material they presented was the need for psychiatric evaluation of the child. Both Mr. and Mrs. D spoke about a specific incident when the child had thrown bricks at another child. Everything about him except this incident seemed to have been blotted out. The worker suggested that they talk more about the child's behavior and tried to relate this discussion to a more generalized concept of what is normal or abnormal behavior. When the parents were able to focus on a more educational approach, which in itself did not have as much pain for them since focus was taken away from their own child, they were able to comprehend that some of his behavior was serious and to accept the plan necessary to help the boy.

4.   *Transference and countertransference.* In a joint interview, the worker has to be keenly aware of the multiple transferences that take place. One must remember that when two people are interviewed together, they naturally present two differing sets of evidence. Hence, the worker has an opportunity of observing the interaction between the marital partners. We have found that, if the caseworker is not aware of his own involvement and his own reactions, he is more susceptible to manipulation by the marital partners than would be true in a one-to-one relationship. If the worker takes sides or succumbs to the more controlling marital partner, the treatment process is adversely affected. Since it is quite easy for the worker to leave the non-verbal partner completely out of the discussion, he should be mindful that he may have to divide his time between the marital partners so that each receives equal attention from him. If he is aware of his own feelings and

reactions to the clients, he is able to understand more fully the types of logical resistance that occur in the treatment process, since these are not blurred by the illogical resistances that occur because of his counter-transference reactions. As the clients progress in treatment, the worker continues to re-evaluate the transference and countertransference reactions.

> Mrs. E was a controlling, depreciating woman who seemed to antagonize everyone. The worker's initial reaction to her was a feeling of being over-whelmed. He appeared to be controlled by her just as her husband felt he was. When the worker realized how he was reacting to Mrs. E, he was able to handle her attempts at control in a non-rejecting way, thus affording Mr. E the opportunity of presenting his ideas and opinions in the joint interview. The worker tried to bring Mr. E into the discussion by asking him, "Do you have something to add to this?" or by suggesting, "I'm sure this is of concern to you, too."

Terminating Treatment
with the Use of Joint Interviews

In terminating treatment, the joint interview can be used not only with clients who have previously been interviewed together, but also with marital partners who by design have been seen in individual interviews. It is our opinion that if the focus of treatment has been on marital and family relationship problems rather than on individual personality problems, the joint interview may be validly used at the point of termination regardless of whether the treatment design has involved joint or individual interviews by the same worker.

A joint interview at termination gives focus to the problems the marital partners have worked on; it also permits the worker to summarize for both of them together their efforts in reaching a solution. It affords an oppor-tunity for the worker to verbalize the gains and the successful use the marital partners have made of casework treatment. Too frequently, caseworkers think that terminating a case should end their contact with the clients they have helped. It is our feeling that joint terminal interviews should be related to the positive interaction in the marriage. If, in the future, the partners should need help they can both be assured that the agency considers each of them equally important to the health and welfare of the family. Their knowledge that the agency feels that they used help well will enable them to return, should the need arise.

> At a point where Mr. and Mrs. F were feeling much more comfortable together and positive about their marriage, it seemed appropriate to terminate treatment. Two joint interviews were held after two years of regular individual contacts with Mr. and Mrs. F by the same worker. Mr. and Mrs. F told the worker separately, and then together in the last interview, that their marriage was much improved but was still no bed of roses. Each felt that he understood the other person better, as well as himself. They could talk together about their problems with some tolerance and without a need to become angry. We all felt that this was an appropriate time to discontinue treatment.

Contraindications for Joint Interviews

There seems to be a variety of factors involved in the failure of joint interviews. It has been our experience that these factors seem to fall into three main categories: the accuracy of the caseworker's diagnostic understanding of the two clients involved, the caseworker's own comfort in using joint interviews, and the quality of interaction between the two clients.

In consideration of joint interviews as a treatment method to be used over a period of time, the diagnosis of each client involved needs to be carefully considered. Joint interviews should not be used, for example, when one client is extremely narcissistic or has an oral aggressive character structure. The need of such a person to be given attention as an individual is so great that he cannot use a joint interview for solving a problem that is of concern to another person as well.

> Mr. and Mrs. G were being seen by the same worker individually about a marriage problem involving Mrs. G's inability to trust her husband to pay the bills and Mr. G's refusal to share his financial worries with her. Each expressed a desire to continue the marriage and felt that their problems stemmed from financial difficulties. Each felt that if they could come to some agreement about how to spend their money their marriage would be happier. The caseworker attempted joint interviews because of their expressed mutual concern. In the joint interviews each accused the other of untruthfulness and they drew farther apart. Each began to phone the caseworker in attempts to build himself up and to tear the other down. Mrs. G was diagnosed as having a hysterical character disorder. She viewed herself as depreciated and long suffering. Mr. G had an oral aggressive character structure with some anal features. His financial manipulations were somewhat dishonest, he had extensive debts, and he withheld from his wife, as long as possible, all information about money.
>
> Although the G's expressed a mutual concern, they could not make use of joint interviews at the particular time these were introduced. Mr. G's pattern of keeping information from his wife was his method of punishing her for her inability to gratify him or to satisfy his dependency needs. His need for a one-to-one relationship made it impossible for him to tolerate sharing the caseworker. Mrs. G's need to depreciate both herself and her husband was too strong for her to put the joint interview to use.

The caseworker must always be aware of his own feelings of competition, his degree of anxiety about expressed hostility, and his countertransference feelings toward both clients in joint interviews. Most workers are uneasy about joint interviewing, since this is not only a seldom used technique but is one that involves a different use of oneself. They are sometimes tempted to plunge into joint interviewing without full evaluation of all the factors involved (as in the G case above) because the couple seems so clearly to have a sustained mutual concern.

The quality of interaction between two clients needs to be evaluated carefully before the worker attempts joint interviews. The difference between success and failure in the use of this technique seems to lie in the degree of competitiveness between marital partners. Hence, sound diagnostic understanding is extremely important. All-pervasive competitiveness disrupts the interaction and prevents success in joint interviews. Such competitiveness can represent a demand for the caseworker's attention in terms of attempting to gain gratification or to depreciate the partner in the caseworker's eyes. If the caseworker is to succeed in keeping the interview focused on the area of mutual concern, the clients must be able to tolerate having their competitiveness put to constructive use. If the greatest need of one or both partners is to ally himself with the caseworker against the other, joint interviews will fail.

> Mr. and Mrs. H came to the agency because Johnny, age 7, was failing in school. Mr. H rejected him completely since he was Mrs. H's illegitimate child, while he lavished affection on his own three younger children. Although Mr. and Mrs. H both expressed concern about Johnny they quickly focused on their stormy marriage. Joint interviews were attempted. However, the high degree of competitiveness outweighed their mutual concern and each partner battled for the caseworker's attention. Each picked at the other in a depreciating fashion, in a seeming attempt to destroy the other person in the eyes of the caseworker for the purpose of gaining all the caseworker's love and attention for himself. After a trial period contacts were discontinued.

Evaluating Progress in Treatment

There are several clues that one can use in evaluating the progress made in joint interviews. One is the manner in which the marital partners start to ignore the caseworker in the conversation. As they begin to relate more and more to each other, are able to contain their anxiety rather than to act it out, and can focus on the problem about which they are mutually concerned, there is not only less distortion in the way they relate to each other but also less and less argument. Moreover, they are able to talk about improvements in their situation and to look directly at each other as they talk. Sometimes they even turn their chairs to form a circle with the worker so that each is more obviously included in the conversation. The more passive, quiet, nonverbal partner becomes a little more vocal, and expresses his feelings and attitudes without provoking the wrath of the more vocal, controlling partner.

> Initially Mr. and Mrs. B literally sat with their backs to each other talking to the caseworker as if the other marital partner were invisible. As treatment progressed they started to face each other, then to talk to each other, and finally they left the caseworker out of their conversation entirely.

Summary

Because the family service agency is concerned with marital interaction and its effect on children and the total family unit, it should consider using joint interviewing as one treatment technique. This technique may help to restore the marital balance so that marital partners can mobilize all their strength to handle crisis situations. In the final analysis, it may assist in restoring family balance.

We have found that the ability of each marital partner to maintain an interest in, and put to use his concern about, the couple's mutual interests is the greatest single factor in the success of joint interviewing. The diagnostic clues and treatment techniques offered here have been developed on the basis of our experience in using joint interviews with clients who have diagnosed character disorders. We are not sure that the same would hold for the treatment of clients with neurotic problems. We realize that our formulations require further study and practice. We feel, however, that we have been able to demonstrate the effectiveness of joint interviewing in a small number of cases and trust that our findings will be useful to others.

Casework with Older Persons

Ruth G. Cohen

Traditionally, older persons have always come for help to the Jewish Family Service of Philadelphia. This agency has had a long-standing interest in the aging although at times this concern has been relegated to the background. As long ago as 1936, one of our workers wrote: "The private family agency recognizes in casework with the aged that its objective cannot be personality growth or a good social adjustment in the same sense in which we hold this to be an objective with younger clients. The psychological problems of old age have not until now engaged our attention as have the problems of childhood and adolescence. We cannot overlook psychological factors in working with the aged any more than with any other group of individuals. The aged have emotions—loves and hates—as have others, and in addition they have long established habits of conduct. The aged person does not change easily. At present we are being guided in the plans we make in providing for the living arrangements of aged couples and individuals by their own needs and preferences. Clearly, our objective in working with old people is their comfort and happiness and our efforts must be shaped toward this end."[1]

The Nazi persecution and the influx of refugees diverted our attention from this interest to alleviating the suffering let loose upon the world. But then, about three years ago, the agency picked up where it left off—when a district office was converted to services for older persons. This was done not only in recognition of the needs of older persons but also of our own professional need to gain additional understanding in giving them help.

They Are the Same—Just Older

The essence of this experience, though not startling or dramatic, is that aging people are complete human beings who have all the emotions and needs of any other group—with the additional factor of age. We have

[1] "Casework with the Aged," a paper presented in 1936 at the Jewish National Conference by Mrs. Beatrice Muller, current case supervisor, Jewish Family Service of Philadelphia.

Reprinted with permission of the author and the National Association of Social Workers, from *Social Work*, Vol. 2, No. 1 (January, 1957), pp. 30–35.

learned that our basic casework concepts are as generic with this group as with any other group; that older persons are individuals in their own right and their needs as diversified as any other group coming to the private family agency for help.

Most important of all, we have learned how desperately they want to feel important and to be wanted—above all to be loved, not cared *for*, but cared *about*. The atrophy of hope, of not being productive, of not feeling their own personal worth are as painful and almost as debilitating as the chronic illnesses that may beset them.

Dr. Maurice Linden wrote recently that:

> growing old is the most unrewarding aspect of our way of life. Our culture is a juggernaut of youthful ideals consigning to dust whatever does not move with it. Our values have been the values of youth—vigor, physical beauty, motion, quantitative productivity and, to some degree, arrogance. Contrasting and unfamiliar to us are the values of later maturity—reliability, wisdom, stability, quality, and humility. Surrounded by contrary attitudes our aging have little choice but to feel that reaching maturity means realizing social rejection. The half-tolerance, offhand acceptance, and disinterest towards the aged constitute social exclusion. And it is this emotional deprivation suffered by millions past sixty that is one of the main forces operating towards making them social dependents, embittered souls, and ultimately physical and emotional incompetents.[2]

In working with older persons in a concentrated and specialized way, we have learned that only as we extend ourselves and accept them as we do our other clients can we see them and their needs in a more individualized way. For, as is characteristic of any group that possesses similarities, there is also a wide range of differences.

Setup of Division

The Division of Services for Older Persons averages 80 to 100 applications monthly, the greater number being met through short-time contact. All the services of the agency are available to the older person in meeting his request—individual and family counseling, financial assistance under certain circumstances to alleviate social and economic problems, and homemaker or domestic service for the disabled to help them remain in their own homes. In addition, new services have been created to meet expressed needs—specifically *1]* a private residence placement program designed to provide supervised placement in a private home for the older person who wishes to enjoy family living for as long as he is able to do so; *2]* a placement planning service that is a casework service for the older person who wishes or needs to change his living arrangements (implicit in this is a specialized knowledge of existing community resources); and *3]* the newest service, the use of volunteers who, with the caseworker, become a team in offering and sometimes performing services for the client of which, in the

[2] Maurice Linden, "Emotional Problems in Aging," *Jewish Social Service Quarterly* (Fall, 1954).

absence of a family member, he would otherwise be deprived (this often takes care of the problem of loneliness).

Staff Must Like Older People

In achieving our objectives in working with older persons, it is vital to presuppose skilled, mature personnel who are interested in older people. Unfortunately, there is a dearth of trained workers who feel the same challenge and interest in working with older people as they do in working with the more youthful, but it is essential to have staff who see this group as individual human beings and not as a category. The caseworker serving older persons needs to be able to impart to them a deep feeling of interest and concern to which all people, but particularly the elderly, respond. Their capacity for change needs to be paced to a tempo related to their individuality, which may be slower than that of a younger person. A positive response to the older adult must not be marred by the factors of their illness, slow pace, or a certain amount of rigidity.

There is excitement and challenge in the kind of strength and life that the older person possesses. Indeed, it is their great strength and ability to cope with life's problems that have enabled them to reach this stage in their lives. When a more youthful client expresses hostility, the caseworker is gratified to know that enough of a relationship exists between them so that the client can feel free to risk that much feeling; yet in dealing with an elderly client who has the courage and the strength to express negative feeling, the same worker may say "Old people can be so cranky!" In working with older people, we have found that if we are alert, we can recognize signals of their great strength—"crankiness" itself is sometimes a sign of vitality, a flag of "no surrender" flying in the face of what might often seem hopeless odds. This quality of strength and the will to live are exciting and challenging.

A Normal Phase of Life

In addition to a real liking for older people, the skilled caseworker must also possess a belief in the positive aspects of this phase of a person's life. If all she sees is senility and a "fading away," if the older person's slower pace irritates and annoys her, then she cannot truly be a real helper. The interested caseworker can experience the dynamic quality and challenge that exist in working with the older person through developing special qualities and skills. She needs to experience in herself a process in relation to the entire concept of old age—first viewing it intellectually, then rejecting it because of her own personal pains and fears, and, then hopefully, coming back to its acceptance in a truly positive way. She must accept old age as an inevitable process, another phase in living, just as childhood and adolescence are a natural part of the life process, with the pain and beauty that go along with maturity.

Only if the caseworker is geared in this positive way of working with older persons can she bear the frustrations that may occur in her daily practice. Only then can she help the older person or his adult children in coping with chronic illness and mental deterioration, or discuss the funeral arrangements older people are prone to talk about—the last reality all of us inevitably face.

The caseworkers in the Division of Services for Older Persons were assigned because they expressed and demonstrated an interest in the older person, a factor that has made it possible for us to live through frequent frustrations in our day-to-day jobs.

Finding a Balance

Keen judgment, too, plays a very important part in working with older persons. Finding the neat balance between "doing for" and "doing with" is *most* essential—something as simple as knowing when to call the public agency to arrange for the initial appointment and when to have the client call for his own appointment. Older persons display amazing inner strengths at times and the caseworker's judgment is always necessary to help them use these strengths to the full and, at the same time, to give them the necessary warmth and support in their efforts to effect positive change. Judgment must be constantly exercised in many other areas as well—when to support defenses of a lifelong pattern or to risk putting in a question or to inject one's own difference that may begin to break up these defenses? Or when to allow the older person to be dependent on the caseworker in meeting his dependency needs and when to put some of this back on him so he can feel his independence? There is the client who is marking time and the client who is racing against time to make his peace with the world before life ends. One of the hardest realities in working with older people is their awareness, and ours, too, that for them time is running out.

Frequently, the caseworker, out of her desire to have her client's remaining years as happy and comfortable as possible, may push the client in a direction he is not yet ready to go, or permit him to jump at a solution rather than slacken his pace and work through a constructive resolution. For the older person, each new experience carries more fear and resistance; for having lived longer, there is more of the known to give up.

A couple in their seventies found it necessary to move from their home where they had lived for over forty years. They were moving into a housing project because of their ill health and inability to climb stairs. The worker's support through this experience was immeasurable—her awareness of what this experience meant in giving up the old and risking the new, in helping them to express their fears, and in supporting the rightness of their feelings. There was great reward when they told the caseworker several weeks after they were settled in their new apartment: "We never could have done this if you hadn't been with us through this." Often this is as much as can be given or is needed—a warm, supportive relationship that helps the client into a new experience with a minimum amount of pain and fear or that helps him sustain the old, knowing that change is neither feasible nor possible.

Frequently, the older person deposits a myriad of problems with the caseworker: "I don't know what to do with myself. I'm so unhappy—my children don't care what happens to me. I can't live alone any longer—I'm too sick. Please tell me what to do." Tremendous self-discipline and judgment are required by the caseworker to select out the part of this reality that she and the client can begin to work on together and within which some change can take place. The dynamics lie in the creative use the caseworker is willing to make of herself in meeting these needs and in helping the client to bring about the desired change.

Adult Children Are Involved

There are many situations in which the deepest use of one's self as a helper is required. This may be particularly true in the counseling help which extends to the adult children of older persons, as well as the older person himself. In some situations. pathological changes, with gradual loss of memory and subsequent deterioration, may cause parents to be totally dependent for planning, as well as support, on their adult children. In such instances, the work may be entirely with the children. In other situations, the older person is capable of participating in the casework relationship, sometimes only to a limited degree. Conversely, when the older person applies, the question of involvement of the adult children—how, why, and at what spots—calls for keen judgment on the part of the caseworker. Aspects of relationship problems between the older person and his adult children that have roots in the past as well as in the present complicate many situations. Adult children, attempting to meet crises in the lives of their parents, are often torn between their feeling of responsibility to them and to their own families. They are often so emotionally involved in their own difficulties with marital partners and/or children that they feel helpless and unable to know where their responsibility to their parents begins or ends. The following case is an illustration.

When Mr. L came to the JFS in April he was troubled about making a living arrangement for his 74-year-old mother. He warned the caseworker he had no intention of becoming "emotionally involved"; all he wanted was "concrete help" in planning for his mother. He described Mrs. L as partially paralyzed, unhappy, difficult to talk to, and unable to adjust to any living arrangement which had been made for her.

His parents had been divorced when he was less than a year old, the father taking the older brother and sister with him, while Mr. L, as the baby, remained with the mother who suffered a stroke shortly after the separation. He had seen his father, now deceased, only once, and his brother and sister, who were brought up in private boarding schools, only twice in his whole life. He contrasted their life of ease and plenty with his own deprivation. He had moved about frequently with his mother, often living in undesirable surroundings. As he grew older and secured employment, he provided a home for his mother with whom he continued to live until he entered the armed forces. At this time he married and upon discharge did not rejoin his mother. Five years ago Mrs L suffered another stroke and was no longer able to live alone. He placed her in various "homes" but she could not make an adjustment, could not find friends, and was constantly complaining and making life miserable for both of them.

It was obvious from the very beginning that this young man was torn with conflict. He needed help not only in planning for his mother but in understanding and resolving his own feelings of resentment and hostility toward his parents, brother and sister. He felt a strong sense of guilt because he preferred to live with his wife and child in the home of his mother-in-law, rather than provide a home which would include his mother. As he was able to unburden himself to the caseworker, in spite of saying that he did not wish to be emotionally involved, he talked about the past and how he was never quite sure of his real feelings toward his mother and father, because he was sorry for his mother and knew only the bad things she told him about his father. He never had the courage to talk about his family relationships.

With the caseworker's help and encouragement, Mr. L could, for the first time, let his mother know that he was concerned about her and because of his concern had come to the JFS for help in planning a different living arrangement for her. He suggested that she, too, come to the agency, which was a different experience since in the past he had engineered it all.

While Mrs. L could only talk about how wonderful her "boy" had been to her, there was an undercurrent of resentment against the son upon whom she felt she had lavished all her love and affection because, as she said, he "was always bringing me the ready-made plan where I had no choice." She was now surprised that he talked to her "like I counted for something." She was surprised at the caseworker's interest in her. Although she had difficulty in walking and her son feared she was deteriorating mentally, somehow this aged woman found the strength to keep appointments with the caseworker as well as the hospital clinics. We learned from the doctor that Mrs. L was "clear and not senile." Mr. L was helped to discuss frankly with his mother his inability to have her live with him and she could then begin to consider the possibility of living in a group boarding home suggested to her by the caseworker. In September she moved to an approved group boarding home where she found companionship with men and women her own age and with whom she had a common bond.

By November Mrs. L had made a fairly good adjustment to her new environment and had acquired several friends. Mr. L said he felt closer to his mother now than ever before and yet felt emancipated, not "tied" as he had previously. He and his wife and child were now visiting Mrs. L regularly in the boarding home and even had her visit them occasionally. Mrs. L who was rejected and deserted by her husband in the prime of her life, had lived in fear of losing her son. She now could believe that her son was interested in her and concerned about her welfare. What was so enabling was his ability and the caseworker's, too, to believe in and permit Mrs. L to use her own strength in living.

A Tricornered Relationship

As in this case, the adult child frequently comes to the agency for help, either with "the solution in hand" or wanting an immediate answer. The impact of needing to involve the parent in this vital planning is at times too much, and here the service may be one of giving information regarding resources which the adult child is free to use as he sees fit; but the way is always left open for him to return for help should he change his mind—and frequently he does. The "why" of involving the parent does not require explanation for this involves a basic casework concept—the individual's right (whatever his age) to plan for himself. To the adult child, however, it may feel belittling, stir up guilt feelings, or be more than he can bear to face. It is one thing to plan *for* another person and quite something else to plan *with* another.

In this tricornered relationship, the caseworker has a unique role—the balance which needs to be achieved between the caseworker, adult child or children, and parent, with the caseworker trying to meet and support the needs of each, both in terms of separateness and being together, and always with the focus of helping parent and adult child to work through a plan that hopefully is satisfying to all concerned. Again, the sensitivity of the worker, her keen diagnostic skill and her sympathetic understanding need to be exercised to the fullest. Some very exciting and dramatic changes may take place, but the caseworker may also meet her greatest frustrations in this kind of relationship. The adult child whose problem of guilt is so deeply rooted that he is immobilized; the controlling, domineering mother who is determined to keep a hold on her child or children at whatever cost; the bewildered, rejected father who cannot understand why after these many years of sacrifice to his children he cannot live with any of them; the adult children who are constantly at odds with each other, based on earlier sibling rivalries, and each having different ideas of plans for the parents—all present a veritable maelstrom of confusions, anxieties, pain, and guilt-ridden feelings. But to offset this there is the sense of satisfaction that comes from working out a sound living arrangement out of chaos, or helping the children to accept the reality of what exists, or enabling them and the parent to work on the problems existent in their relationship.

Collaborative Efforts

There are problem areas beyond the immediate scope of the case-worker. These, however, belong to the community. The inadequate Department of Public Assistance grant, the inability to purchase good nursing home care for the chronically ill whose financial resources are limited, the lack of employment facilities (either part time or full time for the older person who has been discarded by industry), the lack of adequate facilities for the senile person, the need for protective services for the older person—

these are only some of the major unmet needs in the community that often block the caseworker in offering effective help to the older person.

One other vital aspect that is not only true of casework with older persons but of social work in general is the importance of collaboration. The value of collaborative effort has proved immeasurable in working with older persons. In almost every aspect of her work, the caseworker needs to combine her efforts with those of another professional. In planning, there is the medical social worker or the worker in a home for the aged; in helping with financial assistance, there is the public assistance worker; in the area of helping the family plan for the senile or mentally disturbed client, there is the hospital psychiatric social worker; in trying to alleviate the older person's problem of loneliness, there is the group worker; in working out a plan for the chronically ill client, there is the public health or visiting nurse; in the area of employment, there is the employment counselor—all these and others combine to form what we hope to achieve, namely, an integrated program of services for the older person. Only by collaborgtive effort of the highest degree can we begin hopefully and helpfully to meet the needs that exist among older persons.

Whether we are group workers, medical social workers, or family counselors, there is a real challenge in working with older people. We know through our professional and personal experience that not only activity, but creativity, is possible as long as there is life. Social work can and should help to provide the milieu in which such activity and creativity can thrive, flourish, and survive. The community must be educated away from the idea of the utter helplessness of old age and toward a better understanding of growing old, but this cannot become a reality until more members of the profession begin to feel differently themselves. Only if we regard the aging group in a positive light can we develop a program that will meet their needs and has in it all the dynamic, forceful, and alive qualities to which all other aspects of social service in sound, community planning aspire.

Casework with the Older Person and His Family

Margaret Milloy

In casework with the aging, as in any other area of casework, the worker's primary goals are to develop a sound psychosocial diagnosis and to carry out a satisfactory plan of treatment. Many new ideas are being discussed about the diagnosis of the older client, but little has been done

Reprinted from *Social Casework*, XLV (October, 1964), pp. 450–456, by permission of the author and the Journal.

either to incorporate these ideas into the treatment process or to provide a conceptual base for current practice. I plan first to discuss some diagnostic considerations and then to try to relate them to ways of helping older people and their families.

Perhaps social workers have tended to provide less than equal service to the older person because they have geared their actions to his reality needs or those of his family without undertaking a proper diagnostic study of his total situation. Their conscious or unconscious conviction seems to be that the older person can progress in only one direction—down. Seeing only death in his future, they wonder, What is the use . . . ? They often appear to feel that it is more worth while to work with a younger person in short-term ego-supportive casework than to work with an older person whose needs may be similar. This is not to say that they are unconcerned about the older person, his health, and his general welfare, but rather that the new task they face is to make their concern for him more effective by deepening their understanding of him.

Developmental Tasks and Role Functioning

The concept of aging as a developmental stage related to previous stages and carrying with it certain specific tasks is particularly important in thinking about diagnosis. According to Robert Peck, old age poses three tasks: the achievement of ego differentiation as opposed to work-role preoccupation, of body transcendence as opposed to body preoccupation, and of ego transcendence as opposed to ego preoccupation.[1] Charlotte Buhler, as paraphrased by Margaret Blenkner, seems to see one goal in the last stage of life as "finding an inner fulfillment, an inner meaning and integrity,"[2] that enables the individual to face death with the sure knowledge that he has contributed to the future of his family and to society.

Obviously, it is the rare client who comes to a social agency having achieved this goal, and here is where the worker's diagnostic and treatment skills become most important. To what extent can the caseworker help him accomplish the tasks before him? What kind of help, aside from that geared to reality needs, does he require? What capacity does he have for mastery? In this regard, Blenkner makes a plea for social workers to be less concerned with the older person's defenses and more concerned with his capacity to cope with the myriad changes taking place within himself and his environment, which form the basis for the developmental tasks mentioned above. She asks the social worker these questions: "If one accepts the development frame of reference, what is more important to diagnose or evaluate in an

---

[1] Robert F. Peck, "Psychological Developments in the Second Half of Life," in *Psychological Aspects of Aging*, John E. Anderson (ed.), American Psychological Association, Washington, D.C., 1956, pp. 42–53.

[2] Margaret Blenkner, "Developmental Considerations and the Older Client," a paper presented at a Symposium on the Relations of Development and Aging, Fifteenth Annual Meeting of the Gerontological Society, 1962, Miami Beach, November 8–10, 1962 (unpublished).

older person; his particular resolution of the Oedipus complex or his philosophy of life? Which is more likely to offer you a dynamic you can use in treatment?"[3]

What does the caseworker diagnose, which of his tried and true methods can he use, and how can he expand his conceptual framework to include age categories that, for the most part, he has dismissed with a pat generalization? In this connection it might be helpful to make use of Stanley Cath's concept of depletion and restitution in the middle and later years and his construct of the "omnicon."[4] The omnicon includes "not only the total personality (ego, superego, and id) but also the physical structure of the organism down to the cellular level (the body) and the socio-economic, ethical and purposeful environment. This designates that it is the total human being and his personal cosmos that is involved in various phases of the depletion and restoration."[5] Cath speaks of certain basic anchorages that people form throughout life: *1]* an intact body and body image, *2]* an acceptable home, *3]* a socio-economic anchorage, and *4]* a meaningful purpose in life. These four anchorages provide the structure within which the individual performs the required developmental tasks at various stages of life; and the degree of success with which tasks are performed and crises met spells the difference between good and impaired health.

Cath states that throughout life, but particularly in the latter years, a balance is struck between external and internal depleting and restorative forces; and that all these anchorages are vital to the individual's ability to maintain balance. From these anchorages also comes the "feedback"—the memories, relationships, and so forth that reinforce the individual's sense of his own worth and help to maintain his balance. In a sense Cath is talking about the nature of the ego and its capacity to cope with both internal and external stress, and about ways in which its functioning can be strengthened. In terms of casework with the older person Cath's formulation implies that the worker's proper concern is not so much the pathology of the client as those ego and life forces that are still intact or capable of restoration. The caseworker needs to acquire a longitudinal view of the client in order to determine the strength of his anchorages, how well they have served him, and how adequate they are in the present. In other words, if the worker views aging as a developmental stage, he needs to evaluate both the individual's success in mastering the tasks and crises of previous stages and the residue of unsolved problems complicating his mastery of current crises.

Much of the foregoing also can be viewed in terms of the adequacy and continuity of the older person's role functioning at various age levels. To what extent are previous role discontinuities affecting his current problems? How much conflict is there between his and society's expectations in regard to his role performance in his various statuses—for instance, his

---

[3] Blenkner, *op. cit.*
[4] Stanley H. Cath, "Some Dynamics of Middle and Later Years," *Smith College Studies in Social Work,* Vol. XXXIII, February 1963, pp. 97–126.
[5] Cath, *op. cit.,* p. 100.

performance in his roles as husband, father, son, older person, unemployed man—and in regard to his roles as related to his race and religion, his education, and his occupation? As a husband and father, a man is expected to be strong, supportive and giving—the employed head of a household who is active in decision-making. As an old, unemployed man, he is expected to be cheerful, nonassertive, and satisfied with his income from Old Age Assistance, Social Security, or his children. Perhaps he is expected to be a baby sitter for his grandchildren; perhaps a substitute homemaker if he is a widower, or a household helper to his wife if he is a husband. Obviously, the transition from one set of roles to the other cannot be accomplished without great pain and anxiety, not only for the older person but also for those who are affected by his role definitions or participate in them as does the adult child when he feels he should assume the role of a parent to his own parent. It is the caseworker's responsibility to understand this problem area and gear the treatment to it.

Inherent in this discussion are questions that have to be answered about the client's character, his ego-functioning, and past and current traumas to which he may be reacting. How much depletion is irreversible because of the death of loved ones and an inability to cathect substitutes or because of the loss of health? To what extent can the caseworker hope to help the client restore his capacity to function? What objects in the environment can be used as cathectic substitutes? If there are children, how can the worker help to free them and the parent from the old, unsatisfying, unworkable ties and strengthen the positive aspects of their relationship?

It is not easy for the worker to accomplish these aims of casework with the older person, particularly because so many older people seek help only at a point of considerable crisis. Often, unfortunately, they seek help only when there has been so much irreversible loss that the worker can do no more than assist the family in making a plan for the client. The points that follow, however, need to be given consideration in treatment.

Treatment Considerations

The first point concerns the worker's own attitude toward old age and his ability to empathize with the needs of his clients. In order to be able to help older people, the worker must first have resolved his own feelings about death, not only the death of his loved ones but also his own. Much of old age relates directly to real losses—of family and friends, of job, of money and status—to impairment of the body or body functioning, and to antici-pated death of oneself. Unless the worker can recognize the client's losses and empathize with his sense of bereavement, he cannot be tuned in to the client's need to deal with these losses, to cathect new objects or face an irreparable loss realistically. The worker has to be able, moreover, to tolerate the extreme—sometimes overwhelming—social and emotional isolation in which so many older people live and not to be drawn into it if, as sometimes happens, he perceives in the client what he fears to be his own future. This aspect of countertransference, which has perhaps not been recognized or dealt with sufficiently, certainly deserves much consideration.

It is important for the caseworker to understand the handling of grief and mourning. The client may express specific grief reactions or a generalized depressive reaction. For whom or what is he mourning? Is he reacting to a former or a current loss? Is his grief reaction "normal," or are there aspects of morbidity present? If it is a normal, acute grief reaction, perhaps the best help is empathic listening and recognition that the client may need to withdraw temporarily because he is preoccupied with guilt; if someone close to him has died, he may seem to have lost an "anchor," a habit pattern of daily living related to the lost person, and he may appear not quite oriented. But he will not have lost touch with reality, and he will need reassurance, expressions of interest from those around him, and help in making new connections.

As a person progresses from normal grief, where the preponderant feelings toward the lost object are positive and warm, along a continuum of increasing ambivalence, intervention may be needed to help him release negative feelings of loss and desertion. If he can really "suffer" the loss, he will be much freer afterward to express hostile feelings and will have less feeling of guilt in connection with them; through this experience he will be able to withdraw his tie to his lost object. If, however, he is encouraged by family and friends to repress his feelings of loss and "keep a stiff upper lip," resolution of the negative feelings will be extremely difficult, if not impossible, because of the repressed guilt associated with them.

With the majority of older people, mourning is a reaction to both current and past losses. The caseworker's task, then, is to support the client's capacity to master the current trauma. After sensitively exploring earlier experiences of loss, the worker relates these to the current situation by responding either verbally or in a kind of "double talk"—that is, responding to deeply felt emotions at the same time that he discusses conscious feelings. To the degree that the client can be freed emotionally from his ties to the lost object, he will be able to reach out and form new ties to living objects that constitute a measure of restitution.

Developing a Relationship

The worker has to make an unusually heavy emotional investment in the older client—not a personal one, but a feeling, professional one— through which the client learns that he, his thoughts and his feelings, are truly important. If the worker fails to make this kind of controlled investment, the client may interpret his various attempts at ego-restoration as empty reassurance, attack, or pressure to do what seems impossible. If the worker is able to make the investment, he can use supportively many techniques that are effective with younger clients—confrontation, clarification, and interpretation, for example—to help the client accept his world and cope with it. The difference between working with the young and the old in this respect is a quantitative one; the aging person, in comparison with the young person, usually has much less energy to invest, partly because he expends so much in coping with his everyday problems of living. Moreover, unlike the younger person, he tends to despair and to have relatively little hope that what he does will benefit himself in the future. A larger emotional investment by the caseworker is therefore necessary to achieve the same results.

The client-worker relationship is achieved as a result of various types of communication. Extraverbal communication, described so movingly by Helen M. Lambrick, is one extremely important type in work with an aged client: "Often the only way in which we can communicate our continued interest and concern to very sick patients is through touch—and a sensitive worker can always tell when this is appropriate or when it would be too threatening for an inhibited patient."[6] This point is particularly relevant for those who work with older people, and it becomes increasingly important when these clients become ill and have to deal with their fear of death. Even with the younger aged, physical contact can be a kind of social-emotional interaction that tells the client the worker is concerned about him. Social workers have always been taught that physical contact with clients, except young children, is unprofessional; but with the aged and sick it should be regarded as a specific technique of treatment that springs from the worker's empathy with the client and a desire to let him know that he matters. Without this empathy, this controlled emotional investment, physical contact is a gesture that is meaningless or one that may even be harmful.

Although the worker needs to make an investment of feeling, he must be alert to the dangers of overinvesting himself to satisfy his own personal needs. Helen Sholtis has written a provocative article on countertransference in marital problems, due to unresolved oedipal problems of the worker.[7] The same kind of problem can occur in working with couples. Overinvestment in older clients can occur also as a result of the worker's transferring onto them some of his pregenital feelings toward his own parents. Such a manifestation of countertransference is a problem for both him and his supervisor and must be recognized and dealt with before the client's needs can be properly perceived.

The Proper Use of Community Resources

So far, the provision of psychological services has been discussed, but many older persons have also an acute need of concrete services. Probably the more varied the agency services provided, the more social workers are able to reach out to people in need. Homemakers, foster homes, supplementary financial assistance, and protective care are vital to many older clients. Obviously other community resources, such as group work services

---

[6] Helen M. Lambrick, "Communications with the Patient," *The Almoner,* Vol. XV, October 1962, p. 199.

[7] Helen S. Sholtis, "The Management of Marital Counseling Cases," *Social Casework,* Vol. XLV, February 1964, pp. 71–78.

and nursing and custodial homes, are also important complements to a well-rounded service.

Social workers should use the special services available for old people with discrimination. The two most important criteria for utilizing any services (with the exception of protective services) are *1]* Will using the service increase or maintain the client's capacity for mastery? and *2]* Will it tend to lessen his sense of isolation and increase his feeling of being needed? For instance, a part-time homemaker can help an isolated person maintain his independence and so delay or obviate the necessity of providing domiciliary care. This is a very important service to him and the community.

Family agencies should have both a philosophy and a policy regarding the protective care of older people. LeRoy Levitt points out the great importance not only of making "an adequate, flexible, utilizable medical diagnostic evaluation"[8] before taking any legal protective measures but also of recognizing that certain disorders fluctuate and change after a diagnosis is made.

> A knowledge of symptomatology is not as important as information about the modifiability and the medical, environmental, or emotional changes required. The double play of quick diagnosis, then disposition to hospital, commitment, nursing home, or guardianship is interfered with by such an attitude. It is medieval to think of a psychosis at any age as a problem of competency or confinement, just by virtue of the diagnosis. There are as many kinds of senescent problems as there are people with such problems.[9]

Levitt goes on to comment on the reparative capacities of the aged and the seriousness of depriving a person of his civil rights, a move that should not be made without plans for regularly reappraising his initial state of incompetency and the new clinical condition. This principle is just another aspect of concern for the older person, carried forward to a period when he has suffered greater depletion and possibly organic change.

Questions about plans for living arrangements often arise in working with most older people. Can the older person live in the community? If so, with what protections? Does he need institutional care? If so, what kind? Can he use a foster home? What kind of protection does he need? Inherent in all questions in this area is the fact that each person is different from all others; he is a product of his own unique life experiences and has to be understood in that light. Therefore, plans for living arrangements should be based on the principle that as long as a person gains more gratification than pain from living in the community, it is better to help him remain there. Many older people seek entrance to an institution at a point of crisis occasioned by the death of a spouse, a caretaking child, or an important

---

[8] LeRoy Paul Levitt, "Health: Current Practices, Responsibilities, Resources, Problems, Issues, Gaps, Recommendations," a paper presented at a general panel session, Seminar on Protective Services for Older People, Arden House, Harriman, New York, March 10–15, 1963, in *Seminar on Protective Services for Older People,* National Council on the Aging, New York, 1964, p. 110.

[9] Levitt, *op. cit.,* pp. 110–111.

friend. The point of crisis may follow the onset of a disabling illness, with the result that the distress of the client is aggravated by a fear of encroaching weakness. In these circumstances he is apt to regress and focus on his weaknesses and his need for care. The social worker, then, must carefully evaluate all indications, however minor, of his interest in the world and his wish to participate in it.

When a person enters an institution, it becomes the center of his world, and outside relationships take on a lesser meaning. In even the best institution, independence and a sense of mastery must be curtailed. Therefore, by supporting him and by assuring him he will be helped to enter an institution when he needs to, the social worker encourages the older person to live independently as long as he can safely manage it. The words *safely* refers not only to physical safety but also, more important, to emotional well-being.

One client was so hostile and attacking in her overwhelming need to be given to that she drove one person after another way from her. The consulting psychiatrist thought that even though living alone in miserable surroundings was physically dangerous to her, her hostile attempts to meet her insatiable needs could be managed better in the community than in an institution where she would probably "use up" everyone available quickly.

Another client took in a roomer who helped to care for her house. Her need for independence was fierce and unrelenting. She was in great danger of falling or of having some other serious accident, and the social worker consulted a psychiatrist and a lawyer to determine the medical and legal responsibility of the agency for initiating proceedings for protective care. The psychiatrist thought that the client's denial of her dependency longings was one of her most important defenses. To break down this defense would literally destroy her; she had to be allowed to live alone until an incapacity forced her to recognize her need for care.

In both instances the social worker kept in close contact with the clients and made plans for them to be institutionalized when the change was indicated.

Lest the worker consider his responsibilities in working with the older person global, he should recognize, as he does with younger clients, that when personality damage is too great there may be nothing he can do to ameliorate the situation, at least with the current state of knowledge and staff pressures. The worker must make a moral judgment about the use of his time and, after proper evaluation of the needs of the client, either discontinue service entirely or, when necessary, provide only tangible service without psychological treatment.

Working with the Adult Children

The world is full of families in which there is a minimum amount of discord and a maximum amount of respect and love between generations. The older person participates in the total life of such families, and they usually do not seek treatment at social agencies unless the advanced age of the parent creates an acute problem. However, many of the people who come to social agencies have severe intergenerational conflicts, sometimes dormant until the need for plans for care of the parent becomes critical. For many years social workers have been struggling with the question of how to reach out and help adult children with the feelings aroused at this point by the needs of their parents. The whole gamut of unresolved parent-child relationships can be stirred up again in such situations. With as much skill and sensitivity as social workers can muster, they have not been able to help these clients appreciably.

The adult child who is usually able to use casework help in relation to his unresolved conflicts about his parents is an individual whose role as a son or daughter has become secondary to his role as marital partner or parent. He requests help in solving marital or parent-child problems, and some resolution of his own ambivalent tie to the parent is a necessary ingredient to his getting help and managing his current roles more effectively.

What of the adult child who comes seeking help for his aged parent? There is a popular notion that as parents become less capable there is a reversal of roles between parent and child. I do not believe that the roles are reversed. Rather the older person and his child undertake new roles, and they both must learn to cope with the new situation. As the adult child assumes a new primary role with his parent, he may not have the energy to invest in an introspective, uncovering type of treatment. Both internal and external pressures are so heightened when he feels he has to take responsibility for his parent that he cannot afford to dissipate his energy in other directions. Assuming a new role is fraught with much conflict, partly because of the adult child's need to hold on to the cathected object that, in reality, has undergone considerable change through the aging process. If he allows his own strong, negative feelings to emerge, he creates an intolerable situation not only for himself but also for the aged parent, whose realistic problems must be dealt with positively. At this time the adult child's primary task is not to engage in introspection but to help the parent meet his reality needs.

If this formulation is correct, the adult child who asks for help in relation to an aging parent can be assisted in several ways, short of involving him in treatment for himself. One of the most important is in separating reality from the mass of feelings that color it. The social worker can be most supportive if he can help the client understand that his parent is not a child for whom he must assume complete responsibility: the parent is an adult, who, although suffering from serious limitations, has a right to make decisions and to take responsibility for the consequences of those decisions. The worker can lift a great burden from the adult child by helping him see that he does not have to act as if he were omnipotent. He also can help him look at alternatives realistically and share the responsibility of decision-making with the parent. By insisting on discussing plans directly with the parent, the worker can strengthen the adult child's ability to support his parent and to refrain from taking on too much responsibility.

In conclusion, it is worth while to repeat a warning against stereotyping older persons simply because they share one common characteristic, advanced age. Older people differ in their personalities and needs, in their internal and external resources, and in their capacity for change and growth. If social workers are to help them make the most of their remaining years, they must deal with them as individuals and not as undifferentiated representatives of a social category.

Helping the Dying Patient and His Family

Nathalie Kennedy

Helping the dying patient and his family can be a most distressing experience for the social caseworker. It is an area of practice that demands the highest caliber of professional discipline and skill. Paradoxically, it can also be a most gratifying experience, since in offering this kind of help the caseworker is called upon to give as unselfishly of himself and his service as at any point in his professional life.[1]

General Considerations

Regardless of the setting in which the social caseworker practices, there will be a time in his professional life when he will be called upon to help, either directly or indirectly, the patient who is approaching death, and also to help the family members who are close to him. Especially in today's culture, there may be times when he will have to help a patient who has no relatives or who is friendless—as one author says, "friendless when the final test of friendship is made."[2] As a result of his own background and experience, the caseworker may want to ignore or brush aside the summons to offer help; but in his professional role he cannot resort to denial or avoidance when the dying patient requests help or when another colleague makes the request in his behalf. Recently, as a supervisor, I was sorely tempted to counsel a young caseworker, who had an unprotected caseload to "use avoidance" when she described three referrals of dying patients which had been made to her in a forty-eight-hour period. They were all young

---

[1] The author is indebted to Drs. J. M. Natterson and C. W. Wahl, psychiatrists (Los Angeles), and Dr. Joseph Eaton, sociologist (Pittsburgh), for the opportunity to consult with them and to review their papers on certain aspects of death. Moreover, the staff of the Division of Social Welfare, UCLA Medical Center, Los Angeles, furnished many stimulating ideas and data.

[2] E. M. Bluestone, M.D., "On the Significance of Death in Hospital Practice," *The Modern Hospital*, Vol. LXXVIII, No. 3 (1952), p. 86.

Reprinted from *Casework Papers* (New York: Family Service Association of America, 1959), pp. 120–129, by permission of the author and the Association.

mothers suffering from advanced cancer. But, as Harriet MacLaurin expressed it so well, "Members of the social work profession, with its particular set of values, cannot turn their backs on the dying person. It becomes, among other things, a matter of ethics."[3] The significance of what the caseworker does in the process of helping the dying patient is partially dependent upon his own personal philosophy about death and how he can allay his own anxieties.

Social workers in hospitals come face to face with death, as well as with the threat of death, more often than those in other settings. The very frequency with which they encounter death has a profound emotional effect upon them. No one can be dispassionate in the presence of impending death. It may be possible for social workers in community agencies to keep death, and thoughts about it, nearer the periphery of awareness; yet, even social workers in psychiatric clinics, in family and children's agencies, and in other health and welfare agencies inevitably encounter death and the numerous reactions that may accompany it.

Because of the very nature of the setting, social workers in hospitals have had the opportunity of learning a series of lessons in how to help the patient during various phases of his fatal illness—before, during, and after a diagnosis had been made and, often, in the last stages. During these various phases hospital and community agency social workers may work collaboratively in the patient's behalf. For example, when one hospital worker was helping a patient during a seven-month period, from the beginning to the end of her fatal skin disease, scleroderma, one of the many services given was to assist the patient, a proud and self-sufficient person before her illness, to accept referral to the public assistance agency while she was still able to function outside the hospital. This facet of service entailed several telephone conferences with the worker in the Bureau of Public Assistance. Removed as the public assistance worker was from an intimate contact with the patient's illness, nonetheless she could not avoid the impact of the patient's death sentence which affected her profoundly.

After the initial period of mourning and grief has passed, social workers in various community agencies can play a major role in helping close relatives deal with their feelings and with old problems that have become magnified or new ones that have been triggered by the death of a family member. It has been found that even when the physician, nurse, clergyman, and caseworker have given the dying patient and his family the most intensive and skilful help at the time of death, a family may seek help months later with feelings and problems directly related to death. In a recent medical student seminar, Dr. A. H. Parmelee, Jr., Associate Professor in the Department of Pediatrics of the UCLA Medical School, reported on several instances in which, as long as a year after a child's death, the parents had returned to the physician for help in dealing with their guilt feelings and for reassurance and support. Undoubtedly, there are other families

---

[3] Harriet MacLaurin, "In the Hour of Their Going Forth," *Social Casework*, Vol. XL, No. 3 (1959), p. 139.

who seek help from a pastor, who undertake psychiatric treatment, or who ask the help of community clinics and casework agencies long after the death of a family member.

The Hospital Setting

I should like now to discuss the social worker's role with the dying patient and his family, using as the basis of discussion the experience of the social service staff of the UCLA Medical Center. The Center is comprised of the Schools of Medicine and Nursing, a University Teaching Hospital, and a Neuropsychiatric Institute. Its objectives are the teaching of medical and paramedical groups, and medical research. Patient care is provided in relation to these objectives. Hence, patients are accepted on the basis of the Center's teaching or research interests. Accordingly, the objectives of the Division of Social Welfare, of which Social Service is a part, are also those of teaching, research, and service. Unmarried mothers, cardiac children, child-amputee patients and other pediatric cases are routinely referred by the hospital staff to Social Service; other cases are referred on a selective basis. The social workers in the 320-bed University Teaching Hospital are assigned to the Departments of Medicine, Obstetrics-Gynecology, Pediatrics, Radiology and Surgery to provide casework services to both in-patients and out-patients. The services of a psychiatric consultant, assigned from the Department of Psychiatry, are available one hour weekly. However, we are fortunate in also having other psychiatric consultants, not specifically assigned to Social Service, available as needed. There is no organized chaplain's service but clergymen from certain denominations maintain regular visiting schedules while clergymen from other religious groups are on call. There is an organized volunteer program, under professional direction, which is an invaluable resource.

Helping the Mother of a Three-Year-Old Patient

Casework services were given to the mother of 3-year-old Cheryl for an eight-month period beginning one month before the child's death. Interviews were held almost daily for the first five months. During the remaining three months, interviews gradually became less frequent until the case was closed. Cheryl died three years ago, but there is still a warm and friendly relationship between the social worker and the mother, Mrs. S, who drops by to see the worker when she takes her other children to the Medical Center for care. All the evidence we have gleaned leads us to believe that casework services have had a lasting effect. Medical care has been sought early for the other three children and apparently the experience of Cheryl's death has not been overwhelming to the family.

Mrs. S, aged 30 years, was referred to the caseworker at the time Cheryl, aged 3 years, had her right eye enucleated because of a retrobulbar tumor. Prognosis was poor. The intern referred the mother because she was upset and was exhibiting explosive behavior on the ward.

Mrs. S, an intelligent but distraught woman, was resentful and angry about the referral. Initially she saw the worker as a police officer. Once Mrs. S was able to express these feelings, the worker could convey to her the reason for referral—that the staff was genuinely interested in helping her and recognized she was upset with good reason. Although Mrs. S had a realistic understanding of the nature of Cheryl's illness and the poor prognosis for life, she found it difficult to accept because the onset had been so sudden and Cheryl had been the healthiest, brightest, and most outgoing of her four children. She saw in Cheryl a replica of herself as a child. She anticipated "the worst" and expressed herself as being grateful for each day and week that Cheryl lived.

Part of Mrs. S's difficulty in getting along with the nursing staff seemed related to her conflict about her roles as mother and as trained nurse. She was a registered nurse by profession. When the worker cited various examples of problems professional people encounter when they attempt to assist family members with whom they are emotionally involved, Mrs. S gradually began to see that, as a mother, she could not maintain the same professional attitude and objectivity that were possible when she cared for a person unrelated to her. She was then able to look at what she had been doing, to turn over some of the responsibilities to nursing staff, and to be less critical of them. Her relationship with the medical staff members also improved.

In the meantime, the close-knit community in which the family resided had rallied behind the family, and neighbors were helping care for Cheryl's sister, aged 5 years, her brother, aged 4 years, and little sister, aged 6 months. Mr. S, aged 41 years, was thus enabled to continue working as an engineer for a large aircraft firm. Mrs. S, although grateful for the neighbors' help, expressed some feeling about having to accept it. The worker helped her to see that there is value in being able to receive as well as to give.

As the relationship developed between the worker and Mrs. S and as Mrs. S. became increasingly able to handle her own anxieties about Cheryl, she focused her concern on her husband, who she felt needed help in facing Cheryl's illness. The marital relationship was a good one, but Mrs. S was anxious for the worker to talk with Mr. S since she felt that he was being protective of her.

There was one lengthy interview with Mr. S who expressed some dissatisfaction with the medical care Cheryl had received. He was encouraged to talk about what was troubling him. He was helped to see that his anger, which he directed toward the doctors because of the delay in performing the enucleation, was related to his own feeling of helplessness in the situation. The worker suggested that he discuss his feelings with the doctors and raise the questions he had outlined to her. She arranged for him to talk with the chief resident, as he had been the one who had followed Cheryl through all her hospitalizations and could best pull the findings together. She also told Mr. S about his wife's concern for him and encouraged him to discuss with Mrs. S more about how he felt and what he thought. The worker did not plan to see him again but suggested he feel free to contact her if any further questions should arise.

Later Mrs. S reported that the interview with Mr. S had been helpful to her, as well as to him, and that they were reaching out to each other for more support and comfort.

Cheryl continued to decline, and during the last days of her life the worker and parents spent considerable time talking about the imminence of her death, the parents' feeling about this, and how they could prepare the other children in the family. As she had done earlier, the worker again suggested the possibility of religious counsel, but the parents rejected the suggestion. When Cheryl died, both parents took her death fairly well.

As time went on, Mrs. S had less need for frequent interviews with the worker. She became involved with the activities of the other children and with community affairs, such as the community chest drive and political campaigns.[4] Whenever she was at the Medical Center, she came by to see the worker. At one point, there was some question as to whether Sue, the 5-year-old, had a neurological disorder. This was later ruled out, but the worker felt that Mrs. S faced quite well the difficult period of uncertainty about the diagnosis.

In summary, the worker stated that although 30-year-old Mrs. S initially had been resistive to the referral to the social worker, she was able to use the offered help not only in relation to facing Cheryl's serious illness and subsequent death but in relation to other problem areas for her, such as her feelings about herself as a woman and her relationship with her mother which had been a difficult one all her life. Mrs. S had evidenced good ego strength and had been able to handle, on her own, subsequent crisis situations. Although Mrs. S and the three other children remained under Medical Center care, no further problems had arisen when, after eight months, the case was closed.

Helping a Young Woman with Cancer

Casework services were first given to this 33-year-old, single woman, a school teacher of Danish background, when she was an out-patient and sought help. After two interviews, the hospital social worker and the patient reached a mutual agreement to discontinue, with the understanding that the patient could return later. Four months later the patient was hospitalized at the Medical Center for surgery. At this time the resident physician consulted the social worker because the patient was depressed. From that date until two months later when the patient died, the worker had daily interviews with her.

---

[4] This behavior is not unlike "certain changes suggestive of sublimation" which were observed in one group of mothers of leukemic children in a study of "death fear" recently completed by Drs. Joseph M. Natterson and Alfred G. Knudsen, Jr., at City of Hope Medical Center, Duarte, California. It was suggested these mothers were better able to integrate the child's death and loss because a period as long as eight months had elapsed between diagnosis and the child's death.

Louise R, 33 years old, with a diagnosis of cancer of the lining of the uterus, was undergoing radiation therapy following surgery when she initiated contact with the Psychiatric Clinic of the Neuropsychiatric Institute. After an exploratory interview, it became obvious to the psychiatric social worker that the patient's present emotional symptoms were closely related to her medical problems. The clinic physician concurred, and the patient accepted referral to the social worker on the Surgical Service.

In the initial interviews, Miss R expressed the feeling that her current pain symptoms were functional. As a result of her ambivalence about her fiancé and the recent termination of her engagement, old doubts and fears about herself had been reactivated. She also expressed feelings of anger and bitterness about the doctors previously consulted elsewhere who had said that her illness was "functional." She said that she was relieved to have a definitive physical diagnosis. She believed that the prognosis was favorable (which was true at that time), although some doubt and fear were evident in her avoidance of certain subjects and in her uncertainty about the effects of radiation therapy.

With some spontaneity, the patient told about her early background. After her father's death, her mother, an excellent cook, had worked for families of high social postion. Louise had lived with her mother and had played with the wealthy children in the neighborhood. She remembered no unhappiness or worry during that period although she felt that her dependency on her mother had become fixed at that time. Miss R had good intellectual recognition of her feelings and, although she indicated that she felt lonely and friendless and sought major social gratification from her work as a teacher, in the second interview she decided that she had clarified her feelings sufficiently to discontinue contacts with the caseworker.

Four months later, Miss R was hospitalized since it appeared that there was a massive spread of cancer affecting the kidneys and ureters. The resident physician then consulted the social worker, because surgery had been scheduled and the patient was very depressed.

Although neither Miss R nor her 75-year-old widowed mother had requested social service help, the worker resumed contact. When the worker visited Miss R, she was upset, frightened, and crying. She said that she was aware that the "disease" had spread. Again she expressed anger that the original diagnosis had been delayed. Her rebellion was combined with resignation. After ventilating her feelings, she concluded that more surgery was necessary but was most fearful of the radiation therapy to follow. This time she expressed the opinion that her previous symptoms had been non-functional. She implied that her tendency to seek answers within herself, on a functional basis, had been self-destructive and had contributed to her present situation.

After the above interview, the social worker met Miss R's mother in the hallway. She was crying. The worker introduced herself and took the mother to her office. The mother had only recently become aware of the seriousness of her daughter's condition. She was her only living relative.

The mother was conflicted as to whether or not she should have the surgery done by the private physician on the case or as a teaching patient at considerably reduced rates. The worker helped the mother clarify her need for financial help and consulted with the private physician who reassured the mother that Miss R's hospital status would not affect the kind of surgical and medical care she would receive. Following surgery, the medical staff requested psychiatric consultation. The consultant noted the patient's reactive depression. He recommended that the social worker continue to see the patient regularly to offer her much needed emotional support. He said that he would be available for consultation as needed.

Since the senior medical student had observed that the patient was affected adversely by her mother's anxiety it was agreed, also, that the worker would schedule some regular interviews with the mother in an attempt to drain off some of her anxiety. These interviews did not take place, partly because the mother was beginning to display less anxiety. Two possible reasons for the lessening of her anxiety were that she was more active in caring for her daughter at this time, and that a Lutheran pastor, a friend of the family, had begun to play an active role.

In the daily interviews with Miss R, the worker's chief goal was to help her retain a sense of individuality and identity. The worker listened to Miss R's day-to-day symptoms and to her expressions of hostility about the spread of the disease. However, her fear of death was never verbalized as such. During the interviews, the worker and Miss R shared their intellectual and cultural interests. For example, both had visited Scandinavia and were interested in those countries. Miss R lent the worker a book and some pamphlets about Sweden. Although the worker suggested that Miss R let her know when she wanted them returned, she never asked for them. At the end of each visit the worker would say that she would return the next day.

During her downhill course, Miss R clung physically and emotionally to her mother, like a small child. The mother was able to accept Miss R's regressive behavior which has been quite upsetting to the nursing staff. From her knowledge of Miss R's history and background, the worker interpreted to the nursing staff the patient's need for the kind of care the mother was giving her. Previously they had been blaming the mother for Miss R's regressive behavior which included soiling and incontinence. During this period when the worker visited Miss R and they continued their discussions, temporary improvement in Miss R's behavior was apparent to the worker and to other members of the professional staff. After two months of hospitalization, Miss R died.

Some months after Miss R's death, the worker made a final entry in the chart as follows:

> This was an extremely difficult case for me to handle. The patient's age, social situation and intellectual interests were close enough to mine to arouse great anxiety in me and identification with her. Each time I visited her I was very much aware of the danger of over-identification for I felt grief and pain at her suffering which I did not want to transmit to her. . . . I did want to do

my part in helping her retain a sense of individuality and identity. . . . I never did return the book and pamphlets about Sweden feeling they were, in a sense, a gift from the patient to me. But after her death I made a home visit to her mother and returned them then. We talked about Louise and her mother talked about Louise's death with resignation. Her grief was controlled and since she was a stoical, realistic woman who had come through this experience with great dignity, I respected her wish not to share her feelings. She showed me her house, her garden, and some of Louise's art work, speaking with pride of her daughter's creativeness. . . . My own feeling was one of humility.

Conclusion

In the clinical material presented above, there are many of the same elements of casework practice to be found in any area of service, but with one additional disturbing ingredient—the approaching death of the client or a close member of the client's family. Eleanor Cockerill has said: "The social casework method of helping individuals to deal with problems they meet as they move through life is primarily directed toward the objectives of implementing or strengthening the individual's own inherent resources and strength, and of helping him to attain satisfaction of his needs as a human being."[5] The social worker, along with other helping disciplines, helps the dying patient to retain his dignity and not to feel abandoned as he moves out of life. Although each individual situation is unique, there are some aspects of the helping process which teach the worker how to be helpful to each succeeding patient, just as is true in helping the patient or client who is being restored to health and usefulness.

If the caseworker can bring himself to look at his own fear of death and can develop a high degree of awareness of his own feeling, he can manage to sustain an intensive relationship with the patient and his family. If, during the periods when he is helping the dying patient and his family, he can maintain balance and perspective through working with patients who have hopeful prognoses, the experience may be less trying. It is important that the supervisor or administrator recognize that, during such periods of stress for the caseworker, even the advanced and experienced worker, who is accustomed to operating independently, may seek and need more frequent consultation. Concurrently, the worker may need help from the psychiatric consultant, either in relation to the patient or to his own feelings. In the hospital setting, assistance and support can also be supplied by other helping persons close to the patient and with whom the worker has congenial working relationships.

In conclusion, if it is possible for all the helping professions involved in the dying patient's care to look toward the future and to recognize that the skilful, compassionate help given to one patient or a family member may mean better help to many, they may feel some sense of satisfaction in that they are contributing to the prevention of emotional illness and to the furthering of sound mental health.

[5] Eleanor Cockerill, "The Social Worker Looks at the Cancer Patient," undated mimeographed material, page 6.

Part 2

Psychosocial Pathology

In recent years, the social work methods of individual and group treatment of persons with problems in psychosocial functioning have developed and have taken their place in the psychotherapies. Thus, the psychodynamics of clients have received considerable attention in the professional journals. Recent trends in the literature have shifted to a heavier emphasis on the social aspects of man's behavior. This does not imply, as at times is suggested, that the psychological dimension should in any way be minimized; or that the two dimensions of psyche and social should be considered mutually exclusive spheres examined by different persons with different professional identities. Neither does the present emphasis on the social aspects of the client presume that we have exhausted all there is to know about the treatment of the dynamic aspect of a man's human make-up. On the contrary, although a heavy emphasis on the practice-oriented literature written from a psychodynamic viewpoint was observed, the coverage has been far from exhaustive. Some areas have been given special attention; others have been overlooked.

Selecting a framework by which to order the articles was difficult. This was not surprising as the various categories of personality disfunctioning are not always mutually exclusive nor a part of one conceptual understanding of personality. For example, frequent reference is made in the literature to the treatment of the alcoholic. Such a person could also be classified as a character-disordered person or borderline personality; each of which is a separate category.

Terminology presented some difficulty in selecting and classifying articles in this section. For example, in searching for articles on the treatment of sociopathic conditions, Maxwell Jones' article was originally located under the heading of character disorder. This, of course, is the extreme end of the character disorder continuum but does require a special emphasis.

The question of character neurotics, character disorders, and borderline personalities create similar problems of classification depending on the viewpoint of the author.

The treatment of neurotic clients was the original basis from which Freudian theory was developed, and which in turn greatly affected the development of social work theory. Clients with various neurotic problems are frequently included in the caseloads of social workers. It was, therefore, surprising to discover that few articles in the social work periodical literature had directly addressed this type of client. Of special note is Mrs. Austin's article, a classic in the professional literature. This is of particular importance, because of our interest not only in the developmental dynamic problem itself but the problems in psychosocial functioning stemming from it; this for the client himself as well as significant persons in his life. Richard Sterba's paper presents an important review of the historical development of the "neurotic" concept and a reminder of the more diffuse form of neurotic behavior frequently observed in clients whom he designates as "character neurotics."

Character disorders and their treatment have been the focus of much recent attention. Although the articles chosen here approach the topic from a variety of viewpoints, there are unifying themes. Over and over again, the authors indicate we must reorient our treatment viewpoints from the traditional neurotic basis to a broader scope to suit the particular needs of these clients. Especially we must avoid working too quickly, if at all, towards a goal of insight or use uncovering techniques with this kind of client. The first article by Jackel examines the concept and the difficulties involved in making it clear and precise. Otto Pollak next develops some problems which he sees as pertinent to social workers, and which must be addressed in the treatment of these clients. In the last article the treatment of a particular kind of character-disordered client is developed.

From the numerous articles about the treatment of the alcoholic client two have been chosen. These emphasize the critical importance of the first contact with this type of client. Since community attitudes to them are negative and the problem in many instances so apparent, initial rejection is anticipated and frequently provoked. The authors stress that social workers must be aware of the family constellation of the client and as often as possible include one or more members in the treatment process. Thus, flexibility in our choice of treatment techniques and methods is essential. Group treatment is frequently elected for these persons and their families. Experience has indicated that with this type of client wide variations in group composition are possible.

Problems of drug addictions receive considerable professional and popular attention. The article selected presents a less pessimistic view of the effects of therapy than is commonly observed. Frazier stresses the necessity of institutionalization as a part of treatment in conjunction with psychotherapy in which there is an educative and control-building component.

Included in this section are articles on dependency, sociopathy, sexual deviation, and borderline states—all important diagnostic variables frequently encountered in social work clinical practice. None of these has been exhaustively considered and all require much more detailed attention.

A study of the literature for articles suitable for this section revealed divergent opinions concerning the extent to which social work treatment deals directly with sexual problems or sexual deviations. It is obvious that some aspects of clients' sexual lives are of direct concern to the social worker. It is equally certain that treatment geared to the uncovering and resolution of the unconscious origins of some sexual problems is not usually considered within the profession's general competence. Evidently all treatment of persons with sexual problems should not properly be aimed at such resolution; significant gains can be made from the viewpoint of improved control, changed attitudes, and enhanced growth. There are, as well, the beneficial effects on functioning resulting from the reduction of anxiety, fear, and guilt accompanying such problems. The first two articles included suggest that many social workers are not comfortable with sexual material; when present this discomfort proves detrimental to the treatment of the client. This idea is supported by the fact that few articles were located which directly dealt with sexual problems of any kind. Yet, current practice experience indicates that clients frequently bring such problems to agencies. The latter article discusses the use of group treatment for specific sexual problems; it suggests that this approach has important possibilities for other problems in this area. These therapeutic ideas are presented as tentative possibilities and not definitive prescriptions. The authors emphasize the need for further experimentation.

Depression, frequently misunderstood and overlooked in our practice, has rarely been specifically addressed in the literature. The article by Hank Walzer is an important contribution.

The final group of articles in this section deals with the treatment and management of psychotic behavior. Apart from the treatment of the schizophrenic client, which will be discussed, there is a remarkable absence of consideration of other forms of psychotic behavior. For example, the manic-depressive client and the paranoid client are rarely mentioned. Although the true paranoid is not frequently met, persons with paranoid tendencies and mild forms of paranoid schizophrenia are frequently found in the clientele of agencies. There appears to be as much oral tradition of how not to deal with such persons as there is absence of articles and formal discussion of their management. Some references to dealing with paranoid ideas are included in the articles on schizophrenia, but these are only incidental to the main theme. I suggest there is no group of clients which arouses more discomfort and uncertainty than these persons. Many of them continue to function at a level which keeps them out of institutions; but their constant difficulties in social adjustment still bring them and their families to agencies. Thus, a most important contribution could be made by bringing together the practice experience of our colleagues in dealing with such individuals.

As indicated there has been a considerable amount written about the treatment of schizophrenics. I consider this an interesting finding, as a large segment of practicing social workers would consider this group of clients beyond their competence. Esther Marcus suggests in the first article that such clients make up a "large proportion of caseloads in community agencies and clinics." This paper then reviews and examines the current thinking on this great problem, pointing out the vast dimensions of the concept. The four articles dealing with direct treatment of the schizophrenic all emphasize the theme of reality-oriented relationship therapy. Each discusses this from a slightly different viewpoint. The final article addresses the question of schizophrenia from the viewpoint of its impact on the family of the patient. Again this article serves as a reminder for us to see our therapeutic responsibility more broadly than the individual client.

Conclusion

To aid clients effectively to achieve improved psychosocial functioning, it is essential to address their psychodynamic functioning. Although the professional literature indicates that a high degree of attention has been focussed on this area, it is clear that coverage has been far from thorough; it thus requires constant updating and examination for gaps and omissions.

Dynamics and Treatment of the Client with Anxiety Hysteria

Lucille N. Austin

The first attempts to utilize psychoanalytic psychology in casework were associated with the neurotic client and his punishing superego. Guilt-relieving techniques, together with permissive and nonjudgmental attitudes on the part of the caseworker, came to be accepted casework procedures. Over the years, there has been a tendency to use these procedures in an all-inclusive way, rather than selectively. It is now clear that treatment techniques must be based on a clear understanding of the relationships between the various parts of the personality structure and of the underlying unconscious conflict, and that these dynamics differ in different clinical entities. In the various neuroses, as well as in psychoses and the character disorders, there are wide variations in ego strength, the severity of the superego, defenses, symptoms, and characteristic modes of behavior.

A re-examination at this time of treatment formulations about casework with the neurotic client, and particularly those with anxiety hysteria, may be useful. Although there are indications that the caseloads of social agencies and clinics are made up increasingly of clients with character disorders and "borderline" problems, it seems likely that a large number of clients are still in the neurotic category. In many instances, these cases are incorrectly diagnosed as character disorders. I believe, too, that anxiety hysteria is sometimes confused with compulsive neurosis, to the disadvantage of persons in the former category.

In this paper, I shall highlight the clinical features of anxiety hysteria and then discuss   *1]* the nature of the problems that clients in this category present in initial contacts;   *2]* the typical features of the life history as a diagnostic aid; and   *3]* some treatment considerations.

Reprinted from *Ego Psychology and Dynamic Casework*, edited by Howard J. Parad and published by the Family Service Association of America, New York, 1958. (Originally published in *Smith College Studies in Social Work*, XXVII (June, 1957), pp. 167–187). Permission granted by the author and the Association.

The Clinical Picture and Dynamics of Anxiety Hysteria

In Freudian terms, the central conflict of all the neuroses is the oedipal conflict.[1] Capacity to love is established but remains partial under the influence of the oedipal ties to the parents and the incomplete resolution of the problem of bisexual identification; the neurotic does not accept masculinity or feminity. His ego is relatively well organized and developed, but it is weakened by the conflict between the demands of the id and the prohibitions of the superego.

Whereas the compulsive neurotic reacts to the oedipal disappointment by regression to the anal level of operation and manifests problems of anger, the anxiety hysteric reacts by regression to the phallic period, that is, the conflict remains focused in the psychosexual sphere. In the phallic stage of development, heterosexual desires are strong but they are blocked by castration anxiety, fear of punishment, and oedipal guilt. Furthermore, the genital organ of the heterosexual love object is refused full recognition, as if recognition of the difference would be an admission of inferiority. The hysteric handles these conflicts by maintaining bisexual identifications, repression of sexual strivings, and the development of symptoms that are, in themselves, abnormal sexual expressions. Sexual feelings are also displaced on nonsexual relationships and situations, so that a kind of pseudo-sexuality pervades all activities and contacts.

The problems of aggression in the hysteric are predominantly those of erotic aggression, rather than the hostile aggression of the pre-oedipal stage. In the child the aggressive and sexual feelings are intertwined when he perceives his parents as a couple; his resulting anger is in response to the oedipal situation and not to frustration because of unmet dependency needs. Some of the aggressive feelings are conscious or preconscious but they may be somatized or turned against the self.

The characteristic defenses in anxiety hysteria are repression, displacement, and projection. The characteristic symptoms are pervasive anxiety; anxiety as a neurotic symptom attached to a special situation that represents the neurotic conflict; conversion symptoms; fear of abandonment, death, and mutilation; phobias; and sexual inhibitions ranging from shyness with the opposite sex to impotence and frigidity.

Hysterical "acting out" is a marked feature. It is a turning from reality to fantasy and is an attempt to induce others to indulge in daydreaming in order to obtain some relief from anxiety and guilt or to evoke punishment. It is sometimes confused with the "acting out" of the character disorders; in anxiety hysterics, the behavior is neurotically determined by the oedipal wishes.

[1] Otto Fenichel, M.D., *The Psychoanalytic Theory of the Neuroses*, W. W. Norton & Co., New York, 1945, Ch. XI; Helene Deutsch, M.D., *Psychoanalysis of the Neuroses*, Hogarth Press, London, 1932, Parts I and II; Sigmund Freud, *Collected Papers*, Vols. I and II, Anglobooks, New York, 1952, *The Problem of Anxiety*, W. W. Norton & Co., New York, 1936.

In character structure the anxiety hysterics are in many respects most nearly "normal." They show vivid dramatic qualities associated with the excitement and exhibitionistic features of the neurosis. They have lovable qualities, based partly on their fear of losing love which makes them eager to please others. They are more capable of love than the ambivalent compulsive, who provokes rejection as a justification for his own hatreds. Hysterics have considerable charm, imagination, feeling, and sensitivity. They may indulge in chaotic behavior but it has a romantic and colorful flavor. The extensive fantasy life, which they develop as a refuge and as a substitute for unpleasant reality, gives color to their conversations and actions. Their child-like qualities, such as seeking protection, are often acceptable and appealing, particularly in women. Their many real strengths and abilities, combined with a defensive capacity to simulate more adequacy than they feel, enables them, more often than not, to conceal their illness.[2]

The degree of character disturbance ranges from the relatively outgoing person to seriously repressed, restricted, disorganized, helpless, and anxiety-ridden individuals whose neurosis is not held in bounds. In some cases, pregenital factors are in the foreground; in others, compulsive features are mixed with hysterical features, making for a more complicated illness and character structure.

Etiologically, anxiety hysteria may be based in part on a constitutional predisposition but is chiefly rooted in sexually stimulating events—in infancy and in the period between three and seven years—which make for sexual precociousness. Childhood sexual seductions, which are reported in the life history as conditioning factors, are kept secret by the hysterical child because of guilt about his complicity and his wish for sexual excitement and pleasure.[3] His attitude is different from that of other children who speak more freely of sexual matters because they were not responsive to seduction. Karl Abraham says, "The tendency to experience sexual traumas repeatedly is a peculiarity which we can often observe in adult hysterics. . . . Hysterics are those interesting people to whom something is always happening. Female hysterics in particular are constantly meeting with adventures. They are molested in the public street, outrageous sexual assaults are made on them, and so forth. It is part of their nature that they must expose themselves to external traumatic influences. . . . People of this kind have a similar tendency in childhood."[4]

In all neurosis there is suffering; the suffering, combined with the

---

[2] Karl Abraham, *Selected Papers on Psychoanalysis*, Hogarth Press, London, 1949, Ch. XXV.

[3] Freud's original formulation concerning sexual trauma and childhood sexual seduction (*Collected Papers*, "The Etiology of Hysteria," Vol. 1, p. 183) was later altered (*Collected Papers*, "Sexuality in the Neuroses, " Vol. 1, pp. 276–277) to take cognizance of "the deceptive memories of hysterics concerning their childhood" and the fact that often a fantasy of seduction was a defense against the memory of sexual activities practiced by the child himself, for example, masturbation.

[4] *Op. cit.*, p. 57.

transference capacity of the hysteric, provides the leverage for both case-work and analytic treatment. It is possible to work with the ego if the ego feels pain and the person senses the irrationality of his feelings, symptoms, and behavior.

The case records of these clients show certain clinical features and the influence of the neurosis on their social functioning. I shall now present some material on the nature of the expressed problem and conflict in the initial contact, and the typical features of the life history.

The Nature of the Expressed Problem and Conflict

In the initial contact, these clients show marked anxiety, ranging from an acute anxiety state to diffuse and pervasive anxiety feelings. The anxiety is accompanied by feelings of inadequacy and inferiority, of not being loved and appreciated. In general, the anxiety hysteric, at the point of the intake interview, gives an appearance of being sicker than he is, while the intact paranoid schizophrenic or the person with a character disorder may appear healthier than he is.

The presenting problems may take the form of difficulties in family relationships, in the job situation, or in personal adjustments. They have a special meaning, however, for the anxiety hysteric. The external event which touches off the anxiety can be seen to be overdetermined by the neurosis. To the anxiety hysteric, certain problems with a child, a marital partner, an employer, or the circumstances of a physical illness, loss of work, and so on, signify a psychosexual danger. He anticipates the loss of love and the veri-fication of his unfitness and inadequacy as a whole man or woman, as well as punishment for trying to exercise sexual rights and privileges. The com-pulsive neurotic, in contrast, tends to interpret similar events as attacks or as attempts to weaken his controls and to expose his anger and retaliative wishes. Because the hysteric has not regressed to the same level, his psycho-sexual conflicts are partially conscious or, when repressed, are thinly dis-guised. In the treatment of these cases, the caseworker must endeavor to bring the conscious sexual conflicts into focus, since the client will continue to suppress, project, and displace them until he is given permission to talk openly about them.

The hysteric frequently presents his marital problem in terms of differ-ences and incompatibilities in all areas other than the sexual. He usually states that the other partner is the one at fault.

In a typical case, a wife reported that she had decided to separate from her husband because they could not agree on ways of raising their children and quarreled over money. She said she had lost interest in sex because her husband had hit her several years before. Only later could she talk about her sexual problem and the fact that she had grown up without a father in the home. She had heard only negative talk about men from her mother and she did not know how to relate to them. She said she had not learned to give herself in the sexual relationship and achieved an orgasm only occasionally.

Many times these clients will make a beginning contact and then become frightened. They minimize the problem they came with or make a "flight into health" as a resistance to going on with treatment.

> In one case, after a few interviews the woman said that "it is best to forget it all" and that she was doing all right and did not want to continue. With encouragement from the caseworker, she was able to tell about an early sex experience in which "a man took advantage of her when she was intoxicated." Then she was able to tell that she was the aggressor in current sexual relationships with her husband, and that he was often impotent, which was disturbing to both of them. Later she arranged for him to come to the clinic for help.

Sometimes the conflict is expressed in terms of not being able to choose between a home and a career.

> One woman at the beginning of contact was in an acute anxiety state. She said she had a wonderful home, husband, and baby but that she "felt cooped up and as though there were no escape." She had become pregnant immediately after marriage and had had to give up an art career. In later interviews, she described her childhood and told about her father's violent temper. Her mother had been an unhappy woman who felt tainted by sex and she had conveyed these ideas to her daughter who had always been afraid and inhibited sexually. Going to work, obviously, was safer than being a wife.

Some women express their problems initially in terms of feeling pulled between husband and children or between the husband and mother; others have conflict about managing money and difficulties in homemaking.

A man's problem may be expressed in the work situation. The conflict is often centered on employers who, he thinks, belittle him; or he may have anxiety about not doing his job well or feelings of dissatisfaction because he has not found himself vocationally. This group of cases, because of the clear displacement of the oedipal rivalry with the father onto the employer and the sexualization of the work situation, might well be classified as "work difficulty—oedipal type."

In child guidance cases, where the mother's predominant concern is about the child's sexual interests—whether he is four years old or adolescent —the problem is unmistakably a displacement. If the child is young, the mother is fearful of injury to him and is overanxious about his illness. If he is an adolescent, she fears he will get into sexual difficulties and therefore frowns on heterosexual friendships. These mothers often take pride in being frank about giving sexual information to their children but reveal that they are either inhibited in answering questions or seductive in their overemphasis on sex and in their discussion of inappropriate sexual material. The compulsive mother, on the other hand, usually focuses the problem on her fear of losing control over the child and her fear of his aggression and destructiveness.

In the medical social work setting, hysterical clients tend to be difficult and fractious. They shop from clinic to clinic when the doctors find nothing wrong organically, or when they cannot accept a diagnosis and relax under competent medical care. Illness produces undue anxiety because it is associated with castration fears. Sexual fantasies are clearly evident in their exaggerated fears of body injury. Illness is also viewed as punishment for sexual pleasure.

In the initial interviews, the client is not likely to mention symptoms other than his anxiety. He does not think of phobias, conversions, or obsessive thoughts as symptoms but as idiosyncracies. He may not mention situations he completely avoids, but in talking about less dangerous situations he may reveal the presence of organized symptoms. Phobias particularly are obscured by the avoidance measures which he uses to keep them quiescent. Incidentally, I think the caseworker's failure to recognize symptoms and to inquire about their presence frequently results in inadequate data for use in psychiatric consultations. The absence of data may be a contributing factor to the idea that symptom neuroses are not frequently found in agency caseloads.

The client in early contacts often succeeds in leading the caseworker away from the path of building a sound treatment relationship into a morass of transference gratifications. His neurotic need for love and his phobic need for protection form the basis for an initial positive transference. The hysteric often shows marked improvement even after the first interview. His appearance improves and he is vocal in his gratitude for the help he has received. He does this to create a bond between himself and the caseworker as well as to ward off further work on his problem. He usually has extensive fantasy about the worker. Through permissible flattery and conventional interest, he tries to satisfy his curiosity about the worker as a person. As he weaves his fantasies, he is able to blot out any facts that he wishes to ignore. A transference goal—to be loved for himself—supersedes the goal of securing help with his family relationships and other problems of adult adjustment.

The narcissism and the defense of wish-fulfilling daydreams lead the hysteric to an avoidance of hearing anything he might construe as negative criticism; the compulsive, in contrast, provokes criticism and rejection. The hysteric has a tendency to volunteer only a few factual details and has difficulty in giving a consistent, coherent account of what is actually going on at home or at work. He skips from topic to topic. He talks in such a vivid, interesting way that the caseworker may fail to note that he is giving an exaggerated dramatic version of what happened. He demonstrates that he is a talented person, worthy of love and recognition. He produces feelings, not facts. This way of communicating differs from that of the compulsive neurotic. The latter chooses words carefully. He underplays rather than overstates, and gives detailed facts without apparent feeling because the feeling has been isolated.

In many respects, at the points of early contact as well as later, the hysteric seems to be repeating much of his early behavior with his parents. In childhood he had to pretend innocence in order to keep the parent from knowing how much he knew about sexual matters and how intense was his sexual life. An element of scorn for adult stupidity is also reflected as a transference response, especially when he senses naivete and repression in the caseworker.

The client tends to hide his negative transference reactions because he cannot take the chance of losing a source of gratification and protection. When he does venture a negative response, it is often in the form of a childish attempt to let the caseworker know he is displeased. These responses take the form of play in order to disguise the extent and reality of the negative feelings.

As a last comment about problems in the initial contact, I should like to note that it is not always easy to recognize panic anxiety or acute anxiety states. Certain common errors are made in diagnosis. The caseworker may think the client who cries and expresses despair is deeply depressed. The degree of depressed affect, however, cannot be measured by the amount of anxiety expressed. The hysteric's tendency to exaggerate—to believe that all is lost and the worst has happened—must be taken into account; often self-pity, rather than depression, may be the prevailing affect. The phobic client who is seeking protection may give the impression of being a deeply dependent person. Immobilized by his anxiety, he seems uncertain, childlike, and helpless, and, at first, gives no evidence of his real ego strength. In some instances, the caseworker may suspect that the hysteric is psychotic; he may talk wildly and excitedly, show signs of disorganization, and express fears of insanity. A premature referral of such cases to psychiatrists will only add to their fears.

In the early interviews with hysterics, the caseworker should remain calm and supportive, in order to test out the client's ability to regain his ego strengths and to get treatment started with a correct diagnostic appraisal.

The Typical Features of the Life History

The life history is an invaluable tool in the formulation of both the clinical and the psychosocial diagnosis of persons suffering with anxiety hysteria. I therefore will present some typical features of their histories.

Childhood

The life history of these clients usually reveals the presence of the neurosis in childhood. They were fearful, anxious children. They were afraid to go to school, afraid to be away from mother, afraid of the dark, and afraid of new experiences. The women frequently speak of themselves as "good little girls, too afraid to be anything else." They were frequently depressed and moody and took things hard. Toys and pets were overinvested with libidinal significance. The men were often enuretic into latency. They were onlookers rather than participants in sports and frail in physical build, at least in their own comparison to their fathers. They were mothers' boys, not just in the passive, effeminate sense, but "mother's little man" with good manners and consideration for the mother's friends.

Most of these clients remember some of their sexual curiosity, fear, and preoccupation. They express anger because their parents did not give them sexual information. Most of them remember being discovered masturbating and being caught in sexual experimentations with siblings or playmates. These memories are still sources of guilt in adult life because of the parents' excitement, threats of punishment, and predictions of dire consequences. They were sometimes taken to a doctor for examination and were often the object of family concern. The client's memory of such events sometimes goes back only as far as his adolescence, but it seems likely this is a screen memory covering earlier sexual traumas and experiences. These memories, because they are fraught with guilt, are usually brought up only when treatment has advanced and the relationship to the worker is well established.

> One man, who later became mentally ill, had an overdeveloped sense of responsibility for his young sister; he was obsessed with a feeling of responsibility for not having told his family about a man who molested his sister when she was 11 and he an adolescent. He had come downstairs at dusk and saw a man attempting to rape his sister. The man ran and he chased him. He knew him but he did not report the episode to his parents or to the police. Sex was a tabooed subject in his family.

The women often report being molested by men in the neighborhood or by relatives.

> A woman client reported that she remembered being taken to a doctor at the age of 6 or 7. The doctor gave her an internal examination and she felt a sharp pain in the genital region; she had always believed that he pierced her hymen. He had become hostile because her neck was dirty. Her mother had come in at this point and, instead of siding with her, had sided with the doctor. She had always wanted to express her anger at her mother for not protecting her. She thought her husband had always suspected that she had had sex experience previous to marriage. She was not able to tell her mother that she was pregnant with her first child until after three months. She showed shame and anguish in telling these incidents.

Adolescence

The life histories of both men and women in this group show a difficult adolescence. Menstruation for women and pubescence for men were fearful experiences.

> One woman, who began menstruation at 14, had no difficulty at first; she said it proved her womanhood and she used it to get out of housework. Then she began to have little fainting spells, but was not clear about the details. In adulthood she still felt depressed and irritable during menstruation.
>
> One man reported that he was completely unprepared for changes that took place in his body when he approached puberty. He said that he had grown up in complete ignorance about sex. When nocturnal emission occurred for the first time, he did not know what it was. He had earlier been enuretic and thought the emission was a form of the same thing. As it continued he became worried about his health and at last mentioned it to his father who merely shrugged and said, "Well, now you're a man." A kindly family doctor later explained the matter to him.

In adolescence both sexes were shy, had marked feelings of inferiority, and had problems in dating. The girls had crushes on teachers and older women which were more intense than is usual for girls of their age. They had more girl friends than boy friends, and in several cases the girl dated only the man whom she subsequently married; frequently he was an older man. The husbands are described as gentle and understanding, "not sexual like a lot of men." The woman usually seemed grateful to the man for marrying her, feeling that it was unlikely that anyone could have loved her.

The men also had been slow in dating and showed a tendency to separate sexual and tender feelings in their discussions of premarital sexual relationships. They often married women who were sexually inhibited. Neither the men nor the women were promiscuous before marriage and generally did not have extramarital relationships. Rather they would form strong nonsexual attachments which aroused guilt because of their oedipal nature.

These clients have many fears about the effects of adolescent and childhood masturbation, including the fear of insanity which often continues into adult life. The women clients usually do not talk easily about masturbation, but they give evidence of their guilt.

> One woman, early in contact, mentioned her fear of becoming psychotic. She had marked feelings of inadequacy and had always felt second to her brother, who had graduated from college. When she finished high school, she felt unable to decide anything for herself and had been unable to make her wishes about employment or possible further education known to her parents; she felt hurt because of their lack of interest. Through an aunt she obtained a job as an attendant in a state mental hospital, remaining there for a year and a half. She frequently felt panicky and spent many sleepless nights wondering whether she would become psychotic. She pictured herself as socially awkward and dumb.

Relationship to Family Members in Childhood

From early childhood the relationship of the hysteric to the parent of the same sex is characterized by hostile competition, with an accompanying overdevotion to the parent of the opposite sex. Both sets of feelings are guarded through defenses of rationalization and projection. The woman frequently says, "No one liked my mother," and "Everyone loved my father." Overdevotion to the parent of the same sex is a defense against the underlying hostility. The oedipal feelings toward both parents are usually so apparent that caseworkers have difficulty in believing that the clients themselves are not conscious of them.

It is not uncommon for a woman to recall incidents of being embarrassed in adolescence because her father was mistaken for a boy friend. In some women, the negative feeling toward the father may be high, particularly if he had deserted the mother and the daughter; if he remarried, the daughter feels it as a double insult. In one case, the woman said that her father had beaten her with a strap and connected her fear of being a woman with her father's treatment of her. Yet she vaguely sensed that she loved him.

In general, the complaints of the hysteric against his parents are in terms of their unwillingness for him to get ahead, rather than in terms of neglect, which is the chief complaint of borderline and psychotic clients. The hysterics believe that the parents stood in their way. The women feel that their mothers did not train them in housework, did not prepare them for marriage, and did not give sex information. Basically they feel that the mothers did not want them to marry or to have babies.

In many cases, these clients are still in touch with their parents; after marriage many live near them and often live with them for a period. They usually are psychologically overinvolved with them; they are concerned about the affairs of family members and dependent on them for advice in making decisions. The women clients often resent the closeness to their mothers and what seems like their interference, but are unable to tell them so. They sometimes neglect their own families to help their parents.

Sibling relationships are also marked by extreme rivalry, since a particular brother or sister often plays a role in the oedipal conflict. The hostility toward the sibling may carry over to their relationships with their own children, particularly if one child becomes identified with the hated sibling. In the case of women, we find the birth of a brother often had increased penis envy and made feminine adjustment more difficult. Both men and women show strong reactions to having had a crippled or retarded sibling, since the actual presence of handicap heightened their castration fears.

Health Histories

In all age periods of the hysteric, health problems are prevalent. These clients have a tendency toward illness and they overemphasize ordinary illnesses when they occur; after illness, they usually require a long convalescence. Childbirth is fraught with changes for the women and surgery is frightening for both men and women. They have fear of cancer, tuberculosis, and various infections. They worry about nourishment and their weight; obesity is a frequent problem. Some are afraid to go to doctors and others go at the first sign of any sickness.

School Histories

Learning difficulties are frequent in latency and adolescence as a result of sibling rivalry and of preoccupation with daydreams. Also, learning itself is sexualized since it is connected with childhood sexual curiosity.

Work Histories

The choice of a career is complicated by rivalries with parents and fear of competition. Work that involves exhibitionistic qualities, or that calls attention to the person, is often given up in favor of a more anonymous role; if it is not given up, it is carried with anxiety. Work activities are sexualized for both men and women, with resulting anxiety. When the person does succeed in school or work, he feels that something is wrong. He believes that he does not merit the success, or that he got it by cheating, or that his superiors did not evaluate him correctly. The women are torn between homemaking and having a career, often alternating between them and unable to combine them comfortably.

In the women, the motivation to work is in part a masculine identification, but in part a defense against the fear of the feminine role. Their frequent use of their mothers to care for their children while they work is again related to the oedipal conflict; they feel they must turn the children over to their mothers. At work the women are competitive with men but not in as revengeful a way as the compulsive women.

Friendships

The woman hysteric often maintains a friendship with an older woman, or with a series of them in turn. Such friendship is motivated by an over-compensated hostility to the mother. Others find women friends dull and prefer the company of men; with them they may be provocative and flirtatious or they may establish platonic friendships. The men maintain relationships with other men through clubs or informal groups which have in them a strong, unconscious sexual element. The marital partner in both instances senses a threat to the marriage and is likely to quarrel about the other's friends.

In summary, the life histories of persons with anxiety hysteria have similarities to histories of persons with other disturbances. On the whole, however, persons in this group have a stronger tendency to grow and develop than many other clients. They make achievements in spite of problems, largely because there is less ego impairment. Oedipal problems, rather than pre-oedipal problems, are predominant in childhood, in adolesence, and in adult life. Fear of sex and preoccupation with sexual matters and the separation of sexual and tender feelings are their chief problems.

Treatment Considerations and Techniques

The treatment of this group of clients, in general, should be designed to help them to develop some self-awareness as a means of strengthening the ego. Not all, of course, have the ego strength, the motivation, or the supporting favorable conditions to make such treatment possible; these persons, however, can benefit markedly from supportive treatment because of their transference capacity. The choice of treatment should be determined by the evolution of the content and the extent of the neurotic conflict and of the transference and countertransference factors.

I should like to discuss first the countertransference problems that enter into the treatment of these clients.

Caseworkers often have difficulty in engaging clients in a discussion of sexual problems. In a way, caseworkers have acted as if all of sex is unconscious. Since caseworkers do not work with the unconscious, they have tended to rule out sexual matters. Hostility seems to be an easier topic for them to discuss, perhaps because the values of helping clients express anger have been more adequately formulated. The caseworker is able to elicit anger with a feeling of safety and with assurance about the correctness of his technique. Also, the extensive experience in working with the compulsive neurotic has added to the sense of safety; the compulsive's many defenses against complying with the caseworker's suggestion that he vent his anger serve as a protection. The caseworker in these cases may "chip away" at the hostility, but it comes forward so slowly that nothing very frightening happens.

In any event, the hysterical client, with his emotionality and sexuality, appears to frighten the caseworker. The current generation of caseworkers, as well as clients, have been brought up by parents who retained the repressed attitudes of the puritanical previous generation, even though many give lip service to new sexual freedoms. Thus client and worker alike are likely to be wary of talking about sex. In working with the hysteric, whose central neurotic concern is sexuality, the worker should focus on sexual matters relatively early in treatment. If this is not done, the client is likely to terminate contact, using whatever help has been given to relieve his guilt and raise his morale. Such help may be useful but it does not have the value of sustained treatment of the core problem.

When we read case records, we see that the hysteric is seldom able to take the initiative in talking about sex. He hints at it or reveals it through projection or displacement. For example, a client talking about his work frustrations may also be expressing feelings about his sexual inadequacy. The caseworker, therefore, must feel free to ask about possible sexual problems, thereby giving the client permission to talk about them. In order to do this, the caseworker must overcome any feeling he may have that sex is a fearsome topic or that talking about sex is a form of seduction. If the caseworker fails to give the client an opportunity to explore his disturbing sexual problems, he will represent the disapproving or repressive parent who made the child feel guilty, or sent him elsewhere for help, or forced him to hide his sexual concerns.

Handling the anger of the oedipal conflict is doubtless more frightening to the caseworker than handling the hostile aggression related to the pre-oedipal period. Since there is considerable justification for the anger of the client who was deprived in his earliest years, the caseworker can agree with his feelings and offer sympathy. The "unjustified" anger of the neurotic presents more complex problems, for both client and caseworker. The caseworker's own anger, fear, and guilt associated with the oedipal situation may block his ability to help clients with their feelings. He must be able to tolerate his own anxiety and guilt if he is to help them reduce the power of their punishing superego.

In the treatment of the hysteric, the transference relationship is of particular significance. Freud identified the hysterical neuroses as transference neuroses and therefore amenable to standard psychoanalytic procedures. In casework treatment, the positive transference response of the hysteric places the caseworker in a position of primary influence. Certain standard casework techniques, therefore, may have a deeper influence with this group of clients than with others. I shall discuss briefly four techniques: *1]* manipulation,   *2]* emotional release,   *3]* clarification, and   *4]* selected interpretations.

1. Manipulation

By manipulation, I refer to the technique delineated by Dr. Grete Bibring.[5] The main elements are the construction of a corrective relationship and intervention in the client's environment.

The anxious or phobic client needs a calm and consistent relationship because his own anxiety and his tendency to misconstrue or distort relationships keep him stirred up. He needs to be sure he is appreciated and respected, since he feels inferior and unworthy of love. He wants love so badly that frequently in his life he has paid too high a price for it; he often sacrifices his own individuality and his reality wishes. He will tend to repeat this pattern in his relationship with the caseworker. He needs a relationship in which sacrifice is not demanded of him; instead, he needs attention and an opportunity to voice his hopes and aspirations as well as his despairs. The caseworker should construct a relationship that will contain the elements both of a corrective parent and of a kindly person who operates on an objective reality level. A link with the ego, with the person's strivings to improve his functioning, should be established early. The client's problems in functioning must be defined and the goal of working on them must be established and kept in the foreground in order to give a boundary to the treatment and to help in controlling the transference.

The sex of the worker may be an important consideration in casework with these clients, but this question needs further study. In some cases, there has seemed to be a readier response when the female client has been assigned to a male worker.

> In one case, after an initial embarrassed beginning, a woman client clearly responded positively to a nonseductive man worker, who showed respect for her as a wife and mother and who encouraged her to improve her relationships with her husband and son. She believed that her father had belittled her and as a result she had felt unattractive and unable to compete as a woman.

In another case, it is probable that improvement was accelerated when a man client was assigned a fatherly caseworker.

> The client's current work difficulty was tied up with his rivalry with his father. He had repressed his negative feelings about his mother, who died when he was 17, and spoke of her in idealized terms. The worker played the role of an encouraging father who wanted the client to succeed; he made active job suggestions that were in line with the client's capacities. Later he also had contact with the wife so that she could continue to give her husband the support she had given him during the courtship and early days of the marriage. A woman worker might have reactivated a complicated attachment to the mother.

[5] Grete L. Bibring, M.D., "Psychiatric Principles in Casework," *Journal of Social Casework*, Vol. XXX, No. 6 (1949), pp. 230–235.

If a woman worker works with the woman client, careful steps must be taken to prevent the client from regressing into an overdependent attachment. Such an attachment can best be avoided by dealing with her as a grown-up woman and a mother. She should be supported in her maternal role and be helped to work out conflicts that interfere with her assumption of it. Problems of child rearing can be profitably discussed with the expressed aim of helping her be a better mother. If the problem is a marital one, the caseworker should make it clear that the aim is to help her get more out of her marriage. If both partners are involved in a treatment relationship, separate workers may be desirable to avoid recreating the oedipal triangle.

The caseworker's intervention in the management of family life can serve a useful function in both marital and child guidance cases.

> In one case where the mother was reacting to her son's growing independence and attempts to free himself from her seductive love, the worker encouraged the father to become more active in doing things with the boy. The father's participation in the boy's life not only supported his attempts to develop normally, but it also brought relief to the mother by reducing the temptation to cling to her son.

Giving advice about such matters as moving away from irritating parents, changing jobs, and the use of social resources can be psychologically helpful. Changes in their reality situation can give clients protection from phobic stimuli and can reduce the opportunity for neurotic gratifications. When this kind of advice is offered in a reasonable way, these clients do not react with the same degree of negativism that compulsive neurotics do. Often they feel relieved when the caseworker gives advice that is at least partially in line with what they want; usually they can carry out the advice with the sanction and support of the worker. The worker must, of course, guard against becoming an omnipotent figure; the best safeguard is to base his activity on the conflicts and discomforts described by the client.

2. Emotional Release

The skilful use of guilt-relieving techniques usually bring about a cessation of acute anxiety in these clients. Symptoms subside or become less disturbing. Since the neurotic has introjected the ambivalently held love object, the conflict continues in the superego. The conflict can be modified through identification in the course of a meaningful relationship with a parental surrogate. The new introjection can reinforce the positive side of the ambivalence and effectively overpower the negative. A continuing warm relationship gives added strength to the positive identification.

In some cases, the power of the superego may be further reduced by the development of new ego defense mechanisms. Interpretations can be made that result in depersonalization of anger and in new displacements and rationalizations. The client can also gain substantial relief from anxiety if he is permitted to discuss his current sexual inhibitions and fears, as well as his memories of adolescent sexual conflicts that are conscious or near conscious. Being given permission to talk about these problems, in itself, reduces their danger. Guilt can also be reduced if the caseworker universalizes the problem; many of these clients have never discussed sexual matters with their own age group, either as children or adults. The superego of the hysteric is harsh, but it is not as implacable as the superego of the compulsive neurotic.

3. Clarification

Clarification techniques, ranging from simple educational discussions to the more elaborate process of separating reality and fantasy, should be utilized. Specifically, these clients need to be helped to make a new appraisal of their reality situations, which are usually relatively good, and to find new opportunities for enjoyment. Even when reality difficulties are present, they are usually not as serious as the hysteric fears them to be. The caseworker must recognize that these clients have been trying to escape internal danger by attaching the danger to reality situations. In many instances, the caseworker is drawn into handling the reality problems only to find that the client produces a new set. Sometimes, of course, help can be given only with each adverse reality problem as it appears. However, in situations where the ego is relatively strong and the neurosis not too pervasive, the client can develop some degree of awareness as he is helped to see his repetitive behavior patterns and to make connections between childhood feelings and current adaptations.

4. Selected Interpretations

Certain interpretations of the meaning of the client's behavior can be made in the later stages of treatment. These interpretations should be of the kind that will help the client realize the undue influence of his parental ties and his childhood feelings on his current functioning. The connection between his typical ways of reacting to situations and his need to work against his own best interests can be pointed out. Further discussion of his sexual problems and the way they interfere with his personal relationships may also be helpful. Some modification of sexual conflicts often takes place under the influence of the transference. Also, hysterical clients can be helped to gain useful insights through discussion of conscious and preconscious feelings and experiences; the deeper oedipal material, of course, is not touched. By working with the social components of the instinctual conflicts, the caseworker can help the client achieve considerable emotional relief. For example, a man's fear of sexual intercourse is frequently lessened after he has discussed his fear of being dominated by his wife. A discussion of the client's feeling of personal and social inadequacy can carry deeper meanings, thereby relieving the underlying feeling of sexual inadequacy.

> In the case of the mother and son mentioned previously, the mother became angry because the boy's caseworker gave him a present. She expressed her anger to her caseworker after the latter had talked with the father and advised him to associate himself more actively with his son. The worker raised the question of jealousy and the mother, in this interview, admitted her jealous

feelings and then talked freely about her close relationship with the boy during his first four years while her husband was in service. She was able to see that she had subtly kept him from developing a good relationship with his father during the subsequent years. She brought out feelings of anger against her husband for leaving her alone during these years, although realistically she knew he had been drafted and had no choice. She also reported that she never had a satisfactory sexual relationship with her husband. The caseworker suggested that she might be withholding in the sexual relationship to punish her husband for leaving her and that she accused him of being unloving, whereas this might be her problem. The woman in subsequent interviews was able to make connections between her anger at her husband and her childhood feelings of being insufficiently loved by her father, who preferred her brother. Her relationship with her husband improved during contact and she gained considerable self-confidence.

In another situation, a married woman, who had been in treatment for some time, started an interview by saying that she should never have married. Her mother had told her that men cannot be trusted. Her mother, even now, would like to take care of her and her children, and put Mr. R, her husband, out of the house. She made these statements in a half joking way. When the caseworker asked whether the mother knew that things had been going a little better, Mrs. R looked startled and said she had not discussed her affairs with her mother recently. She then asked whether she would be disloyal to her mother if she allowed herself to be more fond of her husband. The caseworker commented on the incongruity of the question, and soon after Mrs. R began to report about the good times she was having with her husband. Later she started to look for a new apartment, stating that they needed a pleasant place to entertain friends. She also said that she knew it is important for a father and children to be close to each other. In one interview she said that, if her husband would be patient with her, she believed their sexual problems could be straightened out.

In general, clients with anxiety hysteria are relatively well on their way to adult adjustment. Their capacity for a certain degree of love for the marital partner and for the children, and their ability to be partially satisfied and succesful in work, can be considered positive indications for treatment. The strong urge to equal their parents, even on a neurotic basis, is an active conflict which can be used to motivate treatment. Usually the material about their parental relationships comes early in the contact and is accompanied by deep feeling. Their overinvolvement with their parents and the influence of the parents in their current reality situation make the central problem readily available for discussion. Also, their current relationship problems with the marital partner and the children provide many opportunities for fruitful discussion.

Conclusion

It is important to conclude this discussion of treatment with the note that sometimes casework treatment should be viewed as preliminary to psychoanalytic treatment. Although casework treatment may be the method of choice in some cases, in others such treatment can only bring partial or temporary relief. Psychoanalysis is a specific treatment for this neurosis and offers possibility of resolution of the basic conflict. Analysis should be considered, if possible, for young persons, particularly young adults, who have such pervasive anxiety and symptoms as to prevent marriage, disturb a marriage, or interfere with their successful functioning in parental and work roles. It should also be considered for young women who are fearful of childbirth or have been traumatized by the birth of their first child. It should be considered also for all clients who are symptom ridden to the point where the only avenue to treatment is to work with the unconscious content of the problem.

The adults who suffer from anxiety hysteria are handicapped in the performance of their social and sexual roles. Since this neurosis is rooted in an unresolved oedipal conflict, its resolution often requires analytic treatment. Casework treatment, however, can serve to reduce the client's anxiety and to restrict the influence of the neurosis on the client's functioning. If the caseworker identifies the neurosis and understands it dynamically, he can help many of these persons live satisfying and productive lives.

Character Neurosis

On "Character Neurosis"

Richard Sterba

Character neurosis is a very young term in our science; only 25 years ago it was introduced by Franz Alexander, who presented a paper on the "neurotic character" at the International Psychoanalytic meeting in Innsbruck. Since then, this term has been increasingly used in the diagnosis of certain neurotic disorders, particularly in recent years. As a member of the Membership Committee of the Psychoanalytic Association, I examine the applications for membership which give the diagnoses of the cases treated by the applicant during his training. More than 20 per cent of the neurotic patients treated for didactic purposes—and therefore carefully selected according to their treatability—are diagnosed "character neurosis."

I consider the frequency with which the diagnosis "character neurosis" has been applied in recent years to be an indication of the progress of our insight into the neurotic process and of our advanced therapeutic approach to neurotic disorders, for it indicates the shift of the focus of our psychodynamic interest from the symptom to the total personality. When Sigmund Freud started his study of psychoneurosis, he had to begin with the obvious manifestations of the neurotic process, with the symptoms. He was soon able to recognize the traumatic origin of many symptoms and their significance as markers, as it were, of strong emotional experiences of the past which had themselves been eliminated from conscious memory. The primitive form of psychodynamic therapy which he first established corresponded to this rudimentary and partial insight into the genetic origin of the neurotic symptoms. This therapy consisted of lifting into consciousness the memories which had disappeared into the depths of the unconscious and in whose place the symptom had established itself in the conscious personality. *Dissolution of symptoms into memories* was the first therapeutic formula. It was of a topographical nature. Correspondingly, the formula of the genesis of the symptom was: Hysterical persons suffer from reminiscences. But almost simultaneously with this first topographical formulation, a *dynamic* one was expressed by Freud and Breuer, namely: The therapeutic process consists of the discharge of pent-up emotion. The "abreaction" of

Reprinted from the *Bulletin of the Menninger Clinic*, XVII, No. 3 (1953), p. 81–89, by permission of the author and the publisher.

dynamic quantities soon became the aim of therapeutic endeavors. With these concepts modern dynamic psychopathology was initiated.

The failure of abreactive therapy, of the so-called "Katharsis," led to further examination of the genetic forces of the neurotic symptom. The tendency of the symptom to reappear, after it has been removed by abreaction, led to the recognition of the permanent sources of energy supply for the neurotic symptomatology. This necessitated the establishment of the concept of *instinct*. The instinctual sources, the vicissitudes of the instinctual energies, and the counterplay of their forces within the mind then became the most important objects of psychodynamic study. This resulted in the discovery of the successive steps of instinctual development and the possibility of regression to fixation points along the course of this development. The fixation point determines the symptomatology to a considerable degree. The distance of the regressive withdrawal from the completed development of maturity thus became the diagnostic criterion.

At the time when I studied psychoanalysis at the Vienna Institute, almost 30 years ago, the diagnosis depended on the careful study of the developmental level of the libidinal energy which supplied the symptomatology. Hysterical symptoms corresponded to the phallic level, compulsive and obsessional symptoms to the anal-sadistic stage, paranoic symptomatology to the anal-expulsive stage, melancholia to the oral-sadistic, and schizophrenia to still earlier developmental fixation points. The diagnosis was based upon the results of the study of *instinctual development.*

The gradual insight into the participation of the aggressive instinct in all forms of neurosis blurred this relatively distinct concept of a diagnostic scale. The development of the aggressive instinct is not so clearly defined, and we are not quite able to fit stages of aggressive development into a developmental schedule. A more significant disturbance of the simplicity of the diagnostic scale based on instinctual, or rather libidinal, development came from another area of psychoanalytic investigation. I am referring to ego psychology.

The earliest topographical and dynamic insight had already necessitated the establishment of the concept not merely of forces that oppose each other, but also of mental areas to which we allocate these opposing forces. The division of the mental apparatus into different parts, or systems, became a conceptual necessity. Ego psychology is the result of this investigation which tried to find the answer to such questions as what the instinct-opposing part of the mind consists of, what motivates it to oppose certain instincts, what determines the selection of the instinctual manifestations against which the opposition is raised, and what are the ways and means which are applied in the struggle for defense. Up till then, we had perceived only the instinctual drive that forces its disguised expression upon the ego and makes it suffer by the intrusion of the foreign body which we call the symptom. Now it was recognized that the ego participates just as much in the creation of the neurotic process. The total personality, therefore, had to be taken into consideration for the study of neurosis. In this way psychoanalytic character-studies were developed with the focus of interest, of course, in *pathological* characters.

Sigmund Freud opened the field of character studies with his famous description and libido-theoretical explanation of the *anal character*. This was soon followed by further studies of the same character pathology by Jones and Abraham. Abraham added the concept of the *oral* character in a paper devoted to this subject at the International Congress in Salzburg in 1924. Rather unsuccessful attempts to establish the concept of a urethral and genital character followed soon afterward. These studies are still based on the psychoanalytic findings concerning the development of the libido, and correspond to the chronological shift of primacy from one erotogenetic zone to the next. It was an important step in our theoretical and technical progress when it was recognized that the same specific instinctual demands for gratification which cause the neurotic symptom can also permeate the ego in the form of character traits. The best studies of this type were made in connection with the so-called anal character. They consisted in the description and understanding of the *systematic* relationship between this type of character and the activities and aims of the anal zone. These activities and aims of gratification can be directly continued into the character trait. A striking example of this is the anal pleasure of fecal retention, which plays an important role in a compulsive symptom and is continued at the same time on a somewhat higher level, and therefore egosyntonically, as pleasure in collecting and as miserliness.

But in his first paper on the subject of a pathological character, which was written in 1908, Freud already had pointed out that some character traits have to be considered as *reaction formations* against instinctual demands. Whereas some character traits were found to be the continuation of instinctual trends, made syntonic by an upward shift to more acceptable aims—we could say by simple ego passage—with others the participation of the ego in the formation of character traits is much more extensive. It was observed that certain infantile activities and attitudes connected with the gain of pleasure from the anal zone, for example, disappeared in the course of development and were replaced by character traits that aimed in exactly the opposite direction from that of the original instinctual gratification. Extensive anal pleasure in dirt, for instance, might lead to the development of the opposite character trait of a passion for strict cleanliness. Here we can no longer speak of a simple ego passage; a much more complicated ego participation has to be postulated if we attempt to explain this transformation of instinctual activity and aim into a character trait with the opposite sign and direction. The absorption of instinctual and aim-directed energies into characterological opposites, which we call reaction formations, could only be understood when the concept of complete desexualization and disaggressivation—of instinctual "neutralization," to use Hartmann's term—was developed. This concept has recently become very important in our ego psychology.

However, the neurotic characters which were established in these early studies were those whose pathology, in the form of exaggeration of otherwise relatively normal trends, were based upon the intensity of certain instinctual demands originating in one of the erotogenetic zones. We might point out also that the anxiety reactions of the ego were considered to be transformations of libidinal energies, since in Freud's theory at that time anxiety was the result of the repression of libido. Libido was thought to be transformed into anxiety through the mechanism of repression, like wine into vinegar.

A new approach to characterological problems as we meet them daily in our clinical work was made possible through two new steps in the progress of psychoanalytic knowledge. The first step was the examination of the nature, the position, and the mechanism of the ego. I am referring mainly to Freud's paper, "On Narcissism: An Introduction" (1914), and to his book, *The Ego and the Id* (1923). The ego's specific ways of dealing with the demands made upon it by its three taskmasters, the id, the superego, and reality, form essentially what we call the "character" of a person, since they present the main features by which one personality structure is differentiated from others. The second step was taken when the theory of anxiety was corrected by Freud, and the concept of "signal anxiety" established. Only with the recognition of anxiety as the motive-power of repression and other defensive measures, and with the insight into the "signal" character of anxiety produced against inner dangers, was our science able to progress to the more refined studies of the "innumerable transformations, distortions and deformities of the ego which are in part the accompaniment of and in part substitutes for neurosis." (Anna Freud.)

Since we attempt to approach our subject historically, we cannot omit mentioning two minor contributions to psychoanalytic character pathology. I am referring here first of all to Franz Alexander's study of the "neurotic character." In his paper of 1927, Alexander described as neurotic characters those personalities whose neurotic pathology does not express itself in circumscribed symptoms, but who deviate from the norm in their general conduct of life. These are men or women of action as compared with the more or less privately suffering neurotic. Their actions and behavior, however, deviate from the normal in that they are the obvious expression of an inner conflict. This conflict might even become conscious if a person of this type is irresistibly driven to perform a certain action against his better insight into the irrationality or immorality of his behavior. More often the inner conflict expresses itself in such a way that the instinctual gratification provided by action and conduct, leads to damage to the ego and, in extreme cases, even to irrational self-destruction. Alexander refers here mainly to the types of personalities who suffer from a fate- or destiny-neurosis. Their neurosis expresses itself in pathological "acting out": in these personalities the conflict between id and superego, though it has become egosyntonic, is still obvious in the irrationality, intensity, and finally in the destructive result of long-range action and behavior. Though the presentation of this type of personality by Alexander in his Innsbruck paper is clear and enlightening, the term "neurotic character" or "character neurosis," as it is used nowadays, covers other types of character pathology as well. That part of Alexander's description of character neurosis which retains its validity, therefore, covers only a fraction of what is designated by this term today.

The second contribution is even more important. It was made in the late twenties by Wilhelm Reich, who at that time was still a psychoanalyst, and it was based on his theory and technique of psychoanalytic therapy. By then it had already been recognized that the single neurotic symptom was only an exacerbation of a more general unbalance within the mind which was brought about by the disharmonies between the different provinces of the mental apparatus. Reich focused his interest on the resistance during treatment. He claimed to observe that the initial transference expresses itself in a specific form that is characteristic for the personality of the patient. To Reich, the important feature of this resistance is not the content, which may be the same with different personalities, but the *form* in which it is expressed and in which it is experienced and sensed by the analyst. He further claimed that this resistance form, as for example a specific way of aggressiveness, or of superiority and coldness, or of suspicion and mistrust, or of submissive passivity, is characteristic of the personality in that every further resistance takes the same form. Since Reich considered this form of resistance characteristic of the individual who offers it, he called it "character resistance." The analysis of this resistance form, systematically through the layers of its historical development, Reich termed "character analysis." From this position, Reich makes a bold assumption. He considers the whole character of a person to be a resistance against inner and outer stimuli. With this step, Reich left the ground of clinical reality, and we cannot follow him any further. But his characterological attempts have a definite value. He focused the interest of clinicians on resistance *forms*, on the genetic exploration of these and on their connection with characteristic attitudes. His description of certain neurotic characters like the masochistic, the instinct-ridden, the passive-feminine, and the genital-narcissistic, for example, are of definite clinical value, and the analytic exploration of the origin of more or less permanent resistance-attitudes is a real contribution to character pathology. His greatest merit is that he stimulated further investigations of the defensive measures of the personality. The result of this stimulation was Anna Freud's brilliant book, *The Ego and the Mechanisms of Defence*. The step which was taken with this book is one from narrow resistance-analysis to general defense-analysis.

All of our ego studies are based on Freud's contribution to ego research. But while Freud's ego analysis was concerned with the ego's dynamic structure, its composition, and the development of its organization, Anna Freud's ego analysis is a study of the ego's *activity*, namely *defense*. Only after the study of the ego's defense activity was added did psychodynamic psychology become an all-round science of man's mind and its working.

Anna Freud's work, as well as the latest studies in the field of ego psychology by workers like Hartmann, Kris, Hoffer, Loewenstein and

Greenacre, to mention a few, has had considerable influence on psycho-analytic characterology. For the character of a person is to a great extent determined by the ego's activities and avoidances, which means by the ego's ways of dealing with claims made upon it by instinct, conscience, and reality. So far, the results of clinical studies from the standpoint of more recent ego psychology have not progressed far enough for a more detailed nosological classification. We cannot yet make as clear a distinction between different character types from the ego standpoint as was possible at the time of libido-developmental character formulations. Our studies are still in flux. Many findings in the realm of early ego development and their relation-ship to instinctual development have not yet been sufficiently absorbed to enable us to make classifications in the form of distinct pathological character types. This justifies us in using a term with a relatively indistinct connotation. "Character neurosis" serves this purpose very well. It indicates the advanced standpoint of our diagnostic studies which takes ego consideration into account, and at the same time, it avoids the distinctions of a closer typology for which we have not sufficiently progressed.

Finally, we will have to try to give the rather difficult answer to the very important question of what kinds of cases we diagnose as "character neurosis." Character neurosis is a big diagnostic pot into which all kinds of psycho-pathology types are thrown. The classical character-pathological syndrome of the anal and the compulsive character might be diagnosed nowadays by some clinicians as character neurosis. The acting-out personalities which Alexander described, whose lives are repeated dramatizations of infantile experiences, trends, and conflicts, are counted as belonging to the character neurosis, although it was only for these that the term "neurotic character" was originally used by Alexander. (There is, it seems to me, no definite distinction between "neurotic character" and "character neurosis.") These are the more obvious neurotic affections of the characterological manifestation of a personality. But minor disorders in the contact with social surroundings, and the different types of more or less obvious disturb-ances in the object relationships of a patient are today likewise readily diagnosed by this term. The famous Wolf-man whom Freud described in his "History of an Infantile Neurosis" would be diagnosed by many of us today as a character neurosis.

We further consider as belonging to the diagnostic entity of character neurosis the manifold pathologically exaggerated *defense activities* of the neurotically afflicted ego, the inhibition of its normal activity and expansion, its diffuse flight reactions from danger situations, and its different patho-logical transformations of instinctual trends into their opposites. This type of case is of particular interest for refined studies of the defenses of the ego. They provide the field in which we can investigate the relationship between instinctual satisfaction and defense, examine where and in what manner instinctual gratification serves the very purpose of defense, and the ways in which the defensive attitude provides instinctual gratification. Through these studies we become aware that what we could call collectively for the purpose of this discussion a "noncharacter neurosis" always involves also the general character reactions of the patient. This recognition of the diffuse permeation of the ego by the same neurotic conflict which feeds the symptoms makes the limits of the term "character neurosis" so fluctuant that the difference between character neurosis and symptom neurosis is in many respects merely one of degree.

Needless to say, the majority of cases that were formerly diagnosed as "psychopathic personalities" are now termed character neurosis, since the more general acceptance of the genetic approach in psychiatry has reduced the validity of the diagnosis "constitutional psychopath."

The readiness to use the term "character neurosis" to the extent that it is done nowadays, although its content is relatively indistinct and comprises such a variety of clinical pictures, is the result of a change in our approach to patients in recent years. Our attitude in the very first interview is different than it was 20 to 30 years ago because of the influence of our ego-psychological insight and understanding. If we have to evaluate a patient today from a diagnostic and prognostic standpoint in an interview situation, we do not rely to such an extent on the symptomatology which he reports to us. Almost automatically we observe the patient's general behavior, the peculiarities of his attitude toward us, his mannerisms, and the mode and inflection of his speech. As we are aware of all these manifestations we use them for evaluation of the neurotic trends which permeate the behavior, for they indicate to the experienced therapist the extent and manner in which the neurosis afflicts the total personality and therefore the character. For our therapeutic expectations and the prognosis of our therapy we almost depend more upon our experience with the pathological character type to which the patient seems to belong than upon the otherwise manifest symptomatology. Being on the lookout in this way for pathological behavior- and attitude-manifestations makes us, I think, more inclined to use the diagnosis "character neurosis" despite its obvious vagueness and indistinctness.

We might mention another understandable, though not quite legitimate, reason for applying this diagnosis to a patient. It is not infrequently used to explain and excuse psychotherapeutic failure. Ambitious psychotherapists, who feel frustrated by the fact that their efforts to cure a person with a neurotic disorder have been unsuccessful, often feel relieved if they can make the patient's character responsible for the lack of therapeutic results. The diagnosis "character neurosis" comes in handy then as an assuagement for the therapist's feelings of incompetence and frustration at his thwarted efforts, for character neuroses are well known to be not very easily accessible to quick and easy therapy.

This short review of some of the different clinical pictures which are subsumed under the diagnosis "character neurosis" does not exhaust the subject. The different nosological syndromes which are covered by this indistinct and not very well circumscribed term each deserves consideration in a separate paper.

The very indistinctness, however, of the term which is used for such a variety of neurotic disorders has one definite advantage. It is a safeguard for the student in his therapeutic approach, for it prevents him from linking diagnosis and therapeutic procedure too closely and too rigidly. It is a very understandable desire of the psychotherapist to have the therapeutic procedure prescribed by the diagnosis of the patient, as we find to be the case in general medicine. We would all like to be able to establish a "grand strategy" of therapeutic approach which is determined from the start of therapy by the diagnosis. It was hoped that the result of investigation of cases with the same diagnosis would provide us with a map that could orient and guide us simply in our task of exploring the dark continent of conflicting mental forces. If this could have been accomplished we should have had a fast and easy way of finding the essential psychodynamics of a neurotic disorder provided that the therapist had begun by making the correct diagnosis. But this ideal of patterning the therapeutic approach upon the symptomatology and the diagnosis based upon it is an illusion. Psychotherapy still is an extremely individualistic procedure, and our ego studies confirm more and more the determination of many ego attitudes by various and *specific events* which the patient experienced in early and earliest childhood. Through its very vagueness the diagnosis "character neurosis" helps to destroy the illusion of planned, quick, and easy therapy. This is a definite advantage of this diagnostic term, and therefore I am in favor of using it at present.

We should remind ourselves, however, that the diagnosis "character neurosis" reflects not only the change in our psychodynamic and genetic concept and our therapeutic approach, but also a change in the general manifestations of neurosis. The nosological picture of neurosis has definitely changed since Sigmund Freud began his first psychodynamic studies. We rarely see the clearly circumscribed symptomatology of a case of classical hysteria or a well-defined compulsion neurosis.

The manifestations of neurosis nowadays are much more diffuse and much less concentrated in outspoken symptoms. Without any special effort or intention on our part, their exploration leads us to the patient's personality and its permeation by neurotic trends in the form of fixations to the past, repetitions of traumatic events of early childhood and of the defense patterns acquired at an early age. It might be difficult to decide to what extent the progress in our psychodynamic studies and our better knowledge are responsible for this change in our diagnostic pictures. But there can be no doubt that the sociological and ideological changes of our era are also responsible for the change in the manifestation of neurosis. Whether, and in what way, this is an expression of the general unrest of our time connected with the disintegration of values in so many fields of human activity and thought is a question of a sociological nature and therefore beyond the scope of this paper.

Character Disorders

Clients with Character Disorders

Merl M. Jackel

In the present state of psychoanalytic knowledge, the classification "character disorder" is subject to a great deal of confusion. One can readily understand why this is so if one remembers that at the turn of the century psychiatry as a whole did not even accept the concept of a psychogenic cause, as opposed to organic causes, for mental illness. Except for psychopaths, whose condition was generally thought to be constitutional and hereditary, persons with what we now diagnose as character disorders were not considered to be in need of treatment by a psychiatrist. Thus the psychiatric classification "character disorder" has actually been a result of the scientific investigation done by psychoanalysts. The concept that a person responds in accordance with certain repetitive patterns that push him into characteristic difficulties has been developed only in the past thirty years. Also relatively new is the idea that these patterned responses have a marked bearing on an individual's choice of career, choice of mate, marital unhappiness, and antisocial conduct. Because these conceptualizations are new, our knowledge is still scattered and our classifications unsatisfactory.

Before discussing the difficulties of identifying and understanding character disorders, I should like first to define *character* and then to make some observations about character traits. One dictionary definition of character is as follows: "those peculiar qualities impressed by nature or habit on a person which distinguish him from others." This is a broad, descriptive definition that I think is useful. Perhaps it could be made more explicit as follows: Character consists of those characteristics or qualities impressed by nature or habit on a person which individually or in their relationship to each other both distinguish him from others and make him resemble others.

Most analysts define character on the basis of ego functioning. Fenichel says: "Thus the ego's habitual modes of adjustment to the external world, the id, and the superego, and the characteristic types of combining these modes with one another, constitute character."[1] Nunberg defines character

[1] Otto Fenichel, *The Psychoanalytic Theory of Neurosis*, W. W. Norton & Co., New York, 1945, p. 467.

Reprinted from *Social Casework*, XLIV (June, 1963), pp. 315–322, by permission of the author and the Journal.

as "a synthesis of many traits, habits and attitudes of the ego."[2] For myself, I am inclined to agree with those who question the soundness of defining character solely in terms of ego functioning. English and Finch use a broader definition, including under character "the sum total of an individual's behavior which is peculiar to him."[3]

I consider character to be a composite of many traits, which are usually established in childhood and which remain more or less unmodified throughout life. These character traits are highly heterogeneous, and a delineation of them will vary in accordance with the frame of reference in which they are viewed.

Factors Influencing Character Formation

Although it is impossible, in a brief presentation, to list all the many factors that influence the formation of character, I shall enumerate a few of them to show that character cannot be regarded merely as a collection of defense mechanisms.

Heredity

Certainly heredity is an important determinant of character formation. First, it is an important determinant of the individual's intelligence and physical characteristics. How important this is to character formation can be seen in the effect on a person of being unusually tall or short, unusually good-looking or ugly, unusually intelligent or dull. Probably, also, heredity plays a role in the potentiality for ego development, the strength of instinctual drives, and the strength and choice of ego defenses.

Constitution

Mothers report, and scientific observation has confirmed, that siblings often reveal marked differences even immediately after birth. For instance, infants may differ in their response to loud noises as early as the second day of life. Some children are more irritable, others more passive. There are undoubtedly constitutional variations that help or hinder the individual in dealing with all the problems in the development of the id, the ego, and the superego. Such variations may determine the extent to which a particular child is traumatized by the demands of his mother or of his environment.

Rate of Physical and Physiological Maturation

Children develop physically and neurologically at different rates. As a result, a certain demand may be readily accepted by one two-year-old, for example, and be obviously traumatic for another. Again, the child who is

---

[2] Herman Nunberg, *Principles of Psychoanalysis: Their Application to the Neuroses*, Madlyn Kahr and Sidney Kahr (trans.), International Universities Press, New York, 1955, p. 303.
[3] O. Spurgeon English and Stuart M. Finch, *Introduction to Psychiatry*, W. W. Norton & Co., New York, 1954, p. 232.

able to talk at an early age does not require as much action as a child who is late in talking. The former child may attempt to deal with frustration by thinking and talking; the latter is forced to act in order to get what he wants, and acting rather than using words may become an entrenched pattern. Similar examples can be cited in relation to early or late muscular co-ordination, bowel control, and so on.

Congenital Defect or Early Illness

The effect of congenital deafness or blindness on character formation need not be emphasized. Congenital deformity, even if corrected, can be traumatic. For instance, an infant's being in a cast throughout the first year of his life or an eighteen-month-old child's experience of prolonged physical pain may produce a profound effect.

Identification

Identification plays an important role in the formation of character structure. The ability to imitate and identify develops early in a child's life. In the course of maturation a series of identifications takes place, most significantly with one or the other of his parents. These identifications are largely unconscious and are somewhat indiscriminate. They are modeled on the child's own understanding of the person with whom he is identifying and not necessarily on what the person is really like. His identifications determine much of what becomes his conscience and his ideals in life. When he is older, his conscious ego may reject or struggle against identification. For instance, a boy may struggle against his identification with his mother. Similarly, my adult woman patients often express the following idea: "The one thing I don't want is to be like my mother, but every day I find I am becoming more and more so." Sometimes the struggle goes on unconsciously and the person behaves compulsively in a way opposite to that of the person with whom he has an unconscious identification.

Psychosexual Development

One of the basic contributions of psychoanalysis is the concept of the influence of psychosexual development on the formation of character. Many factors affect psychosexual maturation, and hence character formation, but I should like to stress particularly the fact that it culminates when the oedipal conflict is resolved (or when the person fails to resolve it). It is at this time that significant regressions occur, identifications are established, and modes of defense become crystallized.

Defense Mechanisms

The term *defense mechanisms* is at present not clearly defined. Anna Freud, who introduced the term, limited its scope to defenses developed by the ego to protect itself from dangers arising out of the instinctual drives. Since the ego is capable of using concurrently a wide variety of mechanisms to defend itself, agreement on which are defense mechanisms and which are not is difficult to obtain. It is probably simplest to include only the ten that Anna Freud specifically mentioned.

In the process of erecting defenses—an entirely unconscious process—the ego always undergoes changes that are either modifying or inhibiting in nature. It should be emphasized that defense mechanisms are not pathological per se; on the contrary, they are important determinants of normal character formation and serve the purposes of adaptation and maturation.

Character Traits

Character traits, in general, are habitual modes of reaction. They differ widely, however, in accordance with the clinical diagnosis of the individual. Thus the character traits in character disorders have certain qualities that distinguish them both from psychoneurotic symptoms and from "normal" character traits.

Normal Character Traits vs. Psychoneurotic Symptoms

Normal character traits can be said to have existed all of the person's adult life, and their dynamics can be traced back to childhood. By contrast, psychoneurotic symptoms usually have a more limited history, and a patient can often state more or less accurately when they began.

Character traits involve broader, more complex reactions than psychoneurotic symptoms do. Compare, for instance, the compulsive neatness, orderliness, and cleanliness of the housewife with a limited symptom such as a hand-washing compulsion. Character traits also have the quality of predictability. It is this quality to which we are referring when we say that a person is or is not acting "in character." It may also be present in pathological character formation—for example, in the girl who repeatedly falls in love with the wrong man or in the man who marries three or four times, each time a woman who turns out to be frigid.

Finally, *character traits are ego-syntonic whereas neurotic symptoms are ego-alien.* This differentiation is of special importance in making a diagnosis.

Normal Character Traits vs. Character Traits in Character Disorders

There is a rigidity in the reactions or behavior of a person suffering with a character disorder that is not present in the character traits of the normal person. For example, the normal person may respond with anger in a work situation where he feels he has been injured. At the same time, he can co-operate with authority figures without feeling he is being submissive. The person with a passive-aggressive character disorder cannot respond in this manner. He is rigid or "fixed" in two ways. In the first place he sees everyone around him as trying to dominate him; he is unable to discriminate between his boss, his wife, and a Hitler. This makes him angry, either consciously or unconsciously. Neither can he distinguish accurately between situations in which anger is justified and those in which it is not. Furthermore, his reaction to his own anger is also fixed; he may, for example, react passively to any situation that might elicit his anger. This rigidity or in-flexibility, this inability to discriminate among various kinds of stimuli and react to them appropriately, distinguishes the pathological character traits from the normal.

Rigidity of response can take any of several forms. There may be a fixed emotional response to a variety of situations, to a specific emotion, to any situation that would precipitate a specific emotion, or to a specific situation. An example of the first kind of response is found in the person who reacts in all situations as if he were being humiliated. I recall a woman of this type. If she was accosted by a man, she felt humiliated. If she was not, she felt humiliated. If she was told what to do, it was humiliating. If she was not told what to do, she was being ignored, and this too was humiliating. If she was not able to do something, it was humiliating; if she was, it was humiliating that she had to perform such undemanding tasks. Regardless of the situation there was only one emotional response available to her.

A fixed reaction to a specific emotion is exemplified by a woman I knew who never recognized or exhibited feelings of jealousy. In situations that might stimulate such feelings, she would react with feelings of pity. She was never jealous of other women but pitied many of them.

My last example is of a fixed response to a specific situation. The patient, a twenty-six-year-old single woman, described going to a moderate-sized business firm to apply for a job. In the office she saw a young man to whom she felt attracted. As soon as she was told he was the boss, her feelings changed to anger, and in her mind she became critical of him—her "characteristic" attitude toward bosses.

Problems of Definition and Classification

I should like now to suggest a definition of character disorders and to discuss some of the reasons for the widespread confusion that clouds our understanding of this category of emotional or behavioral dysfunctioning. *Character disorders form a large and heterogeneous group of emotional or develop-mental disturbances that are usually ego-syntonic and that evidence themselves primarily by abnormalities in the person's habitual pattern of behavior.*

One of the reasons why the term *character disorders* is often confusing is that, as has been suggested, it is used to cover such a very wide range of emotional and behavioral difficulties. In discussing one particular type of character disorder, a speaker or writer sometimes gives the impression that his remarks apply to all character disorders. Obviously, if he has in mind the "actor-outer," his remarks will not make sense to a person who has in mind a compulsive personality. It is important to be as specific as possible about the kind of character disorder one is discussing. Any attempt to deal with character disorders as if they were a homogeneous group of disabilities leads to insurmountable difficulties.

Another source of confusion is that a variety of terms—*personality disorder, neurotic character, character neurosis, behavior disorder, actor-outer*—are used synonymously with *character disorder*. It should be noted, too, that the American Psychiatric Association, in its official classification of mental and emotional diseases aimed at promoting the use of common terminology among psychiatrists, uses the term *personality disorder;* it does not recognize the term *character disorder*. None of the terms used is completely satisfactory, but a social worker should be familiar with all of them. It is particularly important that he know the exact kind of character disorder an author of a professional article is discussing.

One further source of confusion in attempting to classify the character disorders should be mentioned—the fact that several different frames of reference can be used. One, for example, is the level at which libidinal fixation has occurred. The classic example of this is, of course, Freud's description of the anal character: the character traits of orderliness, obstinacy, and parsimony were found to be preponderant in persons whose instinctual life is fixated at the anal level. Similarly, one can speak of oral and phallic characters. But there are other frames of reference—defense mechanisms, social standards, or descriptive similarities.

It is of great importance in understanding nomenclature to appreciate the difference between a primarily descriptive approach and a dynamic approach. A *descriptive* approach has to do with a mode of behavior or the characteristics of a symptom or group of symptoms as they are seen clinically by an observer. A *dynamic* approach has to do with the motivation of these symptoms or of a particular piece of behavior, conscious or unconscious. The same behavior may have several different kinds of motivation, just as a particular motivation may be manifested by various types of behavior. In the official nomenclature of the American Psychiatric Association a third frame of reference is used—one based on society's reaction to the behavior of the person. This classification, the "sociopathic personality disturbances," includes such entities as antisocial reaction, dyssocial reaction, the sexual deviations, and the addictions. Thus, variations in the frame of reference lead to a lack of homogeneity in diagnostic classifications.

Fenichel attempts to classify character disorders according to the reaction of the individual (ego) to internal needs.[4] One group is classified on the basis of how the individual reacts to his conscience (or superego); others are defined by how the individual reacts to his sexual and aggressive drives. These groups are then subdivided. Such an approach makes for a cumbersome number of individual character disorders and at the same time fails to cover the field.

Such confusion emphasizes the fact that psychoanalysis is still a developing scientific endeavor and that analysts are not as yet clear enough about character disorders to be able to establish a satisfactory classification. We might settle for the idea that we are studying various aspects of human personality and that in different character disorders certain factors are more significant than others. It follows that in studying a particular aspect one

[4] Fenichel, *op. cit.*, pp. 463–540.

frame of reference may be more rewarding than others. It seems to me, too, that the frame of reference should also be determined by the purpose for which the classification is being used. For some purposes a purely descriptive approach will be satisfactory, whereas others will require a dynamic approach.

Acting Out

One of the terms frequently associated with character disorders, *acting out*, originated in psychoanalysis. Analysts noted that some patients, instead of remembering and verbalizing the traumatic situtations of their childhood, would unconsciously "act out" these early situations outside the analytic hour. As might be expected, many of these patients were people who in their daily lives tended to use action as a means of dealing with tension. As a result, common usage soon broadened the term to include all such people. The major characteristics of the person who acts out are one or more of the following:

1.   An inability to tolerate tension is general, accompanied by a need to discharge tension by action. Frustration tolerance is minimal, and post-ponement of gratification is impossible.

2.   An intolerance for *any* unpleasant affect. When threatened by such a feeling, he must immediately do something to get rid of it.

3.   A pervasive misunderstanding of the present in terms of the past. People in present life are not perceived or responded to as they actually are but are used as stand-ins for the re-enactment of childhood conflicts and defenses.

4.   A tendency to repeat again and again the same experiences or behavior patterns.

The third of these characteristics is apt to lead the caseworker to mis-interpret the client's reaction as either a transference reaction in the analytic sense or an attempt at manipulation. Superficially, the reaction of the person who acts out may resemble the typical transference reaction of the neurotic. On closer examination, however, it is found to be much more indiscriminate. Often it takes place with people the client scarcely knows. The relationship lacks depth, is based on the role or function of the other person rather than on the person per se, and is readily exchanged for other relationships. This distinguishes it from typical transference. In a sense, the client does try to manipulate the worker, but the manipulation is not usually conscious and is not simply a struggle for power. Rather, it results from his misunderstanding of the present in terms of the past. Unconscious dynamics always underlie the client's manipulative attempts.

The fourth characteristic—repetition—represents the person's attempts to somehow master traumatic events that he failed to master in childhood. An excellent example of how complicated the process may become and how the original drives and defenses may be transformed is a case reported by Alexander in 1930.[5] I should like to cite it to illustrate the four broad types of pathological reaction that are possible for an individual confronted by a traumatic situation.

As a boy, the patient had persisted in taking his milk from a nursing bottle up to the age of at least five. His siblings teased him for it. As a compensation for this teasing he developed the ability to ride his bicycle in the street alone—a feat somewhat beyond his age. He still took his milk from the bottle. In the patient's adult life, these traits persisted as follows: He expected his wife to guess his every need and satisfy his desires without being asked (the bottle); in business, however, he was capable, daring, and successful (the bicycle). This equilibrium was satisfactorily maintained until a new boss was appointed, who dominated and used the patient. In essence, this removed the patient's defense (bicycle). He then "seduced and had as his mistress" the wife of a superior. This, then, was the new defense, the re-establishment of masculinity (the bicycle). At home, he continued the usual demands on his wife (the bottle).

At the point where the new boss was introduced, this patient could have reacted in one of four ways:

1.   Developed a *psychoneurosis.* For example, he could have developed a street phobia that kept him at home and thus have avoided being exposed to the new boss.

2.   Become *psychotic.* For example, he might have become paranoid about his boss.

3.   Developed a *psychosomatic* symptom. For example, he could have developed colitis or a stomach ulcer, which would have allowed him to avoid his boss on days of particular distress.

4.   Solved his conflict by a complicated piece of behavior, in which he used people to re-establish a defense. By reacting in this way, the patient revealed that he had a *character disorder.*

Borderline State

I think it important to make a few comments about the "borderline state." This term, which is essentially descriptive rather than dynamic, has come into common use as psychiatrists and caseworkers have been seeing

[5] Franz Alexander, "The Neurotic Character," *International Journal of Psycho-Analysis,* Vol. XI, 1930, pp. 300–302.

more and more people who are seriously ill but not clearly psychotic. Three points of view on the borderline state should be noted:

1.   Some psychiatrists maintain that the term *borderline state* expresses the therapist's ignorance of the correct diagnosis when he has not made an adequate examination of the patient. They assert that, at best, it is only a temporary diagnosis—one that can serve until a definitive diagnosis can be made. Knight, who has written extensively on the subject, points out that difficulty in making a diagnosis is based in part on the fallacious assumption that a patient must be either psychotic or neurotic.[6] Actually, schizophrenic patients frequently complain about symptoms that are clearly psycho-neurotic—for example, compulsive rituals or extensive phobias. If the psychiatrist looks beyond the patient's presenting symptom, the schizophrenic process becomes obvious. I have always maintained that a full psychiatric diagnosis includes the patient's character structure—for example, a phobic reaction in a passive-aggressive personality, or schizophrenia with phobic symptomatology.

Knight further points out that it is entirely possible for some ego functions to be severely damaged while others remain relatively intact. In most borderline patients the ego functions that are impaired are integration, concept formation, judgment, and realistic planning. Their defenses against the eruption of id impulses into consciousness are also weak. On the other hand, their more general intellectual functions, their conventional adaptation to the environment, and their ability to sustain superficial object relationships may be well maintained. These people can be highly successful in their vocations, but usually their accomplishments are not in line with their abilities.

2.   The second point of view is that certain persons are overtly psychotic at certain times and latently psychotic at others. In other words, such a person has sufficient ego to be in contact with reality, adjust to it, and use good judgment at certain times. However, the ego adjustment is so tenuous that a seemingly minor upset can result in a psychotic break. At a time when such a person's condition is severe, he may be diagnosed as having ambulatory schizophrenia or latent schizophrenia; when it is not as severe, the pre-psychotic state may be regarded as either a character disorder (less disturbed) or a borderline state (more disturbed).

3.   The third point of view is that mental health and psychosis represent the two extremes on a continuum; there is an area in between, in which a person is not psychotic, not neurotic, and not healthy—he is "borderline." The differentiation is based on the extent to which psychotic thinking has invaded the ego. Hence, the difference between character disorder and borderline state is one of degree.

[6] Robert P. Knight, "Borderline States," in *Psychoanalytic Psychiatry and Psychology: Clinical and Theoretical Papers*, Robert P. Knight and Cyrus R. Friedman (eds.), International Universities Press, New York, 1954.

Treatment Considerations

Treating the client with a character disorder is a difficult task. One of the primary reasons is that a character trait is acceptable to the ego; in other words, it is ego-syntonic. Usually the client has no urge to do anything about his pathological character traits because he is not conscious of their making him suffer. A client may, for example, ask for help with a marital problem, feeling that he has chosen the wrong mate and that if he had a different mate he would have no problem. He has no idea that he himself is emotionally disturbed. Another client, like a person I knew who wanted the therapist to help him get rid of feelings of guilt when he cheated or stole, may want to rid himself of a normal reaction and retain a pathological character trait. In brief, one can say that treatment of the client with a character disorder should have as an initial aim making the ego-syntonic trait ego-alien or ego-dystonic.

It is sometimes said that clients with character disorders lack motivation. This is certainly not true. Clients are *always* motivated, but the caseworker may not assess the motivation correctly. For example, a client may come for casework treatment with the conscious goal of working out a marital problem but with the unexpressed need to prove that she was in the right in her conflict with her husband—in order to counteract unconscious feelings of guilt. She may then interpret the worker's efforts to improve the marital relationship as efforts to show that she was in the wrong. Thus, she may react in the treatment situation with indifference or resentment. If the caseworker fails to recognize the basic motivation, which has been frustrated, he is likely to interpret the client's reaction as a lack of motivation.

One of the caseworker's first tasks in treatment is to establish a relationship with the client. To do so, he must have an understanding of the client's conscious and unconscious motivations for coming to the agency. Having established a relationship and accurately appraised the client and his situation, the worker can then use the relationship and his understanding to convert ego-syntonic behavior gradually into an ego-dystonic symptom. If before this happens the client succeeds in changing his environment or by other means getting rid of his presenting discomfort, he is apt to lose interest in treatment. Until the client is helped, through treatment, to become aware of having a problem that requires him to make a change in himself, little can be accomplished.

Occasionally it is important for the caseworker to determine early in contact with the client whether a particular piece of behavior is a psycho-neurotic symptom or a character trait. One example is the client who is late for his first few appointments. Is his arriving late a character trait, or is it a transitory symptom related to his anxiety about coming to see the worker? If lateness has been a problem all his life or if he is late for any appointment even when he is looking forward to it, the worker can assume that his behavior in this respect is a character trait. As such, it has a complicated set of dynamics, is apt to be overdetermined, and serves an important function in his psyche. Interpreting to him that he comes late because he is angry at the worker or because he fears what will emerge in the interview can have no meaning to him, even though the interpretation may have elements of truth in it. Interpretations of this kind often lead to fruitless arguments that use up all the interview time, and the client leaves the session frustrated and resentful. He is likely to miss his next appointment or to discontinue treatment entirely.

This kind of client is extremely difficult to work with. The worker must, however, accept the client's lateness as a part of his character; any attempt to "attack" it or modify it by direct interpretation is doomed to fail. There is no one solution to the problem of dealing with it, but the worker must be flexible in his approach. Sometimes the interview hour may be prolonged so that the client can feel he has got something out of it. Or the worker may explore how the client has dealt with the problem in the past and reinforce the solution the client has worked out. Knowing what techniques to use and choosing the most appropriate depend on the worker's psychodynamic understanding of the client.

Another problem for the caseworker is to avoid being misled by what the client presents as reality. Since his character traits serve many different functions in preserving him from anxiety, the client tries desperately to arrange his outer life so as not to disturb them and his inner life so as to justify them. For example, a man may report that his marriage to a frigid woman is creating a sexual problem for him. It may be true that his wife is frigid; but it may not be true, as he is implying, that he would have no sexual problem if he were married to a more responsive woman. Because a client with a character disorder is inclined to use rationalizations, the worker must be careful not to assume that the reason he gives for doing something is his real reason.

I should like to add one final caution in relation to treatment. Once the client progresses to the point that his behavior is no longer ego-syntonic, he is likely to become depressed or anxious and may develop neurotic or psychosomatic symptoms. If the worker fails to recognize that the appearance of these symptoms does represent *progress*, he may become frustrated and angry at the client at the very time when the client is beginning to improve. After evaluating the ego-dystonic symptoms and the client's reactions to them, the worker can help him by letting him know that his new discomfort represents progress. As appropriate, the caseworker can then help the client use the discomfort to become motivated to improve his social functioning or to reach a decision to get psychiatric treatment.

Conclusion

One of the complications in understanding character disorders is that often the therapist sees only the end product of a series of vicissitudes in the development of a character trait. For instance, a character trait may start as a source of gratification; but as the child develops, it takes on several additional values, a series of defenses, and perhaps secondary gains, which make an understanding of the total personality an impossibility without a thorough analysis. By way of reassurance, I should like to stress that a caseworker is not an analyst; he cannot know all the analyst knows about dynamics and, at the same time, know something about social work. Part of the caseworker's confusion about character disorders is due to five important facts: *1]* the study of character disorders is a developing scientific endeavor; *2]* such knowledge as has been formulated is scattered, lacks integration, and is not clear even to those who specialize in the field; *3]* the classifications that have been developed are designed for more or less severe character disorders and not for the more normal character development to which they are sometimes inaccurately applied; *4]* caseworkers are apt to develop anxiety about not knowing, even in cases where it is not possible to know; *5]* caseworkers often set their treatment goals too high. Recognition of these facts may help the worker avoid unwarranted frustration.

There is just so much a caseworker can know about the dynamics of character disorders, since even the specialists have not yet been able to organize their formulations into a sound theory. However, the caseworker should recognize that no one can attempt to formulate dynamics until he has an accurate and detailed description of the person's behavior in a variety of situations. He can get this most satisfactorily by studying the client's *present* rather than his past. Too often workers are inclined to substitute extensive dynamic formulations of childhood, which must be largely speculative, for a clear description of the client as he *is*, of how he came, and of why he wants treatment.

Treatment of Character Disorders: A Dilemma in Casework Culture

Otto Pollak

In the treatment of character disorders, social caseworkers deal with three groups of difficulties. The first concerns the nature of the condition itself. The main difficulty in work with persons with character disorders is that, because of the primitive ego structure of the persons afflicted, the therapist and the client must engage not only in a process of unlearning faulty reaction patterns but also in a process of diversification and creation in social development. Clients require a type of therapy which emphasizes

Reprinted from *Social Service Review*, XXXV (June, 1961), pp. 127–134, by permission of the author and The University of Chicago Press. Copyright, 1961 by the University of Chicago.

psychological nurture more than gains in understanding, identification with the ego of the therapist, and therefore acceptance of limitations rather than liberation from maladaptive restrictions. Sometimes the course of therapy shows movement even through the development of a neurosis as a step toward health.[1]

Second, the nature of our civilization not only seems to elicit the development of character disorders in an increasing number of people but it also lends support to the persistence of such disorders. From individualism to egotism there is only one step. From romantic love to unrealistic expectations regarding gratifications that can be demanded from the marriage partner there is equally only one. And from such unrealistic expectations to the limitation of one's own giving and the resultant violation of reciprocity in marital interaction the distance is not long either. In a materialistic society id gratifications are prominently offered in overt and hidden form, while the waning power of a generally accepted morality leaves superego forces unsupported. That under such conditions all compromise between id and superego should be weighted on the id side need not be surprising. Most of all, however, a society that mistrusts authority and extols rebellion is likely to furnish many rationalizations to a person whose psychic structures leads to acting out rather than to internalization of conflict.[2] In this cultural framework, psychoanalysis, with its liberating impact upon conventional restrictions in the expressions of sexuality and hostility, has become overextended in the popular mind. Our current civilization, therefore, continually feeds new strength into the resistiveness to treatment of clients who are afflicted with character disorders.

The third complex of difficulties which caseworkers encounter in their therapeutic efforts with this group of clients stems from their own professional culture. These difficulties will be presented here in hypothetical form as a basis for scrutiny and discussion by practitioners. The central thesis presented is that caseworkers have made their greatest professional advances in an orientation of theory and practice concerned with the treatment of the classic symptom neuroses and with character disturbances accompanied by guilt, while they are now faced with clients who exhibit character disturbances which are relatively guilt-free and which lead to conflict in interaction with other people rather than to intrapersonal conflict in the client. Caseworkers find themselves, therefore, sometimes entrapped by the principles of a method of casework which does not appear appropriate for the new group of clients who seem to dominate the case loads of family welfare

---

[1] Rosemary Reynolds and Else Siegle, "A Study of Casework with Sadomasochistic Marriage Partners," *Social Casework*, XL (December, 1959), 545–51; Effie Warren, "Treatment of Marriage Partners with Character Disorders," *Social Casework*, XXXVIII (March, 1957), 118–26; and Otto Pollak, Hazel M. Young, and Helen Leach, "Differential Diagnosis and Treatment of Character Disturbances," *Social Casework*, XLI (December, 1960), 512–17.

[2] Otto Pollak, "Social Factors Contributing to Character Disorders," *Child Welfare*, XXXVII (April, 1958), 8–12.

agencies today. Apparently every success in fighting discomforts in the social sphere is followed by new discomforts which could not have been foreseen. Success in the fight against infant mortality necessitated increased concern with the management of sensory disorders which survived perinatal injuries. The gain in survival of the middle-aged has brought into focus the problems of degenerative diseases. And apparently our successful fight against the symptom neuroses has increased our difficulties in finding means of effective treatment of character disorders.

In order to clarify the nature of these difficulties, it may be helpful to describe the syndrome from which clients with character disorders seem to suffer. The constellation commonly described as a character disorder, as distinguished from a character neurosis, seems to present a constellation of massive projection, ego-syntonic behavior, insistence on self-justification and the need for change in others, insensitivity to the needs of others, hopelessness, and inefficient exploitation of others.[3] Mere inspection of this constellation of characteristics will suggest that casework help oriented to guilt and discomfort in self-perception will find itself without points of easy contact with clients so afflicted. It may serve, however, the task of reorientation which diagnostically oriented casework requires if the difficulties in this respect are elaborated and analyzed. That "therapeutic techniques that are effective with neurotic clients are not appropriate with character disorders"[4] has been clearly recognized and frequently stated in the literature. What has to be elaborated and presented to the profession is the fact that the principles of casework appropriate for the treatment of neurotic clients have by and large been generalized in the subculture of the profession so that principles appropriate for the treatment of character disorders present problems in the professional culture as it has developed. These difficulties will be presented under the headings of relationship difficulties, difficulties in setting goals, and difficulties in treatment methods.

Relationship Difficulties

The outstanding difficulty in establishing a positive relationship with clients afflicted with character disorders stems from the fact that professional training and experience of social caseworkers produce a personality which is the opposite of the personality encountered in such clients. A high degree of self-awareness, sensitivity to the nature of his interactions with others, and ability to give of himself for the benefit of others are the attributes which we find and welcome in successful caseworkers. The client suffering from the impact of a character disorder upon his relationships with others is a person who uses projection, is insensitive to the need of others, and is unable to give

---

[3] Pollak, Young, and Leach, *op. cit.*, p. 513.
[4] Beatrice R. Simcox and Irving Kaufman, M.D., "Treatment of Character Disorders in Parents of Delinquents," *Social Casework*, XXXVII (October, 1956), 388.

in interaction with others. Since the essential quality of a positive relationship is a feeling of "at-oneness"[5] with somebody else, it can easily be recognized that there will be difficulties in the initial interaction between the caseworker and such clients. Opposites have little chance to establish rapport from the start. It is therefore understandable that Effie Warren has found it necessary to publish a warning to caseworkers against the temptation to expect such clients to volunteer facts about their own part in the marital relationships and to cut short such persons in the first interview by bringing them back to a consideration of their own behavior.[6] This, however, is only a consideration of the problem as far as the caseworker is concerned.

It is probable that the client also becomes consciously or unconsciously aware of the contradiction between his own personality and that of the caseworker. On the conscious level, at least, the very personality of the caseworker may present a reproach to the client with a character disorder. Very few of us are able to perceive a person as being helpful if he is very different or if he is actually the opposite of what we are. The client would much rather sense in a therapist a fellow sufferer than a person who is a stranger to his condition. On the other hand, the therapist probably finds it easier to treat a person whose condition he has experienced than one whose experience he has never known. Since self-selection, screening in admission interviews, and professional success in social casework probably have resulted in selection of personnel more inclined to neurosis than to character disorder, the sympathy created by similarity between therapist and client is unlikely to exist between the caseworker and the client with character disorder. The only at-oneness which may come quickly is the id stimulation which the caseworker receives from the client, i.e., the acting out stimulation, the vicarious gratification of receiving without giving, of expressing hostility and hoping to get away with it. Against this type of at-oneness the professional caseworker will be on guard, of course, but even being on guard presents a special strain and for that reason may be the cause of still another difficulty in establishing a positive relationship with this type of client.

Always exploiters of human relationships, clients with character disorders will be tempted to exploit the caseworker by using his skills for their own pathological needs. Such clients have probably come to the agency because they have found their exploitative efforts in human relations ineffective. What they want is first of all an increase in the accessibility to exploitation in their marriage partners or children. Unconsciously, at least, they want to become better exploiters rather than more giving persons. Even though they accept the need for self-change, they want most of all to free themselves only of those aspects of their behavior which interfere with their raid on the personal resources of others. The caseworker will not be able to accept either of these goals and thus by professional conviction about health in human relationships will become in fact an opponent of the client.

[5] Helen Harris Perlman, *Social Casework: A Problem-solving Process* (Chicago: University of Chicago Press, 1957), p. 66.

[6] Warren, *op. cit.*, p. 120.

Casework culture extols reciprocity in human relationships; character disorder defies it.

This basic difference expresses itself also in an incongruity between the perceptions of the client and the perceptions of the caseworker. As a result of the fruitful contact which social casework has had with dynamically oriented psychiatry, the professional perception of caseworkers is geared to individual diagnosis. The caseworker wants to understand the client who presents himself to him as a person in a situation; the client with a character disorder perceives only his situation as unsatisfactory and is entirely concerned with the part that others play in his interpersonal relationships. The client sees what he does not get; the caseworker sees—largely—what the client does not give.

Within recent years the perception of caseworkers has shown signs of reorientation toward the diagnosis of interpersonal relationships and family groups. Yet all these understandings and diagnostic formulations are based on individual diagnoses of the persons involved. In consequence, it is extremely difficult for a caseworker to establish a common frame of reference with such clients from the start. Even, for instance, if the caseworker manages to keep in diagnostic focus two marriage partners with character disorders, the two will be concerned only with what they do not get while the caseworker will be concerned with what both of them do not give. This contest makes it difficult for the caseworker to establish a common goal with the client early in the contact, even though establishing such a common goal is elementary.[7]

The caseworker must learn to be patient with this client group and to be satisfied with agreement with the client on the desirability of certain subgoals which from the point of view of casework cannot be accepted as the sum total of desirability. In the last analysis, of course, the caseworker must see the goal in such cases in the capacity of the client to meet the needs of others. The suggestion made by Rosemary Reynolds and Else Siegle[8]—to connect with the client's narcissism in a logical discussion of behavior changes which will make things easier for him—presents for the caseworker the difficulty of trying to use a condition in the client which represents immaturity and pathology. In this respect some reorientation will probably be necessary to make the suggestion by Reynolds and Siegle an easily workable procedure. The solution may lie in the proposition that maturity and immaturity are designations of conditions which in their purity are unlikely to be found in clients. People are more or less geared to reciprocity, more or less self-concerned, and the caseworker must learn to use the client's potential in these respects without the mental reservation that he is actually fostering the undesirable or is arresting the client's development.

Perhaps most significant, however, is the fact that clients with character disorders are prone to attacks of depression and hopelessness which make

---

[7] Lenore Rivesman, "Casework Treatment of Severely Disturbed Marriage Partners," *Social Casework*, XXXVIII (May, 1957), 244.

[8] Reynolds and Siegle, *op. cit.*, p. 549.

them need persistent encouragement and support from the caseworker. In this respect the culture of casework makes the helping task difficult. Caseworkers notoriously underestimate their effectiveness and are therefore cautious in predicting or promising significant improvement to the clients. It might be worth investigating how many cases are lost after one or two contacts simply because caseworkers hesitate to hold out definite hope to depressive clients. While it may be impossible, due to the nature of the condition, to establish with the client a framework of common understanding and common goals, it may be possible to establish with him a framework of common expectations regarding his improvement and to renew such a framework when the client has a relapse into depressive moods.

Goals

There is no aspect of the helping process in which the culture conflict between a caseworker and the client with character disorder expresses itself more clearly than in treatment goals. If it is correct, as is often assumed, that most therapists have a neurotic personality basis, then it is within their own professional and, perhaps, therapeutic experience that the treatment process is liberating rather than binding. Guilt and anxiety are decreased, spontaneity is increased, self-blame and self-restriction are eased. The client with a character disorder, however, brings to the casework process a personality structure which requires binding instead of liberation, the creation of a measure of guilt and anxiety rather than emotional release from such conditions, restriction of behavior in place of maladaptive spontaneity. To the caseworker who considers these treatment goals it must look therefore as if he were about to take from the client something which he, the worker, has achieved at the price of great effort and emotional investment. People who have become liberated find themselves in a position in which they are to set up limitations for the client and in which they have to help the client toward an internalization of limitations.

In the treatment of character disorders, there is a surface implication of taking away rather than of giving which is in direct contradiction not only with the culture of casework but with our culture in general. Having grown out of material giving, casework still wants to "give" to the client in emotional and psychological respects. Actually, treatment methods appropriate in character disorders demand more such giving than any other type of diagnostically oriented casework, but this giving is method, not goal. The goal is one of taking away from the client his spontaneity in acting out his needs for gratification and expression, his freedom from guilt, his unconcern with others. What the worker does take away from the client in goal-setting is something which we all somewhat regret that we have lost in our upbringing and development—freedom for the id.

Furthermore, social caseworkers sometimes are still under the impact of the goal definition in the *Report on Scope and Methods* of the Family Service Association of America which was formulated with an orientation to people suffering from an excess of guilt and the resulting disabling conditions. It will be remembered that the report identified two treatment aims of social casework: *1]* to support and maintain the client's current strengths by helping him mobilize capacity and resources to meet his current life-situation, and *2]* to modify the client's attitudes and patterns of behavior by increasing his understanding of himself, of his problems, and of his part in creating them.[9] Neither of these two aims seems to meet the needs of the client with a character disorder. Support and maintenance of his strength are not appropriate because the client does not have enough strength. In modifying attitudes through increased understanding, the emphasis is on cognition; the client is to be helped to become the scholar of his misery. In the character disorder, on the other hand, treatment aims at more than either of these goals suggests. It aims at growth of motivation. To achieve this requires a much greater investment by the caseworker than helping the client to maintain strength or to increase understanding. The report is an invitation to do either too much too soon or not enough. What the client with a character disorder needs is, to borrow a term from computer language, "input" which will enable him in the long run to produce emotional and interpersonal "output." He must be invested in to become able to pay interpersonal dividends. Before such an investment is fully made, understanding will not be accessible to him, and what glimpses of understanding he may gain will probably be abused as the rationalization of further acting-out. In terms of goals, then, understanding will never be enough to help these clients; before they can become able to gain understanding they must be motivated to interact with others in a giving rather than in an exploiting way.

Treatment Methods

As far as treatment methods are concerned, the life-history approach, particularly the dwelling upon childhood experiences, is likely to prove of doubtful therapeutic value. Eliciting of childhood experiences and the feelings which accompanied them is necessary for liberation from morbid anxieties, but is not indicated for the creation of a readiness in the client to accept limitations and restrictions. In the person with a character disorder there is nothing to be gotten rid of because there is not enough there. Delving into the past can bring the client into stronger contact with his id impulses. What is appropriate in order to undo the impact of an overstrict superego is contraindicated in the absence of an adequately developed one. In a way both client and caseworker are deprived of the intellectual gratification resulting from a genetic diagnosis. Since this gratification, however, would furnish for the client only justification for his non-giving and exploitative behavior, the caseworker in turn must learn to get along without it.

[9] *The Scope and Methods of the Family Service Agency: Report of the Committee on Methods and Scope* (New York: Family Service Association of America, 1953), p. 7.

If caseworkers are concerned about a relatively low degree of success in work with character disorders, they must remind themselves that they start with many handicaps created by past learning. Perhaps one of the out-standing therapeutic reaction patterns which caseworkers have had to learn is permissiveness. In a world in which everybody has evaluated the client and has shown him various degrees of dissatisfaction with his performance, the at least overtly non-critical attitude of the caseworker has made it easy for the client to distinguish between therapist on the one hand and spouse, parent, employer, and members of the peer group on the other. In the treatment of character disorders this clear-cut differentiation is likely to be lost. Since a strong element of nurture and personality rearing has to be incorporated into the therapeutic effort, the setting of norms and limits, at least indirectly and later on directly, has to enter the complex of therapeutic interaction with the client.

"Rearing" demands more giving—and more denying—than conventional therapy, be it supportive therapy, clarification, or insight therapy. Along with permissiveness, the caseworker must abandon inactivity. Clients with character disorders require praise for even very minor achievement, for sporadic even if abortive effort. When they break appointments, they require more reaching-out from the caseworker than a simple letter or a telephone call. They require sensitivity and response to their hopelessness; they require advice and guidance.[10]

On the other hand, there are certain conventional patterns of casework influence which seem inappropriate. Feelings are not to be elicited because the client already suffers from too great a flow of feeling into action. He is "acting out" and suffers the consequences. To release his feelings further and thus to increase his acting out might bring him into conflict with the authorities, might lead to the breakup of his marriage, or might induce panic.

Setting limits, on the other hand, may furnish an easy cover for the countertransference of the caseworker. Since these are clients who are likely to tax the potential of the caseworker for empathy, countertransference is perhaps a greater danger here than in the treatment of other types of pathology. To be forced into a limit-setting relationship by the nature of the disorder is likely to make it more difficult for the caseworker to become aware of the emergence of non-therapeutic reactions on his part to the client.

There is also the trying demand for prolonged—and renewed—therapy which the elements of nurture and rearing in this type of treatment present. Our general culture has come to value speed as a sign of efficiency. Casework, as well as psychiatric treatment, has not remained unaffected by this tendency. Treatment of clients with character disorders, however, does last longer and moves less perceptibly than even long-term treatment which caseworkers, who do not yield easily to cultural pressure, have defined as standard.

[10] Warren, *op. cit.*, p. 123; Reynolds and Siegle, *op. cit.*, p. 549.

Professional Maturity and Social Change

The caseworker who has read this paper may well be left with the following impressions: *1]* that he has heard all these treatment suggestions before, and *2]* that there is no peace in the development of treatment techniques and of theoretical clarifications. Both impressions are correct, but the implications of fatigue and impatience which they carry may be based on an erroneous assumption. It has always been part of our culture to believe that one final effort might free us from burdensome aspects of human existence. We accept war only as a means to end all wars. We buy blue chips in order to be able to forget all about them. We court a person who might make a desirable mate and after marriage abandon efforts to further his affection and positive responses. In reality there is no peace and there are no final solutions. Every effort creates new problems, and every solution of these problems creates new ones in turn. Caseworkers appear frequently to be exhorted to return to methods of treatment and to approaches which one or two decades ago they were called upon to abandon. Such exhortations are not recantations, they are not the abandonment of fads, they are not the expressions of artificial obsolescence. The ability of the helping professions to remain aware of the swings of the social pendulum and to be able to respond to them seems to be the sign of a high degree of professional maturity.

A Study of Casework with Sado-masochistic Marriage Partners

Rosemary Reynolds and Else Siegle

Can a couple whose married life is a continuous physical or verbal battle, or at best an armed truce, be helped by casework treatment? If so, in what ways? Which casework methods and techniques seem to be most effective? In an effort to find the answers to these questions, a study of a group of cases in which a marked sado-masochistic pattern characterized the relationship between the marriage partners was undertaken in the Community Service Society of New York. The term sado-masochism is used here to describe the simultaneous existence of submissive and aggressive traits in each spouse which lead to a high degree of destructiveness in the marital

Reprinted from *Social Casework*, XL (December, 1959), pp. 545–551, by permission of the authors and the Journal.

relationship. In other words, the partners tend to suffer and to inflict suffering on each other.

After perusal of seventy-five cases in which certain sado-masochistic characteristics had been noted, the following criteria were used to select a group of comparable cases for more detailed study: *1]* marked sado-masochistic aspects in the personality structure of each partner, which interact in the marriage relationship, had been confirmed by the same psychiatric consultant; *2]* extreme verbal or physical hostility, or both, had been employed by the partners throughout the marriage; *3]* at the time of application to the agency, the marriage had existed at least a year and there had been no prolonged separations; *4]* both husband and wife had had casework treatment in the agency. Nine cases that met these criteria were used as the basis of this study. Extensive information was available in the case records. Selected study findings on the following topics will be presented: *1]* significant social and psychological characteristics of the couples and their families; *2]* the casework goals set and the degree to which these goals were achieved; *3]* the treatment method and techniques used in these cases.

Social Characteristics

The social characteristics of these nine couples were markedly similar. All were attractive men and women in their late twenties or early thirties. The average length of marriage was five years, and eight of the nine couples had either one or two children, only one of whom was over ten years of age. These adults were intelligent and had had more than the usual amount of education, since seven of the eighteen clients were college graduates and only three had not completed high school. All nine couples were self-supporting, and two-thirds of the husbands earned more than one hundred dollars a week. Eight men were employed in professional, white-collar, or skilled artisan work and their steady employment records and regular raises indicated at least average job functioning. All but one family lived in a comfortable four- or five-room apartment. Two wives were working outside the home at the time of application to the agency.

What had led these intelligent young couples, with incomes adequate to provide security and comfort for themselves and their children, to apply to a social agency? Five of the nine couples came because of marital troubles, the other four because of difficulties with their older child. No couple applied immediately following a fight in which one or the other partner had suffered physical injury. Each applicant and referral source agreed that the situation had remained essentially the same over a period of time. The intake interviews with these clients were characterized by each person's concentrating on his or her own needs and voicing repeated complaints about the spouse's failure to understand or to be helpful. These complaints were the dominant theme even when the central presenting problem was a child's difficulties.

In fact, fighting and quarreling between husband and wife remained the central theme throughout the casework contact. The marital relationships in these nine families appeared never to be truly calm and relaxed although there were brief lulls between storms. Any subject—children, relatives, sex, money, food, or laundry—could precipitate an argument. The relationships between these husbands and wives seemed to be dominated by their continuing struggle to gain control over each other. The husbands complained bitterly that their wives belittled, nagged, bossed, and criticized them; and the wives objected strenuously to their husbands' leaving them alone, not helping them at home, and not telling them everything. Verbal and physical quarrels were the result. The caseworker observed that it was during the period of relative calm between "big fights" that one partner would choose to do something known to provoke the mate—the husband would stay out until midnight when his wife expected him to come home for dinner, or the wife would neglect to have a suit pressed for her husband when he had an important business engagement. However, although each spouse complained of the other's unreasonable behavior and temper, and frequently threatened to leave the partner, only four of the nine couples had ever separated, and the longest separation had lasted only two weeks.

The tenacity with which these men and women clung to each other appears even more noteworthy when one considers that, on the surface at least, all aspects of each marriage seemed rife with irritation. In no case was there joint planning and handling of the family income; consequently, arguments about money matters were frequent. Most of the wives actively disliked being homemakers and left the responsibility for doing the housework, in large measure, to the husbands. The couples had no mutual interests or close, comfortable relationships with relatives or friends. Their sexual interest and response were far below the average for couples in their twenties and thirties; the majority of the women were frigid and most of the men had potency difficulties. In each instance, contraception posed a problem because neither partner was willing to accept responsibility. The coming of children had been unplanned in most instances and their arrival had increased the tension between the partners. The children's development and adjustment were seriously hampered by the strife between the parents. Particularly the older child, when there were two in the family, showed marked disturbances such as learning problems, stammering, thumb-sucking, excessive masturbation, inability to make friends, and so forth. In addition, there was clear evidence that more than half of these older children had become enmeshed to some degree in the parents' sado-masochistic behavior. Provocative behavior between parent and child, similar to that which led to parental fights, occurred consistently and, in turn, ended with the child's being severely punished and scolded.

To these nine couples, strife within the home was not a new experience. Each of these clients had come from a home torn by dissension, quarreling, and bitterness between his parents during his childhood. Affection had rarely been shown and punishments had been frequent. Each had left home at an early age to become a wage-earner because either the parental home was broken up or space was needed for a younger family member. Nevertheless these men and women had not entered marriage after only a brief acquaintance; the shortest courtship period had been nine months. In fact, seventeen of the eighteen clients had had grave doubts about marrying the present spouse, because they had known during the courtship that they did not share the same expectations of married life. Each had gone ahead with the marriage because he had expected the partner to change. Instead the partner had not changed and, as could have been anticipated, the home life of these nine couples and their children had been fraught with dissatisfaction, irritation and quarreling.

Psychological Characteristics

The psychological characteristics of these eighteen men and women were as markedly similar as were their social characteristics. The clinical diagnoses all lie within the range of severe character disorder, borderline schizophrenia, or schizophrenia. Examination of the ego functioning of these clients revealed that, aside from having better than average intelligence, other important aspects of ego functioning were seriously impaired. All of them showed distorted judgment, unsound reality testing, and extremely low tolerance for frustration. Since they were highly narcissistic, they had only a limited capacity to form mature object relationships. Their over-use of the defense mechanisms of projection and rationalization tended to create situations in which each felt isolated and misunderstood; their superego functioning appeared to be childlike and sometimes defective. Since their behavior was often determined by the fear of being caught, they tended to engage in questionable behavior when external controls were lacking. The absence of a mature ego or superego in these parents adversely affected their children's character development.

As a group, these were extremely impulsive, dependent men and women who lacked the ability to perceive the effects of their behavior on others. Sixteen of the eighteen frequently experienced great anxiety, but the areas in which anxiety was manifest were quite diverse. Varying types and degrees of depression and many types of psychosomatic difficulty were the most common symptom formations.

Sado-masochism was present in a high degree in all these eighteen clients. Each of these individuals revealed both sadistic and masochistic aspects, but the balance of sadism and masochism varied with each couple. In fully half of the families the husband was the more masochistic, but his sadistic side was also in evidence. The extent to which each spouse openly provoked the other was striking. A wife who knew that her husband liked a well-run house would allow dirty dishes to accumulate for several days and would forget to do the marketing. A husband who knew that his wife was possessive, insecure, and jealous would leave poems written to another woman where his wife would find them, and would stay out late without explanation. Often these individuals could describe specifically what had aroused the angry and cruel behavior in the other partner, and yet repeatedly would do that very thing. It appeared that each person had a strong underlying need to maintain this sado-masochistic relationship.

Achievement of Treatment Goals

When faced with such self-centered, impulsive clients who act out their hostility in such an extreme fashion, caseworkers often despair of effecting any beneficial changes in the family situation. Yet the findings[1] of this study revealed that substantial improvement had taken place in seven of the nine families. It should be noted that no basic personality change was attempted or brought about through casework methods, but it was possible to modify the destructive pattern of functioning of these men and women. The length of the casework contact with these families averaged twenty-two months; the longest period was four years.

The following are the four treatment goals most frequently selected for casework activity with these couples. *1] Improvement of the marital balance through modification of the sado-masochistic relationship.* This was a goal in seven cases in which the couples expressed concern about their marriage. In all seven families the provocative behavior between husband and wife lessened, and in six cases the degree of change was marked. Physical abuse stopped almost entirely in four of the five families where this had been a serious problem. *2] Improvement in the children's situation, particularly that of the older child, by reducing the parents' sadistic attitudes and behavior toward the children.* This was a goal in eight of the families. In five of them better parental handling of the children resulted. The gains made by these older children were confirmed by reports from school teachers, doctors, and group leaders. *3] Improvement in sexual adjustment, when the wife's limiting the amount of sexual activity had been extremely upsetting to the husband.* In two of the three cases in which this was a goal, both husband and wife confirmed that noticeable improvement in this area has taken place. *4] Increase in the ability of these couples to manage their current reality situation.* This was a goal in all nine cases; in six, better care and management of the home, finances, and health were clearly evident.

Importance of a Positive Relationship

The fact that it was possible for casework treatment to influence favorably the functioning of most of these couples warrants closer examination of the factors operating and the methods employed to bring about these

---

[1] The evaluation of the results of casework treatment was based on the expressed statements of the clients, the opinions of the caseworker and supervisor, and the conclusions of the study team. As had been found in other studies of the effectiveness of casework service, clients gave a higher rating to the value of the help received than did caseworkers.

changes. The material in these records clearly shows that a positive relationship between client and worker must exist if the desired shifts in behavior and attitudes are to take place. It is recognized that in every treatment relationship more effective results can be brought about if the client-worker relationship is essentially positive. With these sado-masochistic couples, however, a positive relationship appears to be one of the major determinants of the degree of success that can be obtained through casework. The experience of having a person—the caseworker—continue to be interested in and solicitous of their well-being in spite of their ill-advised behavior, seems to have made it possible for change gradually to take place in these highly narcissistic, dependent individuals who had always felt unwanted and unappreciated. When such an essentially positive relationship between worker and client was absent, the sado-masochistic acting out appeared to have become accentuated. Yet, the very traits that characterize these sado-masochistic clients frequently tend to arouse either negative reactions or negative countertransference in a caseworker. Unless a caseworker is continuously alert to his own reactions, and plans early and frequent supervisory conferences and psychiatric consultations in cases of this type, he is apt to find himself responding negatively in three areas: *1]* against the partner who is more obviously abusive and cruel, because of his own identification with the more mistreated spouse, not fully recognizing the latter's less obvious provocative behavior; *2]* against the parent's open abuse of a child, because of his own identification with the child; and *3]* against the great rigidity, self-righteousness and projection of the markedly compulsive and ambivalent clients.

In view of the importance of sustaining an essentially positive client-worker relationship in spite of provocative behavior, the question has been raised as to whether it is preferable to use one or two workers in treating sado-masochistic couples. The findings of this study are not decisive on this point since both plans were used in these nine cases with varying degrees of success.

It is also extremely important for the caseworker to ascertain each client's true situation and manner of functioning in this type of case. Owing to the characteristic way in which such clients project and distort, the caseworker needs to employ a variety of means to ensure that his own thinking is based on as correct an appraisal of facts as possible. Only under these circumstances is the caseworker in a position to help the client learn to evaluate reality factors more accurately.

Factual Data

This study highlighted the importance of having simultaneous casework contact with both husband and wife in order to obtain necessary factual information and even to approximate the reality of the situation. The frequency with which either partner is seen may vary periodically. Simultaneous contact also enables the worker or workers to understand better the family balance and to base casework treatment on it. At least one home visit is indicated since this, too, provides the worker with an opportunity to see for himself the actual interaction between various family members in the home setting. For instance, one worker had tended to discount a compulsive husband's complaints about his wife's poor housekeeping, until she visited by appointment in the afternoon and found soiled diapers on the living room floor, the room bare of curtains and pictures and the table loaded with unwashed dishes from several meals.

Collateral contacts are also essential. Through visits to schools, doctors, and others, the worker is able to correct for himself the client's inaccurate perception of the situation and can open the way for the client to make more fruitful use of such outside resources. Recognizing that sado-masochistic persons frequently tend either to deny or to exaggerate facts, the worker needs to use every available opportunity to correct his own impressions and thinking.

Four Supportive Techniques

Supportive treatment was the method selected by the caseworkers for dealing with all eighteen clients in this study. In the light of the clinical diagnoses of these men and women—from severe character disorder to schizophrenia—one would anticipate the use of this method. Although many techniques are used in the supportive method, only four proved to be the cornerstones upon which successful treatment of these clients was based. The four techniques[2] employed most frequently and with best results were logical discussion, advice and guidance, the setting of realistic limits, and reassurance. These techniques are particularly appropriate for use with sado-masochistic clients who, as has been stressed earlier, show seriously impaired ego functioning and childlike superego development. Through the consistent use of these techniques by a worker for whom the client feels trust and respect, it was possible to help these persons learn to assess their current life situation in a more realistic manner and, to some extent, to curb their self-damaging acting out.

Logical discussion was the technique most frequently used and most effective with all these clients. Since these were intelligent men and women, they themselves at times raised questions about their impulsive behavior. They responded well when the worker helped them again and again to appraise the true situation and anticipate the consequences of their behavior. For example, after one husband had given numerous illustrations of quarrels with his wife, the caseworker suggested to him that if he wanted peace at home, as he had said so many times, he would do well to stop making teasing and sarcastic remarks to his wife which he knew always upset her. Although

---

[2] A more complete presentation of various techniques employed in the supportive method of casework treatment will be found in *Method and Process in Social Casework*, Report of a Staff Committee of the Community Service Society of New York, Family Service Association of America, New York, 1958.

this man had not been able to reach this conclusion by himself, he gradually accepted the idea and quarrels at home became less frequent. Certain clients seemed able to make use of logical discussion in some areas and not in others. One wife made good use of points discussed in relation to her health and use of money, but anything discussed in relation to her older son had no apparent effect on her behavior. Since these were highly narcissistic persons, the use of logical discussion was most effective when the consequences to themselves were highlighted by the caseworker. It was thus possible to bring about considerable modification in their tendency to project blame on others and, also, to lessen the extent of their provocative behavior.

The technique of offering advice and guidance was also particularly well suited to the needs of these individuals. In order for the client to make use of direct suggestion, however, the worker had to proceed slowly and patiently and only after an atmosphere of trust and confidence had been established. Advice and guidance were found to be especially useful in working with these women in areas such as budgeting, household management, and care of the children. Here, too, when the worker's suggestions were made from the point of view of the woman's self-interest, they were more readily accepted. The emphasis had to be placed on "this will be easier for you" not on "this will be better for Jimmy."

The setting of realistic limits by the worker was demonstrated to be an important part of the treatment process in certain instances where a client showed markedly uncontrolled behavior and poor judgment. For example, after hearing from one woman the details of how she would hit, scratch, and bite her husband when angry, and after the husband had come to the office with a black eye and nail-raked face, the caseworker told her that such behavior could not continue. She pointed out to this woman that she was no longer a small child, and that a grown woman does not behave in such a manner. The worker also reminded her of her husband's frequent threats to leave her and added that some day he might do this. After this interview the client did curb this form of acting out, and the husband commented with relief that he was gratified that his wife had stopped attacking him. Improvement in the couple's situation can be furthered by such direct intervention on the part of a worker but, obviously, this technique should be employed sparingly and with discrimination. It should also be noted that when a worker who has an underlying critical attitude toward a client attempts to set such limits, further destructive acting out may be anticipated, since the worker is viewed by the client as a critical parental figure.

Similarly, the technique of giving reassurance, when used realistically and with restraint, proved beneficial. In the treatment of these dependent, self-doubting individuals, well-timed reassurance, when offered by a person whose opinion was respected, frequently lessened anxiety. For example, when the caseworker reminded one mother that a recent physical examination had showed her son to be in good health, the mother's worry about his poor appetite decreased. Although giving reassurance did not touch the client's fundamental problem, it still brought some relief to these men and women who had only a minimal ability to judge facts and feelings accurately for themselves.

In summary, these four techniques proved to be particularly suitable in the treatment of these clients, since they are designed to assist a person to perceive and appraise reality more accurately, to anticipate consequences, to make wiser decisions, to restrain dangerous impulses, and to develop the capacity for behaving in a more rational manner. The intent of casework treatment with these persons was to improve defective ego and superego functioning to whatever degree was possible.

Another technique, ventilation, was used to some degree with all these clients. Many times it was appropriate to encourage these men and women to speak freely of things in their home life with which they were so preoccupied. In certain cases, however, ventilation was encouraged to a greater extent than was advisable, considering the treatment objectives. This occurred under the following circumstances: when too much sado-masochistic gratification was engendered through the detailed description of events; when such telling encouraged the client's tendency toward projection; when there was danger of stimulating borderline schizophrenics to bring out repressed material. Material in this study indicates that the technique of ventilation should be used cautiously with sado-masochistic clients whose diagnoses range from severe character disorder to schizophrenia, since the encouraging of too much emotional release may lead to further breakdown in the client's already precarious functioning.

It was observed in a few instances that when the worker had attempted to secure and use early childhood material in an effort to give the client more understanding of causative factors in his situation, the client's current functioning deteriorated. It is understandable that such a person, whose sense of reality was poor and whose defense structure was fragile, could profit from obtaining some dynamic understanding of his current reactions but could not make use of a genetic approach. When treatment was focused on the present, observable improvement took place.

Conclusion

From the study of these nine cases, it was possible to indentify certain common characteristics of the sado-masochistic marriage pattern. The study also throws light on what treatment goals may be achieved, the effectiveness of certain treatment techniques, and the dangers to be guarded against when working with this type of marital relationship. Treating couples whose marital relationship is predominantly of a sado-masochistic type requires a large investment of time, skill in casework, and great self-awareness and self-discipline on the part of the caseworker. This study indicates that, although no fundamental change in the underlying sado-masochistic pattern can be brought about through casework methods, the pattern of functioning can often be modified. This finding becomes even more significant when it is recalled that the study shows that the sado-masochistic pattern of the parents frequently becomes the characteristic pattern of the children, particularly of the older child. Unless the sado-masochistic responses and behavior of the parents are reduced in extent and degree, the children are likely to relate to other people in this same destructive manner. Consequently it is extremely important that appropriate casework treatment be made available to such persons, not only for their own benefit but in order partially to interrupt this pernicious chain reaction from generation to generation.

The Social Worker's Role in Handling the Resistances of the Alcoholic

Robert Strayer

William Kephart's study of 1,434 divorces in Philadelphia from 1937 to 1950 reveals that 21.1 per cent of the cases involved excessive drinking.[1] Pittman's and Gordon's study of a sample of "chronic drunkenness" offenders shows that "public intoxication was responsible for 2,387 arrests of the sample population and accounted for 77.5 per cent of all their recorded arrests."[2] These two statistics emphasize the grave social implications of the alcoholic's drinking problem, implications which make this type of patient very difficult to treat.

Community attitude toward the alcoholic is generally judgmental, moralistic; the alcoholic is frequently viewed as a social leper who must be cut off from community living. Often rejected by his parents as a child, he finds he is once again being rejected—this time by society in general. He resorts to withdrawal and hostility as a defense against an apparently hostile environment, and liquor becomes his primary support in reducing the tensions of day-to-day living.

The psychiatric social worker, more than any other professional person involved in treatment of the alcoholic, is directly confronted with the backwash of problems—broken homes, emotional and economic deprivation, marital conflict—created by the alcoholic's inability to stop drinking. He operates as part of a treatment team generally comprised of a psychiatrist and a psychologist and, in some instances, an internist. The alcoholic, whose first contact at the clinic is with the social worker, frequently has conflicting desires: he wants to be helped but cannot bear the thought of a life without the support of alcohol. He feels anxious, threatened, and scorned by society. The social worker, then, in order to help the patient achieve sobriety, must overcome the patient's resistance to being helped and try to satisfy his elemental need for acceptance. By relieving immediate pressures, the social worker can reduce his client's need to drink.

[1] William Kephart, "Drinking and Marital Disruption," *Quarterly Journal of Studies on Alcohol*, March, 1954.

[2] David J. Pittman and C. Wayne Gordon, "Criminal Careers of the Chronic Police Case Inebriate," *Quarterly Journal of Studies on Alcohol*, June, 1958.

Reprinted from *Crime and Delinquency*, IX (January, 1963), pp. 39–45, by permission of the author and the publisher.

The alcoholic's basic self-involvement makes it difficult for him to give of himself in a therapeutic relationship. "To be able to keep the patient in treatment we must make him feel he is getting more than he is giving. The technical problem is how to make the giving constructive."[3] To do this, the patient must see himself as an active partner in the therapeutic relationship, not merely a passive recipient of the clinic's services. His recognition of this role depends, in large measure, on the effectiveness of the worker's rapport with the patient. Very often, the patient will come into the clinic with a severe hangover. His primary purpose in seeking help is to find relief from his hangover symptoms. At this point the patient weighs the opportunity for continued use of the clinic's services against the manner in which the clinic responds or does not respond to his need at the time. Thus, it is important for the social worker to meet his patient's need for medical attention by referring him to the clinic physician. Through this simple act of referral, the patient can perceive the dependability of the clinic. In time, the "reliable referral" may form the groundwork of the patient's trust in and acceptance of the clinic staff—making casework and psychiatric service easier for both the worker and the client.

Despite this inroad, however, the patient quite frequently fears and resents the psychiatric help he is receiving. He sees in it the possibilities of being diagnosed as a psychotic and being "sent away" to a state hospital as part of the treatment. He may openly express these feelings (which are sometimes based on early experiences in hospitals or clinics), or he may rationalize and thus evade them. The social worker is responsible for handling these resistances, for allaying the fears, and for clearing up the misconceptions so that the patient is prepared for psychiatric referral. If this is not done effectively, the patient may terminate contact with the clinic.

At intake, too, the patient often attempts to counter the worker's efforts to motivate him to constructive use of the clinic's services. He expresses this resistance in a variety of ways—for example, by denying or underplaying the severity and extent of his drinking habit, by putting the blame for his difficulties on an unsympathetic wife or an exploitative employer, or by assuming a hostile, aggressive attitude as a means of putting the worker on the defensive. Because he may identify the worker with some punitive or domineering person from his traumatic past, he may attempt to use or manipulate him, in the same way he has handled other people, as a means of getting the worker to cater to his needs or insatiable demands. It is not unusual for a patient to threaten to continue drinking, go into the d.t.'s, or commit suicide unless he is admitted to a hospital immediately. Or, if the social worker cannot get him back the job he lost because of his drinking, it is not unusual for him to threaten to discontinue treatment.

Most patients enter a clinic under some form of coercion—by an irate wife, for example, or an authoritative social agency. The worker must take this into consideration and give the patient an opportunity to ventilate

[3] Jean Sapir, "Relationship Factors in the Treatment of the Alcoholic," *Social Casework,* July, 1953.

his feelings and to identify the problem as he sees it. Aware of his patient's torment and inner conflict, the worker must listen to him with patience and understanding, at the same time avoiding emotional over-involvement in his severe problems. The patient coming to the clinic under duress is apt to identify the worker as merely another person in authority—similar to those who pressured him to come to the clinic in the first place. Thus, the patient is likely to resent the worker or "test him out" as a means of provoking rejection—an outcome that would justify his belief that he is misunderstood and unwanted. Nothing would give him more satisfaction than "finding out" that the worker, like the rest of the community, doesn't want any part of him, for then he could, with a clear conscience, terminate contact with the clinic and continue drinking.

The worker must neither be taken in by this approach nor react to it with counteraggression. Instead, he must help the patient identify and recognize his hostility; if he doesn't, he will be adopting the patient's own methods. Then the patient might well ask whether the worker is interested in punishing him or helping him. The very fact that the patient can express himself without fear of being judged or punished is in itself a means of enabling him to see the relationship in its proper perspective.

Testing Out the Worker

The alcoholic commonly understates the extent of his drinking: of course he drinks, but not like some people he knows. His wife makes too much of it. An occasional highball never hurt anyone.

Here, the worker must get through to the facts inadvertently revealed by the patient during the course of the interview. Often, these facts *directly* contradict the patient's claim to "moderate" drinking: How often is an "occasional" highball? Why should his wife "make too much" of his so-called moderate drinking? If his drinking is less serious than is alleged, how does he account for his excessive absences from his job? From here, the worker can lead the patient further: How does he use his alcohol? Is his drinking associated with situational stress? Does he have any history of blackouts and, if so, how does he see it in relation to his drinking? Very likely, the patient has never given much serious thought to the implications of any of these questions.

The essential part of this kind of reality-testing is that the patient should begin to see the facts as they really are, not as he would like them to be. For this reason, the worker himself must be familiar with the facts of his patient's drinking pattern and behavior so that he can offer him help in working through these harsh realities. This technique can be particularly effective with the patient who is not quite certain of the seriousness of his problem. It is extremely important to point out to the patient not the fact that he is "an alcoholic" but rather the manner in which alcohol is affecting his life. To the clinic, "alcoholic" is merely a diagnostic label; to the patient, it is a stigma. Being shown how alcohol has affected his life, on the other hand, emphasizes the reality of his situation.

As further means of manipulating the worker or testing out his accept-ance of him, the patient may attempt to get the worker to arrange for restora-tion of his driver's license (which may have been suspended because of drunken driving). Or, making a show of conceding that drinking in a tavern may lead to mischief, he tries to obtain his wife's permission, through the worker's intercession, to do his drinking at home. In these situations, the patient must be made to understand the role of the clinic and how the clinic functions with respect to that role. Is the worker who complies with his patient's requests subtly endorsing the latter's drinking habits? Does the patient's desire to drink at home rather than in a tavern indicate that he has little or no need of treatment? As far as restoration of his license is concerned, the worker might be wise to ask the patient whether he feels his drinking has any effect on his driving ability. The patient's recognition that it does might be a first step in helping him see that through abstinence he can possibly regain his license.

The threat to go out and drink again is another tactic the patient will use as a means of testing out or getting a hold over the worker. Instead of being thrown off balance by this threat so that he tries to counter it, the worker should analyze with the patient the reason for this threatening decision. In this situation, the worker's task is twofold. He must guard against becoming too involved with the patient, but must be able to analyze the patient's behavior in order to resolve it. The worker operating under a threat usually feels some anxiety about losing the patient. But this is an ever present risk. If he succumbs to his own anxieties and confuses his needs with those of the patient, he will be even more apt to lose the patient.

During treatment, a patient will, from time to time, break appoint-ments or terminate contact with the clinic—especially when he has been drinking quite intensively. Upon the patient's return to the clinic, the worker will have to explore the reasons for his return, at the same time indicating his continued interest and readiness to render service. The patient, for his part, should be aware that unless he makes some effort to cooperate and participate in the treatment, the worker cannot give effective help. Such cooperation can take the form of anticipating, if not actually prevent-ing, a drinking episode.

Making Use of the Patient's Feelings

Use of the patient's feelings of anxiety usually is most effective when the alcoholic coming for treatment has developed really harmful physical side effects, such as avitaminosis or liver cirrhosis, as a result of prolonged drinking over a long period of time. Where the alcoholic is aware of his poor physical condition, the worker may directly—even didactically—analyze the implications of the illness and its relation to alcohol. Part of the interpretation should always consist of informing the patient of the salutary effects of the sobriety that can be achieved through treatment. (These salutary effects, of course, should be stressed only if the patient's physical deterioration can be arrested.) The facts of a patient's physical condition can also be used in "reality testing"—i.e., what reasons does the alcoholic himself give for his physical ailments? Where the patient is worried about his job (as in the case of a person referred to the clinic by his employer for chronic absenteeism due to drinking), the social worker can exploit this anxiety-arousing situation by helping the patient analyze the relationship between his alcoholism and job tenure. Here, too, with the help of a few factual questions, the worker may enable the patient to understand his employer's position in the matter. Any decision the patient makes is, of course, his own; and the social worker must either make sure his client sees things that way or else run the risk of having his patient become completely dependent on him.

In like manner, the social worker can put his patient's feelings of guilt to good use. For example, suppose the alcoholic was referred to the clinic by the court for neglecting his children. He comes to the clinic loaded with resentment, hostility, and feelings of self-righteousness. In this situation, the social worker's duty is to help the patient see the effect of his drinking on the children. Here, too, the technique the worker employs is not one of accusation but of interest in "hearing out" the patient. Only then can the worker "feed back" the patient's own story as a means of pointing out the compulsiveness of his drinking and his need for help. The worker can also constructively channel the patient's feelings of guilt by pointing out the positive aspects of his parental behavior when sober as compared with his parental behavior when drinking. Helping the patient to see the difference can motivate him toward making a decision in favor of sobriety and continued treatment. Often, however, the very threat by a referring agency to remove the children from the home will be enough to motivate the alcoholic to taking a good look at himself in terms of his excessive drinking. At any rate, this is only part of the reasoning that goes into a treatment session with the psychiatric social worker.

Sometimes, the worker can stimulate more action by *avoiding* analysis of anything directly related to the drinking problem and, instead, by offering help with a problem only indirectly related to it. Once the patient feels more at ease and his confidence is won he may be more accepting of the worker's attempt to deal with his drinking problem and may even welcome it. The worker who helps the patient secure public assistance by referring him to the proper source can alleviate some of the pressure he is under, assure him of the worker's interest in him, and help place him in a more favorable position for examining his problem.

The patient seeking help after much procrastination and pressure has mixed feelings abour surrendering his freedom to choose between renunciation or continuation of his drinking. Finding his ego damaged by various crises in his mode of living, he will probably be on his guard, defensive—resentful of his helplessness yet anxious to assert himself. As we have seen, he may even be hostile. By supporting the patient through job placement, shelter, and removal of environmental stresses, the social worker can "set him up," so to speak, for a deeper involvement in the therapeutic relationship.

The Case of Mr. G.

The case of Mr. G may demonstrate more fully the types of resistances the worker must deal with. Mr. G, single, thirty-three years old, came to the clinic as a court referral, having been arrested for breach of the peace. A self-employed and fairly prosperous upholsterer when his drinking began to affect his capacity to work, he left the management of his business to his foreman. When he came into the clinic, his bloodshot eyes, flushed face, and tremulous hands testified to his recent drinking. He initiated the interview by berating the police who had arrested him and the judge who had lectured him. "Why was I sent here?" he inquired. "I'm not a Skid Row drunk." The worker allowed the patient to ventilate his feelings, interrupting him only to ask an occasional question or to clarify a point of information. Mr. G had at one time been employed by his father, also a self-employed upholsterer. This father, also guilty of reprimanding and scolding him, had once told his son that he would never amount to anything, that he was "a no-good drunk." Mr. G finally left his father's employ, first because he could not tolerate his nagging and second because he wanted to prove he could make it on his own.

All these facts gushed forth in a spontaneous expression of feeling. Once having finished with them, however, Mr. G glared in challenge and expectation at the worker—whereupon the worker then asked Mr. G whether he expected to receive still another lecture at the clinic. At first Mr. G hesitated. Then he smiled and remarked, "I hope not. At first I thought you were going to behave like all the others."

Having thus identified the basis of Mr. G's hostility and having set up a beginning rapport, the worker went on to explore with Mr. G the reasons for his referral to the clinic. Mr. G admitted to excessive drinking but identified the term "alcoholic" with the Skid Row type of drinker. Here, the worker, using a strictly informative approach, indicated to him the distinction between the actual meaning of the word and some of its more pejorative connotations. Mr. G's response to this was equivocal. He doubted whether he drank enough to require treatment. True, he put away a pint of whiskey a day but there were others who did the same thing and *they* were not alcoholics. Anyway, he drank only because he was nervous and had a lot on his mind and a lot of responsibilities. At this point, upon encouragement from the worker, he went on to discuss his need to prove himself to his father. He described the pressure under which he functioned in business—meeting deadlines, making decisions. When the worker inquired, "Do you think drinking is a good way of handling pressures?" Mr. G smilingly stated that he realized it wasn't, but what could he do about his nervousness? "Look at me now," he said, raising his tremulous hands for the worker to see. "I'm a nervous wreck. The booze is doing this to me. I don't eat, I can't sleep, I feel all wound up." The worker then asked Mr. G whether he wanted some help in working through some of his pressures. Mr. G agreed that he did but couldn't see how he might be helped. Referral to the physician for medication was suggested to him as a means of securing immediate relief from his symptoms. In addition, the worker offered to discuss Mr. G's problems more fully at a future date. He emphasized that any decision Mr. G might make to do something about his problem was entirely his own—not the court's or his father's—and added that the clinic would be glad to help him if this was what he wanted. To this Mr. G consented.

An analysis of the dynamics of this case makes it quite clear that the patient was confused not only about his drinking problem (in which he failed to accept himself as an alcoholic) but also about the identity of the social worker, whose image he unconsciously replaced with that of his punitive and domineering father. This misconception or "transference," as it is called, could be cleared up only through the worker's nonpunitive, permissive attitude. Also, the worker did not make an issue over whether Mr. G was or was not an alcoholic, but merely accepted him on the patient's own terms, offering service in proportion to the need as Mr. G saw it. No matter what technique is used, however, the worker must always be flexible and responsive to his patient's individual needs.

Combined Individual, Joint, and Group Therapy in the Treatment of Alcoholism

Florence Bush Preston

Perhaps the original title of this paper, which was shortened for practical purposes, may clarify more definitively the subject for discussion: namely, "The Effectiveness of a Selective Combination of Individual, Joint and Group Therapy in the Treatment of Personal and Intra-family Relationship Problems in an Alcoholic Clinic." In this context, joint therapy, in contrast to group therapy, represents therapy with two members of a family as compared to several individuals, not necessarily members of the same family, as characteristic of the group therapy situation. The joint therapy in this discussion involves marital partners.

The idea of selectively combined individual, joint and group therapy,

Reprinted from *Mental Hygiene*, XLIV (October, 1960), pp. 522–528, by permission of the author and the publisher.

tailored, so to speak, to meet the psychological and social needs of the individual patient may, indeed, be new to many of you.

The individuals under discussion include men and women patients who were problem drinkers themselves or were spouses of problem drinkers.

Some mention of the philosophical framework should be made here with regard to symptomatology and dynamics generally. The sympton of alcoholism itself, it is fairly generally agreed, appears to be determined by environmental and cultural factors. The individual who has reacted to a long-time stress situation with excessive drinking may previously have made an adequate or satisfactory adjustment to life; however, he may, over a period of time, regress to a level, in terms of psychological and social functioning, similar to that of the so-called chronic problem drinker or compulsive drinker who reveals more severe pathology originating in an early period of his life and evidenced by difficulties in family, school, work situation, etc., from an early age. This has led many clinicians who have worked with alcoholics therapeutically, to the conclusion that the absence of a significant emotional relationship early in life or its counterpart, the presence of warped, inconsistent, or pathological relationships, contributed to the psychological and behavioral picture presented by the alcoholic.

This premise is substantiated by the problem drinker himself once he is engaged in therapy; the therapeutic relationship appears to meet, in some degree, the insatiable need as expressed by the symptom, and this can result in continued abstinence or a considerable modification of the drinking pattern upon his entrance into therapy and as he becomes better integrated and more mature. One young father of twenty-eight, with three children, who sought help when his wife was about to leave him because of his excessive drinking (begun in adolescence) was able, throughout a year of therapy and subsequently, to maintain abstinence and relieve excessive tension as he resolved many personal and family relationship problems. In this family, the nonalcoholic wife's personality problems were such that the prognosis for the future marital relationship appeared questionable, not from the standpoint of the husband's drinking problem, which no longer existed currently, but from the standpoint of the wife's emotional difficulties which began to be expressed in excessive social drinking and for which she could not bring herself to seek help. This is also an example of how one marital partner may become sicker in an ailing and yet sustained marital relationship as the spouse improves through individual therapy.

Just as some problem drinkers have a basic, long-time personality difficulty which the compulsive drinking symptom expresses, and other problem drinkers seem to have regressed into excessive drinking in periods of crisis or tension, so the nonalcoholic relative represents a similar gamut of personality difficulties. The personal and interpersonal relationship problems presented by family members of the alcoholic may or may not be related to the alcoholic's drinking symptom. Some family members may be as sick or sicker emotionally than the alcoholic, but the drinking symptom itself and accompanying uninhibited behavior are so prominent that social nonacceptance (and prejudice) immediately give it primary importance to the community at large as the focus of all the family ills.

Some mention should also be made of the community facilities in relation to problem drinkers and their family members. Although there is not an alcoholic clinic in every community, there is an increasing number of social and health agencies where help can be found for the problem drinker and family members who seek it. In most communities there is an Alcoholic Anonymous organization whose members provide valuable help to the alcoholic and generally co-operate with existing agencies in facilitating treatment. The nonalcoholic wife may get help from A.A. through its Alanon group, and often this meets her needs, just as A.A. may meet the needs of her husband. The inspiration-repressive mechanism involved in this approach is effective and very helpful to many many people. Here they find a philosophy of life and people with whom to identify and discuss mutual problems. Sometimes this leads to an interest in professional help, which they may seek for several reasons: *1]* The husband's sobriety may not solve their marital problems as they had hoped it would; for instance, many wives discover difficulties in the relationship after sobriety that they had not been aware of before; *2]* The sobriety itself might end; *3]* Frequently, even after a successful period in A.A., one or both partners may feel uneasy, perhaps because of current stress in the life situation and fear that the heretofore smooth adjustment or sobriety is being threatened, and they feel the need of psychological help to avoid recurrence of the previous pattern. This help would be available through private psychotherapists and community agencies such as psychiatric clinics, family casework agencies, child guidance clinics, etc.

In discussing combined therapies, I plan to present, briefly, the main principles involved and the observed developments as they occurred.

To begin with the groups: two consisted of mixed groups of men and women problem drinkers ranging in age from the early thirties to the early fifties. Some members of the first group, which had started almost a year before the second group, continued in group therapy for a total period of 24 months. The second group met for a period of 14 months. The average regular membership in each group ranged from six to ten persons; this was true, also, of the nonalcoholic wives' group which terminated at the end of six months, according to prearranged plan. A fourth group consisting of two young married couples in their twenties met in regular group sessions over a period of three months while in concurrent individual therapy or joint therapy. One-third to one-half of each group membership were in concurrent individual therapy. Although a certain amount of group attrition resulted from the patient leaving the group to continue with individual therapy exclusively, there were some who would not have been able to enter into and sustain an individual therapeutic relationship without the preliminary of concurrent support of the group therapy experience. Individual sessions were available on request to any members not in regular individual treatment. Such sessions were requested for the handling of stress situations when the patient felt he needed help and felt unable to wait for the next group meeting (held weekly) or felt unable to discuss something in the presence of the group. The availability of such sessions seemed to serve a particularly valid therapeutic purpose; the patient could come as near or stay as far away as he chose from closer involvement. Even the occasional, and particularly the regular concurrent, individual therapy sessions demonstrated over and over again how a piece of insight or self-understanding could be helped to "break through" as a result of the patient discussing, in individual therapy, some problem or interaction which had occurred in group therapy. It sometimes happened in reverse.

Although the therapeutic principles applicable in individual work are basically part of the group process, the multiplicity of interactions and interrelationships between the various group members and the therapist provide for additional therapeutic experience not possible in a "one-to-one" relationship, such as when one member, through identification with another member's expressed feelings, is able to be freer of his own constrictions or, in reverse, by mobilizing control of emotional liability. The group is also an excellent medium for reality resting. The group setting makes it possible, particularly with concurrent individual sessions, to observe what is occurring psychologically and behaviorly with each member of the group with regard to: 1] individual dynamics,   2] the meaning of interaction of each member with every other member in the group, and the therapist, and   3] meaning of the group entity as a whole to each individual member.

Since the group setting offers rich opportunity for "acting out," the question may arise regarding the possibility of a group member arriving in an intoxicated state. It happened rarely, but it does occur. It can be a therapeutic experience for the person and the group. An example of this is the woman, a shy person with difficulty in expressing herself, who had had seven months of individual therapy before entering the group. One of her problems had been that of solitary drinking, which had not yet interfered with her responsible, long-time position. She had been under considerable stress and, on one occasion, drank before coming to a meeting, arriving quite intoxicated. She expressed pride at having "made it" to the meetings as well as remorse for her condition. She also expressed herself fully regarding the crisis situation which was troubling her and described her feelings regarding various members of the group. The group identified strongly with her because of their appreciation of her limited ability to express herself and accepted her and her behavior, althought after her departure the group needed help in handling their reactions to the experience. In another instance, a man arrived mildly intoxicated and requested concurrent individual therapy after the meeting, which he used well, maintaining abstinence subsequently. There were good immediate therapeutic results from these two drinking episodes. It is my feeling that this kind of "acting out" behavior requires tolerant but firm and consistent handling. It was made clear to the therapist, both individually and in the group, that the person was accepted, the drinking was understandable in that particular instance, but that there was no approval of further drinking. Other group members made one or two comments of a testing nature regarding drinking, which were handled in the same way: namely, that drinking was not acceptable in the group. This can be conveyed, effectively, nonverbally as well as verbally.

Perhaps it is because of the severity of the personality difficulties and interpersonal relationship problems in these patients that a varied intensification of therapy appears as a possible solution. One alcoholic patient who had been receiving both group therapy and individual therapy, concurrently, seemed unable to make much progress in terms of her disturbed marital relationship. Her husband, who had also expressed interest in individual therapy, requested it with his wife's therapist in a desire to work not only on his own personal problems (he was nonalcoholic) but also on his marital problems. Such a plan was made, and later on, joint therapy with husband and wife together was added.

The timing for joint therapy was important, inasmuch as it was at this point that the husband was becoming aware of his vicarious satisfaction in the dependency needs and "acting out" behavior of the wife because of his own unresolved problems in these areas. It was not long after this that the wife's group therapy could be terminated. It was felt, in this case, that the joint therapy was chiefly responsible for the resolution of the marital difficulties because of the direct therapeutic attention to the marital relationship in the joint sessions.

Various combinations have been utilized, with a specific goal in mind. For instance, the two young couples with anxiety about parent-child relationship problems, who met together for a three-month period, were enabled, through interaction with each other, to handle the anxiety of the two alcoholic members (a man and a woman) sufficiently to motivate them strongly to work on their disturbed marital relationships; both couples subsequently did this in joint therapy.

The use of the joint sessions has served a two-fold purpose: that in which it was the preferred form of therapy with limited goals and that of implementation to individual therapy or group therapy as described. In two instances, two couples—one in their thirties, with three children, and one in their fifties—utilized joint therapy *only* with remarkable success in a relatively short period: the first couple in a period of three months of therapy and the second in a period of six months of therapy. In both of these cases, the crux of the therapeutic interaction in the course of the joint sessions was the handling of the irrational projections and distortions of one marital partner. The unreal elements in the personality conflicts of the partner reacting in this way played the main role in disturbing the previously functioning complementarity of the marital relationship.

Nathan W. Ackerman, in "The Diagnosis of Neurotic Marital Interaction" in *Social Casework*, April, 1954, states: "The conflict between the partners" [moreover] "bears a special relationship to the structure of intraphysic conflict in each partner. The very first question to arise is: What part of the conflict is real, what part unreal and determined by neurotic perception and motivation? Further, how does the unreal part secondarily distort the relatively more real aspects of marital interaction?"

There appears to be increasing recognition in the literature on marital interaction by all the professional disciplines, that the disturbed marital relationship itself may not necessarily benefit, therapeutically, by either individual treatment of one partner *or* by individual treatment of both partners by different therapists working separately. The experience of therapists in this area indicates that attention to the multiple factors influencing the relationship are fundamental to the understanding of its complementarity and reciprocity of satisfactions within the relationship. As is true of the relationships in a group, the marital relationship is more than the sum of the personalities of the partners. The relationship can influence each partner, which, in turn, can change the relationship.

The criteria for selection of patients for any of the three forms of therapy, i.e., individual, group, or joint, included one or more of the following, in addition to clinical considerations: *1]* awareness and recognition of need for help for self in terms of own personality problems; *2]* awareness of self-involvement in marital relationship difficulties; *3]* awareness of self-involvement in parent-child relationship problems. With regard to admission to group therapy, other factors were considered, such as the patient's ability to participate in a group and, particularly, his comfort or desire for comfort in expressing himself in a group. Some were more shy and isolated socially than others. The therapeutic goal, generally applicable to all three therapy forms, was better understanding of self (in the life situation) and/or better understanding of self in relation to spouse or children.

In the alcoholic groups, because of fewer current close interpersonal relationships (many were divorced, separated, or single) these people were motivated for changes within themselves and/or their behavior. With those who did maintain meaningful close relationships, there appeared to be less conscious anxiety in this area.

In the nonalcoholic wives' group, all were mothers of young children and/or teen age children. Motivating factors which all had in common, without exception, were: anxiety regarding the marital relationship and desire for help with parent-child relationship problems. In this particular group, apart from individual changes, there were some universal ones experienced by everyone (whether the husband was in treatment or not); *1]* decrease or disappearance of anxiety and hostility toward alcoholic spouse; *2]* increase in self-interest and in external satisfactions; *3]* decrease in symbiotic relationship with spouse—seeing themselves as separate persons; *4]* recognition of own dependency needs and how handled, including both met and unmet needs; *5]* actual working through of some parent-child relationship problems, resulting in partial or total resolution of specific problems in the children.

By contrast, the results in the alcoholic groups were more individualized, although there were some common realizations by different persons at different periods in treatment, such as: reduction in impulsivity or emotional liability; understanding of patterns of reaction and behavior involving hostility, perfectionistic drives, self destructiveness, etc. One alcoholic patient who terminated at the end of one and one-half years of group therapy and one year of concurrent individual therapy, revealed, as gradual and increasingly adequate functioning occurred (i.e., psychological and behavioral functioning) the following change in pattern: "I have failed again—I give up—I blame my hated stepmother" to "I have succeeded—I can do it again—I understand why I hate my stepmother—I am responsible for my own behavior."

In joint therapy with married couples, there were the following positive prognostic indications in terms of the couples' ability to utilize help:

The initiation of the request for help was made in each instance by the spouse whose current "acting out" (i.e., drinking) symptom had precipitated anxiety and motivation within himself (or herself) to do something regarding his own personal problems as well as marital relationship problems. Subsequently, as predicted accurately by the applicants, their spouses were found, when interviewed, to be as interested in help for their own personality difficulties, in varying degrees, and also interested, and this primarily, in better understanding their part in the marital relationship difficulties; each spouse who had children asked for the same kind of help with regard to his relationships with his children. The nonalcoholic wives involved wondered to what extent they encouraged, consciously or unconsciously, the drinking problem of the spouse.

One of the chief values of the joint sessions appeared to be the immediate availability, through observation, of the kind of interaction which could throw light on the nature of the relationship as well as on the personalities of the marital partners. The joint interaction proved valuable diagnostically and prognostically as well as simultaneously therapeutic. The experiential nature of the verbal and nonverbal interaction shares some characteristics with both individual and group therapy.

From the patients' standpoint in joint therapy, all, without exception, expressed, aside from any attitudinal or behavioral changes, that early in the joint sessions they were able to discuss problems which they could not discuss at home because of upset and angry feelings. Much later in the sessions, they described increasing facility in communicating with each other at home, without tension in the area discussed earlier in the joint sessions, as the marital relationship became relieved of its stresses and strain. The focus here is as much, at times, on the relationship as on the individual patient and since social as well as psychological processes are involved, the resulting development of emotional communication between the partners is facilitated.

In concluding, a word should be said regarding the importance of the initial contact and/or beginning therapeutic period with the person who has a drinking problem. An attitude of acceptance and respect for the individual as a human being is important on the part of every staff member who comes in contact with the patient. In our center, which is a multidisciplinary setting and which includes both a medical and a psychiatric clinic, it is felt that the psychological atmosphere, so to speak, is contributed to by the total staff, including the receptionist at the beginning contact. The giving to and doing for the patient, which appears to be vital initially, is represented by the giving of symptomatic medical treatment. In initial psychotherapeutic contacts, the more active (*than usual*) participation of the therapist is essential. And as all social workers know, the quality known as warmth in the personality of the therapist is almost as, if not *as*, important as technical skill. And, finally, I would like to stress the importance of considering both the problem drinker and the relative who seek help, as human beings with just as individualized a personality and life experience as any other person who, in effect, is saying that he is unable to cope with his life situation without some help. If the alcoholism itself is seen as a symptom rather than unacceptable social or moral behavior, it is easier to find the human being who is enmeshed in its entanglements.

Addictions—Narcotics

Treating Young Drug Users: A Casework Approach

Thomas L. Frazier

A solution to the problem of narcotics addiction does not necessarily appear because of the demand for it or even as a result of vast legislation in its behalf. In fact, it is remarkable that in the face of so much interest and concern so little is known about the psychological, social, and cultural aspects of addiction, and even less about the methods of helping the addict overcome his problem.

Traditionally, it has not been customary to treat narcotics offenders through any sort of therapeutic relationship. Perhaps this is because professional workers are not customarily in settings where they are forced to deal with the addict, or perhaps it is because of a pessimism about the results of such treatment. The faulty or weak personality structure of the addict dates back to the earliest stages of infancy, making any personality changes extremely lengthy and painful, and his typically inadequate drive gives him little capacity to benefit from orthodox treatment methods.[1]

In order to understand fully the many implications in drug addiction, it would be desirable if such disciplines as sociology, psychology, medicine, and law (both judicial and enforcement) could coordinate their efforts into an efficient over-all program. Within such a program individual casework treatment can play an important role. It has been the author's experience that through intensive casework services one is able to evolve a clear diagnostic picture of the drug user and reach those areas of personality from which his conflicts and anxieties arise, to the degree that he is helped to control his impulses and gain some insight into his feelings. As casework attempts to adjust the drug user to society, however, it is equally important to attempt to deal with those community and social pressures from which his personality emerges. It is in this field that legislation would seem to be most effective.

This paper is limited to only one vector approach which reflects the

[1] Otto T. Fenichel, *The Psychoanalytic Theory of Neurosis* (New York: W. W. Norton & Co., 1945).

Reprinted with permission of the author and the National Association of Social Workers, from *Social Work*, Vol. 7, No. 3 (July, 1962), pp. 94–101.

author's experiences over the past six years in the casework treatment of young drug users. The cases described are of some thirty California Youth Authority inmates at Deuel Vocational Institution who were seen in individual one-hour interviews (in some cases supplemented by group interviews) once or twice a week on an average of between thirty and forty times. The diagnostic and treatment methods were also tested in brief intake interviews with about three hundred other young drug users.

At Deuel there is a unique opportunity to attempt the casework treatment of narcotics offenders. It is generally agreed that the most effective treatment of a young drug user can take place in an institutional setting where his basic needs will be met and where, of course, the drug is unavailable, so that he has to find some other means of dealing with his conflicts.[2] In this institution trained and experienced caseworkers have been available to help him find other means. The young drug user arriving at Deuel has been using narcotics for no more than a year or two, so that though his personality may be severely disorganized, he had not yet developed a long-standing physical and psychological dependence on drugs. Furthermore—as is generally true of offenders in this age group between 18 and 21—he has passed the extreme emotional turmoil and imbalance of early and middle adolescence and is now searching for a workable equilibrium before settling into a fixed life pattern. Finally, he is still evolving his relationships with his parents to that he is ready to enter a relationship with a worker.

Beginning the Relationship

The drug user, who is unusually fearful of relationships and who knows instinctively that counseling and the casework process have something to do with getting him to give up his one satisfying experience in life, will usually be very adverse to the idea of help. Therefore, a relationship with the caseworker must be established as early as possible.[3] More often that not the inmate brings some concern even to his first interview, but no matter how superficial and insignificant this concern may appear to be, it should be handled. Since drugs are not available in the institution, the inmate hopefully will decide to try this new approach of interpersonal relationship to help him handle his conflicts and anxieties. As he increased the dosage of heroin during the past months or years to keep going, so he now has a supply of the caseworker's understanding, acceptance, warmth, and trust that he can use in increasing amounts as his capacity for an interpersonal relationship increases.

In the drug user's past experiences with his parents a close relationship has meant becoming overdependent, being found out, getting hurt, or

---

[2] *See* Spurgeon O. English and Stuart M. Finch, *Introduction to Psychiatry* (New York: W. W. Norton & Co., 1954), p. 278.

[3] Walter C. Bailey, "The Supervision and Treatment of Paroled Drug Addicts," an unpublished paper presented at the Eighth Annual Training Institute for Probation, Parole and Institutional Staff, University of California, Berkeley, August 1956.

incurring rejection, and as his relationship with the caseworker develops he may defend himself by seeking flight into silence or intellectualization, or by withdrawing from treatment completely. If he can be helped through this stage and go on to learn that he is accepted with his shortcomings as well as his strengths, he will venture more and more into a discussion of his real feelings. At first these may be associated with his experiences surrounding his use of drugs. Most users are anxious to talk about their drug experiences, thus revealing a great many clues that point to their underlying feelings: "My mom always harped on me, and I got mad. So I went and fixed." "Stuff sure took care of my nerves and it felt good." "Junk makes you feel like Mr. Big." Sometimes the caseworker suggests a structure around which the inmate can express feelings.

> In a first interview, H defined counseling as "discussing problems," but he insisted that he had no problems. He did admit to a large drug habit, but felt this was merely a matter of his own happiness which he was able to achieve through drugs. "I did it just for kicks. It made me forget my worries."
>
> After a brief pause he wondered what he could talk about with the worker. When the worker said he could talk about anything that might seem important he could not think of anything and asked for suggestions. The worker said he might, for instance, tell of his experiences and feelings just before he takes an injection of heroin, or he might tell how he feels about people, and whether parents play an important role in our lives. Perhaps he has some special plans for his future after he leaves the institution. H became quite thoughtful, and he left the office after deciding to come back the following week, "just for kicks."

Insight Development

The task of emotionally re-educating the addict is a difficult one at best. The institution's experience with these young drug users has been to use two approaches. In the first, a covering, supportive approach, the goal has been to teach the user control over certain impulses and behavior. Although emphasis has been on treating the symptom, he can learn through the relationship to control some of his impulses that have hurt society and himself.

The second approach has involved the use of the relationship to gain insight into intra- and inter-personal conflicts. Here the treatment tools have been used to uncover and to analyze. Although it is important for the caseworker to understand the dynamics of the addict's infantile deprivations, emphasis can be on handling feelings as they appear in the present life situation. This tends to avoid lengthy and time-consuming discussions about childhood memories which often tend to take on intellectual content and thus lose their therapeutic impact.

Most addicts have guilt feelings about their dependency. In the past, parents and society have not gratified them sufficiently, but have, instead, usually deprived them of things they desired. The treatment at Deuel has been to *give* in those cases where the addict has been deprived and to let him lean on the caseworker when he cannot stand on his own two feet. As he becomes less guilty about this dependency on the caseworker, limits can then begin to be set to his oral demands. Through the relationship he can then venture into self-determined activities and turn his energies toward more constructive endeavors.

At this stage the feelings of distrust, anger, fear, and the wish for dependency are expressed more openly and directly toward the caseworker. A drug user may wonder whether counseling will work or whether he should see a psychiatrist, or he may fear rejection when the caseworker is a few minutes late. Slowly, as these fears are broken down, he may make cautious attempts at identification and begin to accept the worker's own shortcomings, such as being late for the interview. He may begin to use the self-confidence gained in this relationship with the caseworker to stand up for himself in the institution.

Because the conflicts of impulse neurotics originate in the early stages of childhood, rarely has the young drug user acquired an adequate basis of operation, pattern of behavior, or standard of conduct which he could follow throughout life. Libidinal drives have not been sufficiently sublimated, the ego has remained weak, and the conscience has not developed adequately. As the relationship develops, the caseworker tries to expand strengths and provide standards of behavior which the addict's parents did not provide. Again, a *doing* relationship is often indicated because the addict is not sophisticated or mature enough to discuss his conflicts as they appear in the interview on a verbal level alone. Therefore, a discussion involving his feelings about events and relationships in the institution will make a close relationship with the caseworker less threatening and will tie together his emotional experiences in the office interview with those he has elsewhere.

In the last stage of insight development—which is seldom if ever reached during the nine months or so of casework treatment—the drug user openly and consciously expresses his feelings toward the caseworker. He learns that the caseworker differs from people he has known before, and he is able to modify his feelings and behavior on a more or less conscious level. His libidinal instincts are beginning to be exposed and the ego and superego can now learn to come to better grips with them.[4] He learns to understand himself a little better and to be able to solve some of his problems with his parents on a more practical basis by becoming more independent of them in the manner he has learned to be more independent of the worker.

Relationship with Father

Generally, the role of the father has been overlooked in the treatment of the drug user, perhaps because society does not assign the father an important role in the psychological development of the young child, and specifically because the fathers of most drug users tend to be nonexistent, very distant, or known only through the hostile eyes of the mothers. How-

[4] Anna Freud, *The Ego and the Mechanisms of Defense* (New York: International Universities Press, 1946), p. 68.

ever, experience has revealed that the drug user's feelings about authority (as it relates to the father figure) are quite near the surface, and they are frequently an excellent vehicle for expression and handling of hostility in the first few interviews.

Anger toward the father seems somehow more "permissible" than anger toward the mother. Feeling adequate as a man in comparison with the father can be discussed more readily than the feeling of inadequacy in the presence of, or in the relationship with, the mother. The wish for a strong father can be expressed more openly than the hostility for a domineering, rejecting mother. Although the identification with the father figure is, at best, shaky and laden with hostility, many drug users will make such remarks as the following quite succinctly and early in the treatment process: "Even though I hate his guts, I can understand him better than my mother." "I know why I hate him." "I swore I'd never be like him, and yet I am." "My dad and I are both weak: he gets high on liquor, and I take a fix."

One of the aims of treatment is to help the drug user be at peace with his parents and thus with himself. This goal is quite attainable where his feelings toward his father are concerned, for as he talks about "the old man" he is really talking about himself. The recognition of an identification with the father, no matter how superficial it may be, can serve as a pivot around which many feelings of conflicts can be discussed if not solved. For instance, since the addict's symptom (use of drugs or other impulsive illegal behavior) gets him into difficulties with society, he can learn to control his behavior even though he may not fully understand the underlying conflict. The ability to check impulses, to control feelings, to endure some pain, to feel a little more adequate as a man will figure largely in the inmate's ability to get along on parole. Having recognized more clearly the positive factors in his identification with his father (through a transference relationship with the caseworker), he can now use this insight as a base to delve into similar feelings he has toward his mother. For instance, he may begin to point out how the mother sometimes drove the father out of the house. He may even side with the father against the mother, and if this happens at all on a feeling level, he may eventually try to express some feelings of hostility toward his mother.

In the final stages of treatment the caseworker is compared with the father before he is compared with the mother. At first the addict may recognize his father's weaknesses and say he would like to have a father who has the qualities of the caseworker. When he recognizes that no one can be just like the caseworker he can then separate his father's "good points" from his "bad" ones. Finally, through the caseworker's acceptance he will accept his father and thus himself. When his transference conflicts toward the caseworker begin to be resolved, this may be a sign that he is beginning to be reasonably at peace with his feelings toward his father. Some insights into this relationship have to be dealt with again and again at varying depths, and associated with various experiences in the interview and elsewhere in the institution.

The following case record illustrates how an addict made a distinction between the worker's and the father's authority.

> B compared himself to his father who had also used drugs. "I've been just like my dad, but I could never look up to him." B had expected the worker to be like his father, with lots of authority, to tell him all sorts of things and try to get him to stop using drugs. Things had turned out differently but B still felt the worker was "phony." Surprisingly, he had found himself talking about feelings that really mattered and as he did so he began to feel more adequate, in a way he had never been with his father. The worker asked whether his authority was more understandable than the father's and B felt uncertain but thought perhaps it was a different kind of authority. "If I didn't show up for one of these interviews you wouldn't let me get away with it or bawl me out, but we'd have to discuss it." He felt there was a distinction between getting angry and setting firm limits. He is often reminded in these interviews of how his father abused his position as the head of the family even though he failed miserably as a provider.

Relationship with Mother

The development of the drug user's relationship with his mother can be traced throughout the treatment process. Diagnostically, drug users generally have experienced a long history of emotional deprivation dating back to the earliest stages of infancy. Frequently, a tense, dominant, autistic, unhappy mother forced the child into becoming an adjunct to herself rather than allowing him to develop as an independent person.[5] The feeling of hostility toward the mother and the inability to form any close satisfactory relationships date back to these earliest years. The addict's conflicts reflect this oral deprivation in an infantile helplessness, and the drug helps him regress to a "happy" infancy that was never really happy. The effects of the drug handle his hostility and reduce the tensions which are symptoms of these life-long conflicts. The hostility toward the mother generally remains unconscious, but it is expressed through the use of the drug, which not only "destroys" the user but also symbolically destroys the mother whom he has incorporated through identification.[6] As the drug user rejects his mother, and thus the world, he becomes a lonely, autistic person who lives, eats, drinks, sleeps, and dreams the only salvation that he knows: his next fix.

> C, who had avoided talking about his mother for five months, finally mentioned her casually one day and smiled as he did so. When the worker asked him what the smile was about, C said that he had the feeling that the worker had often wanted him to talk more about his mother. "You probably think my mother isn't quite so hot." The worker suggested that perhaps he had some feelings on this whole subject and that he had left out any discussion of a very important member of his family. C began to talk. Whenever he wanted

[5] Leon Brill, "Some Notes on Dynamics in Treatment in Narcotic Addiction," *Journal of Psychiatric Social Work* (New York: Columbia University Press, 1954), pp. 70–71.

[6] Ernest Simmel, "Alcoholism and Addiction," *Yearbook of Psychoanalysis*, Vol. 5 (New York: International Universities Press, 1949), p. 251.

to do anything, his mother stood over him and suggested what he should do, and when he had any ideas of his own she would always tell him to do something else. Finally, he decided to go out and do exactly the opposite of what his mother said. However, he found that he was not quite strong enough to go against her wishes, until he discovered drugs, which made him feel strong and independent. He associated his freedom from his mother with narcotics. Once, he ran away from home after he had written two bad checks, and, before he got his next shot of heroin, he moved into an apartment. As he stood there he thought to himself, "Now I am really free." The worker repeated, "You felt free?" He nodded affirmatively, and then suggested, "If only I could be free without having to take dope."

The drug user longs for the mother who never provided him with real security, but his feelings toward her are not generally discussed at first. After many months, he may begin to express guilt feelings: "If I love her so much why do I hurt her by using stuff?" Later, hostility may emerge in dreams or by recalling relationships with girls or older women who were suppliers of drugs rather than true love objects. As he recalls past experiences of his mother's possessiveness and rejection, his ambivalence toward her and toward the world may cause his anxiety to reach the limits of his endurance. He may daydream about "getting a fix" and try to regress from his institutional responsibilities and achievements.

D denied any resentment toward his mother. In an interview he stated: "The other day I got a letter from my mom. She told me I was her darling baby son and she wished she had done more for me when I was a baby or that she could do more for me now." He had become so upset he tore the mattress and pounded the walls; generally he thought he had "blown it." He said, "My mother is all wrong! She took wonderful care of me. She was a perfect mother!" Although he denied any hostility he was able to see in subsequent interviews that his reaction to her letter indicated he was entering a sensitive area and he was able to face this later on.

Sexual Development

Sexual development undoubtedly plays an important role in creating an addiction to drugs. Many authorities suggest the addict's psychosexual development has been arrested at a pregenital level,[7] but the author's findings suggest that most addicts have reached the heterosexual-genital stage of development prior to or soon after their introduction to drugs.[8] This distinction is important in the treatment approach to the addict's sexual problems. It seems more likely, as Simmel[9] and Fenichel[10] point out, that a partial retreat or regression from the genital stage takes place as addiction becomes more severe, making genital sexuality less important and fusing largely into an oral, receptive adjustment. The drug then provides an experience which is more accessible and more satisfying to the addict than

[7] Donald L. Gerard, M.D., "Intoxication and Addiction," *Quarterly Journal of Studies on Alcohol*, Vol. 16, No. 4 (December 1955), p. 60.
[8] *See* English and Finch, *op. cit.*, pp. 278–280.
[9] Simmel, *op. cit.*, p. 246.
[10] Fenichel, *op. cit.*, p. 376.

the heterosexual feelings and relationship he may have had earlier in adolescence. Thus, eventually the "fix" takes the place of the sexual experience on a physiological as well as a psychological level. Finally, a sexual impotence develops which reduces not only heterosexual relationships but masturbatory activity as well.[11]

Although there is a need for further clinical exploration, experience has shown that an impressive number of drug users have homosexual tendencies. This is partially a defense against heterosexual relationships, but it arises also out of the fear of being inadequate as a man or as a person. However, overt homosexuality is not always present in drug users, and it may be one of the by-products of a generalized sexual pathology which is concomitant with the desperate need for the next "fix."

> E said the noisy guys in his unit were making him nervous and a couple of punks (homosexuals) were bothering him. He thinks he looks funny (he is physically well-proportioned) and he had this same feeling as a teen-ager. He really wanted a girl friend but he just wasn't up to the whole thing, and he began shooting dope; now there is no hope for such things.

Few of the drug users at the institution are without some kind of heterosexual identification or longing. They feel inadequate and would like to change this. Here again, the wish to be normal, the will to make a change, play an important role in treatment procedure. Because of the short time for treatment and the limited capacity of most inmates, this worker generally refrained from discussing the deep sexual pathology and tried to deal with the dynamics of the conflicts on an unverbalized relationship level or through sublimation. Support of small achievements in vocational shop, school, sports, and the like can help to decrease the fear of inadequacy. The growing identification with his father can make the addict feel more adequate as a man, and as negative feelings toward his mother are repressed or accepted, he can become free to direct his energies toward a more masculine identification.

> F opened the interview by showing some snapshots of old girl friends with whom he used to "shoot dope." He felt he was still quite involved with them and his enthusiasm was reflected on his face. He was free to talk about this kind of girl just as he is free to talk about anything with the inmates. However, when it comes to talking to his girl friend or his mother or having a close relationship with them, the "tension switch is turned on" and he feels helpless.
>
> He wondered whether his girl friend was really aware of this "messy situation." "Perhaps she wants something from me that I am not able to give." He surmised she wanted him to be strong and masculine and independent so that she could lean on him. He wanted to take care of her, and yet he has the feeling that he wants to be the dependent person himself. For the first time he was able to say that he would like to be more sure of himself, and he would like to feel that he is a "pretty adequate kind of person." The worker supported this wish, and pointed out his progress in the interviews as well as his achievements in the training program of the institution.

[11] Sandor Rado, "The Psychoanalysis of Pharmacothymia (Drug Addiction)," *Psychoanalysis of Behavior—Collected Papers* (New York-London: Grune & Stratton, 1956).

Anger and Hostility

There is a noticeable difference between the hostility expressed by the young drug user and that expressed by the more aggressive kind of offender. The armed robber, for instance, is aware of his hostility toward his victim or the world; he generally has little difficulty discussing it and therefore, hopefully, little difficulty in handling it in the treatment process. This may be one reason why his prognosis for recovery is far greater than that of the addict.

On the other hand, the young drug user who robs is seldom aware of any anger toward the victim or toward his parents who originally generated his hostility. The drug has handled the hostility, and his main interest in criminal activity is to obtain more drugs. The actual crime (burglary, theft, and—infrequently—armed robbery) is far removed from the original seat of hostility whereas the use of the drug is one step closer to it.

Quite frequently the drug user will illustrate the fact that he had been aware of a good deal of anger welling up, but that he had had neither the strength nor license to express it. "She [the mother] always had to have the last word on everything. So, before I got mad, I'd go out and fix." The hostility, then, is directed against himself. The drug becomes a vehicle for self-destruction, self-hate (including the hostility for the introjected image of mother), and self-abnegation. The ideal goal of treatment would be to help him direct these feelings toward the caseworker or toward others, but, unfortunately, this is seldom possible in a short-term relationship.

> G came to the office right after seeing his mother and father, his wife and new baby. He described his mother as a "wonderful person" but said he didn't have any real feelings about any of the family. He then began to describe in an equally bland way a robbery he pulled to get dope. The gun was at the head of the old grocer and the barrel was beginning to turn so that it would be fired in a split second. He was ready to shoot the old man although he felt absolutely no hostility toward him.
>
> Three months later G recognized his feeling relationship to the caseworker in that he became uncomfortable if not annoyed before each session. He did not talk then of anger toward the caseworker but of anger toward his wife. During one tirade, the worker kept quiet and after a considerable pause, G said, "There's a lot of anger inside me that is there all the time."

Conclusions

This approach to the problem of the narcotics offender is the result of only one perspective arrived at from the viewpoint of one worker's particular experience.

Although there is no guarantee for the success of short-term casework treatment to effect a cure of drug addiction, individual inmates at the institution have undergone changes in those areas which have brought about addiction, and many drug users have developed some insight and controls. In three hundred brief intake interviews, this diagnostic approach has been proved helpful and the means of gaining relationship has led almost all those inmates interviewed from a hostile disbelief in counseling to a demand for it. Through treatment, drug users have been helped to express feelings and to handle conflicts which have previously evoked only extreme anxiety or the concomitant use of drugs.

The following ideas, then, though they represent only a partial approach to the narcotics problem, can, the author believes, be used as a basic frame of reference for treatment on an individual or group basis, whether inside or outside of an institution.

1.   The use of narcotics is the symptom of an unresolved oral conflict which centers around an individual's early relationship with his mother.

2.   Although the mother has played the most important part in the development of pathology, the father's role, which is generally neglected, can be quite important in the diagnostic and treatment considerations. The feelings of conflict and identification around the father figure are more immediately available in the treatment procedure (particularly in the areas of sex and anger).

3.   Although drug users have regressed from the heterosexual-genital stage of development, there are certain dormant heterosexual longings which can be reactivated and strengthened—partially by strengthening father identification.

4.   Drug users express their anger through the use of the drug (in a sado-masochistic way). When they rob on rare occasions they are not expressing anger directly.

5.   Insight development with drug users is a difficult and lengthy procedure and, in most cases, young drug users can best be helped by teaching them to control their impulses and by providing experiences which are *at least* as rewarding as the effects of a shot of heroin.

6.   The institution can be effective only when all the various phases of the program are coordinated to help the inmate and when both inmates and staff work together on the common task.

There are many other approaches to the narcotics problem. For instance, the control of the importation or sale of narcotics in this country would certainly be one dramatic solution. However, as is true of all delinquent behavior, the use of drugs is a symptom of individual and social maladjustment and the person who is now a narcotics offender would probably—even without drugs—remain in some degree a malfunctioning member of society.

Benefits of "Combined Therapy" for the Hostile Withdrawn and the Hostile Dependent Personality

Edrita Fried

The range of questions which we are posing in the field of psychotherapy has grown significantly. To inquiries concerning the causes of pathology, that is, to the preoccupation with psychodynamics, a barrage of more and more articulate questions is added which are directed at problems of psychotherapeutic techniques. Today in the field of psychotherapy two sets of problems are studied simultaneously: (a) what is wrong with the patient and (b) which therapeutic techniques should be applied at what times to bring about desired changes in personality structure.

The present paper deals with a psychotherapeutic technique which can be described as "combined therapy."[1] I understand by "combined therapy" an arrangement under which the patient is seen by the same therapist, in regular alternation, in individual therapy and in group sessions. In the cases in which the following observations are based, an analytic form of treatment was applied in both the individual and the group treatment. The therapist operated on a long-range plan designed to bring about a reconstruction of the personality of the patient. Analysis of the transference both toward the therapist and toward other group members played a central role in the therapeutic procedure.

The value of combined treatment derives only in part from the fact that if a patient is seen both in group and individual sessions we have put together two good forms of treatment and thus come out twice as rich as with only one therapeutic procedure. Benefits are due partly but not primarily to the fact that the therapist knows more about the patient because he sees him twice as often and in two settings. I do not want to minimize the fact that individual sessions are of great help in understanding the complex network of defenses, the manifold infantile frustrations, and the pattern of interpersonal relations which determine the pathological character structure.

[1] Cf. Edrita Fried, *The Effect of Combined Therapy on the Productivity of Patients*, Internat. J. Group Psychotherapy, 3: 1–4, 1953.

Reprinted from the *American Journal of Orthopsychiatry*, XXIV (July, 1954), pp. 529–537. Copyright, the American Orthopsychiatric Association, Inc. Reproduced by permission of the author and the Association.

However, the primary value of combined treatment derives from the fact that certain basic processes characteristic of individual treatment and certain basic processes characteristic of group treatment impinge upon each other. In other words, the fundamental questions concerning combined treatment should deal with the cross-fertilization which takes place when two forms of treatment are combined.

In the following discussion I shall limit myself to describing the effect of combined treatment on two types of patients: *1]* patients with hostile withdrawn character structure and *2]* patients with excessive dependency strivings, a syndrome frequently referred to as hostile dependency. Combined treatment has made personality reconstruction possible in such cases in considerably shorter periods of time than would have been the case with either group treatment alone or treatment only in an individual setting. Other categories of patients, too, have been definitely helped through combined treatment. Surprisingly enough, benefits are great for overt homosexuals and impulse neurotics. I shall not deal with such cases in this presentation. However, many of the emotional problems of the two patient categories to be considered are found in other types of patients, since the various syndromes are distinguished by differences in emphasis and patterning of problems, rather than by the existence of fundamentally different strains and stresses. Thus I hope that the discussion will be of general value.

Among the patients with a hostile withdrawn character structure we include personalities with severe affect withdrawal, distortions of reality and infantile destructive impulses. These could be characterized as borderline cases or ambulant schizophrenics. The treatment of such patients in existing clinic setups is often so time-consuming that on account of limited therapeutic facilities they present a grave problem. Many hostile withdrawn patients are very unproductive in individual therapy exclusively and in group therapy exclusively. One reason is that conscious experiences are restricted owing to their limited contact with others. Their environment is narrow, almost nonexistent. Moreover, the primary reaction which is elicited is a destructive hostility of such intensity that the patients partly repress it, partly give it expression in the form of projections, and partly attempt to conceal it consciously from the therapist. It is often difficult in once-a-week psychotherapy—the kind of treatment available at best within a clinic setting—to help them reveal anything but stereotyped reaction formations in the form of meticulous politeness. In individual therapy, as against classical psychoanalysis, limited time allowance prevents the patient from making a realistic evaluation of the therapist. For instance, it is hard for the patient to assess the therapist's ability to assert and defend himself if necessary. The hostile withdrawn patient is unconsciously aware of the enormity of his hostility. Moreover, his infantile ideas of grandeur lead him to believe that his impulses occupy a place of singular importance and weight. As a result of both the existing and imagined destructiveness as well as on account of the limited familiarity with the therapist's stamina, hostile withdrawn patients fear frequently that they might injure the therapist, were they to allow themselves to give vent to their emotions. This attitude was revealed by a patient who said to the therapist, "When you offered me the last session in your evening schedule I got scared even though I wanted a late hour. I thought I might be violent. Maybe rape you, or kick you, or something. And there wouldn't be a patient after me to help you."

Observations lead to the conclusion that approximately one third of the hostile withdrawn patients overcome their inability to produce and to articulate their destructive impulses when they are placed in group treatment alone. The majority, and we may add, the emotionally more deeply disturbed, remain inarticulate. The group acts as a stimulant for their hostility and often they come close to a boiling point, but nevertheless they remain silent for months, even years. Their silence is due to a fear that the destructive impulses might prove too overwhelming or else that retaliatory measures by other members might destroy them in turn.

Under conditions of combined therapy, these patients begin to articulate fairly soon. No longer is it true that they exist in a vacuum, since the group represents an environment evoking in the presence of the therapist many interactions which can be relived and analyzed in therapy. The responses need not be admitted and examined on the spot; this can be postponed for subsequent individual sessions. By that time, the impact of the patients' primary reaction, their hostility, has weakened. This makes the initial work possible. Combined treatment gives the patient a chance to build up defenses, to form resistance, through the belated and somewhat emotion-drained examination of hate responses as well as libidinous reactions. With borderline and schizophrenic patients whose impulses have remained savage, this is exactly what is necessary. Eventually, after such belated examinations of hostility have gone on for some time, they become capable of releasing hostility on the spot in group and individual sessions.

During the period in which hostility remains inarticulate or hardly articulate, it is usually not advisable to attempt removing projections and other distortions of reality. The projections and distortions are defense formations caused by the patient's sense of rejection and hostility. The patients are not able to dispense with them. In group treatment premature attacks by group members on the patients' projections are unavoidable. The therapist, aware that hostility should be worked through before projections are attacked, is nevertheless not able to convey his own sense of timing to the group members. The latter are aroused over the distortions of their hostile withdrawn paranoid colleague and attempt to prove how irrational they are. This fact serves to emphasize how important it is in such cases to have a chance through parallel individual treatment to help the patient acknowledge and work through his hostility.

The type of patient whom I am describing has been traumatized in infancy by the most severe rejections. As a consequence he has developed a self-protective caution which sensitizes him to the most minute rejections by his fellow men.

One patient in the hostile withdrawn category, who incidentally has improved greatly through combined treatment, felt deeply rejected after two group sessions following which the therapist, contrary to her usual custom, did not reach for her notebook to enter the record of the session. The patient arrived late for the next group session, sulked and took out a notebook of his own to make entries. It was clear that he took his revenge. It may be added parenthetically that in a manner of speaking he was right as such persons are often intuitively right. The group meets fairly late and the therapist had been too tired in both instances to make the entries. This can be construed as a form of normal rejection. Healthier individuals, of course, would either not notice it or else not react in the same manner.

I have gone into this detail to illustrate how the magnified, ever-present fear of rejection increases the suffering of the hostile withdrawn patient. This is true particularly in the group setting, where frustrations, criticisms and competition are the order of the day. The therapist's attention and caution in individual treatment are the refuge to which the patient looks forward when the group rejections become too painful.

The primary defense mechanisms of the hostile withdrawn patients, besides depressions, are projection, isolation and dissociation. These operations remove them from their own feelings and, as already pointed out, reduce productivity. The patients tend to report on current or past events without reproducing concomitant feelings. Their reports are drained of emotion and the same experiences are milled over again and again. No benefits accrue from this repetition, since mastery over emotional traumata is not accomplished by repetition unless the original emotions are slowly worked through. If the therapist points out the sterile repetitiveness of the patient's productions in individual treatment such interpretations are experienced as contempt for the patient's offerings. The patient is reminded painfully of the disinterest his rejecting mother showed toward his creations. By contrast, if repetitiveness and emotional sterility are pointed out by other group members, the sense of rejection is not as great as when the parental figure of the therapist is involved.

The extensive use of the defense mechanisms of isolation and dissociation enables the patients, if therapy is conducted in an individual setting exclusively, to ward off the emotional impact of insights achieved. The patient dissociates one session from the subsequent one. Following a session in which an understanding was obtained, he comes to the next meeting as though nothing at all had happened. It looks as though he were starting therapy anew. If, at best, previous therapeutic events are recalled, the patient is likely to give merely a literal rendition of the words which were spoken without an affect equivalent. We may say that the resistance of these patients is due to their immunity to words. Owing to their infantile organization words mean little, while action weighs heavily. This immunity to words is reduced in combined treatment because of the action character that attaches to events in the group situation. A young woman tried in vain, while in individual treatment, to detach herself from her new boy friend whom she described as worthless. Her inability to break with him was due partly to a transference phenomenon. The therapist in individual treatment was auto-matically transposed into the role of the patient's mother, whom the patient was accustomed to defy by maintaining love relationships with worthless men. However, it also appeared that in the individual sessions the patient uttered her words of condemnation against the worthless boy friend in an empty manner. After she was placed in combined treatment she began to express her contempt of her friend in more vivid form. She added, "Now I want you to talk about this to me. I was glad when Helen made a grimace of disgust when I talked of Tom [the boy friend]. It is good that Richard [a group member] raised his fists. That makes it all so real, my being fed up with Tom." The action character of the communications in the group made it possible for this patient to fuse emotion and verbal content, and to become emotionally aware of her resentment against her lover.

It should be emphasized that the processes described do not take place separately in each of the respective treatment approaches. Rather, there is a constant cross-fertilization from group to individual and from individual to group sessions. The impact of emotional experience in each type of session is gradually widened and heightened through interaction between the two forms of treatment. Thus, the therapeutic progress of the patient is furthered.

We set out to consider the development of two types of patients under conditions of combined treatment. The second type comprises persons with excessive, usually overt, dependency needs, the so-called hostile dependent personalities. As in the case of the character paranoias, a major problem which these patients raise refers to the fact that the treatment process is likely to be protracted. In these cases, too, combined therapy seems to accelerate the therapeutic process. The basic frustrations of the dependent patient, his defenses, and his methods of coping with his environment differ from the syndrome discussed previously. Accordingly, curative factors as well differ partially from those operating with the character paranoias.

The dependent patient also resists release of aggressive feelings steadfastly in individual treatment. In this instance the reason is that he does not wish to endanger his dependency on the therapist. As in his everyday relation-ships, he attempts untiringly in the treatment process to secure protection from a supposedly omnipotent figure. He wants to hoard love "supplies," to use Fenichel's term, so as to have something to fall back upon in the case of frustrations and emergency situations. Because of these love demands, which are truly insatiable, the dependent patient imposes on his ego the task of continuous vigilance. The ego is to permit only expression of love and worship and to repress hostility. As a result, reaction sequences, in individual treatment, become frequently monotonous. The therapeutic process is brought to a standstill because of the patient's monotonous protestations of devotion. Exhibition of positive feeling constitutes his most potent form of resistance. In once-a-week therapy it takes a long time to reduce such resistance.

Under conditions of group treatment alone, the patient with the hostile dependent symptomatology frequently conducts himself as he does in individual treatment as far as his relation toward the parental figure of the therapist is concerned. He reveals hostility toward those in the group whom he considers his siblings or peers, but he clings tenaciously and monotonously to his love for the therapist. He plays the role of the therapist's pet, and it becomes as difficult to attack this static condition in straight group treatment as in straight individual therapy. The dependent patient wants to preserve the *status quo* at all costs. Every change produces anxiety to a point where defenses may rupture. The fluidity created by shuttling back and forth between group treatment and individual treatment, as is the case where these methods are combined, seems to have exactly this disruptive effect. The vigilance of the ego is reduced and the transference monotony is abolished. Under conditions of combined treatment patients can be observed to spread their capital around, as it were. They invest their devotion now in one, now in another figure. With a variety of transference figures present their ambivalence finally comes to the fore.

For instance, a female patient who was seen in individual treatment exclusively told the therapist repeatedly that she envied all other patients who could come to see the therapist. She wanted her sister, who was undergoing treatment, to change over to the patient's therapist. Seven weeks after the patient had been placed in group treatment also, her first expression of hostility occurred. In a sharp voice she said after the therapist had given an interpretation to one of the male group members, "You needn't have told him that. I myself could have pointed it out and anyway Bob [the male patient] has enough awareness to know himself what's cooking."

The patient with a hostile dependency, if placed in group treatment exclusively, not infrequently develops depressions which are too intense to be therapeutically acceptable. This happens when interpretations of other group members force him to realize abruptly that his customary methods of securing love are ineffective in the group setting, which is equated with the family setting. Among these methods a sulking kind of withdrawal, adopted with the intent of persuading others to coax the patient back into group activity, plays a prominent role. The intensely dependent patient, when faced in straight group treatment with either the indifference or the intolerance of his colleagues to his methods of ingratiation, is overwhelmed by feelings of helplessness, abandonment and rage. Where these feelings are particularly intense, depressions are apt to develop which cannot be safely enough reduced on the spot.

It is necessary that in cases of deep-rooted dependency needs the infantile excessive oral drives be partially gratified if they are to be eventually reduced. In the individual sessions of combined therapy the patient is given a chance to "act out," that is to say, to gratify his dependency needs. This is done, for instance, through his claim upon the undivided attention of the therapist. Partial acting out, accompanied by analytic interpretations, is one prerequisite for breaking the vicious cycle of frustration, withdrawal, increased dependency needs.

Another step necessary in order to shelve a dependency orientation is the realization, on a conscious level, that hoarding of love is not an adequate method of obtaining emotional security. In this respect the group proves to be most helpful. The negative and critical responses of group members to the patient's attempts to lean, in the face of frustration and danger, on protection by a supposedly powerful figure act as a reality pressure. The patient finds that he will earn the respect of the other group members by developing a certain tolerance for frustrations.

We have seen that in the case of patients with hostile dependent character structure, as in the case of those with hostile withdrawn character structure, group therapy exclusively as well as individual therapy exclusively presents certain problems which can be overcome only through protracted treatment. Combining these two types of therapy seems to offer special therapeutic benefits and has shortened the treatment process. This is true to some extent because each form of treatment produces specific therapeutic advantages. However, the primary gains to be expected from combined treatment derive from cross-fertilization. That is to say, the two approaches, over and above being supplementary, are *complementary*. Applied together they yield increased therapeutic benefits and help to avoid certain pitfalls during therapy in a manner paralleled neither by individual treatment nor group therapy, if each is supplied separately.

Discussion

HYMAN SPOTNITZ, M.D.: Edrita Fried has presented us with an important paper rich in observations and understanding. She has addressed herself to the psychotherapy of severely disturbed individuals such as paranoid characters and dependent personalities and has made the significant observation that she is able to obtain a more rapid rate of improvement when she treats these patients with a combination of individual and group psychotherapy than when she treats these individuals by either method alone. It does not necessarily follow, however, that similar therapeutic results would obtain if these patients were treated by someone other than Dr. Fried.

In the first place it requires a certain type of personality and unusual skill as a therapist to deal with these severely ill individuals successfully in individual treatment alone. In the second place, it requires considerable skill to handle these individuals successfully in the group setting. Many therapists have failed here. If we have a gifted individual such as Dr. Fried who is skillful in dealing with these patients both individually and in the group setting, it is inevitable that combining both methods would have even more fortuitous results and it is good for us to learn today that this is the case. It is to be recommended that whenever possible these types of patients should be treated on a combined basis, individual plus group therapy, by therapists who have skill and training in using both these methods.

What is the important factor that is added when patients of the paranoid and dependent type are handled with combined therapy? As is well known, borderline cases have fairly well fixed defense mechanisms which are difficult to resolve successfully. There are many methods for resolving these defenses when they occur as resistances in the course of therapy.[1] Unless the need for the resistances is met the individual in therapy cannot give them up; he cannot understand them, resolve them and integrate them so that they become an appropriate method of adjusting to reality situations.

What does combined therapy specially do? It must meet the needs which maintain the resistance patterns in some unique way that is not true in individual or group therapy alone. I asked one of my patients, a borderline case of many years' standing with alcoholism and schizophrenic trends to her personality, what it was that the combined method had done for her. She said that of course in individual treatment she had learned that she was exhibitionistic. She had also learned that she was shy. However, she had not *recognized* that she was *both*. Combined therapy—seeing the same material in both individual and group therapy—gave her a *combined perspective* that she had not been able to achieve previously. She therefore decided to resolve her conflict about exhibiting herself and being shy at the same time by sublimating her exhibitionism in her activities as a schoolteacher. Now she was able to show off her knowledge while teaching school; she was able to enjoy teaching school whereas previously she had hated it so.

Combined therapy greatly facilitates the *release of instinctual tension* if it is administered by a therapist who is skilled in working with both methods: individual and group therapy. Tension release and tension building as they meet the needs of the client are assisted by combined therapy. Sometimes release can occur only in a bipersonal situation; sometimes only in a multipersonal situation. Sometimes tension building requires a multipersonal situation; sometimes a bipersonal situation. The combined therapeutic method makes it possible to meet the successive needs of the individual patient in a more appropriate way and thus helps the patient toward a more gradual and less stressful type of personality repair and rebuilding.

In closing, I want to congratulate Dr. Fried on her excellent work with the patients whom she describes. She has made many valuable and significant observations.

[1] Hyman Spotnitz, (a) *A Psychoanalytic View of Resistance in Groups*, Internat. J. Group Psychotherapy, 2: 3–9, 1952; (b) "Group Psychotherapy as a Specialized Psychotherapeutic Technique," in *Specialized Techniques in Psychotherapy*, edited by Gustav Bychowski and J. Louise Despert (Basic Books, New York, 1952).

Sociopathy

The Treatment of Character Disorders

Maxwell Jones

Psychoanalysis and allied group treatment methods are accepted as the treatment of choice in the neuroses. Training in psychoanalysis is available to any suitable candidate who can afford to pay for it, and more and more analysts are turning their attention to the problems of general psychiatry, short-term methods of treatment, the special problems of institutional treatment and so on. However, there is as yet no certainty regarding the most appropriate treatment for certain types of character disorders of the sociopathic or inadequate types. The lack of capacity to form social relationships, relative inability to empathise, and unwillingness to accept the fact that they need help makes it difficult to hold them in out-patient, psychoanalytically oriented psychotherapy. For some of these cases at least it would seem that in-patient treatment specially designed to meet their needs offers a more promising approach.

In Britain the Mental Health Act, 1959,[1] enacts legislation which makes possible greatly extended treatment facilities for this type of patient and places the responsibility for their treatment on the medical profession. Perhaps unfortunately, they have chosen to use the term "psychopath" which they define in the widest possible terms as ". . . as a persistent disorder of personality . . . which results in abnormally aggressive or seriously irresponsible conduct on the part of the patient, and requires or is susceptible to medical treatment." The Act provides for the treatment of persons with character disorders (or psychopaths) whether they have broken the law or not and legislates for the transfer to treatment centres of suitable cases from the courts and from prison. Treatment may be arranged in mental hospitals, state criminal mental institutions, prisons, in special units for the treatment of psychopaths, or by probation procedures. It still remains to be seen how successfully this legislation will be implemented. In Britain as in the U.S.A. there is a strong resistance on the part of psychiatrists to this type of patient. This attitude stems from the supposed untreatability of many of these cases.

The great difficulty seems to be that the psychopath calls for treatment techniques which differ from those which apply to the neuroses. Moreover,

[1] London: H.M.S.O. 1959.

Reprinted from the *British Journal of Criminology*, III (1962–1963), pp. 276–282, by permission of the author and the Journal.

relatively little attention has been given to this topic compared with the treatment of the neuroses, and all too frequently the problem is by-passed by rationalizations which say, in effect, why bother because these people are untreatable anyway. In this connection, it would be interesting to know how many professors of psychiatry in the U.S.A. or Britain at the present time give their students any encouragement to think of this type of case as amenable to treatment. Indeed, one is tempted to go further and raise the whole question of our cultural attitudes towards this theme.

The first point I wish to stress is the psychopath's symptomatology. These symptoms belong to the so-called alloplastic group (see Eissler, 1955) where the impulse is "acted out" and results in a change in the external reality situation. In the autoplastic disorders the impulse is opposed by the individual and the conflict or tension dealt with within the psyche with resulting symptom production as, for instance, in conversion hysteria. It is the alloplastic nature of the symptoms which makes them so difficult to recognize as aspects of an illness. Stealing, lying, embezzling, etc., evoke quite different responses in people compared with the autoplastic symptoms (e.g., headache and other conversion symptoms). Moreover, the symptoms of the alloplastic disorders cause little or no displeasure or anxiety. More important, however, is the fact that the psychopath appears to show relatively little concern regarding the effect of his behavior on other people and seems to have comparatively little awareness of social values. This would appear to be related to the psychopath's inability to empathise. (Parker, 1957.) Piaget (1932) has shown that this process of social learning is characteristically found in children's games and behavior around the ages eight to ten. In the psychopath, however, group values have never become an integral part of his personality, and this defect is given none of the interest or understanding shown to other forms of mental defect which are unquestionably recognized as "illness." Along with this anomaly of growth is found the essentially "selfish" characteristics of the psychopath where the achievement of instinctual gratifications without delay and the apparent absence of conscience loom large.

Society may be loth to label the psychopath as ill, but certainly the psychopath himself is even less willing to consider himself in this light. This is not surprising when one considers the inability to form object relationships which characterizes this condition. He feels isolated and unwanted but sees *others* as misguided and hostile rather than himself. There is considerable evidence to support the view expounded by Bowlby (1951) and others (Gesell and Amatruda, 1947; Spitz and Wolf, 1946) that these unfortunate people lack the stable parent figures which are essential for the early development of object relationships and for the incorporation of such figures in the development of a relatively benign conscience. All this contributes to the initial difficulty in treating the psychopath. How can one help him unless he himself wants help? Even if the fear of punishment drives him to seek help how can one help him to form a relationship with the therapist when he cannot relate for any length of time with anyone? How can he talk about intimate things with the therapist when part of his problem is his inability to communicate subjective matter? How can he accept help from a doctor who is clearly associated with authority, and this is particularly true of prison doctors or cases referred for treatment from the courts?

It is because of the above considerations that most of us who have to undertake the in-patient treatment of these people prefer to do so in an environment which has many of the characteristics of a therapeutic community.[2] In such a setting the aim is to offer the new patient a peer group where authority is minimized and the opportunities to form relationships maximized. The more the patient can come to identify himself with the treatment unit the more will he be prepared to examine his own behavior and compare his own norms of behavior with those of the group. Moreover, many of these patients have never felt that they "belonged" anywhere and everything should be done to achieve this feeling. By elevating the status of patients and giving them the greatest possible number of role-playing opportunities, including active participation with the staff in group treatment and other responsible activities, we can do something to overcome the feeling that the staff are privileged, distant people who speak another language and are identified with authority rather than with the patients. Above all, we have got to find ways and means to overcome the individual's inability to form relationships. All staff and patient roles are important in this respect and we feel that *any* relationship can help provided the danger of defences such as "pairing off" or other special and often neurotically determined relationships can be avoided. We believe that treatment can be aided by a generally accepted "feed back" system, so that communicated material comes back to the group with trained staff present. We go even further and feel that the therapeutic culture is enhanced if the majority of staff and patients come to feel that no communications should be automatically regarded as privileged and any relevant material made available to the group if it is thought to be in the patient's own interest.

We are considering patients who are, in the main, unwilling to participate in treatment. The social climate in an established therapeutic community helps to overcome this resistance. "The therapeutic community is distinctive among other comparable treatment centers in the way the institution's total resources, both staff and patients, are self-consciously pooled in furthering treatment. This distinctive way implies above all a change in the usual status of patients. In collaboration with the staff, they now become active participants in the therapy of other patients and in other aspects of the overall hospital work tasks—in contrast to their relatively

[2] See Jones (1959). There are several units for the treatment of character disorders and other types of patients which have the characteristics of a therapeutic community. Examples include Atascadero State Hospital and various projects in the Department of Corrections in California; in Europe, Dr. Landers and his colleagues at Wormwood Scrubs Prison in London, Professor Baan and his colleagues at the Van der Hoven Clinic in Utrecht, Dr. Stürup at Herstedvester near Copenhagen, and the Social Rehabilitation Unit at Belmont Hospital near London, now renamed Henderson Hospital.

passive, recipient role in conventional treatment régimes. (Jones, 1959.) The establishment of an appropriate therapeutic milieu alone will not overcome the communication difficulties and emotional estrangement of the individual who has never been able to form social relationships. It seems fairly certain that these "affectionless characters" need skilled psychotherapy, but whether this should be on an individual or group basis or both is still an open question. Our own preference is a combination of community[3] and group methods, with a minimum amount of individual contact between doctor and patient. The doctor or treater[4] lends his skills to the understanding of the current scene. The therapeutic culture exerts pressures to talk about feelings and examine behavior not only in the formal group treatment setting but in informal situations too. It also approves the examination of the motives behind behavior, particularly deviant behavior, and the implication that any patient can give as well as receive treatment. All these pressures contribute opportunities for the treater to exercise his skill. He does so not only in the daily group of his own patients but also in the community meetings with the other doctors and core staff present. This procedure means that day after day the whole community examines the deviant behavior of some of its members and the implication is that such behavior should and can be modified. Such a belief clearly helps therapy but cannot be maintained unless patients are aware of the improvement in their social relationships not only in the relatively artificial atmosphere of the institution but also in their relationships with people in outside life. Family groups within the institution can help this process, as can frequent home visits at the rehabilitation stage of the treatment.

To be able to communicate with patients with severe character disorders the doctor or therapist needs to be able to relate to them at a feeling level. These patients are frequently not able to express abstract ideas or conceptualize, and for this reason as well as their difficulty in forming a positive transference they cannot easily benefit from individual therapy. They act out their feelings on their environment and this form of immature communication must be understood and used in the therapy. Also, the therapist in a therapeutic community is a real person with personality characteristics which are well known to the patients. In these circumstances it is difficult for a patient to maintain a transference image for long, and indeed it becomes extremely difficult to know what *is* transference in these circumstances. The fact is that, even more than in small therapeutic groups, transference tends to become diluted in various people in the total community. Nevertheless, the recognition and handling of transference and counter-transference does have an important place in treatment, particularly in the later stages. Another factor determining the doctor's treatment role is

[3] By community we mean the involvement of all patients and staff in treatment in both the formal and informal sense.

[4] There seems no reason why a psychiatrist should be the therapist. The important considerations are training and personality and not the possession of a medical degree.

his association with real life situations, in which he is quite unlike the psychoanalyst. We cannot play an objective, neutral, purely therapeutic role but have to take on realistic and restrictive roles at times. We cannot, as in the case of the psychoanalyst, leave this to be dealt with by the police and outside society. As delinquents, particularly those with a low social maturity rating (see Grant, 1959), tend to respect individuals who can manipulate their environment to suit their own ends, the treater has to be ready to "outsmart" the patient and unhesitatingly call his bluff, expose his deceit, etc. This kind of relationship is essential early in treatment but is not limited to the doctor-patient relationship. Few doctors have sufficient familiarity with the domestic or cultural milieu of the patient to be able to play this role with any marked degree of success. Luckily, in a therapeutic community this role relationship is frequently met by one of the patient's own peer group.

Once the patient has begun to identify with the community, treatment becomes more circumscribed. He now begins to internalize many of the values held by the group and begins to be aware of the effect of his behavior on other people. (This represents a transition from alloplastic to autoplastic behavior.) This phase is familiar to the patient population themselves who often refer to it as "so and so is coming into treatment" or more indirectly as "one has to get worse before getting better." At this point treatment takes on a much more familiar picture. The treatment challenge represented by the type of patient we have been discussing is to get him to the point when he can form social relationships and identify with a group. From the administrative therapeutic point of view this is the point at which controls from without should increasingly give way to controls from within.

In brief, the therapeutic community as I have attempted to describe it in very general terms affords, at the early stages of treatment, a milieu where the new patient, isolated and unable to form relationships, suspicious and fearful of authority, can relate to his peers sufficiently to test out possible ways of altering his behavior and attitudes. The skill of the therapist lies in his ability to communicate and feel for the patient and achieve status in his eyes by being smarter than he is. Having achieved this he then has to help the patient to see what there is for him in social change. At a later stage in treatment the therapeutic community affords the patient increasing role-playing opportunities and puts pressure on him to supply his own controls from within.

Bibliography

Bowlby, J. (1951). *Maternal Care and Mental Health*. Geneva: W.H.O. Monograph Series No. 2.

Eissler, K. R. (1955). *Searchlights on Delinquency*. New York: International Universities Press.

Gesell, A., and Amatruda, C. (1947). *Developmental Diagnosis: Normal and Abnormal Child Development*. Second Edition. New York.

Grant, J. Douglas, and Grant, M. Q. (1959). "A Group Dynamics

Approach to the Treatment of Nonconformists in the Navy." *Ann. Amer. Acad. Polit. & Soc. Sci.* 322, 126–135.

JONES, MAXWELL (1959). "Towards a Clarification of the 'Therapeutic Community' Concept." *Brit. J. Med. Psychol.* 32, 200–205.

PARKER, SEYMOUR (1957). "Role Theory and the Treatment of Anti-Social Acting Out Disorders." *Brit. J. Delinq.* 7, 285–300.

PIAGET, J. (1932). *The Moral Judgment of the Child.* New York: Harcourt Brace; London: Routledge.

SPITZ, R. A., and WOLF, K. M. (1946). *Genet. Psychol. Monogr.* 34, 57.

Sexual Deviations

Casework Treatment of a Homosexual Acting-Out Adolescent in a Treatment Center

Sidney Wasserman

In this paper I should like to focus on an adolescent whose primary symptom was homosexual acting-out behavior. The main attempt will be toward demonstrating that casework techniques can be applied in such cases, with encouraging results. In addition, the treatment of this adolescent is within the milieu and controlled setting of a residential treatment center.

Because of the severity and deep-rootedness of the problem, the treatment should be done only under close casework supervision and psychiatric consultation. Conferences between the caseworker, casework supervisor and psychiatrist were held to determine the applicability of casework to this boy.

Because of our limited knowledge in the treatment of sexual deviations such as overt homosexual behavior, we caseworkers approach individuals of this symptomatology with understandable reluctance and hesitancy. Certainly the significance and handling of such a symptom in an adult may differ considerably from that of an adolescent. This is specifically so because such behavior in adolescents is frequently part of the normal adolescent conflict.

We know that with the onset of puberty the adolescent is torn asunder. At this stage of life there is an upsurge of libidinal energy which breaks down the rapport that had temporarily resulted between the ego and id (during latency). Impulses (aggressive and sexual), which during latency were brought under balance, at adolescence create an onslaught which overwhelms the ego and superego. The adolescent suddenly indulges in activities which heretofore had been considered taboo and he (or she) begins to resist and rebel against all forms of authority.[1]

The adolescent whose behavior is manifested by the symptom of homosexual acting-out presents a unique problem. It is at this period of life that the

[1] Anna Freud, *The Ego and Mechanisms of Defense*, 158–70.

Reprinted from *Mental Hygiene*, XLIV (January, 1960), pp. 18–29, by permission of the author and the Journal.

adolescent is seeking identifications. Frequently the young person forms an attachment to another of his or her own sex and age which takes on the form of passionate friendship and love. Because of the pressing conflict of instincts, the attachment may be expressed by overt homosexual behavior. It is therefore difficult to determine at what point the adolescent is forming a homosexual, pathological adjustment which may become a fixed pattern and perhaps be irreversible, and what is merely the "temporary" acting-out which will gradually be replaced by stronger inner controls and defenses.

In working with this particular adolescent boy, it became extremely important that the psychiatric recommendations and suggestions be such that they could be implemented by casework technique and the environment. Because the homosexual problem in this case had become a conscious matter to the youngster, the casework treatment needed to be geared to reality and ego support. The amount of ego needed to be determined as well as the degree of reality assessment and inner anxiety. Sublimating outlets for the aggressive and sexual impulses and activities that would be supportive and stimulating to the ego had to be provided by the environment.

This is the case of A, a tall, sandy-haired green-eyed, sharp-featured, bright, handsome young man of 19 with a well-built body of almost classic proportions. He was placed at the treatment center when he had just turned 14 years old. At the time, he appeared older than his age owing to his almost mature-looking build, his outward poise and politeness and his well-dressed appearance.

He is the eldest of three boys and one girl, his brothers being four and a half and six years younger, his sister seven years younger. He comes from a mixed marriage; his father is Jewish, his mother Gentile.

Since the age of five (according to the parents) A presented problems. He lied and stole, and was uncooperative in any routines such as eating, washing, family rules, etc. For periods of time he was enuretic. In general, he was very immature, even infantile, and tended to isolate himself from both peers and adults. Occasionally he was extremely provocative to younger boys and sought out opportunities to beat them up. In spite of superior intelligence, he did poorly in school, failing in several subjects and receiving gratuitous D's in others.

A severe and hostile atmosphere existed between A and his mother, who was controlling, aggressive, ambitious and competitive with him. She had a strong need to mold him into a submissive, polite boy. The marital situation was a poor one in that the husband was most passive and reluctant to assume a more assertive role as husband and father. He worked in a factory and was consistently reminded by his wife of his inadequacy as a successful breadwinner. In all, the role of disciplining the children was left to the mother, which was undoubtedly overwhelming and frustrating for her. A had particular difficulty with his next younger brother C, whom he described as always being favored by his parents, particularly his mother. A seemed almost indifferent to his other siblings.

As his behavior progressively deteriorated, it became of extreme necessity to remove him from the rejecting, tense environment of the home. On his arrival at the treatment center he made a most promising, appealing, initial impression, but underneath the clean-cut, wholesome look was a deeply angry, damaged, frightened, sensitive, unloved child who had, in a large sense, given up on himself.

In brief form this, then, is the history of A and some of the presenting problems. It did not take long to observe that the pleasant, seeming out-goingness of this boy was superficial—and he didn't allow relationships to develop beyond the superficial. During the first six months of casework interviews, A handled all reality discussion by flights into fantasy. He insisted on talking about jet guns, model rockets and "super bathyspheres." He denied any reason for being at the treatment center except difficulty in school and escaped all discussions as to feelings around placement and separation from home.

During this period, it was decided through supervision, psychiatric consultation and a staff planning conference that the caseworker should hold up reality whenever possible. It was felt important that in order to reach this boy the caseworker should talk at some length with him about rockets, jet guns, etc., and of his plans to construct such projects. The psychiatric thinking, at the time, was that such inventions might be a projection of himself and the telling of these inventions to his caseworker might be his way of wanting the worker to be his friend. Talking to A about rockets and guns was seen as a means of establishing a relationship with A and of break-ing through his defense of being totally self-reliant, independent and self-sustaining. By so doing, we hoped that A's feelings would then come to the fore and the desire for a relationship would take hold.

At the end of the first six months there was the first discovered incident of A's engaging in homosexual play with one of the younger boys of another cottage. This was then followed by A's first admission that he "hated" the center. His homosexual acting-out with younger boys increased. When con-fronted with this by cottage personnel and the caseworker, he was vigorous and hostile in his denial. With the emergence of this acting-out came increased overt hostility along with frequent withdrawal and isolation. However, there was a decrease of fantasying, especially with the adults in the cottage, and as he gave up the fantasying, the overt homosexual behavior continued. Throughout the first year of casework contacts, A's defenses seemed to be primarily projection and denial manifested by flights into fantasy. He was also suspicious, and frequently accused others of spying on him.

Throughout that fall he developed a strong, homosexual attachment to a 12-year-old boy. A freely admitted that he "loved" the boy very much, "more than he ever loved" his parents or brother. At this time it became necessary to set up extra controls and supervision for A to protect him as well as the other boys. He was not allowed in the younger boys' cottages (unless accompanied by an adult) and he could not invite them up to his room.

The group contagion of the problem, because of the normal existence near the surface of such feelings in adolescents, can present considerable difficulties in maintaining outer controls and limiting the acting-out whenever possible.

The previous summer, I had worked as a counselor with A in his cottage. By the end of the summer he had told me of his homosexual feeling toward the 12-year-old boy to whom he had such a strong attachment. In the fall when I returned to the center as a caseworker (A's worker was leaving) A was assigned to me.

In his first interviews with me he referred back to the previous summer when he admitted his homosexual problem to me. I accepted what he said but did little or no exploring except to underline that this was a problem and that he seemed worried. Over a series of interviews he admitted his concern more and more and began to bring out that he feared he could not control his acting-out. This admission came after I took a definite stand to the effect that having and talking out these feelings was all right but that acting them out was unacceptable. This became the theme of our contacts for about six months.

During this period, on the basis of the presenting material the psychiatrist pointed out that A could be treated only if he felt more anxiety. This caution was based on the fact that A was acting-out and showing little concern about his behavior. The acting-out interfered with treatment and it would have to be brought under control before he could be reached. The lack of anxiety, it was stressed, made treatment of such overt behavior unpromising. However, it was decided that I continue to try to stir up his anxiety by pointing up his behavior as unacceptable and by telling him that he was expected to learn to control it. The need to hold up reality to him and to support his weak ego whenever possible was stressed by the psychiatrist.

With the implementation of these suggestions and direction, A became noticeably anxious. He began to hide his face, when talking to me, shielding his eyes with his fingers and looking down at his feet. He spoke of how "ashamed" he was and said he would "rather be dead" than talk of his homosexual feelings. I had to assure him that talking was right. When he spoke of his fear that he would not be able to control his feelings, I was reassuring but firm. I let him know these feelings were rough on him but said he was expected to learn to control them; this was what society and the center expected of him. Furthermore, I told him he didn't help himself by acting-out as he involved another person, and this was serious. I underscored my concern for him. His behavior could only bring trouble and hurt and unhappiness. He had been hurt and unhappy enough.

With this kind of empathizing, A slowly started to bring out his negative feelings toward his parents, particularly his mother. He felt his parents did things wrong and said he couldn't stand it when his mother yelled and screamed at him. He recalled the constant arguments in the home and said he was always fighting with his mother, sometimes with his father, and practically all the time with his brother. He brought out that his parents had often sent him away. He recalled that when his brother C was born he was sent to an institution for six weeks. He was mistreated there and, according to him, his parents didn't seem concerned. He felt he had been tricked into coming to our center. He had thought he was coming to a "glamorous" setup and had not been told that this was an institution for emotionally disturbed children. He hated his parents for sending him here. It seemed to him that the only children who came here were those who were "useless and whom nobody wanted." He wondered if "this is really life?"

By that winter A began being extremely hostile to me. One day after I had watched a basketball game at the center's gym, in which A participated, he came for his appointment and blasted me. I was "spying" on him. He didn't want me ever to come to the gym again. When he calmed down he was able to admit that seeing me outside the office was upsetting to him. In the next moment he exploded and insisted that I was "not curing" him. The only reason he was coming for his interviews was to let me know how much he hated me.

Concurrent with these expressions of intense hostility toward me, there were rather dramatic changes in the cottage. A became an active participant in group activities and was thoroughly enjoying the participation. He began to stay with the group and to take on a leadership role. The boys showed a real respect for what he had to say and offer, and his ideas started to be "picked up." He appeared to be more genuine and friendly. Most of all, there were fewer and fewer incidents of overt homosexual behavior. Though his sexual behavior was better controlled, he was most stimulated in the evenings when the boys took showers. He would wait until all showers were taken and then he would sneak into the bathroom. If sexually aroused when accidentally seeing a boy in the nude, he would start to yell, have a temper tantrum, and then bring himself under control.

In his casework interviews, his hostility, after about six months, began to lessen. He spoke of feeling better and talked about being in a "neutral zone," of not feeling sexually attracted to either boys or girls. For the first time he recognized that he was being helped, and the tone of his conversations began to change from "I can't be helped" to "I have been helped." At one point he said: "When I came here, I knew right from wrong but it made no difference to me, for I had no past and I didn't feel I had a future. Now I can look at my past a little bit and I feel I have a future. I was like a little boy in a big world and I felt very lost."

After two and a half years of failures and marginal work in school, A completed junior high school with D's and some C's. His greatest difficulties were in concentrating, in his short attention span and in continually daydreaming. However, the first signs of a freer, spontaneous manner appeared and there were the beginnings of achievement.

Late the following summer A was seen by the psychiatrist (in order to verify casework impressions). It was felt that he was showing better control of his sexual problems. He refused to discuss his sexual problems with the psychiatrist, which was indicative of having built up some defenses around this. He related on reality subjects, which suggested increased ego strength. The psychiatrist felt I should allow A to talk about his homosexual problem as much as he wanted.

Around that period, A was also re-tested by the psychologist. Two and a half years before his tests revealed a picture of a boy functioning intellectually in the bright normal range (full scale IQ 114). Now his intellectual level was in the superior range (full scale IQ 121). Two and a half years before he resisted any forms of self-expression by maintaining a rigid guard and refusing to expose himself. Now he was still somewhat restricted but he showed a remarkable change in the freedom and spontaneity of expression within the bounds he had set up. He showed a neurotic type of adjustment but more social awareness.

For the next six months however, A seldom spoke of his homosexual feelings except to say that from time to time he got aroused and anxious. But he was able to keep these feelings under control. With the internalization of his anxieties and the controlling of his acting-out, he showed more concern about his physical health. Through most of his interviews, he kept telling me that his heart was beating too fast and that he feared it would stop or that "a bubble or something like it" was trying to pass through his heart.

As he spoke of his life, he said: "What can I do? I can't live with my parents. I have no future, my life is ruined, there is no one to love and if I can't love my parents, there's no one." I acknowledged his concern around this and also pointed out how far he had come, particularly in showing better control of his behavior.

With the lessening of verbalization of his homosexual feelings, and the revealing of increased inner controls, the diagnostic picture changed. It had been about a year and a half since the psychiatrist had indicated that A could be treated only if his anxiety became apparent and that this could occur if his acting-out could be brought under control. Now homosexuality was seen as a neurotic symptom; the boy would require intensive treatment. The psychiatrist suggested that I point out to A that he could talk to me about his sexual problems but that he might someday need more intensive help from a psychiatrist. He felt it important that I point out to A those goals and areas in which I could be of help to him. A's signs of increasing ego strengths, according to the psychiatrist, made the prognosis more favorable.

At the same time, in supervisory conferences, it was felt important that I help A to see his parents more realistically, to see that they were confused and unhappy. I might point out that as a child he couldn't help reacting the way he did—with anger. It was important, however, that he realize he had his own life, that though he couldn't change the past he had a responsibility to himself about the future. We needed to help him develop a concept of self and to recognize himself as separate from his parents. The symbiotic and seductive relationship with his mother could be countered by helping him to see his separateness and to see that what he wanted and did with his life rested with him.

In the months that followed I began to initiate and implement the plan that evolved in the shared thinking of the psychiatrist, supervisor, staff conferences and myself. By the following winter A was letting me know that I wasn't "giving him enough." He kept expressing the wish that I were a psychiatrist, and spent much of his appointment time wanting to know why I didn't become a psychiatrist. He informed me that he was still occasionally bothered with his feelings toward boys but said he could control them, adding that sometimes he didn't even have to think about controlling them— "it just comes natural."

Around that time he showed a strong interest in hypnotism and insisted he was going to hypnotize other boys on campus. I was definite in stating that hypnotizing other boys was very serious and was prohibited. A exploded, demanding that I allow him to hypnotize others. He insisted that I never allowed him to do anything. A few days later I was visiting in the cottage when A called down from his room and asked me to come up. When I arrived I found him in the process of hypnotizing one of the boys. I asked the boy to leave. After the boy left A raged at me. When he calmed down I pointed out that he was not a physician, that he had done something illegal and dangerous, and that I did not want any harm or hurt to come to him.

In a pathetic, grateful manner, he answered: "When I lived at home my parents never allowed me to grow up or do anything for myself. Sometimes I did things behind their backs and then I felt bad inside. Because you mean so much to me and I don't want to feel bad I won't hypnotize others."

Somehow I felt this incident may have paralleled in A's mind the time his mother walked in on him and his brother C when they were involved in homosexual play. A couple of weeks earlier A had recalled this episode in an interview with me. He remembered how hysterical his mother had become and how she had screamed at him about his "naughtiness and filth." Furthermore, she had protected A's brother and had blamed A entirely for luring his brother into it. This was devastating to A.

Early the following spring A began talking to me of his feelings toward girls. He said he was no longer so shy, and found it easier to talk to girls. He began to hang around the girls' cottage and started to learn to dance. Several girls showed a pronounced willingness to get closer to A, but their eagerness frequently made him withdraw from them. He talked then of being more interested "in photography than in girls."

His hostility toward his parents lessened. He was seeing that although his parents were no different, he could get along better with them during his periodic visits home. One day he said: "Before I came here I just existed, but now I am a person." He asked me if I knew the "turning point" in his life and then added: "When you became my caseworker." After telling me this, he became demanding and angry, and maintained that I never did anything for him. He wanted a car. Why wasn't I a psychiatrist? At one point he asserted that I was a "nice guy" but as a caseworker, "you stink." At another point he yelled at me: "Don't you realize that what you say affects my life? You make me sick. Every time we talk I go back to the cottage with an upset stomach and a headache."

That fall, four years after coming to the center, A began speaking of leaving and going home to live, "where school is easier." He started hypnotizing boys from my caseload. In psychiatric consultation I stressed the feeling that A seemed distressed about his feelings toward me and that aside from anger he somehow wanted to run from me. The psychiatrist pointed out that A was expressing homosexuality through hypnotism and was having a homosexual relationship with me by hypnotizing boys of my caseload. He needed to deny my importance to him and I needed to bring it out. It was felt that I should point out to him the defense and denial of his feelings. By so doing I would be supporting his ego and at the same time pointing out that it was one thing to have these feelings and another to act them out.

As I did this with A, he insisted that he was upset because I was a "lousy caseworker" and not important to him. I brought out that it was all right for him to have feelings toward me. If I weren't important to him I couldn't help him. Slowly he mellowed and said: "When I was a homosexual I used to believe I could not be cured. You told me you thought it was too early to tell and you thought I could have feelings toward girls. At first I didn't want to have feelings for girls, but now I have and maybe you can help others the way you helped me."

During that winter A continued to address himself to his leaving the center and to his future. He showed considerable concern about his inability to function on a higher academic school level. He was less sure that he could learn in school "if he wanted to." He became most angry at me whenever I pointed out that he had big ideas about his future but did nothing about them. For example, he spoke of going to college but didn't study. I questioned his desire to go to college. He insisted that he did and pointed to his parents' desires and expectations. When I wondered what his desires and expectations were for himself, he showed confusion and anger. I had, consistently, to separate him from his parents and to emphasize the importance of formulating his own goals according to his own needs and desires.

What was most noticeable in his interviews from about the fourth year of treatment to his discharge after five and a half years of treatment was that his homosexual problem no longer became the focus of our discussions. I slowly moved from defining what was permissible (talking) and what was not (acting-out) toward emphasizing that the past could not be changed but that if he wanted to do something about his present and future, he could.

Significantly, during the spring before discharge, when he was particularly anxious about his feelings of separation from me, he said: "I'm afraid that you see me by my past and as I was." He justified the changes that had come about in him by saying: "Each person has a pattern. If one is raised in a pigsty, he lives like a pig. I grew attached to my mother and I had problems. I didn't know another way of life. Then I came here, and I wanted to change. It wasn't easy. I had to fit into a different pattern, the right one. Lots of times I didn't think I could change, but I did, and now I've learned to do things that give me satisfactions. I don't have to slip back."

The summer before his discharge, A was active in the campus council. He also had but one more semester to go before completing high school. During the summer he went to his home community to be with his parents as his father had been paralyzed. A's mother brought considerable pressure on him to stay home and assume the "father-husband" role. In conflict, A returned to the center and began his final semester of school. He needed assurance that it was all right for him to plan for himself. I recognized that, as unfortunate as his father's illness was, taking on the responsibilities of the household was too much to ask of the boy. A took a part-time sales job in one of the local department stores; he felt he had to help his parents financially.

As he became calmer about the home situation, he once again focused on himself. He spoke of being able to enjoy "little things like people and everyday occurrences." He went on to say that he accepted the fact that he would "never be a very happy person." He spoke of graduation, and of going home to live and then on to college at the start of the fall semester. At one point he said: "Don't worry. I'm not going to stay home indefinitely. I'll go to college and then the service. You see, I am really thinking of myself."

A few months before discharge A addressed himself to the changes that had occurred during his five years of treatment. Interestingly, he summarized: "I knew reality but I didn't want to change. I did it for you, but I think the environment may have been just as important as you. It's like one big experiment all mixed together, and it came out well. One thing I can say for myself: I think I like life, and that feels good."

At the time of his graduation, during one of his last talks with me, he summed up his treatment: "There are three things that happen to a kid in treatment. First, he needs to be removed from the environment that was making him unhappy. Second, he comes to the center where he is shown new ideas and a better world. And third, he has to want to change. But once he is shown that he has problems, he usually wants to change." He ended by telling me that what he wants most in life is "knowledge" and that only by "learning" does he truly think he'll ever be "happy".

It would be deception to conclude that A is now "cured." His problems around aggression, sexuality and inadequacy continue to plague him, but his ego has developed sufficiently that he can cope with these conflicts and use his abilities more adequately. It is very likely that at some later time in life he may very well need additional help and treatment.

At the point of discharge he had become quite the "lady's man" and enjoyed a more comfortable social relationship with girls. As he became involved with a particular girl, however, he frequently or eventually dropped her, feeling he couldn't trust her.

His fear of rejection by girls and women often provoked him to reject them as a means of defense. He sensed the capacity for love and the potential to give within women but feared the possibility of their withholding or withdrawing love. Whether he could work this out sufficiently to make an adequate adjustment remained to be seen.

A came to the treatment center consumed with hate and guilt. At the time, his homosexual acting-out was an attack against all the deprivations and injustices that had been inflicted upon him against his will. Each agressive sexual act only increased his guilt and created further anxiety, necessitating further acts and additional guilt. Such a socially unacceptable and threatening symptom brought on considerable environmental hostility for him. He was in desperate need of love, acceptance and understanding, and the symptom of homosexuality was, in a way, a defiant act and manner of gaining love at any level, as well as a symbol of his tremendous castration anxiety and the fear of taking on a more masculine role. It is interesting that his homosexual partners were invariably younger boys (about his brother C's age). Because C as well as his brother J and sister B were so favored in A's mother's eyes, is it any wonder that A sought what made the younger ones, particularly C, so loved, adored and acceptable? At the same time, he could hostilely bring his brother and all "younger brothers" down to his level (which, according to A's self-image, was of the lowest form).

Perhaps the greatest all-encompassing quality which prevailed within A was his engulfing feelings of unending loneliness. He was in frantic need of a relationship, one that could accept him and maintain social standards which gave him the control that he lacked and longed for. The giving up of the symptom was more than he bargained for but it became possible because of his desire to please a loved adult. In attempting to control his acting-out, he became noticeably more anxious and conflicted. His ability to suppress and later repress these impulses began to increase, however, and his inner controls became effective in coping with outer stimuli. With the ability to control came stronger feelings of enhanced self-worth and confidence. Having an opportunity to express his anxiety, fears and self-hate not only alleviated the pressures and served cathartic purposes but enabled him to rebuild his defenses and redirect libidinal energy into culturally acceptable modes of behavior.

It is interesting to note that the facing of the homosexual symptom and the conflict concerning it led to discussion of A's basic feelings of hate and retaliation, which he harbored and repressed against his parents (particularly his mother). What emerged was an overwhelmed, damaged child who had identified, to a great degree, with the aggressor (his mother) in order to avoid complete annihilation. He had endowed her with magnitudes of power and even admired this all-powerful force which had become almost a monster in his life.

On the other side of the coin was his anger at his father. He looked to the male of the family for the protection he sought from his mother, but he found an uninvolved, passive, frightened man who allowed the mother to rage and lash out without stopping her. To A, this could only mean further rejection and abandonment.

In treatment, the caseworker played a constant and consistent ego supportive role. At times he became the target which absorbed the anger projected and transferred on to him by the boy, whose hate needed to be released and accepted without retaliation. As A began to see to whom his hostility was directed, he began to bring his parents, especially his mother, down to human-sized proportions. Slowly he learned that women were not necessarily female Cossacks who flung sabres about on helpless boys. This became most evident when he began to relate on a closer level to his female resident cottage counselor, a kindly, intelligent, non-threatening, maternal woman. This was not done without months and even years of testing inter-mingled with all sorts of accusations and verbal attacks. This was A's pattern in every attempt at relating. He needed to provoke and reject others because he himself feared attack and rejection. Even today he sometimes resorts to this method of relating, when he is limited by someone in authority or when he senses his need for acceptance by a person in authority.

After years of testing the counselor, one day he told her: "Do you know that you and my caseworker are the two most important people in my life?" At that point he endowed the counselor and caseworker with all the qualities that he felt lacking and that he wished for in his own parents.

A crucial point in A's treatment was when he re-enacted through his worker the homosexual acting-out with his brother C, in the presence of his mother, by hypnotizing another boy when it had been defined (by the worker) that this practice was unacceptable. A was needing to re-live and undo this traumatic experience and was attempting to master it by repeating it. According to Thompson:[2] "In the transference, the patient repeats his childhood experiences, both good and bad. It is further observed that not only do people tend to repeat earlier life situations in the transference, but there is a general tendency to repeat life patterns over and over again. Human behavior is dominated even more powerfully by the tendency to repeat former patterns of life than by the pleasure principle." With the re-enactment A was finally able to see that the adult was interested in pro-tecting him and wanted no harm to come to him. The worker did not condemn and reject; instead, he limited A's action because of his concern for A's well-being, which to the boy was an indication of love and acceptance. What followed was a recognition on A's part that he had done things behind his parents' back that made him feel "bad." He now felt that he no longer needed to resort to this pattern of behavior. He was now freer and able to use his resources much more adequately.

At no time in treatment did the caseworker interpret to A the boy's fears of castration, homosexual-masturbatory or incestuous fantasies. Such an interpretation would generally be avoided in casework. (The caseworker may

[2] Thompson, Clara, *Psychoanalysis: Evolution and Development.*

not be able to select his clients but he can be selective in how he deals with them. A variety of casework approaches can be applied.) Instead, in this case the worker chose to provide casework that was ego-supportive, on the theory that this had much to offer an adolescent whose primary symptom was homosexual acting-out. It was an educational process in which the worker held up reality to the adolescent and thus supported his weak ego. He pointed out the unacceptable behavior (homosexual acting-out), conveyed the feeling that the adolescent could control this, and supported him when he did show control.

For example, to bring the homosexual acting-out of A under control and to bring his anxiety to the surface, the worker had to take a definite, firm, non-punitive stand based on his concern and his desire to protect. To have been indefinite and non-committal would have been permissive and would almost have encouraged further acting-out. Such an approach might unconsciously have meant to the adolescent that the worker lacked standards, and eventually the acting-out might have become a delinquent interplay with the worker. By being firm and insistent, the worker practically coerced the adolescent into facing his anger, hate and anxiety. A was given confidence through the relationship and as a stronger ego developed, he saw that he could function successfully in many areas (as a campus council participant, athlete, cottage leader, student, salesman, etc.).

Empathy and acceptance were also important. A needed to know and understand that the worker was aware of the existence of his feelings and of how difficult they were to live with. As treatment progressed, the worker focused on the concept of self and supported the healthy part of the boy's personality. He helped him to see his separateness, to evaluate his parents more realistically, and to see, first through the worker's interest and then through other relationships, that he could be liked.

Today A manages to live with his parents and is about to enter his freshman year at a state university. There is every indication that he will be able to make an adequate adjustment to life. However, if his problems again overwhelm him, he has strengthened himself enough to know that help is available to him and he will seek it.

In such a case, psychiatric consultation helps the caseworker to understand the diagnosis, to delineate the problem and the dynamics involved, and to set realistic goals within the framework of casework methods. The casework supervisor guides the worker toward helping the adolescent learn to accept his parents, to emancipate himself from them, to develop a concept of self and to use his potentials. This combination of effort—psychiatric consultation, casework supervision and casework—brought this case to a successful conclusion.

Bibliography

Bychowski, Gustav, "The Ego and the Introjects," *Psycho-Analytic Quarterly*, 24 (1955), 516–26.

———. "The Structure of Homosexual Acting Out," *Psycho-Analytic Quarterly*, 23 (1954), 48–61.

Freud, Anna, *The Ego and Mechanisms of Defense*. New York, International Universities Press, 1946.

Freud, Sigmund, *Basic Writings of Sigmund Freud*. New York, Random House, 1938.

Grauer, David, "Homosexuality and the Paranoid Psychoses as Related to the Concept of Narcissism," *Psycho-Analytic Quarterly*, 24 (1955), 516–26.

Johnson, Adelaide M. and S. A. Szurek, "The Genesis of Antisocial Acting Out in Children and Adults," *Psycho-Analytic Quarterly*, 21 (1952), 323–43.

Kolb, L. C. and Adelaide M. Johnson, "Etiology and Therapy of Overt Homosexuality," *Psycho-Analytic Quarterly*, 24 (1955), 506–15.

Lewinsky, Hilde, "Features from a Case of Homosexuality," *Psycho-Analytic Quarterly*, 21 (1952), 344–54.

Litin, E. M., M. E. Griffin and Adelaide M. Johnson, "Parental Influences in Unusual Sexual Behavior in Children," *Psycho-Analytic Quarterly*, 25 (1956), 37–55.

Sperling, Otto, "Psychodynamics of Group Perversions," *Psycho-Analytic Quarterly*, 25 (1956), 56–65.

Thompson, Clara M., *Psychoanalysis: Evolution and Development*. New York, Hermitage House, 1950.

Casework Treatment of Sexual Confusion in Character Disorders

Beatrice Simcox Reiner

In a large proportion of cases of marital conflict, uncertainty about his psychosexual identity is a problem presented by one or both partners. According to its severity and the ways it is expressed, this problem is referred to as sexual confusion, sexual distortion, failure to fulfill the sexual role, or sexual role reversal. Caseworkers often approach such cases with natural uneasiness because of the seemingly random expression of psychosexual maladjustment and the fact that they have been exposed to a variety of generalizations on the subject. One of these generalizations is that sexual disorders cannot be treated by caseworkers. Another is that lack of psychosexual identity is caused by a combination of cultural influences and individual factors[1]—an explanation that, without more clarification, may convey a

[1] Sue Vesper, "Casework Aimed at Supporting Marital Role Reversal," *Social Casework*, Vol. XLIII, June 1962, pp. 303–304.

Reprinted from *Social Casework*, XLIII (December, 1962), pp. 538–545, by permission of the author and the Journal.

discouraging sense of inevitability. Perhaps it would be worth while to examine the effect on casework practice of various generalizations about psychosexual identity, and to see if some of its expressions may be viewed in a more meaningful way.

An Unscientific Approach to Sexuality

No other generation of caseworkers has been so subject to the temptation of succumbing to easy generalizations as is the present one. Evidence may be found in Morton Teicher's article "The Culture of Concepts" and in the letters to the editor it stimulated.[2] In spite of the heat engendered, however, the correspondents seemed to agree that it is imperative that concepts be formulated and that the most important issue is the way the caseworker uses them. A similar conclusion was reached by Victoria Olds in her clarifying article about role theory.[3] Caseworkers are influenced, however, not only by concepts drawn from psychology and sociology that are finding their way into casework thinking but also by some much less specific sociological generalizations that have gained currency in the mass media. These latter generalizations represent oversimplifications that can become clichés or catchalls preventing the caseworker from engaging in further questioning. In the end, too-ready acceptance of theories that have no scientific foundation may lead the worker to adopt an attitude of hopelessness about the possibility that individual clients can change.

Caseworkers should be suspicious of "popular" sociological theory that offers too pat an explanation of human phenomena. One of the best ways of achieving understanding about the relationship between cultural change and individual psychosexual development is the traditional method of case exploration. Within any conceptual framework we employ, it is only through careful case-by-case study that we can understand the similarities and differences that occur and the backgrounds of the characterological phenomena we see. We tend to forget that, as caseworkers, we have access to more dynamic case material on these issues than any other professional group, since our clients represent a cross section of American life and since our interview material has a high degree of validity because clients give it in the context of a meaningful relationship.[4] In this period of extensive generalization we must retain our curiosity, value our observations, and re-evaluate our own attitudes. We should not forget that significant new knowledge usually gives rise to more questions than answers.

[2] Morton I. Teicher, "The Culture of Concepts." *Social Casework*, Vol. XLII, December 1961, pp. 491–93. "Readers' Comments." *Social Casework*, Vol. XLIII, February 1962, pp. 86–88.

[3] Victoria Olds, "Role Theory and Casework: A Review of the Literature." *Social Casework*, Vol. XLIII, January 1962, pp. 3–8.

[4] Beatrice Simcox Reiner, "Some Meanings of Identity for Casework." *Smith College Studies in Social Work*, Vol. XXXII, October 1961, pp. 1–19.

At a recent meeting attended by family caseworkers,[5] Otto Pollak speculated that caseworkers are operating on the basis of Victorian or pre-Victorian concepts of masculinity and femininity, and tend to be disturbed by unfeminine women or unmasculine men. As a result, they may be working against the cultural stream and be unreceptive to the possibility that new cultural modes of expression of the relationship between the sexes are emerging. Perhaps Pollak's analysis is correct. Are caseworkers suffering from a separation between thought and feeling that permits them to believe that personality is a mixture of male and female components while their emotional reactions are still influenced by an outdated "norm" of sexual behavior?

Moreover, caseworkers should give up the naïve belief that somewhere in the world there are large numbers of "normal" families, unknown to them because they come in contact only with pathological families. Irving Harris has done his best to explode this myth.[6] In recent mental health surveys of mid-Manhattan and of a semi-rural county in the Maritime Provinces of Canada, it was estimated that the mentally "healthy" in these areas represented 18.5 per cent and 17 per cent of the population, respectively.[7]

Another possibility for confusion lies in the fact that Western culture not only blurs the differences between what men do and what women do but simultaneously makes us acutely aware of the male or female "image" created by certain external signs. The power of advertising is such that the average client has become adept at reproducing the proper image and the average caseworker is unconsciously influenced by it. Assessing the male or female identity of a client is not a simple task; the most feminine-appearing woman may be the least motherly or sexually adequate, and the most virile-appearing man may be able to love no one but himself.

Sexual Identity and the Character Disorders

Psychoanalytic theory holds that true male or female identity is achieved only when the oedipus conflict has been resolved; therefore, most persons with neuroses or character disorders are confused about their sexual identity and role. Caseworkers are familiar with some of the sexual aberrations associated with the neuroses, but they are less knowledgeable about the sexual confusions manifested by persons with character disorders. I should like, therefore, to review briefly the problems of sexual identity associated with various types of character disorder. I shall place special emphasis on

[5] Middle Atlantic Regional Institute of the Family Service Association of America, Bryn Mawr, Pennsylvania, June 1961.

[6] Irving D. Harris, *Normal Children and Mothers*. Free Press of Glencoe, New York, 1959.

[7] Reported in *Mental Hygiene News*, New York State Department of Mental Hygiene, May 1962; based on a paper by Dorothea C. Leighton, John S. Harding, and Charles C. Hughes, of Cornell University, presented by Dr. Leighton at the annual meeting of the American Psychiatric Association, Toronto, Canada, May 7–11, 1962.

the anal-erotic and the phallic-urethral types, since many of the obvious and marked problems of sexual identity are to be found in persons fixated at these levels of psychosexual development.[8]

In the oral-erotic character disorders, sexuality represents the gratification of thinly disguised oral needs, including the need for closeness and for kinesthetic pleasure. Sexual promiscuity in a person with this disorder may indicate that these needs are insatiable and that he is engaged in an endless search for the all-gratifying lost mother.

The person who has an oral-sadistic character disorder also expresses his oral needs through sexual behavior, but his affect is somewhat different. In contrast with the oral-erotic person, his early experience of severe oral deprivation has made him pessimistic, angry, and convinced of his unworthiness. Through a form of identification with the aggressor, he has come to believe that he does not deserve much. As a result, his love relationships often have a masochistic quality, as if he has no right to expect anything better, or he gets vicarious satisfaction from a relationship with someone even more needy than himself. Within this group of severely deprived persons are to be found the addict and the potential addict.[9] The sexual role is relatively unimportant to the person with an oral character disorder, since all his relationships are basically those of mother and child. Only with resumption of the growth process can we expect any change in his psychosexual behavior.

The person with a character disorder of the anal-erotic type, which represents fixation at the earliest stage of toilet training, is engaged in rebellion against controls. To such a person, masculinity and femininity are synonymous with strength and weakness, independence and dependence. He shows signs of being bisexual and is unwilling to give up either aspect of sexuality. A parent with this disorder often wants to fulfill both the maternal and the paternal roles in relation to his children. Furthermore, he has a somewhat confused identification both with the parent who controls and with the child who rebels. Rebellion against control may be revealed in rebellion against all accepted standards, as is the case with the "beatnik." It may also be expressed in difficulties with employers or, more constructively, in unusual or creative approaches to artistic or practical problems. The lack of a clear sexual orientation frequently results in a broken marriage or in competition with the spouse over which should assume the male role and which the female. The client with this type of character disorder resists discussing his sexual confusion as such, since he knows it is socially unacceptable; at the same time, he does not find it entirely ego-alien.

Casework treatment of the client with an anal-erotic character disorder consists in helping him form a relationship with the caseworker that can

[8] Beatrice Simcox Reiner and Irving Kaufman, *Character Disorders in Parents of Delinquents.* Family Service Association of America, New York, 1959, pp. 37–65.

[9] "Report of a Three Day Conference on Narcotic Addiction and the Teenager: Prevention, Control, Treatment." In-Service Training Department, New York City Youth Board, New York, October 1959.

permit a resumption of emotional growth through new identifications. Resumption of emotional development is a slow process, but it can activated if a treatment relationship can be established and maintained. Treatment consists, in part, in helping the client form new concepts of masculinity and femininity that do not include the old stereotypes of strength and weakness, exploiter and exploited.

A person with an anal-sadistic character disorder, for whom sexuality has a strong sado-masochistic component, usually holds rigid ideas about the proper sexual role for a man and for a woman. When he has some doubt about his own masculinity or femininity, he adheres to these rules of behavior even more strictly. If his marital partner has an anal-erotic or a phallic-urethral character disorder and is inclined to make his own rules, the marital conflict is intensified.

The Phallic-Urethral Character Disorder

Problems of sexual identity often emerge with particular clarity in the treatment of the client with a character disorder of the phallic-urethral type. Since he is fixated at the pregenital level of development dominated by the penis, he is acutely conscious of sex differences and inclined to be preoccupied with them. Characteristic traits of this type of client include exhibitionism, competition, motility, and facility in manipulation. He wants to have the best or the most of everything, and he wants to be admired.

Although the phallic period of development encompasses the oedipal phase, the person with a phallic-urethral character disorder has predominantly pre-oedipal characteristics. For the most part he does not reveal the neurotic symptoms, the hysterical behavior, and the preoccupation with triangular relationships that characterize the person struggling with unresolved oedipal conflicts. Occasionally he may have transitory hysterical symptoms, especially if he presents a "mixed" type of pathology. For the most part, however, he resembles the child who either has not yet reached the oedipal phase or has retreated from it.

Why does a person become fixated at the phallic-urethral stage of psychosexual development? As is true of earlier pregenital fixations, one or more of three important factors are likely to have affected his development: loss of a parental figure, marked inconsistency of early handling, or family troubles affecting the parents that coincided with a crisis point in his psychosexual development. One frequently finds that he has suffered from particular kinds of loss or inconsistency: absence of the father or of a father-substitute during the phallic period; identification with the mother through close and intimate contact with her; reversal of roles by father and mother; insufficient maternal tenderness coupled with brutal rejection on the part of the father; a tendency for the parents to bribe the child by giving him "things" instead of affection; or the parents' need to equate the child with a phallus and stimulate his showing off, combined with failure to meet his needs on his own level. Such a child experiences no true latency, but continues to indulge in sexualized aggressive behavior throughout childhood and into adult life. As an adult, he is primarily narcissistic and has poor capacity for establishing relationships, although he may be charming and seductive.

Since the person with a phallic-urethral character disorder has an infantile superego structure, consisting of partial and inconsistent identifications with the parents, he suffers from objective anxiety rather than guilt. In other words, the sources of his anxiety are external rather than internal. Like persons with other types of character disorder, he allows himself to feel very little anxiety; he avoids it by seeking gratifications (chiefly some form of personal aggrandizement), by experiencing speed or motion, or by manipulating others. Power and possessions are important to him. Caseworkers may be misled by certain similarities between this client and the anal-sadistic client, but the differences between them must be accurately assessed if treatment of either one is to be successful. The person with a phallic-urethral character disorder seeks *power* to promote his own ends; the person with an anal-sadistic character disorder seeks *control* to defend himself from his own forbidden impulses (and those of others) and from his projected aggression, thereby assuring his own safety. Similarly, the phallic-urethral person's use of possessions for conspicuous consumption is different from the anal-sadistic person's investment in owning things as a protection against need or as a self-reward.

The person with a phallic-urethral character disorder is well attuned to our culture. He is aware of what others think of him. He is prone to use effectively the advertised trappings of sex (perfume, cosmetics, jewelry, clothes, and cars) in order to create the impression he regards as male or female. This behavior is part of his search for identity. To the woman of this type, holding a job may be an assertion of her femininity rather than a sign of masculinity. She wishes to be admired as a woman, and a job may put her in contact with men who treat her as a sexual object, who "kid" with her, or who are fatherly to her. In certain jobs she may also get vicarious feminine pleasure—for example, by making other women beautiful. Before the caseworker decides whether the woman client's wish to work has primarily a male or a female connotation, he needs to know what the job means to her, possibly on several levels.

Case Illustration

In the case of the J's, discussed below, the caseworker's failure to understand the meaning of Mrs. J's problems of sexual identity resulted in slowing up the casework process.

> The J family came to the attention of a family service agency when Mr. J complained that his wife was spending more and more time in a dress shop owned by her parents. After several interviews the caseworker was inclined to attribute Mrs. J's behavior to childish dependence on her mother and to a

rejection of femininity. It was some time before the worker secured sufficient additional material to clarify the real meaning of Mrs. J's behavior. In her relationship with her mother, Mrs. J actually revealed few of the characteristics of a small, dependent child. Rather, what became evident was her fixation on her mother as the primary love object (inverse oedipus) and as her major source of identification. Moreover, this line of work reassured Mrs. J about her own femininity through her identification with her mother, who worked to make other women beautiful, and through her modeling in fashion shows.

Mrs. J's lack of interest in housework was not based on rejection of the feminine role. In her childhood, the household chores had been done by a neat, unglamorous aunt who was restrictive with Mrs. J and against whom she had rebelled passively. Therefore, in Mrs. J's mind, doing housework was not associated with being feminine. Her mother's only interest in the house had been in buying furniture. One of the chief battlegrounds between Mr. and Mrs. J was what Mr. J regarded as his wife's extravagance in furnishing the house.

Mrs. J's father had been the more maternal parent. It was from him that she had developed a certain potential for parenthood, but it had been obscured by her struggle to be loved by her mother. Like her mother, she had returned to work as soon as possible after the birth of her baby, leaving his care to paid housekeepers. During his infancy, she had often lingered at work to avoid his feeding time because she felt that his poor appetite was a sign that he rejected her.

Mrs. J had always been embarrassed when her husband demanded a show of affection from her in front of her parents. Her reaction was not the inhibited response of the girl with an oedipal conflict who fears her mother's disapproval of her affection for any man who represents the father. Rather, it was caused by her perception of the competition between her mother and her husband as the primary love object. (The inverted oedipus represents the early passive oedipal attachment to the mother that, in the case of the girl, precedes the active oedipal wish for the father. The combination of a seductively dominant mother and a disappointingly passive father can contribute to the girl's failure to develop further. When treatment of such a girl is successful, oedipal wishes begin to emerge.) Mrs. J's intense jealousy of her younger sister, toward whom her mother had developed a seductive attitude after Mrs. J had stopped working, provided some confirmation of her attitude toward her mother. Mrs. J was also depressed, since she was cut off from all her main sources of narcissistic supplies.

Mrs. J had married a man who was passive like her father and who appeared easy to manage. However, he also represented some aspects of her mother, especially the disapproving, punitive ones. The fighting between Mr. and Mrs. J was described by the caseworker as a battle for "control." Actually it was more than that—it was a fight for "power," a fight to establish who was the boss. The words "control" and "power" may seem to be synonymous, but clinically they hold different connotations for treatment. The fight for power is typically phallic-urethral in its competitiveness, whereas the fight for control suggests anal-sadistic anxiety about control of the impulses.

Some Aspects of Treatment

Once the problem of sexual identity was opened up in the casework interviews, Mrs. J showed her eagerness to work on it—a reaction character- istic of many female clients with phallic-urethral character disorders. Some of them are avid readers of "confession" magazines or other forms of popular literature that offer them some comparisons with their own lives. Such a client is likely to say, "I could write a book myself." Many of them have had a history of lifelong oral deprivation combined with disappointment in the father who was lost or who submitted to the mother's domination. (There is some indication that having a father who was "lost" leads the woman to act out more extensively the ambivalent wish for a father.)

The woman who has a phallic-urethral character disorder suffers from low self-esteem, which must constantly be bolstered through her interaction with others. She has an intense longing to be understood, which is often the key to establishing a casework contact with her or losing her as a client at the very beginning. She is sensitive to conventional platitudes that miss the essence of her feelings. There is wide variation among such clients in the depth of their sensitivity and, therefore, in the length of time before they can trust the caseworker. The client whose character disorder has a strong anal-erotic component may quickly reach the point where the caseworker can, with a light touch, hazard a guess as to what is going on, in the knowledge that the client, whose basic wish is to do everything herself, will toss the suggestion aside good-naturedly if it is incorrect. Another client, however, for whom being understood is a primary aim, will feel that a wrong explanation by the worker creates a barrier in the relationship and is evidence that the worker is just like her mother. In spite of this strong wish to be understood, the woman with a phallic-urethral character disorder often has a fear of closeness that is related to losses she suffered in childhood. This fear should alert the caseworker to the importance of being always available to the client but not letting the relationship become an intense one.

The strength of the phallic-urethral fixation and the extent and kind of acting out are always related, however, to the severity of the client's early losses and the patterns she evolved in adolescence for dealing with them. The chief hazard in treatment lies in her tendency to become depressed, which may, in turn, lead to increased acting out, if not to attempted suicide. In many instances, the acting out itself is motivated by strong self-destructive impulses.

The male client who has a phallic-urethral character disorder is frequently more difficult to engage in treatment than his female counterpart, because his search for psychosexual identity so often takes a more symbolic form, such as preoccupation with making money or with "hot rods." He tends to be less articulate, since in our culture talking about oneself and philosophizing are regarded as feminine. The threatened break-up of his marriage sometimes keeps him in treatment, and it is then possible to form a relationship with him that will permit discussion of his defensive behavior. For example, in the J case discussed above, Mr. J was able to see how his attempts to "prove" himself by undertaking "impossible projects" were related to his lack of identification with his father and had been intensified by an incapacitating illness at a critical time in his childhood.

Other Manifestations of Phallic-Urethral Disorder

The phallic-urethral character disorder has a wide variety of manifestations. For example, Mr. or Mrs. J, both of whom are "uneasy", resemble the early adolescent who is attempting to establish himself as a person. Another manifestation is to be found in the blatantly exhibitionistic "psychopath," who exploits any situation for his own ends and seems devoid of conscience, guilt, or conflict. Included in this diagnostic category are many "call girls"[10] and Don Juans. The proverbial "psychopath" is someone who appears "larger than life" because of his mobility, his unconflicted aggression, and his ability to charm. His lack of genuine sexual identity and his inability to establish relationships are betrayed by the trail of broken marriages and liaisons he leaves behind him. Only rarely does a person with this severe type of phallic-urethral character disorder come for help to a social worker or sustain the contact if he does come. The problems for the caseworker who has such a client are finding a casework goal that will seem worth while to him and controlling his tendency to manipulate the worker. An excellent example of this process is to be found in Nathan Ackerman's description of his treatment of Jim.[11]

Another type of phallic-urethral character disorder is characterized by ego restriction. To the person with a restricted ego, sexual expression and open aggression are taboo. He denies the desire to compete with others and emphasizes the virtues of getting along with people. In contrast to the exhibitionism and the fondness for conspicuous consumption displayed by the "psychopath," his tastes are subdued and he underplays the importance of possessions. The person of this type has a fear of whatever is different from himself and shows a tendency to marry someone with whom he can identify. This behavior resembles a characteristic, transient stage of early adolescence—the stage of denying sexuality and of loving only a person who is like oneself. A married couple who share this disorder maintain a kind of "collusion"[12] to deny sexual differences; thereby, envy, anxiety, or aggressive feelings are avoided. Sexual relations either are severely restricted or merely give the partners a sense of becoming one. In such a marriage, the crisis comes when one partner begins to have feelings, possessions, or activities of his own—in other words, when he resumes the interrupted growth process. Children are often regarded as alien intruders into the marital relationship.

Erik Erikson has ascribed ego restriction, in part, to the abdication of parental roles; the male ideal is exemplified by the maternal grandfather rather than by the father, who is more like a big brother. Sexual rivalry with

---

[10] Harold Greenwald, *The Call Girl*. Ballantine Books, New York, 1958.
[11] Nathan W. Ackerman, *The Psychodynamics of Family Life*. Basic Books, New York, 1958, pp. 240–246.
[12] *The Marital Relationship as a Focus for Casework*. Family Discussion Bureau, Tavistock Institute of Human Relations, Codicote Press, London, 1962.

the father is thereby excluded from consciousness.[13] Margaret Galdston Grunebaum has made a further contribution to the understanding of ego restriction in her discussion of the frequency with which such clients have "secrets." These may be the client's own or their parents' extramarital affairs, the physical or mental illness of relatives, or business difficulties that involve legally questionable practices.[14] Such secrets are undoubtedly a factor in a surprising number of cases, if one can judge from the difficulty encountered in getting more than scraps of history from many of these clients. In some cases, childhood sexual experiences—incestuous or other—may comprise the secret.

Anna Freud has suggested that restriction is one of the methods adopted by the ego for the avoidance of pain, especially by that of the older child, whose greater freedom of physical movement and increased powers of psychic activity enable his ego to avoid such stimuli without performing so complicated a psychic operation as denial. Her examples include children who refuse to compete because of the hopeless rivalry of the oedipus phase and those who want to avoid the disagreeable realization of the differences between the sexes.[15]

Fulfilling the Parental Role

A marriage based on ego restriction in both partners may appear to be a mutually satisfactory one, and the pathology may be revealed only through the children. The parental failures in such a marriage are illustrated by an episode in a case served by a family service agency.

> Mr. and Mrs. D were referred to the agency by their family physician, to whom they had complained about the behavior of their seven-year-old daughter, Helen. They were ashamed of her boastfulness about possessions and of her fantasy of the military heroism of an uncle. Her behavior was the exact opposite of their own refusal to be ostentatious, competitive, or aggressive. They were also worried by her lack of friends and her tendency to stay in the house and read. In the third interview Mrs. D described Helen's behavior with the new puppy they had just given her in the hope that it would force her to go outdoors. In the middle of the night Helen had heard the puppy crying. She had taken her pillow downstairs, lain down beside the puppy's pen, and talked to it, but had made no attempt to pick it up. The caseworker asked Mrs. D, "Do you know what she said to the puppy?" A startled expression came over Mrs. D's face as she replied: "Yes. She was telling it what it should do and what it shouldn't do." Mrs. D was an intuitive woman who had not succeeded in restricting all her feelings; she did not need to be told that Helen's concept of parental tenderness was one of "telling what to do and what not to do." She did, however, need help in translating her intuition into action that would enable her to share the child's feelings and relax some of her own restrictions.

[13] Erik H. Erikson, *Childhood and Society*. W. W. Norton & Co., New York, 1950, pp. 267 ff.

[14] Margaret Galdston Grunebaum, "A Study of Learning Problems of Children: Casework Implications." *Social Casework*, Vol. XLII, November 1961, pp. 461–68.

[15] Anna Freud, *The Ego and the Mechanisms of Defense*. International Universities Press, New York, 1946, pp. 100–113.

The inability of the parent with a severe phallic-urethral character disorder to understand his child's feelings points to the basic fact that his own have never been valued. It is frequently found that in his childhood he was rewarded handsomely with possessions or privileges for disregarding his own feelings and allowing himself to be manipulated in accordance with his parents' desires. His relationships are therefore shallow and he tries to allay his loneliness with glamour, speed, money, and power. As Hans Morgenthau says, "The lust for power is, as it were, the twin of despairing love. Power becomes a substitute for love. What man cannot achieve for any length of time through love he tries to achieve through power: to fulfill himself, to make himself whole by overcoming his loneliness, his isolation."[16]

Treating Sexual Confusion

Although the individual variations seem endless, clients who suffer from sexual confusion do present recognizable patterns that have meaning to caseworkers. The sexual confusion of a person with a character disorder, like his other ways of behaving, thinking, and feeling, is likely to bear some relation to his fixation at a pregenital stage of development. In this respect his sexual behavior differs from that of the neurotic. The neurotic's behavior is dominated by defensive activities of the ego that are designed to reconcile the demands of the superego and of the id. The most familiar neurotic manifestations are, perhaps, the symptoms and behavior of the hysteric and the perversions and undoing rituals of the obsessive-compulsive. The traditional prohibition against the caseworker's dealing with sexual problems can readily be understood, since the neurotic manifestations, involving deep unconscious mechanisms, were recognized and understood by psychiatrists much earlier than the character disorders were. The treatment of the sexual confusions of the person with a character disorder depends, however, not on analyzing ego defenses and increasing the client's tolerance in handling the demands of the id but on helping him resume the growth process through a relationship with the worker.

When he has made a sound diagnosis, the caseworker can help marital partners who have phallic-urethral character disorders to establish improved male-female relationships, in which the husband and the wife supplement each other rather than compete for the male and female roles. A valid diagnosis depends on both a sound conceptual framework and the caseworker's development of an intuitive diagnostic sense based on his perception of qualitative differences in client attitudes. Through the study of individual cases, caseworkers may also make a significant contribution to an understanding of the sexual problems common to our culture and of the process by which cultural change takes place.

---

[16] Hans J. Morgenthau, "Love and Power." *Commentary*, Vol. XXXIII, March 1962, p. 249.

Some Observations of Group Psychotherapy with Paedophiles

Valdemar Hartman

Since the early days of mankind, children have been playing an important part in the lives of adults. According to time and culture, attention has been shown to them by individuals as well as by social institutions. It may be generalized that children are almost totally dependent upon the social environment and that adults are the ones who shape the environment, *eo ipso*, the onus for providing a suitable environment for their development rests upon the significant adults in the child's life. Opinions about "a suitable environment" may vary according to time and culture. Thus, in ancient Greece with its emphasis on the free, uninhibited expression of sexual instincts, a paedophile may have been regarded as "a man with refined tastes." In our culture the paedophile's choice of a child as an object of sexual interest is not condoned. It is viewed as a threat to the child's physical and emotional development—and also violates our Judeo-Christian ethical principles.

One of the cornerstones of our legal system is the protection provided for those unable to protect themselves according to the doctrine of *parents patriae*. Thus the paedophile may face not only society's strong disgust but also prosecution and severe penalty under the criminal code.

Historically, methods of dealing with paedophilic behavior vary. In medieval times such severe punishment as burning alive was meted out. More recently, we find incarceration and asexualization. However, the aim has remained the same: to curtail paedophilic behavior in the interests of protecting our children and preserving our ethical norms.

The new insights into human behavior and motivation brought about a search for more effective methods of controlling paedophilic behavior. It brought, also, emphasis on the doer's personality as the basis factor in motivating this behavior. The rehabilitative idea, having as its focus changes in the offender's attitudes, was seen as a compromise between the emphasis on individuality on the one hand, and our need to maintain social conformity on the other. This rehabilitation idea is becoming a part of a basic philosophy in dealing with our fellow citizens whose behavior grossly deviates from our accepted norms and is perceived as threatening and therefore evoking repercussions from society.

Reprinted from the *Canadian Journal of Corrections*, (October, 1961), pp. 492–499, by permission of the author and the publisher.

One of the relatively recent developments in the search for such effective methods of dealing with paedophilics is the application of group psychotherapeutic techniques for the investigation and treatment of paedophilia. Such research-oriented group psychotherapeutic sessions have been established at the Forensic Clinic of the Toronto Psychiatric Hospital.

The following remarks are gleaned from my experience as the therapist of this group, which has been in existence for the past fourteen months. The limits of this paper make necessary highly selective reporting, and an occasional oversimplification is unavoidable. The report is based upon direct observation in leading the group and also upon discussions of the transcripts and the tape recordings which take place at the regularly held group psychotherapy seminars at the Forensic Clinic. Attempts will be made to recapitulate some significant material pertaining to individual dynamics and group interaction as well as to present some tentative conclusions.

In reviewing the literature, there appears to be agreement about the definition of Paedophilia ("love of children" in translation). It denotes sexual interest in children; the emphasis being on the immaturity of the sexual object. Regarding the etiology there is a wide divergence in emphasis. The inferred dynamics often appear to be contradictory. No studies pertaining to group psychotherapy of paedophiles appear to have been published. Generally there is a paucity of writings referring to this form of sexual deviation.

It is understandable that in establishing this group, our objectives were to learn more about paedophilia and group interaction while at the same time helping the patients to effect better controls over their paedophilic urges.

In order to facilitate the optimal therapeutic group interaction, the proper selection of group members is of extreme importance. In selecting members for this group, the main criteria were patient homogenity in psychopathology and roughly equal intelligence levels. Soon, it became necessary to limit the group to heterosexually-oriented paedophiles only. As for homosexually-oriented, the discussions were too anxiety-provoking and intolerable. Also, to avoid a too-great age discrepancy, the age limits were arbitrarily set from 20–35 years. A variety of occupations were represented. The I.Q. of the group were bright normal or in the superior range, one was a university graduate. The majority were married with small children of their own.

All were previously assessed by a clinical team consisting of a psychiatric social worker, a psychologist and a psychiatrist as having capacity for psychotherapy. There were doubts expressed regarding their motivation for treatment, however. While all of them had acted out their paedophilic urges for a number of years, one over a period of fifteen years, none had previously thought of seeking help. Their present attendance at the clinic was made compulsory by a court order or a threat that charges would be laid unless treatment was initiated. All of them were currently experiencing paedophilic urges. The majority of them experienced quite compulsive urges and most were acting them out. The relative absence of guilt was observed as common to all the members of the group. In general, the patients were anxious, mildly depressed and dissatisfied with life.

In deciding upon the treatment approach, the integration of the presently available knowledge of individual dynamics regarding paedophilia, together with concepts derived from analytic group therapy, was regarded as an ideal to be strived for. Thus, while the group itself was seen as the therapeutic tool, no group goals were externally imposed. Treatment was individually oriented with reliance on unrestricted verbalization in the group. Evidently, since this was a research oriented group, the sessions were not limited to alleviation of the symptoms but were aimed at uncovering of the underlying causes, clarification and insights.

In determining the role of the therapist in the group, it was evident that the traditional permissive catalyst is essential to ensure uninhibited discussion. But we faced a group where for the majority of the members their deviating sexual urges had already become to a great extent ego syntonic despite the reality factor that even an attempt to act out these urges would bring serious social consequences. The decision was made to show firmly on which side the therapist stood as a reality tester. Evidently there also was a need for an equally firm show that the disapproval of their paedophilic urges did not imply that the therapist was chastising or condemning them as human beings. While it may be said that this stand appears not to have interfered with the sessions, it should be indicated that an ever-present danger existed in the form of possible identification as a forbidding authority figure, with the threat of a possible loss of the therapeutic effect.

Essentially the group sessions could be looked upon as a continued process of investigation and clarification. The main reliance was on inter-action, unconscious and conscious, verbal and non-verbal, between group members present at the sessions, and on reactions to the purposeful activities of the therapist as a catalyst and reality tester.

In the development of the group several phases could be observed. Of these phases, the beginning or integrative phase is arbitrarily selected for a more elaborate description. Before discussing this phase, it should be remembered that none of the group members had been a self-referral. All had been subjected to compulsory attendance at the sessions. Thus it is not surprising that their initial attitudes in the group ranged from overt resentment regarding the enforced attendance, to benevolent noncommittal attitudes with regard to the help that was offered. This resistance and resentment at being involved was later aptly described by a probation officer to whom a group member on his reporting day had confided that "you can make me attend but you cannot make me talk."

This may partly explain why the integration of the group as a meaningful therapeutic instrument took some four or five months of weekly one and a half hour sessions. During this period, absences and late coming, as well as demonstrative nonparticipation in the sessions and testing of the therapist, were common features. The most frequently used defence mechanism was that of primitive denial. For example, that there was no sexual element in their urges and does not everyone love children? This was followed by rather generalized projections of guilt. Later, very slowly and cautiously, dissatisfaction with life in general started to develop as group themes. Yet avoidance of any sexual theme was a common feature. Around the third month, their dissatisfactions became more concrete assuming the form of highly emotional criticism of their wives as well as deep resentment, bringing out their own lack of a normal degree of aggressiveness. The use of projection in blaming the sexual attitudes of the wives for the gradually acknowledged urges toward children as sexual objects was instrumental in undoing the denial. Around the fourth month, the group was intensively engaged in exploring the reasons for their sexual attraction to small children. There was full attendance at nearly every session, and the group became well-motivated, learning why they are not able to control their paedophilic urges.

It is reasonable to question what had happened and why such a startling change had taken place in a relatively short period of time. The answers are to be looked for in the already available knowledge about group dynamics. In a simplified way, it may be said that the experience of the new relationships provided by the group with the supportive and anxiety-reducing influences implicit in this treatment approach made possible the reduction of the individually employed defences to the point where introspection became possible with developing self-awareness and the wish for a change. This wish for a change had been an important development since in treatment where benefits are to be achieved by psychological means, adequate motivation for change appears to be the condition *sine qua non*. Evidently, the significance of the supportive aspects of the group cannot be over estimated.

A more detailed observation of this phenomenon was possible some ten months later when a totally unmotivated paedophile under court order to attend, was added to the group. It was most striking to see how the group members' attitudes, most of them on an unconscious level, dealt with the new member's resistances and finally absorbed him into the group, in a surprisingly short period of time. That the achieved motivation has been a lasting one could be evidenced by the fact that of the original group, all members continued their attendance well beyond the legally imposed obligation to attend the clinic (in most of the cases this had been for a period of six months). One member left the group after an attendance of eleven months while the others are still attending.

In describing the individual roles in the group constellation, it could be said that the members had a great tendency to relate to each other and to the therapist as they presumably had related socially in childhood experiences of the past. Thus the significant features were sibling rivalries and distorted attitudes about meaningful figures of an early period of development. While this was utilized for information-getting as well as effecting better reality testing, the emphasis was on "here and now." As already mentioned, the therapist was not a neutralist from the very beginning of the sessions. It was made clear that he does not approve the paedophilic acts even if he tries to understand them. At the beginning stage it was also assumed that a direct prohibition might have to be applied after the neurotic material had been verbalized in the group and some understanding achieved. Such prohibition, in fact, never had to be imposed by the therapist since it came from the group itself and in much stricter form than the therapist could have possibly applied successfully.

In discussing the content of the sessions, certain dominant group themes could be well distinguished by their frequency and intensity. The changes and developments individually and groupwise could be clearly noticed by the changed emphasis and content of the themes. Thus, after reduction of the basic defences, the group's attentions were focused on their sexual difficulties. The slowly emerging insight that sexual difficulties are only a part of their interpersonal difficulties, focused the group associations on the total personalities of the members with the realizations of their own personality inadequacies. No doubt, this was provoking major anxiety and again support of the group as well as the part-identification with the therapist should be stressed as a factor in making the tensions tolerable and in not provoking withdrawal from sessions.

More specifically, the prominent group themes were: dissatisfaction with wives (all but one member were married); concern about paedophilic urges; dissatisfaction with self for not being sufficiently aggressive; apprehensions about adult women and the need to master them; curiosity about the female genitalia, and apprehensions about impaired masculinity.

In the therapist's evaluation, the central theme of the discussion was the perception of adult women as an unspecified danger (the castrating element appeared to be only one aspect) and the rationalization that the group members could not face an adult woman because of the certainty of refusal and ridicule on her part. The resulting anxiety appeared to be discharged by what to them was a total mastery of a paedophilic object via some form of sexual contact with the female child—not necessarily intercourse, however.

While the focal conflict no doubt remained paedophilia, the elements of other sexual deviations, such as exhibitionism, fetishism, voyeurism as well as some confusion about sexual identity, by no means always remained peripheral in the discussions.

It may be of interest to note that in the discussions of the group I currently have in therapy, a new theme is emerging, namely, the search for a connecting causative link between paedophilic urges and the satisfactions they provide in terms of feelings of mastery and masculinity.

In comparing the individual assessments with the findings in the group, in every case the assessment by the clinical team could be confirmed. The disturbance in normal childhood development had been a prominent feature. All the members of the group had experienced either a physical or psychological absence of the father. The mother had taken the dominant role in the family. In every case, this had resulted in an actual or perceived trauma and the real or perceived attitudes of the mother appeared to haunt each patient's life in an exaggerated form.

In placing emphasis on the possible influence of mother's attitudes in the individual dynamics, this should not be regarded as a monocause for paedophilia nor evidence that mother had been a monster. No evidence could be found that the group verbalizations indicating disturbances in mothering could be the result of mother's own psychopathology or were created by father or by a neurotic interaction in the marriage unless a thorough psychosocial assessment of the parental family as a unit had been made. Of a more immediate therapeutic concern was the impression gained from the session, that the group members' present family situation actually could be regarded as a continuum of childhood experiences. The description of their attitudes, the persistent slips in mixing up the mother and the wife and the occasional flare-up of a power struggle in the marriage, even with due allocation for the possible distortions in perception, gave some indication of the intensity of the remnants of the childhood experiences.

At the Forensic Clinic, we offer the wife of the patient a continuing professional contact. In the cases where the wife attended, little progress was made with her due to extreme defensiveness on her part. In some cases we noticed that she attempted to make it difficult for the husband to attend the sessions. For example, she might choose the day when group meetings were to take place for entertaining guests or shopping. Evidently this is an area for deeper exploration.

In returning to the stated objectives in the establishment of this group at the Forensic Clinic, namely, to learn more about paedophilia and group dynamics and to provide immediate treatment for patients, the experimental nature of this undertaking is stressed, and that evaluation of this experiment is based on clinical impression (social functioning being the only external measurable criteria). It is felt that the group sessions are an excellent research media, at the same time providing a possibility for effecting changes in patients' attitudes towards their paedophilic urges. While clearly we cannot talk about "a cure" of paedophilia we can talk about reduced paedophilic urges and ability to control these urges, and over-all improvement in functioning in the community.

In a simplified way, it can be said that there were different degrees of improvement. All group members appeared to have lost the compulsive nature of their paedophilic urges and to be more or less capable of restraint.

Considering further these limited gains, we had the experience of two patients acting out after imposing adequate self-restraint for over half a year. This was precipitated by stress related to personality dynamics regarding which the patient had gained little insight. The group, with the member present on each occasion, were able to explain the acting-out behavior with reference to significant events in the patient's early life together with activating factors in the development of the group.

In concluding, it is emphasized that the purpose of this paper is not to uncover new insights about paedophilia or group techniques nor to depict group psychotherapy as a panacea for curing individual and social ills. It is intended to stimulate some thinking about the possible pragmatic value of this technique, as well as to indicate the need for further extension of the concept that treatment may be a substitute for incarceration, by showing that group treatment of paedophilics is feasible. Does this bring us closer to the idea that legal responsibility should not necessarily be associated with punishment by imprisonment?

Bibliography

ABRAHAMSEN, D. *Who are the Guilty?* New York: Grove Press Inc. 1952.

———. *Report on Study of 102 Sex Offenders at Sing Sing Prison.* Utica: State Hospital Press, 1950.

BAK, R. C. "Aggression and Perversion" in Lorand, S. and Balint, M. edit. *Perversions: Psychodynamics and Therapy.* New York: Random House, 1956.

FOULKES, S. H. and ANTONY, E. J. *Group Psychotherapy.* Toronto: Penguin Books, 1957.

FRIED, E. *The Ego in Love and Sexuality.* New York: Grune & Stratton, 1960.

KARPMAN, B. "A Case of Paedophilia", *Psychoanalyt. Review*, 37:325, 1950.

———. *The Sexual Offender and His Offenses.* New York: 1954.

SLAVSON, S. R. *Analytic Group Psychotherapy.* New York: Columbia University Press, 1950.

Borderline States

Supportive Casework with Borderline Patients

Richard Stuart

Patients diagnosed as borderline are appearing in increasing numbers in all types of social agencies, yet at the same time "classic" neurotics are showing up in fewer numbers. Is this because our skills at diagnosis have improved? Is this because there is more serious illness? In either case, it is clear that a large number of patients diagnosed as borderline account for a vast proportion of treatment time in family agencies, mental hygiene clinics, public assistance centers, and the like. Therefore, to make the best use of available resources and to insure the highest quality of service, it is essential that the meaning of the diagnosis and the treatment considerations be formulated carefully.

The goal of this paper is to suggest a casework approach to help the patient adapt more successfully to his environment. First we shall describe the behavior and personality characteristics of the borderline patient. Then we shall attempt to describe how specific aspects of the therapeutic situation lend themselves to the use of certain techniques. This will include a description of general treatment considerations and various sources of potential change. Last, we shall suggest a cluster of techniques designed to aid the patient in strengthening his hold upon reality.

The borderline state is a stepchild of diagnostic thinking. There are some who regard it as a point on the classic continuum between neurosis and psychosis while others regard it as a separate entity.[1] In the first view, the borderline state ranges from severe, complex, and somewhat disabling neuroses to relatively benign psychoses. The condition is regarded as somewhat flexible with the patient moving back and forth between neurosis and psychosis in response to inner and outer pressures.

In the second view, the borderline state is seen as a stable, precise

[1] Jerome Weinberger, "Basic Concepts in Diagnosis and Treatment of Borderline States," in Howard J. Parad, ed., *Ego Psychology and Dynamic Casework* (New York: Family Service Association of America, 1958), p. 112.

Reprinted with permission of the author and the National Association of Social Workers, from *Social Work*, Vol. 9, No. 1 (January, 1964), pp. 38–44.

diagnostic entity which, while it resembles both neurosis and psychosis, has features that clearly differentiate it from both. While there may be shifts in the severity of his symptoms, the borderline patient has difficulty in perceiving his environment accurately, but he does not display the kind of thought disorder characteristic of the psychotic. In the literature dealing with the treatment of the borderline state, this second point of view prevails, as it does in this article.[2]

"Borderline state" refers to a group of symptom patterns whose common denominator is a predominance of narcissistic control with a resultant weakness of secondary ego processes.[3] These patients have a sense of inferiority that leads to a deep dependency upon others who appear omnipotent in contrast to their own sense of powerlessness. They have a tendency to retreat from object relationships,[4] although this withdrawal may be temporary and partial.[5]

Because of the chronic tension of aggression and anxiety, these patients have had too much pressure to be able to consolidate ego gains. As stated by Knight:

> Some ego functions have been severely impaired—especially, in most cases, integration, concept formation, judgment, realistic planning and the defending against the eruption into conscious thinking of impulses and their fantasy elaboration. Other ego functions, such as conventional (but superficial) adaptation to the environment and superficial maintenance of object relationships may exhibit varying degrees of in-tactness. And still others, such as memory, calculation, and certain habitual performances may seem unimpaired.[6]

Despite the defects in secondary ego processes, there are no clear breaks with reality in the form of hallucinations, delusions, or ideas of reference. The clinical picture is often dominated by the presence of either strong neurotic symptoms such as hysteria or obsessive-compulsivity, somatic complaints, and/or severe and frequent manic-depressive shifts. These patients thus have a proneness to narcissistic injury with impulsive attempts to re-establish equilibrium characteristic of the infantile personality, showing an unevenness of development and an inadequate self-image.

[2] Adolph Stern, "Psychoanalytic Investigation of and Therapy in the Borderline Group of Neuroses," *Psychoanalytic Quarterly*, Vol. 7, No. 4 (1938); Leo Stone, "The Widening Scope of Indications for Psychoanalysis," *Journal of the American Psychoanalytic Association*, Vol. 2 (1954), p. 582: Robert Knight, "Management and Psychotherapy of the Borderline Schizophrenic Patient," in Robert Knight and Cyrus Friedman, eds., *Psychoanalytic Psychiatry and Psychology*, Vol. 1 (New York: International Universities Press, 1954); Melita Schmideberg, "The Borderline Patient," in Silvano Arietti, ed., *American Handbook of Psychiatry*, Vol. 1 (New York: Basic Books, 1959).

[3] Robert Knight, "Borderline States," in Knight and Friedman, *op. cit.*, p. 102.

[4] Edith Jacobson, "Transference Problems in the Psychoanalytic Treatment of Severely Depressed Patients," *Journal of the American Psychoanalytic Association*, Vol. 2 (1954), p. 597.

[5] Otto Fenichel, *Psychoanalytic Theory of Neurosis* (New York: W. W. Norton & Co., 1945), p. 444.

[6] Robert Knight, "Borderline States," in Knight and Friedman, *op. cit.*, p. 102.

Behavior and Personality Characteristics

Despite the severity of their pathology, borderline patients may present themselves as relatively intact persons because of their use of obsessional defenses, denial, omission, projection, and so forth, or they may fashion eccentric environments which provide at least partial gratification for their extreme needs. The illness may be diagnosed through the use of such "soft signs" as frequent blocking, peculiarities of word usage, obliviousness to implication, or oversuspiciousness. An inappropriateness in feeling tone is also found. Expressions of feeling are sudden in onset and cyclic in patterning. Frequently they are out of proportion to their stated causes with the effect often being "undone" by an inappropriate gesture such as a smile or a peculiar concern with detail. In presenting their initial problems, borderline patients may move off from a specific statement in an associative manner without returning to their starting point. Logical errors are common, particularly in deductive processes, and some self-effacing conclusion is almost inevitable. They often refuse to accept responsibility for their own actions and see themselves as the mere pawns of events. This has the effect of reducing their responsibility for the past and serves as vindication for dependency in the present. There is an ahistoric quality to their view of themselves, with an inability to accept the role of the past in their present lives and a constant hope for, and fear of, the future.[7]

Because of the combined impact of depression and anxiety, borderline patients often feel that they cannot mobilize themselves to meet any new challenge. They receive little reinforcement from others in their personal lives because of their proclivity for surrounding themselves with persons whose resources are as limited as their own, and because their demands are unreasonable or insatiable. Owing to their dissatisfaction, they often withdraw and their frequent complaint is one of loneliness or isolation in a world which is angry partly by projection and partly as a response to their provocation. The view of a hostile, uncaring world leads to counteraggression, which causes conflict because it also coincides with dependence upon others. In the writer's observation such conflicts partly explain the frequently bizarre speech mannerisms and the tic-like patterns which represent the intrusion of strong impulses into object relationships. Consistent with the apparent paradoxes they display, these patients usually have some degree of insight into the nature of their conflicts and can clearly express it, although they lack the appropriate affective understanding which would make their insights useful.

General Treatment Considerations

The treatment of choice with borderline patients is an ego- and reality-oriented supportive method. It is generally agreed that psychoanalytic procedures are contra-indicated. This is because the patient has difficulty in controlling the

[7] Jacobson, *op. cit.*, p. 600.

temporarily induced autism and regression, because the semidelusional form of thinking undermines secondary ego processes, and because the somewhat detached attitude of the analyst (which serves as a catalyst for transference) can reinforce the irrationality in the interpersonal relationships of borderline patients.[8] This point of view prevails even though it has been argued that nonanalytic procedures are directed to the less mature aspects of the patient's personality[9] and that the only means of achieving true personality change is through genetic understanding.[10]

However, it must be pointed out that the ability to use interpretation leading to insight presupposes the ability to make cause-and-effect connections and to use symbolism in thought which serves as a delay function. Borderline patients are notably weak in these areas. They cannot take sufficient distance from interpretations to convert them into useful insight, and tend to react to the interpretation as thought it were censure leading to a narcissistic wound. This reaction may provoke more acting out.

Relationship is a central factor in any supportive treatment, and with borderline patients it is particularly important. Conditioned by life experience to think of themselves as inferior to others in their world who are viewed as having great power, these patients tend to establish an illusory and magical transference which leads to great dependency and is based on fear and aggression.[11] The borderline patient's hypersensitivity and negative expectations lead to a suspiciousness and a tendency to overreact to imagined rejection which makes his assessment of the caseworker's countertransference as crucial an issue as is the transference phenomena in the treatment of neurotics.[12] Indeed one of the chief problems is the worker's ability to handle his own feelings of defensiveness and emotional strain which prolonged exposure to the patient's provocation must produce.[13] The factors that can negatively influence the relationship are the excessive demands of the patient and the reaction of the worker if his approach tends to be inflexible. The most effective rapport is one which reveals the caseworker as a flexible, alive, and reasonable person with definite views when problems of human values are concerned, and with reliable reactions to stress situations. It is only then that the patient can experience the worker directly, with a minimum of fantasy elaboration. The patient can use the worker's sense of calm and assurance to reinforce his own more reasoned approaches. Through

---

[8] To the author's knowledge only Gregory Zilboorg, "Ambulatory Schizophrenias," *Psychiatry*, Vol. 4, No. 2 (May 1941), advocates the use of unmodified psychoanalysis with borderline patients. Because of the lack of clarity in diagnostic thinking, however, comparison of treatment approaches is hazardous.

[9] Stone, *op. cit.*, p. 588.

[10] Frieda Fromm-Reichman, *Principles of Intensive Psychotherapy* (Chicago: University of Chicago Press, 1950), p. x.

[11] Jacobson, *op. cit.*, p. 599.

[12] Silvano Arietti, "Aspects of Psychoanalytically Oriented Treatment of Schizophrenia," in Samuel C. Scher and Howard R. Davis, eds., *The Outpatient Treatment of Schizophrenia* (New York: Grune and Stratton, 1960), p. 115.

[13] Stone, *op. cit.*, p. 597.

an effective relationship it is possible to being to overcome the patient's sense of helplessness and confusion and to minimize his defensiveness and hostility. The patient then is able to use the worker as a source of active help in organizing energy to overcome pressing problems and he will be willing to experience the anxiety of some degree of self-examination perhaps for the first time.

Three Sources of Change

The focus of treatment of the borderline patient is to provide experience which will reinforce secondary ego processes in order to help the patient develop more effective means of meeting his own needs in a socially acceptable manner. This requires simultaneous work with both implicit and explicit therapeutic processes.

First of all there is the *formal* aspect of the relationship. The process of establishing a therapeutic relationship has change value in and of itself. Borderline patients almost invariably enter treatment with a subservient attitude which is abruptly changed into an aggressive defensiveness when any pressure is brought to bear on making a closer examination of his life situation. This reaction can be minimized when the worker succeeds in helping his patient to see that the process is exploration and not condemnation. If the relationship can survive this period of testing, the patient is likely to have a fairly strong, positive feeling for the worker because of the all-or-nothing nature of his functioning. This positive relationship is associated "with the repression of overwhelming patterns of experience."[14] Implicit in the treatment situation is a new set of operations which requires that the patient come regularly for interviews in which he sits and talks about his problems, rather than act them out impulsively. He must forego the wish for immediate gratification of instinctual desires in favor of discussing means of obtaining more permanent future rewards. He must set aside his wished-for immediate gratification from the social worker. In so doing, he implicitly accepts some responsibility for his unhappy state and also some responsibility for initiating changes. In addition, he accepts an implicit accountability for his actions as they are to be discussed with the worker. Thus the establishment of a treatment relationship calls into play such ego forces as communication, reasoning, delay of discharge, realistic perception, and control of hostile and sexual impulse both in and outside the casework situation.

In addition to this implicit, formal aspect of the relationship which helps the patient control himself there is a second element of change, namely, implicit *informal* acceptance, which is an important therapeutic factor. Freud suggests that there are three sources of self-regard: the residue of childish narcissism, the residue of experience which serves as a fulfillment of the ego ideal, and gratification of the object libido. The borderline patient intermixes the last two sources superimposed over faulty early development,

---

[14] Sigmund Freud, "On Narcissism," in *Collected Papers*, Vol. 4 (London: Hogarth Press, 1957), pp. 58–59.

and thereby induces a self-fulfilling prophecy of failure. Acceptance of the healthy, adaptive enterprise of the patient contributes to what has been termed a "developmental relationship," at the same time that it helps him contain the aggressive and sexual elements which have complicated his interpersonal relationships in the past.[15] In discussing the therapeutic implication of his observation, Freud remarks that patients will become attached to "whoever possesses an excellence which the ego lacks for the attainment of the ideal," and will seek the "cure by love which he generally prefers to the cure by analysis."[16] This points up a central casework problem: the need to balance acceptance with provocation to change. The worker must avoid the pitfall of unqualified acceptance of the maladaptive behavior of the patient for this can reinforce the patient's feeling of hopelessness. To do this, one must build into the interviews a spirit of examination which emphasizes the areas of potential change.

The third source of change is found in the consequences of the *supportive procedures*. Support is implied when the caseworker probes for new information or offers some form of advice. Furthermore, focusing the patient's concern upon a particular problem not only demonstrates the caseworker's interest, but it also reinforces perception of the problem, which forms the basis for developing a new defense. At the same time it creates a channel for directing activity. This idea is embodied in Freud's comment on various nonanalytic procedures which are "not concerned with the origin, strength and meaning of the morbid symptoms, but instead emphasize something—a suggestion—and expect this to be strong enough to restrain the pathogenic idea from coming to expression."[17] Edward Glover developed this idea further, viewing the process as "neglect combined with counterstimulation."[18] The patient must do or think something new (such as obsessional ceremonial or fixed idea) or take up some counterattraction (anticathexis, cancellation, undoing, expiation). This process is backed by "strong transference authority, which means that . . . by borrowing strength from the suggestionist's superego, a new substitution product is accepted by the patient's ego. The new 'therapeutic symptom construction' has become, for the time, ego-syntonic."[19]

These new defenses are adopted provisionally at first and can only become truly established after considerable time. If treatment is cut short or interrupted, they are likely to evaporate, and this is their chief limitation. When the positive transference is of sufficient duration and intensity, a process of incorporation occurs, consistent with the narcissistic orientation of this group of patients, with the patient taking over the caseworker's suggestions.

[15] Weinberger, *op. cit.* p. 116.
[16] Freud, *op. cit.*, pp. 58–59.
[17] Sigmund Freud, "On Psychotherapy," *Collected Papers*, Vol. 1 (London: Hogarth Press, 1957), p. 254.
[18] Edward Glover, *The Technique of Psychoanalysis* (New York: International Universities Press, 1955), p. 360.
[19] *Ibid.*, p. 361.

The goal of this supportive treatment is the formation of new defenses which will enhance adaptation and improve the means of satisfying narcissistic needs. *No attempt is made to modify the patients' basic personality patterns*, although if changes in adaptation can be maintained long enough, some alterations are likely to occur.[20]

Improving Secondary Ego Processes

The efforts to improve rational control are founded upon techniques that will both control anxiety and reinforce secondary ego processes. Among the techniques are logical discussion, labeling, focusing on the present, anticipatory transference clarification, and reassurance. While borderline patients are not amenable to so-called "insight treatment," this does not preclude their gaining some measure of new self-understanding. The patients are quite capable of understanding the *processes* of their functioning, while at the same time they may be unable to gain insight into the dynamic *structure* of their personalities. The structure includes the underlying infantile conflicts, the process includes the manner in which these conflicts are expressed in daily life. The borderline patient may consistently misrepresent the world around him, may rush immediately into action without delay, may fall to pieces readily or repeat self-destructive rituals: these are process considerations. In work with personality structure the social worker is concerned with *why* certain objects are chosen over others, in work with process with *how* the individual behaves with respect to the objects which he chooses.

A crucial aspect of a psychological process is the cognitive component. George Kelly suggests that "a person's processes are channelized by the ways in which he anticipates events."[21] By this it is meant that all men have a reasoned conception of how the world behaves and how they can best integrate themselves into that world. This conception is partly within awareness and partly not so. It is psychological in nature, and therefore not necessarily logical—with key dimensions ignored or distorted consistent with momentary need. The pattern of its reasoning tends to be somewhat stable and can therefore be studied so that consistent patterns may be brought to light. A knowledge of these patterns can then be used by the individual to guide his own behavior.

Once the casework relationship is established, it is possible to explore with the patient the inner consistencies of his behavior and to elucidate the patterns of recurrent dysfunction. Merely establishing connections between previously isolated instances of behavior "makes the ego relatively stronger

[20] Florence Hollis, "Analysis of Casework Treatment Methods and Their Relation to Personality Change," *Smith College Studies in Social Work*, Vol. 32, No. 2 (February, 1962).

[21] George Kelly, *The Psychology of Personal Constructs*, Vol. 1 (New York: W. W. Norton & Co., 1955), p. 46.

in its relationship to the deeper forces within [the] personality."[22] Establishing these connections in the treatment situation helps to limit the self-punishment which is generally associated with the introspection of borderline patients and establishes a pattern for self-study. Once the patterns have been identified, they may be labeled, and once labeled they become more easily recognized and useful in future planning.[23] The label also helps to distinguish what is and is not included in a pattern. For borderline patients this has the effect of further reducing self-deprecation and it is then possible to see the relatively healthy areas of functioning more clearly.

Labeling is a simple matter once the consistencies are known. When a patient has a tendency to see all authority figures as hostile or to foresee personal failure as an inevitability, labels such as "childish fearfulness" or "dismal-Dan approach" may be applied. The labeling process implies a value judgment that certain behavior does not work, or, in the patients' terms, is "bad." It is thus made ego-alien or encapsulated.[24] This moves it away from what the patient identifies as his core identity, his "me." This is reinforced by the worker's selective support of the healthy aspects of the patient's ego, and by the patient's identification with the worker who is analyzing the patient's thought and behavior.

In this approach, attention is focused on the present all the time, with discussion of the background minimized as much as possible. An understanding of the present is far more useful to borderline patients than a rehashing of the past, which often leads to a recurrence of guilt and despair. Furthermore, the caseworker has no "authority" in matters of the past so this limits him to an ex post facto, verbal process. The most emotionally meaningful level of existence for the borderline patient, whose approach is ahistorical is the present success or failure of his attempts to obtain narcissistic satisfactions. Therefore, the worker can establish a meaningful contact with his patient by limiting it to the focus on the present. Furthermore, it is necessary to keep in mind the totality of current functioning of borderline patients, since they are more sensitive to changes in equilibrium than most patients. Thus, before attempting to modify any bit of behavior, the worker must evaluate its adaptive significance in addition to its immediacy and salience. In an active approach such as this, when the patient's self-dosing is slightly curtailed, there is a danger of unleashing more acting out because of poor timing or indiscriminate activity.

Since the general focus of concern is the patient's interpersonal relationships, both the worker-client relationship and the various extra-therapeutic transferences may be examined during treatment. An important mechanism for keeping treatment going is "anticipatory transference clarification"

[22] Otto Fenichel, *op. cit.*, p. 555. These connections have also been termed "integrative interpretations" by Lee Stone, "Psychoanalysis and Brief Psychotherapy," *Psychoanalytic Quarterly*, Vol. 20 (1951), pp. 215–237.

[23] John Dollard and Neal Miller, *Personality and Psychotherapy* (New York: McGraw-Hill Book Co., 1950), Chap. 18.

[24] Paul Federn, "The Analysis of Psychotics: On Techniques," *International Journal of Psychoanalysis*, Vol. 15 (1934), pp. 209–215.

which helps to offset the acting out of narcissistic wounds.[25] Because the casework relationship is an aspect of the patient's current reality, it may be the subject of discussion, but not in terms of its analog to the patient's formative experiences. Rather it must be regarded as an arena for the operation of patterns that have been labeled and which dominate the patient's general adaptation.

A great deal of reassurance may be required at the start of treatment and at key periods of anxiety. As with all patients, reassurance must be realistic and must also be directed toward healthy parts of the personality. An attempt should be made to shift the focus of reassurance from the patient himself to his accomplishments in adjustment as these accrue. The self-assurance that results from perception of successful, mature experience will be far more durable than the self-assurance that depends on the transference relationship.

Conclusion

Borderline pathology has been defined as *1]* a variety of generally impulsive symptom patterns *2]* whose common denominator is a pre-dominance of narcissistic control *3]* with a resulting weakness in secondary ego processes. These three factors influence the treatment method which is quasi-educational in nature and based upon engaging the healthier parts of the personality in an attempt to improve the level of adaptation. An initial attempt to reduce harmful tension and to reduce the impact of depression is designed to provide sufficient motivation for the patient to move into a limited amount of self-scrutiny under the worker's guidance. Then an attempt is made to introduce rational delay mechanisms as a means of coping with stress. These mechanisms take the form of anticipatory labels of either impulsive activity patterns or their cognitive representations: they become ego-alien and can be reckoned with by the patient in tempering his own reactions.

While this procedure draws upon intellectualization and isolation as defenses, it derives emotional meaning from three sources. First, it is the existence of a strong casework relationship the formal aspect of which makes the treatment possible and which lends considerable emotional significance. Second, as the relationship begins to be effective, the patient starts to derive reinforcement from his improved control, which allows a more self-fulfilling redirection of energy. Third, some energy is gained from his habitual faith in, and reliance upon, magical measures. The introduction of new defenses makes positive use of this tendency. The treatment is limited by the fact that considerable time is needed to integrate the new growth experiences and by the fact that it is dependent upon a continuous relationship with the worker and may deteriorate upon separation. If dependency is skillfully controlled during treatment, however, and some provision is made for sustaining contacts, the latter problem can be minimized.

[25] Stone, *op. cit.*, p. 231.

Casework Treatment of the
Depressed Parent

Hank Walzer

A parent's depression may have a devastating influence on his child's development. The psychiatric literature has amply described the pathological effect on a young child of physical separation from the mother-person.[1] Emotional or psychological separation may produce equally tragic consequences. Such separation may take place when a parent is depressed and his feelings and thoughts are turned inward, away from his child. Casework treatment of the depressed parent should therefore be of particular concern to those working in the interests of children.

In keeping with the current trend toward family-centered treatment, the Children's Division of the Department of Psychiatry at the University of Colorado Medical Center has stressed the need for including both parents in the treatment. The Division's approach to treatment of the child tends to be holistic, that is, to recognize the interdependence between the child's treatment and the treatment of the family as a unit. In this article the focus is on techniques that are useful in modifying parent-child relationships when the parent has the particular problem of depression. Many parents who seek treatment for a child come to the clinic in a helpless, depressed mood that has resulted from the stress created by the child's problems. This is a common condition. The parents considered here, however, are those whose depressive symptoms cause disturbances in the parent-child relationship, although the parents are not so severely incapacitated that they need psychiatric treatment.

[1] John Bowlby, *Maternal Care and Mental Health*, World Health Organization Monograph, Geneva, 1951; Anna Freud and Dorothy T. Burlingham, *War and Children*, International Universities Press, Inc., New York, 1943; René A. Spitz, "Hospitalism: An Inquiry into the Genesis of Psychiatric Conditions in Early Childhood," *The Psychoanalytic Study of the Child*, Vol. 1. International Universities Press, Inc., New York, 1945, pp. 53–74.

Reprinted from *Social Casework*, XLII (December, 1961), pp. 505–512, by permission of the author and the Journal.

Definition and Symptoms of Depression ˎ

The depressed person suffers from an undue sadness or dejection that impairs his ability to sustain vital relationships with others and severely restricts or inhibits important life activities. A depression may be characterized by feelings of discouragement and downheartedness, or it may be a hopeless despair. Bowlby states that not all depressions are pathological. For example, a bereaved person's grief may be a perfectly natural reaction to a realistic loss. Bowlby defines pathological depression as "depressive illness," or "melancholia."[2] In melancholia, as contrasted with normal grieving or sadness, the real source of the emotion is largely unknown; the person reveals a strong attitude of self-depreciation. When an individual is in this state, his lowered spirits may bear little relation to his external circumstances.

There are several common symptoms of depression. The depressed person makes vague complaints of fatigue that impedes normal functioning regardless of the amount of sleep or rest he obtains. He seems to be saying, "I'm tired of all the demands people make on me; I have nothing left over to give them." He may experience insomnia at night and may awaken early in the morning, or, conversely, he may sleep excessively as a means of escaping from the troubles that beset him. His appetite may diminish, with the result that he loses weight. Shifting somatic complaints may plague him, and changes in behavior such as withdrawal, indifference, or boredom often occur.

Dynamics

The person who is depressed suffered in infancy some disappointment, loss, or abandonment at the hands of the cherished love object or mother-person upon whom he was totally dependent. His resultant rage was repressed for fear of further rejection or retaliation by the mother-person. Abraham has called attention to the reactivation of the early infantile pattern of deprivation brought on by a correspondingly serious loss in the current life of the adult.[3] Freud discovered that the depressed person's self-reproaches are chiefly directed against the image of the lost love object.

> [The self-accusations] fit someone else, some person whom the patient loves, has loved or ought to love. . . . So we get the key to the clinical picture—by perceiving that the self-reproaches are reproaches against a loved object which have been shifted on to the patient's own ego.[4]

[2] John Bowlby, "Grief and Mourning in Infancy and Early Childhood," *The Psychoanalytic Study of the Child*, Vol. XVI. International Universities Press, Inc., New York, 1960, pp. 9–53.

[3] Karl Abraham, "The Infantile Prototype of Melancholic Depression," *Selected Papers on Psychoanalysis*, Basic Books, Inc., New York, 1953, pp. 464–70.

[4] Sigmund Freud, "Mourning and Melancholia," *Collected Papers*, Vol. IV, Ernest Jones (ed.), Basic Books, Inc., New York, 1959, p. 158.

The love object has been introjected, and the anger has been turned inward upon the self; depression is the result.

To the depressed parent, the child may unconsciously represent a significant figure from the past. The parent may then attempt to use the child to meet his own unfulfilled need to be mothered. The child who is tied to the parent in this way (partially because of the parent's needs and partially because of his own ambivalence) may actually mother the parent. On the other hand, the parent may also gratify his own need for nurturance by infantilizing the child. Since the child cannot possibly gratify the parent's needs, the parent feels frustrated, and the child becomes to him an ungiving person.

In some instances, the depressed parent perceives in his child the bad part of himself (the introjected figure), and he repeats the mistakes of his own childhood in the current parent-child relationship. One father said, "I see John hating himself for things I hate myself for—not having friends, being easily hurt, and so on. So maybe I hate John when I see him act that way because I hate those things in myself."

Bibring has theorized that the structure of depression is complicated by the ego's awareness of its helplessness. He has likened the ego's feeling of helplessness to the helplessness of the small infant who is totally dependent on the mother-figure for gratification. Therefore, any experience that intensifies feelings of helplessness and loss of self-esteem may create a predisposition toward depression.[5] The dynamics of each case vary, however, in accordance with the individual's life experiences. Bibring has cautioned that not all depressions are the result of loss of dependency gratifications in childhood. However, " 'the orally dependent type' . . . represents perhaps the most frequent type of predisposition to depression. . . ."[6]

Bowlby, too, has pointed out that not all depressions have the same dynamics. He has emphasized the importance of separation or loss of close contact with the mother as a major factor in depression. Yet, he has questioned the "assumption that the syndrome . . . can be explained only on the supposition that an essential in its dynamics is aggression directed against the self. Could it not be due simply and solely to the rupture of a key relationship and the consequent intense pain of yearning occurring in a young child?"[7] The problems of the depressed individual cannot be attributed solely to unresolved childhood conflicts, either. The current family situation of the parent may also be a significant factor in the intensification or reduction of depression. The family of a depressed person is often unable to tolerate or cope with the person's failings and inadequacies, and the members may react with bewilderment and anger as their own needs are not met.

[5] Edward Bibring, "The Mechanism of Depression," *Affective Disorders*, Phyllis Greenacre (ed.), International Universities Press, Inc., New York, 1953, pp. 13–48.

[6] Bibring, *op. cit.*, p. 36.

[7] John Bowlby, "Grief and Mourning in Infancy and Early Childhood," *The Psychoanalytic Study of the Child*, Vol. XVI, International Universities Press, Inc., New York, 1960. p. 35.

These reactions, in turn, further damage the depressed person's self-esteem. As Gomberg has stated, ". . . the diagnosis of the individual [should] . . . not be in a vacuum but rather within the context of the social and emotional environment in which he lives, adjusts, suffers, fails, or succeeds."[8]

The Child Guidance Problem

When the depressed parent comes to our Child Guidance Clinic, he is usually at the stage where he feels overwhelmed and immobilized by the demands his child is making on him. He often speaks in a helpless, self-condemnatory manner about his inability to cope with the child. An excerpt from an initial interview typifies this kind of problem: "I don't know what to do with him (the patient) anymore. Anything I say is wrong, and nothing I do works. I don't know what to do. Maybe I'm too lenient. I don't know anything anymore. He thinks he's a hot-shot; he's too bossy."

The depressed parent often fears that the child will criticize him or stop loving him unless he meets certain demands. His underlying fear of rejection and his fear of his own hostility provoke the child into attempts to manipulate and control him. Frequently, the child tries to manipulate the parent by confronting him with his own ambivalence. The child will say, "You hate me" or "You don't really love me." The guilt-ridden parent will then continue to appease or mollify the angry, unsatisfied child while suppressing his own growing resentment. The unrelenting guilt, nourished by smoldering resentment, perpetuates the vicious cycle of inconsistent, ambivalent handling of the unfortunate child who then acts in such a manner that his parent's guilt is increased.

Supportive Treatment

Depression may interfere with normal functioning to such a degree that the parent has difficulty in meeting the requirements of his parental role. Even everyday tasks may become a burden. The caseworker, therefore, should give the parent a good deal of support in the form of encouragement, reassurance, and praise. The basic ingredient of supportive treatment is the worker's communication of warm concern, understanding, and acceptance of the parent's problems.

Guidance and Environmental Manipulation

One means of enhancing the parent's self-esteem and decreasing his feeling of helplessness is the worker's judicious use of advice and educative techniques. For example, a guilt-ridden, highly intellectual mother who

---

[8] M. Robert Gomberg, "Trends in Theory and Practice," Part 2 of "Family Diagnosis," *Social Casework*, Volume XXXIX, Nos. 2–3 (1958), pp. 73–74.

suffered from fatigue "could not get things done" because she constantly had to interrupt her housework to be with her preschool child. The worker suggested to the mother that she give the daughter play materials and invite her to play in the same room in which the mother was working. On another occasion, this mother complained about having to put the daughter to sleep in the parents' bed because the child was so frightened. The worker explained why this was not good for the child and proposed that the mother, who was an avid reader, try reading in the daughter's bedroom until the child fell asleep.

The depressed parent often feels burdened by his child's demands. Utilization of various community resources, such as nursery school, summer camp, or youth group, can relieve the parent of certain pressures. At the same time, the child can form constructive relationships with his peers and with adults other than his parents. However, the worker should wait until there has been some lessening of the parent's guilt before he broaches the matter of using community resources. Otherwise, the parent may feel too guilty to permit the child to be separated from him.

The Handling of Anger and Guilt

The technique of universalization, in which the worker generalizes about emotional reactions, is an important method of reducing guilt and lessening the demands of a severe superego. The depressed parent can benefit from the worker's universalization of the emotion of anger. At times the worker's therapeutic questioning of the parent's need to be self-condemnatory can alleviate some of his guilt. The worker must be careful, however, not to create more guilt by offering too much sympathy. One chronically depressed mother remarked helplessly that whenever her son became angry she felt she was an utter failure. She castigated herself because she believed that if she had handled the situation properly he would not have had a temper outburst. The worker questioned whether the child's anger necessarily implied that the mother was a failure, and said that all children become angry at times. The mother then told of an instance in which she had handled the child well, and the worker was able to offer his support. The caseworker must be aware that the depressed person wishes to be punished and expects to be rejected, especially when he receives dependency gratifications. The worker's support of the parent may release a good deal of guilt, which the worker must then deal with. One mother, temporarily adopting the role of the worker, asked anxiously, "How are things going?" When the worker pointed out the mother's concern, she expressed guilt about not having been able to give sympathy to a sick friend. As a result, she felt bad about receiving support from the worker. The mother wondered whether the worker planned to continue seeing her and spoke about past rejections. She wept as she voiced her fear that the worker, too, would let her down.

The Recognition and Ventilation of Hostile Feelings

When a positive relationship with the parent has been established, the worker may be able to help him externalize the hostility that he has turned in upon himself. The worker must be careful not to liberate too much hostility in the beginning phases of treatment because the depressed person has had to employ tortuous defenses against expressions of anger and resentment. The worker should avoid using such terms as "mad" or "angry," and should instead use words like "disappointed," "let down," or "annoyed." Sometimes, through the use of an incident unrelated to the parent's family life and its emotion-laden relationships, the worker can help the parent recognize that he does have angry feelings. For example, Mrs. H, who was active in scouting, felt deeply criticized when she was "bawled out" by a scout leader for "being eight minutes late" to a meeting. Mrs. H remarked that it "was a hell of a thing," and she laughed with relief when the worker jokingly pointed out to her that perhaps she wished the leader to "go to hell."

I have found that the ventilation of anger can be made more acceptable to some depressed parents when I use mildly aggressive words such as "heck," "hell," and "damn," which are used commonly in everyday conversation. Through identification with me, the parent can use these words as vehicles for his own anger. It is important for a caseworker to be able to sense correctly the client's readiness for the use of this technique. Moderate and appropriately timed use of the vernacular can become an integral part of supportive casework treatment when intermingled with encouragement, reassurance, and suggestion.

The afore-mentioned Mrs. H complained of her inability to cope with her nine-year-old daughter, Virginia. Whenever Mrs. H attempted to control the child's behavior, Virginia would say, "Mother, you're angry with me," and would have a temper tantrum immediately. Mrs. H would then experience a typical depressive reaction. She would turn her resentment against herself and helplessly back down in her demands on Virginia, or she would go to bed because of her deep feelings of failure and guilt. At times she infantilized her daughter by combing her hair, brushing her teeth, and bathing her. She felt that Virginia was "so sweet" at these times, and caring for the child gratified her own dependency needs. Virginia, in turn, would wait upon her mother when she was ill and would bring her medicine, tuck in the blankets, caress her forehead, and verbally console her. Mrs. H received very little emotional support from Mr. H, who also suffered from periodic depressions and an undiagnosed gastrointestinal disorder. He often berated his wife for "letting the kids run her," but he undercut her shaky authority by telling their two daughters to "take care of your mother" when he went off on business trips.

During the four years immediately preceding her casework treatment,

Mrs. H had been seen monthly by a neuropsychiatrist for supportive treatment and drug therapy because her feelings of depression had been intensified by a hysterectomy. Deprivation in her early life was a major factor in her continued predisposition to depression. She described her mother as a narcissistic, critical, selfish person who "did not care for us," and her father as a shadowy figure who was chronically ill and who had died when she was 16 years of age. A sister three years her senior had cared for her and had assumed almost full responsibility for her. In order to communicate with her mother, Mrs. H had had to go through a chain of command: her older siblings had acted as intermediaries between her and her mother.

As Mrs. H experienced the acceptability of her feelings within the casework relationship, she was gradually able to bring out her anger toward Virginia. Some of the supportive techniques discussed earlier are illustrated in the following series of excerpts from interviews with Mrs. H:

> Mrs. H proudly related how she has learned to be more consistently firm about the limits she sets for Virginia. She laughingly told of one incident when Virginia accused her of being angry with her. Mrs. H said she had retorted, "You're right, I'm damned angry." During this hour Mrs. H reported that she no longer found it necessary to bathe and dress Virginia, and that the child was doing this herself.
>
> In an interview a few weeks later Mrs. H reported that Virginia had had a temper tantrum over Mrs. H's refusal to write a Thanksgiving story for her as a part of a homework assignment. Mrs. H had handled Virginia's underlying fear about her inability to write the story by exclaiming, "Hell, you can do it if you try." When Mrs. H remained firm, Virginia was able to write her own story. Mrs. H then read it and complimented Virginia on what a fine job she had done. The child responded by saying, "You're the best mother." Mrs. H had some lingering guilt feelings that she had been too "forceful" with Virginia about the story. The worker pointed out how Mrs. H had brought out the best in Virginia, and discussed the meaning of the child's accomplishment in terms of a growth experience.
>
> In the next interview Mrs. H reported humorously that after using a cuss word with Virginia, the child had remarked with surprise in her voice, "Mother, I wouldn't talk that way, but I like it when you're so hardhearted." The worker helped Mrs. H to see how important it was for Virginia to sense her mother's firmness and strength, and how, in turn, this contributed to the child's security.

Experiential or Relationship Therapy

In a subsequent interview, Mrs. H recalled the time when she had been pregnant with Virginia. She revealed a good deal of guilt-laden material concerning her shock and anger at discovering her unwanted pregnancy. Her reliving of this experience during the interview, and her use of the casework relationship to become more constructively assertive with her daughter, indicated that she had moved into a more intensive treatment relationship. This shift in relationship at a certain point during supportive treatment takes place in many instances of casework with depressed parents.

Alexander and French,[9] Austin,[10] Kaplan,[11] Levine,[12] and others have labeled this intensification of the relationship and its therapeutic implications "experiential," "relationship," or "intermediary" therapy. According to these writers the relationship provides a "corrective emotional experience." The client finds that the caseworker does not respond in the manner the client anticipates as a result of his earlier relationships and experiences with parental figures. This new kind of relationship provides a model for healthier identifications. As one parent commented, "Now when things aren't going well, something you have said flashes through my mind." The goal of experiential therapy is the modification of the client's personality pattern, or some change in his behavior which will decrease his vulnerability to external pressures. Restrictive ties to parental figures are loosened by the reliving of certain feelings and attitudes that have caused problems in the past. In some instances "casework carried out with an understanding use of the transference relationship, plus attempts at clarification and at giving the client intellectual awareness of the way the past interferes with present functioning, can result in the development of degrees of insight which will lead to better integrative behavior."[13] In many cases, however, the therapeutic relationship can lead to change even when the client does not have intellectual awareness.

Use of the Casework Relationship

I have found that it is frequently necessary to undertake experiential therapy as part of the casework treatment of the depressed parent if important changes in the parent-child relationship are to occur. Perhaps this is because deprivation in the parent's earliest relationships is a major factor in his depression. Mrs. T, the submissive, depressed mother of Mary, a pre-school child, illustrates this point. During Mary's infancy Mrs. T's depression had contributed to the child's affect deprivation, which had caused a serious disturbance in the child's ability to develop meaningful relationships with her parents, teachers, and peers. Mr. T was a coldly intellectual man who was almost completely involved in his own career and who had been unable to give his wife the support she needed when she had been overwhelmed with the care of the child.

> During her interviews, Mrs. T commented on how tiring it was for her to be alone all day with Mary because of her own need for companionship and understanding. Her forced smiles quickly dissolved into tears, and she

[9] Franz Alexander and Thomas Morton French, *Psychoanalytic Therapy*, Ronald Press Co., New York, 1946.

[10] Lucille N. Austin, "Trends in Differential Treatment in Social Casework," *Journal of Social Casework*, Volume XXIX, No. 6 (1948), pp. 203–11.

[11] Alex H. Kaplan, "Psychiatric Syndromes and the Practice of Social Work," *Social Casework*, Volume XXXVII, No. 3 (1956), pp. 107–12.

[12] Maurice Levine, "Principles of Psychiatric Treatment," *Dynamic Psychiatry*, Franz Alexander and Helen Ross (eds.), University of Chicago Press, Chicago, 1952, pp. 307–66.

[13] Kaplan, *op. cit.*, p. 111.

cried frequently. She would do housework all day and then go to bed exhausted. There was a striking parallel in her relationship to her own mother, who also was described as having done housework all day and having been "too busy" to play with Mrs. T when she was a child. Mrs. T cried softly as she spoke of her deep need for "someone who would be a companion to me, who would laugh and talk with me"—someone who would be different from her cold, over-controlling mother who was "so much older."

Following the ventilation of these feelings, Mrs. T reported that she and her daughter had played store together, using a makeshift cardboard box. Mrs. T had saved empty food containers for the "store." Mary would delightedly buy and sell food, and Mrs. T would take on the roles of customer and grocer as her daughter wished. Mrs. T improvised play money to add an extra touch to the game. She also had tea parties, using Mary's toy cups and saucers, but real tea and cookies.

Thus, as Mrs. T relived some of her feelings about past deprivations, she was able gradually to become more spontaneous and giving toward her child. She did not make any insightful statements about how the repetition of past problems had affected the mother-daughter relationship of the present. She did, however, experience this insight emotionally as she became more able to find new ways of relating to her child.

A parent can use the casework relationship to test new ways of behaving in an assertive manner, ways that can then be used in other life situations. For example, in a later interview Mrs. T reported that she felt tense whenever she decided to use her own judgment rather than follow the worker's advice in a particular situation. The worker stressed that it was all right for her to disagree and to make her own decisions. Mrs. T commented, "I'm learning that," and in a subsequent interview reported that she had taken the initiative in organizing a Great Decisions group.

The Recognition of Dependency Needs

The parent may be helped to gain a measure of insight into how his own wishes to be mothered are satisfied through the child. In pointing out to the depressed person that he has passive-dependent wishes, the worker must be tactful and must offer reassurance that these wishes are acceptable. The parent may then become aware of his ambivalence toward significant figures who have in some way frustrated or exploited his dependency needs. For example, in one interview Mrs. H, who was discussed earlier, brought out painful memories of her own mother. This subject had been touched off by a visit from her mother, who was making the rounds of various relatives' homes. Her mother suffered from a heart condition and required Mrs. H's constant attention when she visited her.

Mrs. H related sadly that she had always had the feeling that "when mother is around you should be quiet and keep away." She felt that her mother was more like a grandmother to her because of a wide age difference, but that there had always been a distance between them. Mrs. H wanted to "make it up to Virginia because of the attention I lacked." The worker explained that mothers often give their children the love they themselves have missed and in this way also "make it up to themselves." The worker reminded Mrs. H of the sensation of warmth and closeness she felt when caring for Virginia, and gave examples of her infantilization of the child. Mrs. H reflected on this and realized she had "always looked for a mother." She described how utterly dependent she had become on a close friend, to the extent that the friend had often taken Virginia (as an infant) to the doctor and had even arranged the appointments. On one occasion the doctor had angrily asked both adults, "Who is the mother here?" Later the friend had died of a heart attack. Mrs. H commented significantly that "I was almost relieved after her death because I felt freer." Later in the hour Mrs. H was able to acknowledge her anger toward her mother, who also made many demands on her and yet was unable to assume a maternal role toward her.

Insight into the Sources of Anger and Guilt

Once a parent is encouraged to feel that the emotion of anger can be appropriate or justifiable, the worker may be able to move into the area of feelings of anger and guilt that are inappropriate in the present because they are related to childhood experiences. Kaplan indicates that "a degree of insight" can be achieved with clients who have fairly good ego strength. He succinctly states the following general rule as a guide: "The weaker the ego strength, the more supportive the casework; and conversely, the stronger the ego strength, the more intensive the casework."[14] Therefore, when a depressed parent exhibits relatively good ego strength, it may be possible to uncover the source of his anger in a childhood situation and relate it to current relationships with his child and other family members. In this way, restrictive ties to the past are loosened so that the parent is able to obtain some degree of insight into his relationships with others. The effort to decrease the severity of the superego, however, must go hand in hand with the client's increasing awareness of his anger.

Mr. R constantly berated himself, thought himself worthless, and felt helpless in dealing with the significant people in his life. His relationship to his mother had been marked by a seductive dependency and overcloseness. He reported that when his mother died he went into a reactive depression lasting a year. Since then, despite his predisposition to depression, he has been able to hold a responsible position as a district manager of a large wholesale store. His wife contributed to Mr. R's need to berate himself. She had a belittling, provocative manner of relating to him, in contrast to a seductive way of relating to an adolescent son. The family seemed to be paired off; Mr. R. had a "special bond" with nine-year-old Teddy (the patient) and an almost maternal overconcern for the child's welfare. Whenever Mr. R returned home from work feeling blue, he would sit up late and watch television with his son on his lap.

In casework treatment Mr. R needed to paint with heavy black-and-white strokes the picture he gave his parents. He described his father as the angry and punitive villain, while his mother was depicted as saintly and all-giving. When the case was taken for psychiatric consultation, it was decided that Mr. R needed to explore his ambivalent feelings toward his mother. Gradually Mr. R was helped to recognize that his feelings of helplessness and his wish

[14] Kaplan, *op. cit.*, p. 112.

to "stay under the covers" were related to his mother's overprotection of him. He recognized that his mother "had taken something away from him" by her over-solicitous behavior. His mother's role in keeping him apart from his father, as well as his guilt in having his mother all to himself, became evident. He brought out his fear that his adolescent son might displace him in his wife's affections much as he had displaced his own father in his mother's affections. Mr. R began to have a clearer picture of his father as a weak person who was, analogously, dependent on Mr. R's mother and a rival of Mr. R for her attentions. Mr. R was helped to clarify his fear of losing his mother: "Mother was my entire world, and I couldn't go against her." His need to feel close and safe made it necessary for him to suppress his anger lest he be rejected or suffer retaliation. The theme of his introjected guilt concerning his mother was, "How could I be angry with you? Look at all you have done for me." In an earlier interview Mr. R had said, "When I married my wife, I was very mean to her and cross all the time." Now he saw that the reason for this behavior was that he had been unconsciously asking himself, "Why is this woman keeping me from Mother?" He recognized his ambivalent tie to his mother, who would say, "Come live with me; you're sick, you need my help." Mr. R summed up his feelings by saying, "That's why I always had to feel I was bad." He then related this material to his fear of making the same mistake with his son, and was able to recognize that he must permit the boy to grow up.

Conclusion

Supportive techniques of encouragement, reassurance, guidance, and utilization of community resources can be helpful in fostering attitudes of self-respect and adequacy in the depressed parent. As the casework relationship is intensified, the "corrective emotional experience" can free the client from certain feelings and attitudes that have caused disturbances in the parent-child relationship. The parent is then enabled to try out newer and healthier modes of relating to the child.

Although casework treatment will vary according to the client's motivation for change and the degree of his ego strength, the worker should not make an "either/or" choice between supportive treatment and insight therapy. Both types of treatment, and the techniques appropriate to each, can be utilized profitably in casework treatment of the depressed parent.

Psychosis—Schizophrenia

Ego Breakdown in Schizophrenia: Some Implications for Casework Treatment

Esther S. Marcus

The last decade has seen considerable increase in systematic attempts to understand the dynamics of schizophrenia and to apply this understanding to the treatment of schizophrenic patients. As the over-all knowledge about schizophrenia has grown, there has been increasing recognition of the numbers of people—people without florid symptomatology—to whom this diagnosis applies. We now know that the schizophrenic personality structure has many manifestations and that the degree of social functioning can vary enormously. In some individuals, the diagnosis is fairly obvious; in others, only careful clinical evaluation and perhaps the use of projective tests can detect the thought disorder pathognomonic of schizophrenia. Some individuals can live a lifetime with the ego defect covered over. In others, increasing dysfunction may be stimulated by any number of inner and outer stresses. Frequently, it is the manifestation of the problem in social and interpersonal areas which causes these people to seek help—and to seek it at a social agency. Under the diagnostic labels of ambulatory, incipient, latent, or borderline schizophrenics, they make up a large proportion of the caseloads in community agencies and clinics. In addition, caseworkers frequently have contact with acutely disturbed schizophrenics, either by assisting in hospitalization or by later collaborative treatment in the mental hospital. The posthospitalized schizophrenic may also be receiving casework help. The worker's role and the goal of treatment naturally vary from case to case and are influenced by the setting. It is hoped, however, that increased understanding of some of the dynamics of schizophrenia and of the principles of treatment will make more effective the help given all these clients.

The subject of schizophrenia is vast, and the areas of new and helpful knowledge are many. However, I shall limit myself in this paper primarily to a discussion of the structural changes that occur in the schizophrenic personality in the process of breakdown and their significance for understanding the communications and treatment needs of the schizophrenic. I shall also consider some implications for casework treatment.

Reprinted from the *American Journal of Orthopsychiatry*, XXXI (April, 1961), pp. 368–387.
Copyright, the American Orthopsychiatric Association, Inc. Reproduced by permission of the author and the Association.

Dynamics

The pioneers in the psychological treatment of schizophrenia started with their ability to sense intuitively what the patient was attempting to communicate. Once there was recognition that schizophrenic productions have meaning and can be understood, there was increasing effort to find a key to an over-all understanding of schizophrenic manifestations. This particular aspect of the study of schizophrenia (and its application in treatment) was given considerable impetus by Paul Federn, whose work was published in comprehensive form in 1952 (3)*. Federn saw the loss of cathexis of the ego boundary, with its attendant loss of a sense of personal identity, as the central feature of schizophrenia. He saw the ego boundary as having the function of a sensory organ that separates the individual from the outside world. A person with a well-functioning ego boundary senses clearly what is inside—whether thought, memory, or fantasy—and what is outside, i.e., a real object or event in the external world.

Freeman, Cameron, and McGhie (4) applied Federn's concepts to their study of a number of chronic schizophrenic patients. They found that regardless of the etiology of the disorder, this "disturbance of the development and maintenance of adequate ego boundaries [is] . . . the central feature of the schizophrenic disease process" (p. 49). With the disruption of the ego boundaries, the schizophrenic experiences uncertainty as to his own existence. He loses a sense of himself as a distinct entity, separate from the external world. He can confuse himself, and parts of his body, with others or with objects in the immediate environment. There may be a vague unclarity as to whether an experience pertained to him or to someone else.

This loss of a sense of personal identity affects not only current experience, but also the patient's capacity to experience himself in a continuum. Although the memory of events may continue, the sense of order and duration is often lost. Intervals in time and place lose their meaning. Events of the distant past may be felt as having just taken place. For example, an apparently coherent, although scattered, woman complained bitterly in an intake interview about the difficulty of having her 90-year-old mother to care for. The interview was well advanced before the worker became aware that the mother had actually been placed in a nursing home four years before.

In the breakdown of ego boundaries and the dissolution of an integral ego, the secondary processes and functions of the ego become impaired. Such functions as perception, memory, and ability to synthesize, to integrate, to comprehend, to organize are affected to varying degrees. What emerges is primary process thinking. Logical thought processes give way to archaic, infantile ways of dealing with the world. Rules of logic, of time and space, of cause and effect cease to exist. The world is perceived in terms of magic and wish fulfillment. Instead of orderly, reality-oriented thought

*References will be found at the end of the chapter.

processes, there is the use of the primary process mechanisms of displacement, condensation, symbolic thought, and concrete thinking. The impairment of the capacity for abstract thinking is a major feature of the thought disorder. It is seen, for example, in the literal interpretations of proverbs frequently given by schizophrenic individuals.

> One fairly intact, well-functioning woman, when asked the meaning of the proverb "People who live in glass houses shouldn't throw stones," replied that the glass might break.
>
> It is illustrated in the behavior of a young man with an extremely high IQ who was, however, failing in college. He was amazed and uncomprehending when he failed a one-credit "snap" course because of overcutting. It was finally possible to discover that he had not kept track of his absences in this course because in the first session the instructor had told the students that the course was so easy they could "pass it without coming to class"! This same young man could not understand why he received a zero on an essay question in which he was asked to discuss the effectiveness of the inflationary measures utilized during the depression. His answer that "they were fairly effective"— showing both concrete thinking and condensation—seemed to him a satisfactory response.

The loss of a sense of personal identity, the fusion of the inner and outer world, with little ability to localize and organize stimuli arising from either source, and the replacement of secondary thought processes by primary process thought mechanisms help explain much of the bizarre behavior of the psychotic schizophrenic. I shall examine only a few of the grosser manifestations, keeping in mind the fact that to a lesser degree the same process operates in the less acutely disturbed schizophrenic. There is the "schizophrenic's susceptibility to environmental stimuli, which he is [however] unable to perceive in their proper order and context" (4, pp. 61–62).

> An example of this was a client who was engaged in an apparently jumbled and incoherent conversation. As she was listened to, it became apparent that the talk was in part a response to inner stimuli; i.e., as a thought came into her mind she might express it or she might counter it as if responding to someone else's voice. This talk was interspersed with responses to external stimuli not immediately obvious to the interviewer. For example, there were responses to snatches heard from other people's conversations. There was an apparent response to the blowing of a car horn, which must have implied to her that someone was double parked, because she then admonished the imagined culprit, etc.

Freeman et al. (4, p. 62) found that "this incorporation of random stimuli into the patient's stream of talk was very common and explained much of the apparent bizarreness and lack of purpose in the speech content."

The phenomenon of hallucinations can be understood when viewed in terms of the breakdown of the outer and inner ego boundaries. Freeman et al. point out that the breakdown of the ego boundary and the "reduced awareness of the mental and bodily ego, leads to an experience of the thought processes as divorced from the control of the individual, and therefore as alien and externally located. . . . Thus the patient's own thoughts, lacking ego feeling and therefore a sense of inner 'belongingness' are perceived by him as externally located auditory and visual experiences" (4, pp. 64 and 65).

The breakdown of the secondary process mechanisms also helps explain the formation of delusions. The *purpose* of the delusion, as pointed out by a number of authors (1, 2, 3), is to cope with the havoc caused by the breakdown of the ego boundary, when the world becomes strange, chaotic, fragmented, and incomprehensible. There is an attempt to explain the confusion caused by the perceptual disturbances and to make some order out of chaos. This is done, however, in terms of a false reality, i.e., a reality in which rules of logic, cause and effect, etc., do not exist. For example, if the schizophrenic feels that people know his thoughts, he might explain this by the existence of a machine that reads the mind—or, on a somewhat higher level—by the fact that his wife must be telling his secrets.

> One client, a butcher, complained that there was a conspiracy to drive him out of work (otherwise, how explain that he lost one job after another?), that he was being given conflicting information about prices, that his fellow employees frequently pushed his arm so that he cut the meat incorrectly, and that he was being distracted from his work by whisperings regarding his personal life. It was quite obvious that these delusional ideas were his attempts to explain increasing periods of lack of contact during which he became oblivious to his surroundings and to the passing of time, engulfed in his own unintegrated past. His confusion made it impossible for him to remember which prices were in operation at the moment, and he might cut the meat in response to an order given three days before.

Important for our purpose is some consideration of the course that the illness takes. Eissler says that "the schizophrenic process may take its full course or may come to a standstill at any point of its development" (2, p. 164). Federn indicates: "The personality disintegrates slowly, reality perception still controls the more important falsifications, and a rather good adjustment may last for many years with a very slow change to the better or the worse. Therefore psychotherapy has a good chance to protect an individual against recrudescence of the disease" (3, p. 170). He makes a distinction between latent schizophrenia, i.e., a personality in which the underlying structure is a schizophrenic one, but overt psychosis is kept in check, and early or incipient schizophrenia. He says that "the therapeutic aim is to prevent a latent schizophrenia from becoming a manifest one. For this reason the diagnosis of latent schizophrenia should be made early. Even though it may be impossible to prevent the outbreak, the attempt is worth our while since the outcome of schizophrenia is unpredictable in any case" (pp. 169–70).

Eissler says that preceding the acute outbreak of the illness there is frequently a period of withdrawal. "It seems as if the ego has fought a long time to keep up its interest in the world, then a sudden collapse sets in. . . . More often the period of withdrawal is clinically mute, long lasting and not noticed by the patient's environment, often not even by the patient himself" (2, p. 160). In the second phase, that of collapse, the patient feels confused, dreamlike, disorganized, unable to comprehend what is going on around him; the ego is fragmented; everything is unreal and chaotic. In the state of restitution, when the ego again pushes toward reality, one finds the delusional system setting in—the attempt to explain the psychotic perception of the world. These three stages are separated thus primarily for purposes of discussion. In actuality, it is not always possible to tell whether the delusions are part of the initial phase or the postacute phase. Eissler has pointed out that a patient may be in all three phases at the same time. In addition, he has found that some patients do not go through the second stage, but form delusions in what he calls a "short-cut" manner (p. 160).

In evaluating the seriousness of a patient's illness, Eissler says that he is "convinced that a prognosis . . . cannot be made in terms of whether the patient is smearing feces or is orally fixated. The decisive point is the extent of regression in the ego and possible destruction of higher ego functions" (2, pp. 160–161). In considering the effect of the illness—i.e., whether the higher ego functions have been preserved, temporarily impaired, or permanently damaged—it is necessary to know the extent to which these functions had been developed prior to breakdown. There is considerable variation. For example, in some individuals executive ego functions may be highly developed; in others, very little. Even after acute breakdown, some schizophrenics may show considerable residual capacity for synthetic thinking—even when this thinking is coupled with a defective sense of reality as manifested in delusional ideas.

Although these dynamics have been described in terms of the acutely disturbed, their understanding is important in working with the less disturbed schizophrenic; the variations we find are of degree rather than kind.

Treatment

Many writers agree that the earlier in the course of the illness the patient receives treatment, the more favorable the prognosis. However, establishing and maintaining contact with these individuals present special problems. Some of the problems in initial contact have been discussed elsewhere (7). We know that frequently these clients do not ask for help in the usual sense. They present themselves, and their communication needs to be understood. More than with the neurotic client, the decision about appropriate activity rests with the worker. The schizophrenic client has little ability to synthesize an entire situation, to know what is wrong, and to present some formulated solution—no matter how potentially unhelpful—with which he requests help.

> For example, in one rather extreme case, the client began, in the intake interview, by talking aimlessly, could not say what was wrong or why she had come, and finally said that she did not know what to prepare for dinner. The worker, realizing the degree and nature of disturbance that this behavior portended, began to clarify, in a simple and active way, what the woman's

living situation was. What emerged from this and subsequent contacts was that this schizophrenic woman and her two children had been cared for by her mother, who had recently had a stroke. The client stated that she had no one other than her mother. While not factually true, her statement was psychologically true. Her siblings had at first provided a housekeeper, but when the mother improved slightly, withdrew her on the assumption that the client could take over the tasks. In a state of helplessness and abandonment as acute as that of a young child, and just as incapable of visualizing a solution, she presented the immediate and crucial problem confronting her—without her mother, she and her children were in danger of starvation. The worker gave simple instructions regarding food, provided assurance that the agency would stand by and work out some plan to help, and kept in telephone contact over the weekend, in order to hold the situation together pending exploration of other plans.

Sometimes these clients are able to ask for help with a specific problem. Less frequent, however, is the request for help with personality difficulties. There is little sense of "This is me, this is how I function in relation to situations and people, these are the people I cannot get along with, these are the situations I cannot cope with." In addition, any suggestion of a personal problem (i.e., of there being something wrong with the individual) generally is devastating, and too intolerable to face. As they continue, withdrawn clients generally have little ability to state what they are getting from contact or why they want to go on. In several cases in which clients had shown evidence of considerably improved functioning and a decrease in withdrawal, and in which the relationship with the worker was extremely important, there was no concomitant ability to verbalize this. While in their own indirect way they all indicated a need for continued contact, their comments were typified by the vague "I think you helped me with my thinking." Some could point only to concrete reasons. For example, one client was not ready to stop seeing the worker because he still had a problem—his parents had not yet moved out of their junk-filled apartment! However, even his ability to state definitely that he needed to continue represented considerable progress.

Much of the treatment activity is determined by the extent to which the schizophrenic's communication is understood. The difficulty in grasping the communication varies, depending on the extent of destruction of higher ego functions, and the extent to which the communication is in primary process language. With some clients the communication is fairly direct; with others less so.

> For example, one client, the butcher earlier mentioned, in an acute psychotic state and in need of immediate hospitalization, telephoned while his wife was being seen and told the worker that he was thinking of buying a cemetery plot for himself, his wife, and their children. He said that until now what had kept him from killing his wife was the thought that his children would be left alone. He had decided that perhaps it would be better if they all went together, and he was going ahead with the arrangements. But he was not going to let anyone put him in a hospital. The worker assumed that he was letting her know that the flimsy controls over his impulses were breaking

down. His spontaneous comment about hospitalization indicated that somewhere there was some awareness that he was ill and in need of it; and his comment was in response to this inner awareness. The worker then went on the assumption that he would be relieved by hospitalization. She was positive in suggesting it to the wife, who arranged for an ambulance. When the police and the ambulance arrived, the wife was quite surprised by her husband's meekness, but even more so by his lucid statement that if she was really arranging to take him to the hospital, then he was glad to go because he wanted treatment. This was a startlingly lucid comment in the midst of days of acute paranoid disturbance.

In another situation a posthospitalized young woman with a well-developed delusional system revolving around her religious beliefs complained to the worker that a demon in the form of a bird had been recently alighting on her shoulder and singing popular songs—something which was against her strong religious convictions. The worker surmised that this was an expression of emerging conflict over her rigid morality. She therefore worked with the client on the idea that some very religious people saw God as not frowning on lighter things like popular music and that it would be understandable if she as a young person was interested in it. The "bird" shortly thereafter disappeared.

Two major aspects of work with schizophrenics are the need to establish affective contact with the individual and the need to strengthen his enfeebled ego. The two are separable primarily for purposes of discussion, because generally the establishment of affective contact is the framework for all other treatment principles. The patient must in some way begin to experience an emotional connection with the therapist. This in itself is an important part of treatment, is ego strengthening, and is essential if further work is to be done. Eissler, in discussing the break with reality, has pointed out that in the course of it "a real person [the therapist] can be cathected by the patient with narcissistic libido and at that point the breakdown of the ego boundary, the fusion between ego and world, can be at least temporarily stopped" (2, p. 145).

Much has been written in psychiatric literature about the qualities in the therapist that bring about this situation. Sechehaye (8), Fromm-Reichmann (5), Hill (6), and others have emphasized various aspects. Whatever method one uses, the wish to penetrate the isolation of the individual and to establish a connection with him is important. The therapist's need to be there for the person, to become part of his life and his world, and to feel that he, the therapist, will stop the internal destruction that is taking place, is vital. Eissler points out that the doctor "should believe in his own omnipotence; the patient's recovery must be of high emotional importance to him" (2, p. 164). Whatever the therapist's underlying motivation, the need to "rescue" the other individual must be strong.

Care must be taken to avoid activity or behavior that is likely to arouse negative feelings toward the worker. The capacity for object relationships is poor, and the relationship with the worker can easily be disrupted by a negative reaction. The effect of this disruption is greater and more far-reaching than it is with the neurotic client.

For example, after an extended contact with one well-functioning, borderline schizophrenic woman, the worker pointed out that the client had difficulty in seeing something new if it came from the worker, and that this apparently interfered with the gratification that the client was getting out of her newly found and growing ability to see and understand her own behavior. Although the client was able to see this intellectually, her emotional reaction was that the worker was trying to take something away from her—this new-found area of gratification—and therefore the worker temporarily became the "evil mother." In spite of a very positive relationship, the client went through a period of increased disorganization, re-experiencing some feelings of estrangement and of increased helplessness, none of which had been in evidence for some time previously. With a neurotic client, although the reaction of annoyance at the worker might be similar, one would not expect the same kind of total effect on the client's functioning.

The same care should be applied in dealing with any significant object relationship. Negative reaction to parental figures should not be elicited precipitously. In spite of the destructiveness that may exist in the parental relationship, or may have existed in the past, the tie, however tenuous, to the object, i.e., the parent, may be crucial in maintaining a connection with reality. In addition, unconscious identification with parental figures may make premature emphasis on their negative qualities narcissistically destructive.

Much of the treatment activity aimed at ego strengthening is determined by the schizophrenic's lack of awareness of subjective feelings, difficulty in separating the internal from the external, and general impairment of the sense of personal identity. These clients need help in knowing what they are feeling, what they are reacting to, what others are feeling. The most obvious surface feelings such as sadness, hurt, annoyance are frequently not perceived and not expressed directly. Suggesting, for example, that the fidgety client is feeling restless, and may want to leave, may appear simple but can be meaningful to a person who has little tangible sense of himself. They need help in identifying symptoms of the illness in order to counteract secondary threats to the ego. Where there has been impairment or destruction of the secondary functions of the ego, such as ability to concentrate, to organize, to work—the client may see this as laziness, incompetence, or stupidity. Recognizing these changes as symptoms can help counteract the guilt, self-criticism and feelings of inadequacy. Identifying the various symptoms that make up anxiety or depression can also be of considerable relief to an individual who sees them in a fragmented form and experiences the reactions as mysterious and frightening. In relation to any symptom, the hope can be held out that with treatment it could be modified.

The executive and synthesizing functions of the ego having been disrupted in the process of breakdown and as a result of it, anything that encourages a feeling of mastery and of ability to cope with internal and external pressures is vital. Activity aimed at helping cope with internal pressures is frequently related to reducing guilt and anxiety, counteracting feelings of helplessness and helping the person deal with the conflicts which are overwhelming him. What these are is frequently conveyed through the fantasy, delusion, or hallucination, which is a communication in primary process language. Once the process of breakdown has begun it is accelerated by the emergence of unacceptable and previously repressed impulses and fantasies, or as Federn holds, improperly decathected previous ego states. Freeman et al. point out that "the hallucination or delusion is invariably stimulated by the patient's present experiences . . . such activity is closely related to the patient's earlier experiences, but fully understood only when its relevance to the present events is appreciated" (4, pp. 70 and 71). This means that "listening sympathetically" to this kind of material and at the same time looking for the first opportunity to shift to "reality" matters is not necessarily the most helpful way of dealing with the situation and overlooks opportunities for understanding, and helping the client understand what is going on for him.

This does not mean that the emergence of fantasies should be encouraged and that efforts should be made to obtain details for their own sake. If, however, the material that is presented is examined for its specific connection with the individual's immediate life situation, this scrutiny will of necessity determine the detail that needs to be elicited.

> For example, in one interview a posthospitalized client spoke in an agitated fashion, reliving the horror of her pregnancy and delivery ten years before. The worker focused first not on what had been so disturbing about that pregnancy, but on what was stimulating this material at this particular time. She was able to obtain sufficient facts to conclude that it was probably connected with the woman's having had intercourse without contraceptives the night before. Although, in response to the worker's comment, the client claimed that she was sure she was "safe," actually the thought had occurred that she might conceive. Once the fantasy was there she responded to it emotionally as if it were fact, and all the old unintegrated terror was evoked. The worker pointed out that she was reacting as if she were pregnant, and reinforced the realistic appraisal that it was very unlikely, and that even if she were to conceive, a pregnancy now need not be the same as the previous one. When her agitation diminished, it was possible to help her examine somewhat more dispassionately what had gone on during her pregnancy ten years before that had made it such a nightmare for her.

Even in the acute period of the disturbance, when "the patient's ego feels itself at one with the schizophrenic symptomatology" (2, p. 131), some vestige of reasonable ego remains. The fact that the client does not spontaneously share regressed or bizarre fantasy or activity may be part of the attempt by the remaining intact portions of the ego to continue to keep it in check. If, however, the material is agitating to the client and arouses anxiety about "insanity" or some other self-critical reaction, ignoring its existence is not helpful, for these reactions themselves serve as an undermining force. If the client provides any indication that such a force is operating, the worker needs to get enough of an idea of what is going on to counteract the secondary reaction. This does not mean that the behavior or preoccupation should be sanctioned by the worker or the client. The recognition that there is something wrong with the ideas or behavior can be tacitly affirmed, while the self-flagellation is converted to an interest in understanding the purpose—frequently defensive—that the ideas serve.

> For example, a woman whose husband was dying felt guilty about her fantasies revolving around her contemplated life after his death, and frightened and disturbed by the fact that she had recurrent fantasies about his corpse. Without eliciting details about the corpse fantasies, and thus inadvertently encouraging the preoccupation, the worker brought out the mere fact that she had them. The client was considerably relieved to have the realistic horror in her husband's impending death affirmed, and her fantasies explained as one part of her attempt to make the unknown future less frightening.

Frequently, behavior that the client is distressed about and that the worker himself may question can be dealt with as an effort on the client's part to cope with his life, thus avoiding trouble with either the client's or the worker's superego and the undermining of healthy—as against archaic—superego reactions.

> For example, a client who had been married chaotically to several deteriorated men was able, with help, to free herself from the last. She went to work for the first time in her life and, in addition, established a much quieter and less destructive relationship with a man who helped support her. She began to berate herself for allowing this relationship to continue and yet was obviously unable to give it up. The client's self-criticism, focused on its lack of permanent satisfaction and the damage to her growing child, was not disputed. However, the worker highlighted both its improvement over previous relationships and its representation of a growing ability, in the face of a difficult situation, to do something about it. Instead of returning to her psychotic mother, as she had done in the past, she had been able this time to find someone to help take care of her while she needed this help. The various other ways open to people in her situation, which she might eventually be able to use, were discussed. The worker in this way bolstered the ego ideal by pointing up the client's own implied more mature standards, and by retaining them as a goal. The client can be told that as he feels better, less frightened, and stronger, he will more and more act in accordance with a realistic ideal.

A vital part of treatment is to diminish feelings of helplessness. Frequently these are heightened by the client's feeling that a decision has been taken out of his hands or that he is at the mercy of others. The recognition of this in itself can offer some relief, and where possible, helping him see his contribution to the specific situation can counteract the feeling of helplessness. This effect can be achieved, for example, by pointing out when there is enough specific evidence that the client had something to do with another's negative response to him, or with the termination of a relationship. Helping the person cope with frustration and tolerate intense feelings is ego strengthening. The fact that a need, for example, is great can be recognized. However, the extent of the need can sometimes be explained as being the result of the degree of deprivation suffered as a child. This can help diminish somewhat the overwhelming reaction when the need is not met. In general, recognizing painful feelings but conveying the conviction that these can gradually be examined, understood, and coped with, can afford relief. All this allies the client with the worker and mobilizes the ego to work on the reaction instead of merely continuing to be overwhelmed by it. At the same time, it offers a sense of the worker's support.

> For example, in an interview with a woman who was expressing extreme feelings of unworthiness and a sudden inability to deal with the smallest routines, the focus was first on clarifying the onset of the current reaction. It appeared to have been stimulated by a rejection she had experienced the previous week from her husband. Pointing out that her feeling about herself hinged almost totally on others' reactions to her—in this case, her husband's—and that she experienced no sense of self-worth apart from others' approval, directed her interest to this reaction as a mechanism, as something that had its roots in her past and did not need to remain that way. This was pointed out as part of her problem, one which could with time be worked through, so that she could then cope with other people's reactions to her without being overwhelmed.

The worker needs to align himself with the healthy part of the ego, to help the client combat such manifestations of the illness as paranoid reactions. Federn says:

> In treatment, those parts of the ego which still function with adequate distinction of thoughts and reality must be employed as allies. Only with their help can the repair of the deficient part be accomplished (2, p. 167). The latent schizophrenic who begins to become psychotic learns . . . to resist his inclination suddenly to attribute the character of certainty to previous ideas of reference. He himself undergoes the experience that his conscious, critically directed attention is able to correct the beginning falsifications (p. 193).

The focus in the foregoing discussion has been on the intraphysic aspects of treatment aimed at ego strengthening. Space does not permit a discussion of the very important topic of the role of family interaction in either disturbing equilibrium and accelerating the process of breakdown, or in supporting improved functioning. The separation between "internal" and "external" has been made for purposes of discussion, and with complete recognition that it is an artificial one, since the personality is always dually oriented to internal processes and the social environment. Intraphysic and interpersonal processes can generally be defined only in relation to each other—as the last example demonstrates. Nor is it possible to discuss here the wide range of environmental and social measures, and the dynamics of family-oriented treatment. I would like to touch briefly, however, on one aspect relating to external pressures, and relevant to our present topic—considerations in the worker's decision regarding direct involvement in the environment.

One factor in this decision is the client's awareness of his external situation and whether he can keep the worker informed of what is going on.

> For example, the young man who thought he could pass the course without coming to class had no awareness of whether or not he was functioning effectively. He rarely grasped what was expected of him. In the midst of failure, he had the impression that he had done all his assignments or that he had done well on an examination. When he began to express some interest in wanting to do better, the worker established regular contact with the teachers

and kept informed of his actual performance. It was possible in this way to interpret reality to him, help him cope with its demands, and prevent the accumulation of additional avoidable failures.

In general, when there is any indication of difficulty in functioning and when the client is a poor informant, the worker's being "in on" the client's life is important.

> For example, the client who "had been helped with his thinking" had a good possibility of obtaining a very suitable job. He presented no anxiety about the coming job interview. It was only the worker's very specific interest in how he was planning to handle it that revealed that he was probably going to talk himself out of the job, because of some involved reasoning about not wishing to show how desperately he wanted it. By being in on this situation, the worker was able to help him approach the interview much more effectively.

Direct intervention is usually indicated when the client cannot deal effectively with the situation, when it is of importance in his life, and when the worker's intervention will not be experienced as destructive. In one case, intervention might have saved a job for a client, but he felt too threatened by the exposure involved to justify intervention.

The worker's attitude about the environment is important. To be effective he cannot be immobilized by feelings similar to those of the client. He must not feel that the environment is immovable but, on the contrary, must have the conviction and zeal of the mature parent: he nurtures all evidence of growth and maturation; he helps the individual cope with the demands that are made on him; he helps him avoid or postpone situations that he is not ready to cope with and that will be ego weakening; he can sense what disappointments are tolerable and which are intolerable, trying to help avoid the latter and cushioning those he cannot prevent. And when a situation becomes too much, he takes over—if the client permits.

In ego strengthening, the use, emphasis, and timing of any of the treatment principles described vary with the needs of each client and the specific nature of the ego problem. For example, helping the client become more aware of *what* he is feeling seems to be important in early contact with withdrawn clients—the ones who are losing contact without anyone's being aware of what is taking place. The more agitated client who is involved in a more active internal struggle and who shows more evidence of such secondary symptoms as delusions and hallucinations usually requires a more complex approach, involving the counteracting of feelings of helplessness and the diminution of the intensity of some of the conflicts. The case of Mrs. A exemplifies one set of needs and the treatment derived from the principles discussed above.

Mrs. A came to the agency after not following through on two earlier applications. A woman in her early twenties, she had been married twice. The intake worker saw no evidence of serious illness. Mrs. A described a severe marital problem, but placed the blame for all the difficulty on her husband. She was annoyed when the intake worker alluded to Mrs. A's own feelings, and she insisted that it was only Mr. A who needed help.

She subsequently telephoned to refuse the appointment offered by the con-tinued service worker, stating that her husband had changed his mind about using the agency's service. She sounded somewhat incoherent. The worker made an effort to help her come in at least once, but Mrs. A refused.

When Mrs. A called back two months later, she did not ask for an appointment but went into a tirade against her husband. When the worker finally suggested that it might be a good idea for her to come in to see her, she hesitatingly agreed, with interpolated comments that she did not see what for, etc.

In the first interview, her disjointed, rapid-fire monologue bordered on incoherence. She seemed hostile, out of contact, and talked as if the worker were attacking her. She alternated between tirades against her husband and angry defense of herself. She gave information and then had no recollection of having shared it, wanting to know suspiciously how the worker knew these things about her. She did not respond directly to clarifying questions asked by the worker, but would lapse instead into what appeared on the surface to be an unrelated tirade. It was apparent, however, that she had heard what the worker said but that the questions evidently evoked un-bearable feelings with which she attempted to cope through her outbursts. For example, the worker's asking whether she and her husband were still together or apart was apparently intolerable, because Mr. A had left her. She could not state this fact because it was too painful, and she responded instead with an outburst about what a disturbed person he was.

It was apparent that Mrs. A's ego boundary was poorly cathected. She felt internal accusations as coming from the outside. She was confused about the meaning of others' behavior, responded to isolated statements, and was unable to grasp anything but the literal meaning. She had appar-ently been behaving in a panicked, impulsive, aggressive fashion. She was suspicious and somewhat fragmented.

The worker's focus then shifted to an attempt to reach Mrs. A, diminish the agitation, and establish a connection with her. The internal attacks had to be diminished, and she had to be strengthened so that she could cope with what currently felt like an intolerable situation, arousing intolerable feelings. In some way, she needed to be helped to perceive the worker as a supportive figure—one who would help her in her struggle against the encroaching illness.

The worker gave up any attempt to obtain the simplest facts. Instead she responded to the underlying panic—indicating awareness of how frightened, alone, and deserted Mrs. A must have felt and must still be feeling, and how little way out she saw. She was told that such feelings would account for some of the things she had apparently done in the marriage. (Without being specific to Mrs. A, the worker guessed from the latter's defense that she apparently, among other things, had locked her husband out, gone home to her mother, and refused sexual relations.) There was recognition of her inability to comprehend her husband's behavior, and simple explanations were offered as to what he probably meant. There was an attempt to diminish the self-critical reactions which were intolerable and experienced as coming from the outside. She was offered the possibility that with help from the worker she could learn to understand why she did things, could exercise more control over what happened in her life, improve her judgment, and eventually lead the kind of life she wanted for herself. The idea was that initially the control and improved judgment would be a result of the worker's "being in on" her life with her.

During the initial interview—and a number of the early interviews— Mrs. A's shifting and fluid "ego feeling" was graphically in evidence. As she felt relief and some sense of mastery, she quieted down, was aware of the worker, and gave information directly. When this became too painful, she reverted to a defensive tirade and appeared to be out of contact. Her struggle to cope with her feelings of abandonment was evident as she grasped eagerly at the worker's suggestion that she might again at some time in the future be in a position to *choose* a man.

At the end of the first interview the suggestion of further appointments was made on the basis of the worker's desire to help with the many problems and decisions facing Mrs. A, and without allusion to any personality diffi- culties contributing to her problems in her marriages. Mrs. A, who was temporarily relaxed and in contact at the end of the first interview, agreed to return on the basis that she thought the worker understood her. If the worker thought that she could help her and she should return, she would.

As the contact progressed, a clearer picture of Mrs. A's personality emerged. Evidence of the thought disorder and of the poorly cathected and fragmented ego boundaries pointed to a diagnosis of schizophrenia, but there were indications that the process was not far advanced. Her ability to inte- grate experiences was quite faulty. Her behavior was random and impulsive: she had no ability to evaluate her behavior or to connect it with subjectively experienced emotions. Feelings were unintegrated, and behavior was deter- mined by whichever feelings erupted. Judgment of other people was ex- tremely poor. Her sense of self as separate from other people—as a distinct entity both in the past and present—was also poor. For example, there was constant fighting among all her relatives; between her mother and her father, who had separated when Mrs. A was two, but were not divorced; and between her mother and the latter's married lover. When Mrs. A was involved by the others in these arguments, she responded as if she was one of the other family members. Mrs. A's excellent grooming represented a positive carry-over from a time when she took pride in her appearance. Currently, however, it was apparently being done automatically and she was surprised when others commented on it, since generally she felt dirty and unattractive. She frequently spoke of herself in the third person. She would talk to herself as one would to a child. As the contact with the worker progressed, she would imagine what the worker might say to her in a specific situation and she would talk to herself in that way.

Mrs. A had paranoid ideas, with shifting insight into them. When con- tact was advanced she told the worker that she was afraid she had ideas of persecution, with awareness that her reaction was not rational. At other times, particularly at points of severe distress, she had minimal insight into her delusions, which, however, were never florid and did not get out of hand. For example, she thought that someone, "a man", came to the house during the day as evidenced by an unflushed toilet and by a disappearing skirt; and that there were mysterious phone calls which were really from her husband, who was calling both to upset her and to communicate with her. She went as far as considering going to the district attorney's office, but decided to discuss it with the worker first.

She felt little connection with people. As contact progressed, she put into words the dreadful sense of isolation—of being all alone in her own barren world—that she frequently struggled with. She felt confused by much of what went on around her. After two or three months of contact, she had no recollection that her worker was not the same person who had seen her in intake. However, by the time she left treatment, she recalled her much more specific response to the intake worker: that the latter talked in a way which Mrs. A was unable to understand, doing so deliberately to confuse her, because she was against her—"as I felt everyone else to be at that time." Here we see the paranoid reaction to explain her inability to comprehend.

Mrs. A's terror of helplessness—of being under someone else's control—was often in evidence. She had had a paranoid reaction when she had entered a hospital for minor surgery. An extremely traumatic event in her life had been her temporary placement in a shelter at the age of three, during which she had screamed constantly.

The executive functions of Mrs. A's ego were least impaired, and this had probably been important in counterbalancing the disintegrative process. At points of stress, when a situation felt unbearable to her, she *did* something. The behavior might not be thought through, or it might not be the best way of coping with a situation, but she at least acted to relieve the pressure temporarily. She had left home at 17 when the situation there had become too much for her. She became a band singer, going through all the steps involved in interviews, auditions, etc. She opposed her parents in her decision to marry her first husband shortly thereafter; then divorced him. When she felt herself on the verge of a breakdown during the chaotic and tumultuous breakup of her second marriage, she decided that she had to be able to support herself outside show business, and so forced herself— to the extent of muffling her phone—to study stenography until she was able to obtain "respectable" work as a stenographer. However, in many of these situations as she recalled them, she had no awareness of what had motivated her behavior, and, even more, she had the feeling at times that someone else was doing these things, not she.

When she came to the agency, she had nowhere else to flee. She was staying with her mother, who sounded like a rather unrelated, helpless person, somewhat afraid of her daughter, and tending to be controlled by her. She felt herself degraded by two broken marriages, so that fleeing from her mother into the arms of another man when her tension mounted at home was no longer a solution. At the time, she was actually more clinically disturbed than she had ever been.

Mrs. A did not need help in dealing with her external situation in the way schizophrenic clients often do. She was quite capable of getting a job, for example, or of getting any legal information she needed. When she finally decided to move with her mother to another community, she made all the arrangements for housing and employment transfer. What she did need help with, however, was in acquiring a sense of herself as a person, beginning to tolerate, experience and be aware of feelings, and integrating these both currently and in relation to her past relationships. Goals were to help her develop better judgment and to diminish the tendency toward impulsive behavior with its destructive results.

In working with her there was, initially, a cautious attempt to arouse her interest in understanding the reasons for her behavior. For example, when it was obvious that she had no idea why she had left home at 17, the fact that something must have been going on to bring about this move was presented for her consideration. Her curiosity was stimulated by the very fact that she had no idea as to what this could have been. Since she did tend to take on as her own other people's reactions to her, emphasis was put on expressing the worker's goals for her. For example, she did not have to rush into meeting other men. She was young and needed to choose carefully; the worker wanted her to gain sufficient understanding of her life, so that she could avoid other mistakes, etc.

Mrs. A did have a capacity for awareness. Whenever the worker pointed out that she was reacting as if the worker were accusing her and asked where these accusations came from, Mrs. A would, with amazement, agree and puzzle about herself. This tendency to puzzle, to try to understand herself, was encouraged. Mrs. A experienced considerable pleasure when she began to *feel* reactions, look at them, and understand them, rather than strike out impulsively. For example, she described a visit with her sister, with whom she generally became embroiled in upsetting and incomprehensible quarrels. She was aware of her usual feeling of anger but then realized that it was aroused by her mother's playing favorites rather than by anything her sister had done. The anger dissipated, and she did not follow her usual pattern of lashing out at the sister without knowing why. Mrs. A stated that even if this one realization were the only change she experienced as a result of her interviews, it would have been worth the entire contact. The importance to her and to any individual of this sense of mastery, of knowing what is going on inside himself and what he is reacting to, and the sense that reactions are then under control rather than mysterious and uncontrollable, cannot be overemphasized.

Mrs. A gradually moved from the feeling that she had initially expressed —that she found herself saying things in the interview that she did not want to think—to the attitude that she incorporated from the worker: she wanted to understand herself and some of her unhappy feelings so that she would not have to continue her life in so impulsive a fashion.

Her delusional reactions were generally handled by touching on the conflict behind them. By the time she brought these in it was possible to suggest, for example, in relation to the mysterious phone calls, that perhaps, in spite of her anger at her husband and her disappointment with him, she missed him and at times wanted him back. It was interesting (and showed Mrs. A's attitude toward feelings) that the first time she became aware of positive feelings toward her husband, she brought this to the worker as something that she thought she could tell the worker, but that no one else would understand; she thought her mother would be angry with her if she knew that Mrs. A felt this way. There was constant interpretation to Mrs. A of emotional reality and explanation of her own and others' reactions; i.e., what she felt, what a relationship was like, how people reacted. Her recognition that the odd behavior of her family was psychologically rather than genetically determined was important in counteracting her conviction that she came from bad stock.

During the course of the contact, as her annulment was becoming final, she experienced increasing tension that she would now be under her mother's "jurisdiction." Concurrently, the mother was hospitalized after a minor accident. The latter's increased self-absorption and demands on Mrs. A stimulated an increase in Mrs. A's feelings of both being abandoned and unappreciated by her mother. The old impulse to run away from home came to the fore. This time, however, it was possible to get to all the feelings of rejection, of abandonment, of anger at the mother, of being consumed by family quarrels. She was able to recollect for the first time the similar feelings that she had actually had prior to previous flights from home. She was aware that she would have fallen into the arms of any man who offered to take her out of the chaos and confusion that she associated with life with her family. Yet this time she recognized that this was no solution and that it only led to further difficulty. She also began to separate the confusion outside and the confusion inside. She began to recognize the sense of help-lessness at not really understanding the adult world. She began to grasp that others' reactions to *her* were frequently a response to her behavior and feeling toward *them*. During the contact, she quite on her own did some volunteer work at a foundling home. Discussing in detail with the worker the reactions of the children was a reliving, and an attempt to integrate, the feelings that she had experienced when she had been placed.

She terminated contact after about a year by moving with her mother to another city. Aside from her own desire to go to a new community, Mrs. A, who had planned this move over a period of months, felt that it would finally enable her mother to obtain a divorce. She planned to contact a local agency, should she feel the need for further help. At the time she left, psychiatric evaluation, which had been utilized twice in the early months of treatment, indicated that the disintegrative process had been arrested and reversed, with expansion in healthy ego taking place. She was not at all out of contact. She looked back both on the past year and on her life with much greater awareness and understanding. There was less impulsive behavior and she controlled this tendency when it arose. She had begun to learn to deal with the psychotic portion of the ego. There were no current delusions. Although there were transient paranoid reactions, she usually identified them and could frequently see what went into them, so that she could move from the reaction to the underlying feelings. She could tolerate and look for mixed feelings. She was aware of her difficulty in sensing what people were like. Although the thought disorder was still there, she had been helped to weather a difficult situation, without acting out as she had before. Hopefully, the gains she had made would help her cope with her ongoing life somewhat more effectively.

Mrs. A's leaving was hard on the worker, who was left with a feeling that the job was not completed and with the wish that—like a parent—she could have guided her charge into greater development. In addition there was a retrospective doubt as to whether the decision not to try to see the mother—which had seemed so valid—had really been sound. But the worker needed to be satisfied with the growth that had taken place and the hope that, should there be signs of increased difficulty in the future, this young woman, having had a positive experience with the worker, would again turn to a professional person for help.

Conclusion

The subject of schizophrenia is vast; the patients are many; the symptoms are varied; their needs are different. Schizophrenia has been described as psychiatry's number one riddle. The theories of etiology range from organic illness of an as yet unknown cause to a disturbance brought on by early traumatization in the child's relationship with his parents leading to subsequent behavioral maladjustment. The theories of treatment vary. At one end are those who see only organic therapy, the prognosis remaining poor. At the other end are those who see no essential difference between the schizophrenic and the neurotic patient. The theory of the latter group has to some extent been a reaction against the hopeless attitude toward schizophrenic patients that was frequent in the past.

Casework practice has to some extent reflected the attitudes prevalent in psychiatry. Some agencies have in the not so distant past still held that they would not take on schizophrenics for treatment—on the assumption that little could be done for them or that they belonged with psychiatrists. Others have assumed that there was no essential difference between the schizophrenic client and other clients. The treatment approach in these latter instances frequently did not take into consideration the special problems and so often came to grief.

The intent of this paper has been to highlight some of the recent theoretical explanations of schizophrenic manifestations. Schizophrenics are neither hopeless nor are they like everyone else. An understanding of the nature of the ego structure of schizophrenic clients is important for caseworkers because it makes clear that caseworkers can be of help, but that the help must be based on a clinical grounding that considers the client's special treatment needs.

The factors to be considered in deciding which clients appropriately belong with the caseworker and which need to be treated by a psychiatrist are complex and have not been discussed here. Once the schizophrenic client is in our office, however, it is important to establish contact with him, irrespective of what his long-range treatment needs may be. There is a wide variety of help that clients can get from any treatment. For some, lasting integration and change takes place, with increased capacity for coping with their lives. Others may not experience permanent personality change. Treatment may have helped them weather a difficult period and may have been a preventive of possible deterioration. The help given any schizophrenic individual is important, for it may affect the ultimate course that the illness takes. At times, this help needs to be offered without active verbal participation on the part of some of these clients, because, in spite of their desperate need, some can never acknowledge verbally either their need for help or their need for another person. But for any caseworker, in whom the need to "rescue" is strong, the knowledge of the help he has given can carry emotional meaning for a long time. A relationship implies the involvement of two people, and, as the worker remains a part of the client, so the client remains a part of the worker.

References

1　ARIETI, SILVANO. *Interpretation of Schizophrenia*. New York: Brunner, 1955.
2　EISSLER, K. R. "Remarks on the Psychoanalysis of Schizophrenia," in Eugene B. Brody and Fredrick C. Redlich (eds.), *Psychotherapy with Schizophrenics: A Symposium*. New York: Internat. Univ. Press, 1952.
3　FEDERN, PAUL. *Ego Psychology and the Psychoses*. New York: Basic Books, 1952.
4　FREEMAN, THOMAS, JOHN L. CAMERON and ANDREW McGHIE, *Chronic Schizophrenia*. London: Tavistock Publications, 1958.

5　FROMM-REICHMANN, FRIEDA. *Principles of Intensive Psychotherapy*. Chicago: Univ. of Chicago Press, 1950.
6　HILL, LOUIS B. *Psychotherapeutic Intervention in Schizophrenia*. Chicago: Univ. of Chicago Press, 1955.
7　MARCUS, ESTHER S. "Initial Contacts with Incipient Schizophrenic Clients." *Soc. Casewk.*, 39: 551-559, 1958.
8　SECHEHAYE, M. A. *Symbolic Realization*. New York: Internat. Univ. Press, 1951.

Casework Treatment of Ambulatory Schizophrenics

Laura Farber

This paper deals with some theoretical aspects of casework with ambulatory schizophrenics, and with a number of specific treatment techniques that are particularly applicable to work with these persons, although they are also used with other diagnostic groupings. The discussion is focused on one aspect of casework with the schizophrenic person—direct treatment in which the objective is improvement in his social functioning. The techniques described are based on the understanding of ego functioning. Since this presentation is drawn from the writer's experiences as a caseworker in both the in-patient and out-patient services of Hillside Hospital, the word "patient" will be used throughout.

Because the number of schizophrenics living in the community seems to be increasing, their treatment is a problem that confronts not only caseworkers in psychiatric clinics, but also caseworkers in many other settings. Clients with similar, if not identical, problems come to the attention of all community social agencies. If caseworkers are to be effective in their work with schizophrenics and are to be dealing with more and more of them, it is imperative that they have adequate clinical knowledge of the nature of the personality disturbance called "schizophrenia." Such knowledge will influence the way in which cases are handled since it will enable the caseworker to know in advance the problems he is most likely to encounter.

The term "schizophrenia" has not been clearly defined. It holds different meanings for different people; there are wide areas of disagreement about it and no single treatment approach can be proposed. Although there are characteristic modes of schizophrenic functioning, and schizophrenic patients resemble one another to some degree, they can actually be distinguished from one another in respect to the degree of their affective thinking, and behavioral disturbances.

We are primarily concerned with what is generally called ambulatory schizophrenia. The term as used in this paper includes individuals whose ego functions are not so markedly impaired that they cannot maintain themselves with some measure of effectiveness in the community. A large number of patients known to the Out-Patient Clinic of Hillside Hospital fall within this group. For the most part they show none of the dramatic symptoms, such

Reprinted from *Social Casework*, XXXIX (January, 1958), pp. 9–17, by permission of the author and the Journal.

as hallucinations, delusions, and bizarre behavior, which commonly are diagnostic indicators of schizophrenia. However impressive, these are but accessory symptoms, characteristic only of the more advanced stages of illness, and they may be altogether lacking in the ambulatory patient.

Characteristic Symptoms

The characteristic symptoms of the ambulatory schizophrenic patient are those that are fundamental to schizophrenia, in that they are always present but in varying degrees. As outlined by Bleuler, these symptoms are: disturbances of association, disturbances of affectivity, the predilection for fantasy as against reality, and the inclination to divorce onself from reality.[1] These disturbances constitute failures in acquired ego functions. In the later stages of schizophrenia these symptoms may be readily discernible, but their manifestations are more subtle in the ambulatory patient and often not immediately recognizable. For example, after several interviews, it becomes apparent that many of the patient's verbal communications, regardless of specific content, consistently lack a certain vital clarity. Or, while listening to a patient, one may suddenly realize that a sentence or two, flowing smoothly along with everything else that he has said, is inappropriate to the context.

It is important to note the extent of impairment in the ego functions of the ambulatory schizophrenic; specifically, impairment in the areas of judgment, perception, organization, self-preservation, synthesizing of experience, and reality testing. Not all these functions may be uniformly affected in any one patient. Since a failing ego has but limited "coping" energy, defenses are created in order that some degree of cohesiveness may be maintained and disintegration avoided.

A schizophrenic may thus be viewed in part as a person who is to some degree regressed and who, like the infant whose boundaries between himself and others are vague, has intense needs, lacks controls, and is sensitive to slight indications of psychic danger. In reality, however, he is not the infant who is moving ahead on the road and who has not yet learned to differentiate himself from the environment. He is, instead, the adult on the path back, having undergone life experiences, many of which have created anxiety so painful that he has had to withdraw into himself from the world about him. His disorder is thus an ego-defensive function.

The ambulatory schizophrenic's tolerance for pressure may be decreasing as he struggles with unconscious impulses threatening expression. Because his feelings are so easily stimulated, getting close to external objects is a risky business, and the patient maneuvers to maintain distance. Such patients often complain, during initial interviews, that the world seems cold,

<hr />

[1] Eugen Bleuler, *Dementia Praecox; or, The Group of Schizophrenias*, translated by Joseph Zinkin, International Universities Press, New York, 1950.

empty, strange, and alien. Other parts of the schizophrenic's personality may be intact, however, and in a number of respects he is like others rather than different from them. The caseworker should relate to and thus strengthen these stable parts of the patient's personality. At the same time the caseworker should be respectful and accepting, although not encouraging, of the existing impairments since these are also part of the patient's unique differences and individuality. It may be necessary first to meet the patient's infantile needs to some degree in order later to strengthen his more mature drives.

Preserving Ego Defenses

The casework process is primarily one of reorienting the patient to his present social reality, rather than one of attempting to help him resolve internal psychological conflicts. Although casework treatment with schizophrenics may frequently be geared toward the maintenance of present levels of functioning, in order to prevent further deterioration, it need not exclude the possibility that some degree of modification in adaptive behavior may be achieved. Treatment goals as well as treatment techniques should be flexible. The basic casework approach to schizophrenic patients rests, however, upon attempts to nurture carefully and to preserve their ego boundaries and defenses. The worker's efforts are directed toward massive support of ego defenses and reinstatement of ego functions with particular emphasis on reality testing if this is failing. The degree to which these efforts are successful depends upon the establishment of the worker-patient relationship. Casework with schizophrenics is based upon the traditional broad techniques of support and clarification, and within these wide categories a variety of specific approaches may be used. Caseworkers achieve good treatment results with these patients even though the techniques employed may vary from worker to worker. Choice of specific techniques frequently grows out of the uniquely personal manner in which a particular caseworker relates to an individual patient, and it was from individual experience that the writer arrived at some of the following formulations.

The formerly warranted prudence of many caseworkers in attempting to work with schizophrenics—a prudence that resulted from the potential dangers and unpredictable nature of casework treatment of them—has blossomed into anxious caution which may be limiting and incapacitating. Although schizophrenics make challenging patients, they also inspire pessimism, precisely because they are difficult to treat. A pessimistic attitude in itself may handicap a caseworker in attempting to achieve results that are realistically possible. If the casework goals set are flexible and considerate of the patient's limitations, the worker can afford to be optimistic. Because the treatment course with the schizophrenic is often stormy and, by our usual standards, the gains are relatively small, caseworkers are often ready to call the patient "untreatable" or "unreachable." Although this may be true at times, it is preferable in the beginning for the caseworker to be as flexible as possible in relation both to treatment processes and to goals, rather than for him to begin with the assumption that the patient is beyond help.

Reality-Oriented Treatment Approach

Some caseworkers treat many patients, including ambulatory schizophrenics, by means of what may be called the laboratory method. They are advocates of "objectivity" and "neutrality," who seem to regard their function as that of providing a screen for the patient on which he may safely project a wide range of thoughts and emotions, which the caseworker then "interprets." The development of this method may in part be attributed to the early development of casework in analytically oriented settings where caseworkers were brought into close contact with the ideas of classical analysis, some of which were then modified for casework purposes. Although this approach is desirable and effective with some patients, it may be not only useless but even harmful with schizophrenics, since it may foster an impersonal and passive attitude on the part of the caseworker.

A passive casework approach may encourage both regressive withdrawal and anxiety. The atmosphere of remoteness which it creates serves perfectly as a setting for the silent patient, or for the patient who is introspective. The schizophrenic patient, on the other hand, needs actual direction in turning his attention toward externalities. The simple fact of the caseworker's "being there" is of particular benefit to the schizophrenic, but it may not be sufficient in itself. The necessary atmosphere of mutuality resulting from the interaction of two human beings will not be achieved if the caseworker's contribution and participation are limited to his merely being present or occasionally punctuating silent listening with a few words. The caseworker cannot establish the effective relationship through which all treatment gains are achieved if he sits in remoteness from the human struggles confronting the schizophrenic patient.

In working with the schizophrenic patient, the caseworker should utilize an active, reaching-out, reality-oriented approach in which he establishes what can be called a "controlled" involvement—controlled, that is, by the realistic limits of the worker-patient relationship of which he never loses sight. An active casework approach will furnish the schizophrenic—a person whose perception of the external world is blurred as a result of his anxiety and whose ego boundaries are ill defined—with what he needs, the opportunity of relating himself to a real person from whom he can gain a clear and dependable image. The nature of the schizophrenic's problems demands that the caseworker represent a segment of reality, and thus the worker must allow his own feelings to be acknowledged in order to enter into his relationship with this patient.

The caseworker's genuine emotional responsiveness to the feelings of the schizophrenic may evoke in the patient a variety of personal feelings toward the worker from which he may build a fantasied relationship which transcends professional limits. Problems may arise if these feelings exceed the level of moderate strength. It is usually desirable for the patient, although he is characteristically ambivalent, to have predominantly positive feelings for the caseworker, since there is less danger of serious difficulties resulting from overpositive than overnegative feelings. If a patient reveals strong feelings of affection for the caseworker as a person, it is extremely important that such expressions be graciously and respectfully accepted. To the schizophrenic patient these may be represented by a cautious offering of a precious gift. Interpreting them as "transference" feelings, truly meant for another person, as might be done with non-schizophrenics, can be devastating to this vulnerable person and may be experienced by him as harsh rejection.

It is often difficult, yet necessary, to discover ways in which it is possible to reject the feelings but not the patient. It is possible to accept expressions of positive feeling and then to translate them into broader terms. For example, a man in his twenties expressed affectionate feelings for a female caseworker and made references to being sexually attracted to her. The caseworker accepted his feelings as meant for her, and since she knew him to be a shy person with strong feelings of isolation, commented that he seemed to be really telling her that he was beginning to feel some closeness toward other people, which was a healthy gain. She added that she was pleased to hear this and that, although he seemed to feel attracted to her as a woman, she felt that he needed her most, and that she could help him best, as his caseworker. In doing this, the caseworker refused the role of girl-friend, yet she did not reject the patient since she made clear to him her desire to continue to relate to him in her professional role.

On the other hand, strong negative feelings toward the caseworker can create serious problems as they can disrupt the treatment relationship. In his active role the caseworker is bound to display some of his own individual personality characteristics, some of which the patient may dislike and respond to with anger. These negative feelings must first be listened to and accepted; but it then is helpful for the caseworker to intiate discussion of the circumstances relevant to their being expressed—why the patient is preoccupied with his dislike for the worker at this particular time. His preoccupation may be a reaction to something the worker has unwittingly said or it may simply be a means by which the patient can avoid talking about himself. Generally speaking, in order to assist the patient in identifying the reason for his feelings, and in order to reduce the possibility of distortion, the caseworker has to be free enough to disclose his own feelings and the meaning of his actions so that they may be objectively examined. The frequently used casework technique of responding to questions with questions —for example, asking "why" when the patient asks a somewhat personal question—must frequently be discarded with the schizophrenic, particularly if negative feelings are to be kept within reasonable limits.

The Patient-Worker Relationship

It is important that the beginning phases of treatment be concerned primarily with the establishment of the vital patient-worker relationship, particularly since the schizophrenic is often unusually resourceful in defending himself against interpersonal involvements. The manner in which the early interviews are handled may either greatly facilitate the development of the relationship or make it practically unattainable. It may be added that the schizophrenic patient who has established any degree of relationship will repeatedly test the caseworker's ability to remain constant, the extent of his interest, and his capacities to tolerate the patient. The relationship, once established, is, in any event, but precariously maintained. During the early stages of contact, the ways in which the patient tests may often be subtle. His attitude may be one of quiet scrutiny. If, so to speak, the caseworker passes the first tests and the relationship moves forward, the testing becomes more direct and piercing, and may produce in the caseworker anger, helplessness, or anxiety, none of which are comfortable feelings. Although it is distressing to witness the schizophrenic's need to confirm the caseworker's reliability over and over again, it is also painful at times for the caseworker to be in the position of test target.

Where the work setting offers a time-limited period of treatment, it is even more necessary for the caseworker to provide the stimulus and assume the initial responsibility for establishing the relationship, as this cannot be left to chance nor delayed until the patient makes a move. Each caseworker must make continuous efforts in his own individual manner to emerge as a solid object on which the patient can focus and to which he can also cling at times if necessary. Fundamental attitudes such as empathy, warmth, and respect are often insufficient, particularly with those patients who are constricted or detached. These attitudes must be accompanied by energetic efforts to induce the patient to direct his attention away from himself and toward the external world in the person of the caseworker. In addition to the highly important non-verbal communications such as glance, gesture, and posture, these efforts include verbal communication in which it is not only what the caseworker says that matters, but, equally important, how it is said.

The effectiveness of speech very much depends upon the tone of voice and the feeling qualities that accompany the words. The caseworker, on certain occasions, should have a suggestion of conviction, firmness, or insistence in his voice. Language is a potent means of communication and may be used freely, although not as the sole means. Not only should the caseworker be actively inquiring by continuing to ask questions despite sparse answers, but also he must be active in responding by commenting frequently upon the patient's remarks so that the patient at least knows that he is being heard. Although schizophrenics are persons for whom non-verbal communication assumes special significance, they frequently need to have the worker's support, interest, and attention demonstrated in words.

Exploring the Patient's Problems

Casework usually starts with an exploratory phase during which the nature and scope of the problems confronting the patient are determined. Casework with the ambulatory schizophrenic places emphasis on the problems the patient is encountering in his handling of current reality situations; thus the initial focus should be on the facts and feelings surrounding the circumstances of the patient's coming for help. Although these facts and feelings may seem obvious, the obvious can often be obscure. The caseworker cannot assume that these are at all clear to the schizophrenic patient, but rather should assume that they need to be both established and clarified. Thus, it is often valuable for the caseworker to put what appears to be the obvious into words. Many schizophrenics are unable to verbalize concretely their need for help, and the caseworker must often do this for them. The caseworker takes his cues in doing this from what the patient has thus far said and from his non-verbal attitude, and thereby attempts to convey some understanding of the patient's feelings.

It is possible to anticipate the patient's probable attitudes toward seeking to help because his fears, doubts, confusions, and expectations are not basically different from those of other patients although they certainly may be more intense. Many of these patients cannot be expected to focus on, or even to identify, their problems. The caseworker may have to identify the patient's unexpressed concerns and, at times, emphatically state them. During this process the caseworker does not depend solely upon verbal explanations; he acts out his function, thereby demonstrating to the patient how casework operates. He conveys something of what his help involves, and what he and the patient may attempt to do together, so that the patient's expectations of him will not get so far out of touch with what is actually possible of achievement in the situation that the patient becomes angrier and more frustrated.

As a result of the caseworker's verbalizing for the patient and bringing some of his feelings into the open, the patient may visibly experience relief of tension. It seems to be enormously encouraging to the schizophrenic to feel that another person has managed to understand at least a part of what he is feeling and has shown respect for him by communicating this to him. The fact that he can be understood implies further to him that his feelings are not unusual nor are they beyond the pale of human understanding. In addition, the schizophrenic is very concerned about whether the caseworker is a competent person. For example, during an initial interview a patient, in a challenging manner, said to the caseworker: "If I tell you my problems, what more can you do for me besides giving me empathy?" This attitude of infantile defiance is not uncommon, and it may be wiser for the caseworker to answer such questions directly as they arise than to postpone or avoid answering them.

Encouraging Verbalization

One technique that may be used to encourage the schizophrenic patient to verbalize involves the caseworker's giving him something specific to which to relate. For example, a patient reported that he attended a family social function which he did not enjoy. He could not on his own say why it was so unpleasant, nor could he answer the caseworker's questions. The caseworker then made use of his knowledge of this man's characteristic difficulties and suggested a possible reason why he had failed to have a good time. The worker suggested that the patient did not feel comfortable because he felt obliged, as he usually did when his mother was present, to limit his freedom of action for fear of evoking criticism from her. As a result of the caseworker's stating this one possibility, the patient had a specific factor on which to focus and to which he could respond. He then said that he had actually been made uncomfortable by something else—the presence of a fellow employee whom he had not expected to be present. This comment was pursued and led into a discussion of the patient's interpersonal relationships on his job—an important area of functioning which it had not previously been possible to discuss.

Something may be gained, also, from the worker's venturing an opinion regardless of whether it eventually proves correct. A need on the part of the worker to be correct most of the time hinders vital spontaneity and defeats the objective of bringing the patient's thoughts, feelings, and attitudes into the open where they may be realistically appraised. A possible error or what may actually be a difference of opinion helps the schizophrenic to separate his attitude from his total self as he considers the different ways in which a situation can be viewed and described. If the caseworker can acknowledge being wrong without being defensive, the patient is provided with the opportunity of seeing the worker more accurately and realistically as another fallible human being. As a result he may not need to regard his own mistakes as unique or devastating, and may be freed from some feelings of inadequacy. For example, a patient in her early thirties was involved in a chaotic marital relationship and vehemently denied that she in any way contributed to the violent battles that took place regularly. She projected the entire responsibility for these scenes onto her husband, thereby stabilizing her own rage toward him. For many months, while viciously criticizing neighbors whom she felt were pitying her, she nevertheless presented herself to everyone as the victim of her husband's abusiveness.

At the beginning of the contact there were but few attempts made to discuss these projections with her since the casework relationship was tenuous. As the relationship developed, so did an identification with the worker, and the patient gradually revealed more specific information as to how these arguments arose. During one particular interview, the caseworker managed to elicit details that indirectly revealed that the disagreement under discussion had resulted from her insisting to her husband that she had been right in her evaluation of a particular situation when she had actually not been. She was able to examine realistically the circumstances under which this argument had arisen when she was reminded of some of the mistakes the caseworker had made during the contact and was then asked why she found it so hard to admit the possibility of human mistake in herself.

Holding the Patient to Reality

Since certain schizophrenics are vague and confused in their thinking, it is important for the caseworker to consider ways in which the patient may be held to discussion of important realities so that the interviews do not become "much ado about nothing." These patients readily escape into irrelevancies and generalities, avoiding topics of significance by all sorts of circuitous means, and some become more anxious as they become more confused. The caseworker must listen intently to the patient who rambles, or the one who talks compulsively, in order to understand what he is trying to convey and in the hope of picking up at least one significant statement which then may be pursued. If a patient dwells on a circumstantial narrative about a situation that is irrelevant to his difficulties, it is the caseworker's responsibility to direct his interest elsewhere. This may be accomplished by referring back to an area discussed previously, bringing it to the patient's awareness in a general way so that the topic does not appear to be abruptly changed. Once it is in front of the patient it may be followed by a question that requires a more specific answer. Sometimes a patient resents the worker's firm attitudes in interrupting his verbal wanderings, and he feels thwarted and angry. Since such feelings may hinder further communications, the caseworker should help the patient realize that his anger is related to the worker's activity and that this reaction is understandable.

Dealing with Anger

Most schizophrenics suffer from pervasive or chronic feelings of rage to which the term "unassuageable anger" has been applied.[2] In his struggles with rage, the schizophrenic will feel more secure from his own impulses if the caseworker's strength or control serves to reinforce his own impaired ego. Although the caseworker may feel more comfortable in being permissive, he must often be firm and even demanding since the patient needs external controls. The caseworker must set limits, but not arbitrarily, and these limits may be more acceptable to the patient if he is given reasons as to why they are necessary. A 20-year-old patient, whose grandiose schemes

[2] Karl Menninger, M.D., "The Diagnosis and Treatment of Schizophrenia," *Bulletin of the Menninger Clinic*, Vol. XII, No. 3 (1948), pp. 96–106.

revealed poor reality testing, frequently expressed anger toward the case-worker. One day, during a period when she was particularly distressed, she became furious with the caseworker when the latter refused to comply with a request to write a letter to the patient's sister in her behalf since the worker felt that the patient was capable of handling this on her own. Feeling helplessly angry, the patient grabbed a small ash-tray from the caseworker's desk. The caseworker did not wait for the minute to pass during which the patient might have returned it to its place, but instead ordered her to put it down and gave as the reason the fact that she would not allow the patient to hurt either one of them. When the patient did not respond even after the caseworker repeated this, the caseworker reached over and removed the object from the patient's hand. The patient was shown that the case-worker possessed the control the patient lacked.

The schizophrenic is caught up in a circle of anger; the original anger, after being expressed, brings guilt, which in turn creates additional anger. Whether the verbal expression of hostility is subtle or blatant, it is wise to clarify it at once since otherwise the patient may be left with discomforting guilt. This unmitigated anger of the schizophrenic may be a further problem in treatment since he may project a good deal of it onto the caseworker and thus may readily feel that the worker is attacking or rejecting him. In addi-tion, by verbally attacking the caseworker and attempting to disparage him or to prove him worthless, the schizophrenic attempts to prove that he in no way needs the worker, and thus he increases his provocative testing as the relationship assumes importance and his anxiety mounts.

Dealing with Paranoid Ideas

A large number of schizophrenics, particularly when under stress, develop paranoid ideas which serve to ward off anxiety but in many instances create social difficulties. Since new experiences are frequently terrifying to the schizophrenic, he may develop suspicions regarding the intentions of others. Whether the expression of the paranoid idea is directed toward the caseworker or toward another person in the patient's environment, immedi-ate handling is nevertheless called for lest the distortion become more involved. The caseworker neither agrees nor disagrees with such ideas, but accepts them as what the patient is experiencing. If the caseworker disagrees with a distortion, the patient may become more cautious or may be forced to elaborate.

One way in which the caseworker may deal with paranoid distortions is illustrated by the following brief case excerpt. A 20-year-old man was being seen regularly with particular focus on his problems in employment and residence. A few weeks after beginning a new job that was potentially promising, he told the caseworker about his idea that co-workers were laughing at him as he passed their desks; hearing the murmur of their voices as he reached the other end of the office led him to believe that they were also talking about him. The caseworker first approached the patient's reactions to what he perceived, which were feelings of fear, anger, and rejection. With persistence she then attempted to elicit factual material about the circumstances under which his ideas had arisen. She asked questions about the office situation in general, about particular people of whom the patient was suspicious, and inquired as to whether the patient had ever felt this way before in any other situation. At the same time she attempted to create some doubts in the patient's mind and to have him consider alternative meanings, through questions such as, "What other explanations might there possibly be for their laughing?" She did not deny the validity of the patient's feelings, but indicated that she was dubious about the validity of his perception.

In order to strengthen the patient's reality-testing ability, the case-worker should elicit details of the reported situation. With these details the caseworker can then review the relevant circumstances step by step, trying to pull them together into some sort of objective sequence of events, so that the patient can become aware of the relationship between the actual situation and his feelings abouts it. In this case, the patient was helped to relate his own feelings of humiliation resulting from a public criticism by his supervisor, to his later feeling of being laughed at by others. Since effective reality testing depends to some degree on the identifications supporting it, it may be advisable for the caseworker to assume a position of critically examining the patient's attitudes toward the worker himself so that the patient may then assume a similarly critical attitude in relation to his own actions and those of others. The caseworker should be explicit, frank, and detailed in his discussions with the suspicious patient in order to prevent some, although certainly not all, of his potential misinterpretations. There should be no tacit understandings with these patients, and absence of comment regarding a distortion may mean to the patient that the worker is tacitly giving consent.

Conclusion

The casework approach outlined in this paper can best be called "directive." Some of the difficulties that frequently arise during casework treatment of the schizophrenic patient have been described, and techniques for handling them have been suggested. It is recognized that this is a complex area of treatment in which further exploration and experimentation are needed. Although one cannot suggest final answers to many of the questions posed, caseworkers should be willing to be flexible in experimenting with various, and possibly new, treatment techniques.

"Reaching Out" Therapy with Schizophrenic Patients

Barbara K. Varley

"Reaching out" therapy is neither presumed to be, nor offered as, a new concept of treating schizophrenic patients. In many respects this therapy is similar to that done by Fromm-Reichmann (4)*, Rosen (5), Diethelm (2) and others, except that the frame of reference is psychiatric social work. The major emphasis is on relationship with the therapist; there is no attempt to deal directly with deep intrapsychic conflicts, although knowledge of these dynamics aids the therapist in planning treatment. Diethelm states: ". . . alleviation of anxiety and of other disturbing emotions may frequently be necessary for progress in a reintegrative psychotherapy. In many patients this is the essential goal that can be obtained" (2, p. 423). In this process the therapist need not wait for patients to initiate the "reaching out" or seeking-help process. Instead, she may be the one to reach out first and express in words, feelings or actions the desire to be of help to them. This method requires considerable patience on the part of the therapist, who has to be willing to give without requiring much in return.

The present study is based on work over a 5-year period with 20 female schizophrenic patients, hospitalized on a 24-bed psychiatric unit in the Salt Lake General Hospital. The diagnosis of the patients was established by the psychiatrist in charge of the unit. Most of the patients were in their thirties; the youngest was 18 and the oldest 44. Their psychiatric histories varied widely, some having been ill for years with several hospitalizations, and others only several weeks. The majority of these 20 female schizophrenics had somatic therapies concurrent with psychotherapy. Perhaps the only common factor was that all patients at the start of treatment were still overtly psychotic with delusions or hallucinations, or both. The process of "reaching out" therapy was used in every case, with patients being involved in treatment from six months to two years.

Initially, most patients were seen three times a week on the ward. This allowed contacts to be more casual and friendly than would be the case when interviews were held in the more formal setting of an office. Almost without exception, frightened, lonely patients are fearful and distrustful when an interest is expressed in them by the personnel. But given time and

*References will be found at the end of the chapter.

Reprinted from the *American Journal of Orthopsychiatry*, XXIX (April, 1959), pp. 407-416. Copyright, the American Orthopsychiatric Association, Inc. Reproduced by permission of the author and the Association.

an opportunity to assimilate the feeling tone of the therapeutic environment, they gradually begin to trust the staff. If in the beginning the therapist does not focus directly on the patients, as in a formal interview, they then have an opportunity to risk responding to the therapist as a person within the treatment milieu, avoiding, until more comfortable, the intensity of one-to-one contacts. Frequent brief, informal visits are made to patients in the early stages of therapy. These prepare the way for formal interviews later, when patients are able to tolerate the closeness involved in a psychotherapeutic interview.

As Scher observes: "If perceptual intrusion is regular and reliable, as in the case of repeated visits by the same therapist, it may become a reference point on which other data may be hung and may give the psychotic a greater readiness to accept other percepts" (7, p. 179). Without question this process is of considerable significance as an early step in establishing rapport. Repeated visits by the therapist allow patients opportunity to reduce gradually their resistance to involvement. Without risking or giving much in return, patients are able to observe, sense, and comprehend the interest of the therapist, who is "reaching out." English (3) supports the theory that patients will gradually respond to the therapist who is willing to give of himself.

Essential in treatment with schizophrenics is the idea described by Whitehorn: ". . . manifestations of an attitude of respectful and sympathetic independence, on the part of the doctor toward the patient, combined with an expectation that the patient also has potentiality for respectful independent action, and that neither patient nor doctor needs to submit to the other" (9, p. 421). The therapist must have real empathy for patients; otherwise patients sense a pseudo interest and the desired goals of treatment become more difficult to obtain. Schizophrenics are highly sensitive and are keenly aware of the emotional response of others to them. This sensitivity is characteristic of their premorbid personality and becomes intensified during the psychotic period.

As a result of the complexities of psychosis, the responsibility for beginning treatment rests with the therapist. Supported by her motivation to "reach out," the therapist can start the process. The motivation for recovery, however, rests with patients and must be present even though slight. The therapist's decision to begin therapy depends on an assessment of the patients' past histories and a recognition of defense mechanisms which may hide the patients' desire for help. The therapist must be able to see beyond these subterfuges and recognize them as devices operating to protect patients from further ego insults.

The therapist must be prepared to accept steadfastly patients' repeated testing of the expressed wish to help. Thus, the therapist must respond with a constant, unwavering desire to understand and assist in their recovery. Toleration of patients' testing is a measure of the therapist's maturity and objectivity—two highly essential attributes in the treatment process. Since the therapist must personally participate with patients, Fromm-Reichmann

(4) stresses the importance of the therapist's being a mature, secure, and emotionally satisfied person, who does not need the therapeutic relationship with patients as a means of satisfaction, direct or indirect. Without such confidence and security, the therapist is likely to find psychotic patients' activities anxiety-provoking. The therapist's anxiety, whether directly or indirectly expressed, can create a block in the therapeutic process and may upset the patient, who intuitively recognizes these feelings. Honesty regarding the feeling of the therapist is important when working with schizophrenics. Better therapeutic progress is made when the therapist is able to acknowledge her own feelings when a question is raised. This may occur throughout treatment, but seems to be strongest during the initial phases.

If the actions of patients make the therapist angry, at times the therapist should honestly state this. Honesty in expression by the therapist aids patients in understanding their part in interactions with others. The traditional bland accepting approach may actually be detrimental to patients, who are unsure of their ability to communicate or to evoke reactions in others. The weakened ego of a schizophrenic is not able to abstract meaning and insight from the nondirective techniques usually employed in psychotherapy.

> One patient, after five months in treatment, suddenly became resistant because she was nearing the point of discharge from the hospital. After attempting to handle this many times, I did become irritated, for I felt she was afraid to trust her own strengths. One day she stated to me that she knew I was angry at her. I acknowledged that I was angry, not at her, but at her behavior, for I felt she was capable of more effort than she was currently showing. The patient responded well to my direct answer, talked about her fears of discharge, and began to do things to help herself.

When patients are reluctant to talk during interviews, I have frequently suggested they write instead, recognizing that they are fearful of telling me things about themselves because they fear my reaction to the information. If patients are able to write material which they have been unable to verbalize, this is then used during subsequent interviews to help them discuss the problems.

> One patient, who was transferred to me after her previous therapist left the service, was extremely reluctant to speak in interviews. She was silent most of the time she was with me, and although she was not catatonic, she was sufficiently disturbed so that I could not handle her as one might a neurotic patient. She was able to use the device of writing, and the following material is quoted from a note she wrote about a month after beginning therapy with me.
> "I really don't intend you to ever read this, but it helps to put things down on paper. I have a lot of things bothering me, more than I talk about or write about. I am ashamed of some, although I shouldn't be. You know it's funny to want to do something, but can't even though you know it will help you. Something has come back that used to bother me before. It all started with a dream. Who the woman was, I can't recall, but in the dream I wasn't ashamed or embarrassed. I feel cold towards my boy friend again. Very cold. I hope I am not beginning to like my own sex better, yet deep down it is a feeling of I don't care. I don't feel as though I want sex play. No, all I feel that I want

is just to be close to someone, that alone satisfies me. You know, deep down I would just love to have you get hold of this, but you would probably want to talk about it and I don't wanna. Do you think I can ever adjust to really being happy and enjoying life again, and do you think I could break away from home and manage without too much trouble? It would sure make things better if I could stay with you for about an hour and really talk over a lot of things. You really don't give me a chance. I think I could talk if we got started and weren't pressured for time. I am very time sensitive or conscious. The way you rush me in and out, I wonder if you're really interested. I almost doubt it. Of course, how do I know, maybe I just don't understand you. I am very conscious of people around me and how they feel towards me. That makes it difficult sometimes. Oh well, sometimes I don't like myself. I'm going to leave this lying around, maybe you'll get it and maybe not. Hope if you do, you can read it, it sure is sloppy."

The patient revealed in this note more about herself than had been previously known. This additional information facilitated treatment significantly. There were other such notes; some she would hand to me, others she just left lying on the ward. They helped me to understand her and to know the problems which were currently disturbing her.

An interesting experience with another patient was the reverse of the preceding one.

While the patient was overtly psychotic, she often questioned whether certain things were happening for specific reasons. For instance, one morning she asked me if the newspaper on the ward was printed especially for her. I told her this was the same paper that was distributed throughout the city and that a copy was delivered daily to my home. She asked me to write on a piece of paper, "I have a copy at home," which I did. She carried the piece of paper with her all day to help her maintain contact with reality. She repeated these same requests several times, but eventually was able to master this confusion through verbal questions.

During the initial phase when patients talk about their delusions and hallucinations, the therapist need only listen. Eventually, the therapist will be able to comprehend the patients' feelings regarding these ideas and then it becomes possible to assist them in grasping reality more firmly. Only after rapport is established with patients can one begin to question their delusions directly. Many patients are frightened by their delusions, particularly grandiose and paranoid ones. They are fearful of their own imagined power as well as the power they attribute to others. After the therapist has a good relationship with patients, who are frightened by their grandiose ideas, it frequently is beneficial to take a stronger, more forceful position, stating that they are not able to influence others as they feel and fear they can. With the therapist constantly holding to reality, patients will gradually begin to test reality for themselves and to question their own delusions.

When patients are overtly upset, they may reach for the therapist with a physical gesture, such as wanting to hold her hand. For some patients it is therapeutically beneficial for the therapist to allow this. However, one must be sufficiently aware of the patients' dynamics to understand the meaning this action may have to them. A physical gesture may convey better than words to some patients the therapist's knowledge and acceptance of their emotional turmoil. To other patients even a minimum of physical contact may be very frightening and must be avoided. Since traditionally the therapist is schooled in verbal communication, it becomes more difficult to learn and use nonverbal communication with sureness and competence.

Either accompanying the delusional phase or immediately following it, patients express considerable hostility. They need to be encouraged to ventilate the hostility which they have felt toward people in their lives who they feel have contributed to their disturbance. If this hostility is expressed against the therapist, she must be prepared to cope with the situation so that patients do not suffer another destructive emotional experience. Since this hostility, like an infection, must be relieved before progress can be made in treatment, the security of the therapist is the important element. Visitors to patients are a practical matter to be considered, especially during the time patients are expressing hostility. Because they are so emotionally involved with the patients, families may not understand nor accept sudden outbursts of hostility unless they are being seen routinely by a staff member and understand the treatment process. Without this, it is very likely that family members will counter in kind and leave the patients more disturbed. If personnel shortages make it impossible for the significant family members to be seen regularly, until the patients achieve more control it may be advisable to deny them visitors. Although this procedure may not be acceptable to either patients or their families, further complications of family relationships can be prevented by such an authoritarian stand.

For several reasons I deliberately attempt to create a dependent situation with patients. Experience has shown that they have never been able to resolve, handle, or face their dependency needs and the fears created by these needs. Their earlier experiences have been with people who were disturbed or immature and unable to fulfill the patients' emotional needs. Perhaps, in the premorbid personality of schizophrenic patients, there were so many intense needs that few people could have fulfilled them. As they begin to describe their early emotional experiences, it becomes apparent that mother, father, and others were unable to meet their demands. While talking about these experiences they frequently abreact with the therapist. The therapist can then provide patients with a "corrective emotional experience" (8, p. 426) so that patients can partially resolve the feelings surrounding the past difficulties. They have never formed a healthy identification, since frequently their parents are emotionally unhealthy. Thus, their own self concept is poor and no clear mental picture of themselves is established. The self-image is blurred, as though mother, father, and other significant people are incorporated. They cannot see themselves as separate, distinct entities.

Working with female patients allows me to encourage them to imitate me in the beginning and later to establish their own separate identity. Much of this interaction takes place on a nonverbal level which is difficult to identify. However, I have observed patients holding their hands in positions which would be similar to mine or beginning to smoke after treatment has started. Some of the younger patients have copied my hair style or clothing. Subsequently, many patients relinquish these imitative mannerisms and return to behavior patterns more characteristic of their own personality. With a few patients, I have felt improvement was directly related to their working with a female therapist. At times, we have social conversations, during which topics are discussed such as how a girl behaves on a date; what she does when a fellow makes sexual advances toward her; how she handles her own sexual impulses; and what she should do about them. These discussions are geared to what is socially acceptable. Since the patient is disturbed by her sexual impulses and does not want to be promiscuous, the therapist needs to help her learn to handle them, to accept the fact that they are healthy, normal impulses, and to exercise some control over them. Mainly, one must attempt to reduce the patient's feeling of being "bad."

During treatment, the therapist should accede to many of the patients' demands, but at the same time endeavor to help them recognize realistic limitations. Therapist's contributions are restricted although most patients will desire a more personal relationship. Many patients want to see the therapist more than once a day. I tell them that if they are disturbed later, they can ask the nurse to call me and they will be seen briefly before I leave for the evening. One patient became extremely demanding of my time. She would have the nurse call me and then not want me to leave. At no point did I remain beyond a few minutes, but reminded her that we had had our interview for the day, and that although I was sorry she was upset I could not remain. She was encouraged to use the nurses and aides to help her calm her fears and to learn there were others in the environment who could help her. When patients make such demands, interviews are focused on the needs which necessitate the requests. The therapist can reassure patients of her interest, but at the same time remind them of her limitations. Most of my patients are aware that I see other patients and live a life of my own. However, occasionally patients can be seen more than once a day, if this becomes necessary.

Interpretation is usually limited to the therapist-patient relationship. When patients are reluctant to talk about themselves because they are fearful of the therapist's reaction, the question of why they are fearful should be pursued. Generally, their response relates to their fear of not being liked. They fear that the therapist will see them in the same "bad" way in which they see themselves. They also feel that parents see them as "bad" individuals, so that it is important for the therapist to continue to remind patients that she is not their parent. One patient was convinced I would respond as she assumed her mother would if she had told her about an abortion she had years before. I reassured her that I was not her mother, that I did not feel as she thought her mother did, and that I wanted her to feel free to tell me anything. Most patients can accept the therapist's understanding after repeating the testing process a number of times. Once having found that they can say anything, they begin to talk in detail about their past lives and emotional reactions to past experiences. It is a verbal catharsis. At times, depending on the patient's ego strength, a few interpretations of some of the material can be made. However, the majority of these patients cannot accept interpretations and at the same time incorporate them emotionally. Therefore, one needs simply to accept what they say and help them to feel comfortable, focusing constantly on the present interpersonal relationship. If within this frame of reference a patient indicates an ability for more extensive exploratory psychotherapy and if the patient's ego strength allows it, she then may be helped to transfer to a psychiatrist.

After two or three months of intensive relationship, some patients begin to pull away. If they are unable to explain the withdrawal and there do not appear to be any environmental reasons, the therapeutic relationship is then re-evaluated. Freudian theory provides considerable understanding of schizophrenic patients' sexual confusions. During therapy some of this confusion may come to the foreground and patients may fear the therapist will see them as sexually abnormal. They fear that the therapist will interpret their attachment as a homosexual one. When patients are able to verbalize this conflict, no attempt is made to deal with the psychosexual dynamics. Instead, it is helpful to view the situation as a reaching out for a relationship with another person. Patients usually express this fear as being "queer" or "abnormal." In such instances, it is often necessary only to reaffirm that affectionate feelings are permissible and normal. One patient, who stated her concern about her sexual adjustment, told of a dream in which her sister had been nursing at her breast and spontaneously associated the dream to her relationship with me. In this situation, it seemed better to reassure her that such fantasies are common, that affectionate relationships with other women, including the therapist, are not pathological, and that the combination of these feelings does not make her "sexually abnormal." After several sessions spent discussing confused sexual feelings, patients will find relief from them and be able to move forward toward recovery.

During the period of overt psychosis, the therapist assists in making decisions for the patients concerning activities, visitors, etc., and as they begin to improve, they must be encouraged to make their own decisions. At times, it may be necessary for the therapist to insist that they do so and to reassure them that they are capable of it. One must watch lest they make decisions which might be harmful, but short of this, they should be given freedom.

While patients are in the hospital the administrative psychiatrist has responsibility for medical and environmental management. He makes decisions concerning drugs, occupational therapy, visitors, etc. The therapist is then free to help patients explore feelings evoked by the doctor and to relate these to lifelong behaviorial patterns. Sometimes a dependent patient finds the hospital environment and therapeutic situation so gratifying and the prospects of departure so frightening that she refuses to consider leaving. It then becomes necessary for the administrative doctor to set a date for discharge. Generally, the patient is able to mobilize the necessary strengths to meet the situation, and with therapeutic help, even profits from the experience.

My constant efforts in interviews are focused on the interpersonal relationship created by therapy. I use myself as a specific person in their life to help them experience, for perhaps the first time, a positive consistent relationship—one where they can talk freely, express their hostility, expose hurts, reveal guilt and admit positive feelings. They are frightened by their own intense emotions, both hostile and affectionate, and in treatment they must learn to handle positive feelings as well as negative ones. Patients are frightened because they do not know how others will react to them. As Bateson and others (1) indicate, the schizophrenic patient was caught in a "double bind" very early in life—the mother-child relationship was plagued with double meanings. The mother's expression of love was always repudiated by contradictory words or actions. A strong father, who could intervene and correct the situation, was not present and the child grew up confused by the chaotic communications. This state of bewilderment results in a feeling of rejection.

As a part of their therapeutic experience patients are encouraged to broaden their contacts. They must learn to form healthier friendships with people, where their ideas are accorded respect and their feelings are recognized. They are encouraged to speak more frankly not only to the therapist, but also to their families. The purpose is to help them establish themselves as individuals separate from the therapist, from the mother, from the father, and everyone else. Patients will say that for the first time they begin to see themselves as independent people with ideas and feelings quite different from those of their parents or spouses. As progress continues, patients are given longer leaves of absence. During this time, interviews are focused on the social situation and interactions with families.

Finally, when patients are ready to leave the hospital, the discussion centers around plans for them at home, on the job, at school, etc. Except for the patient previously mentioned who had to be pushed toward discharge, most patients have consciously wanted to leave the hospital to return to a more normal type of life. The therapist must be aware of the ambivalence felt by patients—the wanting and not wanting to leave the controlled yet warm, giving environment of the hospital. The patients' concern regarding adjustment when out of the hospital can be met by an assurance of help on an outpatient basis, by stating that the therapist is there to help, and by pointing out that the hospital is there should they become overly upset—if necessary they can return to it. Having been given this assurance they are then followed on an outpatient basis for as long as may be necessary. This stabilization period usually lasts from four to six months. Gradually patients begin to want to try on their own without further interviews. Even though patients express such a desire, the therapist must gauge the patients' readiness and terminate treatment only if advisable.

Before therapy is concluded, I attempt to teach them how to recognize early signs of emotional upset. Usually they ask for elaboration, because they want to know how they can prevent future hospitalizations. I emphasize that psychotic symptoms, with which they are familiar, will recur when they are under too much pressure. They need not be concerned about the symptoms, but must try to think through what it is that is upsetting them. I tell them their symptoms are like the fever which is the indication of an infection and that they will have to try to recognize the source of their trouble. I express the idea that there will be times when they may again need professional help and that they should not be reluctant to return for more interviews when and if it becomes necessary.

Occasionally I ask patients who have the ability to do so to summarize what has taken place in therapy. I believe this recapitulation is beneficial to them if they can understand even part of the process which has taken place during treatment. Ruesch and Bateson state: "Differences which exist between the patient and his contemporaries are reduced through efforts of therapy; paradoxically this is achieved by making the patient accept the fact that he is different from others; after his acceptance of this difference he no longer feels threatened, and gradually learns to accept the fact that he is like other people" (6, p. 167).

Summary

Material has been presented to illustrate a method of therapy with schizophrenic patients used by a psychiatric social worker without dealing directly with deep intrapsychic dynamics, although this knowledge is essential. The therapist must be a mature, secure, and emotionally satisfied person, who can personally engage in the therapeutic relationship. The therapist may begin treatment by "reaching out" to patients. Honest expression of feelings by the therapist is important and aids progress in treatment. Nonverbal communication is a meaningful exchange between patient and therapist, but more difficult to use with sureness and competence. The therapist becomes a specific person in the lives of patients, and interviews are focused on the interpersonal relationship created by therapy.

References

1 BATESON, GREGORY, DON D. JACKSON, JAY HALEY, and JOHN WEAKLAND. *Toward a Theory of Schizophrenia*. Behav. Sci., 1: 251–264, 1956.

2 DIETHELM, OSKAR. *The Psychopathologic Basis of Psychotherapy of Schizophrenia*. Am. J. Psychiatry, 111: 422–425, 1954.

3 ENGLISH, O. SPURGEON, and STUART FINCH. *Introduction to Psychiatry*. New York: Norton, 1954.

4 FROMM-REICHMANN, FRIEDA. *Principles of Intensive Psychotherapy*. Chicago: Univ. of Chicago Press, 1950.

5 ROSEN, JOHN N. *Direct Analysis*. New York: Grune & Stratton, 1953.

6 RUESCH, JURGEN, and GREGORY BATESON. *Communication*. New York: Norton, 1951.

7 SCHER, JORDAN M. *Perception, Equivalence, Avoidance and Intrusion in Schizophrenia*. Dig. Neurol. Psychiat., April, 1957.

8 SEMRAD, ELVIN. *The Treatment Process*. Am. J. Psychiatry, 111: 426–427, 1954.

9 WHITEHORN, JOHN C. *Hateful Self-Distrust: A Problem in the Treatment of Schizophrenic Patients*. Am. J. Psychiatry, 111: 420–421, 1954.

Group Casework with Relatives of Adult Schizophrenic Patients

Philip Mass and Jeanne Odaniell

All of us who work with schizophrenic patients are aware of the complexities of the illness. While great strides have been made in understanding its origins and treatment there is still no unanimity among psychiatrists which would with finality permit them to say, "We understand schizophrenia." Instead, we find that there are some who emphasize possible organic factors while others stress the psychological aspects. Therapy consists of drugs, shock treatment and/or psychotherapy, which may range from almost complete passivity to a "total push" program.

If schizophrenia is perplexing to the therapist, imagine how confusing and exhausting it must be for the relative who cares for the patient, is much more emotionally involved and has many emotional problems of his own to contend with. How should he react to the peculiar mannerisms and illogical reasoning? If he is too lenient, the patient's demands may become insatiable. If he is harsh or abrupt, the patient may feel rejected. In addition to this dilemma he may be limited in his quest for help. Usual sources of guidance and support—such as other relatives, friends, ministers and physicians—may not be able to offer the necessary assistance. Prejudice, judgmental attitudes, lack of specialized knowledge, and failure to appreciate the needs of the individual hamper the outsider in offering services.

When the relative comes to the clinic he may be quite helpless in reacting properly to the patient, full of doubts, filled with overwhelming guilt and apprehension. Sometimes as a defense he insists that his methods are correct without need for change, but generally he hopes to get direct advice.

This article is based on experiences with two groups which met two years apart. There were differences in the management of each which had important effects on group activity and reactions. The first group met once monthly over a period of four years. The same male caseworker supervised both groups. In the second group, which lasted for six months and met weekly, another social worker acted as recorder. She did not actively participate in the group, but performed a most valuable function in discussing after the meeting her objective impressions and opinions of the group activity; the members only rarely responded to her overtly. The more

Reprinted from *Mental Hygiene*, XLII (October, 1958), pp. 504–510, by permission of the authors and the Journal.

frequent meetings served to facilitate group interaction and relationships and created a more dynamic and faster moving situation. The addition of a recorder freed the group leader from taking notes and allowed him to respond more fully to the group process.

It was necessary for the group leader to be mindful of the total treatment program, to give proper consideration to the patient's treatment and to the casework needs of the relatives. Special emphasis was placed on the inter-relating factors between the relative's background and the patient's personality structure as seen in the following examples.

Mr. B, an unmarried 27-year-old veteran, was in the service for two years before his discharge for inaptitude and enuresis. Following his return home he showed irrational thought, bizarre behavior and poor contacts with reality. His improvement after two months of private hospitalization was not maintained, and he was brought to our clinic for treatment.

He was the third of four siblings. One older sibling is married and apparently has not presented any serious emotional problems. The older sister is unmarried and still lives in the parental home. The youngest brother was described as a mental defective. Shortly after birth the veteran developed jaundice and required more care than the other children. This special attention persisted as he was often ill throughout his childhood and displayed numerous emotional difficulties such as enuresis and difficulty in adjusting at school.

Both parents had a deprived economic life and a difficult emotional background in Europe and faced problems of readjustment after they arrived in the United States. Mr. B's father was especially troubled and seemed to resent the attempts of his wife to enjoy herself. They lived in one room even after the children were born and there were constant financial pressures to contend with.

Mrs. B was overprotective towards her son throughout his life. This was apparent in her contacts with us. She insisted upon accompanying him to the clinic, although she was discouraged from doing this since he could come alone. Intellectually she could understand the reason for her actions, but emotionally she could not give up the mother-infant relationship even though it often involved considerable personal sacrifices. She would almost compulsively repeat actions which were designed to intensify the veteran's feelings of inadequacy. His often helpless manner encouraged her in this respect. In our earlier dealings she showed a lack of conscious concern about overtly bizarre behavior and constantly stated, "He'll be all right . . . It just takes time . . . He really likes us." etc. Her actions belied her pollyannaish approach to her son's illness. She kept up a never-ending vigil which allowed only disturbed sleep, and she became tense, anxious and physically exhausted.

Mr. F was a 35-year-old unmarried patient who was hospitalized while overseas because of marked confusion and bizarre behavior. He made stereotyped responses to questions, he was manneristic and his speech was illogical and disconnected. At times he showed catatonic behavior with mutism. He was discharged from service and transferred to a VA hospital where he was given shock treatment and later was placed on trial visit status.

The patient's early history indicated no known special problems as far as his physical development was concerned. He was very closely attached to his mother and became known as a "mamma's boy" by his sisters. He was bashful and withdrawn and had no close friends of either sex. He completed three years of high school, then quit because he lost interest. He had several jobs which included house canvassing for information, messenger work and bottle washing.

Both his parents were born in Europe, his father in Germany and his mother in the Ukraine. They had many financial difficulties, especially when the patient was fourteen and the father lost heavily through poor investments. There were two younger sisters, one of whom married a minister and left town. The other sister was a member of our relatives' group. The mother was too ill to come to the clinic.

This sister was 34 at the time, single and closely attached emotionally to her mother, although she was not aware of the degree. She was a steady worker, participated in church activities faithfully and in many ways was overly conscientious in doing the "right thing." In her relation to her brother she was uncertain and befuddled. She wanted him to go out socially with her "because it was good for him," observed his movements very closely and became upset at minor, as well as gross, bizarreness, not recognizing that her own feelings interfered with her ability to evaluate the situations concerned.

Reasons for a Group

Through talking with the patients we became increasingly aware of the important roles played by their relatives, and we developed an interest in possible modifications which might take place in the patient's condition if some form of treatment was also extended to the relative.

Several factors were taken into consideration in electing to see the relatives in a group. Previous interviews with relatives gave indications that they had strong guilt feelings about the patient's condition. There was a tendency to feel the responsibility for precipitating the illness as well as perpetuating its present state. In one of the group sessions this attitude was discussed along this line:

Mrs. B turned to Mrs. S and pointed out that she did not think Mrs. S should feel that her son's illness was her fault as one person is never completely to blame. Mr. S felt they spoiled their son, while his wife remarked that she didn't want to put her husband "on the spot" but there never was any cooperation in the family. Others in the group made reassuring comments. Mrs. B said her husband wanted to stay home and help his younger son dress for the Boy Scout meeting, but she insisted that he come to the group meeting because "this boy must learn to care for himself." She didn't want to make the same mistake again.

Although it was not considered beneficial to attempt to suppress these guilt feelings, it also was necessary to avoid situations which tended to create more guilt. It was believed if the individuals were included in a group the existing feelings could be handled and the possibility of arousing more guilt would be lessened. Only in a group situation could they have the opportunity to meet and discuss their difficulties with several people undergoing similar experiences. This would offer an advantage of numerous reassurances from other group members and an opportunity to accept their own feelings in a more realistic perspective.

It was also believed that a feeling of "oneness" and sharing of a common goal would arise out of the similarities of their situations. In a group each participant would have an opportunity to identify with others.

The relatives were expected to be ambivalent about the acceptance of the part they played in the illness. Because of this and their own unconscious needs they tended to perpetuate patterns of behavior which were destructive to the patients. These patterns might be more easily recognizable to the relatives if they could see similar patterns reflected in the behavior of others. Interpretation by the group members was expected and it was believed it would prove more meaningful than if given solely by the caseworker.

Composition of the Group

The composition of both groups indicated a broad cultural range which included widely different national origins, diversified economic backgrounds and certainly a variety of temperaments and emotional reactions. For example, in the first group there were members of Irish, Negro, Jewish and Austrian extraction. The three major faiths were represented in both groups. Religious differences were never considered to handicap group interaction at any time. The number at the group meetings varied, but there seemed to be more action when six members were present.

An interesting development, which occurred in the second group, seemed to arise spontaneously from the needs of some of the members. The fathers of three of the patients were encouraged to attend the meetings by their wives and by the patients. The two men who assumed a more passive role in the family situation remained in the group while the one who was a controlling, overtly rejecting father and who could not face his role in the patient's illness discontinued after three sessions. His wife, who became very upset when the group discussed emotional aspects which were frightening to her (associated with failure in her role as a mother), also discontinued at the same time.

There were three single sisters in both groups. They carried the primary responsibility for the patient's care. Early in contacts with them individually a particularly confusing relationship with the patients was noted. In a sense they assumed the roles of mother, sister and wife simultaneously. They had little insight initially and were often unduly upset by some of the patient's actions. For example, Miss F was quite perturbed because her brother did not take her to parties and dances. Miss A watched through the keyhole while her brother masturbated in the bathroom and wanted assistance in keeping him from engaging in this practice. Miss S constantly threatened her brother with return to the hospital because he went out at night without telling her where he spent his time (even though he was never involved in any trouble).

Group Process

Since each potential group member had been seen individually for the purpose of explaining the group, no effort was made to give further interpretations of the group's function during the early meetings beyond the explanation that the illness was viewed as a problem common to all, thus the reason for meetings. The relatives at first seemed uniformly to believe that focus should be kept on problems which they viewed as directly involving the patients, and felt they should limit themselves to "reports" on the patients' behavior.

In the early meetings most of them centered their discussion on a descriptive account of the veterans' symptoms, stressing those which contributed to difficulty in relationships at home. They questioned each other a great deal and seemed to seek mutual similarities in their situations. This early phase was also characterized by a tendency to seek direct advice from the group leader and by attempts to gain the clinic's impression of the patients' conditions. As the participants became more comfortable in the group, and some of their resistances were met, this type of activity diminished and focus was more on their means of handling various difficulties created by the patients' behavior. This continued to be an important issue throughout the meetings, but through the direction of the group leader they were also able to examine their own feelings about the patients. In the later meetings some of the members displayed ability to bring out their own problems which were independent of the patient and his problems. The focus here was not to treat them intensively, but to enable them to evaluate their role and more effectively increase their ability to see themselves in relation to the patient's current needs and demands.

Resistance of one type or another was present throughout the sessions. Several relatives displayed resistance to being in any way associated with the veteran's illness or treatment by refusing to take part in the meetings, either by not attending or by remaining silent while there. Most resistance was accompanied by a defensive hostility displayed by the relatives and seemed to center around accepting their roles in the behavioral difficulties of the patients and around discussing themselves. Hostility was often directly expressed toward the group leader and by the relatives toward each other with very direct interpretations and criticisms. In the early sessions they occasionally demanded that the group leader explain in what way they were to be helped by the group and cited the group's failure to provide the type of help they felt they needed. At much later periods there were more expressions of appreciation for the group. To demonstrate the above mentioned points and their relatedness some of the group interplay is included in the following example:

The group discussed the handling of hostile feelings by one of the patients toward his parents, who were both present in the meeting. The group leader said he felt that Miss A wanted to say something. She sighed and said that it wouldn't take her long to make up with someone. Mrs. S responded by saying they couldn't do this because that would indicate to her son that they were wrong. Also they didn't want him to return to their home, because she had "enough to make her nervous" with her husband there all the time. Miss A retorted that she did not come here to get help with her difficulties, but she tried to think about them and solve them herself. Mrs. S wondered why she did come here and at first Miss A laughed and said, "To listen to other people and maybe help them with their problems." Mrs. S· responded sarcastically that this was fine and they certainly appreciated her help. (Actually Miss A did discuss her background at another session.) She continued by being critical because Mr. and Mrs. S didn't take their son back to live with them. Mrs. S became quite angry, yet said that was "fine" and that she was "glad" to get any advice she could. She turned to the group leader and remarked she often needed advice but "he said nothing." He said she sounded dissatisfied with the way things were going. She agreed, then—directing her remarks to each member individually—implied that their advice was no good. Some of the group members offered suggestions, including the group leader, who tried to direct attention to the atmosphere in the home rather than any specific occurrence, but she denied that there was tension in her home. She turned to the group again saying she was quite comfortable with them and wanted advice (which she was ready to reject) but later suggested that they change the subject and talk about someone else.

Intragroup relationships developed early in the meetings and were of great importance in their effect on the group and its individual members. As a whole, they seemed to be aware of the individual's need for support and acceptance. As reported earlier, when one group member talked of guilt feelings about her son's illness, all supportively assured her that they too experienced similar feelings. Another mother in conflict about accepting recommended hospitalization for her son was encouraged by the group to use the group meetings to work through this conflict, although this meant that for a period of several weeks little time was left in the meetings for consideration of their problems.

A type of "family relationship" seemed to develop which often resulted in sibling rivalry-like activity, but which also allowed the relatives enough mutual support to express themselves freely and to gain more benefits from the group activity.

Role of the Group Leader

The group leader approximated an authoritative figure who was kindly and firm, understanding but not overly sympathetic. He needed to direct the different personalities and forces occurring in a group to keep the discussion meaningful and useful, and to protect individual members from poor advice or excessive hostility directed by one or more of the other group members. It was important, subtly or directly as the need arose, to sift the meaningful from the unnecessary, and to encourage more passive members to have their say. Pauses seemed longer, similar opinions expressed by several persons seemed to have more impact and in general group casework was more fatiguing to the group leader. Counter transference certainly needed to be considered and handled, and for that reason discussions with the recorder were especially helpful. A group rapport needed to be encouraged and fostered in keeping with the ultimate goals of helping the relatives and patients. It was important to understand the group processes and dynamics which produce more intensive and complex feelings than is usual in individual casework.

Evaluation of the Experience

The most impressive results from the meetings of both groups were the great reduction of irritating occurrences between the patients and family members, and the more comfortable and relaxed atmosphere in the homes. It is certainly significant that in the three years since the termination of the first group and in the the 16 months since the last contact of the second group only one relative has called in an alarmed manner to seek help. From the patients, most of whom still come to the clinic, there also has been a noticeable diminishing of complaints about home conditions, except in one case where the parents did not continue in group casework.

The following factors, we believe, contributed to these improvements. As mentioned earlier, the relatives were able to gain information about handling the patients' problems, primarily from others who experienced fundamentally similar difficulties. As a corollary to this point, the relatives were able to distinguish between minor (or imaginary) and major difficulties. Mrs. B learned that it was not so important for her son to drink his milk as he did as a child, but later did accept the recommendation for hospitalization. Mr. and Mrs. S were unduly upset by the patient's hostile remarks—"What did we do to deserve this?"—but eventually, although with great reluctance, they accepted his need to assert his own personality, and moved away from him.

The recognition by the relatives that they had emotional problems, many of long duration and exclusive of those presented by the patients, served to lessen the intensity of their hold on the patients and relieved more basic anxieties they possessed. This was difficult for the group members to do and much resistance was met, but enough material of this nature was discussed to prove useful and meaningful. It was important for the leader to proceed gingerly because this was perhaps the major defense and most feared subject which confronted the group. This fear of exposure of their own "faults" undoubtedly played an important part in frightening away several members who did not participate regularly and quit after a few sessions.

One may ask: Would group orientation meetings with a speaker, followed by group discussion, serve the same purpose? We do not believe that this approach is as soul-searching nor as personally meaningful to the members as group casework. If one assumes that the feeling tones, subtle as well as overt in expression, which occurred between the patient and his parents influenced the development of his illness, then it would be logical to assume that if the key relatives developed more insight into their own problems, along with a more general educational process, they might become sources of support to the patient.

The key which unlocked the door to a real change in behaviour and attitude turned when the members spoke about *themselves*—often with great emotion and relief. Some of our fears about arousing such feelings were unfounded; we learned, for example, that resistance did not necessarily mean unwillingness to talk about themselves. As in individual casework, care was taken by the group leader to give necessary support as more personal defenses were exposed; even more important, the group members supported each other on these occasions.

Perhaps the most important sidelight to our group experiences was the greater appreciation that we gained of the relatives who tried so hard and were basically so sincere in their efforts to do the right thing, though these efforts were accompanied by personal pain brought on by actual unpleasantness and their own sense of failure. This was not easy because of our own prejudices and because of actually witnessing the results of their earlier unknowingly destructive actions. They seemed much more human and understandable as we became better acquainted with them.

Part 3

Physical Handicaps

The physical state is one of the important areas of the client's total situation which the social worker must consider. This is not to suggest that a medical assessment of the client is the social worker's responsibility. Rather, his task is to assess the extent to which the life and patterns of psychosocial functioning presented by the client are affected by his physical condition.

This responsibility rests both in the assessment phase and in the selection of treatment goals and methods. It presumes therefore some knowledge of physical functioning. Certainly in every case the obligation to individualize must be kept in mind; a therapist would seriously err to consider that all clients with a particular handicap or disease entity were to be treated the same. The necessity to individualize does not imply that we cannot acquire some understanding of clients and indicators for their effective treatment by considering the common factors of their physical condition. For example, only when we understand how much a particular blind client is like other blind clients can we, in fact, individualize him and thus understand how he is different.

There is a further reason for considering the client's physical state. Frequently, our work with people will involve helping them understand and accept various physical problems of other family members. As well as assisting in this recognition and working through of feelings in order to understand better, as part of our responsibility we often aim at helping them to cooperate with and at times participate in the treatment of the afflicted family member. As suggested in the articles presented on the mildly retarded and other forms of brain-damaged children, there may be a considerable amount of resistance and denial on the part of the family, loath to accept such a diagnosis. This in turn frequently limits the potential progress of the client. To involve other significant persons appropriately in treatment requires that the social worker understand the nature of the physical condition and its manifestations. There are several difficulties which can arise from a failure to understand the client's physical condition. Some of these are to support the parents' denial of a diagnosis, to overlook manifestations of illness, or to fail to see changes in a situation.

Although it is not our primary task, we do have a responsibility to recognize obvious physical problems. Certainly I am not implying that we should be diagnosing medical conditions. Nevertheless, we have a responsibility to be aware of some of the possible physical conditions and their manifestations which clients themselves might not recognize. Again, we can use the example of a mildly brain-damaged child. It would be tragic if because of a lack of awareness of easily recognized patterns, such a child were treated as a reaction type of problem to a family situation instead of as a child with a physical handicap. In the Krupp-Schwartzburg article, it is suggested that some of these children can go unrecognized for some time because of unawareness of the therapist and of the patients' families. In multi-professional settings the cooperation and amalgam of several disciplines assist in this regard, and social workers are more attuned to these areas. It is much more difficult, and yet much more crucial, for social workers in nonmedical centers to be equally aware of physical symptomology.

With the growing importance and prevalence of social workers in health fields as well as an increased social orientation in psychiatry and medicine, it is evident that social workers are going to be involved much more with persons suffering from, or recovering from, various physical illnesses. The increase of shorter hospital stays, home care for patients, widespread rehabilitation, retraining programs, and publicly supported insurances, will all demand that social workers be more physically oriented than has been our custom in recent years. There are some indications from the early literature of more general involvement in health issues than at the present time. Now, medically oriented social work has tended to be a more restricted field. Just as all social work must, in fact, be "psychiatric," in the same manner all social work must be "medical."

The selection of articles presented in this section is not all inclusive. It does represent the principal areas of physical functioning addressed in the recent literature. Some early articles were located dealing with polio and tuberculosis, but they were not included because they were outside of the time span covered in the book. Also, there has been dramatic progress in the control of both of these diseases; thus the content of the articles was outdated.

Many of the articles included in this section were of a "one of a kind" category; that is, they were not selected from a large group of several articles dealing with the same topic. I mention this point to emphasize the irregular and almost haphazard pattern of writing in this area of our literature. A beginning search was made into the principal medical journals to locate articles of direct relevance to social work. Two things were quickly observed: first, the overwhelming amount of medical data covering the vast variety of topics both microscopic and macroscopic; two, the almost total lack of social work contribution to these journals although other disciplines such as sociology and psychology have contributed.

It was observed that a larger number of articles dealing with physical handicaps are directed to child patients than to adults. I am not fully clear what this indicates. It might mean that medical social workers are more prevalent in children's services than in adult services.

Two areas which have received some emphasis are the fields of retardation and blindness, especially blindness in children. Again, the reason for this is not clear. It may be that these conditions are generally untreatable and to a great extent unchanging for the person afflicted. Thus, the principal difficulties are in the area of necessary psychosocial adjustments for both the clients and their families. Of these two areas mental retardation had by far the greatest number of articles. Beyond the four used in this section there were five others which could have been utilized as well as several more not selected for other reasons.

In the first part of this section articles are grouped dealing with various forms of cerebral disfunctioning. A common trend can be observed throughout them: one, the necessity for understanding the nature of the handicap; two, its effect on the psychosocial development of the person; and three, its effect on the significant others in the client's life. The authors all emphasize the relationship capabilities of these types of clients, and the danger of underestimating potential for improved functioning.

As mentioned above, social work treatment of retarded clients and their families has been given heavy emphasis in the literature. Several approaches to the many problems presented by these clients are discussed in the articles included here. In all of them emphasis is put on the necessity of knowing our own attitudes towards retardation and their possible interference with therapy. The theme of individualizing and building our treatment on diagnosed strengths rather than presumed limitations is highlighted.

The remainder of the articles in this section are listed in alphabetical order. As mentioned above, the social work literature has been sparse and haphazard in regard to specific physical and medical problems so that topical classification was not possible except in the first section. The format of the articles in this latter division is varied. Some articles contain a detailed analysis of the particular symptom under consideration and the treatment implications; others discuss the analysis of a particular approach to treatment; others outline a program of service; and still others offer the analysis of one or a few cases. As a totality they do present a thorough overview in a general way of social work treatment of physically handicapped persons.

Some of the concepts raised in the group approaches to either the epileptic or cardiac patients have equal applicability to other forms of illness and limitations. The concept of adjustment to the crises of blindness and the analysis of the adjustment process can be applied to similar crisis situations resulting from the onset of illness or disease. The themes of denial of the illness and damage to the concept of body image and adequacy are well discussed in Ballak's article on tuberculosis. These themes are repeated with varying degrees of intensity in other articles.

The social work responsibility of helping the client with decision-making in relation to surgery is examined in Bondy's article on cardiovascular surgery; it has direct application to some other forms of surgery. Attitudes to terminal illness and the dying cancer patient are examined as well as our responsibilities in these situations. Although many commonalities in the treatment implications of physically ill and handicapped clients are stressed, the necessity for particular and specific knowledge is in no way minimized. The social worker will in each case be utilizing his common skills, individually adjusted to the needs of each client or group of clients. This requires a balance between a general orientation to the effects of illness on functioning and attitude, as well as detailed knowledge of the present situation. The articles on hemophilia and quadriplegia clarify this dual responsibility.

Although each topic discussed in these articles points up the necessity for specific knowledge, only one underlines the need for specific skills. In Chough's article on deafness the need for different forms of communication skills is discussed. The author emphasizes the desirability of some social workers developing knowledge and skill in communicating directly with the deaf. The frequently used method of utilizing interpreters or translators is discussed and the familiar problems, frustrations, and limitations associated with this method are highlighted.

Conclusion

This group of articles is interesting, important, and useful. Yet it is thought that a wealth of additional knowledge and skills, both generic and specific, has been accumulated within the professional cadre concerning the treatment of the psychosocial ramifications of physical handicaps. This material should be made available to the general stream of professional literature. In the last four years, many student research projects for the master's program in different schools of social work in Canada and the United States have been directed to particular disease entities and the psychosocial implications for the patient and his family. It is hoped that this is an indication of a growing interest in this dimension, and that more such articles will soon be presented in the journals.

The Brain-Injured Child

The Brain-Injured Child: A Challenge to Social Workers

George R. Krupp and Bernard Schwartzberg

The brain-injured child has been given little attention as a treatment entity by social workers in the fields of child welfare, family casework, foster care and adoption, and psychiatric casework. In recent years, however, several agencies have discovered that an increasing percentage of children under care or referred for service seem to fall within this category.[1]

The social worker can be of considerable assistance in the recognition of this disability, and in getting the parents to accept the diagnosis. In the agency, the parents can obtain the counseling they need, and also can be directed away from inappropriate casework therapy for the child. When a total therapeutic regime for the child is required, it can be planned and followed through within the casework setting.

In considering the caseworker's role with the parents of a mentally retarded child, Kelman notes, "A particularly crucial function . . . is that of guidance or treatment of parents. . . . they have a right and a responsbility to participate closely in planning for [the child's] care. . . . Some parents have experienced profound difficulties in caring for their . . . child, owing to the nature of the child's condition, to their own subjective difficulties, or, as is usually the case, to a combination of the two."[2] He adds that they should be encouraged to particpate in planning, not only for humanitarian reasons but also to ensure that the treatment program instituted may be carried on appropriately in the home. These proposals also are sound in regard to the parents of the brain-injured child.

The social worker's role in helping the brain-injured child is   1] to provide counseling and guidance for the parents, and   2] when desirable, to provide the child with direct help, including the necessary therapy when the agency is equipped to give it, or appropriate referral when the agency

---

[1] The source material for this paper was drawn from the experiences of the authors when they were associated with the Family Service Association of the Five Towns, Woodmere, N.Y.

[2] Howard R. Kelman, "The Function of a Clinic for Mentally Retarded Children," *Social Casework*, Vol. XXXVII, No. 5 (1956), p. 239.

Reprinted from *Social Casework*, XLI (February, 1960), pp. 63–69, by permission of the authors and the Journal.

is unable to provide direct service. The family service agency, whose case-work treatment is family oriented and which can provide a range of services, lends itself well to such a program.

The parents' feeling of bewilderment and confusion concerning the child's behavior is a crucial problem. Special attention should be given to the fact that many of these parents have not been able to accept the diagnosis of brain injury, despite their having been advised of it—sometimes years before—by various doctors, clinics, and special educational resources. Because of their anxiety and lack of knowledge, the parents frequently fight against the acceptance of this diagnosis. They often mention the child's highest level of performance as proof that the child is not retarded or damaged, and ignore other areas in which the child functions poorly. This tendency is not surprising, since the brain-injured child's behavior is almost always erratic or spotty. Hence, the parent rationalizes and cites scores of examples to disprove the previous diagnosis and recommended course of action. Invariably, in the first contact with the caseworker, the parent will deny the child's condition, and complain that the case has been mishandled in the past.

The brain-injured child is frequently brought to the attention of the social worker either by the parents because of his poor school adjustment, or by the school itself because of his poor educational achievements. Some-times the referring school or parent is also concerned about the child's high degree of volatility as well as by his lack of any real social adjustment.

It has been estimated by various authorities that the incidence of children suffering from this condition is much larger than the public realizes. For example, Weir and Anderson note that a large proportion of the 5 per cent of failing children in the school system in Rockford, Illinois, was suffering from the results of brain injury.[3] That such a comparatively large proportion can go generally unrecognized may be due, in part, to the fact that the parents see the children primarily in the protected environment of the home. When the child goes to school, he is then observed in relation to his learning ability and in new social situations that create anxiety. His atypical behavior leads to a recognition of his condition. Frequently the school and the family are in conflict because the parents do not accept the school's observations and recommendations. The social worker should not be involved in this struggle, but must maintain his focus on the meaning of the child's behavior.

Behavior Characteristics

The particular behavior defect that the brain-injured child manifests depends upon the area of the central nervous system that is damaged. If the intracranial centers that initiate and co-ordinate muscular activity are the

---

[3] Homer F. Weir, M.D., and Robert L. Anderson, M.D., "Organic and Organizational Aspects of School Adjustment Problems," *Journal of the American Medical Association*, Vol. CLXVI, No. 14 (1958), pp. 1708–1710.

areas involved, the consequence may be cerebral palsy. If the areas of the brain that are concerned with intelligence are affected, one consequence may be mental deficiency. The injury of the particular areas that control speech and sight may result in distorted sensory perception. Disorders of other areas may produce epilepsy. If the damage occurred early in life and the involvement is diffuse, the result may show itself in altered behavior in relation to many functions. It is the child who falls within this last category who is of primary concern in this discussion—the child who usually has no gross motor or sensory disturbance and whose intelligence is average or even above average. It is this child whose disability often goes unrecognized. Frequently, such a child is diagnosed as having a severe behavior disorder, as being mentally defective, or as suffering from schizophrenia. Once the clinician is familiar with the clinical picture, brain injury is not difficult to recognize, but proving the diagnosis is often difficult.

No behavorial act is the result of a single preceding or predisposing event; and every act has both conscious and unconscious components. A particular symptom may have both physiologic and psychodynamic determinants. Although the organic factor is one of several factors that influence the child's total adjustment and personality, the behavior patterns of brain-injured children reveal a distinctive similarity. The parents, too, reveal a distinctive similarity in that they are almost always anxious and worried and usually give a confused and contradictory description of the child's history and present functioning.

The common behavior characteristics of the brain-injured child have been described by numerous authors.[4] He is different from others of similar age and development. He tends to be outside, or on the periphery of, the group and presents a strikingly erratic performance. This erratic and inconsistent performance is what causes the parents (and frequently the social worker and the school teacher) to be perplexed. This erratic quality has resulted in their describing the child's behavior as poorly integrated, variable, unco-ordinated, inconsistent, strange, queer, and lacking in stability. The child tends to be hyperactive or hyperkinetic. He is often described as overactive, hypermotile, or driveless. His behavior is often characterized by sudden rages, irritability, lability, and uncontrolled impulsivity. The lability in the intellectual sphere is evidenced by his poor concentration, distractibility, and short attention span. Frequently such children have difficulties with number concepts and with arithmetic owing to their difficulty in conceptualization. Instead of grasping number concepts as a

[4] See particularly: Harry Bakwin, M.D., "Cerebral Damage and Behavior Disorders in Children," *Journal of Pediatrics*, Vol. XXXIV, No. 3 (1949), pp. 371–382; Alfred A. Strauss and Laura E. Lehtinen, *Psychopathology and Education of the Brain Injured Child*, Vol. I, Grune and Stratton, New York, 1947; Lauretta Bender, *Psychopathology of Children with Organic Brain Disorders*, Charles C. Thomas, Springfield, Ill., 1955; Edgar A. Doll, "Mental Deficiency vs. Neurophrenia," *American Journal of Mental Deficiency*, Vol. LVII, No. 3 (1953), pp. 477–480; and Charles Bradley, "Organic Factors in the Psychopathology of Childhood," *Psychopathology of Childhood*, Paul H. Hoch and Joseph Zubin (eds.), Grune and Stratton, New York, 1955, pp. 80–104.

whole they will count out the number. An example is a five-and-a-half-year-old who, when asked how many coins (4) were shown to him, had to count each coin separately to the total of four; he could not perceive the four as a whole.

Another characteristic usually noted is perseveration or the tendency to repeat behavior whether or not it is appropriate. This tendency is frequently assumed to be a form of negativism, particularly when the child refuses to give up or shift his activity.[5] Because the child's attention may be distractible but also highly perseverative the behavior picture is confused. Another trait frequently found is low tolerance for stress and frustration. The child may be attentive when it pleases him to be so, yet hopelessly inattentive when efforts are made to control him. For example, a ten-year-old child was able to sit and listen to records at home for long stretches of time but was unable to sit still at school for more than five minutes. Moreover, the brain-injured child is almost invariably ostracized by other children. Often, he has poor muscular co-ordination and finds it difficult to ride a bicycle, tie his shoelaces, or engage in sports.

If the clinician specifically asks about the types of behavior described above, it is astonishing how frequently the child's behavior will then be described in these terms. One of the bewildering aspects of his behavior is its sudden and frequent change. The child will have periods during one day or for days when everything goes well and he appears to be relatively bright; then there will be periods when everything goes wrong and he appears and acts quite stupid. His anxiety readily becomes intensified and disrupts his performance; his conduct is unpredictable and alternates between infantile and more mature behavior. His ability to establish rapport alternates with inaccessibility, and his affectionate acceptance of others alternates with negativistic withdrawal.[6]

Authorities have advanced various hypotheses to explain these behavorial phenomena[7] in terms of the basic brain injury. In summary, they all seem to agree that these children have the following defects which the uninjured do not have: *1]* Faulty powers of inhibition and control, motor and emotional; the child is forced into actions that are not intended. *2]* Disturbances of perception. Perception is more than receiving stimuli; it is an act or a process in which meanings are attributed to the sensed stimuli. *3]* Predisposition to anxiety due to impaired organization, confused interpretation of the environment, and early postural reflex disturbance. The child has impaired visual-motor performance, with a corresponding inability to distinguish foreground figures and background details. There is a sort of confusing-the-forest-for-the-trees response. Distortions of body image are also present. *4]* Secondary psychological defense mechanisms related to the repeated frustrations (anxiety) encountered by the brain-

---

[5] Charles Bradley, *op. cit.*
[6] Edgar A. Doll, *op. cit.*
[7] See especially Alfred A. Strauss and Laura E. Lehtinen; Lauretta Bender; Edgar A. Doll; Charles Bradley, *op. cit.*

injured child and his parents. These may be character reactions such as meticulousness, clinging or withdrawal; psychoneurotic reactions such as phobias, obsessions, and compulsions; psychotic reactions such as schizophrenic thinking disturbances and specific disabilities.

Diagnosis

Despite the ease of making a diagnosis in typical cases of brain injury, clinicians frequently fail to make it. One of the reasons for this failure may be the erroneous assumption that this diagnosis implies a hopeless future. The fact is that such a child tends to improve as he grows older and develops greater ego control. An accurate diagnosis can be made if the clinician bears in mind the six following considerations. These are given in what seems to be their order of value to the clinician.

1.   The composite picture described above and the developmental history. These distinctive patterns must be present. They constitute the soundest basis for making a diagnosis of brain injury.

2.   The child's performance on judiciously selected psychological tests. These must be administered by a psychologist *sensitive to the special problems of the brain-injured child.* In our opinion the psychological test is almost always more significant for the diagnosis than the neurological examination. Without positive findings on the psychological tests a definite diagnosis is difficult to make.

3.   Past medical history. Prenatal factors, such as toxemia, abnormal vaginal bleeding, maternal infection. Prenatal factors, including trauma, anoxia, prematurity, Rh incompatibility. Postnatal factors, including trauma, meningitis, encephalitis, convulsions, cerebral hemorrhage.

4.   Neurological investigation. The presence of neurological disabilities strongly supports the diagnosis. Pediatric neurological examination should emphasize postural reflexes, eye convergence, motility, and the manner in which the child relates to other individuals. Such evidence may not be present if organic factors are in operation. Thus, Silver notes, "Fully 20 per cent of all children seen in the Bellevue Hospital Mental Hygiene Clinic suffer from organic defects incurred during prenatal, paranatal or neonatal life. . . . In them . . . classic neurological examination . . . gives essentially normal results."[8]

5.   Consideration of the family background and of other members of the family. If the child is extremely disturbed, but the family is well adjusted

[8] Archie A. Silver, M.D., "Behavioral Syndrome Associated with Brain Damage in Children," *Pediatric Clinics of North America*, Vol. V, No. 3, W. B. Saunders Company, Philadelphia, 1958, p. 688.

and the mother in particular is not schizophrenic, rejecting, or controlling, the clinician should consider the possibility of an organic defect.

6. Electroencephalogram. This is of limited value, since it can be positive when organic findings are absent and negative when they are present. Much too much emphasis has been placed on this diagnostic procedure.

The child who has suffered a severe brain injury in early life, and the child who presents typical schizophrenic symptoms (autism, bizarre thinking, merging with the environment, withdrawal from people) following a period of normal development are not too difficult to distinguish diagnostically. There are, however, many children for whom a differential diagnosis is not easy to make. Some children seem to have both conditions. Many workers in the field feel that the same cerebral defects or dysfunctions associated with mental retardations or brain injury may and do induce certain patterns of disorganized thinking which are termed schizophrenic.[9] The authors agree with this but use the term "schizophrenic" only when no organic factors are revealed in the clinical picture, the psychological tests, and the history.

The Role of the Social Worker

In working with the brain-injured child and his parents, the social worker should have three main objectives: *1]* recognition of the brain-injured child; *2]* formulation of a treatment plan for him and his family; *3]* offering assistance in carrying out the treatment plan.

Recognition

The social worker needs to acquire a basic understanding of the clinical entity known as the brain-injured child, and the meanings of each aspect of the child's behavior. He should recognize not only the individual elements of the syndrome, but also the combination of factors which characterize this diagnosis. He needs to know both the emotional and the physical reasons for the child's behavior and for the lack of impulse control. Above all, he needs to understand the relationship of the organic brain damage to the child's educational and social adjustment. This knowledge enables him to help the parents to understand the child better, and to work out a treatment plan with the school and other community resources.

Paramount in the worker's mind must be the fact that the brain-injured child has specific disabilities in the area of perception, and that his ability to conceptualize is impaired. This child finds it difficult to master two and

---

[9] See Max Pollak, "Brain Damage, Mental Retardation, and Childhood Schizophrenia," *American Journal of Psychiatry*, Vol. CVX, No. 5 (1958), pp. 422–428; and Joseph Wortis, "Schizophrenic Symptomatology in Mentally Retarded Children," *American Journal of Psychiatry*, Vol. CXV, No. 5 (1958), pp. 429–431.

three dimensions, he responds more to details than to the whole, his motor and emotional controls are poor, and he needs to repeat experiences. When the social worker recognizes that the child's perception is defective and that his learning ability is thus impaired, he will be able to understand better why the parents are so confused in their assessment of the child's intellectual capacities. Many of these children have average and above average I.Q.'s, yet fail miserably in school and in new learning situations. For example, the parents of one child who had been examined by several clinicians could not accept the diagnosis. By making tape recordings of the child's responses to their questions, the parents attempted to prove to the examiners that the child was not so slow and retarded as all the examiners had indicated. When one listened to the tape recording it was quickly apparent that the child had good ability in rote matters and that they had given him indirect clues to the correct answers. Hence, they were overoptimistic in assessing the results. It should be emphasized that in order to understand the child's behavior and his poor learning ability one must recognize his difficulty in abstract thinking and in conceptualization. For example, one child could take measurements of two halves of a table but could not add them together to get the whole.

A social worker alert to this diagnosis will notice the child's gait, posture, and facial expression. He will observe the particular speech characteristics—immaturity, slowness, and an echoing quality. A history of erratic behavior, hyperactivity, impulsivity, and social unacceptability, significant information derived from the genetic history, and the above observations should immediately suggest to the worker the need for psychologic and psychiatric consultation to confirm the diagnosis of brain disorder.

The psychiatrist is in the best position to help the social worker understand the medical and neurological implications of brain injury. He may make his contribution as a member of the staff of the psychiatric clinic, as a consultant in a family or children's agency, or as a teacher of a seminar in which all the members of the casework staff of the agency participate. He may also be used as a diagnostician who sees the child for a diagnostic interview to ensure the validity of the diagnosis made.

Formulation of a Treatment Plan

The worker in a social agency needs to take into consideration the assets and liabilities of the parents, as well as the nature and extent of the injury to the child, and the limitations of the child's functioning because of the damage. In general, however, an appropriate treatment plan includes counseling and guidance for the parents, referral to a medical resource for medical or drug therapy needed by the child, some sort of relationship therapy when indicated, and suggestions for modification of the average educational plan, such as placement in a special class or securing a teacher of the homebound, if this is possible. When the school does not permit any modification of the usual curriculum, or when the parents are unwilling or unable to benefit from a counseling or guidance relationship, it may be necessary to work out plans for the child away from his home—foster care, placement in a treatment institution or in a specially structured educational setting. The psychiatrist usually participates in formulating the plan.

The brain-injured child has a weak ego and a history of repeated failure in handling his own needs and his environmental pressures. Special educational techniques are required to help him develop ego mastery. These are divided into two main groups by Kaliski[10] and include "experiences in everyday living, awareness and interpretation of each other's needs, feelings, forming relationships (adults and peers), getting acquainted with the community, its structure, its resources, its needs, civic responsibilities," and "learning the skills and acquiring the tools necessary to function independently in our culture." An atmosphere in which the child is relaxed and in close contact with the teacher is a most important tool for his educational retraining.

It should never be taken for granted that the child will understand and follow ordinary verbal directions, especially when time and space relationships are involved. The brain-injured child has difficulties in perceiving the relationships and similarities between things in the world around him, which is the basis for abstract thinking. He often perceives things quite differently from the normal person and his attention is distracted by any insignificant or meaningless detail. Therefore, it is important to avoid any unnecessary or distracting stimuli.

At the same time, each task the child is asked to perform must be concretized for him. It must be broken down into its component parts, and each one must be made concrete. For example, the child may be unable to tie his own shoelaces. The special educator, educational therapist or psychologist who is helping him learn to perform this task can do so only by over-concretizing the material. Each step is broken down into its simplest elements. The child learns each step in minute detail, and gradually learns to put the steps together. Or again, the child may know his multiplication tables and spelling by rote. He may know that two times three is six, but he does not know why it is six. The educator may use diagrams and teach him by adding two threes. What he already knows by rote can be used in developing conceptualization in this way; thus, multiplication and division are spelled out.

The child's attention has to be directed through the use of special techniques, because one of his major limitations is his inability to concentrate on ordinary visual or auditory stimuli. This can be done through specially designed visual stimuli such as lights, color, or forms, or through special auditory stimuli. In addition, certain kinesthetic approaches may be used to increase conceptualization. For example, the special educator may hold the pencil with the child, and go over the letter that is being taught, or the letter may be made out of clay, pinned out flat, and then traced with a stick

[10] Lotte Kaliski, "The Brain Injured Child—Learning by Living in a Structured Setting," *American Journal of Mental Deficiency*, Vol. LXIII, No. 4 (1959), pp. 688–695.

or the finger. These and other kinesthetic approaches increase the child's comprehension by moving from the concrete to the abstract. Although special techniques have been developed, educators of the brain-injured child by no means have the final answer for educating him. As Strauss and Lehtinen state, "what we present today is only a vague, preliminary 'scouting' in the field of defect and disease and as yet we do not even know to what extent our efforts toward alleviating disease and defect are efforts in the right direction."[11]

Assistance in Carrying out the Treatment Plan

In establishing a treatment program for the brain-injured child, the social worker must be aware that any plan will involve three groups of people: the school authorities, including the psychologist, principal, and classroom teacher; the family physician or pediatrician; and the parents themselves. Even the child with superior intelligence usually has had a history of failure in school, and the referral to the agency often comes at a point of desperation. Thus, it is vital to secure the co-operation of school personnel in working out a special program, or in securing greater understanding of the child in the regular curriculum if this is possible. Hence, the school psychologist should be included in the plan as early as possible in order to make sure that the other school authorities, including the classroom teacher, understand the child and his problem and work to help him within the school setting.

Second, especially when drug therapy is part of the child's treatment (other than in a psychiatric clinic) the co-operation of the family physican must be secured, since it will be he who administers the drug treatment in conjunction with the consultant psychiatrist of the agency, and relates this treatment to the total physical functioning of the child. His co-operation in the planning should be secured as early as possible.

Finally, the major task of the social worker, that of giving guidance or casework counseling to the parents or parent substitutes, is carried on simultaneously with the other aspects of the treatment plan. The parents or foster parents are thus enabled to accept the diagnosis and plan on a continuing basis and to handle their own personal feelings which may interfere with their seeing the child as in need of special help.

Conclusion

The brain-injured child must be understood in terms of his biological damage, his psychological defense mechanisms, and the environmental forces acting on him. The social worker also needs to be aware that the child tends to improve as he grows older.

The social worker, therefore, needs to be alert to the overt signs which point to the existence of this type of damage in order to carry out his function

[11] Alfred A. Strauss and Laura E. Lehtinen, *op. cit.*

of providing service to the brain-injured child and his parents. He must see his role as one of helping the parents to secure additional direct help for the child when it is needed while providing concurrent counseling. Consultation with or participation by both psychiatrist and psychologist is essential to any social agency considering a program of this nature.

The social worker cannot be expected to assume the responsibility for making the clinical diagnosis of the brain-injured child. He should, however, be able to spot the chief behavioral characteristics and typical history of this type of child, and to understand some of the dynamic implications of the child's psychopathology. Unless he is able to do so, time will be spent needlessly in exploring the possibility of other diagnoses, in interviewing the family members, and often in attempting inappropriate casework treatment of the child. This is not only an inappropriate use of the caseworker's time, but also does the family and child a disservice.

When the social agency clearly sees its responsibility in helping a brain-injured child, and does the job in a professional and competent manner, it can be of considerable assistance to both the child and his parents. In this way, the social worker helps the child, the family, the school, and the community in which the child lives. All benefit from the social worker's efforts, and the child is able to lead a more fruitful and productive life.

Cerebral Palsy

Technical Alterations in the Psychotherapy with an Adolescent Cerebral Palsy Patient

Arnold S. Carson

Within the last decade the practice of psychotherapy has broadened in spectrum and has become sufficiently eclectic to be useful with mentally retarded children, character disorders, sex offenders, stutterers and a variety of other classifications (5)*. With broader application, specialized techniques have been developed.

The purpose of this paper is to add to the continuing effort to develop clinical skills for working with people who are typically considered "poor psychotherapeutic risks." Specifically, the short-term psychotherapy of a 14-year-old cerebral palsy patient will be described with particular emphasis upon obstacles to treatment and the technical alterations which were developed to overcome these obstacles.

Theoretical Considerations

Much has been written about the effects of physical handicap upon the ego and the subsequent adjustment of the handicapped youngster (1, 2, 4, 6, 7, 11, 12, 13). There is little doubt expressed in the literature that the severe physical handicap of a child carries with it, as one of the side effects, some degree of ego impairment. Psychoanalytic theory places special importance on the physical self, both in differentiating the self from others and in the development of the ego.

> In the development of reality, the conception of one's own body plays a very special role. At first there is only the perception of tension: that is, of an "inside something." Later, with the awareness that an object exists to quiet this tension, we have an "outside something." One's own body is both at the same time. Due to the simultaneous occurrence of both outer tactile and inner sensory data, one's own body becomes something apart from the rest of the

*References will be found at the end of the chapter.

Reprinted from *Mental Hygiene*, XLVIII (April, 1964), pp. 249–256, by permission of the author and the Journal.

world and thus discerning of self from nonself is made possible. The sum of the mental representations of the body and its organs, the so-called body image, constitutes the idea of *I* and is of basic importance for further formation of the ego (8, pp. 35 and 36).

Other noted psychologists have commented on the importance of physical self for personality development from different theoretical frames of reference (9, 10, 14). However, Wright cautions theoreticians against presupposing a straight-line correlation between physical handicap and emotional disturbance during adolescence. "Although physique carries a particularly heavy emotional loading during adolescence, it is not correct to conclude that any single physical deviation will invariably or even probably produce distress (14, p. 181).

Ausubel adds: "The psychological consequences of deviation will depend on 'social and individual attitudes toward nonconformity,' the strength of intrinsic attitudes of self-acceptance and the possession of compensatory assets" (3, p. 102).

In addition to the structural aspects of personality development in physically handicapped children, the writer has noted a number of consistent psychodynamic factors which have had particular applicability in the understanding of adolescent cerebral palsy patients with medium to severe crippling.

The physical and social development of the child with cerebral palsy is slowed down. His motility is impaired. Often he is incontinent until the age of 7 or 8 and sometimes dependent upon urinary bags throughout his life. In addition to toilet training, personal responsibility for cleansing, dressing, eating and speaking often need be postponed. Many of these youngsters are carried over the shoulder of their parents to the period of preadolescence.

Undoubtedly these atypical patterns of development predispose them to severe dependency problems as they get older. Consequently, the adolescent cerebral palsy patient in psychotherapy will often fight off a dependency relationship with the therapist or succumb to it so readily that there is little potential initiative manifested.

In their psychosexual development a post-oedipal development is an exception. Most of these youngsters remain partially to totally fixated in the oral and anal phases of development. So much attention and energy has had to be given to the functions of eating and eliminating that they often remain the chief avenues of sexual gratification even in adulthood. Genital sexuality is often hampered until these adolescents can work through their feelings regarding extended handling of their sexual organs by their parents during ages where there should be a quiescence in parent-child intimacy. It is worth noting that the prolonged physical dependency of the crippled child upon his parents sometimes makes it necessary for these parents to ignore some of the taboos essential in the normal child-parent relationship.

A number of obstacles to psychotherapeutic treatment with the cerebral palsied youngster follow from the research, theory and clinical observations:

1. Strong dependency needs continue to be buffered by the ever-present palsy.

2. Affliction at birth precludes the opportunity to develop a more favorable self-image.

3. Self-sufficiency with inadequate personal equipment is a feeble alternative to the gratification derived from being cared for in the bathroom, at the dinner table and in the bedroom.

4. The "why should I be the one who is afflicted?" question is one that tends to set off a severe depressive reaction, while the answer is sought.

5. The avenues for sexual growth and exploration are limited by the lack of motor co-ordination, the rejection by peers of the opposite sex, and the conveyed fears of adults concerning their development in this area.

Case History

Bob T was born in 1947. Mrs. T was anemic during the pregnancy. He was delivered after $7\frac{1}{2}$ months of carriage; labor was forced for $2\frac{1}{2}$ hours; toes were bruised; and legs remained in a triangular position for three weeks. The baby breathed spontaneously at birth and weighed 7 pounds 2 ounces. Bob was a healthy baby and was circumcised a few days after birth. He had the usual immunizations at 6 and at 9 months. He was able to finger-feed at one year and spoon feed at two. Head control was established at three months, and he could roll over about the same time. He began to crawl at three years and could stand without support at four years.

At the age of $8\frac{1}{2}$ months Bob was diagnosed as a "congenital spastic." He was placed on a Prostigmine Regime until the age of two. Loss of eyelid droop and muscle tone improvement was noted. At two the standing diagnosis of cerebral palsy with general loss of muscle control in the abdominal and gluteal muscles was established. Bob was fitted for an abdominal corset in 1952 and long leg braces in 1953. He continues to wear these physical aids. Physical therapy case notes have the following repetitive pattern: slight gains, broken appointments, case temporarily inactive, reopened, slight gains, broken appointments, etc.

Bob's father is a self-made man from an Italian-English, Roman Catholic cultural background. He has attended college over the past 10 years and has gained inservice training in the field of metallurgy. Mrs. T is from an English-German, Roman Catholic background. She has been trained as a commercial artist but is employed full-time in the home caring for her 4 children, of whom Bob is the oldest. Bob, age 14, is followed by a brother, age 13; a sister, age 8; and a brother, age 3.

At the age of 7 Bob was tested with the Stanford-Binet, Form L, and earned a score within the bright normal range of intelligence. He received homebound teaching until the age of 9 when he was placed in a school for handicapped children. At the age of 10 he was transferred to a different school and reacted to the transfer with an episode of soiling his pants two to four times a month. Bob's pediatrician prescribed 10 mg. of Aterax per day to tranquilize the anxiety assumed to be underlying the soiling. Throughout the period of school attendance, Bob was described as being resistant to learning and to the school's physical therapy program.

Bob was referred for psychotherapy because of his underachievement in school and physical therapy, his constant regressions into unrealistic fantasies and general immaturity.

Administration of Treatment

Bob was seen once a week in an outpatient orthopedic clinic. His physical therapy, occupational therapy and social service were enlisted at times as aids to treatment. The therapist was a post-doctoral fellow in the counseling service of Merrill-Palmer supervisors. There were 29 treatment hours with Bob, an equivalent number of supervisory hours, and a total of 5 interviews with Mr. and Mrs. T.

Treatment

The therapist was cautious about working with Mr. and Mrs. T because of their dissatisfaction with previous psychological contacts. They consented to treatment for Bob but were weary of having people telling them how to rear their children. The goals of therapy were to help Bob understand his passive resistance, "smart aleckiness," and find ways of handling his impulses which would not elicit rejection from others.

A second goal of treatment was to put Bob's fantasies to the test of reality. The initial stages of therapy were devoted to establishing a positive working relationship with the patient.

The therapist initially defined the modes of operation with the patient in too-rigid a manner. He expected a boy of 14 with better than average intelligence to be able to utilize verbal therapy on a time-limited basis. It became apparent that Bob (who emotionally was more like an 8 or 9 year old) could not utilize classical methods of treatment.

The first six interviews were a period of no movement. Bob was not willing to trust or reveal himself to someone who was not going to allow him to function in his typical manner. He was only comfortable when he knew the person he was with and could control the other person with this knowledge. He continually asked the therapist personal questions and would test the boundaries of the therapist's discipline. (The patient would open the therapist's drawers and want to read case notes.)

With the advent of no therapeutic movement, the therapist, with the help of his supervisor, made a number of changes in the mode of operation. Play materials such as clay, crayons and games were offered. At times the entire verbal therapy was carried out during a game of checkers or darts. The time limits of treatment were made more flexible so that the patient could determine if he wished to continue treatment or not.

The therapist would help the patient to help himself through a variety of experiences. One that was particularly meaningful to the patient was grasping his hands, fisherman style, and walking down the stairway with him. This activity elicited some anxiety from the therapist and the patient since both were aware that if either slipped they would tumble down the stairs entangled in 60 pounds of braces.

The therapist made a constant effort to help Bob become more aware of his strengths. Bob has a definite asset which he undervalued. Although crippled, he has definite artistic ability. The therapist began talking with him about how he could use his talented hands. Movement became rapid with the newer modes of operation.

Bob brought in his concerns about having his sexually matured body handled, dressed and cleansed by his mother and young female attendants at school. Fortunately, Mr. and Mrs. T had observed Bob's increased motivation in school and loss of belligerent attitude and now were willing to accept help from the therapist in rearing him. The therapist helped the father to accept more responsibility in caring for Bob at the toilet, shower, and other places where physical contact and exposure were necessary.

Bob began to identify with the therapist strongly and would carry the therapist's program of helping him to help himself into the home. Around the middle phases of therapy the patient began expressing many angry feelings toward his father and mother.

Bob's wish to murder anyone who would put him a wheelchair (Mr. T threatened Bob with a wheelchair if he did not carry out his physical exercises) was considered seriously by the therapist. The therapist considered with the patient the possibilities of committing murder within the context of the patient's handicapped motility and lack of finances. Realization of the extent of his handicap elicited the patient's basic feelings of inadequacy. Bob made a plea to sail off to some primitive island where he could live alone.

The therapist considered this plea for alienation again in terms of its possibility. This brought a new surge of hostility from the patient, directed and expressed toward the therapist. Bob believed that as he grew older he would be able to walk without crutches, drive a low-slung sportscar, marry easily, have a family and earn lots of money as a metallurgical engineer. No one had ever delineated for him fact from fantasy and possibility from probability. The therapist worked closely at this point with the orthopedic surgeon, and it was determined that Bob might be able to drive in an especially-equipped car and, from a physical point of view, marriage and sexual relations might be possible. Walking without crutches was pretty much out of the question.

All fantasies that the patient brought in were entertained in terms of their reality value. The patient became very indignant when the therapist called the U.S. Navy recruitment office with him present in order to establish that he could not join the Navy, as he had fantasied.

His unwillingness to accept his crippling was brought to a head during an interview in which Bob and his parents were seen together. The purpose of this interview was to discuss vocational possibilities for Bob. For the first time, during this interview, Mr. T approached Bob with the fact that he could not perform the work of a metallurgical engineer with his handicap. The therapist confronted Bob with the impossibility of his driving a low-slung sportscar. With Bob's anger welling up inside of him, Mrs. T commented sympathetically, "This is a hard pill for Bob to swallow." It was for her, too.

An alternate modality in which treatment was carried out was psychosexuality. Purposeful sex education assured Bob that he could discuss his concerns in this area during the interview. Gingerly, at first, he revealed strong voyeuristic tendencies and an anal conception of birth. At first he depersonalized his drawings pertaining to sex.

The therapist, utilizing knowledge from early experiences with Bob, extended himself by drawing on paper some of his own conceptions of sexuality. Two essential needs emerged from the psychosexual modality of treatment. The patient tried to use the therapist as a procurer of pornographic material and experiences. In some of his more daring hours Bob demanded that the therapist bring his secretary into the office, make her undress and leave him alone with her. The second need, the desire to be nurtured, was brought into the interview in an interesting manner. Bob became very secretive, demanded confidentiality, then confessed that the reason girls shun him is because he cannot use his hands adequately to cleanse himself after defecation. His rationale for being shunned by girls was understood by the therapist as a powerful defense against rejection, buffered by taking on the characteristics of a buffoon in appearance and behavior to ward off inner sadness and to explain the rejection. This interpretation was confirmed when Bob, attending a camp for crippled children, became interested in a girl and soiled his pants seven times in 48 hours in order to explain a seemingly inexplicable rejection from her.

In spite of his reaction to rejection from girls, gains were noted in a number of areas: Bob now looks and behaves more like a 13-year-old than a 9- or 10-year-old. He has lost his "smart alecky" attitude. He is responding well in school and physical therapy. There have been some basic revisions in Bob's self-concept. He realizes much more his physical handicap and his vocational assets.

Generally, his fantasy life is filled with more potentially productive ideas. Specific familial conflicts have been resolved because Bob no longer sits back and instigates fights between other family members. He is more able to express both positive and negative feelings toward his father. The remaining problems in the area of Bob's ability to cope with rejection from peers are still handled by soiling.

Discussion

Bob admitted to no dependency needs, although he depends upon another individual in almost every aspect of his life. After reactive, arrogant independence was given up by the patient, the therapist chose to ward off a severe dependency relationship and afford the client with help in helping himself. This alteration served as a buffer against a too-speedy regression and, at the same time, helped to increase the patient's skills in handling day-to-day situations.

The self-image of a palsied child is based upon his accomplishments during childhood. Unfortunately, the child with palsy is handicapped in those skills which are attributed with primary importance during childhood; i.e., walking, talking, bowel and bladder control, feeding, etc. The inadequate self-image can be countered through "foresight therapy." In addition to having the child recall his past experience, the therapist directs the child into fantasies about himself 5, 10 or 15 years henceforth. Some of these fantasies have proved to be as bizarre as early childhood nightmares.

The fact that "something is wrong with me" is sometimes given to bizarre speculation about how the patient can be "righted" or punished. "Foresight therapy" affords the therapist with the opportunity to correct anxiety-ridden images about the future and to educate the patient on his potential vocational assets.

The difficult problem of how to help the patient part with infantile sexual gratification was encountered in the case illustrated. Although adolescents sense the inappropriateness of having adults of the opposite sex care for them at the toilet and shower when they are sexually mature, the repressed sensual gratification obtained from such care is a powerful deterrent against giving up such experiences. The promise of adult heterosexual relationships is vague for the palsied adolescent. In the case illustrated the therapist did not dwell on the patient's infantile gratifications but instead enlisted the aid of the parents in changing the patient's outlets for sexual gratification. The patient only began to grope for more mature ways of meeting his sexual impulses when father replaced mother as his attendant at the toilet and shower.

The palsied adolescent's question of why should he be the one who is afflicted precludes an intelligible intrapsychic answer since the affliction is not something that the patient wrought. The analogy which might help clarify this answer is that of the brain-damaged adolescent asking the question of why should he be so confused. In both cases their burden is not something they purposely wrought; yet as adults they will be expected to accept responsibility for what they are.

In the case illustrated, the patient was comforted by the therapist pointing out that everybody has burdens to bear to a greater or lesser degree. Dark skin, lack of money, limited intelligence, cowardliness or marital problems are some of the many burdens people bear. He conveyed to the patient that as he matured he would continue to be judged by some fearful people for his palsy, but the primary criteria for his own worth would be his manner of coping with his palsy.

Summary

The purpose of this paper was to describe psychotherapy with a 14-year-old cerebral palsy patient. Particular emphasis was placed on the obstacles to psychotherapy brought about by the physical affliction and the technical alterations which were used to overcome them.

Theories, research and clinical observations in the field of somato-psychology all point to some degree of ego deficiency in medium to severe crippling from birth. Problems specific to cerebral palsy which have previously precluded psychotherapeutic intervention were *1]* the affliction buffering dependency needs, *2]* lack of opportunity for development of positive self-image, *3]* gratification of pre-oedipal sexual strivings by significant adults, and *4]* the seemingly inexplicable rejection of those afflicted.

Technical alterations in psychotherapy were discussed, utilizing a case study to illustrate implementation of technique. The therapist warded off a severe dependency relationship by helping the patient to help himself. Opportunity for developing a positive self-image was afforded by "foresight therapy," a process of exploring and analyzing progressive fantasies in addition to regressive fantasies.

Pre-oedipal sexual strivings were frustrated through manipulation of the familial environment and exposing the patient to a purposeful program of sex education. Actual rejection and feelings of rejection were handled by helping the patient to use his personal assets effectively and to ward off implied or felt worthlessness.

Acknowledgment

The author wishes to express his appreciation to Carolyn Pratt, Ph.D., who so ably supervised the case presented here.

References

1 ADLER, A., *Study of Organ Inferiority and its Psychical Compensations* (New York: Nervous and Mental Disease Publishing Co., 1917).

2 ALLEN, F. H. and G. H. J. PEARSON, "The Emotional Problems of the Physically Handicapped Child," *British Journal of Medical Psychology*, 8(1928), 212–36.

3 AUSUBEL, D. P., *Ego Development and the Personality Disorder* (New York: Grune & Stratton, Inc., 1952).

4 BARKER, R. G., "The Social Psychology of Physical Disability," *Journal of Social Issues*, 4(1948), 28–38.

5 BYCHOWSKI, G. and J. L. DESPERT, *Specialized Techniques in Psychotherapy* (New York: Grove Press, Inc., 1952).

6 CRUICKSHANK, W. M., "The Impact of Physical Disability on Social Adjustment," *Journal of Social Issues*, 4(1948), 78–83.

7 CUTSFORTH, T. D., "Personality Crippling Through Physical Dis-

ability," *Journal of Social Issues*, 4(1948), 62–67.

8 FENICHEL, O., *The Psychoanalytic Theory of Neurosis* (New York: W. W. Norton & Co., Inc., 1945), 35, 36.

9 FITZGERALD, D. C., "Success-Failure and T.A.T. Reactions of Orthopedically Handicapped and Physically Normal Adolescents," *Journal of Personality*, 1(1950), 67–83.

10 HENTIG, H. VON, · "Physical Disability, Mental Conflict and Social Crisis," *Journal of Social Issues*, 4(1948), 21–27.

11 McANDREW, H., "Rigidity and Isolation: A Study of the Deaf and the Blind," *Journal of Abnormal Social Psychology*, 43(1948), 476–94.

12 SHELDON, W. H., in collaboration with S. S. STEVENS and W. B. TUCKER, *The Varieties of Human Physique: An Introduction to Constitutional Psychology* (New York: Harper & Row Publishers, Inc., 1940).

13 WRIGHT, B. A., ed., *Psychology and Rehabilitation* (Washington, D.C.: American Psychological Association, 1959).

14 Wright, B. A., *Physical Disability: A Psychological Approach* (New York: Harper & Row Publishers, Inc., 1960), 13–85, 162–78.

Epilepsy

Experiences in Working with a Group of Seizure Patients

Marguerite Puvrez

In an article "New Approaches to Old Problems," written in collaboration with Miss B. Elliott, which appeared in an issue of *The Social Worker*, we described our reasons for attempting to form a group made up of patients subject to epileptic seizures. We mentioned then what we thought would make it initially difficult for such a group to "jell": that the presence of a medical authority as well as a social worker, with lectures prepared by persons from outside the group, would provide meetings rich in information but poor in free expression.

The goal of the present article is to describe the experiences of social therapeutic treatment, experiences garnered while we guided a group of young epileptic adults at the Montreal Neurological Institute.

Sickness in general not only creates new problems for the patient and his family, but also frees traits of the personality previously dormant, revealing them in broad daylight. One can state that epilepsy presents difficult situations which require a strong well-adjusted personality. We have rarely met such well-structured personalities among epileptics with whom we have come in contact. As in all cases of sickness, the first goal of any medical caseworker is to appreciate the problems created by the new situation, or those which could interfere with the medical treatment, bearing in mind the case of epilepsy that:

1. This is a sickness often hidden because of the blacklisting prejudices of society.

2. It often commenced in the early life of the patient.

3. One can never speak of a cure, but only of a "control," depending always on the cooperation of the person involved.

Reprinted from *The Social Worker*, XXX (April, 1962), pp. 31–38. This article was originally written in French under the title of *Expériences en travail de groupe avec des épileptiques* and was translated by Colin Tisshaw. It is reprinted by permission of the author and the Journal.

No means can then be overlooked which may result in the patient's development of self-confidence and confidence in others, in the development of positive traits of his personality, and in development of the control with which he will employ them in the inevitable crises of the future.

This article aims to point out the positive results of the utilization of group dynamics, that is to say the forces, pressures, tensions, influences, and controls exercised on the individual by the group or by one or more members of the group—influences created by the fact of the group situation that support, modify, or channel the patient's individual energies in social manifestations or his effectiveness in coming face to face with realities. This article is not intended to present a replacement for other methods, not even other methods of group therapy. It does not pretend to be another milestone in the literature of group therapy, which is becoming more and more abundant each day. It is simply the result of our personal experiences, which we found to be interesting and productive but from which we should refrain from drawing hasty conclusions.

Before giving some examples of cases, let us say that the "Open Group of Young French Speaking Epileptic Adults," to which we shall refer under the abbreviated term "the group," was formed in the beginning of June, 1958, at the Montreal Neurological Institute, because of the following considered factors.

1. Our experience in casework with seizure patients showed us that the epileptic must face the most crucial social problems between adolescence and adulthood, i.e., family, friends, work, marriage, and children.

2. Their real or subjective isolation brings about serious personal and social consequences, so that the personal casework is long, sometimes disappointing, and not of the nature to help the patient where he needs help most—in overcoming his isolation.

3. Although we belonged to an English-speaking hospital, from 65 to 70 per cent of the seizure patients followed in the outdoor clinic were French-speaking or were immigrants who preferred to speak French.

4. The percentage of patients between the ages of twenty and thirty were in the relative majority—130 out of 496 in 1958.

The goals which we proposed for our group were as follows:

1. To permit the patients to express their feelings about what they wished: themselves, the clinic, the doctors, the treatments, the medications, their families, and their state of health—sometimes so variable and depressing. It was felt that it was easier for them to relate to a group of seizure patients like themselves, rather than to a social worker who does not suffer from the

same condition and whose secondhand knowledge does not, in their minds, enable her to grasp the total impact of their illness.

2. To permit the patients to be better self-informed on their real condition by having informative meetings from time to time directed by a French-speaking neurologist.

3. To permit the seizure patients to satisfy their needs for affection, a very deep need because of so often being misunderstood and rebuffed.

4. To enable the patients to obtain a social rehabilitation, possibly more rapidly than through private casework, supplementing the latter in every way, prolonging it for the benefit of the client, and gaining time for the social worker.

5. To create a milieu where seizure patients, who had never been able to voice their opinions, would have their own group, with a president, secretary, and treasurer, and would be able to say and do what they wished.

The criteria for the choice of members were as follows:

1. Epilepsy had to be clearly diagnosed and the patient had to have been informed about it by the doctor.

2. The patient had to have attained such an age that any subject could be discussed before him.

3. The patient had to have such a personality as to permit a certain flexibility in changes of attitude.

4. The patient must not have had pronounced mental retardation nor serious psychiatric problems.

5. The medical prognosis for the patient had to have left some hope for control of the seizures.

6. The patient had to have shown proof in the past of having been capable of some social adjustment, either in his family, in school, or with his peers.

Meetings

Since the beginning of June, 1958, the group met once a week, for about an hour in the evening. Certain members who were employed during the day stayed after the session for a more personal casework interview. There was an annual monthly lapse for holidays and also a period in which we organized several informational meetings, at the request of the group, for parents of young epileptic children.

At the time of this writing the group had approximately eighty patients, although the number in attendance has varied widely. Rarely has a person attended for less than a month, and the majority of members came from four to seven months. The number of people at each session varied from twelve to eighteen. A nucleus of seven or eight members who were extremely loyal in attendance also evolved. They helped us greatly in preserving a warm atmosphere, providing a touchstone and initial confidence which enabled new members to be rapidly integrated.

Let us now look at some case examples.

These first cases will show the efficiency of the support of the group in helping a client benefit more from medical treatments or to accept new treatments.

First Case

Claire was a young girl of twenty-six, the sixth child in a family of eleven. She started having convulsions before her fifth birthday and has never been well-controlled. Her parents were good people, capable of love, but who had excessively protected their child. Claire consequently was very dependent, never went out alone, had not even had six years of schooling (and that with irregular attendance), and did not know what it was to make a personal decision. She had been referred to the social service because of recently developed deafness which was threatening her hearing in both ears. The doctors wanted to try to operate on one ear and then the other, but were not able to guarantee positive results. At any rate, they promised that there was nothing to lose. In personal casework neither Claire nor her mother wanted to hear of it. Claire came to the group for two or three months. Her case was the subject of a couple of discussions, a couple of allusions and then was left alone for a while.

One fine day, Claire came to announce to me that she agreed to the operations on her ears. While her hearing is not perfect, it has improved and her position in the family has been enhanced.

Second Case

Louis is a young man of twenty-seven, the only child in a family of two, his sister having been adopted. He started having epileptic seizures towards nine years of age. His parents had been very affected, and their personal relations had not been the best. The child had been overprotected but with a basic hostility which stemmed from his rejection. The parents were "good" as it is generally accepted, and strict. The boy had been put in a boarding school "for his own good." The parents decided what studies he would follow and even the place where he would apply. In due course, when the "child" became twenty-three years of age, he didn't want to have anything to do with anybody and refused one place after another, always relying on the impossibility of his being accepted, to the great despair of his father; and he became openly disagreeable with the family, to the great despair of his mother. Psychiatric treatment was started, but the psychiatrist was not very optimistic and asked that we do intensive casework with Louis. As we were not able to obtain any change in attitude, we tried having him join the group, already well organized at the time, while continuing the personal casework. Little by little we could feel that Louis was cooperating with the casework and was starting to profit from the previously received psychiatric treatment. After about a year, Louis accepted a position—even though it was suggested by his father—and demonstrated to the group how much it was possible to become *independent* in a *dependent* milieu. Another year passed. His situation was stable, and Louis was then part of the nucleus of the group.

Third Case

Gloria was a married woman of thirty-three, who had always been subject to epileptic seizures, more or less controlled. Separated from her husband from the beginning of her marriage, she obtained the custody of their child, a boy, and her husband was supposed to pay her a separation allowance. After several months the husband disappeared, and the mother preferred to earn her own living for her son and herself rather than sue for nonsupport. She placed herself in domestic service and was successful in giving love and a family atmosphere to her son. However, as he was approaching fourteen, he began to show signs of independence, as all adolescents do—refusal to obey, little escapades, poor results in school. The mother was affected by these, and the result was a break in the equilibrium brought about by the anti-convulsant medication; the mother had more attacks, and so the case was referred to social service.

While doing intensive casework with the mother, we also had the intellectual capabilities and the social adjustments of the young man examined. We obtained excellent results, particularly in mathematics, and our advice was for him to pursue his studies in a good school. We requested financial assistance, and his father was found. As he was now well-off and comfortable, he agreed to accept his paternal responsibilities on the condition that he be the one to choose the school; and he chose one far from Montreal. This seemed to be unacceptable to the mother, who became more and more sick. We were in front of a blank wall because the mother refused to see a lawyer, although we provided one free of charge. It was at this time that I thought of the group. Gloria did not need to go for more than a few sessions. The first session was dramatic, with the members of the group direct and insistent in their opinions. After three sessions, Gloria agreed to be helped by a lawyer, and she accepted the separation of her son. She left domestic service temporarily to go to work independently, regained sufficient equilibrium to enable the medicines to take effect, and her seizures were again being controlled.

In several cases the group represented for the patient a milieu of exchange sufficient to provide for a better utilization of his personality potential. The following cases only received a short period of attention in individual casework.

First Case

George was a man of twenty-nine who had only had two attacks when he was little, but who started to have epileptic seizures again when he was twenty-eight. Abandoned by his fiancée, he returned to the anxious and stifling protection of his mother. The group gave him the necessary support so that little by little he educated his mother to protect him less, without hurting her, and he felt capable of becoming more and more independent and sure of himself.

Second Case

Jean was nineteen years old. He came from far away in east Quebec. He had excellent grades and hoped to find a good job in Montreal. He had never had epilepsy previously. Shattered hopes, financial difficulties, and epileptic seizures made him desperate because he felt he was a burden to his sister who already had several children. The group gave Jean the support he needed to adjust himself better to actual realities and to content himself with a less elevated position with the intention of taking up his specialty again when he saw an opening.

Third Case

Jeannine was a young girl of seventeen, who had not passed her ninth year in school because she failed one subject. Discouraged after three tries, she refused to redo her entire year. It wasn't long before the group made her see the advantages of ninth grade and even tenth grade, and Jeannine took up her studies again, followed with interest by the group. She succeeded and then tried to do twelfth year alone at home, because the doctors had not yet found a way to obtain the balance of medication to control her *petit mal* seizures.

For some of those patients who had weaker personalities, the group was a milieu less threatening than medical authority. If supported by personal casework, they had the courage to persevere for a certain continuous time with the group, their difficulties in forming personal relationships seemed to dissolve, they became aware of their own deficiencies without feeling too threatened, and they sometimes accepted the psychiatric treatment they needed.

First Case

Simone was a young woman of twenty-seven, who had three children, looked after by her mother in the country, and who was separated from her husband. She had had epileptic seizures since puberty, but she always succeeded in supporting herself and her children by doing domestic service. However, she often had periods of depression; and when she became pregnant while separated, she had a serious depression and tried to commit suicide. Even at these most critical times she continued to attend the group meetings, and even though the members didn't know anything of her recent condition, she felt a complete and sincere acceptance and understanding there. By personal casework it was not difficult to make her want to regain her previous outlook and to accept the plan of the psychiatrist, which was quite difficult for her. However, the difficult period passed, the psychiatrist felt that the treatment was successful, and the patient took up a happy life near to her children again.

Second Case

Marie was a young woman of thirty, not married, who had had epileptic attacks since a young age. She lost her mother when she was five, and her father remarried and sent her to boarding school. Epileptic seizures caused numerous complaints and difficulties. However, these attacks had never been accepted openly as being epileptic, even at twenty-nine years of age. Even though we knew this patient was trying to accept and follow her treatment, she was not able to admit that she was an epileptic. Several times she tried to come to the group, but each time, after the meeting she would disappear. She was not able to see herself with "all these epileptics"; she preferred personal casework, which was less threatening for her. At the end of a year, and after several tries on her part, she finally could come regularly, accepting herself as one of the others, and at the same time was successful in making friends. Recently, in personal casework, she expressed the desire to be helped by a psychiatrist, a service which had been offered to her some time previously. She wished, she said, to be more like the other members of the group, confident and more sure of herself.

Third Case

The cases were not always successful. Martha was a young girl of twenty-one, who had had a baby at nineteen and who started to have epileptic attacks after the birth of the baby. Referred for support and continuation of treatment at the epilepsy clinic, she was able to put her baby up for adoption after two months of personal casework. Since then she has tried to come to group conferences. Although there she could express much hostility and aggression without being rejected, she was at the time of writing not well enough to maintain regular attendance and benefit from intensive exchanges and support from the other members of the group.

Impressions

1.   Our role has not been that of a director, nor that of an observer. It was more that of a catalyst.

2.   The group represented for each one his greatest need—a family, understanding parents, friends. It was an accepting milieu where the patient found a favorable atmosphere for the utilization of the positive forces of his personality.

3.   The dynamics of the group were, in the majority of cases, more rapid and more effective, more direct and better accepted, than the dynamics of personal casework. It was often thanks to the latter that the patient could utilize the group dynamics more effectively.

4.   The work of the group brought an additional satisfaction to the social worker, which was to see the members of the group developing such qualities as understanding, reciprocal acceptance, the capacity for mutual help and support, and patience toward one another in waiting for changes or modifications in attitudes—all qualities which better prepare them for a fuller life and a more satisfying future.

Conclusions

It seemed to us to be sufficiently interesting and worthwhile to show the usefulness and the many advantages of the utilization of group dynamics as a complementary method to casework, or as a method that can replace casework when the latter is not possible or where the individual approach seems unlikely to achieve the desired results in the available time.

The field is wide open for research concerning:

1. A group of patients such as the one described above, made up of those having both casework and group therapy.

2. A control group receiving only casework service.

3. A control group of patients who would not benefit from any social service.

Mental Retardation

Casework Service to the Mentally Retarded Child and His Parents

Miriam F. Mednick

The attitude of caseworkers toward the mentally retarded client in their concern for his welfare has been undergoing a profound change. Not long ago there was a fairly widespread feeling among caseworkers that there was no point in trying to offer casework service to the mentally retarded person. The fact of his mental retardation loomed so large that it was assumed there was no way of establishing a meaningful relationship with him. We saw the retardation and not the person. In taking this attitude, social workers were no different from other groups in the community. Even the fields of education, medicine, recreation, and vocational training looked upon a normal I.Q. as a kind of passport to their services, and the mental retardate was barred from admission.

How many persons in the United States are mentally retarded? No national accounting of the total number has been done, but estimates can be made on the basis of studies undertaken in certain areas. The best informed guess is that 3 per cent of the population falls within the range of mental retardation, which means that approximately 4,800,000 persons are, to some degree, characterized by an innate lack of mental capacity. By far the largest number are mildly retarded—those who are capable of being trained to assume social responsibility for themselves. The next largest number are moderately retarded—those who can be trained to achieve some measure of self-help, but who still need supervision. The smallest number are severely retarded—those who are so badly handicapped that they will never be able to learn the simplest components of growing up or of being independent; they cannot walk, talk, or feed themselves and will require constant care all of their lives.

It used to be accepted that any individual with an I.Q. below 70 was by definition mentally retarded; those with I.Q.'s between 50 and 70 were thought of as morons; those with I.Q's between 20 and 50 were defined as imbeciles; and those with I.Q.'s below 20 were labeled idiots. As we have learned more about the mentally retarded we have come to recognize that

Reprinted from *Casework Papers* (New York: Family Service Association of America, 1957), pp. 103–112, by permission of the author and the Association.

a rigid classification based upon intelligence quotient alone is not valid. We have now adopted the classifications of mildly, moderately, and severely retarded which take into account the individual's capacity for learning, for self-responsibility, and for social adaptability.

Helping the Parents

The problems presented to the parents of a mentally retarded child are among the most tragic and most difficult that any parent has to face. The mentally retarded child is different from the normal, in intellectual endowment and often in physical appearance; he may never achieve physical maturity, he may always be dependent to a greater or lesser measure on his parents, and frequently he is not accepted by society. By his very existence he can become to his parents a symbol of guilt. So little is known of the causes of mental retardation that few answers can be given to the parent who asks why it happened. Countless parents struggle with the question of what they did that contributed to their having a retarded child.

The caseworker who attempts to help the parents of a retarded child must begin with the realization that he cannot take away from them the pain of having such a child. No matter how helpful he may be in his understanding of them and in his realistic planning for a solution to their problem, he cannot alter the basic fact that they have a retarded child. I do not mean that parents cannot be helped to find a way of handling their problem. This is possible; but parents properly resent the caseworker's attempting to make things right.

Beginning, then, with the realization that he cannot remove this tragedy from them, if he wants to be helpful the caseworker must accept a second basic truth—that the nature of their problem does not make the parents of retarded children "different," "in a class by themselves," or incapable of being helped. A caseworker does not need special training and skill to cope with their special problems. Some specialized knowledge is helpful, but any caseworker in a family agency, a hospital, a guidance clinic, a placement agency, or a school, who has the desire to learn, can secure the specific information he needs. The casework skills required are generic casework skills. They include sensitivity to the parent's problems, helping him express his feelings, offering and interpreting the agency's service constructively, examining with him the choices available in dealing with his problem, and sustaining him in the choice he makes.

The casework help that can be offered to this parent has three basic components. The first is giving him an opportunity to tell a sympathetic and understanding person what it has been like to have to struggle with the care and training of a retarded child. Time and again a parent has said to a worker at the end of a first interview, before anything in the situation has changed, "I feel so much better now." He has been able to get a sense of sharing his burden, and comfort in the knowledge that he is no longer alone in coping with his problems. This is the factor that has contributed so much toward making the parents' organization, the National Association for Retarded Children, such a potent force toward improving the services available to the retarded.

The second basic component of casework help for the parent is a community service that can meet some part of his child's need—whether it be a diagnostic clinic, special educational facilities, recreational opportunities, medical care, specialized therapy, foster care, or institutional care. These resources should be expanded since the most highly skilled caseworker cannot be successful in helping a parent whose child needs a specific service that is unavailable. Although social workers may not be able to induce the community to establish certain services, they can do a great deal toward making existing services available to the mentally retarded by accepting these persons as agency clients.

The third component of casework help for this parent is the caseworker's ability to offer help in a constructive manner. It is not enough merely to identify the problem and offer service. The caseworker must be able to separate himself from the parents and the child enough to permit the parents to look at their problem and their feeling about it realistically and to begin to make some changes. Often this is a painful and difficult experience, but facing the problem and weighing the choices available comprise the first step in meeting one's problems. Unless the caseworker is prepared to use his professional skill with strength and imagination he will become nothing more than a sympathetic listener.

I should like at this point to say something about the question of institutional placement of the retarded child. Twenty-five years ago, in most sections of the country, the only solution possible for care of the retarded child, and not even a completely adequate solution, was institutional placement for life. Today we realize that many such children are capable of adjusting in the community if given proper help. Often our efforts should be directed toward offering help to them and their families at home. Doing this necessitates the expansion of existing community services to include the retardate. But there are some persons within the mentally retarded group who are best cared for within an institutional setting. These include the severely retarded person who needs primarily custodial care and the person who needs the protection of an institutional setting. As long as the need for this kind of care exists, it should be provided under the highest standards and should be given by trained and considerate personnel. Today it would be as much of a mistake to rule out institutional care as one solution as it was formerly to think of institutional care as the only solution to the problem of mental retardation.

Parental Reactions

One of the difficult decisions the parents of a retarded child must make is how best to meet the needs both of the retarded child and of the other children in the family. The retarded child frequently needs so much specialized attention and time-consuming care that the other children are neglected or deprived of their just share of their parents' attention. Regardless of whether the retarded child remains at home or is placed, the parents are faced with a choice. Many parents feel that this particular child needs much more attention than the others because he has so many limitations; they must "make it up to him" out of compassion or guilt and are blinded to the needs of the other members of the family.

Before describing a striking example of this type of parental reaction, I should like to mention the work of the Exceptional Children's Unit of the Philadelphia Department of Public Welfare with which I am associated. The Unit offers service primarily to children and adults who have been committed by the Municipal Court to a state institution for the mentally retarded. The committing court gives the Department of Public Welfare the responsibility for providing interim service. This service may be in the form of help to parents in filing the admission application, temporary foster care until there is space available in the institution, and casework help to the parents and the child with the many problems they face. The Unit is also asked to provide service to some exceptional children who do not need institutional care but who cannot remain in their own homes and need specialized care elsewhere. Not all the children who are committed to an institution for the mentally retarded really need to go there. Consequently, we explore with these individuals and their families the potentials for their developing more responsible behavior in the community and help them to achieve this goal.

The B family was referred by a school counselor. John, aged 10, had become such a behavior and educational problem in class that a recommendation had been made to send him to a residential disciplinary school. The school attendance of three other B children was poor. When the counselor talked with Mrs. B she found her to be interested in John and concerned about his troubles. However, one of the children, Sam, aged 8 years, was severely retarded. He could neither walk nor talk, and had to be tended like an infant. He was subject to convulsive seizures and slept badly, often crying in the night and waking the whole family. He was known to our department. The parents had previously placed him in an institution but had taken him home because they were dissatisfied with the care he was being given. They were devoted to him and had never given up the hope that he would improve. They would even do without things they needed so that Sam could have something he needed. Mrs. B said that when on occasion she had to choose between buying food for the family and buying milk for Sam, she would buy the milk. She admitted that she did not have time to supervise her other children's homework, and did not always know who their friends were or where the children went. Mr. B spent much time giving Sam exercises or soothing him when he was fretful.

When Mr. and Mrs. B came to talk with the caseworker it was a difficult interview for all three of them. As they talked it became increasingly clear that the parents had to choose either to keep Sam at home and let John go to the residential disciplinary school or to accept placement for Sam so that they would be able to give more time and attention to the other children. They went over and over the situation, completely blocked in their ability to decide which to do. The caseworker described the foster home available and left the decision to them. She gave full recognition to the intensity of their feeling and how placement must seem to them like giving up hope. She made them look at something they could not face without professional help—what keeping Sam at home was doing to the other children. At the same time she gave real support to the possibility of their placing Sam by offering, in addition to the concrete service, an expression of her feeling that this was an acceptable solution. At this point in the interview there was a long moment of tense silence and then Mr. B, a big man, put his head down on the desk and cried. He had decided. These parents could not have solved their problem alone. Without casework help they could not have worked through their conflicting feelings about Sam to the point of deciding to place him. The placement worked out well and Sam was happy in it.

Jimmy's situation serves as another illustration. Jimmy's mother had come to the agency in desperation. She wanted to keep him at home, but added that he was driving her crazy, and the only solution she could think of was placement. As she talked with the caseworker it became clear that the problem was not only Jimmy's mental retardation, but her attitude toward him. She could not impose any limits on him and then hold firmly but gently to them. She told of how well Jimmy did in the class for retarded trainable children which he attended. The caseworker helped her to look at the differences between the way the teacher handled Jimmy and the way she did, and she began to realize that if she changed, Jimmy might change also. She decided to try to help Jimmy behave so that he could live with his family. Although improvement has been slow, Jimmy is still at home. His mother is learning that she can say no and that Jimmy can learn to accept it. Of course, learning is more difficult for a retarded child, but with patience, gentleness, and firmness he can be taught.

Casework with the Retarded Child

Since the mental retardate is a person for whom both learning and communication are difficult, it is sometimes assumed that he has no feelings, or at most a limited range of fleeting, lightly-held emotions. The expression "happy little moron" is far from accurate. There is so much sadness, frustration, and fear in the lives of the mentally retarded that the happy ones, I suspect, are in the minority. A retarded individual can feel very deeply and he can participate in a casework relationship. The capacity for feeling is universal and not an attribute only of those who have normal intelligence.

In order to help the mentally retarded person, the caseworker must believe that he is capable of emotion. He can respond to help when it is offered with sensitivity and understanding. A caseworker who meets such a client at the client's level with no prejudice and no impatience will succeed in cutting through the slowness, the shyness, and the timidity to the core of his feelings. There are no specialized techniques, no magic formulas to be learned. If the worker applies the basic principles of generic casework with understanding of the client's particularized need, the client can be helped. It is important to go slowly, to speak simply, to give him time to turn the thought over in his mind and make his own thought connections, not to try to cover too much in one interview, and to be sure that the choice of plan is left to the client.

Although these principles of practice are common to many casework settings, how many times has a child-placing agency rejected a child for placement because he was mentally retarded, in the belief that he would not be able to make use of the placement? How many times has a mental hygiene clinic refused to accept a child or an adult for psychotherapy because he was mentally retarded and it was considered a waste of time to attempt to alleviate his emotional problems because his mental retardation made him incapable of responding? How many times has a family service agency rejected a client or refused to accept a referral of a client because he was mentally retarded and therefore was thought to be incapable of utilizing casework help?

I should like to present some case material to illustrate that the mentally retarded child is capable of feeling and of responding to casework help.

Bobby was 4 years old. He could not walk, talk, feed himself, or take care of his personal needs. His mother wanted to place him because she now had a baby and could not care for both children. Previously she had lavished care on Bobby in an effort to help him and train him. Now that she had decided to place Bobby she wanted to get it over with quickly. She was frankly skeptical of Bobby's understanding what was going on and thought peculiar the worker's suggestion that the mother talk to him about leaving home. When the worker arrived to place Bobby, she was greeted with the statement that Bobby was being "ornery"—as if he understood something was happening he didn't like. Bobby continued to be ornery on the drive to the foster home, hitting the caseworker, squirming like a little eel, and shrieking at the top of his voice. The worker accepted his need to express the fact that he did not like what was happening and told him so. She repeated a number of times what was going on —that she was taking him to live with a different mommy and daddy, that it was not possible for him to stay at home but that his own mommy and daddy would come and visit him, and that she knew he did not like what was happening. Of course, Bobby could not reply. When they arrived at the foster home the worker told him that his new mommy was waiting to meet him and it was up to him now. She asked if he was ready to go. Bobby stopped crying, gave the worker a long, considering look, smiled and held out his arms to be carried. He made it clear that he wanted to ring the doorbell, and he did. Although Bobby was a retarded child, his reaction to a placement experience and his response to casework help were no different from those of a child of normal intelligence.

Barbara, at 10 years of age, had been brought to the city detention home for children because she had attacked her grandmother with a knife and had threatened to kill her. She was an illegitimate child whose mother had completely rejected her. Barbara's mother had married. Since Barbara was illegitimate and also retarded, the mother felt that she could not ask her husband to support Barbara and could not have her live with the family. Although she lived in the neighborhood she had very little to 'do with Barbara. All her life Barbara had yearned to be accepted and loved by her mother. She had been raised by her alcoholic grandmother and had had an extremely deprived life, both emotionally and economically. We placed her in a good foster home although we knew that it was an experiment that might not be successful. At first everything went well, but then Barbara began to run away. Each time she would appear at the detention home—once arriving in a taxicab after she had persuaded someone to pay her fare. Her foster parents came to get her and the social worker talked to her. She promised never to run away again—and then did so. Finally the caseworker decided that she should attempt to discover the reason for this behavior and to help Barbara become more settled in her foster home. From her knowledge of Barbara's life before she was placed, the caseworker surmised that Barbara was trying, by her repeated running away, to get to her mother so that she could stay with her. Barbara had never expressed this wish and the worker knew that it had to be talked over between them if Barbara were ever to be able to move beyond wanting to go back to her mother and be able to accept what life held for her. With patience, gentleness, and firmness the worker talked to Barbara and, what was even more important, helped Barbara talk to her.

The last time Barbara had seen her mother was when she had been at court and had been committed to the state school for retarded children and our department had been given the responsibility of placing her. She had figured out that if she ran away she would be taken to the detention home; she hoped that if she ran away often enough she would be brought before the judge who had the authority to make her mother come to court. Barbara thought that if her mother could see her again, she would feel the love for Barbara which she had never shown and would take Barbara home to live with her.

After the caseworker had helped Barbara to verbalize these thoughts she was then able to tell the worker with tremendous feeling and anguished tears that, in the courtroom, her mother had said that she did not want her and did not care what happened to her. The caseworker permitted Barbara to sob out her hurt and her hopes, and was able to help her face the painful fact that her mother did not want her. Perhaps she could now begin to build her life around the good things she had in it. Barbara is not an easy child to help but I think it is possible to do so. The caseworker would never have known Barbara's need for help if she had not believed Barbara was capable of feeling. She could have shrugged off the runaway episodes with the easy explanation that, since Barbara was retarded, she had poor judgment and reasoning ability and just did not know any better.

Importance of Attitude and Skill

A mental retardate is capable of utilizing the help available to him in a casework relationship in order to change and to grow, to move from fear and dependence on another person to self-confidence and independence. A number of teen-agers and young people in their twenties who at one time were diagnosed as mentally retarded and for whom institutional care was recommended are to be found in the caseload of the Philadelphia Department of Public Welfare. We decided to see what we could do to help these young people find and hold jobs. We discovered that the most important elements of the task were the attitude and skill of the caseworker. If he had a genuine belief in the client's potential capacities and could sustain him through his initial attempts, the results were often amazing. The caseworker must, of course, be prepared to face the client's real limitations, and to modify techniques and expectations accordingly. For example, one 17-year-old boy had never learned to read or write and needed help in filling out job application forms. He also had to be taught how to travel to and from work. But he did get a job and he is now self-supporting. He used his first earnings to buy truly extravagant Christmas presents for his foster parents and the other boys in the foster home, and the caseworker wisely delayed until after Christmas any discussion of budgeting or saving.

Although the foregoing illustrations all represent successful experiences in offering help, the caseworker is not always so successful. Failure may be due, in part, to the fact that caseworkers are only beginning to experiment with ways of reaching these clients. But caseworkers, like educators, are discovering that the retarded person is capable of learning and assimilating new patterns of behavior. Some of his slowness, I believe, is due to his experience with the frustration his life has held and his reluctance to tackle something new which he is afraid will be too difficult for him to master.

The limitation of intelligence which leads to failure in learning is real. The way other people relate to the retarded individual can, however, make a tremendous difference in his ability to learn. If he is not given an opportunity to perform to the extent of his ability, his frustration will be increased by the added artificial limitation. He will then refuse to attempt to learn something new because he has been told in the past that it is too difficult for him to master. The skill and strength of the worker can be invaluable to the client through the support given him in making a choice that may lead to independence.

This approach will enable many adult retardates to adjust to living in the community and many retarded children to be happily adjusted to life with their own families. Too few people know of the advances that have been made in knowledge about the mentally retarded and what can be done to help them. Caseworkers can make a great contribution in disseminating this new scientific knowledge and in helping to expand community services for this group.

There is a vast opportunity for offering casework help to the mental retardate and his parents. If we recognize that we have a service to offer to these parents and that the mentally retarded child is capable of deep feeling and can participate in a casework relationship, we can look forward to a continuing expansion of service to those whose need is so great and whose response can be so gratifying.

Casework with Parents of Retarded Children

Alexander Hersh

It seems to be a sign of the times, a good omen perhaps, that most parents of retarded children are eager to have help for their child, and similarly, for themselves with their own feelings about the child. Like the remainder of the community, however, they feel the need to control the help they receive. They seek it when they want it, take as much or as little as they desire, and focus their use of help in areas which present the greatest concern to them, though these may not be the areas we see as most problematic. As a natural reaction against the intense and interminable quality of their problem, they frequently want to resolve their anxiety precipitously. They seek a simple or comfortable solution. One's first reaction might be to agree with them—agree that their problem is too great and their feelings should be spared. This attitude is a reflection of the feelings of the larger community, which finds the total impact too hard to bear and surrenders to it. This may be exemplified in the "put him away and forget about him" prescription.

These observations are offered because the writer believes that in developing service for the retarded and their parents, one must look at the degree of parental and community responsibility to be borne. Compare, for instance, a service for retarded children to the family, adoption, or child guidance services. Where will you find the degree and duration of such dependency problems, except possibly with severe mental or physical illness? In the outpatient service at the Woods Schools[1] we are always struck by the inevitable question that is asked at the end of a session when we have interpreted the results of our evaluation of the child. "When do you want us to come back?" they ask. Inherent in this powerful question is the hope that maybe next time we will see improvement, as well as the expressed need to have support in carrying the burden.

[1] The Woods Schools are a private residential school for 400 children with mental, social-emotional, physical, and academic handicaps. Children are placed within the school according to chronological age, mental age, social-emotional age, degree and nature of problem. Comprehensive care is given, including special education, diagnosis, psychotherapy, and lifetime care.

Reprinted with permission of the author and the National Association of Social Workers, from *Social Work*, Vol. 6, No. 2 (April, 1961), pp. 61–66.

In our experience, "one-shot" evaluations are of little value. Results are too often denied or distorted by the parents and signal a start on the dreary rounds of looking for someone who will speak the hopeful words they want to hear. A service that carries with it the sincere wish to share the burden of the long-term problem will enable parents to accept a current interpretation of their child's problem. This is not a conscious withholding of information. It is a realization that the true and final expression of a child's handicap and potential cannot be predicted, but must evolve out of the parents' use of our definition of the problem given to them, as well as the climate which they may provide for him. A two- or three-year period, with planned or periodic follow-ups, allows parents time to work on their own feelings, with the specific directions and help given them through the service. The shortcoming of the one-shot evaluation is that it frequently blocks the positive parental feelings from the fullest expression.

Casework Focus

Our own philosophy attempts to transcend direct "counseling" of parents. By this I refer to the oft-used precept of counseling: to diagnose the problem and then divulge it to the parents, together with a specific bit of advice such as "He will always need supervision." This is fine as far as it goes, and represents an important medical responsibility to parents and child. A more meaningful and skillful counseling, however, is directed toward helping parents to use this information, but with sympathetic understanding of their need to develop certain natural defenses such as denial or avoidance. One must recognize the traumatic quality and endless ramifications of their problem. These need to be seen and dealt with one by one as they emerge out of the child's daily life. In this way parents can, with a caseworker's support, organize their feelings to give positively to the child, creating a parent-child relationship that supports the child's growth and development as a person, however handicapped he may be.

Should retardation be seen as the same or different from work in other areas in which social work has traditionally been engaged? One may quote Kelman:

> In the course of the last two decades the dimension and implication of problems of mental retardation have begun to be more clearly understood. The problems of the retarded have now come to be viewed as essentially similar to those of any other major chronic illness or disabling condition and some important advances have been made in recent years in the development of methods of rehabilitation, education and socialization. But despite the striking advance in knowledge and technique over the past two decades, a large gap still exists between what we know and how we have been able to help the parents of retarded children and the children themselves.[2]

[2] Howard R. Kelman, "Social Work and Mental Retardation: Challenge or Failure?" *Social Work*, Vol. 3, No. 3 (July, 1958), p. 40.

Casework counseling of parents of retarded children seems to be a relatively recent innovation, and until now emphasis in the literature has been on the establishment of a diagnosis with its interpretation to parents, generally given with a specific recommendation. In our setting we use the residential placement as a structure for a long-term effort to help parents with their feelings, as related to the child and his problem. The preparation for placement, the decision, and actual placement usually represent the healthy impulse of the parent to help his child. Though this act is guilt-producing by virtue of its inherent element of rejection, it also releases the problem, with relief from guilt, in the sense that the parent has done something which will help the child. It has been our experience—and hence philosophy—that the thorough working through of parental feelings toward a retarded child is a lengthy task demanding both persistence and skill.

Our focus is on help with problems developed in having and relating to the retarded child. These are seen as significantly different from the attitudes of the parent before his child is born. The latter represent the rightful concern of the psychiatrist. The former, constituting ego-derivation from the problem itself, are more concretely the concern of the social worker —the area where he can make the greatest contribution as a counselor of parents.

Unique Problems of These Parents

What are some of the specific or unique problems of the parent of a retarded child? Unique, in this sense, means problems that are quantitatively the same as those present in all families but occur with unusual intensity in the families of retarded children. They constitute core problems in virtually every instance where there is a retarded child. They include disruption of normal ego functioning of parents and therefore disruption of normal family life routines; development of excessive and unusually intense feelings of guilt and personal inadequacy; excessive and long-standing dependency burdens that cause emotional draining in parents; friction in connection with siblings because of stigmata and untenable goals which the family has set for itself; distorted perceptions of the child; and finally, distorted projections on the child. Unfortunately, space will not permit discussion of the latter two categories.

The blow of having a retarded child, or learning later that one's own child is retarded, is severe. Whatever the parents' personality organization, the delivery of a severely retarded child is a terrible shock and disappointment. The disruption to normal ego function in parents, and particularly in the mother, is clearly evident and to be expected. In an unusually poignant paper, Ada Kosier has described the impact of the birth of a baby with anomalies on the parent as follows:

> The threat to him of having produced a child severely malformed may be so great that he may not be able to carry even the most urgent of parental responsibilities. He may try to leave his baby in the hospital indefinitely; he

may deny the baby's need for special treatment; he may neglect the baby physically or he may devote himself so exclusively to the child that he is cut off from other life experiences.[3]

Most parents go on to organize some kind of defense lest the pain become completely unbearable. With or without skilled help they mobilize themselves to make some kind of plan for their child and themselves.

Probably the largest number of parents feel at the time of the birth of their child that he is normal. It is only later, as his development lags, that he is seen as not normal. Still later, however, in recapitulating, many mothers admit that they suspected rather early that their child was different. Statements such as "He was just different," "He was too still," and "He was like a lump of clay" are common and express the extra burden that mothers carry for their closeness to their child. We have known some mothers who fought the world on behalf of their child, almost because they knew too soon that the child was different. They had a secret that acted as a bond between self and child. The invasion of the outer world and its harsh realities could be climaxed in no other way than a pitched battle in which their struggle to maintain the cherished secret was waged.

In attempting to understand these parents one becomes aware of a number of recurring factors. First of all, it is most often the mother who is most threatened; second, it is the mother who may later develop the self-isolating and martyr-like tendency that often identifies the extreme stereotype concept of a parent of a retarded child; and third, the mother usually acts as though she has been insulted by life—as if she could no longer be fulfilled. Whatever the exact nature of the threat to the mother in having such a child, in extreme cases it seems that nothing anyone can do will remove this feeling of mutilation to the self. One mother we know spoke of the "sobering effect"—that she could never look on life in the same way as before. And countless mothers comment on the bitter frustration and their feelings of lack of fulfilment because so much of their love seems to be for naught. Some of them tend to force their mothering on the child because they refuse to be denied this pressing need of their own. It is paradoxical that in one instance a mother may place her child when he is very young and forever feel a sense of emptiness, while another says, "I know I'm being selfish but I'm keeping him at home until I die. I don't care what happens after I'm gone." At the Woods Schools we are more apt to be in a counseling relationship with the former, who feels left out of her child's life. We encourage these mothers to visit and share in their child's care and planning in any way that is practical and psychologically sound. We know of many such mothers who achieve some fulfillment by working for programs for retarded children and by supporting other parents in gaining perspective on their situations. These are important outlets if recognized as giving temporary stop-gap results.

This threat to one's feeling of wholeness that comes from having a

[3] Ada Kosier, "Casework with Parents of Children Born with Severe Brain Defects," *Social Casework*, Vol. 38, No. 4 (April, 1957), pp. 183–189.

retarded child is a difficult thing to work with or even to generalize about. The feelings of guilt and inadequacy are extreme and intense. Much has been written about the parents' feelings of guilt at having borne a retarded child, but little is known about how to relieve these feelings. It is as though this guilt became a part of the parents' character. After a period of time there is no available thread for helpful unraveling. From the caseworker's standpoint one needs to work something through for one's self to develop acceptance of parents who may not be able to see the true nature of their child's handicap and are self-punishing as a result. When a caseworker can do so, parents are less threatened and can come to see him as helpful and supporting.

Should Every Parent Accept the Child's Handicap?

The point of view of the writer, as well as his predecessor[4] at the Woods Schools (and others),[5] is that not every parent can be expected to "accept" the handicap in his child. Perhaps it seems too passive to say that some parents should not accept the degree of handicap because to do so might endanger their mental health. Yet I know of one such case where the child came to be a way for the mother to avoid being grown up and taking on the roles of wife and mother. She and the child are virtual siblings, to the exclusion of the father. The strength of these feelings is evidently great, for many well-intentioned people have been ignored when they have given her "advice." It reminds us of John A. Rose's article on part-time mothering, which points up that each person has a way of solving his own life problem.[6] This, of course, is a psychological application of Cannon's principle of homeostasis.[7]

A caseworker can be of infinite help to parents in this dilemma by being clear as to which parents are motivated for change and can use active help and which must proceed in the darkness, always warding off anyone who seeks to help them change. However, there are many parents who, though severely handicapped by their own guilt, can use the support and warmth of another person. Over a period of time they can come to a greater realization that their role as parent to their handicapped child may always be a partial one, never completely fulfilling, yet with potential for satisfaction, depending on the degree of the child's handicap.

A case in point is a mother who described her own anxiety and terrible disappointment at having her child away from home, but at the same time

[4] Mary Carswell, "Helping Parents in the Private Residential School Setting," *Proceedings of the 33rd Spring Conference of The Woods Schools* (Langhorne, Pa.: The Woods Schools, 1958), pp. 86–98.

[5] Eve Mayer, "Some Aspects of Casework Help to Retarded Children," *Journal of Social Work Process*, Vol. 7 (1956), pp. 29–49.

[6] John A. Rose, "Child Development and the Part-Time Mother," *Children*, Vol. 6, No. 6 (November–December, 1959), pp. 213–218.

[7] W. B. Cannon, *The Wisdom of the Body* (New York: W. W. Norton & Co., 1932).

expressed full realization and acceptance of the fact that he would undoubtedly need to be away all his life. As she spoke she evolved her own
plan, which the caseworker supported, that the child should spend part
of every summer with the family as long as it was practical to do so. We
agreed that this would serve several purposes. It would enable both parents
to feel more fulfilled and take away some of the awful feeling that they were
withdrawing from their child or doing little for him. It would give the
whole family a chance to interact, out of which each could develop his
own relationship to the child and his problem. Finally, it would give the
child a feeling of membership in the family and the support he needed in
using the school placement from year to year.

Fathers

Just as mothers are concerned and responsive, fathers may be equally
so. It would seem that, because of the closer biological tie, the mother suffers
the more intense feelings. In our own setting we find fathers more removed,
less emotionally involved, more objective, and less expressive of their
feelings. It is always harder to understand fathers because we do not see as
much of them. We have made some interesting observations about fathers
who appear extremely guilty. They have been, for the most part, overtly
warm people, nearer to the maternal role than usual; they are more apt
to turn their hurt into aggression because of their inability to tolerate
strong feelings, or to resist stubbornly a working through of these feelings.

One such father harbored a deep resentment against his child for
almost ten years. His own shame at having the child, and fear of his own
strength associated with the child's negative strength, was very great. It
was only after he had expressed much of this deep feeling to the caseworker
that, in his words, he "became a different person." The child felt the difference and responded almost immediately. Whereas in the past the boy had
always detoured around his father, he now began to share many of his
thoughts with him, tested and accepted his strength, and began to identify
with him as his father and as a man. Later, in describing the change, this
father said he could not figure out what had happened—in the past he had
not missed his boy while he was away at school, but suddenly he did!

It is a moving experience to share with a father the moment when he
allows himself to feel the deep emotion of having been tragically struck by
having a severely handicapped son. One father was recently bringing out
his wife's question of whether she should continue to visit their boy, a
severely defective child who has been a student in the school for a few years.
The parents visit faithfully, but the visits have had no apparent meaning
to the child. The father was saying that he hoped his wife would want to
come in to talk to me too, because as we spoke many questions were raised
which needed to be explored. He was particularly concerned about what the
other children at home would feel if they stopped visiting. Then, as if it
were too much for him, he said he would not want to come just once every

five years—the shock of seeing the boy physically changed might be too great. He liked to come for reassurance. He felt better when he came, even if the visits did not mean anything to him or to the boy. When the caseworker suggested that he came because Jimmy was his son, tears welled in his eyes and he could hardly get out the words as he repeated, "Yes, Jimmy's my son; that's why I come to see him." The affirmation, as he acknowledged his son, was in his voice as he spoke.

Fathers also appear to have a particular problem with their retarded child when they have not yet achieved, or are currently working through, their separation from their own fathers. As with mothers at a similar point in development, the ability to carry through in their own role depends a great deal on how liberated they are and feel. It is interesting, for example, to note how often fathers have a problem merely in relating on a level at which the retarded child is comfortable. It seems that the retarded son may create a real puncture in the male ego unless the father is well established as father and husband. This problem is often expressed in aggressive and disapproving action. More subtle and difficult to help is the father who smothers and denies the boy his own manhood. Adolescence is particularly stormy, but affords some basis for confrontation and identification between father and son.

The excessive and long-standing dependency problem presented by having a retarded child may take different forms for each parent. It is usually the mother who seems caught up in the day-to-day burden and the father who presents the greatest challenge in holding to the present in working through areas of feeling. Parent after parent expresses concern and question about "what will be later." We attempt to support the parent in concentrating on the present, but also to respect the problem of the future because it is very real. The relative helplessness of the handicapped child causes much concern about how much emotional and economic investment can be risked and made available at one time or on a sustained basis. Those who have been engaged in long-term foster care will recognize the similarity here. Again, note the interminable quality of the dependency and how deeply it affects parent reaction to responsibility.

Siblings

Concerning the problems that occur in connection with siblings, we have noted clinically that parents frequently give this as a reason for putting the child into an institution. A Mongoloid child is quite acceptable in the home until his sister starts dating, but then becomes a major focus of concern. In many cases families handle this kind of problem by institutionalizing the child, which then stirs much guilt. On the whole, we believe that parents should take things as they come, little by little, year by year. Some problems, however, can be predicted. Casework done with foresight will help families plan accordingly, so that they do not set their total family goals without realizing their full implications. There is thus less guilt and more meaning to steps taken later.

Most parents have a hard time allowing siblings to have their own relationship with the retarded child who is away at school, and supporting them in it. Often, this is because of parental concern with what will happen after they die. It is especially hard for parents to keep from becoming controlling—frequently an expression of their own ambivalence. That is, they unconsciously put the sibling to work carrying their negative feelings. Inevitably, and contrary to conscious parental expectation, this ends up in estrangement rather than healthy compassion between the children.

It takes a unique form when the child has been placed in an institution at an early age—before five, for example. Because the parent has often not had sufficient connection or bond with the child, the separation takes on an absolute quality and the placed child does not view his parent as a parent but merely as a visitor. A parent in this situation is unable to help the sibling with the relationship because his own is so unsatisfactory and unfinished. This, together with the unnaturalness of visits with an institutionalized child, makes it extremely difficult to sustain without guilt and strain.

There is an interesting contrast between parents' use of residential care for their child and their use of outpatient help. Work with both is equally challenging and deeply satisfying. The family whose child is being cared for in a residential school strives to find a part-time relationship in which they and the child can derive satisfaction from one another. The family whose child is at home presents the sharper need for help because their problems are more immediate. They come to identify their community outpatient service as a source of support and direction in understanding their child and his behavior and helping them to meet his needs.

Work with both groups is rewarding and represents to all engaged a challenge to be met as we develop more resources to deal with the needs of the retarded child and his parents.

Counseling with Parents of Retarded Children Living at Home

Sylvia Schild

In the light of the emergent philosophy and prevailing practice of encouraging home care of mentally retarded children, a re-examination of the casework counseling technique with parents is indicated. Until recent

Reprinted with permission of the author and the National Association of Social Workers, from *Social Work*, Vol. 9, No. 1 (January, 1964), pp. 86–91.

years, social workers in the field of mental retardation were primarily located in institutions and the focus of casework with families was usually geared around the problems of placement planning. With the advent of special clinics for early diagnosis and evaluation of retarded children, attention shifted to parental feelings and reactions and to ways of counseling parents more satisfactorily. The need for a sympathetic, supportive approach to the parents has been well established with the recognition that the impact of the retarded child is deeply disturbing to the ego-functioning of the parent.[1] The importance of having as complete a knowledge and evaluation of the child's problem as possible has been accepted as a necessary counterpart to being able to provide a meaningful explanation to the parents of the child's difficulty and to give consideration to the parental questions and emotional involvements related to having a retarded child.[2]

Social workers in specialized clinics and social agencies are now dealing not only with the areas of diagnosis and placement, but with the complex task of helping the family and child live together more comfortably in the home. The purpose of providing maximum benefit to the child needs to be interlocked with minimal stress to total parental needs and family functioning. Both the child and the family are faced with making adequate adjustments to and in the community in which they live. Unless these ends are achieved, maintenance of the child in the home serves little purpose.

Professional workers, in supporting a philosophy of home care for retarded children, must be keenly aware of the responsibility to know how to help families achieve this goal with maximum ease. This paper proposes to examine some aspects of counseling with parents of retarded children living at home that are characteristic of the problem and that may lead to a better understanding of how to work with these families. These observations are drawn from experience in counseling with families receiving services in the Child Development Clinic at the Children's Hospital of Los Angeles. The clinic is a diagnostic and counseling center primarily for retarded children less than age 6. The observations thus are related to the early adjustment of the preschool child and his family, although they may be generic to the problems of the older retardate as well.

Ambivalence of Parents' Feelings

Enormous ambivalence of feeling is evoked in a parent when he learns that his child is retarded. Feelings of rejection, dejection, and disappointment collide with anxious hopefulness, doubt, anger, and self-pity. Strong

[1] *See* Helen Beck, "Counseling Parents of Retarded Children," *Children*, Vol. 6, No. 6 (November–December, 1959), pp. 225–230; and Alexander Hersh, "Casework with Parents of Retarded Children," *Social Work*, Vol. 6, No. 2 (April, 1961), pp. 61–66.

[2] A. Wheeler Mandelbaum, M.D., "The Meaning of the Defective Child to Parents," *Social Casework*, Vol. 41, No. 7 (July, 1960), pp. 360–367.

emotions of guilt mix with protective parental reactions; resentment, confusion, and insecurity become pervasive. It is this ambivalence that characterizes initial work with families of retarded children. Thése conflicting emotions are never completely resolved, as the long-term aspect of the problem and the repeated crises that stem directly from the fact of the child's handicap stir up the ambivalence from time to time. To help the parent, it is necessary to ferret out the positive aspects of the ambivalence and help him to build on these so as to find some answers to the problem immediately at hand. Thus, ambivalence is dealt with in relation to the immediate crisis situation on a reality basis and by focusing on the areas that are conducive to meeting the needs of the family. The following case illustrates this point:

> A young couple had just heard the diagnosis of retardation for the first time. In the hostile tirade the mother loosed on the social worker, she vehemently denied that this catastrophe could be true, attacked the doctors, blamed herself. Toward the end of the outburst, she cried out, "Nothing I ever do is perfect. How will I ever be able to raise this child?" In this plea for help the social worker recognized the mother's immediate fear and denial of the diagnosis as resulting from her shaken confidence in being able to successfully handle her mothering role with the defective child. The positive aspect of the ambivalence, underlying the fear of inadequacy, was her intense desire to be a good mother. This was an area that could be worked with realistically in counseling, since she was indeed performing successfully in her mothering role with her two older children. The husband's support to his wife was encouraged. With help and attitudinal change, this mother was enabled to depend again on her own inner strengths and resources in coping with the child; this in turn paved the way toward better understanding of the child's limitations and freed her to work on other aspects of the problem.

A factor accounting for sustained ambivalence toward a retarded child is that the parents are deprived of the opportunity to project any blame for the problem onto the child himself. It is too difficult in any rational way to blame the child for his own defect. This differs from situations in which, when social pathology exists and becomes reflected in disturbed parent-child relationships (for example, in emotional disturbance and delinquency), the parent realistically is able to hold the child partially responsible for a share of the problem. This serves to alleviate some parental guilt and lowers resistance to accepting help. In the area of mental retardation the self-accusatory parent, who feels that he alone is in some way accountable for his child's limitations, is very well known.

It is an accepted fact that part of the resistance of the person seeking help stems from his feeling of responsibility for the problem. When guilt is intensified, the resistance to help will be proportionately increased. Because of this, those endeavoring to help parents of retarded children must be aware that heightened resistance is usually due to the inwardly projected guilt of the parent. In counseling, this guilt needs to be alleviated and an emphatic understanding of the problem area imparted to lower the parent's resistance, freeing him to benefit from the offered help. Most parents hope to hear an authoritative and sympathetic endorsement of themselves, of their human and parental competence, and of their right to blame them-selves for what has happened.[3]

One way of ameliorating the guilt of parents is to counsel them together in joint interviews. This helps to focus on the mutuality of feelings and responsibility shared by each parent and aids to shift away from individual parents the assumption of self-blame for the problem. The joint interview technique often may help to restore the marital balance around the mutual concern for the child so that the parents are better able to mobilize all their strengths to handle crisis situations.[4] Although mothers are generally en-trusted with the major care of the child, management is a joint responsibility of both parents. Too often the father's role and share of responsibility are overlooked, especially when it is the mother who assumes the task of taking the child for his medical care and transmitting the medical information and advice to her husband. Joint interviewing frequently serves as a device to engage the father actively and to give due consideration to his concerns and attitudes, as well as to those of his wife. Counseling parents together is supportive and enables them to concentrate their energies, not as much on the fruitless searching for why this has happened to them, but more productively on how they can better perform in their parental roles in order to benefit their child.

Changes Required of Parents

The hard reality that needs to be faced is that with the presence of a retarded child the family is no longer the same and it cannot be reconstructed as it was before the arrival and impact of the defective child. Perhaps the area of greatest difficulty that needs to be resolved in the counseling process is the changes required on the part of the parents to meet the special needs of the retarded child. These often conflict with parental functioning that heretofore was considered satisfactory.

Often the management of the retarded child is perceived by the parents as being no different from their performance with their normal offspring. Counseling needs to be directed toward helping parents to see that their attitudes and feelings relative to mental retardation per se have indeed shifted their own parental behavior.

> One mother complained constantly of her child's temper tantrums. The disturbance the child was creating was upsetting to the entire household and the mother felt at her wit's end. The parents were beginning to feel that to keep the child in the home was almost impossible. The mother stated she was handling the problem behavior exactly as she had in the past coped with similar behavior in an older child.

[3] L. Kanner, M.D., "Parents' Feelings about Retarded Children," *American Journal of Mental Deficiency*, Vol. 57 (1953), pp. 375–379.

[4] J. Geist and N. M. Gerber, "Joint Interviewing: A Treatment Technique with Marital Partners," *Social Casework*, Vol. 41, No. 2 (February, 1960), pp. 76–83.

Closer examination revealed that in reality the mother, caught up in her disappointment and her attitude that a mentally retarded child was totally worthless, considered the child not worth bothering to discipline. Also, the father was unsupportive, leaving all discipline to his wife. Hence, the mother responded to the tantrums with anger and helplessness, and was permitting herself to be manipulated by the child. The youngster, having no external controls put on his behavior, became increasingly infantile and difficult. This gave validation to the low value placed on him by his mother.

When the mother gained some insight and understanding that she was reacting differently to this child than to her normal offspring, she began to cope with the problem. Her self-esteem increased with her more effective management of the child. In addition, the father was helped to participate more meaningfully in the child's discipline, thereby giving his wife emotional support. As the child's behavior improved, the parents acquired a new appreciation of him. This in turn helped them to evaluate better the considerable potential latent in their mildly retarded son and to enjoy a more favorable relationship with him in the home situation.

The resistance and ambivalence of the parents in counseling are amplified also by the nature of the new stresses encountered merely by virtue of being the parent of a retarded child. The problem of keeping the retarded child at home is determined by a number of factors, such as sibling relationships, social status, family attitudes, the degree of deficiency in the child, and so on. These are all potential problem areas and the ability with which problems that might arise in these areas are handled and solved vary from family to family, situation to situation.

The new stresses arising from the presence in the family of a retarded child are not pathological as such, but should be viewed as a normal complement of problems for the situation that may affect the parent-child relationship and to which adjustments need to be made. When a pathological situation (i.e., divorce) is imposed on a family and is disruptive to family functioning, the focus in counseling must be directed toward the realistic problems that occur as a result of the pathology.[5] It has been pointed out that the presence of a retarded child in the home is often a precipitating factor in individual or family maladjustment or breakdown.[6] The family that is able to adjust satisfactorily to the impact on it of a retarded child has also to deal adequately with the many normal problems that occur in relation to the situation. Their attitudes, feelings, care and management of the child, and the like must all be taken into account.

These normal problems attending the presence of a retarded child in the home must be dealt with on a reality basis to permit the best possible solutions to be effected. Some of these problems are met often in other handicapping conditions of childhood: the increased dependence of the child on the parent, confusion and lack of finiteness in medical diagnosis,

[5] H. Pannor and Sylvia Schild, "Impact of Divorce on Children," *Child Welfare*, Vol. 39, No. 2 (February, 1960), pp. 6–10.
[6] Robert M. Nadal, "A Counseling Program for Parents of Severely Retarded Preschool Children," *Social Casework*, Vol. 42, No. 2 (February, 1961), pp. 78–83.

crumbling of parental aspirations for the child, rehabilitation and training problems, and the like. However, there are some conditions that occur uniquely in the case of the mentally retarded child and his parents.

One solution, which is culturally sanctioned, is often freely available to parents of the severely and moderately retarded. This is the opportunity to relinquish responsibility for care of the child to an institution if, considering the degree of his intellectual impairment, the child is eligible. Granted that placement holds the parents to a modicum of responsibility and is indeed an appropriate solution in many situations, there still is a need for recognition that this alternative presents conflict for the parents and may impair efforts to effect a successful adjustment in the home. From the time that parents are told that their child is eligible for institutionalization the ambivalence about the child and the problem increases. Again, this ambivalance needs to be handled in counseling, with the focus geared to the positive aspects inherent in the successful fulfillment of parental roles and responsibilities.

Counseling Should Be Spaced

One difficulty occurring in counseling with parents is that the resistance of the parent is sometimes insidiously supported by the behavior of the child himself. The parents may move well initially in shifting to more positive attitudes and methods of handling the child only to be thwarted by the slow movement of the child in responding to improved parental functioning. Although intellectually the parents can relate the slow pace to the child's mental limitations, they often become frustrated emotionally and can react by feeling that the counseling is unproductive. This can cause reversion to easier, more familiar patterns of behavior. The counselor, too, can become uneasy and impatient by the slow pace of the child's response and may fail to support the parents' efforts adequately or project blame on the parents for failure to utilize the counseling.

The most immediate help, consequently, occurs when the parents are having critical emotional distress and help can be directed toward easing their personal difficulty rather than being geared to change in the child himself. Casework for this latter goal, which is focussed around the management and behavior of the child, can perhaps be best provided when spread out over proper and widely spaced intervals to give the child an opportunity to react and develop at his own speed.

A review of the reactions of forty parents to diagnosis and counseling emphasized that the parents needed time to take in the extent of their problem and solutions needed to be worked out step by step. Also, parental questions did not arise in an organized, crystallized fashion but gradually, as the child grew.[7] When the element of time is taken into consideration and work with the family is structured over appropriate intervals, the

[7] Charlotte H. Waskowtiz, "The Parents of Retarded Children Speak for Themselves," *Pediatrics*, Vol. 54 (1959), p. 319.

parents are able to bring into counseling some growth on the part of the child that might not otherwise have been apparent if counseling around the child had been sustained on an intensive basis. In other words, parents need intensive casework help at times of crisis situations but, in addition, they need a continued contact. The latter can be less intensive and made available to them over a longer period of time. Such counseling should be properly spaced and educationally focused, to help the parents with the practical problems of daily living with their retarded child. This help is often crucial in determining if the child can live in his own home and in strengthening and sustaining the mental health of the total family unit.

Counseling related to everyday living experiences with the retarded child helps to sustain the parents' motivation to continue in a program designed to improve the child's behavior and to develop his potential. Parents need to deal with concrete situations—the success they achieve in such common daily experiences tends to ameliorate the problems of living with a retarded child. For this kind of approach the caseworker must have a keen knowledge and awareness of normal growth and development. To help the parents understand their child's behavior, it is important to assist them in relating behavior to normal functioning and expectations of children as well as to comprehend the limitations in their own child and its implications.

Summary

In summary, this paper has discussed some aspects of helping parents who have retarded children living at home. The following points were suggested:

1. Professionals counseling parents to keep their retarded child at home assume an additional responsibility to learn how to help the parents achieve this goal comfortably. This implies not only increased understanding of the problems faced by the parents, but also better awareness and skill in involving and sustaining parents more effectively in the counseling process itself.

2. The key factor to be dealt with in the counseling process is the ever present ambivalence of the parents about their retarded child. Movement toward satisfactory solution of problems is more easily attainable when the positive aspects of the ambivalence are used constructively to meet feelings and to free parents for changes in attitudes.

3. Guilt feelings of the parents are enhanced by the fact that they cannot rationally project any responsibility of blame for the problem on the child himself. These guilt feelings heighten the resistance to meaningful participation in counseling. Involvement of both parents in joint counseling is one

way of alleviating the inwardly directed guilt and of helping parents to focus on more rewarding functioning in their parental roles with the retarded child.

4.   The presence of a retarded child changes the structure of existing family relationships. One area of great difficulty is that former parental functioning may prove to be inadequate in meeting the needs of a retarded child. Parents need help in seeing that their attitudes and feelings relevant to mental retardation per se affect their parental behavior.

5.   There are many new stresses affecting families of retarded children that should be viewed as normal problems for the situation and that need to be dealt with on a reality level. Some of these, such as the easy access to shifting responsibility of the child through institutionalization and the slow reaction of the retarded child to parental teaching and management, are unique and may hamper counseling efforts.

6.   Parents are best helped at times of crisis, but counseling geared to improvement of the child's behavior and to daily living can be structured over spaced intervals planned to compensate for the slow movement and the maturation of the child and to offer sustained support to the parents.

The importance of more and better knowledge about how to help these families has been best expressed by a parent who has written:

> The greatest single need of parents of mentally retarded children is constructive professional counseling at various stages in the child's life which will enable the parents to find the answers to their own individual problems to a reasonably satisfactory degree. . . . We need guidance from someone who can help us to see that this thing which has happened to us, even though it may be a *life-shaking* experience, does not of necessity have to be a *life-breaking* one.[8]

[8] Mrs. Max A. Murray, "Needs of Parents of Mentally Retarded Children," *American Journal of Mental Deficiency*, Vol. 63, No. 6 (May, 1959), p. 1084.

Organic Psychiatric Disorders

Organic Psychiatric Disorders of the Aged: How They Affect Family Relationships

Mayer Fisch

A human reaction to a stimulus is customarily compounded of two elements, reason and emotion, in variable proportions. When the stimulus is of a simple nature, that is, one that neither presents danger nor touches upon a deeply rooted personal need, reason easily guides our response. For example, if we are faced with the necessity of traveling from one place to another, our choice of means of transportation naturally will be determined by logical considerations of time, distance, and convenience. However, even in such a situation there may be instances of phobia in which emotion may raise an insuperable barrier to logical decision. On the other hand, if we are suddenly confronted with an armed stranger in unfamiliar surroundings on a dark night, our response will probably include a much larger emotional component and will show less consistency from one individual to another.

The study of the emotional component in response to a stimulus—or in behavior, as we usually characterize it—has largely constituted the subject matter of psychiatry in this century. Emotional reactions have been found to originate in certain basic needs and strivings, which are modified in the course of an individual's training and development. The modifiers are the immediate family and the larger society in which the family exists. A high degree of harmony between the standards of the family and those of the social group is usually conducive to easier adjustment. When there is significant disparity between the ideals of each, coupled with conflict within the family or marked internal inconsistency in its attitudes, we are inclined to make a diagnosis of a neurotic family structure. The goal of psychotherapy has often been defined as one of minimizing the effects of past unhealthy emotional conditioning so as to leave an individual freer to act in response to current reality. This goal may equally be stated as an attempt to increase the rational component of behavior at the expense of the emotional. To this we may add the usually unspoken, often unrecognized corollary: that we expect the resultant behavior to more or less correspond to established social norms.

Reprinted from *Social Casework*, XXXIV (1958), pp. 503–507, by permission of the author and the Journal.

For the purposes of this discussion, two points should now be stressed. First, that an individual's reaction to an emotionally charged situation is governed to a large degree by his own unique constitution and accumulated attitudes, which are based on past experiences that have become an automatized part of his personality, that is, his unconscious. The second point of special relevance to this subject is that our criteria of good adjustment, or emotionally healthy reactions, are largely socially determined.

Let us view the question of how illness, particularly psychiatric illness, in the aged affects family relationships, in terms of a stimulus-subject-response equation. We see at once that many variables enter the picture at every point. It is obvious that the serious illness of a close relative is always a complex stimulus, and one which is apt to provoke a highly emotional response. When the relative is aged—and I am particularly referring to aged parents—further complications are added. But we must first seek to answer a simpler question. Do we know what we would consider a "healthy" or "normal" response to this stimulus?

Society's Attitudes

Our society presents us with many ambiguities and contradictions. If a patient consults us because of a subway phobia, we usually know our goal even before we learn anything of the patient's inner life or background. The goal is to help him resolve whatever conflicts are connected with this area so that he may ride the subway in tranquility. We would rarely plan to handle the situation by prescribing for him taxicabs or even walking. If a family seeks guidance because of a disturbed child, we immediately form a picture, once again, of what result we would like to see achieved—an adjusted child in a well-integrated family unit. But here we begin to make certain reservations; perhaps a detour or alternative to this ideal will prove wisest. When a couple seeks help for marital problems, we first hope to preserve and strengthen the marriage bond on a more secure footing, but we may, in some circumstances, possibly view divorce as preferable.

What of the family whose presenting problem is an incapacitated older person? In this instance, we have no clear preconceived point of departure, since—in regard both to family and to aging—we live in a culture of changing values. Families are once again in fashion; "the family that prays together stays together" and "togetherness" are familiar slogans. But do these phrases truly reflect our mores or are they the denial, the reaction formation, of a society which has become alarmed at excessive fragmentation? Before espousing the cause of family unity too wholeheartedly, let us remember that not too long ago the tightness of family bonds was often castigated as leading to social rigidity, patriarchy, nepotism, and lack of individual freedom and opportunity. Probably we are in favor of just so much family but not too much.

What are the implications of this attitude for the aging and their families? We consider it abnormal for a child to marry and continue to live with his parents. The young couple are supposed to establish their own household; the middle-aged parents continue on their own. They grow old; they go on and are admired as "independent old people." One dies, the other becomes ill or progressively enfeebled. We often expect the survivor to live with his or her children, who, by this point, are themselves middle-aged. Thus, our social ideal for families at this juncture of life seems to be "in health divided, in infirmity united"—an inappropriate standard.

What do we think about old age per se? We encounter an ever increasing proportion of aged in the population, and with characteristic American enthusiasm try to convince ourselves that it's not really bad. The opening lines of *Rabbi Ben Ezra* are much quoted, but how many of us truly believe that "the best is yet to be"? Alas, few of our aged clients seem to agree. We all know that retirement can be bad—many magazine articles say so. But somehow pressures in Congress are always in favor of lowering the retirement age; and a labor leader who would advocate a contract with deferred retirement would not find his popularity with his membership thereby enhanced.

The roots of this confusion probably lie deep within our social structure. Perhaps the problem of the role of the aged appears new and more striking to us because, in an immigrant society, they were few aged in the first generation. They had often been left behind in Europe. And, of course, the vastly increased longevity of the past generation or two, urbanization, and changing political views as to the relative degrees of responsibility of the state, family, and individual for personal welfare and security all bear upon the question.

Thus, we have no unified social ethos as to what "family" and "aging" connote. This does not, however, imply that various subgroups or individuals do not have firmly fixed notions in regard to these terms. It is vital, therefore, in dealing with such a client family, to ascertain the frame of reference within which we are working before proceeding to the more particular aspects of the case. Perhaps because these problems are so close to universal, we may tend to project to an unusual degree how we would feel or act in the situation, only to discover later that we have not been meeting the family on any common ground. It is needless to add that while these social inconsistencies, or hypocrisies, may confuse a family's reaction, the effect upon the aged person himself is apt to be more devastating.

Organic Disorders

The above remarks constitute the backdrop of this discussion. Let us now turn to the specifics. The stress of which we are speaking is the aging of a family member, aging that will inevitably lead to some degree of infirmity. We need not catalog the manifold disorders to which the aged may fall victim. One group of illnesses, however, carries unique overtones of its own and warrants particular attention—the group of organic psychiatric disorders of the aged. These illnesses originate in a loss of functioning brain cells, either directly via simple atrophy of the brain or secondarily via arteriosclerosis of the blood vessels supplying the brain. The two resultant conditions, senile psychosis and psychosis due to cerebral ateriosclerosis, for all practical purposes, may be spoken of jointly. They are obviously basically organic conditions which, to some extent, are normal and physiological; the point at which we consider them diseases or psychoses is purely a matter of degree. The cardinal symptom of this brain deterioration is loss of intellectual power, readily recognized by impaired memory and ability to concentrate or learn. The phenomenon of disorientation is a direct outcome of this loss.

Clinically, these conditions are far more complex than the above descriptions may imply. First, there is no one-to-one relationship between clinical symptomatology and the extent of brain damage later found on autopsy. A patient with great functional impairment may have suffered only relatively slight brain damage, while another whose brain has been far more ravaged by deterioration may continue to function almost normally. Second, symptoms are not limited to the intellectual area, but may include emotional, perceptual, and personality changes as well. For example, depressions, hallucinations, and paranoid delusions are not at all uncommon in this group of patients. Usually such disturbances, considered as secondary manifestations, appear after the intellectual or memory loss has become apparent. Not infrequently, however, the emotional or personality signs appear first, for example, slovenliness or temper outbursts in milder cases; these provoke quite a different reaction. A recent report from Kings County Hospital showed eighteen cases of elderly people admitted to the prison ward over a period of years, following arrest for murder or attempted murder. Their senile conditions were recognized only upon study during their hospitalizations. Of course, purely functional disorders, especially depressions, also occur in the older age groups and require different treatment, so that we cannot dismiss any signs of psychopathology in an elderly patient as evidence of brain deterioration.

We have come to view the psychoses associated with senile arteriosclerotic changes as not totally different from the other psychiatric disorders with which we deal. The organic loss is an added element of stress, but the entire reaction is equally dependent on the premorbid personality, including any latent neurotic conflicts, and the life situation at the time of illness. This formulation often seems to us to bear the novelty of discovery, yet Plato observed, "He who is of a calm and happy nature will hardly feel the pressure of age, but to him who is of an opposite disposition youth and age are equally a burden."

Family Reactions

With this group of diseases particularly, the impact upon a family is highly conditioned by the specific symptomatological manifestations. The response to incontinence is generally so universal, and the problems posed by it so practical, that we usually do not have to speculate on the manner in which the original Oedipus complex was resolved in order to understand this part of the reaction of family members. However, their notion of the cause of the incontinence will influence their feelings even about this, as do a mother's ideas about enuresis in a child. These are truly psychosomatic illnesses, in that the physical cannot be divorced from the psychic component. But many families do make this separation. For better or worse, society remains far more tolerant of physical, than of psychic, affliction. A family may thus be quite tolerant of physical dependency, almost as tolerant of forgetfulness (which they recognize as due to brain impairment), but openly critical and punitive toward emotional outbursts. The degree to which the one group of symptoms or the other predominates is central in influencing family reaction. When the symptoms are primarily in the emotional and personality spheres, feelings of shame associated with psychiatric illness are often called forth. Shame is exacerbated if sexual acting out or obscenity is part of the picture, and may pose a real problem in the family's relationship to the community. Furthermore, the patient may be fairly well organized and oriented one day, and the next, may disrupt the household routine by inept confusion. The family cannot be expected to understand the variability of cerebral circulation, and is apt to attribute the change to wilful negativism.

Our first duty then is to educate the family as to the nature of the disease the patient is suffering. We probably err too often in assuming that families understand more than they do about these conditions as well as about their degree of reversibility, treatment prospects, and life expectancy. It should be noted that the intellectual loss is generally irreversible, but that the emotional manifestations often can be ameliorated by medication. For management purposes, in cases where emotional disturbance is prominent, it is probably wisest to minimize the importance of premorbid factors and attribute the condition wholly to the brain damage. A family's handling of a paranoid, delusional, senile person will be smoother if they can regard the behavior as the result of a purely exogenous disease, rather than as proof that the mother or father was always excessively surly and suspicious. Our aim is to allay rather than to reawaken the old conflicts which must have been produced by such personality characteristics.

On the other hand, when we see a patient whose emotional tone remains cheerful, calm, and contented despite extensive intellectual loss, it is usually of real comfort to the family to be told that this is evidence of sound emotional health in the past. Almost invariably we shall find, in these instances, a history of good relationships in the family, and so run little risk of contradiction or unfavorable reaction to this statement. Similarly, questions about heredity may be answered reassuringly. There may be some familial tendency to the onset of these reactions occurring at certain approximate ages, but there is surely no consistent relationship, and obviously little can be done about it.

Determinants of Family Attitudes

Just as the clinical condition of a brain-injured older person is derived from three sources—the degree of brain damage, the life situation, and previous personality patterns—so we may view the family's reaction as based on three analogous determinants, all intermingled. The first is the nature and degree of incapacity of the older person, which we have just discussed; the second is the current reality situation; and the third is the past relationship to the patient or client.

The impact of the aged person's illness on the current reality situation differs for each family member. Evidently, the burden is not the same for a single child and for a married one; for the son or daughter and for the son-in-law or daughter-in-law; for the child and for the grandchild. The middle-aged child of the patient in a three-generation family must look cautiously in both directions before revealing an attitude of rejection toward the infirm parent. He may be eager on the one hand to relinquish what seems to be an intolerable immediate burden, and yet be aware that he may be setting an example for his own children vis-à-vis himself in the not too distant future. By contrast, the teen-age grandchild, who is apt to be sharing a room with the troublesome patient, has not this problem to contend with.

We must always be alert, however, to seek beyond the obvious. It may at first appear that the presence of the patient in the home is all that prevents a grown child from enjoying a richer life of his own than he now does. Is this the case, or has the child unconsciously forced the bonds of dependency to be stronger than reality requires them to be as a defense against involvement with his contemporaries? A couple may state that the elderly patient is the sole cause of marital discord. "My husband threatens to leave if I don't get my mother out of the house." Is this so, or has the patient been made the focal point for expression of marital differences which arise in distant, perhaps unrecognized areas? It is our responsibility to investigate the marital relationship as well as we can, to bring such a situation to light if it exists, rather than to wait for the eruption after the patient has been dislocated.

The last determinant of the family's reaction—the past history of the relationship—is the most subtle, but often the most important. This is the source of the most highly charged family feelings. It is the old relationship that is most apt to lead to irrational, emotional feelings and behavior; much of it is deeply buried within the personalities of the individuals concerned, perhaps beyond their conscious perception. Usually information about this relationship is not volunteered, either because those concerned are not aware of its ramifications, consider it irrelevant, or do not wish to discuss it. Furthermore, little is revealed by casual observation of the actualities of the current situation. We may see an intellectually impoverished, physically enfeebled, older person who must rely for his total care and sustenance on a mature, vigorous son or daughter. It is obvious who is dependent on whom. Yet we must picture the situation in reverse, as it was in the different phases of their lives until recently, when parent was parent and child was child. Then we must ascertain what unresolved conflicts, carried over from the remote past, may still be operating in this altered context.

A dependent child may remain emotionally dependent for approval on a parent, perhaps to the neglect of his own family, even though the parent is far beyond the ability to gratify his need. A dominating parent will usually continue patterns of attempted domination, often using illness as an additional lever. How do the children respond? They may continue patterns of complete rebellion or obedience set down in the past or may now, under the pressure of guilt, abandon open rebellion and try to do the "right thing," but show their resentment in a more covert fashion.

To reiterate, the reactions of family members and of the patient to this type of stress are partly derived from the facts of the stress we see before us. But they are also derived from the personalities and past histories of the people involved and from how the stress impinges on other facets of their lives. Tolstoy wrote, "All happy families resemble one another; every unhappy family is unhappy in its own fashion." We must avoid projecting and generalizing. We must learn what are the specific problems of each family and its members, or in what fashion they may be unhappy, and then infer the special significance for them of the illness of the aged relative.

Family attitudes are so deeply ingrained that they are often among the best-preserved elements of a fading consciousness. A totally disoriented patient who had no notion of her whereabouts in time and place, nor of the identity of the person to whom she was speaking, was asked if she lived with her daughter, which she did. However, she corrected the examiner, "No, my daughter lives with me." We rarely hope to alter these attitudes, either in the parents or in the children, in the work we do with these families. But only to the degree to which such attitudes can be brought to light in counseling, and their importance as motivational factors weighed when family plans or changes are being considered, will the plans be built upon a solid, realistic foundation.

Making Hospitalization a Growth Experience for Arthritic Children

Joan Morse

Since John Bowlby focused attention on the traumatic effects of separating sick children from their parents for an extended period, clinicians have hesitated to recommend prolonged hospitalization for children.[1] Treatment procedures in a hospital setting seem especially frightening and painful to children, for their fears and fantasies magnify the real discomforts of the medical milieu.[2] Well-meaning efforts of staff and families to compensate young patients for the discomfort they are experiencing by giving them presents and special privileges may afford them so much secondary gain that they find more immediate gratification in remaining ill than in becoming emotionally committed to the long, often difficult, struggle to regain their health.

The treatment of juvenile rheumatoid arthritis sometimes requires a prolonged hospital stay to achieve remission of the illness or to prevent or correct deformities resulting from the disease. Experience at the Robert B. Brigham Hospital in Boston has shown that, without prolonged hospital care, some children who have juvenile arthritis will inevitably be crippled.

Specialized treatment of rheumatic disease in adults and children has been provided at the Robert B. Brigham Hospital for most of its fifty-year history. Recently, in 1963, with the impetus provided by an initial grant from The National Foundation, a multidisciplinary group was organized for the study and treatment of juvenile arthritis, and members of the Social

---

[1] John Bowlby, *Child Care and the Growth of Love*, Penguin Books, London, 1955, based on the report *Maternal Care and Mental Health*, World Health Organization, Geneva, 1951, pp. 139–49.

[2] Veronica B. Tisza and Kristine Angoff, "A Play Program for Hospitalized Children: The Role of the Playroom Teacher," *Pediatrics*, Vol. XXVIII, November, 1961, p. 841; Edward A. Mason, "The Hospitalized Child—His Emotional Needs," *New England Journal of Medicine*, Vol. CCLXXII, February 25, 1965, p. 408.

Reprinted from *Social Casework*, XLVI (November, 1965), pp. 550–556, by permission of the author and the Journal.

Service Department became particularly interested in examining the psychosocial changes that occur in children requiring prolonged hospitalization.

During the first year of the program five girls required long-term hospital care, extending from seven to twenty-four weeks. By coincidence, each child represented a different age group, ranging from infancy to adolescence. The ages of the girls were as follows: Susan M, one and a half; Rosella J, three and a half; Mary L, six; Barbara T, eight; and Christine F, thirteen and a half. Each child showed marked psychosocial and physical improvement between the date of admission to the hospital and the date of discharge. Thus far, the results of the study demonstrate that long-term hospital care can not only correct swollen joints and flexed limbs but also improve the child's total functioning within the family unit. These dual gains can be achieved, however, only if attention is paid to the whole range of social, emotional, and environmental problems associated with juvenile arthritis.

To accomplish this task, the social worker in such a setting as the Robert B. Brigham Hospital must have broad professional competence, including ability to work intensively with parents, and must have an active interest in modifying detrimental environmental factors and sufficient flexibility to function as a member of the hospital team. The skills needed have been described by Harriett Bartlett as those of "the experienced worker in action not as a caseworker or consultant but as a professional social worker, assessing situations and moving from one appropriate method to another, with full awareness of the nature of the decisions involved and the professional components of each activity."[3]

The Illness and the Patients

Juvenile rheumatoid arthritis is a generalized disease of unknown etiology that runs a variable, often intermittent course. The onset of symptoms, which may be acute or insidious, begins before puberty. These symptoms may include fever, pain, stiffness, and the swelling of one or more joints. Twice as many girls as boys develop juvenile arthritis.[4]

Studies by The National Foundation have estimated there are 50,000 patients in this country with the juvenile form of rheumatoid arthritis. J. Sydney Stillman, M.D., chief of the medical service of the Robert B. Brigham Hospital, suggests, however, that with better diagnostic criteria and more widespread recognition of this disease, a more accurate figure, including children and adult patients in whom the disease developed before they reached adolescence, would approximate 250,000.

The medical regimen prescribed varies with each patient because the

[3] Harriett M. Bartlett, "The Widening Scope of Hospital Social Work," *Social Casework*, Vol. XLIV, January, 1963, pp. 8–9.
[4] Henry K. Silver, C. Henry Kempe, and Henry B. Bruyn, *Handbook of Pediatrics*, Lange Medical Publications, Los Altos, California, 1955, p. 527.

natural history of the disease is unpredictable.[5] Treating patients with severe symptoms requires close co-operation between medical and orthopedic specialists, the patient's intensive use of physical and occupational therapy, and a high standard of nursing care. Although observers have long believed that emotional, social, and environmental factors influence the course of juvenile rheumatoid arthritis, research is needed to validate this assumption.

At the Robert B. Brigham Hospital, a special weekly clinic known as the Clinical Treatment Center for Juvenile Rheumatoid Arthritis was started in December 1963. A social worker interviews the parents, and often the children as well. The Social Service Department assumes responsibility for providing casework services, particularly for the families in which the child requires hospitalization.

During the first nine months, seventy-five patients with a definite or probable diagnosis of juvenile arthritis were examined at the clinic. Most of the children received out-patient care, supplemented by one week of intensive examinations in the hospital; only the five children to be discussed in this article required prolonged hospital care. In addition to having certain general symptoms, they all had difficulty in walking or were unable to walk at all at the time of admission, and they had all failed to respond to previous treatment.

These children came from middle-class and lower-middle-class families. In each case both parents were alive and the father was employed at the time of the patient's admission; none of the families had ever received public assistance. All the parents had been born in the United States; they ranged in age from twenty-four to forty-two. There were two, three, or four children in each family.

The children were provided with ward accommodation. Their pattern of care was somewhat similar although their treatment was individually prescribed. The regular staff provided them with similar nursing service. The children received physical and occupational therapy daily. They were examined by orthopedic consultants, who prescribed casts, traction, splints, braces, and crutches during the course of treatment. All the children were able to walk by the time they were discharged.

The staff members of the juvenile arthritis center met weekly. They were responsible for making treatment recommendations for the hospitalized children and for the out-patients. Two internists specializing in rheumatology, the child psychiatrists, the pediatricians, the physical therapist, the occupational therapist, and the social worker assigned to the center attended the conferences. An orthopedist was on call as needed. These sessions, which were marked by free communication and exchange of ideas, resulted in the formation of united decisions by the staff regarding patient care.

The child psychiatrist who served as a consultant for the inpatients

---

[5] Regina Fiesch, "Counselling Parents of Chronically Ill Children," *Pediatric Clinics of North America*, Vol. X, August, 1963, p. 766.

made suggestions about the ward milieu and the management of the patients, and he was available regularly as a consultant to the staff providing direct service to the patients and their families. Formal psychotherapy, however, was not available to the children during their hospital stay.

Economic Stress

Serious financial burdens are a frequent and disturbing problem for families with arthritic children.[6] A lack of funds for the direct and indirect cost of medical care can threaten the social well-being of the entire family. The following case illustration shows the worker's effort to help one family cope with these burdens.

Susan M's family lived in a rural area of a state where employment opportunities were limited. Her father's earnings were sufficient only for the family's fundamental living expenses. The parents had already borrowed money, using their car, insurance, and furniture as security, to pay for Susan's two-week stay in another hospital. During those two weeks, slender Mrs. M had lost ten pounds "from worry."

Before Susan's admission, when she was eighteen months old, the referring physician told the social worker of the family's limited financial position, and the worker was able to obtain funds for a sixteen-week out-of-state hospital stay from the agency that serves crippled children.

The worker found Mr. and Mrs. M to be thoughtful and considerate of each other's needs and Mrs. M to be warm and loving with Susan. It was not surprising, therefore, that the first person in the hospital to whom Susan responded positively was an exceptionally warm and motherly nurse. As Susan improved, the occupational and physical therapists assumed a major role in her care, using play techniques in teaching her to exercise. Helping Susan to learn new words became a favorite project for the entire staff. She also learned to feed herself.

Since the relationships within the family were good, the social worker focused her efforts on preventing any further distress as a result of the economic and emotional strain of having a child hospitalized far from home for a prolonged period. Money for travel expense was obtained so that Susan's parents and her brother and sister could visit her weekly. Between visits the family was informed by letter of Susan's progress during critical periods of her illness. Before Susan was discharged, funds were made available to allow Mrs. M to live near the hospital for two days while she learned how to help Susan exercise.

Mrs. M was able to accept help without becoming overly dependent on the worker. She was emotionally strong enough to entrust Susan to the hospital in spite of her deep concern for her, and, later, when her daughter was discharged, she was able to resume caring for her with obvious joy.

When Susan returned to the clinic for follow-up care, it was hard to believe that this adorable blonde child who ran about, calling hospital staff members by name, had been described by her doctor as a "pale, unresponsive lump" when she was admitted to the hospital.

[6] Robert H. Manheimer, Katrine R. C. Greene, and Frances Kroll, "Juvenile Rheumatoid Arthritis in New York City, 161 Cases," *Archives of Pediatrics*, Vol. LXXVI, May 1959, p. 181.

Separation Anxiety

Separation from his mother is a particularly difficult problem for the rheumatoid child.[7] Nevertheless, the child's physical separation from the parents during the hospital stay may be viewed as a crisis that can be used to help both parents and child gradually begin to develop a psychological separation from each other.

Rosella J, three and a half years of age, was referred to the child psychiatrist two days after admission because she cried and refused to eat and was vomiting. When Mrs. J. visited the hospital, she would only peep at her youngster through the ward door. Meanwhile, the staff characterized Rosella as "totally unmanageable." In addition to having temper tantrums, she was rebellious, manipulative, combative and resistive.

The psychiatrist thought many of Rosella's symptoms stemmed from anxiety and fright as a result of the way her mother had handled her admission to the hospital. The child had been told she was entering the hospital for a "vacation," and she had come to fear she was abandoned. In consequence of these circumstances, the social worker initiated a long-term relationship with the mother to help her learn more effective ways of assisting her daughter.

Mrs. J had to be helped to accept the need for casts, exercises, braces, and crutches so that Rosella herself would co-operate with the doctors and physical therapists in using these aids. It was also necessary for the worker to win Mrs. J's confidence in him and the rest of the staff so that the mother could visit Rosella without interfering with treatment procedures, criticizing the hospital, or bringing sweets before a meal. Even learning to terminate a visit by assuring Rosella that she would return the next day was difficult for this mother.

In the process of establishing a relationship with Mrs. J, the worker learned the reasons for the disturbed behavior that had provoked Rosella. Rosella, who was the youngest child, was conceived when her mother was expecting menopausal symptoms rather than another pregnancy—and Mrs. J's mother also had given birth to a menopausal child, who suffered from epilepsy and was a patient in a state institution. Mrs. J's father had died shortly before Rosella began to show symptoms of arthritis. Mrs. J had been overwhelmed by her recent loss and by her special fear that Rosella, like her sister, would suffer from a chronic illness.

The mother seemed too volatile and too suspicious of authority to be able to modify her own behavior by self-understanding. The social worker hoped, however, that a corrective relationship would help Mrs. J control her constant interference with Rosella's treatment.

After several informal meetings on the ward, sometimes preceded by the social worker's taking Mrs. J by the arm to help her break away from her clinging daughter, Mrs. J felt comfortable enough to come to the worker's office for weekly appointments. Gradually, she came to enjoy discussing each aspect of Rosella's progress. Her criticism of hospital routines diminished as she began devising ways in which she could use her own energies to work creatively with her daughter and other young patients; for example, Mrs. J helped them make decorations for the Thanksgiving and Christmas holidays.

[7] Gaston E. Blom and Babette Whipple, "A Method of Studying Emotional Factors in Children with Rheumatoid Arthritis," in *Dynamic Psychopathology in Childhood*, Lucie Jessner and Eleanor Pavenstedt (eds.), Grune & Stratton, New York, 1959, p. 127.

The next step was to help the mother gain confidence in her own ability to handle Rosella, before she was discharged. Appointments were scheduled for practice sessions with the physical therapist, but Mrs.ʳ J failed to appear until the social worker helped her understand that she would not be judged by her daughter's performance. Finally, six months after her admission, Rosella was transferred to a day hospital program until she was ready to enter nursery school two weeks later. During this period the staff was able to follow Rosella's progress, and the worker continued to reinforce Mrs. J's decision to allow her daughter to enter school.

When Rosella was interviewed by the nursery school director, he made this statement: "She proved quite delightful, less shy than I anticipated. She shows good signs of responding to our program."

Emotional Constriction Related to Maternal Deprivation

A marked inability to express feelings was observed among the twenty-eight children with rheumatoid arthritis who were studied intensively at the Massachusetts General Hospital from 1948 to 1954;[8] this trait was typically observed in children with a history of maternal deprivation. Such an association of emotional constriction and maternal deprivation was particularly obvious in Mary L, an exceptionally "good" six-year-old child from a small town in Vermont.

Mary rarely complained, although no one visited her. She formed superficially rewarding relationships with everyone she met at the hospital and was soon a "ward pet," surfeited with presents she hardly seemed to notice. Indeed, Mary's ingratiating behavior suggested she was severely deprived to the point of "almost failing to distinguish between one adult and another."[9]

When the social worker first began to see Mary regularly, she talked blandly about nonexistent brothers and sisters. Later, she felt comfortable enough to discuss family pets, her two real younger sisters, and, finally, her parents. Although Mary gave no indication of any family strains, the staff was concerned about her tendency to fantasy and her mother's failure to visit. The social worker telephoned Mrs. L and arranged for her to travel to the hospital for an overnight visit.

Mrs. L, aged twenty-four, looked tired but youthful. She had separated from her twenty-eight-year-old husband after a difficult and troubled winter. The family had lacked adequate heat, clothing, and food because Mr. L had been spending most of his wages from the local lumber mill on liquor. Contemplating divorce, Mrs. L had taken the children to her sister's home in another small Vermont town. There Mary's arthritis, which had been symptomatic for a year, had grown worse. The local pediatrician had referred Mary to the center, and Mrs. L had remained in Vermont with her other children.

Mrs. L had dropped out of high school because of her pregnancy and had been married shortly before Mary's birth. After two subsequent pregnancies, a hysterectomy had been performed when she was twenty-three years old. Mr. L's sister had moved next door, and she had often left her own children with Mrs. L while she and her brother went out drinking with friends.

[8] Gaston E. Blom and Grace Nichols, "Emotional Factors in Children with Rheumatoid Arthritis," *American Journal of Orthopsychiatry*, Vol. XXIV, July, 1954, p. 595.

[9] Eleanor Pavenstedt, "Environments That Fail To Support Certain Areas of Early Ego Development," in *Ego Development and Differentiation*, Vol. II, Forest Hospital, Des Plaines, Illinois, 1964, p. 11.

When Mrs. L mentioned her idea of seeking divorce, the social worker talked to her about making arrangements for the children, especially about her eligibility to receive an AFDC grant. As the mother began to feel less trapped by her hostility toward her husband, it became apparent that she still cared for him. She also began to realize that his presence in the home would mean much to Mary.

By the end of her one day's visit to the hospital, Mrs. L felt she understood her own feelings well enough to make some decisions. She planned to rent an inexpensive apartment in her sister's town, close to a school Mary could attend and close to her husband's work. She planned to encourage him to join them.

By the time Mrs. L had made these plans, Mary had begun to feel comfortable in the hospital; in fact, she was sufficiently secure to be naughty at times. She delighted in "buzzing" into the men's ward in her wheel chair, and she became careless about picking up toys. Mild discipline was established to prepare her for her return home and her experiences in school.

Mary completed the first grade one year after she was discharged. Her social adjustment seemed excellent. She was happy and relaxed as she talked about her sisters and schoolmates, sledding, and birthday parties. Both parents accompanied her to the clinic when she returned for visits during the year. Her boyish, backwoods father was as pleased with her progress as her hard-working mother. At the time of Mary's last visit, the pediatrician noted she was doing well "with just the right amount of co-operation and resistance."

Psychological Illness

Psychosocial factors influence the clinical course of juvenile rheumatoid arthritis in many patients treated at the center. It has been necessary, however, to hospitalize only one patient during the first year of the project because her psychological illness made improvement at home impossible.

Eight-year-old Barbara T could not walk, although the swelling in her ankle joint had subsided as a result of bed rest at home. Frightened, depressed, and apprehensive, she continued to remain in bed, or in a wheel chair, with her leg prominently displayed. Because her doctor feared her leg muscles would atrophy, he recommended hospitalization. In part, he also wanted to determine the effect that separation from her parents would have on her symptom. The information the social worker obtained in interviewing the parents helped the staff plan an effective program of treatment.

Mr. T was a tall, handsome, athletic man. He disliked being employed on the early morning shift at a shoe factory. In the afternoon and evening he cared for Barbara and her brother while his wife went out to work. Because of Barbara's illness, he had had to stop coaching the Little League baseball team on which his twelve-year-old son played.

Vivacious, energetic Mrs. T was a strikingly attractive brunette. After she organized her home in the morning, she left to work from 4 P.M. until midnight at a modern electronics plant. Mrs. T loved her work, at which she excelled, and enjoyed spending the extra money she earned, a good part of which she spent on new clothes and coiffures.

Barbara's health had been good until the spring preceding her hospital admission, when she had begun to feel pain in her ankle. Shortly thereafter, a hysterectomy had been performed on Mrs. T. When the mother had returned to work in September, Barbara had once again spent the rest of the day after she returned from school with her father and brother. Later that fall, the rheumatologist had observed the hot, swollen ankle symptomatic of her arthritis.

A week after Barbara entered the hospital, her spirits improved. In fact, she soon became quite coy. With a disarming smile, she discussed her then normal-looking leg with the psychiatrist.

After considering her psychosocial history and her clinical symptoms, the staff concluded it was dealing with a combination of juvenile arthritis and conversion hysteria. Barbara, perhaps feeling threatened by spending so much time with her father and brother, had wanted her mother to stop working. According to the psychiatrist's speculations, she felt guilty when her mother underwent surgery and temporarily made her wish come true; her inability to walk, even after the swelling of her ankle subsided, might have resulted from Barbara's need to feel punished for wanting her mother to become sick again so that she would have to stay at home.

The therapeutic problem was to establish an emotional climate in the hospital that was sufficiently different from the one at home to permit Barbara to give up her difficulty in walking. The secondary gain Barbara derived from being immobile was decreased by limiting the attention and presents she received from her family. The staff gradually helped her to participate in an active program. The occupational therapist was instrumental in helping her to learn to cook; she had never shared this activity with her mother because her father had prepared the evening meal. In contrast to her father, who showed much anxiety about her illness, her male physician purposely assumed an attitude bordering on indifference.

For seven weeks, until she herself wanted to walk, Barbara resisted all attempts of the staff to help her. For a few days she worked hard with crutches, and then she went home for a trial weekend visit, which was successful. One week later she was discharged. In three weeks, she was playing with her friends and riding her bicycle and had resumed a full schedule of activity at home.

During Barbara's hospital stay the social worker interviewed Mrs. T weekly to help her understand the psychological and physical components of her daughter's illness. Accepting the existence of a psychological component was painful for Mrs. T, since, as a consequence, she gradually had to recognize that the role reversal she fostered at home might be influencing her daughter's symptoms. Yet, by the time Barbara left the hospital, Mrs. T had arranged a leave of absence from her job and was awaiting an appointment at the local child guidance clinic where Barbara might be helped by psychotherapy.

Parental Denial

Denial is perhaps the most common psychological defense mechanism resorted to by orthopedically handicapped children and their parents.[10] When the medication prescribed alleviates the disease, families tend to minimize its intensity and thus delay seeking the best treatment.

Thirteen-year-old Christine F was literally waddling when she was admitted to the hospital. Symptoms of juvenile arthritis had been evident in her ankles, wrists, fingers, elbows, and shoulders for four years. The cortisone medication prescribed by a local doctor had helped this adolescent maintain a level of

---

[10] "Emotional Reactions of Orthopedically Handicapped Children," in *Feelings and Their Medical Significance* (published by Ross Laboratories, Valley Stream, N.Y.), Vol. VII, January, 1965, p. 1.

activity that satisfied her father; Mr. F was pleased Christine had missed only two weeks of school throughout her four-year illness. A self-made man, he proudly described his daughter as "independent and self-negotiating."

Unfortunately, cortisone is a drug that has powerful side effects. Obesity and osteoporosis were two of the more serious side effects that resulted from Christine's use of it. Her osteoporotic bones lacked calcium and strength, and some of the spinal vertebrae had been compressed. Not until the compressed vertebrae caused this usually stoic girl to experience acute agony did the family decide to seek specialized medical care.

Eleven weeks after her hospital discharge Christine was no longer dependent upon cortisone to "keep going." She became less restrained emotionally and cried sometimes, first in an interview with the psychiatric consultant, and later as she talked with the social worker and struggled to gain a more mature understanding of her illness. She continued her excellent study habits and was supervised by a teacher at the hospital and a tutor at home. Christine completed her eighth-grade work on schedule, and she was walking well enough when high school opened to take her place there along with her classmates. She lost weight, adopted an attractive new hair style, and in manner and appearance became a more outgoing teen-ager.

Her parents freely expressed their feelings to the social worker, discussing their previous attempts to obtain medical care for Christine, their disagreement about what should have been done, and their feeling of responsibility for her present handicaps. After improving their comprehension of her illness, the parents were able to arrange a more realistic school program for her, so that all her classes were located on one floor, and allowance was made in her home schedule for adequate rest and appropriate exercise.

Conclusion

Upon admission to the hospital all five children discussed in this article presented evidence of psychosocial difficulties in addition to active rheumatoid arthritis. By the time they were discharged from the hospital seven to twenty-four weeks later, both their social and physical functioning had improved.

Just as more than one factor may have precipitated the onset or exacerbation of juvenile arthritis, more than one factor may be cited to account for the improvement in the total functioning of these children after a period of hospital care. Undoubtedly, the patients did feel better physically. Their parents had had an opportunity to gain from the doctors and the social worker a better understanding of the disease itself and how their attitudes might influence its course. The parents increased their competence by attending teaching sessions on physical therapy and by observing appropriate activity for such children in the Occupational Therapy Department.

Although the family of each child experienced special strain when she was hospitalized, the parents were relieved of the physical burden of providing for her care. Having the hospital assume this responsibility can lessen the guilt of parents who blame themselves when their child's condition deteriorates at home.

Although other factors operated simultaneously, these patients showed the benefit of having participated in an appropriate social work program designed to modify the family response to illness and to preserve family strengths. The parents in this program received both environmental and psychological assistance. Depending on the situation, the social worker offered the parents a supportive or a corrective experience, or she helped the parents clarify the meaning of the child's illness and of the parental role in treatment. In staff conferences the social worker exchanged ideas with other staff members and interpreted the changing needs of patients and their families.

Nevertheless, prolonged hospitalization remains a potential psychosocial hazard to the family and child. Invalidism can be increased, and progress toward maturity can be thwarted by emotionally unhealthy hospital practices. Long-term hospital care is also expensive to both the family and the community. Yet, with some types of chronic illness, such as juvenile rheumatoid arthritis, there are times when there is no alternative if the crippling process is to be arrested or minimized. In cases in which potentially harmful parent-child relationships exist, the crisis of hospitalization may provide an opportunity for therapeutic social work intervention. Appropriate attention to the patient-family constellation can transform the child's stay in a hospital from a possibly damaging experience into one that promotes his social and emotional well-being as well as his physical health.

Casework with Asthmatic Children

Mary Brueton

Casework in a clinic where treatment is for psychosomatic conditions involves consideration of rather different ways of helping than in the more straightforward situation of the Child Guidance Clinic where the parents recognize and ask for help directly with their children's emotional problems and where psycho-medical treatment is implicit and available in the setting.

Thus, at an Asthma and Allergy Clinic, a child with a skin or chest complaint is often regarded by his parents as being only physically ill and referral of these families by the pediatrician to the social worker presents a challenge to formulate a new approach of a more experimental kind, which was possible, and encouraged by the consultant pediatrician in the clinic where the following work was carried out.

Sometimes, although the social worker may have tried to arrange for single interviews, the mother insists on bringing the child as a way of defending herself from what seems to her a threatening situation; her feelings that her mothering is being judged or that she has failed. Again the child may be brought not as a defence against the enemy within but the enemy without; to avoid what the mother may regard as condemnation or questioning by family, relatives or friends of her motivation in coming to clinic without the child. There is also the reality problem of having to bring the child because there is no one around to look after him. In all these circumstances whether the presence of the child is a defence or un-avoidable, an approach has to be devised for the situation until such time as the mother can get enough from the relationship to discard her defences or find a baby sitter.

Sometimes there is so much denial by the mother of anything but a somatic problem that even after a great deal of contact a casework relation-ship can be seen as unlikely to develop. It was in this latter situation, due to my own or the mother's limitations, that as an alternative an attempt was made to work directly with three children from different families; the ages of the children being appropriate and the mothers able to tolerate the relationship. Nevertheless I did see parents at intervals, both to discover how the child was progressing from their point of view and also in an

Reprinted from *Case Conference*, IX (September, 1962), pp. 98–101, by permission of the author and the Journal.

endeavour to prevent them feeling excluded. At no time, however, did I pass on a child's confidence. I acted on the belief that the most useful way of communicating with children was not always by conversation and used drawing materials, plasticine, toys and play to help complement speech. I did not attempt any direct interpretation of anything that occurred because of lack of experience and partly, at the time, feeling it was not a suitable technique for me. Although not specifically referred to in describing the progress of these cases, the children were being treated at the same time by the consultant, with whom they were frequently discussed.

Robin F. aged 8

Robin's mother was referred to me when she brought her 10-year-old daughter, Harriet, to the Asthma Clinic. Mrs. F described a very disturbed relationship with her husband, but eventually said that her chief worry was her younger child, Robin. She told me how she and her husband had attended the Child Guidance Clinic at R. (where they lived until last year) to discuss their attitudes to the children and that as a result of this interview her husband wanted nothing more to do with psychology which he considered to be rubbish. Both children had had asthma for the last five years and Robin in addition was given to destructive behaviour and wetting the bed nearly every night.

Mrs. F discussed her own physical symptoms as well as those of her husband and of the children at length and always used her physical symptoms to avoid talking about her emotional problems in any way other than circuitously.

From consideration of the history and having the impression of the mother as a rather disturbed woman we formed the opinion that she needed to attend a psychiatric clinic, but she said that her husband would never permit her to take Robin to see any psychiatrist. I felt that she was a person with limited ability to form relationships at any level other than a superficial one (or perhaps my experience was insufficient to be able to breech this barrier). Assessment that she was in need of direct psycho-medical treatment was agreed in discussion with the consultant and reinforced during many interviews that followed and with lack of progress, and the pattern of denial and avoidance which emerged, I decided to concentrate on Robin.

Robin was a plump, active little boy when I first knew him in the summer of 1956. He talked freely about his hopes and his wishes, but not much about his fears. It was apparent from the beginning that he was very appreciative of having one person to give him undivided attention for an hour every week (this was the usual duration and frequency of the interviews with the children). At first he showed a fear of hospitals, having spent some months in one for treatment of his bed wetting, but this fear seemed to disappear after we made several visits to the children's ward where he used to ride on the rocking horse. He displayed a talent for drawing which was surprising because his mother and father complained of his manual clumsiness. (His father was a very talented amateur artist.) For a while he drew a picture every week when he came to see me, usually done while we were talking.

When I saw Mrs. F from time to time I emphasized the good things about Robin which came out in my interview with him; she used some of the time to give vent to her hostility to her husband, especially during a period when he was being cited in a divorce case and it looked for a while as though the marriage was in the balance.

By August, 1957, Robin was asthma free and dry at night. (I had in fact never discussed his bed wetting with him.) He had also moved from a "B" to an "A" class; his relations with his father had improved, chiefly I think because his father was now busy with a boat-building hobby which meant he was home less. Mrs. F had decided to forgive her husband for his promiscuity and relations were on a better footing between them. Both the children had made friends. Robin joined the cubs. Harriet's asthma had stopped and she had gained a place at grammar school. This was the situation at the last interview before taking a year's absence from the clinic.

On returning I had a letter from Mrs. F to say that she was in hospital with a skin rash. I went to see her in the ward and found that things had deteriorated very much at home after the previous summer when a boat which her husband had built capsized in the dock and drowned one of his colleagues sailing in it, a young man in his twenties. Since then her husband seemed to be withdrawn, had little to do with his office colleagues and developed stomach pains; their marital relationship had gone from little to less.

Mrs. F in this interview showed that she seemed to have gained some insight, although she was still preoccupied with bodily symptoms. She did, however, consent to see a psychiatrist at last. Robin had gone down to a "B" class and was bed wetting again.

Robin started coming to see me again in January, 1959, and continued until the beginning of 1961. He used to bring pictures which he had painted and showed much progress in this talent, with a more mature ability to criticize his work and appreciate other pictures he used to see in my room. He was very keen to resume our relationship and again showed his desire for someone's undivided attention. He also began to talk about his failures and his fears which he had not been able to do before. During the next year he started to play football for the school which was something in which he did not feel he was competing with his father who had no interest in this game (unlike his drawings). During the summer he came top of the class and moved back to the "A" class. The father's stomach pains were diagnosed as caused by a duodenal ulcer. The family were hoping to move back to somewhere near R where father could resume his boat building and sailing in safer waters.

I found it very difficult to assess what went on in the casework process but Mrs. F seemed to respond to even superficial support in a manner out of all proportion than what would have been anticipated. Robin, who was deeply attached to his mother, seemed to thrive on the extra amount of attention without developing any intolerable conflict of hostility to his mother or her becoming jealous of me (an obvious hazard in casework with children). Mrs. F saw the psychiatrist twice and gradually her skin improved. After many setbacks the family moved back to R from where Mrs. F wrote expressing in very warm terms her appreciation of the clinic's help and news that Robin had a place at the grammar school there.

Maureen C. aged 9

Maureen's mother was a thin, ill-looking woman who seemed much older than her years and gave a history of long-standing asthma in herself as well as her mother, her sister, Maureen and another sibling. Mrs. C did not feel that her health and the care of her six children would allow her to come regularly to clinic for weekly interviews so I decided to try to work with Maureen. Mrs. C was quite willing to arrange for Maureen's fourteen-year-old sister to bring her and she began to attend at the end of 1958.

Maureen was a round faced, timid little girl, third of six siblings ranging from 14 to 3 years of age. At first she used to speak in a whisper and "blocked" frequently in conversation. She used to say she could never think about anything to talk about or to draw. As time went on she became more friendly and able to express herself quite freely. Constantly she used to draw a house and a garden with one little girl and expressed a wish to be an only child. Like Robin she was very aware and appreciative of not having to compete for attention with other children during the interview hour. She told stories about her pictures (in which the sun was always shining) and she made everybody live happily in the end although sometimes exciting and imaginative things happened, like a man being about to drown, just saved by a lifebelt.

A few months after I began to see her, Maureen's grandmother died (supposedly of asthma)—"my brothers and sisters cried, I was the only one that did not". Maureen was very attached to her grandmother and the only school-age grandchild who was not allowed to go to the funeral with the others because her mother thought it would be too upsetting for her. We discussed feelings about death and age and Maureen showed in talking about her grandmother that she felt her grandmother's love still surviving and real as if she were alive. Maureen had fears which she talked about again and again in stories she made up or in relating happenings at school which centred around corporal punishment. We often discussed her feelings about children being hit. Her asthma attacks became less frequent. She did have one severe attack, however, when a boy shut her in the playground after school; in playing with a doll and a cot Maureen expressed her feelings about how frightened the doll would feel if this happened to her.

After about six months Maureen showed something which I could only assume was insight. Whereas before she expressed her fear of her teacher hitting her and other children with the crook of his cane, she now said that he only did this when he was bad tempered and he was only bad tempered when he was ill, and she knew he was ill because she saw him taking Beechams Powders. (I thought a lot of this was transferred feeling about her mother who is rather a sharp tempered woman, but I did not comment.) At this point she began to draw another little girl in her pictures. I think now this was probably why Casework continued until the beginning of 1960 when the family moved to another part of the city to be near Mrs. C's mother (who is a great help to the family during Mrs. C's frequent illnesses) and the journey from there was considered by her mother to be too long for Maureen to make every week. The last news I had of Maureen in 1961 was that she was fairly well but still having some asthma.

Gared M. aged 14

Mrs. M was first seen in the summer of 1956. She seemed a sensitive woman, but like many mothers of asthmatic children rather rigid and much on the defensive; able to talk about her physical symptoms but not about her emotions. She was the survivor of "everything taken away" (hysterectomy) and seemed very early on in Gared's life to have partly rejected him, preferring his younger and more robust brother. Gared's father had suffered from stomach ulcers for many years. I saw Mrs. M several times during 1956-57 in an endeavour to get a better contact with her and visited the home which is in a remote part of one of the Welsh Valleys. However, Mrs. M appeared so threatened by any relationship other than a very superficial one, and because she insisted that Gared's condition was a physical one which had little to do with her "otherwise why would he have had three long spells in hospital away from me?", I decided to work with Gared directly.

Gared started coming for interviews in the autumn of 1958, he was a thin, but lively boy whose asthma had been so severe that he had missed much schooling. It was his eagerness and excitement at travelling more than my persuasion that decided his mother eventually to let him make the long bus ride to the city alone to see me.

After a few interviews when he was rather shy, he talked about his problems more freely, describing his resentment about his mother's domineering and jealousy of his younger brother. We usually began by playing a game of some kind, cards or lexicon and later chess. This was planned at first to help him to feel more at ease, but was continued even when it was no longer necessary. He was keenly competitive, liked playing and always played to win. With some encouragement, during the months that followed (having been shown he could make these visits without mishap or injury to his health) his mother allowed him to play football, and he was soon after chosen to play in the school team. This gave him much satisfaction and prestige, and the confidence gained seemed to be carried over into managing other parts of his life. His school work improved and this gave him more stature in his mother's eyes. She was also able to relinquish the reins on him a little. His attacks of asthma grew less severe and occurred at less frequent intervals. He made his first lasting friendship with another boy and later progressed to making several friends.

When I saw his mother about six months after he had been coming for interviews Mrs. M was very pleased at the improvement in his health which she maintained quite firmly was due to Scott's Emulsion which she had given him during the winter.

Casework was discontinued when Gared left school to take up a job after the summer holidays. That Christmas I received a letter from him in very affectionate terms saying he would come to see me during his annual holidays, that he was now asthma free and working at the local steelworks. The following Christmas another letter arrived with greetings saying that he was quite well and happy and enjoying his work.

It may be that very little happened therapeutically through casework and that Gared would in any case have improved. I find it difficult to assess what happened in the process but looking back on the interviews (which went on for about a year), significant material ventilated centred round his resentments and his fears, his lack of confidence and his hostility to his parents and eventually his acceptance of his ambivalence to his mother.

Reflecting in the light of further experience and a little more professional maturity, while preparing this material, it could be speculated that the security of the casework setting offered an opportunity for emotional growth for these children, who in this relationship with an adult less anxious than the adults in their home environment, found it safe to ventilate fears, aggression and hostility and to work through these sufficiently (in spite of the worker's unself-conscious approach at the time) to develop far enough to be able to accept ambivalent feelings. It is also possible that they would have improved with medication and maturity without casework help. It could also be speculated that they would have gained immeasurably more by psychotherapy, which my approach never reached in depth, being as it was directed to the "here and now" and satisfactions in the real world.

Acknowledgments

In early days at the Clinic I was grateful for consultation with Dr. B. Steinberg (now Consultant Psychiatrist at Fareham and Lecturer to the Southampton Generic Casework Course) until he left Cardiff. I also read everything I could find on social work with children (not very much).

The most helpful book I found was the one by Selma H. Fraiberg, *Psycho Analytic Principles in Casework with Children.*

The children studied were all out-patients at the Asthma Clinic under the charge of Dr. J. Jacobs, Consultant Paediatrician. I would like to thank him for his encouragement and sanction to work freely with his patients and their parents and for reading this material and criticizing it helpfully.

Names and some details have been changed to avoid recognition.

Readjusting to the Onset of Blindness

Frances T. Dover

Caseworkers are continually seeking to deepen their understanding of personality and of the individual's capacity for adaptation to inner and outer stresses. Our knowledge and understanding of how the individual responds to a particular crisis situation are still extremely limited.

The onset of blindness is certainly a severe blow to the total person, shaking to the core his previous life adjustment. Particularly because there is great emotional and cultural significance attached to vision, the blind person is not only faced with the need to learn how to function without sight, but he also has to learn to cope with the reactions his handicap provokes in others.[1] It is only within the last decade that we have begun to stress the importance of individualizing the blind person in respect to his emotional needs.

Historically, the agencies designed to serve the visually disabled have tended to stress the adequacy and variety of programs needed—residential, home teaching, vocational, recreational, and so on. These concrete services have been, and continue to be, extremely important in helping the blind person meet some of the physical demands of his daily living. However, we now recognize the need for appraising and understanding the emotional equipment with which each blind person is endowed and his ability to cope with the varying problems associated with blindness.[2]

Professional caseworkers employed in agencies that serve the blind increasingly have been able to observe individual reactions to the trauma of the loss of sight, and some of the factors involved in the person's way of readjusting to a new set of reality circumstances as well as to a new way of feeling about himself.

We have observed that while the onset of blindness is indeed traumatic, the individual is able in the majority of instances to use the help of the case-

[1] Mayer Fisch, M.D., *Psychotic Reaction to Blindness*, unpublished manuscript, 1950.
[2] Helen Lokshin, "Psychological Factors in Casework with Blind Older Persons," *Journal of Jewish Communal Service*, Vol. XXXIII, No. 3 (1957), pp. 321–327.

Reprinted from *Social Casework*, XL (June, 1959), pp. 334–338, by permission of the author and the Journal.

worker in so realigning the psychological forces as to incorporate his new disabling condition. The readjustment process involves those integrative features that are necessary for the person's continued functioning within the social setting.

Dynamics of Readjustment

This paper deals with the newly blinded adult and some of the dynamics of the readjustive process. It also examines some of the characteristic reactions the newly blinded person exhibits as he copes with his new, extremely difficult life situation.

Isolation

The withdrawn, isolated behavior of the newly blinded is a common phenomenon. It is characterized by blandness, colorlessness, lethargy of an extreme kind, an attempt to remove oneself from the environment, and a cutting off of oneself from social relationships and social activities. The person does not allow any stimulation from the outside world to reach him. This first stage of reaction to blindness has been referred to as "shock" or "emotional anesthesia."[3] Some individuals react as if there has been a total loss of self, and therefore there is nothing left to connect with other human beings. It is as if the person cannot separate the loss of a part of his body from the feeling of total destruction of self. In some persons, the loss of vision is analogous to the loss of a loved object.

The significance of this first reaction to the onset of blindness lies in the fact that it has many disintegrative features, which need close watching and evaluation. The duration and intensity of this phase are important indications as to whether the person is moving toward a healthy adaptation with his handicap or toward further breakdown. The ophthalmologist and the hospital staff have a major responsibility in helping the newly blinded through this initial period and in involving other community resources as quickly as possible. The greatest help that can be given during this period is to stand by the newly blinded person and to help the family understand that this reaction is one of the ways in which the person is defending himself against an intolerable situation and that support will be available both to the newly blinded person and to the family through various sources in the community. The focus of help at this point is on day-to-day problems. No reference should be made to future planning, and there should be no attempt at giving psychological insight.

Depression

Reactive depression does not always follow loss of vision. Usually, when the person is depressed, there is a history of previous disturbance, particularly of low frustration tolerance to stress situations and a marked feeling of low

[3] Louis Cholden, M.D., "Some Psychiatric Problems in the Rehabilitation of the Blind," *The Field of Vision,* Vol. X, No. 2 (1955).

self-esteem. The reaction following the onset of blindness is in harmony with the kind of character and personality structure that existed prior to the disability. Thus, the well-integrated person, who has weathered previous life experiences satisfactorily, is likely not to need to react to blindness with depression. The poorly integrated person, who has previously had difficulties and who has been able to maintain a precarious emotional balance until faced with the acute situation of the loss of vision, may well react with feelings of worthlessness and with great hostility, directed in part toward himself.[4]

Loss of vision, like any other major disablement, is a blow to one's body image and consequently to one's self-esteem. It requires a major reorganization of one's life, particularly in relation to dependency. One's activity is severely limited, and there is an increased necessity for depending upon others. One must re-learn how to perform the simplest, most routinized tasks. Usually, the individual is not able to deal with the feelings of frustration and anger he experiences, and he feels helpless, odd, and undesirable. The prevailing stereotyped attitude of pity toward the blind, which the newly blinded person now has toward himself, is merged with feelings of worthlessness, and together they create an all pervading mood, depressive in character, and affecting the whole person. The outward manifestations of this over-all mood are an inability to sleep, loss of appetite, excessive crying, and an excessive tendency toward expressions of self-pity. It is during this very critical time that the person especially needs support from his environment. If his depression is reactive to the trauma induced by the onset of blindness, it will probably be limited in duration.

During the period of reactive depression, treatment should be supportive in nature, and the client should be encouraged to verbalize his feelings of anger and frustration. Emphasis should be placed on specific planning, although the goals should be limited. Limited rehabilitative measures such as orientation to getting around in the home, the beginning of travel instruction, or some special group work activity should be instituted. The caseworker should be cognizant of, and work closely with, the person's practical needs, before help is given in understanding the emotional problems involved for him. This is the period during which there is great need for the worker to involve the relatives, and to understand and work with some of the familial relationships, the family's confusions, and their dependency struggles.

Projection and Denial

Projection as a mechanism of defense against anxiety is frequently used by the newly blinded person who is trying to protect himself against what he considers an intolerable situation. It is usually coupled with attempts to deny that the condition is irreversible. Denial is frequently expressed through assertions that hope cannot be abandoned, that new medical discoveries are being made all the time and that this condition too may be

---

[4] Unpublished minutes of psychiatric seminars, Social Service Department, New York Guild for the Jewish Blind, 1956–1958.

subject to change by some magical means, and so on. The need to deny loss of vision appears even in the fairly emotionally stable individual in the early period of his disablement. Frequently, however, the newly blinded person directs his anger toward, and attributes his handicap to, the incompetence of the physician in charge of his case. This temporary outlet makes the individual's anxiety a little easier to bear, although it postpones his need to face the reality of his situation and divert his psychic energies into unproductive channels. His own guilt, if he feels in some way responsible for his loss of vision (as in diabetics who have not followed the strictly prescribed regimen), is somewhat alleviated if he is able to place the blame for his condition outside himself. By making someone else feel guilty, he can feel less so himself.[5]

Projection is also used by the newly blinded person as a means of protecting himself against the severe impact of the current stress situation. If projection is recognized as a reaction to the blindness and if the caseworker can deal with it on a conscious level, the person can frequently be helped, by careful and selective use of consulting ophthalmologists, to clarify the medical facts and to understand the nature of his eye difficulty in a way that will dispel his suspicions that someone needs to be blamed for his condition. It is extremely important for the person to have a careful medical assessment so that he may begin to sift out his emotional involvement with the problem. Caseworkers are often stymied by the unwillingness of the medical specialist to share the medical facts with the patient, especially if the condition is irreversible. His confusion about his true medical condition, coupled with the emotional stress of the disability itself, often hinders the newly blinded person from using his energies more constructively soon after his loss of vision. Denial can take a passive form in which the patient verbalizes his acceptance of his condition, but does nothing to adjust to it. He merely lets others in his environment be active on his behalf.

Integration

Integration, as I am using the concept here, is the continued effort to function by incorporating the handicap of blindness into the concept of the self. The person now responds realistically to the demands that daily living imposes upon him as a handicapped person. It is extremely difficult for the sighted individual to imagine the physical difficulties that a blind person encounters. Changes are called for in every activity of living. As each new situation is met and conquered, there is renewed capacity to meet other situations and to accommodate the inevitable frustrations involved in living without sight.

Integration as a social concept also applies to the blind as a group that is generally excluded from many kinds of social and economic opportunities because of the fears and misunderstandings that prevail. As with other

[5] Arthur P. Noyes and Lawrence C. Kolb, *Modern Clinical Psychiatry*, 5th ed., Saunders, Philadelphia, 1958, Chapter IV.

groups in society who are struggling to be accepted for the productive contribution they can make to the whole, so the blind and other disabled persons also seek a healthier social attitude toward their handicap and toward themselves as the bearers of the handicap. The disabled person who has succeeded in accepting and integrating his handicap is generally also the one who can blaze the trail for further social acceptance and integration.

Mobilization

Active mobilization is the furthering of the individual's integrative process and the active use of personal and outside resources for enriching one's functioning on every level. Thus, mobilization implies both active personal adjustment and greater mastery of the environment. For example, the blind person who has received job training through an agency now chooses to seek work outside the agency's sheltered workshop. He is ready to face greater difficulties in working with sighted people and he will also leave an imprint on his environment. He is truly helping to mold his culture. This is the person who will learn to travel unaided, not because his other senses are better developed as compensation for his loss of sight, but because he has confidence in his own capacity and in what he has learned. This is the person who will attempt to lead as normal a life as possible, taking his handicap as part of himself, feeling its burden, but not allowing it to weigh him down.

Individual Reactions

Not every newly blinded person goes through the various stages outlined. All these reactions can be experienced simultaneously, partially, one at a time, or in different combinations. They are also experienced in varying intensity by those who have lost some of their vision and who greatly fear becoming totally blind.

For some individuals, the onset of blindness is not only disabling, but so totally incapacitating as to keep them from functioning in any normal way. Thus, the onset of blindness is often a precipitating factor in total break-down. Such a person does not have sufficient plasticity or ability to maintain a balance between the inner stresses experienced because of the new disability and the impositions of the environment. On closer examination of such a person's past history, one finds that his ability to adapt to previous stresses has been weak. The areas of greatest vulnerability for these persons have been their general social relationsips, dependency needs, and sexual adjustment. The onset of blindness is the last straw when there is little psychic energy left to fight off or to meet new stresses, and a psychotic break may result. Only a small number of the newly blinded individuals who come to the agency's attention fall within this group; obviously they may require immediate hospitalization.

Case Illustration

Miss A, a 50-year-old unmarried woman, was referred by a hospital medical social worker to a specialized agency for the blind, following unsuccessful surgery for a detached retina. She had lost all her vision except for light perception. She had threatened and attempted suicide. She was extremely hostile toward her family, cried constantly, and behaved as if she were totally helpless. This behavior was in great contrast to her previous self-sufficiency and independent manner of functioning. She was described by her family as having been self-centered, controlling, and inflexible. She carried a martyr role in the family, had assumed total responsibility in caring for her aged, ill parents before their death, and had raised two children of a younger sibling who had died a number of years previously.

Miss A was first seen by the worker in the hospital. She was extremely guarded but she stressed her inability to accept living as a blind person, her feelings of uselessness, and her further thoughts of suicide. At the same time, she mentioned her concern for the amount of grief she was causing her family. The worker picked up on Miss A's interest in her family. This was the first sign of the client's moving away from her previous total self-absorption. The worker stressed that the family members were very much concerned about her and were in contact with the agency to find the best way of helping her. The worker tentatively and cautiously made reference to the many services for the visually disabled available at the agency. The hospital had in the meantime arranged for a psychiatric examination. The psychiatric diagnosis was "reactive depression." It was recommended that, since Miss A had sufficient integrative potential, she be offered casework help. She was not considered a suicidal risk at the time of discharge from the hospital.

For a period of almost two years, the caseworker worked intensively with her. During the first two months, help centered on the practical aspects of Miss A's daily functioning. She expressed much pent-up anger about being blind. She still refused to accept the fact that she could not see, and insisted on either trying to function as she had done before the loss of her sight, or remaining completely inactive and in that way withdrawing from the need to face the reality of her blindness. Very gradually, she was able to accept some orientation instruction at home. The intense emotional struggle around acceptance of blindness continued. She would often react with intense nausea, severe palpitations, and extreme sweating, both before and after the orientation instructor's visit to the home. Crying spells continued to recur. During interviews with the caseworker there was a certain blandness in affect and inappropriate smiling.

Although these depressive and disintegrative symptoms remained in evidence, certain features of integration and better adjustment began to emerge. Miss A began to expand her interests by requesting to learn how to knit and type. Whereas earlier she had lost all interest in food and eating, she now asked to be taught how to handle food in a restaurant. She began to resume social contact in a limited way, but refused to involve herself in a group of blind persons.

After several months, Braille instruction was introduced and Miss A began to consider some vocational retraining. However, all social and rehabilitative planning was contingent upon the results of further eye surgery. After several more operations, Miss A did regain partial vision. She felt the need, however, for more casework help. For the first time, Miss A felt that she was being helped to look at herself as the person she was; that she had great dependency needs which she had tried hard to cover up by her self-sacrificing and over-attachment to her parents and siblings. She no longer needed to be the strong, efficient person she thought her family expected her to be. She gradually gave up the unrealistic hope that she could return to her former employment. She then took what she considered the most important step in her life by marrying a man she had known for many years.

Thus, Miss A, who might otherwise never have sought any help for herself, found new strengths that could be mobilized, not only for meeting her visual disability, but in facing other experiences that formerly had held great fear for her.

Conclusion

The special contribution of the caseworker in the readjustment of the newly blinded lies in his acceptance of the person as a *whole* human being. The needs and strivings of the blind person are accorded the same kind of recognition given to any person who is seeking to find the strength to cope with a difficult reality problem. Loss of vision, like any other serious physical disability, requires adjustment to the realistic demands of daily living which are indeed difficult to meet. The emotional strains and stresses are severe; they are different for each individual and each person copes with them in in his own way. The previous life adjustment of the individual, his feelings about himself, his characteristic way of meeting crises, and his capacity for adequate family and social relationships, are all important factors in planning a suitable rehabilitative program for him. The more understanding of the person the caseworker possesses, the more effectively can he help the person find and use available services appropriately. As more is known about the particular needs of the visually disabled, our efforts to create new services will be met with more appropriate community response. Concrete services, including orientation instruction, vocational training, and specialized group work, are exceedingly important and valuable tools for motivating the newly blinded person toward the kind of functioning his individual capacities permit. Above all, the development of casework skills must keep pace with new knowledge and new ways of helping to rehabilitate the increasing number of visually disabled persons.

Revealing Diagnosis and Prognosis to Cancer Patients

Rosalind Jablon and Herbert Volk

The social and psychological concomitants of cancer are profound and extensive, and a treating physician inevitably needs to grapple with these allied issues. Present medical thinking also holds that it is inadequate to treat a "disease." The doctor-patient relationship must encompass concern and activity to help a patient with the anxieties evoked by the illness and the treatment process. Though this philosophy is widely supported, medical practice frequently falls short of the epoused goal. Typically the physician's explanation for restricting his activity to the treatment of disease is that he does not have the time for more than this. It is tacitly assumed thereby that a doctor would have the skillfulness generally to help patients in the broader sense. The authors question this premise and propose that it is rather the other way around. The difficulty in implementing comprehensive medical care arises out of the failure of medicine to understand the problems and skills involved in attaining this quality of service, and as the medical profession achieves greater appreciation of the complexities of treating a "human being," it will find both the time and means to do so. Toward this goal, the ensuing discussion offers some deeper understanding of a critical problem in managing the breast cancer patient. This is the issue of revealing diagnosis and prognosis to the patient.

The thinking expressed in this paper is mainly based upon experiences with breast cancer patients attending the tumor clinics of the Bronx Municipal Hospital Center, a New York City general hospital. The authors believe these patients to be representative of the general breast cancer patient population, but this is an inference based upon observation rather than statistical demonstration. Breast cancer patients include women with operable disease as well as patients with advanced inoperable or recurrent postoperative malignancy. Generally the patient with early operative mammary cancer is a younger woman than the patient with advanced metastatic cancer. However, within our population there is no predictable correlation between stage of illness and age of the patient. In this study

Reprinted with permission of the authors and the National Association of Social Workers, from *Social Work*, Vol. 5, No. 2 (April, 1960), pp. 51–57.

patients are differentiated according to broad age groupings, since it is believed that this criterion is both meaningful and functional; more concretely, it offers the medical practitioner the clearest and most usable guide for dealing with the problem under discussion.

In determining the appropriate type of medical treatment for the breast cancer patient, the stage of the disease is clearly the critical differentiating factor. However, in studying the sociopsychological trauma incident to the illness and the kind of social casework service needed by the patient, the most significant (and readily observable) differential factor is typically the age of the patient. Since our paper is concerned with the latter area, we are classifying our patients into two broad age groups—the first, women in the age range from 35 to 50 years; the second, women 70 years and over.[1] The significance of this specific chronological classification is the differentiation between persons functioning at sharply different phases of the life cycle, and therefore typically carrying very different social roles in living. The age group 35 to 50 is generally made up of women who are actively connected with others in the roles of mother, wife, friend, and working person. These patients are usually aware and mentally alert. The life experience and self-image of this woman is oriented toward being socially and physically adequate and self-reliant. In contrast, the patient 70 years and over has few active relationships, her social role is minimal; frequently she is dependent on other adults (married children) or she is alone in the community. She is a less aware person; her total life pattern, psychically, biologically, and socially, is largely adjusted to passivity and dependence. Women whose age is between these two ranges, 50 to 70 years, constitute the most heterogeneous group, but our studied population showed no significantly different characteristics among these patients as compared with the patients of the preceding two groups. This leads us to include the 50- to 70-year-old patient in either one of the aforementioned patient groups; the appropriate choice will depend upon the grouping with which her particular living patterns are most comparable.

Illness, as any life event, is an experience which occurs within the broader life picture; and the meaning and dimensions of any experience are synthesized out of its significance within the broader whole. The full life picture for the women of 35 to 50 years is radically different from that of the woman of 70, and therefore the social and psychological meaning of disease at these different stages of life will necessarily also be sharply different. In line with this, the treatment role which social casework offers these patients will need to vary, derived from the difference in meaning and impact of the illness in the total life configuration of the patient.

The nature of a social casework service to any person is bounded and

[1] Age alone does not automatically define and categorize the vital qualities of a particular personality and her life involvements. In discussing large groupings of patients, however, age is the most applicable single criterion for classifying patients into homogeneous subgroups based on sociopsychological factors. The writers accept that more extensive study may yield finer or changed age groupings as more precisely significant.

determined by that person's awareness of his situation. The most vital life fact for the cancer patient is his illness; and a casework service will need to be geared closely to the patient's understanding of his medical condition. This pertains both to concrete services which can be offered, as well as to what can be an appropriate focus of counseling help. In illustration, one can only handle irrational fears about cancer with the patient who has been medically informed of his diagnosis.

Should the Patient Be Told?

There have been sharply differing attitudes in the medical profession about whether to reveal diagnosis to a cancer patient. General agreement exists only about the need for sharing diagnosis with a responsible relative. The philosophy opposing sharing diagnosis is the more entrenched and long-standing one, whereas those who argue for greater candidness with patients represent more recent thinking. Advocates of each opinion have written effectively for their beliefs. Each side points for justification to a particular sequence of traumatic eventualities that may ensue when the patient either is made aware of his illness or is "protected" from his diagnosis. It is unfortunate that each school of thought largely ignores the logic and experiences of the other. However, review of the literature, observation of professional practice in the Bronx Municipal Hospital Center, and discussion with medical personnel of other New York City cancer centers reveal that these two opposing philosophies exist more in terms of theoretical speculation than in daily medical practice.

Practicing physicians exposed to both views reject a dogmatic use of any one theory of patient management. They express the need to individualize in giving medical information, recognizing that any piece of knowledge may be helpful to one patient but destructive to another. Medical practice, however, is at a still different point, lagging far behind intellectual conviction—in fact, few patients are told a cancer diagnosis. In view of this dichotomy between conviction and practice, it is important to examine the opinions traditionally offered on the issue, "Should the patient be told?"

Those who believe that it is generally more helpful to conceal a malignant diagnosis from the patient present the following reasons:

1. The awareness that the illness is cancer precipitates too great an emotional burden. The usual patient would respond with panic or depression, thus destroying his capacity for productive living during his remaining span of life.

2. Most cancer patients do not want to know the truth about their illness. Though generally not stated explicitly, the sequence to this is assumed to be: this patient knows what is best for himself, and the doctor will be most helpful by respecting the patient's wishes.

Those who argue for informing a patient of his diagnosis and prognosis point to the following observations:

1. It is virtually impossible to deceive a cancer patient effectively about his illness. His own awareness, the infinite subtle communications brought him in his relationships with others (family and medical personnel), will transmit clues to the truth.

2. Inasmuch as most cancer patients suspect their diagnosis and become aware at some point of their medical course, attempts to conceal it with unduly optimistic statements breed distrust, resentment, and emotional isolation in the patient. The patient needs to feel trust in his doctor, the support and closeness of friends and relatives in bearing his illness; he is deprived of these when fed unrealistic and unconvincing promises.

3. There are patients who have known their diagnosis and who have had the strength to continue productive living. They have demonstrated that there can be greater values and ease in being aware of one's real condition.

4. Most laymen are to some degree emotionally and knowledgeably irrational about illness. A patient suspecting cancer but advised otherwise is also frequently left alone to harbor many irrational fears. To the degree that there is doctor-patient trust and the illness can be discussed openly, a doctor can learn the patient's fears and help him understand his illness more rationally and to take measures in his own behalf.

Each of these points of view expresses a partial truth of human psychic life and human relationships. Still unanswered, however, are two key problems: first, perceiving the unique way in which each patient integrates these strands within himself; and second, judging therefrom the most helpful course of medical management for the specific patient. In essence, we see both views as having contributed theoretical insight; but the task still untouched concerns the skillful management of a therapeutic relationship with an individual patient as this relates to the sociopsychological trauma inherent in malignancy. And in considering the latter, the specific questions now needing re-evaluation are the following:

1. Medicine accepts the validity of comprehensive care and differential management in dealing with the cancer patient. Yet practice continues to conceal diagnosis, and differential management is sparsely evidenced. What factors can explain this? Is existent practice meeting patients' needs?

2. How can one differentiate what should be told to whom? Can we begin to formulate significant criteria to help judge whether a particular patient should be informed of his diagnosis and/or prognosis—or the reverse?

3. In malignant illness where the social and psychological meaning of the affliction is most profound, is it the best practice to place sole responsibility upon the physician for determining the psychologically best course of patient management? Is the medical doctor generally adequately equipped to help the patient with the emotional trauma?

In the Bronx Municipal Hospital Center Breast Clinic, patients are not usually told their diagnosis. Our experience is that many patients, certainly women below age 50, suspect their true illness and carry this terror-laden knowledge only lightly veiled.[2] Most patients are ambivalent about corroborating their suspicions. They demonstrate strong need to avoid exploring their fears; yet, equally tenaciously, they distrust medical and familial reassurances about their illness. Overtly these patients frequently appear to come to the resolution of keeping the truth barred behind a thin veneer of desperate hope. Yet many of these same patients do have the strength on occasion to ask directly, "Do I have cancer?" This situation constitutes the basis upon which it is argued that the cancer patient usually does not want to know the nature of her illness, and that the doctor will be most helpful by following her wishes. However, this thinking needs critical evaluation.

A Psychosocial Approach

The human being cannot bear isolation, and man's psychic structure inevitably strives against this. On conscious and unconscious levels, we devise ways to re-establish threatened interpersonal connections, tenuous as these ways may be. A sense of isolation breeds guilt, inadequacy, and fear, and we search to avoid experiencing ourselves as isolated from others. Death is isolating—not only for the dying, but also for the living. Further, the values of our culture also tend to emasculate man's capacity to deal with the inevitable facts of infirmity and death. Dependence and inadequacy, inherent in any illness, are defined culturally and experienced individually as bad and to be feared. Doctor, patient, and family members are all subject to these emotional forces; and consciously and unconsciously, we will all try to shield ourselves from meeting human mortality and weakness. Thus, the cancer patient who chooses overtly to deny the threat of malignant illness comes to this solution within a milieu which encourages evasion. In infinite direct and subtle ways, we who are well discourage this patient from facing us with his frightening, alienating truth. Should he want to know a malignant diagnosis, he may first need to "help" the living to bear his tragedy before he can be given his own right to do so. Ilse S. Wolff reports just such a situation most movingly. A young nurse recorded her experience with a patient in the late stages of bacterial endocarditis:

[2] This observation is widely confirmed in other studies dealing with the cancer patient's awareness of his illness. A bibliography is available from the authors.

. . . Every day when she entered his room, she felt a strong upsurge of feelings of guilt. She was going to live, while he, of her own age, was about to die. "I know he wanted to talk to me; but I always turned it into something light, a little joke, or into some evasive reassurance which had to fail. The patient knew and I knew. But, as he saw my desperate attempts to escape and felt my anxiety, he took pity on me and kept to himself what he wanted to share with another human being. And so he died and did not bother me.[3]

Need we not ask to what extent our continuing "humane" denial of medical reality with a cancer patient may be protective of our own defenses against the impact of death, inadequacy, and pain? Also, to what degree does our practice reflect intertia? We continue to do what is more familiar, thereby following the path of least resistance—intellectually, psychologically, and socially—for both doctor and patient. Inasmuch as medicine still cannot cure cancer, can this diagnosis cause some sense of guilt and defeat for the doctor, making it difficult for a sensitive physician to reveal a malignant diagnosis? There has as yet been no serious, scientific exploration of the question of what is therapeutically best for the patient himself.[4]

Medical opinion generally agrees that it is necessary to individualize the doctor-patient relationship, but that it is difficult to judge what is best in dealing with an individual patient's anxieties and questions. Truly this is so. Today there exists a large body of knowledge concerning skilled, therapeutic intervention in the social and psychic life of man by means of a trained relationship. Psychiatry, social work, and psychology are all disciplines involved in this content. The general medical practitioner or surgeon can only rarely be skillfully aware of all the many facets of his patient's social and emotional life, yet this doctor is asked to judge and to act with helpfulness in relation to a patient coping with the trauma of malignancy. It is also he who must carry final responsibility for what is told a patient regarding his medical condition, since the physician must be responsible ultimately for the patient's care. It is this situation which necessitates that those trained in dealing with human behaviour and interpersonal relationships contribute to medical understanding of these perplexing problems in patient management.

Professional staff will be better able to evaluate the social and psychological facets of a patient's life when they have some clear and specific criteria by which to guide them. Such objective criteria need to be understood as guides to facilitate arriving at an individualized approach to patients, through highlighting some of the important, common differentials among patients. Guiding criteria must be applied together with careful individualized judgment, never in a dogmatic, mechanical manner. It is within this

---

[3] Ilse S. Wolff, "The Magnificence of Understanding," in Samuel Standard and Helmuth Nathan, eds., *Should the Patient Know the Truth?* (New York: Springer Publishing Company, Inc., 1955), p. 32.

[4] All the studies seen by the writers deal with this major question only in a tangential or philosophic manner. Nevertheless, the data available do tend to challenge the continued widespread practice of withholding diagnosis from the cancer patient.

framework that we have drawn up the following tentative recommendations which have been useful to the authors in evaluating the question of whether a breast cancer patient should be informed of her diagnosis and/or prognosis. Though the specific recommendations which are presented apply only to the breast cancer patient, it is our opinion that this report has wider pertinence in pointing out a useful direction of thinking in relation to all cancer patients.

Recommendations for Interpreting Diagnosis

Unless there are major contraindications, the patient with breast cancer up to 50 years of age for whom there is probability of medical control of the disease for a substantial period of life should be advised of her diagnosis. However, along with this, it is vital that the patient's concepts of the disease are essentially accurate. The patient must be told clearly first, that she is not doomed, and second, the few cautions she will need to observe. The patient between 35 and 50 years is typically a woman actively participating in many relationships; often others are dependent on her. She is an aware, thinking person, whose self-image is geared to being adequate. Such patients almost invariably suspect their true diagnosis; reassurances to the contrary are rarely effective. This person's many active involvements in community and family groups hold the constant threat of temporarily allayed suspicions being restimulated, the truth becoming known, under circumstances in which realistic medical knowledge and assurance are least available.

Such a woman is more probably a person with strong motivations for life, inherent in her biological and social status. The motivation toward life carries with it both the need to feel herself in control and the strength to face trauma. It is these forces that impel the younger woman to express a persistent, though conflicted, desire to know her diagnosis in contrast to the older patient who will usually deny the illness far more effectively. The same drives in the younger patient can, however, also be channelized into other directions if the patient is permitted an alternative. They can be available to the patient in facing her true diagnosis and still reaching out for continued satisfactions in living. It is our experience that the anxiety of the younger patient is frequently interwoven with fears about the welfare of others, primarily her children. Realistically, knowing her illness (when there is still a hopeful prognosis) may release a parent from corroding uncertainty and conflict and free her energies for planning constructively for her child and herself. It is also important to realize that honest, realistic reassurance will generally be more effective and sustained than false over-optimistic hopes. Similarly, our own capacity to deal with the patient's anxieties will be more secure when we are not burdened with gross untruths.

The woman under 50 years whose illness is at an advanced stage presents different problems. Her social roles and emotional and intellectual attitudes have been described. However, the patient's more critical medical status produces grave differences in her emotional resources and needs, as compared with the patient of the same age whose disease is controlled. The advanced cancer patient will be experiencing more or less prolonged debilitation and physical pain, relieved usually only for brief periods. There can be no hopeful prognosis of sustained freedom from disease. Death is advancing inexorably. The patient's accelerating symptoms of pain and disability will intensify anxiety and hopelessness. On an overt level the patient may evidence an intense, desperate desire to live, but one can safely assume that this is far from the entire emotional matrix. At our present point of understanding, it is wiser with most of these patients to conceal diagnosis, but this decision must always be determined discriminatingly in relation to the particular patient—not mechanically out of inertia.

It is pertinent to be aware of two vital considerations with the advanced cancer patient. First, does the patient herself convey strong need to know her diagnosis? Obviously, if she does not want this knowledge, it will not be of therapeutic use to her, but will only increase her anxiety and despair. Second, there are some persons for whom uncertainty and not knowing are intensely upsetting and emotionally draining, since for them unsureness is emotionally synonymous with total loss of control. This patient will press to know diagnosis in an effort to subdue the feeling of loss of control. This is a most difficult patient to manage, since the same unbearable psychological threat of loss of control is also inherent in the patient's medical status. To tell such a person her diagnosis contains the danger of intensifying the very anxiety which drives the patient to demand the diagnosis. The most helpful management may be to share as much real understanding about the illness and prognosis as is asked by the patient, and which can be given without revealing diagnosis or the inevitable fatal prognosis. The disease can be explained, to the extent of the particular patient's understanding, in terms of the organic processes involved (sufficiently broadly as to conceal the diagnosis); as a chronic, inflammatory condition responsive to palliative measures for varying periods of time. With this kind of understanding, the person may be helped to feel a sense of greater control of her life, since understanding is a force which can yield a greater sense of adequacy and active participation.

For the woman over 70 suffering from either operable or advanced cancer, there is generally no therapeutic value in knowing the nature of her disease, and in our experience, this patient rarely requests this. Her biological and social life level is such that she is essentially adjusted to passive, dependent living. She is aware of and accepts the fact that illness and incapacity are virtually inherent in her stage of life. She has both diminished need and strength to cope with life's traumas in an active participating way. To give the patient the knowledge of her diagnosis and prognosis would generally precipitate added anxieties and would serve no useful purpose for the patient's remaining life.

Interpreting Prognosis

What should be told a breast cancer patient requires differentiation between sharing diagnosis and dealing with questions of prognosis. To be aware that one is living with an incurable illness, or that one faces a danger of possible reactivation of disease, does not involve the same degree of psychic threat as is contained in the knowledge or suspicion of inevitable fatality. To the degree that a patient is able to face the realities of her life, her capacity to make constructive adjustments is enhanced. Many who could not bear knowing a diagnosis of cancer can sustain the knowledge that their illness is chronic, or holds the danger of reactivation. In many instances it would be far more helpful to give the cancer patient this kind of realistic, prognostic picture, rather than to permit false or overly optimistic concepts of cure. A case in point would be the young breast cancer patient who becomes pregnant without knowing the risks of reactivating the disease, because of the factors involved in hormone levels during pregnancy.

In our experience we found it advisable to inform the advanced cancer patient that her disease is chronic, though amenable to palliative measures, rather than to permit or encourage her to build hopes of cure. New therapeutic agents which can bring temporary regression of disease may be interpreted by the patient as a cure, regardless of whether the doctor corroborates this. However, the potential dangers in this unrealistic understanding are too great to be justified by the transient value for the patient of believing or hoping that a cure is possible. The patient who anticipates cure is implicitly directed to live unrealistically; she is unprepared for what does occur and misunderstanding interferes in feasible planning for her life. Moreover, when there is protracted illness with periods of clinical relief and then further progression of disease, the patient who has been awaiting cure will become confused, resentful, and distrustful of the medical relationship. She will feel deceived and increasingly isolated from family and doctor as her unreal hopes are slowly shattered by the stark truth of her experiences.

Conclusion

In proposing these beginning guides to differentiated medical management of the breast cancer patient, we emphasize that the criteria used—age and stage of disease—cannot be applied mechanically, without evaluation of their substantive appropriateness to the particular patient. They are to be understood as guides, not substitutes, for differential diagnostic judgment with each patient. The significant individual characteristics of each patient must always be considered.

Cardiac Disorders

Casework with Families and Patients Facing Cardiovascular Surgery

Magda Bondy

One of the dramatic developments in medical treatment since World War II has been the progress of cardiovascular surgery, offering new hope for improved functioning and life expectancy. Its objective is always prolongation of life or improvement or stabilization of functioning.

The broad category of cardiovascular surgery covers a number of different surgical procedures, with differences in their risk, outlook, and potentials. In Beth Israel Hospital in New York City, on whose experience this paper is based, although there is not yet a program for open heart surgery, several different operative procedures are at present undertaken. Some are fairly simple procedures, medically considered comparable in risk with such other well developed forms of major surgery as appendectomy and cholecystectomy with convalescence and outlook relatively uninvolved unless complications arise. There are gradations of risk in the other procedures and in some the expected convalescence can be lengthy, with ups and downs, continuing limitations for some time, and extended uncertainty as to eventual level of stablization in functioning. In her own preparation, the caseworker needs as definitive information as possible from the doctor so that she can be clear about the nature of the integrative process being demanded of the patient who has to decide about the cardiac surgery. This is also essential in helping the patient later with the psychological and functioning processes of convalescence and the problems they create for him.

The cardiac conditions for which such surgery is performed are usually handicapping to personal and family functioning, and contain the potential for additional damage. Although some patients and families appear able to make necessary adaptations such conditions are apt to have disruptive effects. In addition to necessarily changing ways of carrying personal and family roles, they can acquire symbolic value,[1] serving psychological and functioning ends. Thus for one patient, limitations may support a defense

[1] Leopold Bellak, M.D., Editor, *Psychology of Physical Illness*, Grune & Stratton, New York, 1952.

Reprinted from *Journal of Jewish Communal Services*, XXXVI (Spring, 1960), pp. 294–306, by permission of the author and the Journal.

against feelings of inadequacy; in another, similar limitations can disturb established defensive adaptations that have served him well. Many problems related to a person's distorted concept of himself can also be falsely attached to the cardiac illness. The cardiac problem can thus become a pivotal part of the patient's adjustment in living, functioning, and carrying his family role.

The prospect of cardiovascular surgery obviously can raise complicated reactions over and above the realistic ones. Since it offers hope of improved life and functioning, it appeals to the healthy desire for fuller living. Since it is major surgery, it contains a realistic threat of bodily damage and death. Moreover, since it is so new, and goes contrary to traditional inviolability of the heart as an essential to human life, at times it tends to set off fears of death beyond anticipated medical risk.[2] And finally, because of its threat to established adjustments, it endangers defensive patterns. It is because of these effects on capacity to cope with environmental, social, and relationship problems that the caseworker's participation in the programs of cardiovascular surgery offers so rich a service to patient and family alike.

Cardiovascular service at Beth Israel Hospital is basically treatment-centered and research-oriented. From the early days of this service, casework assessment has been part of the comprehensive evaluation which determines whether problems in functioning are complicated by personal and family stresses. A primary consideration too at times is whether the timing of such surgery can or should be modified for minimal disruption of individual and family life or to allow for casework or psychiatric treatment in preparation for surgery. It is to be noted that the Social Service Department makes available the battery of casework services referred to above through its usual referral, application, and case finding devices. The specific aspect is that the cardiovascular team, by administrative policy, provides for casework services as needed in all patient situations considered.

The decision to undergo surgery can be a tremendous one, undermining, as previously discussed, defensive adaptations. The period of convalescence, with its need for continuing protections and limitations, can also be a tense one, creating or exacerbating problems of adjustment and family relationship. The anxiety involved in undertaking activities previously forbidden and now medically recommended may be immobilizing.

The focus of this paper, however, is the initial crucial period when cardiac surgery is being considered by the team, and the patient and the family have to make the decision about it. On the solidity of decisions and the motivation involved rests much of the ability of patient and family to make the adaptations necessitated by the changing medical outlook and the rehabilitation process. Therefore the nature and quality of the decision made may indicate the casework services that may be necessary at various points throughout recovery.

Thus far, we are finding that our early participation in team study

[2] Sir James Frazer, *The Golden Bough*, The Macmillan Company, New York, 1943.

serves a triple purpose. For the doctors it provides relevant data on individual and family functioning, including resources and stresses, useful in arriving at comprehensive medical diagnosis and treatment plans. For the patient and for those significant family members who need it, it provides a supporting, planning, or counseling casework service. The caseworker establishes the beginning differential casework diagnosis determining the services needed now and likely to be needed if surgery is recommended, or alternatively, if no such treatment hope is possible. Central to this evaluation is consideration of the nature and extent of the patient's motivation. The problems of motivation and the differentials within them will be discussed later. Among the questions considered are: Is the patient sufficiently motivated to carry out this type of surgery with understanding of its nature, its hazards, and its potential for improved functioning? If he is not adequately motivated, what is the content of his problem and how can he be helped?

This paper will consider the professional questions for the caseworker in decision-making. It will approach this from the point of view of the developmental level of the patient and the family balance, its modifiability where the balance is inappropriate to developmental level, and the medical considerations. The reason for this is that the nature of responsibility for family decision is different at different stages of growth, and in different cultural settings, even though the legal responsibility in our community remains only the parents' until an unmarried child is 21. Focal periods for discussion in this paper will be children, adolescents and adults.

Parents' Decision for the Young Child

Our doctors inform us that ordinarily surgery prior to the age of four is, for medical reasons, undertaken only on a life-saving basis. Therefore, we have thus far had experience within our team program only with patients four and older. Children in our society are entitled to parental protection when important decisions need to be made. Among the inherent responsibilities of parenthood, for instance, are planning for schooling, living-regime, protection of health, and expectations of acceptable behavior within the family, toward authority-figures, and outside the home.

Therefore, obviously, the significant persons to make the decision for cardiac surgery are the parents. Since they too are part of the culture in which we live, we find that parents of young children almost universally accept this responsibility. In two situations where parents have held adamantly to the child's deciding for himself, we found serious psychopathology. One was a man diagnosed by a psychiatric hospital as psychotic. In the other case, although psychiatric diagnosis could not be obtained because of the degree of the mother's withdrawal and the father's incapacities, the mother never left the house, and gave many other indications of severe mental disturbance.

For practically all of the parents concerned, however, the recommendation for this surgery had great emotional impact, and decision was complicated by their conflicted feelings about it. On the one hand, it promised improvement for the child. On the other hand, it also often carried the fear that the child might die in surgery or that the child could not understand and might hate the parents. It also often reactivated or exaggerated fears of responsibility and difficulty in carrying adult roles and parental authority. Usually where the child was obviously severely limited, the parents could dramatically see the hope of gains. Where the child was only mildly handicapped and could function in many ways usual for children, it was apt to be much more difficult for parents to grasp the functional gains anticipated. The prospect of limited life expectancy, when some years of life were still foreseen, or of a slow downhill course had much less reality for the parents than the child's present difficulties.

Not surprisingly, educational background or intelligence alone were no safeguard against this conflict. Instead, as might have been anticipated, the nature of the individual parent's personality organization, the quality of the marital relationship and relationship with the child, and parental expectations and hopes for him, were more significant.

Usually the parents with good ego strength and healthy relationships were freest to absorb the medical reality, to respond to the child's need, and to utilize, if necessary, a casework service to clarify the steps that would best protect their child.

> One example is the situation of Mr. and Mrs. S, loving, responsible parents of a four year old, who with great strength had weathered much trouble in their wartime experiences. They seemed to have no unusual difficulty in deciding to give Bobby the benefits of cardiovascular surgery when it was recommended. During Bobby's hospitalization and prior to surgery, he developed a mild respiratory infection. At this point the parents became uncertain about the decision for surgery. It developed that Bobby's infection reactivated for them an earlier traumatic experience where their first son died of an infection in a concentration camp. Their earlier grief colored their present reaction, with a gush of fear that surgery might cause infection that would imperil their second son's life. When the caseworker helped them to clarify their confusion through highly focused counseling, they could, much to their relief, rediscuss with the physician the risks involved, particularly with reference to infection. They could then reaffirm their decision for surgery.

Sometimes parents, able to make many major decisions without undue anxiety, are immobilized at the recommendation for cardiac surgery, which seems to them, and indeed can be, a life-and-death matter. Among these are parents whose anxiety is a result of ignorance or confusion about the medical facts. These are people who function well under ordinary conditions of living. For them, clear and specific medical information, geared to their ability to grasp it, can often be sufficiently relieving to free them to make a decision. Sometimes, in addition to this, they need counseling help from the caseworker to evaluate the plan most genuinely protective both to the child and to the family in terms of the balance of gains to be achieved and reality-risks involved. We have already experienced evidences that the broadening campaign of public information in the field of cardiovascular surgery is lessening this particular problem.

Obviously, much more involved problems of personality and relationship can precipitate difficulty in making serious decisions about health problems in parents capable of making other decisions. Often, such anxiety reflects previous experience with an unfortunate aftermath of taking responsibility for close family, as for one parent who had urged his own mother to undergo surgery and she died despite it; or for another who on medical advice had hospitalized her mother in a psychiatric hospital and continued still to bear her mother's constant recrimination. These are situations where the parent is carrying excessive guilt as a result of past action which, however positive its motive, has felt to him like an act against his close relative. People who function essentially well in the usual responsibilities of daily living can often utilize counseling either in one interview or over an extended period to help them separate the present reality from the old situation. They can then carry a parental role in the present reality situation without infusions of old guilt. To do this, it is of course necessary to reopen with the upset parent the old situation contributing to the present confusion. Usually such consideration of the discrepancy between the parent's guilt feelings and the reality of the responsibility he carried and effects of his actions relieves the discomfort with which he has lived so long.

Decision-Making by Disturbed Parents

Thus far the parents described have been essentially well functioning people but who experience exaggerated reactions in health decisions. Parents with impaired integrative capacities have additional problems in coping with these reality decisions. Caught in their own difficulties in being adult and in being parents, they are apt to be immobilized by the anxiety engendered when they are required to make the decision about surgery. They often have a basic problem in taking responsibility for any major decision; with a secondary problem, often not secondary in its consequences, about which decision to make.

Our experience has shown the importance of careful casework evaluation of the problem in making the decision, and the hazard to personal adjustment and family balance that each alternative entails. Without such evaluation, it is possible to overlook the potential supportive values to the parent and to his ability to carry parental role in the experience of having assumed responsibility for constructive action to protect his child. On the other hand, in the absence of such evaluation, it is possible to exert undue pressure to make a decision which could disturb existing adjustments supportive in family life.

This difficulty in making any major decision involves distrust of one's own capacity as well as, in some instances, difficulty in trusting any outside person.[3] This is a problem reflecting so basic a difficulty with authority, self-image, and the weight of adult demands, that an attempt to deal directly with it could only further burden a person pressed by a high level of anxiety in daily living. A more hopeful approach with a potential for offering relief to such burdened people is often to focus on the doctor's essential responsibility for recommending the treatment method of choice under these particular medical circumstances. This entails the doctor's explanation in terms the parents can understand of the values to be achieved by surgery and its potential protections, as well as its risks, and the risks to be anticipated if surgery is not performed. Concurrently, the caseworker protects their defensive patterns, helping them protect the child through her identification both with them and with the medical decision, relieving them of the total burden of decision.

It would be helpful to examine further the nature of this kind of identification and help in choice, so often misconstrued as an extension of medical authority in a so-called *"host agency."*[4] As caseworkers, we know the supportive values to functioning and ego integration of enabling people to take action that bolsters self-image and respect for themselves. The parent who has by default, out of his own problem, not provided adequate protection for his child may well find it increasingly painful to live with his own sense of having failed his child should the anticipated difficulties develop. We are of no service if we sit alongside while he flounders and capitulates to his own weakness out of his own despair. As professional caseworkers, we would want to support basic defenses by enabling parents who need such help to act in ways consistent with what they and the community they live in value in parental protectiveness of children.

Other considerations apply when the problem in decision about cardiac surgery is a result of a pathological relationship between parents and child, an outgrowth, of course, of individual pathology in the parent. Sometimes severe disturbance is shown in extreme over-protection of the child. Sometimes the parent expresses directly, or indirectly, his problem in being a parent. Often, too, casework evaluation shows that he is acutely uncomfortable over his resentment about his child's handicap and the problems it created for him, and is afraid he may agree to surgery primarily to end his own discomfort. We have found it advisable, when indecision is an outgrowth of such a pathologically disturbed parent-child relationship, to defer direct consideration of the basic problem. To open this just when the parent must make a decision, often an urgent one, could create a double problem for him without in the least facilitating a decision.

In these situations some techniques that bypass the pathology at least for the time being have proved more directly relieving and effective. I have previously spoken of clarifying that the choice of medical treatment to be

[3] Maurice Levine, M.D., *Psychotherapy in Medical Practice*, The Macmillan Company, New York, 1945.
[4] Maxwell S. Frank, M.D., "Standards of a Social Service Program in a Hospital," *Journal of Jewish Communal Service*, Vol. XXXI, No. 1, Fall, 1954.

recommended belongs with the doctor. As in the situation previously referred to we provide casework support to the positive in the parent's self-image which wants to meet his own and community standards. We realize that this is also utilizing his existing guilt to the degree that instead of immobilizing him, it enables him to make a choice that will support his own way of functioning, family adjustments, and the child's needs.

Where we find that consideration of the parent-child problem does not assault defenses important to functioning, equilibrium, and existing family adjustments, it may be possible to enable the parent to consider additional help at an appropriate time following surgery. According to diagnostic judgment about the treatment-of-choice, the caseworker then helps him to utilize casework treatment for improvement of the family climate; or alternatively, psychiatric treatment. On the other hand, where it is found that this is likely to constitute a danger to equilibrium, the worker is careful to help him maintain the defenses that enable him to function.

A comparable, but somewhat different, approach has proved helpful where parents are so involved in marital conflict as to consider the needs of the child and what is to be done to help him as secondary. This degree of removal from the child's need reflects individual pathology in the parents. It may well be that decision cannot wait upon the parental determination of whether the home is to be maintained, on what terms, and at what cost. The worker instead handles the way in which the marital situation is interfering without attempting to work out the marital problem itself. Since these parents are virtually always aware of their marital conflict, such discussion is not usually assaultive to unconscious defenses. It is ordinarily possible to discuss directly that they are reacting out of their own marital problem, which is not relevant to the immediate decision on how best to protect the child. Frequently even parents at loggerheads can be helped to combine forces out of their common concern for their child who needs their strength. Help in relation to their marital problem can wait until the medical crisis is over.

In addition to the foregoing diagnostic consideration, help to parents in decision about cardiac surgery raises the question of whether one or both needs the help, and to what extent. During our initial casework process both parents are included, if available. Obviously, it is possible to have clarity on the pattern of family interaction only through discussion with both. In view of the responsibility involved in this decision, too, it is important that both parents participate so that neither carries the full burden. In addition, such diagnostic assessment determines whether both or either parent need ongoing casework help, and to what extent. It is also important when such a problem exists to determine whether it is predominantly the problem of one parent, or both. Although it is true in general that where only one parent is having difficulty in decision, the concentration of casework help is provided to him, we have found it important in the interest of family unity not to exclude the more comfortable parent. The extent to which the second parent is involved depends on the nature of the problem, as already indicated, the mutuality of decision vital to family cohesiveness, and the patterns of carrying responsibility customary to this couple.

Parenthetically, either parent may have difficulty in coping with the processes of recovery, and may need intensive help following surgery to encourage the child to modify activity timed with development in functional capacity.

This discussion so far has emphasized the responsibility parents carry for this decision for children. Ordinarily intensive casework help is not provided directly to the child, as a matter of philosophy and diagnostic thinking, since strengthening the parents to carry their role is more helpful to family living. Limited, highly focused direct help is given to the child usually under certain specific circumstances, as where a child is raising questions about what hospitalization and surgery will be like which the parent lacks experience to answer. The social worker is in a particularly good position to answer questions on admission procedure, physical setup, ward routines, life on the ward, and so on. Another example would be where despite apparently responsible parental handling the child himself is showing evidences of undue anxiety or discomfort for unknown reasons. In one such situation, for instance, casework interview directly with the child showed that he was troubled by his parent's explanation that he needed this treatment because something was wrong with the way his blood circulated. Although this had seemed a comprehensible and adequate explanation, he suffered from acute anxiety when blood was drawn for diagnostic tests. To him, the fact that at times important organs did not receive sufficient blood meant that the blood being drawn might be critical to a vital organ. With this misconception corrected by the doctor, his inappropriate anxiety subsided, and he could go along with the procedures with parental support. Finally, the caseworker may step in to provide direct help in preparation of the child for recommended surgery where diagnostic assessment shows the parents unable to help him sufficiently even with casework help to them. This may mean that they cannot do so even if surgery is scheduled sufficiently in advance to allow for this help; or alternatively that the medical urgency is such that it would be hazardous to the success of surgery to defer it to allow for the counseling help that would make this possible for the parents.

The Adolescent and the Decision for Surgery

The parental responsibility in decision about cardiac surgery is somewhat the same when the patient is an adolescent but has some additional considerations. These are specific to the fact that the adolescent is moving into a more adult role, increasing responsibility for his own life, well-being, and health care, and has more voice in decisions that affect him. Also, he cannot be humored or carried in for surgery against his will as a five year old can. Although it is still the parents' legal responsibility to make so vital a decision to health and well-being, the balance achieved between dependence and independence in family life in other aspects of living affects the balance in this decision too. Where the youngster is involved in acting out his rebellion against parental authority and controls the question of cardiac surgery can become an issue in the family battle. This is consistent with our experience in working with adolescents with cardiac or other handicaps apart from consideration of surgery. For instance, we have often found the cardiac condition utilized as a weapon in the parent-child relationship as when the parent erroneously uses the cardiac condition to reinforce his demand that the child keep appropriate hours or alternatively, when the child uses his cardiac status to demand special consideration not medically required.

Although our experience with adolescents undergoing such surgery has been limited, we have some observations to note. Among those we have worked with has been one group with good ego development, good capacity to cope with health problems, daily living, and relationships, well able to take on quite mature motivations.

> For one 16-year-old patient the risk of surgery was great, the outlook questionable. Limited all his life by a serious congenital heart difficulty, and threatened in essentially good functioning by steadily increasing disability, he was under strong inner stress when he migrated to America alone to join his newly married sister. He was in search of a cure and a future he could achieve here. Raised in institutions since his mother's death in his early childhood, he had been taught a code of values placing a great premium on independence, earning, and self-sufficiency. It was deeply disappointing to him that the doctors felt that surgery could offer only a limited prospect of stabilization or improvement of functioning with considerable risk to life and that they recommended instead intensive effort to achieve stablization through medical treatment and modification of activities to a point consistent with his real handicap.
>
> He reacted to this with some acting-out and testing-out, for the first time in his life as far as we could determine; but also with essential conformity and desire to achieve in whatever ways were possible. Casework support enabled him to see small ways in which he could contribute to his own slow improvement, even though it meant giving up some of his ambitious hopes. He could then use counseling help to make the adaptations in living his disability required—curtailed school hours, with limited school program, special transportation, considerable rest, with modified physical effort in sports and other physical outlets, and a salt-free diet. His ability to integrate recommendations so difficult for a boy his age, with his ambitions and life-goals, represented considerable strength, capacity and maturity. His religious background and education in institutions with a value-system stressing discipline and conformity were helpful to him in this difficult period. Unfortunately, his cardiac condition was so advanced that in spite of all protective measures it continued to deteriorate.
>
> When surgery was finally advised because of the imminent threat to life he swung to the hope of perfect results, expressing anxiety, indirectly, with some withdrawal symptoms. Since it was felt that this served a basically protective function for him, casework help at this point focussed on enabling him to raise some of his questions with the doctors, and hear their realistic information and the moderate improvement hoped for, as well as the risk of surgery. He could acknowledge the risk; express his indecision, take hold of the discussion of his own goals for himself, socially, educationally, and vocationally, and the

help in achieving them that even limited gains in surgery could afford him. His motivation for the surgery became more substantial and realistic, enabling him to tolerate the long preliminary hospitalization and the surgery itself. Within this period the older sister, acting in place of his parents, also needed service to help her in carrying responsibility for decision on surgery. Plans were made also to bring the father from his out-of-town home so that this young woman need not carry the entire burden for decision. This family was also helped to draw on their deep faith in God and in the Church to which they belonged. It was felt that this, and the availability to them within the hospital of a clergyman of their own faith, were supportive sources of inner strength which had helped them in many serious life situations.

Another significant group of youngsters were slowed up in emotional and social development, with family relationships at a level far below what is ordinarily expected at this age. Two patients, whose very dependent behavior and immature social adjustment seemed an outgrowth of seriously overprotective parental attitudes, present a sharp differential in casework diagnosis.

One 16-year-old girl, the only daughter of a family of new Americans, looked and acted much younger than her age. Her cardiac disability, diagnosed many years before as a congenital defect, had led to her becoming the center of family attention, to the detriment of her three brothers. Her parents had lost family during the war; survived concentration camp experience; and sustained great hardship in establishing themselves in this country. They limited this child, over whom they hovered anxiously, beyond medical recommendations; and her after-school social life in the rural area where they lived was confined essentially to the family group, since other visiting would have involved travel and planning. In this situation, the mother took over entire responsibility for decision. The youngster went along as a matter of course, denying conflict. The relationship-problems created by the utilization of the cardiac handicap by both family and patient emerged in her post-surgical hospital adjustment; when casework help could be given them.

Similar apparent immaturity in a 20-year-old girl, however, did not reflect as much individual and family disturbance, because close examination revealed the "excessive" parental limitations were cultural and reflected consistently the specific medical direction given them in Europe. We have felt that this imbalance in family roles, in which adolescents have not begun to participate in decisions affecting them, as is usual in our culture, can not be dealt with at the point of decision-making. At this point, it is a reality in family life to be accepted and worked with. While going along to some degree with the family's way of operating, we have utilized the requirement of some involvement of the adolescent himself to establish in a beginning way that as part of community expectations we expect from adolescents more participation than from small children.

With such help this 20-year-old girl could indicate the preponderance of desire for surgery together with her concern about it. Her anxiety, essentially extremely well contained, was manifested in her objections to the plan to transfer her from Medical Ward, where diagnosis was established, to Surgical Ward, where everyone would be strange. Because we believed her denial of some aspects of her anxiety protected her in carrying through a decision she wanted, casework activity did not break into this. Instead, we reviewed with her her various objectives for herself: fuller school than had yet been possible, a worklife perhaps in an office, ultimately a family of her own; and the ways in which cardiac surgery could contribute to these. She was taken to the surgery ward several times by the caseworker. She was helped to express her reaction to the impact of IV tubes, very ill patients, et cetera. She met a few patients prior to and after their surgery. She used the worker's help to see that for some days immediately post-operatively they were uncomfortable; but also to see how they could ambulate, feel better, eat normally after the initial post-operative period.

These situations have highlighted for us the importance of including both adolescent and family in decision about and preparation for surgery; the obvious importance of differential casework diagnosis; the values of surgery for helping the youngster achieve his own real wishes for himself, his steps toward adult responsibility, and his desire to join with his peer group in activities normal for his age.

We do not as yet have sufficient experience in cardiovascular surgery with the youngster in very early adolescence to feel that we can comment on some of the special features of work on this problem at this stage of development.

Adults and the Decision for Surgery

With children and adolescents, we have discussed the responsibility parents carry in making the decision for surgery. With adults, in contrast, the patient himself inevitably arrives at the ultimate decision, although key family members may, of course, have an important part in it. Important in consideration of casework help needed during the period of decision-making is evaluation of the nature of family balance and the pattern of family interaction and mobilization for problem-solving. This determines whether other family members besides the patient need casework help either because of the impact of the recommendation on them or because out of their concern they are possibly impeding the patient's use of his own vitality for decision on his own behalf.[5]

In our experience, the recommendation for cardiovascular surgery, whether for congenital cardiac anomaly or damage due to rheumatic fever, has usually been made long after the original medical diagnosis, and after many years of medical care and varying adjustments to this health problem. Where the impact of the recommendation is disorganizing to a patient's ability to decide, the practices previously discussed on provision of casework help to arrive at a sound decision apply. However, somewhat to our own surprise many of the patients have come requesting this surgery. Often we find that their hope in doing so was to achieve a complete cure. Sometimes, in their anxiety for a perfect result, they have been unable to consider the possibility of limited gains, and still less the chance that the doctors would

[5] David M. Levy, M.D., *Maternal Overprotection*, Columbia Press, New York, 1954.

not advise surgery. This blocking out can at times leave them totally un-prepared for the post-operative period, the length of convalescence and the protections required during it, the slow improvement in strength and functioning, and the possibility that they may still need to plan for com-promise-adjustments in work and in other activity.[6] Therefore we have considered this kind of apparent eagerness for surgery as unrealistic moti-vation, requiring casework help.

> One such person was a well-functioning man of 40, with a good stable marriage, and a great desire to fill protective roles to his wife and his children. Warned for many years of limited life-expectancy, he migrated to this country in search of a guarantee of normal life-span, full functioning, and good earning potential. Medical findings indicated that reparative surgery could offer only questionable results at its present stage of development; and con-tained serious risk to life. Prior to the doctor's decision against surgery, the worker was handling with him his all-or-nothing expectation, in an effort to cushion the blow should his expectations need to be modified; and to enable him to take in any differences between his own expectations from surgery and the medical realities. This was extremely useful when final medical recom-mendation was that surgery should not be undertaken for the present. During his reaction of discouragement and hopelessness, this could be drawn on. It enabled him to recover equilibrium sufficiently to take steps in working out plans with us whereby his family and his medical condition could both be protected until a later point when surgery was recommended and performed. These plans involved a service to his wife so that she could take on some new responsibilities in the family store. Because of the essentially sound family relationships, she was sufficiently together with him in the whole process of adjustment to medical recommendation so that only this limited service was necessary to her.

The situation is somewhat different when a marriage has been stabilized on the basis of neurotic interaction.

> The L's, a new American couple in their late thirties, were quite panicky when new symptomatology in Mrs. L required hospitalization, with suspected recurrence of old rheumatic fever. Their usual defensive adaptation, with Mr. L turning to Mrs. L to share his problems and to make family decisions, were not conducive to the protection of the defenses she needed to carry through medical treatment, workup, and possible consideration of cardio-vascular surgery. Actually, his sharing of each medical statement raised anxiety undermining the ability she needed to remain in full control. Her own adjustment was already under assault from the reactivation of wartime and concentration-camp traumata that we so often find in the hospitalized patient with this background; and she could not tolerate this additional pressure from Mr. L. Casework service to her concentrated on reinforcement of the current reality that she was getting good medical care and individualized concern in supporting her hopeful outlook. This made it possible to separate the current situation from the reactivated fears of traumatic, experimental medical care in the hostile concentration-camp setting. In order to make this possible the worker provided Mr. L the support he needed and that Mrs. L could temporarily not sustain. For a time, therefore, he brought his questions,

---

[6] James L. Halliday, M.D., *Psychosocial Medicine—A Study of the Sick Society*, W. W. Norton & Company, Inc., New York, 1948.

anxieties, and discussion of each report to the worker, holding back from his wife as his contribution to her well-being. This enabled them to carry through under the pressures of the period prior to decision about surgery.

There is one other factor requiring comment. This is the problem arising in the occasional situation when surgery is essential to the patient's welfare, and yet would have undesirable consequences for the entire family.

In one such case, the patient's long use of multiple chronic physical illnesses to control other family members was such that she would be likely to utilize cardiac surgery to fixate complaints and symptoms and clutch even more tightly at her husband in ways that might well disrupt the marriage both wanted to preserve. In such a situation, when neither psychiatry nor casework service is considered hopeful in stablizing or improving the emotional and relationship pathology, it is necessary for the team to decide which of the limited goals available has the most to offer the family. Where surgery is recommended as essential, casework with the patient and the family members is focused on enabling them to consider the meaning of the recommendation in terms of its life-preserving value. Following surgery, casework help would continue to minimize anticipated disequilibrium and to support those factors that have stablizing effects.

Interaction of the Cardiovascular Team

In our program the decision for cardiovascular surgery is a medical one, since this procedure is considered non-elective and is undertaken only to prolong life or increase functioning in an otherwise deteriorating condition. The caseworker participates in team diagnosis and treatment planning because of the hospital's experience that surgery, successful though it may be without casework, for some patients fails of its objective for one of two reasons. Sometimes the adult, whether patient or parent, in his own panic, runs from necessary medical care. This is quite different from decision against medical recommendation based on due consideration of what the alternatives involve. Secondly, the patient sometimes fails to make the anticipated gains in daily living. Casework is therefore planned to prevent this breakdown.

Without going into detailed discussion of the team's composition and organization, suffice it to say that it represents a variety of diagnostic and treatment personnel, medical, surgical, casework, and, where necessary, psychiatric and other specialities with a structured group meeting on regular schedule and carrying out clearly established procedures. As part of the presentation of diagnostic findings prior to recommendation on surgery, the caseworker discusses her psychosocial findings and recommendations as they relate to this problem. Since increasingly all team members within their training and practice have some knowledge of growth and development, the casework contribution is focused on filling in the gap between the personal and family adjustment, and the functioning they convey to the doctor together with the underlying dynamics and relationships. Such casework material is consistently related to the problem under consideration and the outlook for adjustment and rehabilitation.

Within the ensuing team discussion the caseworker carries professional responsibility for interacting with the other team members. This ensures that final team decisions as to whether surgery is to be done, when it is to be done, and the preceding preparation by treatment personnel include the highly individual knowledge and the specifics of treatment responsibility of casework, as well as of the other disciplines within the team.

As part of her activity in team interaction she makes recommendations about the preparatory process, the casework help patient and family will need to make a valid decision, the timing of surgery to allow for this in the absence of medical contra-indications, and what is foreseen at this point is likely to be needed in the process of convalescence and rehabilitation.

Discussion of the preparatory process may include how the doctor's explanation and discussion with the patient, and sometimes the family, can be related to their level of comprehension and pattern of integration. Sometimes we recommend inclusion of a key person in family decisions within the initial explanation. In one such case, a woman depended excessively on her learned father for major decisions, bypassing her husband at times within this. It was decided on casework recommendation that the doctor could be most helpful to this family in arriving at a decision they could sustain by discussing the recommendations jointly with the father, who was the family symbol of authority, as well as the husband, who had the right to be included in decisions about his wife. In this situation a separate three-way discussion among the doctor, patient, and caseworker was indicated to protect the patient from the unnecessary anxieties likely to arise from her family's fears and questions.

At other times, the team considers how medical findings can be explained in ways the family can grasp in view of the caseworker's findings on family intelligence, education, sophistication, and culturally determined attitudes and values. In one particular situation, the father of a seven-year-old youngster presented himself to the world as an assured, capable professional man. Casework findings were that he became extremely anxious about permitting the child to judge for himself when he was over-tired as the doctors had previously recommended. He therefore over-limited the youngster for fear of over-taxing him. This knowledge enabled our doctors to set up a program of sharing all subsequent medical information in specific terms, taking responsibility for defining permissible and prohibited activities within the general limits possible.

The other major part of this initial team decision in which casework evaluation and recommendation have useful bearing is the question of timing of surgery. Obviously, where immediate surgery is essential, this takes priority. In such situations the worker has to modify quickly her own desire to recommend deferring it from the point of view of emotional readiness and family circumstances. However, even where surgery is urgent, our doctors assure us that usually the caseworker does have at least some limited time to provide highly focused help. It is, of course, more comfortable for the worker, then the time-wait can be closely geared to the process of consolidating decision soundly for this individual family unit. In the situations already reviewed in teams, deferment of surgery has been decided upon for periods up to a year to allow for casework help or psychotherapy or both. Such an extended delay would ordinarily involve a situation where surgery is vital and there are serious blocks in the ability of patient and family to integrate this recommendation sufficiently for a constructive decision.

Finally, we have found it useful in working with children to establish a regular procedure for the caseworker to participate in the conference among the doctor, parents, and sometimes the child, in which the team recommendation is discussed. This serves the multiple purpose of helping the family clarify questions they have difficulty in presenting and of providing a point of reference in future casework service where families out of their own anxiety distort what they were told. This is something we may well want to consider for patients of other age groups as well.

Conclusion

This paper has reported the experience of social service within the cardiovascular surgery team at Beth Israel Hospital, in the area of cardiac surgery which is relatively recent in medical care. It has discussed the functioning of the caseworker within the team while the possibility of cardiac surgery is being evaluated and her role with the patient or family needing help to make a decision about it. Some differentials both in casework diagnosis and in provision of casework service have been reviewed. It is hoped that with more experience, it will be possible to refine further criteria determining differentials in the processes of helping patients and their families face with more assurance the problems of cardiovascular surgery.

Casework with the Deaf: A Problem in Communication

Steven K. Chough

The caseworker dealing with the deaf client faces a frustrating problem regardless of the agency with which he is affiliated. The difficulty in communication is a paramount problem in any social work service for the deaf. In practice, the caseworker as well as the psychiatrist, psychologist, physician, rehabilitation counselor, or other professional is faced with the problem of communication and its distortion at every step in his work with the deaf client. The natural result is difficulty in understanding the client as a person, his problems, his feelings, and his potential strengths. The importance of communication cannot be overemphasized. Without communication the client-worker relationship cannot be established and help cannot be given.

It is difficult to discuss or describe the "typical" deaf person, because people who are termed deaf may vary widely in the degree of hearing loss, methods of communication used, their attitudes toward their deafness, and many other factors. They experience and interpret culturally engendered frustrations or gratifications according to their own personality and developmental history. It is, therefore, not advisable to assume that all deaf persons face the same kind of problems or respond to these problems in the same way. Perhaps emphasis should be placed on the principle that deaf persons are just people and, as such, are subject to the same problems as the unhandicapped.

Keeping this variability in mind, one can note certain general characteristics in terms of "deafness." There is, perhaps, a communicative difference among those who are deaf at birth or become deaf in early childhood, those who become progressively deaf because of gradual loss of hearing in later life, and those who become deaf suddenly in adulthood. The distinction among the communicative ability in these three categories of the deaf is too complex to discuss here. For the purposes of this paper the term "deaf persons" is used to describe both those totally deaf from birth or early childhood and those partially deaf or hard-of-hearing who are unable to understand normal conversation.

Reprinted with permission of the author and the National Association of Social Workers, from *Social Work*, Vol. 9, No. 4 (October, 1964), pp. 76–82.

It is estimated that today there are approximately 250,000 deaf children and adults in this country. "In a representative crowd of 700 Americans, we find no more than one who is deaf."[1] The deaf pass unnoticed and are pretty much lost in the general mass of people. "They have no *visible* characteristics that set them apart. They generally become known only as communication demands reveal their severe disability."[2]

In social work literature, authors discussing work with the deaf usually have focused on persons with partial hearing loss and on communication through the use of a hearing aid; the communication problem in work with severely deaf clients and the need for skills in communicating with them have received little attention. There is a possibility that much is missed with the deaf client in any social agency or health facility when communication is limited. It is hoped that this article, dealing with the effect of communication obstacles, various methods of communication used by the deaf, and the need for skills in communication, will be of some help to social workers in recognizing and dealing with the communication problem in order that the casework method may be utilized with the deaf. When a caseworker is mentioned in this paper, reference is being made to one who himself is a hearing person.

Effect of Communication Obstacles

One of the most basic needs of human beings is to communicate with others.[3] Each of us is aware of the fact that communication is not only the key to intellectual comprehension but also a medium for the expression of feelings and emotions. Dr. Rose Spiegel states:

> Communication is a dynamic process—an experience in itself and also the gateway to other experience. Communication not only is a psychobiologic means, it is also an end—a process whose fulfillment brings its own gratification.[4]

She continues by saying that communication is a process that has, in a sense, some of the quality of growth and maturation, because a person has been shaped as a personality by his specific life experience in communication with others. Of significance, too, is the statement of Dr. Jurgen Ruesch, an outstanding authority on communication in psychiatry, to the effect that

> since man needs a certain amount of gratifying communication in his life in order to learn, to grow, and to function in a group, all events that significantly curtail communication eventually will produce serious disturbance.[5]

[1] Boyce R. Williams and Elizabeth A. Chase, "Deafness: New Approaches," *Rehabilitation Record* (November–December, 1960), p. 17.

[2] *Ibid.*

[3] Robert L. Sharoff, M.D., "Enforced Restriction of Communication: Its Implications for the Emotional and Intellectual Development of the Deaf Child," *American Journal of Psychiatry*, Vol. 116 (November, 1959), p. 445.

[4] "Specific Problems of Communication in Psychiatric Conditions," in Silvano Arietti, ed., *American Handbook of Psychiatry*, Vol. 1 (New York: Basic Books, 1960).

[5] "General Theory of Communication in Psychiatry," in Silvano Arietti, ed., *op. cit.*

Helmer R. Myklebust, a psychologist specializing in work with the deaf at Northwestern University, explains that

> man is highly dependent on his senses. Through his senses come the sensations which contribute to his experience. Upon the information he receives from his senses he builds his world, his world of perception and conception; of memory, imagination, thought, and reason.[6]

The ordinary infant does not first learn how to read but learns to comprehend and use the spoken word; he acquires auditory language. Dr. Edna S. Levine, an authority on psychology of the deaf with rich experience in working with deaf children and their parents, mentions Sigmund Freud as having acknowledged the importance of hearing in the metaphor "ego wears an auditory lobe."[7] Language, depending to a large extent on hearing, is the form that conveys ideas or messages, especially in interpersonal relations. "The existence of speech and language for all human beings seems to be bound to the human propensity for symbol-making."[8] Many scholars have long declared that without language human nature almost ceases to exist. Language is, it is seen clearly, the symbolic reservoir of the feelings, emotions, ideas, attitudes, and motives that are involved in the expression and perception of human experience and behavior.

The emotional development of the deaf, then, can scarcely remain unaffected by the barrier to comprehension. When a deaf child attempts to learn all aspects of language, an auditory sense deprivation limits to a large extent the world of experience. Since learning language, including reading, is initially a matter of hearing, the deaf child in school must work much harder than the hearing child to remember and memorize. Because of the language deficiency created by this sense of deprivation, the deaf child is faced with difficulty in understanding what is put before him and has trouble expressing himself. His vocabulary is built slowly and may be limited. It can be concluded that the lack of language is a great obstacle to thinking itself and to psychosocial maturation. It is, however, a serious mistake to assume that the imperfect language used by a deaf person means defective mental ability.

> An inability to communicate creates barriers to the satisfaction of basic needs. Since the individual's well-being depends in large part on his ability to satisfy his own need harmoniously with the needs of others, the deafened person may experience considerable frustration both from inner, emotional sources and from outer, social situations.[9]

The majority of deaf persons have learned from experience that they cannot avoid meeting further frustration in communication. Because of difficulty in, or in some instances lack of, means of communication there

---

[6] *The Psychology of Deafness* (New York: Grune & Stratton, 1960), p. 1.
[7] *The Psychology of Deafness* (New York: Columbia University Press, 1960), p. 25.
[8] Spiegel, *op. cit.*, p. 917.
[9] Esther W. Fibush, "The Problem of Hearing Loss," *Social Casework*, Vol. 36, No. 3 (March, 1955), p. 125.

can be nothing for some but a life of deprivation, loneliness, and dissatisfaction. It is difficult for the deaf to communicate their problems, their frustrations, their needs, and their hopes.

> In addition, they are apt to be sensitively aware of their own shortcomings, and even more so of the indifference and misconceptions of the hearing world about the need and problem of the deaf.[10]

Sharoff warns parents of deaf children not to restrict them from expressing themselves through natural communication, because such restriction can affect their ability to grow to emotional and social maturity.[11]

When deaf persons' communication with hearing persons becomes extremely frustrating, they are apt to seek ways of defending themselves by withdrawing or aggressively controlling the exchange of conversation. However, for them the real problem is not deafness in itself but the fact of living in a hearing world. Actually they live in mental isolation and suffer the lack of healthy socialization. Most of them are uninformed and misinformed about many things pertaining to the hearing world and even to the deaf world.

Methods of Communication

The communication methods used widely by the deaf in this country are speech, lip-reading, writing, finger-spelling, and sign language. Speech and lip-reading are referred to as "oral communication," sign language and finger-spelling as "manual communication."

Finger-spelling or the manual alphabet is defined as "the regular letters of the alphabet formed by standard positions of the fingers of one hand, and words and sentences are thus spelled out in straight language."[12] Sign language refers to "an ideographic method of expression in which words and ideas are graphically formulated through codified gestures of the arms, hands, and body aided by facial expression."[13] While the characteristics of the sign language are more colorful, lively, and dramatic than other means of communication, it has some disadvantages, especially those of grammatical disorder, illogical systems, difficult expression of abstract ideas, and linguistic confusion.

The combination of oral and manual communication is referred to as "the simultaneous method" or "multiple communication." This is characterized by the use of the sign language and finger-spelling, with the individuals at the same time speaking. By "speaking" is meant either vocalization or movement of the lips without actual speech. In practice, when a hearing person, while using manual communication, speaks, the deaf person to whom he is talking can read his lip movements while watching his hands

[10] Levine, *op. cit.*, p. 40.
[11] Sharoff, *op. cit.*, pp. 443–446.
[12] Levine, *op. cit.*, p. 321.
[13] Levine, *loc. cit.*

as well. When the latter speaks aloud while using manual communication, the hearing person can listen to him. If the deaf person speaks inaccurately or unclearly, the hearing person can move his eyes quickly to the other's hands, picking up his meaning from the sign language and finger-spelling. Understanding the deaf individual's speech depends upon both his ability to speak and the hearing person's familiarity with the speech of the deaf; it is probably best for the later to watch the manual communication as well.

Finger-spelling has some advantages over sign language, especially in that it permits use of the names of people and places, technical or abstract words, and certain words that cannot be expressed by sign language. Its major values are accuracy and exactness. To many deaf persons, however, telling a story or listening to it through the manual alphabet only is slow, dull, colorless, and emotionless. They prefer a combination of sign language and finger-spelling to any one of the other methods. A number of the deaf, as well as the hard-of-hearing, can read lips and speech with amazing skill. The oral method is a desirable medium for those who can understand normal conversation. Unfortunately, though, the majority of the deaf are poor in speech and lip-reading. Just as many people do not have a natural ability in music, many deaf persons do not have a natural talent in the art of lip-reading.

Casework services with the deaf through written communication can be successful but are available to a limited number of highly intelligent deaf persons. Many deaf people confess a difficulty in comprehension when this method is used, admitting that they usually guess at meanings on the basis of familiar words. Just as hearing people prefer oral or spoken communication to written communication, so do almost all deaf people prefer manual communication. The written method seldom can express the emotional tones the worker needs to grasp, and the slowness of this method may affect the flow of ideas and feelings. The less formal education the deaf client has received, the more difficulty the worker may have in communicating with him through the written method alone.

The author agrees with Levine's statement:

> Manual conversation eases the strain of lip-reading and talking in prolonged interviews and enables the subject to relax somewhat while still continuing to converse. This is a particularly important consideration in cases of emotional disturbance, in which the writer has noted a preference for manual communication even on the part of habitual oralists.[14]

In the simultaneous method, if a deaf person misses a word or a statement on the lips, he always has the manual method to fall back on, because manual communication is perceived more adequately than lip movements.

> Even the most expert lip-reader is grateful for the larger visual area presented by the hands when used along with speech. . . . The average deaf person finds himself watching the lips, with his peripheral vision getting assurance from the

[14] Levine, *op. cit.*, p. 166.

hands that he is not missing anything. In this manner we have a communication procedure that is exact and free from guesswork.[15]

In addition, multiple communication can be of great value in developing speech and improving skills in lip-reading.

Need for Communication Skills

Few social workers are trained in the skills necessary for social service to the deaf; still fewer know how to cope with the communication problem in actual practice. Also, hearing workers frequently encounter a feeling of uselessness and hopelessness when assigned to help deaf clients with whom they feel they cannot communicate. Because of the unusual communication skills necessary, the social worker with the deaf has been limited in utilizing his usual knowledge and skill. He cannot talk with the client.

Because of lack of adequate communication, few deaf clients and patients are able to describe themselves or their needs adequately. How can the caseworker encourage the essential dignity and self-worth of these deaf clients? How can they be helped to develop and utilize their strengths? How can they be helped to feel like useful and adequate citizens in the community? How may they be assured of a worker who has both an understanding of and appreciation for the problems of the deaf? If communication is recognized as a prime factor in the caseworker-client relationship, how, then, can the simultaneous method be used by a worker to help the deaf improve their social functioning?

The following is an example of how deaf clients suffer because of communication obstacles and of how they can be helped through use of multiple communication with the caseworker.

Mrs. A was a congenitally deaf woman with two children. Because the father had been out of the home for some time she had received Aid to Families with Dependent Children for six years. An earlier caseworker, unable to communicate with her even through writing because of her limited education, had obtained the sparse social information in her case record from her children and other relatives. Little or nothing was known about Mrs. A's feelings or her perception of her situation. She had been severely isolated much of her life, and limited social and educational experience had followed a traumatic childhood.

Early work with Mrs. A was educational, not traditional casework. She was helped to understand the standardized sign language, improve her knowledge of English and of basic mathematics, and learn to tell time with the aid of a special type of clock. She was encouraged to go out of the house, to use public transportation, and to risk herself in socialization with other deaf people. Eventually she was able to move into a rehabilitation program, learn a trade, and accept employment in competitive industry. Communication with this client was not easy, but the use of the sign language combined with finger-spelling permitted the exchange of thoughts and ideas necessary in the educative and casework process.

[15] Mervin D. Garretson, "The Need for Multiple Communication Skills in the Educative Process of the Deaf," *The Banner*, published by the North Dakota School for the Deaf, Vol. 72 (March, 1963), p. 3.

Some of the general psychosocial factors prevailing among the deaf should be considered. After graduating from a school for the deaf, a great number of deaf persons tend to maintain association with other deaf people through various organizations of the deaf. Their tendency to seek social satisfaction from other deaf persons rather than from hearing people has given rise to a complicated social system. Many deaf persons, although desiring to seek out other deaf people, may for various reasons be unable to do so, leaving them no choice but to withdraw and live in a world of loneliness.

Some clients seems to feel ashamed or uncomfortable in asking help from social agencies, especially the public welfare agency, because they regard their need for public assistance and casework help as an indication of failure. Since deaf people constitute a small group in any given city, they may know almost every other deaf individual, and are likely to feel uncomfortable in the presence of other deaf people if they are known as recipients of public assistance. Capable deaf people have great pride in their own achievements and abilities. More specifically, as a class they are proud of their economic independence. Consequently, many of them are highly critical of deaf recipients of public assistance or have little respect for them. Such facts discourage economically deprived deaf clients from seeking out other deaf people socially. The social worker needs to be sharply aware of this psychology of the deaf in relation to their stereotyped concepts of social work.

Suggestions for Caseworkers

In work with hearing-impaired clients, as well as all hearing clients, the caseworker endeavors to help them lead a useful and satisfying life. The worker should remind himself that he is not treating a deaf client as a disabled person but as a human being whose disability is an integral part of his personality.

The caseworker should accept the deaf client as he is and help him maintain his self-respect and personal dignity. He needs to be able to "give and take" freely with all types of deaf clients in order to establish rapport. He then will be able to enable them to bring out the important feelings, their hopes, and the significant aspects of their lives that they may have had difficulty sharing with others.

Caseworkers can help hearing-impaired clients a great deal through arranging for medical examinations, the purchase of hearing aids, and planning for auditory and speech training. However, it is an erroneous conclusion that a hearing aid and remedial training will soon put everything to rights. Those who are hard of hearing or have a speech defect may need much more help than a hearing aid can give them. What is important in considering any casework service are:

1.   Assessing the factors in the deaf client's personal and social development.

2.   Assisting him on the basis of this assessment, in coming to grips with the reality of his problem and in helping him work toward personally acceptable and realistic goals.

3.   Helping him in locating and using various resources in the community.

4.   Assisting, when necessary, in coordinating the various services available to him in his rehabilitation program.

When the hearing caseworker begins working with the deaf, he is apt to seek a third person who is capable of interpreting for the deaf client. It is not easy, however, for the worker to gain rapport with the client with a third person present. When the interpreter is a parent or other relative, it may be especially difficult for the worker, because the person may perform the role of collaborator by talking *about* rather than *for* the deaf client. In such interviews there is always the danger of the interview becoming a conversation between the worker and the interpreter. It should be kept in mind that the caseworker is responsible for maintaining the focus on the deaf client, not on the interpreter. When the hearing-impaired client gains confidence in the worker though skilled communication, he will often prove to be a highly co-operative interviewee.

The manual alphabet is the unified, standardized method all over this country, but in the sign language there are many "dialects" in different areas, just as in oral communication used by hearing people. In addition to mastering the sign language together with finger-spelling, the worker may need to master dialects as much as possible. When he is faced with unfamiliar gestures used by the deaf interviewee, he may ask him what is meant. The deaf client will usually be glad to explain, for he can thereby feel useful. Too much help requested of the client by the worker may, however, affect the role expectations of each and alter the relationship.

When the caseworker needs to obtain information about a deaf client from other persons, the deaf client must know why the worker wishes to see others, and what purpose will be served. The client should participate to the extent that he gives the worker permission to obtain the information and the worker discusses with him how important other people can be in relation to a better understanding of his situation.

In the case of a joint or family interview while the deaf interviewee is present, the caseworker should continuously let him know precisely what is being discussed. If the client wants to say something, the interviewer should break off his discussions with the other persons and listen to him or explain as well as he can exactly what they are discussing. It should be realized that the deaf client has learned in the most heartbreaking way how to wait. Keeping him involved in the caseworker's thinking and planning will help greatly in breaking down his isolation and impassiveness and enable him to develop more desire to participate in the casework plan.

Summary

The most significant need in the successful practice application of social work with the deaf is the recognition that the great barrier in communication is the first problem encountered by hearing caseworkers new to work with the deaf. In the usual interview situation, the client has a chance to tell his own story in his own way and the worker has an opportunity to hear his problems, needs, and feelings as the client expresses them. On the other hand, there seems to be an inability or natural reluctance on the part of a hearing caseworker unfamiliar with the deaf to overcome the communication obstacles that exist. There is apparently an equal inability on the part of deaf clients to tell their story to the uneasy and awkward interviewer.

As the casework relationship with the deaf client is developed, the worker learns how he feels about his hearing loss and his unsolved problems and finds the range of his motivations, capacities, and opportunities in the process of the social diagnosis and treatment. Deaf people usually place their confidence in a hearing worker who is skillful in multiple communication and who has acquired an understanding and appreciation of the general problems of the deaf. The caseworker, therefore, is urged to learn these communication skills so that he can talk with the deaf in the most relaxing way. As Ruesch has stated:

> If we attempt to explore the secrets of psychotherapy, we invariably fall back upon its first and most important requirement—that, in addition to the patient, there must be another person present who is accessible and visible, who can be talked to, and who is ready to understand and to respond. Once interpersonal feedback is established, the exchange elicits in the patient the sensation of pleasure. To be acknowledged is pleasant; to be understood is gratifying; to be understanding and to agree is exciting. This gratification becomes the driving force which induces the patient to seek further improvement.[16]

Caseworkers who work directly with deaf clients or patients are much in need of preliminary preparation, as are any professionals who specialize in new fields. It is suggested that there should be at least one caseworker trained to communicate with the deaf in a large agency or hospital in which deaf recipients are helped or are designed to be helped. Where can he learn the sign language and finger-spelling? There are many available sign language facilities provided by schools for the deaf and by city clubs, state associations, religious organizations, and fraternal orders for the deaf. The period of learning manual communication depends to a great extent upon the individual's ability and motives, ranging from several months to several years. It must be realized that learning manual communication is an art, just as is learning any foreign language.

It is hoped that the hearing social worker who is confronted with the problem of communicating with deaf clients will use his skills and make a

---

[16] Ruesch, *op. cit.*, p. 904.

real effort to help the clients achieve mutually acceptable and realistic goals. While skill in communication is but one phase of the casework process, it is an extremely important one, basic to the application of other aspects of the casework method. If the significance of adequate communication with the deaf is realized by social workers, more deaf clients may accomplish the reality and gratification of full citizenship.

The Diabetic Client

Mary W. Engelmann

Diabetes Mellitus is a common disease in North America. In Canada alone there are approximately 200,000 known diabetics. This figure will undoubtedly increase as detection methods improve, and as greater medical knowledge enables diabetics to enjoy longer and healthier lives. Social workers in both medical settings and community agencies can expect to see more individuals with this chronic condition in the future.

At first glance it would not seem that this handicap is particularly serious. Diabetes does not have a marked effect on the victim's appearance and no stigma is attached to it. The well-regulated diabetic can, with few exceptions, participate in most activities and he meets with relatively little discrimination in job-seeking.[1] Is it necessary then for the social worker— whether in a medical setting or not—to be concerned about the implications of this handicap? The answer can be found by examining the illness more closely.

In diabetes, more than in any other chronic illness, there is a delicate interplay between the victim's emotional life and satisfactions and his ability to live with and control his condition. The requirements for adequate diabetic control can affect the person's attitude to himself and his inter-personal relationships. Much depends on the previously existing personality patterns of the individual and the interaction of his family life. Those persons who have made reasonably satisfactory adjustments find it easier to cope with diabetes, though even in the best of circumstances, there are periods of stress, anxiety and anger. For the person with problems, whether emotional or environmental, diabetes can be particularly upsetting and difficult.

---

[1] A. H. Kantrow, M.D., "Employment Experiences of Juvenile Diabetics", *Diabetes*, Vol. 10 (1961), pp. 476–481. This article is a report on a survey of the employment experiences of the alumni of the camp for diabetic children in New York.

Reprinted from *The Social Worker*, Vol. 35 (February, 1967), pp. 6–10, by permission of the author and publisher.

Emotional Health and Control

An understanding of the interaction between emotional health and diabetic control, along with an understanding of some of the specific anxieties and problems encountered by the diabetic, should enable the social worker to assist him more skillfully.

There are varying degres of diabetic severity. The older individual who develops diabetes generally has a milder form of the illness and his diabetes can be controlled through diet alone, or through diet and oral medication. In a person under forty years of age, diabetes is generally more severe, requires insulin therapy, and is often much more difficult to control.

Diabetes and Emotional Stress

While diabetes is generally considered to be an inherited condition, due to a metabolic defect, there is some indication that it can be precipitated by emotional stress. Some studies suggest that the onset of diabetes may have been preceded by a period of deprivation, particularly loss of emotional support, unconscious conflict and depression.[2] Obviously, in such situations, the individual is weakened in his ability to cope with the meaning of the diagnosis. The new diabetic may be shocked, frightened, and even have moments of panic. He may feel a sense of despair because he faces a lifelong incurable condition. The amount of technical information he must absorb about diet and insulin therapy can seem overwhelming, and he may have doubts about his ability to care for himself. Along with this great increase in anxiety can come feelings of inadequacy and insecurity as he is faced with the awareness of physical limitation, dependency on insulin and continuous medical supervision.

Parents of a diabetic child have many of the same reactions as the adult diabetic, and often have a great sense of guilt. Irrational feelings of having neglected their child, or of having passed on a hereditary defect are present in almost every instance. The parents of a diabetic child are often overwhelmed by the technical information given them. Parents, at such a time, need the opportunity to discuss their anxiety and receive supportive help in developing their strengths and capabilities.

Diabetes is controlled through a therapeutic regime consisting of a restricted diet, insulin injections, and regular exercise. Adequate rest and regularity in meals are important. As it is a condition which must be regulated on a day-to-day basis, diabetes must be controlled by the patient

---

[2] P. F. Slawson, M.D., W. K. Flynn, M.D., E. J. Kollar, M.D., "Psychological Factors Associated with the Onset of Diabetes Mellitus,"*JAMA—Journal of the American Medical Association*, Vol. 185, No. 3 (1963), pp. 96–100. E. Weiss and O. W. English, *Psychosomatic Medicine, A Clinical Study of Psychophysiologic Reactions*, 3rd Edition 1957, pp. 334–335.

himself or, in the case of a young child, by his parents. The doctor can determine the initial regulation, can advise, and can help in illness or emergency situations, but the diabetic himself is responsible for the actual treatment.

Emotional upsets, in addition to illness, will have a definite physiological effect, actually raising the blood sugar level, thereby adding to an already complicated job.[3] Diabetic coma and insulin reactions are two serious and immediate complications which can develop. In the former, the blood sugar level becomes too high, and the person loses consciousness after a period of time. In the latter, which can come on suddenly, the blood sugar level drops too low, and causes aberrant behaviour and, in the latter stages, results in unconsciousness. Both if untreated, can lead to death.

Control Can Create Resentment

What meaning does this have for the diabetic individual and his family? The diabetic cannot "adjust" to his diabetes and forget about it. In order to control it effectively, he and his family must be constantly aware of and concerned about it. This situation can create resentment and irritation. The other members of the family find that, at times, their lives and social activities are limited by the diabetic's need to adhere to his regime. For children and adolescents this regime will add to already incipient feelings of being different. Diabetic women may have added concerns about their adequacy as it is difficult for them to carry pregnancies to completion. It is obvious that, even in the best of circumstances, there are going to be periods of rebellion, frustration and resentment.

In a disturbed situation diabetes can add to an already charged atmosphere and be used by both the diabetic and his family in an attempt to solve neurotic conflicts. The diabetic regime can become the focus for arguments which usually reflect existing and more deep-rooted personality conflicts. The anger and frustration that all diabetics and their families feel will be exacerbated, added to more basic hostility, and reflected in destructive ways towards self and others. This can result in the diabetic's denial of the illness and in a lack of adequate concern, manifested in deliberate over-eating or neglect of insulin requirements. In this way the diabetic can control, and indirectly hurt, his family. As he becomes ill, he gains attention and sympathy but, at the same time, adds to his guilt feelings of being a burden. All of this can create a vicious cycle of anger, illness, guilt and depression. The immature, dependent diabetic may use his poorly controlled diabetes and resulting illness as a way of meeting his emotional needs.

[3] D. G. Prugh, "Psychophysiological Aspects of Inborn Errors of Metabolism," in H. I., V. F., and N. R. Lief (eds.), *The Psychological Basis of Medical Practice*, New York, Harper & Row, 1963, p. 421.

Personality Patterns in Diabetes

Some observers say that dependent, passive behaviour is a frequent personality pattern in diabetes. Their views are summarized by Dr. David Hawkins:

> While a wide variety of individual personality patterns are seen in diabetes, clinicians have over and over commented on the frequency of marked passivity, masochism, extreme oral dependency, and frequent retreats into illness in these patients. Rosen and Lidz noted that the refractory diabetic patient "reacted to sibling rivalry by regressively seeking maternal attention by becoming helpless and demanding or negativistic rather than through more active measures". It is easy to see that this illness with its emphasis on diet would facilitate regression to whatever oral dependent behaviour was potentially present in the patient, and there is considerable evidence that in many individuals a passive dependent character structure antedated the onset of the clinical disease. Mirsky postulates that there is an inborn, metabolic problem from birth, even though signs and symptoms of the disease do not become manifest until later, and that this interferes with the development of a confident and mature outlook.[4]

Other observers emphasize that these diabetic personality patterns are the result of and not the cause of the disease. Doctors Philip Isenberg and Donald Barnett, in writing about the personality of the juvenile diabetic say the following:

> What we have outlined above suggests that there are bound to be certain similarities in the group of diabetic children because of the traumatic effect of the onset of the disease on most families. The persistent vulnerabilities and character trends which have been studied and reported on are probably the consequence of the disease and not its cause. What has been reported is a certain suppression of emotions, a feeling of being oppressed by a frustrating outer world which forces the patients to subordinate themselves to its demands. As a group they feel somewhat restricted and have been shown to be less spontaneous and free in the expression of their emotions and fantasies. Since therapy aims to control the disease by imposing restrictions on diet and requiring certain routines to be fulfilled many claim this tends to increase the feelings of being oppressed and frustrated.[5]

Insulin injections can carry implications of self-punishment or self-multilation to the diabetic. If injections must be given by a member of the family, similar fears with consequent guilt can result for the nondiabetic. The strict regime may carry the implication of punishment and authority and may reactivate in the diabetic earlier unresolved conflicts.[6] Diet restriction may be linked in the individual's mind to a restriction of love

[4] D. Hawkins, M.D., "Emotions and Metabolic and Endocrine Disease," Lief, *op. cit.*, pp. 274–275.

[5] P. Isenberg, M.D., and D. M. Barnett, M.D., "Psychological Problems in Diabetes Mellitus", *The Medical Clinics of North America*, Vol. 49, No. 2 (1965), pp. 1127–1128.

[6] F. Upham, *A Dynamic Approach to Illness*, New York, Family Service Association of America, 1949, pp. 91–92.

or affection, with the result that he may, denying the seriousness of this for his illness, have periods of over-eating, even gorging himself.[7]

The marital partner, fearing that the diabetic may become totally dependent on him, and perhaps resenting the inevitable partial dependency, may become over-solicitous and concerned, thus accentuating the diabetic's sense of being handicapped. Insulin reactions can come on suddenly, even in the best-regulated diabetic. They can be embarrassing as well as dangerous and can result in the diabetic being at times dependent for life or death on his marital partner, family or occasional associates.

Reaction Manipulation

Reactions can be used by both the diabetic and the non-diabetic for control and manipulation. A beginning insulin reaction has some resemblance to an anxiety attack. There have been instances when a diabetic thought he was suffering from fairly frequent reactions but was actually suffering from anxiety (blood sugar levels were found to be normal or above normal).[8]

A case history reported in *Diabetes*, the journal of the American Diabetic Association, illustrates some of the interaction between neurotic disturbance and the control of diabetes.[9] A young woman diabetic was ensnared in a conflict between her parents and her husband. She was unable to decide whether to be the dependent child of her parents or develop a mature relationship with her husband. In spite of the fact that there were frequent arguments and scenes between all members of the family, the presence of tension was denied.

This young woman was admitted to the hospital five times in one year in diabetic coma, always following a family argument. There was ample evidence that there was no neglect of insulin treatment or diet, and that the comas were her attempt to escape from her problem. She could retreat into the relative safety and neutrality of the hospital and at the same time receive attention and sympathy. Psychiatric help enabled both her and her family to develop some insight and alleviate the tension-producing situations. As a result her diabetes came under much better control.

Much has been written about the particular problems that are encountered in the family with a diabetic child and about the importance of seeing that the child's emotional growth is not blocked by the condition. There are some particular problems that may be encountered when diabetes develops in a family where there is already a disturbed parent-child or marital relationship. All parents have some resentment about the extra care and responsibility required by the diabetic child. However, in some instances, the child himself may be resented and rejected. Parents may show

[7] Lief, *op. cit.*, p. 420.
[8] E. Weiss and O. S. English, *op. cit.*, p. 342.
[9] G. L. Schless, M.D., and R. von Laveran-Stiebar, M.D., "Recurrent Episodes of Diabetic Acidosis Precipitated by Emotional Stress," *Diabetes*, Vol. 13, No. 4 (July–August, 1964), pp. 419–420.

this by using the diabetic regime in a punitive way under the guise of achieving good control. Over-protection and over-anxiety can accentuate the child's sense of handicap and may be an expression of hostility. Parents may, by using the rationalization that the child must become independent, give the child too much responsibility for his diabetic control and then blame him when things go wrong. A history from the records of the Social Service Department of the Royal Alexandra Hospital, Edmonton, illustrates this latter point.

A diabetic child, aged eight years, was the third of four children. There was much conflict between the parents. The mother, a nervous tense woman, suffered from asthma. The father, quiet and passive, was somewhat aloof from the family situation. Neither parent understood diabetes adequately and neither was able to enforce the necessary discipline concerning diet and rest. The child was given a great deal of responsibility for his own diabetic care. When difficulties developed and he had to be hospitalized, he was blamed by his parents for this.

It would appear essential that the social worker be aware of the ramifications of diabetes in working with afflicted clients. Recognizing this the New York City Diabetic Association has set up a special counseling service for diabetics. This service not only works directly with diabetics, but also provides specialized information on diabetes to community agencies.[10]

While many diabetics appear to be able to cope successfully with their condition, there are always a number who fail to do so and stumble through life with an increasing complex of physical and emotional problems. It is these people who are most likely to come to the attention of social agencies, and it is in working with them that a knowledge of the particular problems of diabetes is necessary.

[10] A. H. Kantrow, M.D., "A Vocational and Counselling Service for Diabetics," *Diabetes,* Vol. 12, No. 5 (1963), pp. 454–457.

Some Psychosocial Problems in Hemophilia

Alfred H. Katz

Hemophilia is a congenital, chronic illness, about which relatively little is known although it affects some 40,000 persons in the United States.[1] The medical problems it presents are far better understood than are its psychosocial aspects. The latter have received little attention in this country except for an early paper by Cohen and Herrman and a fragmentary outline for psychiatric research by Poinsard.[2] This discussion is an attempt, based on some years of association with the problems of hemophiliacs, to sketch some of these psychosocial factors, since social workers may encounter persons with this illness in the course of their work.

Hemophilia is a hereditary ailment characterized by excessive bleeding. It is not yet subject to cure, but in the past two decades various therapeutic advances have been made in the direction of stopping or controlling hemorrhaging and in the management of some resultant problems. Genetically, hemophilia is the product of a sex-linked recessive gene which is transmitted by females, but which primarily affects males. It also occurs, but quite rarely, as a result of genetic mutation. In recent years a number of related "bleeding disorders" have been found, which are milder in symptomatology than classical hemophilia, and which can be differentially diagnosed by refined laboratory procedures.

The severity of hemophilia varies from individual to individual although, generally speaking, severity remains comparatively stable among afflicted members of the same family. Some physicians (and patients) believe that there is a cyclical or seasonal variation in the onset and severity of bleeding

---

[1] Although the figures regarding the incidence and prevalence of hemophilia vary and are not definitive, this figure, given by Dr. Armand J. Quick of Marquette University, is the most commonly accepted estimate.

[2] Ethel Cohen and R. L. Herrman, "Social Adjustment of Six Patients with Hemophilia," *Pediatrics*, Vol. III (1949), pp. 588–596. Paul Poinsard, M.D., "Psychiatric Aspects of Hemophilia," in *Hemophilia and Hemophiloid Diseases*, Brinkhous, ed., University of North Carolina Press, Chapel Hill, 1957.

Reprinted from *Social Casework*, XL (June, 1959), pp. 321–326, by permission of the the author and the Journal.

episodes. Others believe that there is no such seasonal change, but that with maturation the affected individual learns to take better care of himself and is therefore less prone to situations where bleeding may be touched off.

With the introduction in the past twenty years of methods of banking blood, and particularly with the development of methods of processing human plasma through freezing or lyophilization, the treatment of hemorrhages has been greatly facilitated and the mortality rate among hemophiliacs has declined sharply. Owing to the volatility of the coagulative factor, the hemophiliac requires transfusions of blood or blood derivatives that have been freshly prepared, if the bleeding is to be stopped.

Although hemophilia is comparatively rare, it poses such severe problems of medical management and of psychosocial stress to the patient and his family that it must be considered a serious health problem for those affected and for the community. Not only does the moderately-to-severely affected individual have frequent, and at times almost uncontrollable, bleeding from external abrasions and sites, but even more serious forms of internal bleeding can occur from no apparent cause. Such bleeding episodes may be extremely painful, and often result in orthopedic problems. Hemophilic arthropathy, as it is termed, arises from such repeated bleedings into joint spaces. Orthopedic abnormalities and permanent damage to muscles and joints can occur from this type of bleeding. The approach of orthopedists and physiatrists to appropriate measures of therapy and correction for such problems still varies considerably, and much of the therapeutic work that is being done is on an experimental basis.

Social Problems in Hemophilia

From this brief review of medical problems it can be understood that, both for patients and for their families, hemophilia reproduces many or most of the psychosocial problems of other forms of congenital chronic illness, but with some added special features. Prominent among the latter are the extreme feelings of distress, guilt, and self-reproach experienced by the parents of newly diagnosed sufferers, especially by the approximately 50 per cent who are unable to trace a history of hemophilia in their families, but who are suddenly confronted with a child bearing this "hereditary taint," who forever after needs special care.

The protective care of the hemophilic infant and young child has to be extremely thorough to prevent the trauma that can result from normal childish exploration of the environment—crawling, body contact with furniture and floor, sharp-edged toys, and so forth. From a tender age the hemophilic infant must be protected from the more strenuous forms of physical contact with playmates and play objects; at the same time normal curiosity, growth, and socialization have to be fostered through stimulation by other means. *Thus the most general and pervasive psychosocial problem for these parents is to give their child physical protection and, at the same time, avoid making him overdependent and eventually a psychological invalid.* This all-pervading problem imposes tremendous burdens on the self-restraint and psychological maturity of the parents, siblings, and others in the hemophiliac's immediate environment. When he reaches school age, these problems are aggravated. The necessity of reaching a viable balance, of treading the narrow line between physical protection and psychological overprotection now involves teachers, playmates, and others in the child's environment.

The possibility of danger to the child is aggravated by the fact that frequently the young hemophiliac offers no external physical signs of his condition and thus appears to other children to be completely normal. Perhaps because of the difficulty of limiting the child's physical activity at this time, the school years are often the period of most frequent occurrence of hemorrhagic episodes. It is common for hemophiliacs to miss many weeks of the school term as a result of requiring rest and immobilization after, or between, periods of hemorrhage. Repeated bleeding can also lead to weakness and anaemia, with their effects on vitality and energy levels. The loss of time in school involves not only possible academic retardation and its important emotional concomitants, but the equally important loss of contacts with other children, of the socializing effects of play, and of the maturational benefits of social activity within a peer group.

It is also clear that if a hemophilic child is born into a family in which other male children are not affected by the disease, he tends to pre-empt major attention in the family, and there is a consequent withdrawal of attention from siblings.

Among the urgent and continuous pressures confronting the parents of a hemophilic child are the threat of being called upon at any moment to secure emergency medical attention for a hemorrhage; the consequent necessity of staying close to sources of such care; and the cost of such attention, not only in relation to the services of a physician, but particularly in relation to the replacement of blood or blood derivatives that may be used in transfusions. On the latter score, in some parts of the United States the American Red Cross does supply blood or blood products for hemophiliacs without requiring replacement by the individual user. In other localities the voluntary organization of hemophiliacs—The Hemophilia Foundation—may assume the responsibility and sometimes can cover the emergent needs of a particular family. Since, however, a hemophiliac may require as many as fifteen to twenty pints of whole blood to meet the exigencies of a single episode —and in the course of a year may require as many as one or two hundred pints of blood—this voluntary organization is usually overwhelmed and cannot meet all the requests. Thus, the drain on the finances and the energies of afflicted families is enormous. In those localities where blood or blood derivatives have to be purchased, the minimum cost to the family is $10 or $12 per unit, exclusive of administration fees. Therefore, the financial drains are constant, chronic, and severe; and these drains have important psychosocial consequences in increasing intra-familial tensions and in promoting shame, withdrawal, and social isolation tendencies.

Other medical costs result from the frequent hospitalizations that are necessary for hemophiliacs. Although many of these families have hospital insurance, it is not at all uncommon that a hemophiliac will require repeated hospitalizations every few weeks and thus exhaust within a short time the coverage by hospital insurance for the whole year. In some states, Crippled Children's programs may carry a portion of the cost of hospitalization, but eligibility for such aid is frequently defined by the state only in relation to the performance of corrective orthopedic procedures and is not available for the simpler procedure of treating a bleeding episode and its sequelae.

Such other emergent costs as those for transportation, ambulances, appliances and braces for those orthopedically afflicted, and special fees of medical consultants are all constant accompaniments of this condition.

As indicated above, the area of schooling and vocational preparation is a critical one for the hemophilic child. In this regard, parents require much help, counseling, and support in order to understand the importance of maintaining the child's independence, autonomy, and self-reliance insofar as possible, and to handle the child appropriately.

Problems of Adults

One of the striking observations regarding the hemophiliacs with whom I had contact was of the number of young adults in the group who lacked a stable occupation. When referrals of young men who were mild or even moderate sufferers were accepted by the State Division of Vocational Rehabilitation, the possibilities of their becoming self-maintaining were found to be excellent. However, this resource was little known and not widely utilized by the families of sufferers. It was my experience that social service assistance is rarely sought by or extended to adult patients in hospitals or attending clinics. The hospital social services for hemophiliacs tend to concentrate efforts on the problems of young children, their eligibility for assistance under Crippled Children's programs, and other such tangible services as camp arrangements, which are helpful and which carry a good deal of meaning for parents.

What has been found lacking, however, has been an approach to the hemophiliac through a program of counseling and advisement that would start at an early age, and that would tend to forestall the development of some of the special problems the hemophilic adolescents and young men encounter. The following case example illustrates some of these problems:

> Harry B, aged 26, a sufferer from classical hemophilia of moderate severity, had lived in a small suburban community of New York all his life. He was a handsome young man, with no orthopedic involvements; yet he had been in and out of hospitals for years for treatment of hemorrhages and resultant internal complications. Harry was the only hemophiliac in a family of four sons. His father was a retired ship-building worker who received a pension. The three brothers—one younger and two older—worked at manual trades.
>
> Of apparently normal intellectual capacity, Harry had finished two years of high school after an elementary schooling that was irregular owing to his frequent illnesses. He was 19 when he decided that he felt awkward with the

younger high school students and simply dropped out. He had had no jobs, but amused himself at home by watching television and playing records. He did not go out socially, but had one close friend, a young man who had taken an interest in him and had attempted to arrange blood donations for him.

Harry played the piano and spoke of wanting to become a musician. He wanted to study at a school where he could learn to make transcriptions for jazz orchestras. He could not, however, afford to attend such a school, and did not know whether, after taking such training, he would be able to get a job in this field.

Harry verbalized his interest in such vocational planning, but had not followed through on suggestions that were made to him of discussing the plan with the State Vocational Rehabilitation Division. This failure to follow through seemed to be a characteristically apathetic approach to his own situation.

It is clear that casework help to Harry and his parents would have had to begin when Harry was much younger if realistic vocational counseling and referral were to take place. In extending casework help to his parents, the caseworker would have had to take into account the special medical and psychological problems experienced by the hemophiliac during various phases of his development. To be helpful, the caseworker would have had to be aware of the very special frustrations and anxieties that both Harry and his parents had encountered. As this case reveals, the caseworker must be particularly aware of the problems associated with the hemophiliac's adolescence. In addition to the maturational stresses of normal adolescence, the hemophiliac experiences growing awareness that he is afflicted with a chronic disease, one that has multiple implications for marriage and parenthood roles and for the highly valued role of worker in our culture.

The adolescent hemophiliac thus may call into question his own adequacy in relation to most of the important adjustment indices in the adult world. Unless he is helped to explore and understand the ramifications of these feelings and reactions by means of a professional relationship, he can easily lose his way, and, like Harry B, retreat into a chronic passive dependency which is not realistically related to his actual medical condition. I found particularly noteworthy the number of such apparently "lost," passively dependent, apathetic, and depressed personalities encountered among young adult hemophiliacs. That I also encountered a relatively small number of comparatively active and outgoing individuals, who had made what seemed to be a good adjustment to their illness and disability, should also be stated. In perhaps a majority of cases there were problems of overdependency and passivity. It should be possible for many hemophiliacs, through skilled casework help, to achieve a better adjustment that will involve coming to terms with limitations in relation to their image of themselves, their possibilities of becoming vocationally active, and their problems of social life.

A readily acceptable focus for such casework help to adolescents and young men would seem to be the area of vocational planning. The possible range of occupations that can be followed by the hemophiliac is limited by several factors: *1]* the innate capacities of the individual; *2]* the severity and frequency of occurrence of disabling episodes; *3]* the presence and degree of correction of orthopedic defect; and *4]* the attitudes of potential employers. Within a framework of such limitations, hemophiliacs have been able to function in the professions, in education, small businesses, and clerical occupations. Generally speaking, severe physical exertion is not advised, although one encounters hemophiliacs who are laborers, bus and truck drivers, machinists, and workers in other active trades. Awareness of the many vocational possibilities open to him and of available community resources for helping him secure employment in one of them can be decidedly therapeutic for the young hemophiliac, even without exploration of deeper, underlying feelings.

The problems of social life are also acute for the young adult who suffers from his constant awareness of the implications of his condition for marriage and parenthood. Awareness of such problems frequently imposes a pattern of withdrawal from group or individual relationships, which in turn intensifies his feelings of loneliness, isolation, and depression. Through simple encouragement, some young men have been helped to try, and have found considerable support from, planned participation in social and recreational activities with other handicapped or non-handicapped persons.

Problems of Female Relatives

One of the most serious areas of conflict is that experienced by the female members of a hemophilic family. Their conflict arises from the fact that they may be carriers of the defective gene, although they are not personally affected by the illness. Genetic data indicate that there is a fifty per cent chance that the daughter of a male hemophiliac will be a carrier of the defective gene. There is a fifty per cent chance that a male child born to a carrier will be a hemophiliac. *All* the daughters of a female carrier of the gene are themselves carriers. Thus, in the well-known instance of Queen Victoria, who was a hemophilic carrier, all her daughters were carriers; they married into the royal houses of Spain, Germany, and Russia, where, among their male children, several hemophiliacs were subsequently found.

There is at present no reliable test which indicates whether or not the daughter of a hemophilic male is herself a carrier of the defective gene. Researchers are continuing to try to develop such a test but so far without success. In view of this, the psychological situation of the potential carrier is understandable. Attitudes range from shame, and the impulse to conceal the possible hereditary defect, to withdrawal from social contacts and extreme depression. It has been found that the daughters can be helped through professional or lay sources to face realistically the alternatives that confront them. Some daughters of hemophiliacs, for example, have been ready to take a chance on marriage and motherhood; they may rationalize their actions by the belief that, first of all, they have a "fifty-fifty" chance of having a healthy son; or that the care of a hemophilic child is not such a tremendous burden and is to be preferred to childlessness; or they may be convinced that the improvements in therapy developed over recent years, and the prospects of current research, give promise of more effective control or even a cure. Some women have sought to adopt children rather than to risk a perpetuation of the defective gene. Adoption has been arranged, to the writer's knowledge, in several instances, both within and outside the structure of social agency services. It is of interest to note that among hemophilic families known to me, there are several with two or more affected sons, and that such multiple-sufferer families are found in religious groups that do not have prohibitions against birth control practices.

Therapeutic Aspects of Help to Hemophiliacs

Like other groups of the specially disadvantaged and handicapped, hemophiliacs and their families can draw great strength from group associations. In those communities where the voluntary agency concerned with their problems exists, these families have been able to work out generally superior arrangements for blood procurement, medical services, and special schooling. The less tangible advantages of participation in such "self-help" groups are also worth stating. Among these are: *1]* overcoming the sense of isolation and overwhelming distress, frequently experienced by parents as a first reaction to the diagnosis of hemophilia; *2]* provision of accurate information regarding problems of medical management, child care, blood procurement, and so forth; *3]* socialization through contacts and exchange of experience with other families who can contribute to knowledge about developmental phases and problems that can be anticipated; *4]* provision of organized or informal opportunities to discuss the parents' fears, frustrations, and satisfactions arising from the particular difficulties of caring for a hemophilic child; *5]* opportunity to discuss broader and longer-range problems that can be anticipated on behalf of the child so that planning can be done; *6]* possibility of securing through group action better facilities of a therapeutic and educational nature for their children; *7]* cathartic effects of such personal participation, which helps to relieve anxieties by channeling them into constructive outlets.

As stressed in the foregoing, it seems to me that casework services are extremely important for both parents and patients, to help forestall and minimize some of the problems that have been described in this article. Such assistance can help to define and resolve for the parents some of the major feelings that may inhibit their handling their child in a way that combines necessary physical protectiveness with maximum psychological self-reliance. Early establishment of a relationship with a caseworker enables the hemophilic youngster to express his own perceptions, fears, anxieties, and wishes about himself, that for one reason or another cannot find adequate expression in his family group. Vocational planning can and should be instituted early in order to assist the hemophiliac to "capitalize his losses" by turning to academic or quiet hobbies, to make up for the fact that he cannot be an active participant in body contact athletics and rough games. Early counseling is particularly imperative for the individual who does not have the intellectual endowment suitable for pursuing academic courses of study, in order to steer him to an appropriate and consistently pursued course of preparation leading toward ultimate employment.

The older adolescent and the young adult need constant encouragement and opportunity to discuss their personal problems and reactions in other than the emotion-fraught home situation. One way social workers can also help in this area by arranging special opportunities for group participation in existing social agencies, community centers, and informal clubs. Posing these problems and needs, however, does not answer the question of who in the community, that is to say, what professional group, will take responsibility on behalf of such patients. From my experience with hemophiliacs, I should estimate that not more than twenty per cent of the afflicted families in a large city have had contacts with social agencies. Although individual situations must be dealt with individually, it is apparent that once the definite diagnosis of hemophilia is made, the resultant psychosocial, educational, vocational, and other social problems of a patient and his family are numerous, diverse, long-continuing, and almost uniformly present. It would seem of great benefit, then, to have centers established for information, referral to appropriate resources, and, if possible, direct casework and related services—such as group counseling—that would utilize specific knowledge of the condition and its effects. The hemophilia associations are not yet strong enough nor do they have financial resources sufficient to provide such services, although they recognize the necessity for them. It would thus seem that in this, as in other fields of chronic illness, the community is in need of a new type of casework service, one that offers comprehensive information and knowledge of resources appropriate to meeting the needs of the chronically ill, along with some direct services of both a casework and a group character. The challenge of meeting the needs of the hemophilic patient and his family is a persistent and urgent one for social workers in all settings.

Quadriplegia

Special Problems Encountered in the Rehabilitation of Quadriplegic Patients

William B. Neser and Eugene E. Tillock

The special problems encountered in efforts to rehabilitate quadriplegic patients will be discussed in this paper. Because the disability of quadriplegic patients is so severe, their problems present a challenge to the doctor, the nurse, the social worker, and the other members of the rehabilitation team.[1] The social worker is the team member who bears primary responsibility for helping patients solve their psychosocial problems. In this article we will present a case summary to depict the typical medical, social, and emotional problems a patient encounters at successive stages of the rehabilitation process. In the course of this presentation we call attention to the range of activities undertaken by the caseworker to help patients solve their problems and achieve the maximum benefits attainable from the total rehabilitation process.

Major Medical Problems

Quadriplegia is defined as paralysis or weakness of the arms and legs. It may be caused by such disorders as poliomyelitis, cerebral palsy, or muscular dystrophy, or by injuries sustained in an accident. A quadriplegic patient requires continued medical care to prevent further deterioration of the bladder, breakdown of skin tissue, and contracture of muscles. The first major medical concern is control of the bladder. In some instances, the bladder retains its tone and an incontinent patient can be trained to void on schedule; in most instances, however, the bladder loses its tone and its control function. A patient who is unable to regain control of the bladder may require catheterization. The patient with a urinary elimination problem is plagued with two constant dangers. He may sustain permanent damage to his kidneys, or he may develop temporary infections in the bladder or the kidneys. Bowel management does not pose such a serious problem. The danger of infection is less, and successful chemotherapeutic management of this condition can usually be attained more readily.

The second major medical concern is the maintenance of the patient's

---

[1] William F. Hartnett and Eugene E. Tillock, "The LPN and Rehabilitation," *Practical Nursing*, Vol. XI, No. 4 (1961), pp. 18, 28–29.

Reprinted from *Social Casework*, XLIII (March, 1962), pp. 125–129, by permission of the authors and the Journal.

skin tone at an optimal level. The breakdown of skin tissue and the resulting formation of decubitus ulcers are not simply a matter of unrelieved pressure, excessive wetness, poor nutrition, faulty enervation, or any specific combination of these factors. Aaron Rosenblatt and Vincent Trovato recently pointed to the importance of considering the effect of psychosocial factors in the formation and perpetuation of bedsores. Either consciously or unconsciously the patient may use these bedsores to manipulate his environment.[2]

The third major medical concern is the maintenance of muscle tone and the prevention of contractures. This subject is well described in rehabilitation literature and requires mention here only to emphasize that, as in the case of skin care, the patient's environment and his psychosocial problems can become crucial factors in preventing the formation of contractures.

Doctors are also concerned about increasing a patient's residual physical capacities. Braces and related orthotic devices are used to increase the quadriplegic patient's motoric capacity. The patient's degree of adaptability to artificial aids is dependent upon his residual muscle tone and control. Existing orthotic devices, however, provide very limited assistance to a patient with a total spinal cord lesion at or above the sixth cervical vertebra. A patient with this degree of disablement is limited to intermittent experiences with verticality on a tiltboard, a dependent wheel chair existence, and the use of devices—such as electric page turners and electric typewriters— which can be manipulated by the mouth or head. Quadriplegic patients with partial lesions who can benefit from the use of supportive arm, hand, and finger devices can achieve a greater degree of independence.

Even with such assistance a quadriplegic cannot live alone, or even remain alone for any length of time, unless he achieves nearly complete return of hand function. All quadriplegic patients who leave the hospital require close care and medical follow-up. The home program may include a very high fluid intake, medication for the control of genitourinary tract infections, daily exercises, and scrupulous skin care. The family and the patient must learn the many details of health preservation if the patient is to maintain the gains he achieved in the hospital.[3]

Characteristics of Quadriplegic Patients

The average age of quadriplegic patients at Highland View Hospital is lower than that of the general patient population. Many patients are teenagers who were injured in automobile accidents or while they were engaging in such athletic activities as diving, horseback riding, or performing on a trampoline. Some patients are young husbands or wives who were injured in accidents at home or at work.

Before World War II, 9 out of every 10 quadriplegic patients died

[2] Aaron Rosenblatt and Vincent W. Trovato, "Evaluating a Medical Symptom with Paraplegics," *Social Casework*, Vol. XLI, No. 3 (1960), p. 131.

[3] Eugene E. Tillock, "Health Oriented Education of the Quadriplegic Patient," *The Bulletin*, The Academy of Medicine of Cleveland, Vol. XLVII, No. 1 (1962), pp. 6, 46–47.

within a year of the onset of their paralysis. Prospects for survival have been greatly increased by recent medical advances. The helplessness of quadriplegics, however, is generally so severe that many of them question the value of survival with this condition. One patient commented that living with his incapacitation was "sheer hell." Quadriplegia has been described as a way of life. It entails a total adjustment for the patient and his family to an extreme form of personal catastrophe.

A quadriplegic patient with a complete lesion of the spinal cord at or above the sixth cervical vertebra is almost totally helpless. The only part of his body over which he retains control is his head. He is completely dependent upon others for the satisfaction of his physical needs. He is unable to perform even such activities as eating, scratching an itch, or lifting a pencil. In his incontinence and physical helplessness he approaches the dependency of an infant.

Patients are often in a state of emotional numbness after the illness or accident that resulted in quadriplegia. They do not comprehend what has happened to them or what the eventual outcome will be. Usually they are hopeful and look forward to a complete recovery. When they come to realize the permanence of their disability they are forced to face the stark reality of their future existence. Many quadriplegics continue to deny the nature of their disability; they look forward to the day when they will be cured by a miracle. A patient generally needs a period of time, which may rage from 9 to 15 months, in order to translate his lack of physical improvement into the psychological acknowledgment that his disability is permanent. His attempt to integrate this knowledge often results in his entering a phase characterized by deep depression and mourning.

The family members of quadriplegics also find it difficult to accept the permanent disability of the patient. Their reassurance often reinforces the patient's effort to deny reality, for they may be even less prepared than he to face the prospects of his grim future. The thought of home care frequently poses such an overwhelming threat to family members that they try to find some escape from its terrifying implications. Relatives are also frightened by the continuing depletion of their financial resources, by the shift in their own social roles, and by their own fears of becoming disabled. The medical social worker assumes a major responsibility for helping the family members and the patient deal with all of these problems.[4]

Case Illustration

The following case study is a record of the supportive treatment rendered to a female quadriplegic patient and her family.

Miss M, 34, was a tall, attractive, unmarried, native-born American who had been injured four years earlier in an automobile accident in France,

[4] Genevieve R. Soller, "The Public Health Nurse and the Chronically Ill Patient," *Texas Public Health Association Journal*, Vol. XII, No. 4 (1960), p. 163.

where she had been teaching. When she was transferred to Highland View Hospital six months after the accident, she was aware of her diagnosis and prognosis. She had a fractured dislocation of the cervical spine resulting in complete and permanent quadriplegia with bowel and bladder incontinence, symptoms of leg spasms, and generalized, profuse sweating. However, she had not completely accepted the reality of her disabilities. She vacillated between putting up a brave front and giving way to her underlying feelings of despair. At times she still hoped she would recover. She spoke of returning to teaching and of making a significant contribution to society. When she realized that she was helpless, she did not wish to go on living. Several times she expressed the wish that the staff would let her die. The only hostility she could express directly was toward the French physician who had saved her life.

Miss M had been the economic and emotional mainstay of her family. Her father had been a marginal provider, constantly preoccupied with his own medical problems. Her mother was emotionally dependent on the patient and had a history of at least one mental breakdown. The glamour of teaching overseas had been only one reason for the patient's departure from her home; she had also been trying to escape from the emotional dependency of her parents. Miss M was upset because she was no longer able to discharge her filial duties by contributing to the financial support of her parents. She was also upset about having to submit to her father's all-day visits. He spent these long hours either talking about his many physical problems or giving her false reassurance about her own physical problems. The father's egocentricity and mild senility were so deeply entrenched in his character that he was unable to understand the negative effect on his daughter of his visits.

All members of the rehabilitation team were worried about the depth of Miss M's depression. They employed every available therapeutic modality to help her. They emphasized the importance of her physical progress, represented by her ability to regain limited use of her arms. This newly won ability presented the patient with the first real possibility of "solving her problem" by committing suicide. A primary objective of the medical social worker was to help the patient recognize her losses, express her sorrow, and make plans for a realistic future.

At about this time the patient reached the stage of being able to manage a home visit. She was now able to sit up in a partially reclining wheel chair for extended periods of time. After the family was carefully prepared for her visit, the patient's physician granted her a one-day pass. The visit was uneventful, and the staff was relieved to learn that she had not attempted any suicidal actions.

Areas of Casework Treatment

After this stage was passed, the patient was seen by a social worker for at least one hour a week during the next two years. Some of the interviews were devoted to enabling the patient to feel free to explain her needs to others; she learned to give others appropriate cues in order to enable them to help her. The caseworker helped her to develop a feeling of limited independence and to gain a sense of control and mastery over her condition.

Other interviews were devoted to improving Miss M's relationship with her parents. The caseworker used the techniques of partialization and interpretation to help her improve her understanding. Once the patient was able to recognize the anger she felt at being exploited by her parents, the case-worker helped her to deal more appropriately with her hostility. He also helped her limit the demands she made upon her parents. By working through problems that arose from impaired interpersonal relationships with her parents, she subsequently gained the ability to accept her dependency without guilt.

Another important problem that called for attention was the handling of urinary incontinence in social situations. It was difficult for the patient to remain continent during physical therapy and visiting hours, and still drink the large quantity of water recommended by the physician. Problems of this nature govern the extent to which a quadriplegic patient may participate in routine and normal activities without inhibition. As a means of supporting Miss M's efforts, the caseworker reviewed with her the procedures recommended for achieving bladder control.

Miss M continued to make progress in her physical rehabilitation. She was able to gain a fair return of function in her arms and she developed a moderate degree of hand control. Eventually she mastered the independent transfer of her body from a wheel chair to other surfaces of similar height. Micturition was sufficiently controlled so that she no longer needed to use a catheter. She continued to have leg muscle spasms; she had lost all sensation and muscle control below the waist.

Plans for Discharge

Before a workable discharge plan could be developed, opposing points of view had to be reconciled and economic obstacles had to be removed. The physicians believed that it was unrealistic to expect the patient to live alone. Miss M believed that life would have no value for her if she could not teach again. The thought of staying at home for any great length of time was unbearable. Plans for her future were complicated by her meager resources. Her family had little financial or emotional support to offer her. The County Welfare Department, which had been furnishing financial assistance, offered the possibility of placement in a nursing home. At this point a series of compromises had to be made with the aim of integrating the recommendations of the physicians for sheltered placement and extensive care, the patient's goal of returning to active teaching, and the limited resources of the family. Only after much effort was the patient convinced that she could not realistically expect to support herself through teaching. This emotional blow temporarily hindered her mental and physical recovery.

During the course of treatment, the patient was evaluated by vocational counselors and psychologists. Their findings provided the caseworker with valuable aids in making effective discharge plans. While she was a patient at the hospital, Miss M, with the assistance of a volunteer group, attended one evening course at a local college. Miss M's self-confidence was bolstered by the experience of attending college successfully and establishing some meaningful social relationships. She also formed relationships with people throughout the hospital. One such relationship was with a friendly visitor, who was recruited by a member of the social service department of the hospital. This friendly visitor was supervised by the caseworker.

With much deliberation, Miss M decided to select a new career in the field of vocational counseling. Her decision seemed to be a sound one when it was evaluated in terms of her intelligence, her counterphobic desire to help others, and her record of academic achievement. The co-operation of the local Bureau of Vocational Rehabilitation and the County Welfare Department was obtained to supplement the costs of education and separate maintenance during a training period.

The patient showed a capacity to implement her vocational goal by obtaining a federal scholarship, by gaining admission to a large state university that was adapted to the needs of handicapped students, and by making her own travel arrangements. The medical social worker completed his primary activity with this patient by making two referrals: The first was to the hospital volunteers, who were asked to outfit her with clothes and linens; the second referral was to the Travelers Aid Society for assistance with any travel problems she might encounter. Miss M was discharged to attend the university in February, 1960, 27 months after her admission to Highland View Hospital.

Follow-up

The caseworker had two follow-up interviews with the patient. In addition Miss M has sent him several supplemental "progress" notes. Her report at the end of the first semester stated that she had received "three A's, two B's and a broken arm," the broken arm resulting from a wheel chair collision with a snowbank. Her motivation has remained high, her depression is completely masked, and her hope for employment after graduation seems to be realistic. She has led an active social life at the university; she is friendly, outgoing, and lighthearted. She has had trying times, but her ability to laugh at her own predicaments has helped her to adjust to difficult situations. Her emotional adjustment seems to be the best one possible under the circumstances; this level of psychosocial adjustment will probably remain intact, barring any radical change in her physical condition.

In summary, Miss M is a young, intelligent schoolteacher who recovered partial use of her arms and hands after she had sustained a cervical injury to the spinal cord which resulted in complete paralysis. After having moved through successive stages of the rehabilitation process, she will probably achieve economic independence in her new career as a vocational counselor.

Conclusions

One goal of the social worker is to enable the quadriplegic patient to make optimal use of his residual physical resources. Heavy demands are made upon the skill of the social worker for the achievement of this goal. He must be able to work with a number of individuals—the patient, members of the family, members of the rehabilitation team, and members of the community. The highest degree of tact and human understanding is required in handling the severe emotional reactions of the patient to his overwhelming physical and social limitations. Diagnostic acumen is needed to help the patient set a realistic goal of vocational aspiration. Treatment skill is needed to help the patient achieve this goal. These abilities are important even when, as in the case of Miss M, the patient is self-directing and is highly motivated to achieve economic independence.

The needs of the family should not be ignored as the patient moves through the successive stages of the rehabilitation process. Family members are deeply concerned with all aspects of the patient's progress. Their co-operation and their acceptance of a treatment plan are essential if the plan is to succeed. Members of the family often need help in adjusting to the changes in their roles and the role of the patient.

The members of the hospital staff and interested members of the community can render valuable services that contribute to realization of the rehabilitation goals; the social worker needs to establish satisfactory patterns of communication with them so that the patient can gain the benefit of their efforts. The social worker also needs to know how to make use of environmental resources to support the patient.

The case of Miss M may be regarded as atypical in once sense: Few quadriplegic patients possess the physical, social, and emotional resources necessary to achieve such a high level of adjustment. Nonetheless, the accomplishments of Miss M reflect an advance in the rehabilitation of quadriplegic patients which would have been considered impossible a few decades ago. As a result of the increasing effectiveness of medical science, more and more people with severe disabilities are now able to survive for longer periods of time. The less they are able to make optimal use of their residual capacities, the greater will be the drain on the health and economic resources of their families and the community. Hence there is a need to use all available medical and social resources to enable each patient to achieve the maximum goals of rehabilitation.

Psychiatric Aspects of Tuberculosis

Leopold Bellak

The interrelationship and co-existence of psychiatric disorders and tuberculosis have long been of interest: a review of the literature revealed a paper on tuberculosis and insanity as early as 1863[1] and in preparation for this paper we encountered more than ninety references specifically concerned with this problem.

The present report deals with tuberculous patients seen for psychiatric consultation and treatment in a casework agency.[2] The author saw only those tuberbulous patients passing through the agency who were considered by the social work staff to be significantly emotionally disturbed. This sample constituted about 10 per cent of the total case load of the agency over about two and a half years.

Forty-six patients were seen by the author for at least one diagnostic interview and the majority for a series of psychotherapeutic interviews. Those seen only once were followed in treatment conferences with workers who continued the contact with the patients. In addition to the 46 patients mentioned above, about 250 were known to the author through casework and treatment conferences, as described later.

Of the 46 patients, 25 were males and 21 females. Their ages ranged from $17\frac{1}{2}$ years to 62 years, with 39 of the group falling between the ages of 25 and 45. They fell under 17 different diagnostic categories, among which anxiety neurosis and hysteria were most frequent; four psychotics were also included.

The factors we observed in our patients nearly universally were: *1]* traumatic effects of diagnosis; *2]* increased secondary narcissism and changes in body image; *3]* increased oral needs, with passivity; *4]* problems of the return home.

---

[1] T. S. Clouston, "Tuberculosis and Insanity," *Journal of Mental Science*, Vol. IX, No. 45 (1863), p. 36.

[2] The Committee for the Care of Jewish Tuberculous.

Reprinted from *Social Casework*, XXXI (May, 1950), pp. 183–189, by permission of the author and the Journal.

Traumatic Effects of Diagnosis

The first response to being informed of the diagnosis was frequently an attempt at *denial*, the patient maintaining that it could not be so. Only in a very few patients was this denial pathologically prolonged. In the majority it was followed by a more or less pronounced *depression*. A *catastrophic reaction* was frequently based on some very primitive concept of tuberculosis, or occurred because it was seen in terms of the experience of another family member or an acquaintance. The most profoundly disturbing effects seemed to exist in those cases with a familial history, where the diagnosis led to identification with the previously affected family member. This was, of course, most traumatic in the case of men identifying with a previously ill mother, militating more or less repressed anxieties. Acceptance of the illness often also brought about a profound *disturbance of the body image*, to be discussed later. In the case of men with a great libidinal investment in their masculine prowess, this was particularly upsetting. (This observation, of course, also holds true for several other chronic diseases, as most observations reported here hold true for either totally incapacitating or chronic diseases, as, for instance, observed in cardiacs by the writer.)

A more specific response to the diagnosis of tuberculosis in some patients was observed as a *tendency to nausea and vomiting*. It was particularly marked in one young man who started this symptom the day of the diagnosis and maintained it for years. In another young man, who in early childhood had associated the idea of being ill with vomiting, this idea became reactivated on his being informed he had tuberculosis. In a third young man, the nausea was associated with anorexia, and he had to be hospitalized due to danger of starvation. A parallel case of fear of tuberculosis manifesting itself as a fear of pregnancy was seen, in private practice, in a female patient. Her father had died of tuberculosis in her childhood, while an older sister died of the same illness during the patient's adolescence. She identified tuberculosis germs and sperms in an infantile fantasy of oral impregnation; all her symptoms were related to this fantasy—the fear of having holes made in her and bleeding to death. In the men, too, neurotic disturbances related to oral-passive wishes and defenses against them.[3]

There was absolutely no suggestion that a particular personality type appeared more frequently among the tuberculous patients than in the general population. The response to their illness could be clearly seen in relation to their pre-existing personalities, varying in basic dynamics as much as in any other group seen by the author. Any similarity appeared

---

[3] Apparently a certain amount of gastric disturbance may occur in pulmonary tuberculosis on a primarily somatic basis. Cohen (in L. Brown, "Mental Aspect in the Aetiology and Treatment of Pulmonary Tuberculosis," *International Clinics*, Vol. III, September, 1933, pp. 149–174) points out that, as the tuberculosis progresses, there is a corresponding significant decrease of free acid in the gastric juices. In this series, 20.8 per cent of over 1,000 patients entering the sanatorium complained of gastro-intestinal symptoms, which he considers a complication rather than a symptom of tuberculosis.

to be a secondary change in response to this threatening disease and the chronic invalidism necessarily imposed for some years, as outlined below.

Increased Secondary Narcissism and Changes in Body Image

A painful organ or one known to be ill attracts attention. If the illness is chronic and of major importance, the ill portion is treated in a nearly anthropomorphized fashion, as a separate being. Special provisions are made for it and care provided, and an attitude is established which closely corresponds to that of a mother toward her child. This solicitous overconcern may, in varying degrees, be extended to the whole person and demanded from the outside world as well as tendered by the person toward himself. In the healthy person, a large emotional investment is made in a (developmentally changing) variety of figures; in the neurotic, an excessive investment in himself has been maintained. A physically ill person makes an increased investment in himself as a defensive measure against further harm. In the neurotic this reinvestment will be greater and there will be more reluctance to give it up when the crisis is passed than in relatively healthier individuals. This reinvestment we speak of as an increase of secondary narcissism.

The clinical importance of the body image was originally described by Paul Schilder[4]: "The image of the human body means the picture of our own body which we form in our mind . . . the way in which the body appears to ourselves." The fact that the child needs to learn to differentiate its own body from the rest of the world hardly concerns us here. What is pertinent is that everyone does develop some concept of his own body, frequently an overidealized and/or a greatly underrated one. Illness distorts this body image. An affected organ may loom so prominently as to affect the body concept profoundly; one is reminded of the humorous map of the United States as drawn by a New Yorker—New York covering two-thirds or more of the entire North American continent.

The clinical manifestations of this increased narcissism and the disturbance of the body image are obvious and familiar: hypochondriacal concern, depression, and many bodily complaints that cannot be correlated with physical findings, persistent self-observation, and anxiety. The more manifestly observed increased oral needs and passivity also result.

Increased Oral Needs and Passivity

The tuberculous patient, then, becomes more narcissistic under the threat to his life. Sanatorium routine makes this almost inevitable. Rest is extremely important and all his needs are taken care of. A premium is put on his paying attention to his health, on his being passive, accepting all but

[4] Paul Schilder, *Image and Appearance of the Human Body*, Routledge, London, 1935.

spoonfeeding; he is generally forced to accept, for the time being, almost the image of being a baby.[5]

It is thus not very surprising that a good percentage of patients have a hard time giving up this attitude immediately upon being discharged from the sanatorium. They have seen other patients return with relapses, and they doubt, with justification, the doctor's criteria of health. The relatively psychologically healthy patients, or those who always had strong defenses against passivity and oral wishes (therefore probably "bad" sanatorium patients) will pass through this stage more or less easily. The more neurotic patients, or those who to begin with had a more infantile attitude or strong oral wishes, will hold on to the regressed position.

In clinical practice these tendencies manifest themselves in difficulty of rehabilitation. In the sheltered workshop these patients progress poorly and when it comes to looking for outside employment they somehow cannot find jobs. Careful examination will reveal either that they do not look very hard or that they unconsciously discourage prospective employers by some subtle means. This sort of patient expects things to fall into his lap. He expects the agency to continue to take care of all his needs, or he may transfer this attitude to public welfare institutions. The ambivalence ordinarily expressed toward the parents may be expressed toward the agency and the worker who represents it, and a more or less painful weaning process sets in.

At this point Freud's concept of the secondary gain of illness becomes useful: since he is an invalid, the patient is unconsciously set to enjoy all the advantages of this state while being taken care of.

Problems of the Return to Family

The patient who has been away from home for a period of from one to three years may have varying problems when he returns. As a father, he may have to adjust to the fact that he is not the head of the family any more, at least for the time being, if he is unable to provide for his family as before. Problems of status become a frequent cause for reactive depressions due to the repressed aggression they engender. That sexual problems exist is obvious. One woman's main problems and reactive depression centered around the fact that her 5-year-old daughter had become estranged from her over the past three years and had become attached to the foster parents.

In our experience, by far the most clearcut problems occur in the return home of the adolescent or post-adolescent patient. The boy or girl may have left home at, say, 17, and finally returned at 20. Many youngsters came from traditionally overprotected or patriarchally-structured families. In the sanatorium they lived under altogether different conditions, in a sexually mixed group of all ages, and were exposed to many ideas. These circumstances, superimposed on the already autonomously revolutionary changes of adolescence, result in tremendous difficulties on returning home. While

[5] It must be noted, however, that the current trend is to decrease the necessary passivity by permitting the patient as much self-direction as possible.

the average family has the opportunity to adjust to adolescent changes in small doses and with the normal amount of friction, our patients are confronted with sudden changes and violent clashes. These may lead to forceful regression with neurotic symptoms, or, if unattended, to a premature separation, with hardships and guilt feelings on both sides. Awareness of the need for special attention to the adolescent tuberculous and their families therefore seems one of the most clearcut results of our experience.

In summarizing, it can be said that about 10 per cent of the patients passing through this agency for the tuberculous appeared psychiatrically disturbed more than the "average" person. Psychiatric study of this sample revealed no specific character type or neurosis. A certain common denominator appeared in the psychological responses to the problem of tuberculosis; these patterns of reaction conform to expectations on the basis of psychoanalytic hypothesis concerning the effect of severe chronic bodily disease. Further factors are added only inasmuch as oral fantasies are more specifically stimulated by tuberculous illness (oral contagion) and the particularly severe incapacitation.

Psychotherapy and Casework

The general approach to the patients' problems was that of brief psychoanalytically-oriented psychotherapy within a casework setting. This connotes not so much an actual procedure as a frame of reference. In taking the patient's history an attempt is made to understand how the person has learned to perceive his environment through early and later experience, how he views the present situation in terms of his past experience; his chief complaints and symptoms must be understood as a compromise between his wishes and the way he perceives the environment, and attempts to help him are made by integrating physical and environmental changes.

If we are able to understand the dynamics of the patient in his present situation we must decide how to go about helping him. We are entirely in agreement with the excellent presentation of Grete L. Bibring[6] who emphasizes that casework and, for that matter, psychotherapy in general, need not use insight therapy, but may often find manipulation, abreaction, or clarification more profitable.

[6] Grete L. Bibring, "Psychiatric Principles in Casework," *Journal of Social Casework*, Vol. XXX, No. 6 (1949), pp. 230–235: "We do not use the term 'manipulation,' as it sometimes is used in casework, to describe the undesirable attempt of the worker to force his concepts and plans on the client. We use the term in a more positive sense. After listening to and observing the client we may use our understanding of his personality structure, his patterns, his needs and conflicts, and his defenses in order to 'manipulate' him in various ways. We may make suggestions as to what steps may or may not help this individual to cope better with his problems; we may plan with him as to his emotional, professional, and recreational activities; we may give appropriate advice to members of his environment; we may modify our attitude and approach to his problems; or we may purposely activate relevant emotional attitudes in the client for the sake of adjustive change. It is in this specific sense that we use the term 'manipulation'."

This viewpoint needs emphasis, since, unjustifiably, a feeling seems to have developed in many conscientious caseworkers that nothing short of a complete psychoanalysis is of any value and that any symptom-directed approach is little more than quackery. We believe, on the contrary, that the full understanding that psychoanalysis gives us should be used to assess the available assets and liabilities in the patient and in the situation, and change those aspects in ways most profitable to the patient. We speak of brief psychotherapy, since circumstances do not permit a great time investment in an individual patient; thus, this time limitation must become part of the therapeutic program, one of the factors to consider in planning the optimal approach. It is true that this approach may not be suitable for every patient, and recourse must occasionally be made to psychotherapy outside the agency, if possible.

The procedure used in the agency is as follows: the social worker works with the patient, requesting a case discussion with the psychiatrist at the worker's discretion. In such an interview an attempt is made to arrive at a diagnosis, to discuss the psychodynamics, to plan further treatment steps, and to arrange a follow-up interview. If necessary, the psychiatrist may see the patient himself for diagnosis—if a differential diagnosis is difficult to arrive at or if the question of psychosis or suicidal risk is involved. If the case is not suitable for treatment by the social worker, the psychiatrist may take the patient on or refer the case to an outside source.

The general frame of reference followed is that psychiatry is to a caseworker a basic science, as anatomy and physiology are to a doctor. Psychiatric principles enable the worker to understand the patient's psychodynamic structure and his clinical casework training equips him to help the patient. His casework training can be compared with the clinical training of the general practitioner, whose knowledge of anatomy and physiology does not give him the special knowledge and skill of the surgeon; similarly, the social worker does not have the equipment to undertake major psychiatric operations. He should have an understanding of them and, possibly, proceed with them under supervision after extensive experience.

This view, I believe, acknowledges the special skill and independent function of the social worker; like the general practitioner, the worker can handle many problems more competently than the specialist, since he is specially trained in casework techniques and generally has a broad view of the problems involved, including the social aspects, knowledge of the family and the social setting, and command of the community resources. Thus, we must see the worker both in juxtaposition and subordination to the psychiatrist for maximal usefulness.

Dealing with the Reality Problem

The tuberculous psychiatric patient differs from the more usual psychotherapeutic patient in that he actually has a difficult reality situation to deal with: his illness or the danger of relapse, lack of earning power, as well as the other features mentioned above. The seriousness of these reality problems should never be forgotten or underestimated. A busy professional person working all day with such serious problems cannot afford to identify too much. At the same time there is a definite danger of not appreciating the actual difficulty of the situation and hiding behind a screen of professional jargon. If the casework aspects of the reality situation are overlooked it is just as bad as overemphasizing these aspects.

In the C.C.J.T., the Altro Workshop provides an opportunity for graded rehabilitation by means of the needle trades, as described elsewhere. [7] Here the patient may harden himself physically, improve his financial status, and, with the help of the caseworker, gradually take over ordinary responsibilities.

The patient with reality difficulties will, of course, blame all his neurotic problems on the reality situation. The way to deal with this problem is *to acknowledge fully his actual troubles, and then carefully to isolate them from the neurotic superstructure,* and to point out the irrational aspects of his reactions. An example I frequently use is the following: If there were ten people in a subway car and you performed the experiment of stepping on the left foot of each one, you would get widely differing reactions; some would give you an angry look, some would smile or ignore it, others would howl, still others would kick back, and some would actually feel guilty themselves. All these people were exposed to the same situation of, say, 180 pounds descending on their left foot. Why does each react to the particular situation the way he does?

We must also attempt to relate the existing reaction to characteristics that existed in the patient *before* his tuberculous illness, and point out to him his propensity for this particular type of reaction—anxiety, depression, and so on. The attitude of the patient toward his problems has to be made *ego-alien,* that is, unacceptable, instead of permitting it to remain ego-syntonic. For that purpose it must be isolated, extrapolated and held up as something pernicious in itself and independent of the reality situation, however difficult.

Dealing with the Transference Problem

What has been said about increased narcissism, oral needs, and passivity makes it evident that the emotional relationship of the patient to the worker is a particularly intense and conflictual one. Ordinarily I like to reserve the term "transference" for the relationship between patient and psychoanalyst; it is characterized by the fact that the analyst does not enter responsively into the situation, and that the patient must gradually relinquish his defense mechanisms in dealing with the analyst, permitting regression and freeing anxiety. This is a condition not ordinarily fulfilled in casework, but it is closely approximated in dealing with the tuberculous patient—more than any other client he has been reduced to a defenseless, nearly infantile pattern

[7] Edward Hochhauser, "Objectives of Sheltered Workshops," *Jewish Social Service Quarterly,* Vol. XXV, No. 4 (1949), pp. 533–545.

in the sanatorium, and he displays attitudes toward people otherwise found primarily in the psychoanalytic situation.

Because of the great psychosomatic lability of the tuberculous, I believe that the transference situation, if we may call it that, needs to be considered with the greatest care. It is best to maintain a primarily positive relationship. I am not interested in creating a maximum of independence in the patient nor in serving the transference situation completely, and never abruptly. I leave the patient with the statement that I believe he is well but that I should always be glad to hear from him, whether he has problems or not. The tuberculous patient is frequently, and justifiably, afraid of relapse and is being threatened by a catastrophic crippling of the ego. He is therefore entitled to a more supporting attitude than many ambitious workers are willing to give. In this connection it is interesting to point out that the incidence of relapse of cases of the C.C.J.T. over two decades has been very small under a regime that in those past decades was only benignly supportive without any psychotherapy or even any specifically psychiatrically-oriented approach. It would be unfortunate indeed if a too-active psychotherapeutic approach would increase the rate of relapse; currently the ideal goal is to improve the individual patient's adjustment and experiences by psychotherapy without overextending his assets.

Dealing with Orality and Passivity

It requires a great deal of tact to discuss with patients their oral and passive wishes. It is necessary first for the patient to accept such tendencies before it is possible to show their existence in him and to deal with them. An example I frequently use is the following: I discuss the feeling nearly everyone has on certain mornings, particularly if it is rainy or cold, when one has to get up to go to work: one feels one ought to go to work, even wants to go, and yet one wishes one could stay in bed. This very human feeling demonstrates the need for passivity in everyone, the wish to be taken care of instead of having to fend for oneself. A similar feeling may persist when one has become accustomed to the protected situation of the tuberculous. We show the patient that it is perfectly reasonable to feel that way but that this attitude is a stumbling block. We may have to illustrate, by careful, detailed analysis of concrete situations, how the patient actually let slip some chance for improvement of his job situation. Limitations of agency funds may constitute the external compelling factor in decreasing the secondary gain of illness, if properly manipulated.

Anorexia and Other Psychosomatic Problems

In dealing with psychosomatic disorders, one of the main problems is to get the patient to accept the fact that emotional disturbances can cause bodily changes. The example of blushing is useful in this connection—embarrassment leading to a dilation of the blood vessels, the skin reddened by the blood shining through. A contraction of the blood vessels may lead to nutritional deficiencies and the ever-present germs may give rise to all sorts of eczemas and furuncles. One can explain that some people blush with the skin of their gut and get diarrhea or stomach ulcers. Many symptoms can be demonstrated to the patient as the result of fast breathing (overventilation) when anxious—causing dizziness, weakness, and so on.

Anorexia and nausea, as has been mentioned, are usually related to unconscious pregnancy fantasies or oral wishes. One can deal with them simply by explaining to the patient that he acts as if he were afraid of swallowing something bad—perhaps germs—and in the case of anorexia tries to avoid it, or he regurgitates them in the case of nausea. Small doses of insulin to produce appetite are used by some physicians with great success, starting with 10 units and increasing by 5 units up to 25 units, two and one-half hours before meals, if the consulting lung specialist does not consider that the increased metabolism may be harmful and if the patient can be watched to avoid coma. In one of our severe cases hospitalization was necessary to prevent physical collapse.

Depression

The tuberculous patient is often depressed. He is in a difficult reality situation, facing oral deprivation on his return from the sanatorium and harboring much latent aggression against the world in general and against family members to whom he is supposed to be grateful, although he often has much reason to feel resentment against them. Demonstrating the aggression and releasing it, by pointing out how emotionally "reasonable" this reaction is, usually proves very successful. In a few more difficult cases a mixture of nembutal and desoxyn or methedrine has proved useful and harmless when used in consultation with the tuberculosis specialist.

The Return of the Adolescent

The adolescent who returns to his family after years of absence has changed a great deal in his behavior and in his reactions to his family's behavior. As with all adolescents, we must gain his confidence, be on his side, and yet represent a parental figure who is not too permissive, lest we increase his guilt feelings. If the disturbance is not too severe, a discussion of the typical problems of the adolescent—his growing up and the family's reluctance to acknowledge it, his ambivalence toward his parents, problems of sex and of occupation inherent in this period—may help a good deal. It is almost always advisable to see the family or to have someone else see them to try to work out their difficulties. Only if the family is markedly pathological and no change can be effected is it advisable to help the youngster toward independent living quarters and a break with the family.

The Patient Who Acts Out

A fair number of tuberculous patients react to their anxiety and their passive wishes with a denial of the illness, ignoring all precautions against overwork, colds, and so on. This holds true particularly for adolescents but also for adults with masochistic character disorders, or for male patients who have to deny their castration fears by exhibiting their toughness. If the acting out is mild it may be simpler and more advantageous not to disturb this pattern of adjustment. If there is actual physical danger, however, it may be necessary to analyze this defense—if possible, precipitating anxiety and an overcautious attitude which can then be dealt with more easily. As in all intra-aggressive, self-harming behavior—and it may have to be designated as such—it is important to identify the object of the original aggressive impulse; the patient may want to punish his mother or someone else by making himself ill again.

Summary and Conclusions

Some psychiatric aspects of tuberculosis, as encountered in a social agency, have been discussed. No specific personality type or psychiatric disorder was observed among the 46 patients seen by the author for consultation or psychotherapy, nor in the 250 patients discussed in detail with social workers.

The psychological reaction to being informed of the diagnosis of tuberculosis is met by a series of defense mechanisms often in terms of pre-existing fantasies, and sometimes experienced as a catastrophic change in body image. With this change of body image an increase in secondary narcissism, oral needs, passivity, and regression is observed as is to be expected on the basis of psychoanalytic hypotheses. The problems of the return to the family after an absence of months or years have been mentioned, with particular reference to the complication of the family relationships in adolescents.

Psychotherapy is aimed at the isolation of the irrational aspects of the responses to an admittedly difficult reality situation—the peculiarly strong transference problems in the patient who is reduced almost to helplessness by his illness. Psychosomatic problems need simple, convincing explanations first, and then further interpretation. In the case of the adolescent, the family usually needs help also and, if this is impossible, his separation from the family needs to be encouraged. Depression and denial of the illness as self-harming behavior need prompt attention.

Part 4

Sociocultural Factors

The sociocultural aspects of client functioning has been the prime focus of many recent discussions. There has been an abundance of written and verbal enthusiasm about these rich and fertile fields. Important and influential as this trend has been on practice attitudes and understanding, the amount of material written by social workers concerning direct practice implications of these data has not been remarkable, at least not if the professional literature is used as an indicator. The need to do more has been frequently stressed; the results have been uneven.

It is clear though that progress is being made. The impact of the Stein and Cloward book *Social Perspectives on Behavior* on social work practitioners, especially recent graduates, has been marked. The Council of Social Work Education has published several case summaries in which treatment was structured to meet various sociocultural elements. Intensive efforts are being made to incorporate the thinking of people like Spiegel, the Kluckhohns, and others into our conceptual framework. Many student projects are examples of this.

Obviously social work is just beyond the beginning point of translating the importance of these dimensions into generalized therapeutic considerations. It is interesting that all the articles located for this section of the book were written after 1959; they are recent articles reflecting the beginning trend to incorporation.

It is evident that the articles in this section point up more gaps in the literature than in the other areas in this book. Nevertheless, these articles not only reflect a trend to increased development of this dimension in our practice but clearly point out the rich potential for treatment which they present. An interesting observation is that this is the only section of the book which does not contain any specifically group treatment articles.

This is surprising. It would seem that some of the diagnostic dimensions of sociocultural factors would be particularly available to group approaches. If, for example, the Kluckhohn work on value orientations is considered, especially the dimension of "relational values orientation," it could be hypothesized that collaterally oriented persons would be expected to involve themselves more easily and presumably more effectively in group treatment than individually oriented clients.

Spiegel has suggested that special variations in the one-to-one relationship is required for those groups of clients from selected ethnic groups in whom he was interested. The articles included under ethnicity although far from exhaustive do give some further indications of how such ethnic considerations will affect both the goals and conduct of treatment. More such data are needed. At this point I am not clear if the need is for a great number of articles from practitioners experienced with different ethnic groups, or immediate work on the development of a more general theory.

The former would require some fifty to one hundred discussions of just the major ethnic groups in North American culture with which social workers are confronted. Obviously a social worker cannot know every group; however, if in fact it is an essential dimension in understanding our client, the profession may have to work towards the development of a bank, or deposit of ethnic knowledge and the accumulation of practice implications, upon which practitioners could readily draw. This, of course, would have to be constantly updated, as such groups are themselves in constant development and transition.

The five articles included in the section on ethnicity examine the question of working with ethnic differences from varying viewpoints. To understand persons requires our understanding of how we are perceived by clients from the context of their own cultural orientation. Floyd J. Neville re-emphasizes the danger of cultural blindness and a strong tendency to view other cultures from our own basis. He uses the Eskimo culture to develop this theme. Externally different as is the way of life of the people he describes, his comments have direct relevance to work with any group of clients from a different culture. In the second article the importance of understanding internal changes which take place in cultural groups is developed. The author, Manheim S. Shapiro, discusses the ramifications from within that result from unrecognized shifts in values and attitudes of a group wishing to find its place in society. The article on the Navaho patient uses a case summary to demonstrate the importance of not only understanding ethnic differences and influences, but of developing skills by which the worker is accepted as a legitimate person in the client's attitudual system.

The final two articles in this Part deal with an ethnic difference from another viewpoint. The problems examined are associated with client-worker relationships in therapy between groups when there is clear and recognized antipathy. Concepts of color blindness, emotional distance, and mutual perception of worker and client are developed. Two important generalizations are made: first, the amount of work still to be done in translating knowledge and awareness of client differences into effective practice; second, the tremendous source of experience and data available in our agencies for learning how to work most effectively within these real and observable differences in clients.

The importance and significance of class factors as a diagnostic variable have been given less attention in the literature than ethnic factors. Of the articles addressed to this variable more attention has been given to lower-class clients than other classes. This is to be expected since this segment of society has long been presumed the special interest of social workers.

All the articles dealing with the lower class emphasize the grossness of this category. Within the term is included a wide range of problems, persons, forms of behavior and differences. There is a tendency in the articles to give most attention to the multiproblem and severely economically deprived families living in submarginal conditions. Implied in this is the erroneous idea that the membership in the lower class presumes the need for treatment. Perhaps we should remind ourselves that it is customary to subdivide the concept of lower class into two groups, lower lower and upper lower. To date most of the emphasis has been on the former.

Florence Hollis acknowledges the usefulness of social class as a diagnostic variable and the necessity for modification of treatment emphases rather than distinct methods in formulating treatment plans. She also stresses the lack of precision of the variable and the danger of letting it become a stereotype. Fantl and Meyer emphasize the necessity to understand the impact of the clients' milieu on their functioning, to avoid seeing psychopathology rather than reaction to stresses and conflicts in the life situation, and to diagnose and treat individually rather than by generalities.

Although emphasis in the literature has been on lower-class clients, some attention from a different viewpoint has been focused on the middle class. Ruth Fizdale discusses one approach to increasing the involvement of middle- and upper-middle-class clients. Just as it has been necessary to alter some of our treatment approaches to lower-class clients, the author suggests we must make other kinds of shifts to involve middle-class clients.

All the authors agree that the variable of class is significant. All stress that at this point we can only be tentative as to the treatment implications.

Obviously, the range of clients receiving social work treatment is widening to include all facets of society. It would be helpful to the whole profession if our colleagues would make more available their experiences with clients from different classes. Perhaps the private practitioners could make an important contribution here, as they are presumed to treat clients from parts of society not always found in the clientele of agencies.

Personal and group values are a dimension that have received particular attention in recent years. To date, work in this area has indicated some most interesting leads for practice which must be given further attention. Some corelation between values and interview content has been demonstrated, as well as value differences between workers and clients. Rather than working within the value structures of the client as has been frequently suggested, one of our treatment goals might be to change a client's values. Such a goal is in itself contrary to traditional social work values but must still be examined.

Conclusion

It is clear that extensive and interesting gains have been made in the profession regarding the incorporation of social science concepts into practice. It is equally clear that much still remains to be done to translate our interests and appreciation of these concepts into operational case-directed activities. Obviously, other dimensions of a sociocultural nature have not been fully explored. For example, it might well be that the occupational roles of clients could develop into patterned areas of strain and stress necessitating similar patterned alterations in treatment. The search for similarities in clients' sociocultural functioning along selected dimensions, which can help us more effectively develop and apply a profile of treatment techniques most applicable to the individuality of the client and his situation, can be observed in all the contributions.

Ethnicity

Casework in an Igloo—Adaptation of Basic Casework Principles in Work with Eskimos

Floyd J. Neville

A rather peculiar sensation bubbles up in most of us when we try to imagine Inuk and King Solomon as contemporaries and co-editors of the multi-featured story of man. If we can afford to be honest about it we may have to admit the sensation is most often one of surprise.

It is difficult to explain surprise in a situation like this because there is indeed sufficient scientific proof to warrant accepting the parallel as historical fact. The explanation is undoubtedly complex but it does suggest, as least in part, an orientation and a prejudice born of cultural conditioning; a conditioning which, of itself, limits the knowledge and appreciation of people and events outside the sphere of one's own culture.

This may be a rather lumpy pill for the reader to have to swallow so soon. On the other hand it may be just what he needs to prepare himself for the even greater shock of seeing Inuk as a client.

The following commentary is a simple and very limited attempt to look at Inuk, the Eskimo, as a person with a problem; and to try to determine why and how basic casework principles can and must be adapted to meet his situation. In the attempt, I have only been able to scratch the surface and in so doing I hope I have not done Inuk or casework a disservice.

The three years of research and practical field experience behind the commentary took place among Eskimos in the Eastern and Central Arctic and more especially in the Keewatin District. The points made have been made with these groups of people in mind, but I believe they would also be valid by and large, when applied to Eskimos in the Western Arctic. Although Eskimos do differ from area to area, they still possess, as a total group, a common and fairly well-defined cultural heritage.

For the most part I have talked in the commentary about casework principles in theory and in practice. I have not gone to any length to explain or even re-define these principles. For the sake of brevity as well as of relevancy, I have had to assume that the reader understands them.

Reprinted from *The Social Worker*, Vol. XXVIII, No. 3 (June, 1960), pp. 5–19, by permission of the authors and the publisher.

From time to time I have introduced actual cases. This was not done with a view to demonstrating the casework process, but rather to highlight certain points having reference to particular principles. I think it is important to remember this so that the reader does not feel frustrated at being allowed to see only part of the picture.

Wherever possible I have also tried to relate my observations about casework in this particular setting to the more conventional casework settings in the south. I feel this tends to bring to life our common belief in the generic content of social casework. I had hoped too, however, that it would throw more light onto the cultural content of the human personality and of all human behaviour and the significance which this has for the further development of social casework.

Basic Casework Principles

I have always found it difficult to academically examine and deal with each of the generic casework principles as separate metaphysical abstracts and to arrange them in some kind of logical sequence of importance. For example, it is not easy to talk about "acceptance" or the "non-judgmental attitude" without also talking about "the right to self-determination", or about "self-awareness". This is an understandable state of affairs however, because while they are indeed separate metaphysical abstracts, they are also vitally inter-related and interwoven in concrete human behaviour.

One has to start somewhere, however, and I think perhaps it is "self-awareness" that can most easily be separated out and recognized as the first and most fundamental of the principles. Self-awareness is knowledge, of the most basic order, upon which the other principles are founded. Using this line of reasoning then, we might say that self-awareness permits acceptance and the non-judgmental attitude, which in turn permits the relationship, which helps the client to direct himself toward adjustment or remedial change. If my logic here is open to question, I can always claim author's licence and say that for our purposes this sequence is good enough. In any event, as Mr. K. would say, this is how we are going to proceed.

Self-Awareness

Not long ago, at Rankin Inlet, I talked with a young Eskimo man and his wife, from the interior of Keewatin. To preserve anonymity, I will call him Kadluk, a name which is about as common among Caribou Eskimos as Smith is among Anglo-Saxons. He was married and had two small children.

Kadluk had moved to Rankin six months before, in search of more opportunities—opportunities for wage employment, better housing, a more stable supply of food; in short, he came in search of a better life.

A few years ago he had been hospitalized in a sanatorium in the south for treatment of T.B. for a period of about eleven months. During that time he underwent surgery and he was not what we would call a strong person. His wife did not have good health either and she suffered periodically from rheumatic pain. Her condition made it difficult for her to walk long distances. The children, when I knew them, seemed healthy enough.

All their lives prior to coming to Rankin, and excepting that period of Kadluk's hospitalization, these young people had lived more or less in the traditional manner of the Caribou Eskimo. They had followed the caribou in the spring and summer and early fall over miles of mosquito-infested tundra, in the heart of the Barren Lands. Kadluk had trapped the white fox through the long dark and bitterly cold months of late fall and winter; for a few weeks each summer he had stevedored at the Post during the period of re-supply.

Their home had always been a tent from late spring through early fall and a snow house the rest of the year.

As long as the caribou could be found and slaughtered—and as long as Kadluk was healthy enough to do this, the family ate simply but well and were warmly clothed. In years when a few men and women in New York or Paris decided that foxes would be worth money Kadluk and his wife were able to buy a better rifle or sewing machine and a little extra tobacco and gum and tea and flour.

In recent years, when the caribou could no longer be found in large numbers, hunger and privation and occasionally starvation have been frequent visitors to Kadluk and others like him.

When he and his wife moved to Rankin last winter with some of their friends, they indeed found a better life. They lived in a wooden house for the first time. It was not large by any standards but it was warm and dry against the pitiless Keewatin winter. Kadluk found a job with a mining company and in return received more money than he knew what to do with, although he did not manage to save any.

For him and his wife and family there was no more endless walking in search of phantom caribou; no more eternities huddled behind a snow block jigging for a few elusive fish; no more dripping igloos, nor sickness without medical attention, nor death without the solace of friends.

Kadluk came to talk to me in May when the sun had rolled back the darkness and the last real blizzard had coughed itself to death. We talked about many things and he told me about the Eskimo love of the land, his love for his land far away in the lonely interior. And finally we came to the point of our conversation and he told me that he wanted to return to the interior with his wife and family, to resume his life there. We talked about this at considerable length and from every angle, but it remained his ultimate decision. I want to conclude the story on this note.

There is a fundamental significance to this story, which should not be missed because it sets the tone to much of what we will consider henceforth. The point is not the wisdom or lack of wisdom in Kadluk's decision, nor whether I was accepting or non-judgmental, nor whether I recognized his right to self determination. Its real significance lies in the very way in which the story itself was presented by the writer and interpreted by the reader and the essential meaning which this holds for me and you and Kadluk. Let me explain this further.

A note of impending tragedy, of irrationality, of contradiction, and of heroism is inescapably written into my account of this situation. For some of us the case may stimulate sensations of pity, maybe even of tremendous sadness; and perhaps it conjures up too, a little of that old familiar sensation called surprise. If Kadluk had written or told this story, the story of his life on the land and his experiences at Rankin, he would have done so very differently. We would most certainly not see his life and his actions and his decisions as heroic or tragic or irrational. Everything about the way in which I related this case, included even my passing reference to Kadluk's extravagance and improvidence, reflects my own perception of reality, the reality with which my culture has provided me, the reality of "western" man.

I want to define "culture" as simply as possible before we go any further so that we will clearly understand how it is used here and the vital relationship which exists between it, the perception of reality, and principle of self-awareness.

Culture is not simply a collection of traits and acts and artifacts, existing in some state of abstraction. The friendly smile, the igloo, the caribou hunt, raw meat, do not constitute Eskimo culture. These things are no more than outward manifestations of a culture. Kluckholn and Kelly define culture simply and clearly enough for our purposes as:

> a historically derived system of explicit and implicit designs for living, which tend to be shared by all or specifically designated members of the group.[1]

In this definition it is the term "designs for living" which perhaps best describes the essence of culture, which gives it its true and full meaning and distinguishes it from brute society. Implicit in culture, as it is defined here, is an evolving, socially transmitted, orderly, intelligent way of life—a way of life which is complete and intelligent in the strictest sense of the term. The process by which a human being adapts to his culture and learns to fulfill the function of his status and role is called enculturation. In the enculturation process what the individual really learns is an organized pattern of behaving and functioning which he abstracts from and applies to daily life situations as they arise.

This understanding of culture, as a concept, is necessarily related to our consideration of the principle of "self-awareness", because implicit in "culture" and the "enculturation process" is the corollary that culture conditions, to a large extent, the individual's perception of reality. In fact, it is no exaggeration to say that in a restricted but nevertheless real sense the worlds in which two different cultural systems live are distinct worlds, and not merely the same world with different labels attached. It is the very

---

[1] Clyde Kluckhohn, and William Kelly, 1945. "The Concept of Culture." In Ralph Linton (ed.), *The Science of Man in The World Crisis*, pp. 76–106. New York. Columbia University Press.

grasp of this reality, the reality of Kadluk's world and my own world, which we are concerned with, in discussing the principle of self-awareness.

> In the way of a specific observation then, I would say that: In work with the Eskimo, self-awareness must be broadened as a concept to include an awareness of the cultural self, the self as a product of cultural conditioning.

In the more conventional social work settings in the south, self-awareness can quite often manage to remain a concept of fairly limited proportions. Let me give you two hypothetical situations to explain what I mean.

A Canadian-born, city-bred social worker, dealing with a Canadian-born, city-bred couple in marital conflict, has no particular need to reflect on cultural patterns in his own or in his clients' background in practising, or in consciously activating this attitude called self-awareness. Nor are cultural patterns as such, likely to be an important clue to the worker's understanding of the dynamics of this situation. The worker and his clients, here, share a common cultural heritage which is mutually understood and appreciated.

If we change this hypothetical situation by merely substituting "a Sicilian-born, country-bred, couple in marital conflict" in place of the "Canadian-born, city-bred, couple in marital conflict", a significant factor has been added. Cultural patterns in the clients' background become an important consideration in the worker's understanding of the dynamics of the situation. Cultural patterns in the worker's own background also become an important factor in his achievement of the kind of awareness he will need to preserve and practice the "non-judgmental attitude", for example.

In the latter hypothetical situation, knowledge of the "cultural" self, the self as the product of cultural conditioning, should become very much a part of the concept of the self-awareness. There is only a difference of degree here too between this situation and that of Kadluk.

There is a general principle here which seems to follow and which I think should apply right across the board—namely that:

> self-awareness, as a concept must be broadened to include the cultural element in human behaviour, especially where there are differences in the cultural background of worker and client.

Acceptance and the Nonjudgmental Attitude

I want to preface my remarks about the adaptation of these attitudes to work with the Eskimo by a brief consideration of the essential purpose of social casework itself—i.e., to bring about self-change on the part of the client. As we proceed I think my reason for doing so will become clearer.

Self-change, especially where and because it involves the uprooting of personal values and learned familiar patterns of behaviour is always a painful and traumatic experience. Pain, in the healthy personality, always conjures up resistance and hostility. Basically, this reaction is just another expression of the fundamental drive for self-preservation. The "change" involved threatens the integrity of the "self", as seen and understood vaguely or lucidly, consciously or sub-consciously, in whole or in part, by the self. Psychiatric medicine and social work were quick to recognize this and to develop skills and techniques to cushion and to handle resistance and to transmute it into positive action on the part of the patient or client. "Acceptance", and the nonjudgmental attitude are good examples of this.

Imposed-change (as opposed to self-change) may also involve the uprooting of personal values and habitual ways of behaving. It is often a more painful experience, because it robs the individual of the freedom of choice in the matter of his change. Here again we have the element of resistance and hostility, just as in self-change. When society imprisons or otherwise limits the freedom of the criminal offender, it imposes change upon him. Inevitably there is resistance to and resentment over this change. As an individual he may at times act out this resistance through personal revolt against the prison authority. As a member of a group, he may join in the group's expression of resistance by participating in a prison riot.

Resistance and hostility, at the individual level as well as at the group level, follow certain learned or habitual patterns as directed by personal experience and the experience of the broader group. Mr. Castro and his followers, for example, are "conditioned" to express resistance and resentment over the changes imposed upon them, through physical violence. Ghandi and his followers, on the other hand were "conditioned" to favour passive techniques.

In the North today many changes are being imposed on the Eskimo and his way of life, directly and indirectly, by "western civilization" as a whole. In the eyes of "western" man these changes may be good or for the better. But they do constitute the phenomenon of "imposed" change. If we admit that the Eskimo is a man with integrity, with a thought and value world all his own, then we have to admit and take for granted that he is enduring pain and that there is resistance to and resentment over this. The wonderful Eskimo smile, his apparent readiness to be directed and "moulded" and to imitate what he sees around him, should not be taken to mean that he does not feel the pain of self-change and imposed-change or that there is no resistance or hostility in him.

I may seem to have gone to great lengths in this preamble, but there is an important point in all of this. If it is missed one can only see half or maybe even less of the picture. The point is that in the casework situation with the Eskimo only part of the hostility which the worker encounters is that normally associated with self-change. The other part which is often impossible to measure is that which derives from the change which western culture imposes directly and indirectly on the Eskimo. Sometimes this hostility is expressed consciously and it may be even personalized. At other times, the Eskimo client may hardly be aware of it or he may express it on a more impersonal basis. The worker has to be aware of this and must try to sort it out some way or other if the client's behaviour is to have any rational meaning at all. I mention this because it is very much related to the principle of "acceptance" and "the non-judgmental attitude".

Fifteen winters ago, a gaunt hungry ghost called Starvation stalked a small group of primitive and very isolated inland Eskimos in the Keewatin District. Before it was trampled to death by the caribou migration of the following spring, it had claimed the lives of many people in the group.

A little Eskimo girl about six years of age and her brother, about five years older, survived the starvation of their parents when they were snatched up by a white trapper and taken to his cabin further south.

Again, for sake of anonymity, because we are dealing with a very small number of people, I will call the little girl Manie and the little boy Aloot.

Aloot, as a young lad of ten or eleven, was just old enough to be lonely and discontented in his new "white" home. He soon remedied this, however, by acquiring a small team of mangy dogs and setting out on his own to rejoin the group—which amazingly enough he managed to do, although it involved a journey of well over two hundred miles.

Manie remained in the white man's home or with friends of his for the next fifteen years. During this period she gained a knowledge of the language and customs of the white man and of course, in turn, lost her own language and customs. She had no contact at all during this period with her brother or other members of her group.

As often happens to youth the world over, who have forgotten or never known their own parents, Manie began as a young girl of fourteen or fifteen to "search" for her parents. She knew, of course, that they had perished during that terrible winter long ago.

The history of this "search" in itself is very interesting from a purely clinical point of view. Unfortunately I will have to pass over most of this because it is not exactly relevant. Perhaps I will say simply that dynamically, Manie had in her search substituted her brother and the other members of her group for her parents, and that her drive to rejoin them was essentially and finally tied up with her own evolutionary philosophy of personal integrity.

Manie's search ended in one sense in the winter of 1958–59. After a good deal of interpretation on both sides (i.e., to Manie and her brother and relatives), she was brought North for a visit with her brother and the group. This, of course, was meant to be a "sorting out" period for her and the others. To say that this was considered advisable before any permanent decisions were made, would be a gross understatement. Manie was by this time a relatively sophisticated young lady of twenty who had never been north of the tree-line since the age of five, and who had quite forgotten what is was to be Eskimo. Aloot and his group on the other hand, except for a few external changes, had remained pretty much what they were before—the most primitive group of Eskimos on this continent; a group whose social behaviour was, in many respects, unintelligible to all but a few outsiders.

The idea of a free-wheeling, sorting-out period for Manie and the group was a perfect example of "western" man's tendency to project his own "reality", his own sense of values and ways of looking at things onto another "reality", and then to be surprised when the two do not coincide.

Once Aloot and his group had accepted her and the reality of her return, it could not comprehend the idea that she was still "free" to choose between remaining with them or going away again. As far as the group was concerned, it was the group itself (and the principals within it) and not Manie, which would make this decision.

In a very short time, her life was like a thread in the fibre of the group. A labyrinthine maze of complex relationships was thrown up almost overnight. A marriage agreement was soon worked out for her by the brother and the parents of one of the young eligible men of the group. Manie was delighted with this.

In the spring of the year she was married to this young man, whom I shall call Timila. Personally, as the caseworker, I had great misgivings about the marriage because of the timing and because it was obvious to me that Manie could still not appreciate how this would affect her position with the group, or in fact, her whole life.

The marriage did indeed mark the end of one phase in this story and the beginning of a new phase. In many respects the new phase was about as dramatic—and as traumatic—as the first.

The honeymoon, spent for the most part with Timila's family, was soon over and Manie settled down to the daily tasks of being a wife. But this did not mean a "wife" in her understanding of the term, but rather in his understanding of the term—a wife to a husband whose language she still did not understand, and whose ways and customs were quite incomprehensible to her. Timila on his part also seemed to quickly settle down to the business of proving to himself and to his wife and to the group, that this young woman was or could be a "wife" in the group's understanding of the term.

I will not go into details here as to the form that this "making-over" process took, except to say that the pressure on Manie to conform to the patterns of the group were tremendous.

About three months after the marriage, the group as a whole moved out of the larger established Eskimo community to a hunting and fishing camp, about sixty miles away.

This move in itself had nothing to do with Manie but it held a great deal of significance and symbolism for the group. It marked the resumption of the old group patterns of behaviour, patterns which it had superficially abandoned because of social pressure while it was part of the larger established community.

Timila began to take most of his meals in his mother's tent instead of in Manie's tent and to pursue the hunt with more gusto than ever. This was customary to some extent but there was a certain element of retaliation here too, which could not be measured but which meant in essence "at last I have you on my own grounds". This indeed was the case because there was no white man within sixty miles who could "interfere". The situation, and the fact that Manie could not speak Eskimo or make herself understood, just about sealed her off completely.

This story goes on and on, but I need not go any further to emphasize the point we are immediately concerned with.

It is relatively easy to academically isolate Manie and her situation, to think of her for the moment as a young girl, an Eskimo legally and in appearance only; and then to consider acceptance and the non-judgmental attitude, as they apply in her case. When one knows a little more about her earlier life experiences it is not difficult to understand the dynamics of her search, the driving motivations that impelled her to do what she did, and the fact that she stuck by her decisions, although in so doing she would appear to have acted unreasonably. In short, because it is within the realm of our own professional and cultural experience to appreciate this it is easier to be accepting and non-judgmental in one's dealings with Manie. The hostility which she expressed in the interview situation does not present any particular challenge either.

When we begin to isolate Timila in the same way, however, something rubs, and that "something" has to do mainly with the fact that we cannot so readily accept and be non-judgmental about behaviour or attitudes which we cannot fully understand. This is particularly true where the behaviour seems, for all intents and purposes, to be at variance with something as basic as our own traditional concepts of "good and right reason".

In Timila's case it was not possible either to always distinguish one type of resentment or hostility from the other. It is the group in this instance, as well as Timila, which provided the key, as I think I have made clear in the story. In summary then:

> Acceptance and the non-judgmental attitude as they apply in this setting, often means that the worker accepts without being judgmental, attitudes and values and customs not only different from his own, but quite outside the realm of his own cultural experience and understanding. It means too that he has to learn to understand and to cope with not just the usual hostility around self change, but that too which is peculiar to a group immersed in a situation of imposed cultural change.

The Use of the Relationship

The relationship in the social casework sense of the term implies more than a knowledge of the client as a unique individual with a unique problem, located in a cultural context and highly influenced by this cultural world. This is still mere knowledge. The relationship also implies the ability, on the part of the worker, to transmute this knowledge through applied skills and techniques—and attitudes, into vital positive action on the part of the client.

The vital content of the casework relationship, of course, implies by its very nature "communication" between worker and client. The more

direct the communication, the greater the "personal" quality of the relationship. This is so generally true that it may be axiomatic, but it is worth
spelling out and developing in the present context because there are some
real communication problems in work with the Eskimo which do effect the
casework relationship.

Communication between two people can be established very quickly
and in any number of ways, depending upon the ability of the two to give
out and receive mutually understood symbols, and upon the elasticity of
the physical and psychic media separating the two. Generally speaking,
however, and for our purposes we could say that communication, in a
restricted sense of the term, can be achieved through verbal and non-verbal
means.

In much of casework practice, and particularly in the establishment
of the casework relationship with a hearing, speaking client, the spoken
word, as a means of communication, is not only quite essential but also
the normal method of proceeding. I don't think we have to belabour this
point. If the client hears, he expects to hear words; if he speaks, he expects
to express himself and his problems and his attitudes through words that
will be understood. The Eskimo client is no different in this respect. Ideally,
he naturally expects communication in his own language. The appreciation
of this situation in itself should be an incentive to learn the Eskimo language.
There is yet another incentive, however, which has a more scientific base,
namely that we learn to understand a culture through understanding its
language. This point should perhaps be developed a bit, because there are
certain implications to it which may not be readily apparent and which
cannot really be ignored.

Although there may be disagreement among contemporary anthro-
pologists as to the precise relationship of language to culture, it is generally
agreed that it is an integral one, i.e., that language is part of the whole and
functionally related to it. Language and linguistic patterns are a guide to
social reality. The real world is to a considerable extent built upon the
language patterns of the group. In essence, of course, this does not mean that
linguistic patterns inescapably limit sensory perception but rather that they,
like other cultural patterns, direct perception and patterns of thought into
certain habitual channels. All of this implies too that language is far more
than a mere tool for the communication of ideas and feelings and
attitudes.

There is a corollary here which follows logically enough and which
is very much related to any consideration of basic casework principles. The
corollary states in effect that in order to thoroughly understand and appreciate a culture and the troubled human personalities within it, one must
understand its linguistic patterns.

Whatever the social worker can learn of Eskimo linguistics and language
patterns will certainly aid in and facilitate his understanding of the group
as a group. We cannot dispute this. On the other hand, social work as a
profession is not especially orientated towards the study of linguistics, nor

does this fall within the range of its primary focus. Moreover, when social work talks about understanding the worker's "self" and the client's "self", it does not mean total knowledge of these selves. Total knowledge is not possible for any of us at any time.

However true the corollary may be then in the rarified air of pure logic, social workers and social work will have to regard the Eskimo language as it does any other language, that is, primarily as a means of communicating and understanding and appreciating ideas and feelings and attitudes in the normal course of the casework process.

As a general principle, good interpreters, as media of communication between worker and client, can be used to advantage in the administration of the social insurances, for example, and in certain other areas of practice where the use of the strong relationship is not of primary importance. In dealing with more personal and complicated problems however, direct communication on a person-to-person basis is more essential. This is certainly true but in a more particular way when applied to the Eskimo.

Shortly after I first went into the North, a young Eskimo woman, by the name of Mage, came to me in a rather agitated frame of mind. She rattled out a story in Eskimo which except for a few words, I was unable to understand. About all I could tell was that she was complaining about her husband. I also understood her to mention a set of women's underwear. These threads of information puzzled me—and needless to say amused me unduly. The whole situation was very hopeless and the woman could sense this. Fortunately, Eskimos have a wonderful sense of humour and we both stopped and laughed hilariously. In spite of the ridiculous light that this put both of us in, this nevertheless was the beginning of the casework relationship with her.

When I had found some semblance of composure again I offered to bring in an interpreter, which I did, and the interview resumed. The only interpreter available in this case was a young Eskimo boy about the same age as Mage and who lived in the same community.

When the interpreter was introduced, Mage's whole attitude changed and the interview took on a stilted, cautious, ambiguous tone. She was able to tell me that her husband would not buy her a set of underwear. I was ready to accept this as the "presenting problem", but she could not be drawn out and it was quite apparent that we had come to the end of the interview. For all intents and purposes she had withdrawn from further help.

Mage was not ready to or able to talk about the personal relationship between her husband and herself in front of the interpreter. There were many reasons for this which I could only assume at the time, but which were confirmed through later experience. To have discussed her situation under the circumstances would have, in her estimation, made it common knowledge. She and her husband would have lost face in the Eskimo community.

When I finally got back to this case months later, after I had learned more of the language and did not use an interpreter, I was able to build up the relationship again. My command of the language was still not fluent at that time, but allowance was made for this. The "presenting problem" of course turned out to be just that and it led into a very complicated marital situation involving the tactful handling of traditional Eskimo feelings about sterility. Mage and her husband were childless. In the way of conclusion, I might add that before I left that community Mage and her husband were the proud adoptive parents of a baby girl.

In this case direct communication and the use of the relationship was much more important because of the problems involved, the kind of "change" indicated for the client, and the necessity of eliciting and dealing with very personal material. A knowledge of the Eskimo language sufficient at least to express oneself accurately and on a person-to-person basis, is essential for real effectiveness in situations like this. The use of interpreters here only tends to water down the "personal" quality of the relationship. Then too, the presence of the interpreter introduces a new factor into the relationship, the precise meaning of which is often difficult if not impossible to decipher. Most Eskimo communities are very small by southern standards and their sociology is such that the interpreter and the client are thrown together in a complex maze of other relationships within the group. We may think of the interpreter merely as a "voice", which does our talking for us, but this is often an over-simplification of the situation.

As far as the use of the relationship is concerned, then, I would say that:

> in dealing with the Eskimo a working knowledge of his language is essential to real effectiveness in those situations requiring use of the strong relationship, because direct communication between worker and client in the interview situation controls and determines the quality of relationship.

This observation has general applicability to similar and nearly similar situations elsewhere although there may be a question of degree involved. I am thinking here, for example, of casework with new Canadians in the South.

Self-Direction and the Right of Self-Determination

The Eskimo, characteristically, is a very pleasant individual anxious to avoid conflict, to conform and to co-operate. This is true of his relationships within the group, as well as with outsiders.

Traditionally, his social-political-economic system was built upon a whole series of inter-dependent relationships which were essentially "gemeinschaft" in quality. One has only to visit the Arctic, to view its emptiness and to sense the precariousness of all life within it, in order to understand how the physical environment in itself has conditioned him to develop these characteristics. Unfortunately, such traits are sometimes, if not often, interpreted by non-Eskimos as signs of personality weakness. One frequently hears it said that the Eskimo has no mind of his own and cannot make sound decisions. Indeed some non-Eskimos in the country really believe this. I would qualify this judgment almost endlessly. Certainly, he sometimes has difficulty making decisions about matters that lie outside the realm of personal and cultural experience. We are no different in this respect. Then too, the phenomenon of "choice", of choosing between various and equally attractive alternatives, was not a common one in the traditionally simple life of the land. He is still learning how to choose. In the "western" enculturation process that is sweeping across the Arctic to-day, the more "primitive" Eskimo is at a distinct disadvantage in the matter of decision-making, not only for the reasons given above but because he is often up against more aggressive individuals who do not always understand him or his situation, nor recognize his right to self-determination.

Let me go back for a moment to Kadluk, the man who left the life of the land for wage employment, and then thinking better of it, decided to return to the land. Kadluk made this decision after considerable reflection and soul searching. There is no doubt in my mind however but that I could have talked him out of this, or influenced him by one means or other to remain at Rankin Inlet. From our point of view, Kadluk's decision to trade the comforts of civilization for life on the land, a life that would mean privation and the possibility of starvation for himself and his family, may seem like sheer madness, an inability to make sound decisions and a contradiction in human logic. When all the factors in this case are weighed and considered in their proper perspective however, this conclusion is not valid. Kadluk's decision was not really a contradiction in human logic, but in the logic of western man. He made his decision and it was the right one for him.

In the case of Manie and Timila the possibilities for interfering with the marriage before and after it took place were numerous and rather tempting to say the least. One is free to question the sanity of Manie's decision, in view of her lack of understanding of what she was getting into. However, one cannot question her right to make this decision, against what would seem to be her better judgment, and still uphold the principle of self-determination.

The same thing applies to Timila. The fact that he did not seem to understand what his marriage would do to Manie and himself and the group does not negate his right to go ahead with it, and to work out his own solutions to the problems which followed. If self-determination as a right is as basic as we believe it to be, then it applies to Timila and Kadluk and Manie just as it does in the case of you and me.

In brief then:

> Self-determination, self-direction as casework principles apply with equal force in work with the Eskimo. It is easier to appreciate this when the Eskimo and his problems are seen in their proper cultural perspective. The tendency among Eskimos to co-operate and to accept help in the matter of decision making is more often related to factors of culture rather than to basic personality weakness.

Summary

When most of us try to imagine Inuk and King Solomon as contemporaries and co-editors of the story of man we become surprised. The explanation for this reaction is complex, but it does suggest, in part at least, an ignorance, an orientation and a prejudice born of cultural conditioning; a conditioning which tends to limit the knowledge and appreciation of people and events outside the sphere of one's own culture. It is important for the social worker whose field of work is with the Eskimo to try to fully understand this because he is dealing with a group of people who are still, by and large, members of a different culture.

Social casework lays claim to a number of basic generic principles which are adaptable to any work setting. The purpose of this commentary is to point up some of the main adaptations called for in casework with the Eskimo.

In this setting, self-awareness, as one of the basic concepts of casework, must be emphatically broadened to include the concept of the cultural self, because culture is a very significant part of all human behaviour and of the total human personality. This point has general applicability to similar casework settings elsewhere.

Acceptance and the non-judgmental attitude as applied to casework with the Eskimo, mean that the worker often has to accept, without being condemnatory, attitudes and values and customs that are not only different from his own, but quite outside the realm of his own cultural experience and understanding. In addition, it means that he has to learn to understand and to cope with not just the usual hostility around self-change, but that which is peculiar to a group immersed in a situation of imposed cultural change.

The relationship and the personal interview are basic to the practice of casework. Communication between worker and client is essential to building the relationship and this is normally done through the use of the spoken language in the interview situation. In this setting, a knowledge of the Eskimo language tends to build up confidence, the feeling of being understood and the sense of confidentiality. This is particularly important where the use of the strong relationship is indicated. In more simple situations interpreters can be used to good advantage. This point also has general applicability in similar settings where language and cultural differences are important factors.

The tendency among Eskimos to co-operate and to accept help in the matter of decision making is often more related to factors of culture rather than to basic personality weakness. Self-determination and self-direction as casework principles apply with equal force in working with the Eskimo. Again it is easier to appreciate this if one sees the Eskimo and his problems and the problem-solving pattern of the group in their proper cultural perspective.

Conclusion

There are only two logical conclusions that can be drawn from this entire discussion. First of all we must conclude that the basic principles of casework apply with equal force in work with the Eskimo, but certain adaptations have to be made. Secondly and finally, it is essentially the cultural factors in the background of worker and client that determine how the adaptations must be made.

Changing Jewish Attitudes—And Their Consequences for Jewish Community Relations Workers

Manheim S. Shapiro

The title for this paper, in itself, reflects some interesting changes. If we go back ten or fifteen or twenty years, I believe we would find that the field of Jewish community relations was operating on the basis of two axioms: the first, that all American Jews were united in the perception of how inequality of acceptance by others influenced their lives; the second, that this inequality could be eliminated primarily by modifying the environment in which they lived, or somewhat differently stated, by changing the attitudes of non-Jews, by affecting the legal and governmental codes which permitted or prevented discrimination, and by changing the social norms of the general American Society.

It is probably a reflection of some desirable changes in American society as a whole that Jews can at least sometimes focus upon the intra-group rather than exclusively upon the inter-group relations. Some of the bread and butter issues (primarily forms of discrimination and *visible* hostility of the last twenty or thirty years) for Jewish community relations workers are considerably relieved, if by no means solved.

Discrimination in job opportunity, which literally made the difference for survival during the pre-war depression, has been greatly reduced. Although there are still particular occupations in which discrimination is a factor, Jews do appear in almost every kind of business and vocation. The problem of college admissions has been sensationally reduced, almost to the point of elimination, and even fraternity discrimination has in large measure been overcome. While there are still pockets of discrimination in housing in

Reprinted from the *Journal of Jewish Communal Service*, XXXVII (Summer, 1961), pp. 405–410, by permission of the author and the Journal.

certain communities, most Jews can in fact obtain homes or apartments of the type they desire or can afford. Even resorts, with their sensitivity to social contact, are yielding to change and it is not uncommon to find Jews visiting the "swankiest resorts," which were once regarded as the exclusive domain of non-Jews.

Even anti-Semitic organization and propaganda seem to be reduced in effectiveness and acceptance, although the tensions arising from the aspirations of other minority groups have had an echo in the revival of anti-Semitic agitations; and the recent shocking wave of desecrations have given pause to any who were being complacent.

Our work with non-Jews is by no means finished. There lie before us still the problems of social discrimination which symbolize an assumption of inferior status for Jews; the issues of executive employment, upgrading and recruitment; the opening of employment opportunities in industries and businesses which remain closed; the complete acceptance of fair housing practises; and a variety of other discriminations. There are still in our midst the Conde McGinleys and the Gerald L. K. Smiths and their spiritual sons, the Lincoln Rockwells and the John Kaspers. There are the forces in the American society which can make it possible for teen-agers to paint swastikas on temples, smash windows, throw bombs and even shoot. There is the attempt of Arab propagandists to drive a wedge between *Americans* and *American Jews* as a means of weakening Israel. There is still the unfinished business of assuring equality for all Americans. There are the constitutional issues of church-state relations and the social issues of inter-religious tensions. In short, there are still tremendous tasks for the field of Jewish community relations in modifying the extra-group attitudes and conditions which affect the lives and future of American Jews.

Cultural Pluralism

However, the theme of this paper is that there is another element—the intra-group arena—which also requires our awareness and perhaps our effort. The proposition before us is, stated simply, that the attitudes, and probably forms of behavior related to such attitudes of Jews also have an impact upon inter-group relations and therefore upon the achievement of our general goals.

Let us briefly examine these goals. We have spoken frequently of "full equality" for the Jew in the general society and I suggest that in speaking thus we meant something more than job opportunity, or access to housing, or admission to college; I think we were talking about equality, not merely "acceptance" or access to facilities which are symbols of *treatment as an equal* rather than equality itself. But equality is an equation, with two sides. And for a Jew to be an equal, he must also feel himself equal. In other words, when we speak of "equality" we posit the notion that when two Americans meet they will evaluate each other on the basis of their identities and qualities as human beings, and avoid the irrelevant introduction into this evaluation of factors of race, creed, national origin or culture, on either side.

On the other hand, there is also implied the mutual recognition of each other's distinctive group identity without invidious inference. In other words, while our definition would deny the irrelevant introduction of group identity, it would affirm the appropriateness of distinctive group identities in relevant contexts.

Closely allied to this latter aspect of our programs has been the social concept of a pluralism which encourages distinctive group cultures as a force to enrich the whole society. Such a concept not only permits but also in a sense obligates each group to bring to the whole society the culture which the group bears; the loss of the culture of any group in the society, is a loss to the whole society. In consequence, the attitudes, the knowledge, the maintenance of a Jewish group culture and the diffusion of that culture in the general society are matters of moment for the continuation of a pluralistic society.

Having stated the proposition, then, that Jewish attitudes are related to our general goals of equality, of relevant group distinctiveness and of a pluralistic society, let us proceed to an examination of changing Jewish attitudes. The American Jewish Committee has been making studies of Jewish attitudes for some years now. The report of the Riverton study is well known. In the last two years, we have been developing related studies conducted with volunteer interviewers and we have completed two such studies in White Plains, New York, and in a Southern metropolis we call Southville. Interviewing has also been completed on a major study by our Scientific Research Division in a midwestern suburb called Lakeville, and a volunteer survey in a major resort city called Bayville.

Rather than repeat the data which are already available in the literature, as a means to provide a basis for futher inquiry, I have elected to present a selected number of propositions, hypotheses and questions. The answers to these questions have a bearing on the potential success of Jewish community relations work and on the ways in which we define and fullfill our responsibilities. However, I am offering these as *open* possibilities. Were there to be a debate on all or any of these propositions, I would have decided views of my own. In this particular case, however, I am doing my best to state the problems rather than offer my own answers. In connection with each, I shall cite in general terms some of the evidence of our studies.

Intra-Group Religious and Cultural Values

Proposition One

That if a religious or cultural group is to contribute distinct values to the general society it must have such distinct religious and cultural values and its members must know them.

This proposition seems obvious on its face. Those who are steeped in Jewish lore would assure us that there are many distinct differences between Judaism and certain "universal" ethical systems, or the Christian ethic. Our studies reveal however that by and large a majority of American Jews are substituting for the traditional beliefs and practises of Judaism, a generalized set of secular humanistic moral and ethical principles and community responsibility. As Marshall Sklare has pointed out on a number of occasions, the precepts of Judaism affecting daily living are being abandoned, and ceremonies which are annual, more or less festive and more or less convenient are being retained or expanded. In almost all the communities we have studied "gaining the respect of Christian neighbors" is ranked above such items as "belief in God," "attending services," or "contributing to Jewish philanthropies" as essential to being a good Jew.

Among some groups of our respondents there are as many who exchange family Christmas gifts as light Sabbath candles. It is interesting that in at least one of the communities, most of our "People of the Book" had no objection to their children's singing Christmas carols or participating in Christmas plays but overwhelmingly objected to their being subjected to Bible-reading in the schools.

While our studies are not definitive on this point, the studies combined with observation suggest that American Jews are comparatively unfamiliar with the precepts of the Jewish religion or the treasury of Jewish culture (with the exception of certain gastronomic delicacies and some Yiddish imprecations.)

What is more, the evidence is that comparatively few of them are doing anything to find out. Not more than 25 per cent claim to have attended any course, lecture, study group or discussion group on Jewish matters. While about the same proportion claims to have done serious reading in Jewish matters, it turns out when they are asked to name the reading matter, that by "serious" Jewish reading they mean the local Anglo-Jewish weekly, an organizational newsletter, or a popular best-seller which happens to be about Jewish characters—and is a book-club choice.

Among the questions we must ask are these: To what extent is the Jewish group prepared to contribute to the complex cultures we hold up as an ideal for a democratic society? Can most Jews hold up their end of a "dialogue" among religious or cultural groups which demands both a knowledge of Jewish values and traditions and a commitment to them? To what extent does actual contact with Jews establish in the minds of other Americans conflict between their *expectation* of Jews as an equivalent *religious* group and their *experience* of Jews as non-believing, a-religious individuals?

Self-Acceptance of One's Group Identity

Proposition Two

That acceptance of one's self and one's group identity is a prerequisite to relationships as equals with others.

When we ask our respondents if they are ever embarrassed by the behavior of other Jews, a majority says "yes." When they are asked to describe the kinds of behavior which embarrass them, it turns out to be the whole catalogue of charges leveled at the whole group of Jews by anti-Semites: "loud, noisy, vulgar, pushing, clannish, moneyminded." Of course, it is always *other Jews* who are guilty of this behavior. But does this not reflect something in the consciousness or subconscious of those who are giving the answer? Does not even the claimed embarrassment of the behavior of *other* Jews reflect a hyper-sensitivity that suggests an uneasiness with the group identification?

In the Riverton Study, an overwhelming majority of the respondents favored the continued existence of the Jewish group. When asked their reasons, they gave such answers as that a group which *had contributed* (and I emphasize the past tense) so much to the world should continue; or, on the other hand, that having survived in the face of unequal odds for so long, it would be cowardly or wrong to give up now. There were virtually no answers suggesting that the group had contributed much to the respondent himself or to members of the group itself.

Is it not necessary to like one's self and one's group before one can like others, or be liked by them? Is there not a necessity for American Jews to find an internal security and satisfaction with being Jewish as a component of having good relationships with others? Can American Jews be freed of the insecurities of centuries of wandering and persecution by discovering significant personal group values in Judaism, without group chauvinism?

Inter-Group Association

Proposition Three

That a readiness by Jews to associate with non-Jews, both in formal organization efforts and informal social contact, is essential to the ultimate establishment of a true multi-group civic partnership.

Jews are, by all statistical findings, much more frequent joiners as a group than the general American population. Our surveys show that as a whole they join about the same number of Jewish organizations as non-sectarian organizations. However, upon closer examination it turns out that many of the non-sectarian organizations they list are business, professional and trade associations which they are in a practical sense virtually compelled to join as a business measure. It thus turns out that Jewish women belong to many fewer non-sectarian organizations than do the Jewish men (and this in itself has many interesting connotations). Furthermore, they are likely to belong in comparatively large proportions to a selected group of organizations (PTA's and in some communities the League of Women Voters are good examples) and to avoid others entirely. Further, in reporting on time spent in organizational work, the time they give to Jewish organizations by far exceeds the time given to non-sectarian groups.

In the matter of residential choice, the majority of our respondents express a desire to live in a neighborhood where the proportion of Jews by far exceeds the proportion of Jews in the community. In one community, where

Jews form 15 per cent of the total population, some of our respondents wanted to live in a neighborhood which is 75 per cent Jewish. In another city where Jews are 2 per cent of the population, the average of their expressed desire was for a neighborhood around 30 per cent Jewish.

Insofar as social contact is concerned, we asked our interviewees about whether they had spent a social evening in the homes of non-Jews in the preceding year, and some 60 per cent said they had done so at least once. That leaves 40 per cent who did not do so *even* once. When we ask the same people if they have had non-Jews in their homes for a social evening in the past year, the percentage falls off sharply, by a margin of about 15 per cent of those who assert they visited non-Jews. In other words, *fewer than half* had non-Jewish guests.

The recital of figures like this can be extended. They serve really to confirm the common observation we all have made that there is a "five o'clock shadow" between Jews and non-Jews.

I think the questions we must probe with respect to this whole area have perhaps been best put by one of our lay leaders who, speaking about this at our recent annual meeting said, "How much of this is a perfectly normal and healthy desire to associate with those of common interest and with whom there is a possibility of appropriate common effort—Jewish education for the children, a temple or synagogue, Jewish philanthropy" (and I add a sense of group identity)? "And how much is a neurotic fear of non-Jewish associations bred by centuries of persecution and a clinging to the isolated security of the exclusive contact with other Jews? To what extent are our Jewish institutions and organizations permeated, as Louis Marshall put it, 'by a distinctly Jewish tendency' and to what extent are they Jewish merely by virtue of the absence of non-Jews? To what extent is the involvement of Jews in Jewish activities and associations the product of an expectation of rejection by non-Jews which may exceed, or mirror, the actual amount of rejection they are likely to encounter?"

I add, is not the question of readiness among Jews for free association with non-Jews a matter community relations workers must consider?

Positives of Inter-Group Association for Young People

Proposition Four

That the encouragement of contact between children and young people of various groups will conduce toward greater mutual understanding in their adulthood.

I am reminded of a study of the attitudes of non-Jews toward Jews which we completed some twelve years ago. One of the most interesting findings was that those who had contact with Jews, as neighbors, as co-workers, as friends, were consistently less likely to express prejudiced views than those who had never had contact with Jews. But those who had had such contacts in their childhood were by far less likely to express such prejudice even than those who had had the contacts in adulthood.

Now, in our studies we find a most interesting, and perhaps to be expected, set of attitudes. Jewish parents want their pre-teen age children, the younger ones, to be in mixed settings (for example, in Boy and Girl Scout troops, in school, and even in friendships); but once their children reach high school age, they would prefer a minimum of contact with Non-Jewish children outside the classroom.

It is of great interest to note that in Southville, 75 per cent of the parents of even the pre-teen children say they do not want their children to have Christian friends of the *opposite sex*.

The inference, of course, is plain: the issue is intermarriage. Apart from the question of whether intermarriage can in fact be forestalled by trying to prevent contact rather than by making Jewishness a positive factor in the lives of the children, there also remains the question of the impact of such separation upon the intergroup attitudes of both the Jewish and the non-Jewish children and the import of such separation to the parents on both sides. Let us grant that intermarriage of our children would discomfit us, both from the point of view of our psychic and emotional uneasiness and our intellectual concern about Jewish survival. Nevertheless, must we not look at this as a problem of viable relationships and practical methods rather than a resort to flight? What guidance can and should Jewish parents have as to raising their children in a multi-group society, fostering wholesome intergroup attitudes and avoiding the prospect of intermarriage which they fear?

Conclusion

It is fairly clear that there is not the unanimity of point of view or understanding that we had among Jews when their major concern was the various forms of discrimination which blocked access to job, a home, education for their children and so on. There is not even the same unanimity there was on certain social restrictions which *symbolized* a social inequity. Now that Jews are economically comparatively secure, live in suitable homes, educate their children in good colleges, and go more or less where they want to, the problem of their intergroup relations is becoming more complex and more subtle.

In the arena of our ideal of cultural pluralism, I think the case is fairly clear that most of today's American Jews are not too knowledgeable about the Jewish culture. Perhaps it is because in the press for Americanization and economic achievement, this was perforce neglected. And perhaps because they came so far so fast economically and in status, they are ready for a rest to consolidate their gains. And maybe because they carry still the effects of centuries of inequality, they either cannot accept or are frightened of actual equality.

Be this as it may, I suggest that we as community relations workers cannot be frightened or indifferent. Whatever we may ultimately decide is our function in this area, or the function of others, one thing, I believe, is clear: we cannot achieve our basic goals only by working *for* Jews in changing the environment so equality is possible. One way or another we must work *with* Jews so that equality can be real.

Cultural Factors in Casework Treatment of a Navajo Mental Patient

Inez M. Tyler and Sophie D. Thompson

Planning aftercare service for a non-English-speaking Navajo Indian who has been a long-term mental patient presents the social worker with two specific kinds of problems. Not only must he deal with the usual problems associated with the discharge of a mentally ill patient, but, in addition, he must deal with problems that are unique to the Indian culture. The case discussed in this article illustrates the importance of the worker's understanding the Navajo language and culture.

The Navajo woman who returned home had been a mental patient for twenty years in a hospital located at a great distance from her family and homeland. The worker showed unusual skill in utilizing her knowledge of the patient's cultural background to help the patient and her family achieve a realistic view of her return home. In this case it is of special interest to note the process by which certain specific cultural beliefs were incorporated in the patient's symptomatology. Before a discussion of the case is presented, however, information is given about the Navajos and their mode of living in order to provide some understanding of their orientation to problems involving health and medical care, and how this sociocultural orientation may affect casework treatment.

Cultural Background

With an estimated population of 90,000 the Navajo is the largest Indian tribe in the United States, living on 14,450,369 acres of land in the states of Arizona, New Mexico, and Utah. Their complex social and economic problems are compounded by cultural and language barriers that separate them from the dominant society. Their poor roads, their inadequate transportation facilities, and their low educational attainment further serve to increase their isolation. During the past ten years, however, there has been

Reprinted from *Social Casework*, XLVI (April, 1965), pp. 215–220, by permission of the authors and the Journal.

great progress in making available to the Navajos an opportunity to be educated in local day and boarding schools and in the public schools of "bordertowns" that lie outside the reservation.

Traditionally, the Navajos are a semi-nomadic people whose principal livelihood is gained from herding sheep. They are accustomed to move with the sheep to new grazing land. They live in octagonal hogans, built of logs and mud; the floors are dirt, and a smoke hole is cut in the roof. The one-room hogan may shelter an entire family composed of from two to twelve or more persons. The Navajos do not live in villages, and the family groups are often separated from one another by long distances. In many instances the members of a traditional matrilineal extended family, including grand-parents, parents, and daughters and their husbands are still found living near one another. In general, however, no more than four or five hogans are located in one place. The hogans lack indoor sanitary facilities and electricity. Neither water nor wood is readily available, and each family must haul its water from a distance, perhaps so much as twenty miles. The storage of hauled water has become less a threat to the Navajo's health since the people learned in a sanitation program supported by the Public Health Service to build platforms for the steel water containers.

The traditional Navajo religion is oriented primarily to maintaining health and curing illness. One of the simplest and clearest statements of Navajo religious thought and its relationship to health was made by Mary and John Collier, Jr.:

> The basis of Navajo religious thought is that the universe and all the earth peoples function according to rules. The misfortunes of sickness and premature death are the result of not following the rules. Navajos hold ceremonials to restore order in the individual by performing exact rituals which will require supernatural forces to withdraw their punishment, or the sickness, from the individual. To be well you must obey the ancient rules, and the chants and ceremonies are routines to re-establish the broken routine.[1]

Medical and Psychiatric Facilities

In 1955 the responsibility for the medical care of Indians living on reservations was transferred from the Bureau of Indian Affairs to the Division of Indian Health, a part of the U.S. Public Health Service responsible for all health services to Indians and Alaskan natives. Six hospitals, three field health centers, and a number of health stations provide preventive and curative health care to Navajos living on the reservation.

The staff of the Division of Indian Health is especially concerned about the high rate of illness among mothers and children and the high rate of infant mortality; they are also concerned about the high incidence of accidents and the identification and care of people suffering from emotional

[1] Mary and John Collier, Jr., "The Basis of Navajo Religion," in *Societies Around the World*, Vol. I, I. Sanders and others (eds.), Dryden Press, New York, 1953, p. 300.

problems and mental illness. Providing comprehensive health services to patients on the reservation is complicated by problems of communication, shortage of staff, and other factors already mentioned.

The Public Health Service contracts with state and private mental hospitals to provide psychiatric care for the Navajos, since psychiatric services are not available on the reservation. In past years mentally ill Navajos were committed to federal hospitals located hundreds of miles from their homes, where, because of the language barrier, they received only limited care. Some Navajos have remained in such institutions for as long as twenty years, or even longer. Recently emphasis has been placed on using psychiatric facilities that are near the reservation. Efforts have been made, when medically feasible, to arrange for patients previously sent to distant hospitals to return to their reservation. Mrs. Y was one such patient, whom the caseworker helped to return home after a long absence. In this instance, the caseworker was the only trained Navajo caseworker on the reservation.

Case Illustration

In the late 1930's Mrs. Y was living with her children in her mother's extended family kinship group. Following the death of one of her relatives in this camp, she was accused—apparently by an aunt and a sister with whom she had quarreled—of killing the relative. The court records do not contain a clear statement of the circumstances surrounding the death of the relative. Mrs. Y was hurriedly convicted, and her mother was unable to see her before she was taken from the reservation.

Mrs. Y could not converse in the prison because no one there understood the Navajo language. She became depressed and resistive and developed symptoms of emotional disturbance, such as vomiting and refusal to eat. As a result she was transferred, within a few months after her imprisonment, to a mental hospital in the East. At this hospital the patient spoke to no one for many years and lay huddled, in a fetal position, in a blanket on the floor. She continued to be resistive and apprehensive, spoke to no one, and refused to be examined. Attempts to speak to her through an interpreter were unsuccessful, but it was not clear whether the problem stemmed from the inadequacy of the interpreter or the inability of the patient to communicate with him.

Gradually Mrs. Y began to show improvement and became less resistive. She spoke her native language, began to smile, ate well, slept well, and was quiet and pleasant. She showed some interset in others about her, and as she continued to improve, she began to take care of herself and to eat her meals with a group of other patients. By then twenty years had passed since she had been imprisoned, and she was over fifty years of age.

After the hospital staff inquired at the Division of Indian Health regarding plans for discharging Mrs. Y, the caseworker on the reservation contacted her daughter, who was then an adult with a family of her own. She also contacted Mrs. Y's mother and sister in order to include them in the planning for her return to the reservation. The family members were pleased to receive news about the patient, and they were also pleased at the possibility that Mrs. Y might return home after such a long separation. During a visit to the social worker's office they tape recorded a message to Mrs. Y, and the tapes, along with photographs taken that day, were sent to her.

The Caseworker Visits the Patient

It was hoped that Mrs. Y could be either discharged or transferred to an institution closer to her home. The reservation caseworker visited her at the hospital on a number of occasions in an attempt to arrive at an accurate evaluation of her condition. On the first occasion the patient eyed the worker apprehensively. The worker said hello in Navajo and told Mrs. Y she had come from the Navajo country to see her. The patient continued to look at the worker and remained silent. The worker asked the patient if she were a Navajo. She replied yes, and then tested the worker's Navajo origin by asking her to name the clan to which she belonged. Because the worker was able to speak in Navajo and understand the patient's feelings and cultural background, Mrs. Y could express her feelings to her freely.

The worker learned that Mrs. Y strongly resented her removal from her home, and she held her family and relatives responsible. With each succeeding visit to the patient, her feelings about having been "hauled away" seemed to increase. "They destroyed me, trampled me in the dirt, stripped away my clothing, took me apart joint by joint." At this moment she pointed to her knees, shoulders, and elbows. "They brought me to shame, they made me nothing. I crawled begging to go back, I had no pride [self-respect]. I am nothing, only a stranger here, I have no will, no thinking, no right to say yes or no, to decide. . . ."

To questions regarding her wish to return home, she replied, "I'm not in authority; that's not for me to decide." Who was the authority? "I don't know." The doctor asked her if she would return home if *he* said she could do so. Again she said it was not for her to decide. She had no right; she was only there. Then she said, "It costs money. How will I pay?" Assurance that her transportation would be paid did not help her to make her decision.

The doctor asked her if she knew she was in a hospital. She replied, "*Hwo'la* (I don't know)." Was she aware of the nature of her illness? "*Hwo'la.*" The caseworker asked whether she knew that she had been sick in her "thinking process." Again she replied "*Hwo'la.*" The doctor then asked her if she had ever killed anyone. She promptly shook her head and replied "No, no." Would she kill anyone? Again her answer was, "No, no." Whenever her family was mentioned, she began a monologue. She spoke about them in a rapid, breathless way, and her set speech sounded like something she might have memorized, something she was repeating automatically. When the worker asked her which members of the family were responsible for her imprisonment, she replied, "All of them." The only members of her family whom she exempted were her children, whom she thought of as small and helpless. She showed her feelings for them when she said she had "nearly died for them." The worker and the doctor thought that if the patient could change or moderate her attitude, she could be discharged and return home. To help her mother's family understand her illness and attitude, they decided that the worker should visit them.

The Caseworker Visits the Family

On the reservation the caseworker discussed the plan to discharge Mrs. Y with the patient's mother, her daughter and son-in-law, and her two sisters and their husbands. They showed interest in the plan and were anxious to have the patient returned to them. The women in the family were an impressive group, attractive, healthy, and friendly; each of them had an excellent sense of humor. Mrs. Y's mother, old but alert and intelligent, was obviously the matriarch of this extended family group. Her rule was not rigidly authoritarian. Instead, she exercised a guiding influence on each of the independent families in the camp. The worker was impressed by the dignity, pride, and self-assurance displayed by the family; it seemed that they might have been descendents of an influential and ancient lineage of medicine men.

The women were very interested in hearing about the patient and asked many questions about her: How did she look? Was her hair turning grey? Did she look "as old" as her sisters at home? What kind of clothes did she have? Could she still speak Navajo? Did she still remember them or the children? What had she said about coming home? Had she commented on their photographs and the tape recordings of their voices? The worker reported her observations of the patient and the feelings she had expressed about the family. They, in turn, told the worker a little of the history of the patient's departure from home. The mother, as head of the household, then took the proper steps to call together community leaders and councilmen and learn their reactions to her daughter's proposed return and to help them understand her illness.

The Patient's Return to the Reservation

It took several months to arrange for the transfer of the patient to a general hospital on the reservation. Mrs. Y was given appropriate clothes and was accompanied on the flight by an attendant. She recognized the caseworker at the airport. From the beginning she was cheerful and in good contact. On the ride from the airport to the hospital she talked in Navajo about her trip: "A morning cab ride to the airport, boarded an airplane, three stops en route, scared, and near the end of the trip, vomited." This experience seemed to remind her of her abrupt separation from her family when she had been taken to prison. She conversed well and spoke of her family when the worker told her that she was on her way home. Mrs. Y said "I didn't know where we were going, but I just stayed right behind her [the attendant]." She said she had suffered "for nothing" for many years and recalled that her mother had not witnessed her removal from home. An aunt had delivered her to the "wolves" to destroy her mentality. They cast a spell over her and took complete possession of her mind to the extent that she could no longer think or feel. In her own words, "I just gave up to them."

Wolf is a colloquial Navajo term meaning *witch*. Clyde Kluckhohn and Dorothea Leighton emphasize the strength of witchcraft beliefs among Navajos, even today, and the deep-seated fears associated with them: "What counts is that belief in witches is universal and that there are deep fears, much gossip and countless and widely current anecdotes."[2]

Throughout her stay at the hospital on the reservation, Mrs. Y's adjustment was satisfactory. She was assigned to a ward occupied by other Navajo women. At first she sat by her bed most of the day, but soon she began to exchange a few words with the women. Later, in talking to them, she said that she had been away from home a long time. She wondered whether she still owned any sheep and whether she retained authority to make decisions in her own home. She enjoyed a ride with the worker around the reservation to look at flocks of sheep, people riding horseback, an occasional wagon on the road, and of course, the hogans. She said that these sights brought back memories of her people. They stopped at the store, and the worker permitted the patient to make her own purchases so that she could learn whether or not Mrs. Y was capable of making decisions by herself. Mrs. Y purchased cookies and candies and paid the correct amount to the clerk.

The patient became aware of the difference between her short hair and the long hair of the other Navajo women, which was plaited in the traditional Navajo knot. Navajo women feel that long hair adds to their attractiveness, and it enhances their self-image. Several times the patient made reference to her hair, and the worker felt that long hair would help her regain her self-esteem.

Mrs. Y's mother, sister, niece, daughter, and two small grandsons visited her the day after she arrived at the hospital. Mrs. Y had no difficulty in recognizing her mother, but the other members of the family had to introduce themselves to her. She readily accepted her grandchildren, hugged the baby occasionally, and inquired about the identifying characteristics of her son-in-law—his parents, clan, origin, and so forth. She was obviously happy to see her family. She said that until then she had been afraid to believe that she was really home. Her mother gave her information about her brothers and sisters and her other relatives and her neighbors. Although Mrs. Y's ability to express herself in Navajo was somewhat limited, she conversed rationally and coherently with the family. When they attempted to plan for her return home and asked her how she would like her clothes made, she kept saying, "I have no authority; I cannot decide." Her daughter told her that

[2] Clyde Kluckhohn and Dorothea Leighton, *The Navaho*, Harvard University Press, Cambridge, Massachusetts, 1946, p. 172.

her refusal to make decisions was part of the past life that she had left behind her. Now she was home, among her people, and she was again entitled to all her rights and privileges. She was a person again. She could now make decisions, and the family would help her.

Mrs. Y, however, still feared members of "the old regime" who had taken her away from her home. Her mother explained that "the old regime" no longer exercised authority over the Navajos, but Mrs. Y did not quite understand this. The patient continued to refer to the aunt who had sent her away, and her family reassured her by telling her that this aunt had died. Mrs. Y asked the worker to tell the officials of her return in order to learn about their reaction. She also talked about a bracelet taken from her when she had been imprisoned.

Mrs. Y was confused about the reasons for her imprisonment. She believed that she was the victim of the jealous, now deceased, aunt who had sought to bring evil upon her. She spoke again of "Navajo wolves" (human beings in wolf skins) turned loose upon her, crawling upon her hogan, and running riot in her mind. Her daughter, who had been ten years old at the time of her mother's imprisonment, remembered these animals crawling on the hogan at night and scaring the whole family. The worker surmised that these ideas, rather than being manifestations of the patient's illness, were a part of the Navajo culture. Kluckhohn describes the way the Navajos believe these "witches" behave:

> Witches are active primarily at night, roaming about at great speed in skins of wolf, coyote and other animals (bear, owl, desert fox, crow). This is one bit of witchcraft lore with which even the youngest Navajo is familiar. Indeed, ["wolf," in the Navajo language] I have found to be the most common colloquial term for "witch."[3]

Since Mrs. Y was able to adjust to life on the reservation successfully, the worker believed she would be able to adjust to living among her people without great difficulty. She still needed help with the unresolved problems of "the wolves," symbolic in Navajo culture of everything evil and to her of her fear in connection with her traumatic separation from her people. She also needed assurance that she had a secure place with her family and in the community. The family could help her with this problem, but the worker thought it advisable to request support from the community agencies for both the patient and her family.

Two months later the worker made a home visit and found Mrs. Y baby-sitting for her niece. She had just finished feeding four children, aged four, three, two, and one, and washing the dishes. She apologized to the worker for not giving her something to eat, explaining that she was not in her own home. She was cheerful and talked of helping her mother with the cooking and other chores; she also helped to prepare the wool for weaving. Mrs. Y was anxious to weave, but her mother had advised her to wait, because she still suffered from nocturnal episodes of vomiting and diarrhea.

[3] Clyde Kluckhohn, *Navajo Witchcraft*, Beacon Press, Boston, 1962, p. 26.

At night she was afraid of something she could not identify, but during the day she had no problems. These symptoms may well have indicated her persisting fear of witchcraft. Her family had arranged for some ceremonies to be performed that were designed to cure Mrs. Y of her illness, and they were planning for more of them. These ceremonies are the basic Navajo method of curing illness, including illness caused by witchcraft. Kluckhohn and Leighton state:

> The most efficacious reassurance for victims of witchcraft is provided, therefore, by the unusual, complicated, and costly prayer ceremonials, with many relatives and friends in attendance, lending their help and expressing their sympathy.[4]

The particular ceremony recommended by the Navajo diagnostician depends on his identification of the supernatural cause of the illness. The ceremonies vary in length from one to nine days. Many relatives and friends gather to participate in them, bringing together the efforts of the community for the well-being of the patient. In this way they provide a positive emotional support for the member of the community who is ill. The Public Health Service doctors have come to recognize the continuing importance to the Navajos of their ceremonies, and in some cases they encourage the use of native methods of treatment along with those of modern medicine.

In a second home visit the worker learned that Mrs. Y had made marked improvement. She was living in her own home and taking full responsibility for herself. She had woven a number of rugs and was pleased to be back on the reservation. Mrs. Y spoke of the "voices inside her," but she recognized them as a part of the past and they no longer guided her in her actions.

Summary

The case discussed in this article illustrates some of the problems social workers encounter in the rehabilitation of patients who have been hospitalized for long periods. Long-term care of patients in hospitals located at considerable distances from their families and communities often fosters the development of symptoms associated with institutionalization. Although the patient's illness may be in remission, his ability to relate to family and community is thwarted by his isolation from them. Members of minority groups may, of course, be even more isolated than patients who are members of the dominant culture.

Some of the problems the social worker encountered in helping a Navajo Indian return to her home after an absence of twenty years were resolved because the worker understood the patient's cultural beliefs and customs and was able to communicate with her in her native language. The worker helped the family understand Mrs. Y's illness and her attitude toward them, which was essential in securing the family's participation in planning for her return home.

Casework service is especially needed in helping mental patients who

[4] Kluckhohn and Leighton, *op. cit.*, p. 175.

have been hospitalized for a long time to bridge the gap between living in the hospital and living in the community. It is especially important to involve the patient's family and community agencies in planning for the discharge of such patients.

The Negro Worker and the White Client: A Commentary on the Treatment Relationship

Andrew E. Curry

When the caseworker and the client are members of different racial groups, the factor of race becomes an important variable in the casework treatment process. In this attempt to examine the subjective reactions and responses of the white client and the Negro worker in the treatment relationship, certain sociological and psychological influences on the relationship will also be considered.

It is a truism that, in casework practice, the worker must understand and exert some control over psychological responses, such as transference and countertransference. It is equally necessary that he take into account the sociological matrix in which the psychological responses occur. The clients' sociological supplies—his values, norms, and reference groups—should be assessed as carefully as his psychological supplies. In spite of the general acceptance of these principles, relatively little systematic attention has been given to their application in treatment of a client of one race by a worker of an other.[1] Casework supervisors, however, frequently have to deal with the profound consequences of this particular kind of client-worker relationship. Consider, for example, the Negro worker with a predominantly white caseload who is overly conscientious about adhering to the fine points of eligibility; or the "socially conscious" young white worker who plans relatively lavish budgets for Negro families only; or the white worker who makes a biased judgement that a Negro mother is refusing to let her mentally

[1] Luna Bowdoin Brown, "Race as a Factor in Establishing a Casework Relationship," *Social Casework*, Vol. XXXI, March 1950, pp. 91–97; Inabel Burns Lindsay, "Race as a Factor in the Caseworker's Role," *Journal of Social Casework*, Vol. XXVIII, March, 1947, pp. 101–107; Eric Layne, "Experience of a Negro Psychiatric Social Worker in a Veterans Administration Mental Hygiene Clinic," *Journal of Psychiatric Social Work*, Vol. XIX, Autumn, 1949, pp. 66–69. For the view that a patient is best treated by a member of his own race or religion, see C. P. Oberndorf, "Selectivity and Option for Psychiatry," *American Journal of Psychiatry*, Vol. CX, April, 1954, pp. 754–58.

Reprinted from *Social Casework*, XLV (March, 1964), pp. 131–136, by permission of the author and the Journal.

ill child enter a psyciatric hospital because her welfare check will be cut while he is there. This short list of examples could easily be extended.

In a pioneering paper, Leonard Simmons discussed a phenomenon called "Crow Jim" and its effects on the practice of a Negro worker. Simmons defined "Crow Jim" as a form of Negro racial prejudice—"animosity, hostility, and bitterness felt by Negroes toward whites and a predisposition of Negroes to descriminate against them."[2] Elsewhere, the transference and countertransference reactions of the members of a treatment group and their Negro therapist were examined in two articles,[3] but aside from these efforts and that of Simmons few guideposts are to be found in the professional literature for caseworkers and supervisors who must deal with the problem.

In this article the relationship between white client and Negro worker is discussed from the standpoints of *1]* the casework relationship and the vicissitudes of rapport (or lack of it), *2]* relevant aspects of ego psychology, and *3]* the nature of the underlying social factors that sustain certain modes of thought, racial tensions, and intergroup conflicts. Each of these has crucial importance for caseworkers and supervisors, educators, agency executives, and others concerned with the refinement of practice skills.

The subject is relatively difficult to examine because of the near-impossibility of gaining sufficient distance from the events of the day to be objective and clear-headed. Everyone seems to be taking part in some way in the current social revolution. For some persons change is occurring too quickly; for others it is not quick enough. Interracial group tensions now permeate every aspect of our contemporary society, and there is no reason to believe that the client-worker relationship is immune to them. The casework relationship, by its very nature, is a product of the mutual perceptions of client and caseworker—perceptions based on what each has been taught to see and what he needs to see.[4] These perceptions cannot be divorced from affects, which are "indices" of the dynamic and economic conditions obtaining in the "psyche."[5] More importantly, however, they cannot be divorced from each individual's attitudes, beliefs, and social norms. Affects and attitudes are embedded in the fabric of each personality and in the ethnic subculture from which each has drawn his values, biases, hopes, and fears. Through careful study of this subject, social workers may obtain "a clearer picture of value orientations based on ethnic backgrounds."[6] They

---

[2] Leonard C. Simmons, " 'Crow Jim': Implications for Social Work," *Social Work*, Vol. VIII, July, 1963. p. 24.

[3] Andrew E. Curry, "Some Comments on Transference when the Group Therapist is Negro," *International Journal of Group Psychotherapy*, Vol. XIII, July, 1963, pp. 363–65, and "Myth, Transference, and the Black Psychotherapist," *Psychoanalytic Review* (scheduled for publication).

[4] See Solomon E. Asch, *Social Psychology*, Prentice-Hall, New York, 1952, Chapter 8, pp. 223–27.

[5] Marjorie Brierley, *Trends in Psycho-Analysis*, Hogarth Press, London, 1951, p. 55.

[6] Herman D. Stein, "The Concept of Social Environment in Social Work Practice," in *Ego-Oriented Casework: Problems and Perspectives*, Family Service Association of America, New York, 1963, p. 74.

may also learn more about the ego's response to the normative structure of the environing community—about how the ego sustains its identity in the flux of social change.

The Client's Image of the Negro Worker

The reaction of a white client to a worker is presented in the following case, in which the worker's sensitive use of the situation enabled him to establish contact with the client despite her initially negative response.

> Miss K was an unmarried thirty-three-year-old white woman who had been diagnosed as suffering from a "schizophrenic reaction: chronic undifferentiated type." She was then on convalescent leave from a psychiatric hospital, having been released as greatly improved. Altogether, she had been hospitalized four times as a mental patient. On meeting the Negro worker in the initial posthospital interview, she explicitly stated that she did not like his race, his looks, or his office. She said she would not return again and that the worker would have to drag her into the few evaluation interviews required by the state. The worker acknowledged his concern and his sympathy for her feelings. He wondered if there might be some subject they could talk about, and he made some general comment about appreciating her frankness and honesty. His efforts failed to engage her at that point, but about three weeks later she telephoned and asked to see him. She said she was "feeling funny again" and was thinking about suicide.
>
> She came to the interview promptly, and immediately said that she had been feeling very bad ever since she had said "those nasty things" to the worker. The worker pointed out that he did not recall her saying anything more than that she did not like Negroes, and he had appreciated her honesty. He reminded her that the function of the agency was to help her and that he had been appointed to see her for that purpose. Miss K, appearing to relax, said that she must have been *thinking* some "funny things"; perhaps she had not *said* them after all; anyway, perhaps she should talk with the Negro worker, since she was always having "dark thoughts." The worker said that he did not know what the "dark thoughts" were but that, if she wanted to help him understand, they could arrange to see each other regularly. Miss K accepted, commenting that maybe she would have something to live for then.

The worker undoubtedly resented Miss K's "attack" on him. Perhaps he was even hurt deeply; however, he never lost sight of her reference to suicidal thoughts. As many workers do, he wondered about the client's social frame of reference as well as about her psychological needs. (One must wonder also about the worker's frame of reference here. Was he more "social worker" than "Negro social worker"? This kind of question, touching on the articulation of professional identity, awaits study.)

In terms of Miss K's response to the Negro worker, what was her "social context of action?"[7] The discussion that follows is concerned not with the broad issues of social psychology and social action but with the

[7] Alex Inkeles, "Personality and Social Structure," in *Sociology Today*, Robert K. Merton, Leonard Broom, and Leonard S. Cottrell, Jr. (eds.), Basic Books, New York, 1959, p. 273.

response of individual clients, since the action of an individual in any situation—particularly a stressful one—reflects personal motivations however much it also reflects the determining influences of the social environment. The forces in the environment, in turn, can be reflected in individual action only to the extent that they are mediated through the personality.[8] The social environment, of course, varies from neighborhood to neighborhood in a community and from state to state in different parts of the country. A client living in Oregon would be expected to respond differently from one living in Virginia because of the differences between those states in the position of the Negro.

The Meaning of "Negro" in a Social Context

Prejudice is often based on a faulty chain of reasoning according to which the world is divided into two groups of people, we and they: " 'they' are different, therefore inferior; if inferior, we are justified in disliking them and in treating them as inferiors. . . ."[9] The treatment "they" receive can be structured and sanctioned by complex and rigid patterns of discrimination. Currently a major effort in the United States is aimed primarily at upsetting the structured patterns of discrimination. Once these are changed, it is thought, then individual beliefs, attitudes, values, and perceptions will also change. This view may be valid, but it should be recognized that many of the attitudes of prejudice are not manifested in institutionalized patterns of discrimination but in the various modes of thought (fantasy and myth, dreams and superstitions) that reference groups nurture. The white Southerner is quick to remind the white Northerner of this subtle point.

In the social context, the designations *Negro* and *white* are emotionally laden signs and symbols that have important sociopsychological stimulus value. Krech and Crutchfield, in considering this stimulus value, stated that there are two different functions that the beliefs and attitudes of racial prejudice can serve: "*1]* There are the beliefs and attitudes of racial prejudice that serve *in defense of the self,* and *2]* there are the beliefs and attitudes of racial prejudice that serve to maintain the individual's *identification with society.*"[10] In the definition that each (self and group) makes of its own integrity, the meaning of *Negro* may be symbolic of something that for some unknown reason can be expressed in no other way. That is to say, there is more meaning in the sign/symbol *Negro* than is expressed in group norms and values. We will need, ultimately, to learn how such meanings come into being. To say that attitudes are socially determined is an inexact way of saying several things. We may agree that the formation and change of attitudes can only take place in the setting of

[8] Inkeles, *loc. cit.*

[9] S. Stansfeld Sargent, *Social Psychology,* Ronald Press Co., New York, 1950, p. 449.

[10] David Krech and Richard S. Crutchfield, *Theory and Problems of Social Psychology,* McGraw-Hill Book Co., New York, 1948, p. 456.

significant social and emotional relations. But one is hard put to know, at this stage of our knowledge, what *significant* means—to whom, when, and in what part of the country.

Using Help and the Response to Authority

The white client often has difficulty in recognizing and accepting the Negro worker's authority and his ability to help him solve his problems. In this context the concept of "Crow Jim" attitudes in the Negro worker may be studied profitably. As a professional helper, the Negro worker encounters the same problems as his white counterpart; he must be able to establish a good helping relationship and empathize sufficiently with the problems and needs of his client. But the Negro worker's professional task is more difficult because he must deal not only with the client's expected psychological resistances to using help on the terms prescribed by the agency's function but also with the sociocultural and characterological resistances stimulated by his being a Negro.

These resistances are different for the client in a Vermont family family agency and the client in a Georgia public welfare agency. It may be easier for the Vermonter than for the Georgian to associate the Negro worker with authority. Because of the social traditions in Georgia, however, it may be easier for the client there to percieve the Negro as one who gives service; he will screen out the authority aspects of the worker's role. In both situations, the white client's perceptions need to be observed and studied on two fundamental levels: his perception of *Negro worker* and his perception of *Negro*. When the white client has little difficulty in perceiving that the Negro worker possesses the authority vested in him by the agency, the community, and his profession,[11] it is evidence that the client's ego is able to manage an extremely complex situation. Difficulties arise when the worker's and the client's subtle responses to *Negro* and *white* begin to spill over into the professional contractual relationship between them. Stable interaction is most likely to occur when client and worker share the same norms and expectations and when optimum cathexis exists between them. The social distance between client and professional worker[12] is being carefully studied by social scientists. These may also be an "emotional distance" that needs equally careful study.

Much supervisory time is undoubtedly spent in tackling this complex issue. Typically, both the client and the worker make a great emotional investment in the casework relationship. Their perceptions, biases, likes and dislikes, fears, and fantasies each influence their reality-testing and self-observation, their identity and self-image.[13] When the variable of race is added,

[11] Andrew E. Curry, "The 'On-Call' Contract with the Schizophrenic Leave Patient," *Napa State Hospital Quarterly*, Vol. IV, January, 1963, pp. 18–21.

[12] Charles Kadushin, "Social Distance Between Client and Professional," *American Journal of Sociology*, Vol. LXVII, March, 1962, pp. 517–31.

[13] Roger R. Miller, "Prospects and Problems in the Study of Ego Functions," in *Ego-Oriented Casework, op. cit.*, pp. 108–126.

it seems to function like a Rorschach card capable of stimulating a wide range of reactions that indicate the underlying emotional frame of mind of the helper and the person being helped.

Emotionally Distorted Perceptions

The reciprocal responses of Negro worker and white client should not, however, be conceived of as transference reactions. *Transference* is a psychoanalytic construct used to denote an irrational and infantile attribution of characteristics to another person and a response to him in terms of these attributes. When complex symbolic processes, fantasies, fears, and counterphobic reactions are motivated by characteristics the other person does possess, such as a black skin, such responses are not transference reactions. Rather, they are residuals of fairy tales, folk tales and children's stories that deal with darkness, bogeymen, badness, and evil. Their psychodynamic import is great, and they complicate still further the already complex problem of dissolving racial tensions based on prejudice. For example, if either *white* or *Negro* signifies threat, the ego can deal with this *external* perception by avoidance. The person can pattern his social relations in accordance with the doctrines of segregationists and restrict his social activities with Negroes. The *internal* perceptions, however, give the ego no such possibility of escape.[14] Even if extensive sociological changes occur (desegregation, integrated services, open housing practices, and so forth), subtly distorted perceptions can still persist in the psyche, beyond the reach of conscious control.

The Negro worker must be willing to allow himself to recognize the existence of these emotionally distorted reactions in the client and in himself. He must also be willing to risk discovery that his clinical practice is being affected by his own insidious reactions. He must make this effort because he is professionally responsible for the establishment of a therapeutic casework relationship. He may gain a measure of comfort and security from knowing that his profession and his agency have made clear their belief in such values as the dignity of the individual, equal opportunity, and social justice. But all the social-psychological information in the world will not produce sound, conflict-free casework practice unless the Negro worker has examined his own emotional reactions.

There is no getting around the fact that a great deal of emotion is interwoven in the fabric of interracial relationships. The Negro worker and the white client (and the white worker and the Negro client as well) will find that their interactions are highly charged with emotions that they may not be completely aware of or are not able to handle. The consequences of being a Negro, in relation to the range of responses a white client may make, are not at all equivalent to those of being fat or bald or ugly—the symbol *Negro* has much more affect and stimulus value. It is both incorrect and clinically unsound to argue that the dynamics of the casework process are not affected

[14] Angel Garma, "The Genesis of Reality Testing," *Psychoanalytic Quarterly*, Vol. XV, April, 1946, p. 161.

by the worker's race. Both the worker's and the client's responses to it, whether deeply unconscious or preconscious can stimulate or impede the establishment of a sound casework relationship.

Transference and Countertransference

The fantasies and fears developed by the white client because his worker is a Negro can have a crucial effect on the eventual manifestation of the transference, as it is related to resistances and the working through of resistances. The white client's reactions are also influenced by the counter-transference of the Negro worker, his self-image, and his reactions to the white client. Because of the regressive pull in the accompanying fantasy systems of both client and worker, great anxiety can be stimulated in the worker, especially if he harbors neurotic resistances to identifying himself with his race. If the client becomes aware of the worker's reactions, the resulting interference with communication precludes effective treatment.

Countertransference phenomena are probably present in every treatment relationship. The worker habitually deals with them in various non-verbal ways. Often, however, they are either ignored because the worker does not know what to do with them or repressed because he responds to them by first developing anxiety and then defending himself against the anxiety. On the conscious level, Negro-white relationships are directly related to a person's values, ethics, group norms, and social-political philosophy. Some interesting dimensions of countertransference are revealed, however, by focusing on the unconscious and preconscious power of *black* and *white* as symbols that appear in the fantasies of the Negro worker.

When the Negro worker's reactions to his own race are unresolved and overly complicated and the white client's reactions to him are hostile or unfriendly, the worker's reactions take two distinct, though not unrelated, forms: *1]* the countertransference of defensiveness, which is derived from the unconscious conflicts about his color; *2]* the countertransference of interaction, which is derived from the white client's negative reaction to the worker. In either case, the Negro worker's reaction is based upon his unconscious need or wish not to be a Negro, not to be what he is. His un-willingness to allow the white client to accept him as he is further interferes with the progress of treatment, since this acceptance is essential in therapy.

The white client's whiteness as an image for fantasy may constitute a difficult situational exigency with which the Negro worker is unable to cope.[15] The Negro worker's counterresistance and counterphobic reactions to his blackness may actually be manifestations of his questioning his own sense of identity. When the white client becomes aware of these reactions, he is called upon to bear too heavy a burden. In one sense, he is called upon to "treat" the feelings of the Negro worker who has failed to work through his feelings about his color. In another sense, the client may find himself being

---

[15] See Gert Heilbrunn, "Comments on a Common Form of Acting Out," *Psychoanalytic Quarterly*, Vol. XXVII, January, 1958, p. 88.

used as an audience before whom the Negro worker plays out his own fantasy, or personal myth, that he is really a "Negro white". Uncomfortable with himself and preoccupied with his own hatreds and fantasies about blackness and inferiority, the Negro worker inevitably arouses tensions and anxieties in the white client. If the worker is able to recognize his effect on the client, he can take advantage of it, as was illustrated in the case of Miss K, to further the process of treatment; in other words, he can use race as an important tool in treatment. He cannot do so, however, if he is not ever mindful of "Crow Jim" attitudes and countertransference contaminations of what could prove to be an advantageous situation. Working through the client's displaced reactions to the therapist or caseworker is the *sine qua non* of all the psychological therapies.

When the worker's race is used by the white client as the point of departure for an attack on him, it constitutes a source of great anxiety for the worker. He may get anxious about the threat to the client's ego identity, which may result in hypercathexis of the client's ego defenses.[16] He may get, anxious about the threat to the client's ego-ideal, superego commands, or reference group norms, which may result in the client's overvaluing these commands and norms. Or he may get anxious about the meaning of *black skin* in the fantasies of the white majority and in their evaluation of minority groups. Such an attack creates resistances in the client and counterresistances in the worker that neither of them may be able to overcome.

It is important to remember that in the history of psychoanalysis, the phenomena of transference and countertransference were understood before there was a comparable understanding of character. As a result, transference phenomena and character were for a long time considered separately. It may well be that with further developments in the study of character and ego psychology, the phenomena of transference and countertransference will become clearer, particularly as they are affected by race.

Summary

Because social workers practice in a wide variety of settings, they are in an ideal position to observe and study the effects of the client's race, ethnic group, and reference group on several important aspects of the treatment relationship—on his perception of the worker and of the agency and on his utilization of service. They are also in an ideal position to observe and study their own attitudes, values, and prejudices, which affect their perceptions of clients. It is hoped that the thoughts presented here will contribute to such study.

[16] See Erik H. Erikson, "Ego Development and Historical Change," in *Identity and the Life Cycle* (*Psychological Issues*, Vol. I, No. 1, Monograph 1), International Universities Press, New York, 1959, pp. 18–49. Erikson points out that "the suppressed, excluded, and exploited unconsciously believe in the evil image which they are made to represent by those who are dominant" (p. 31).

The White Worker and the Negro Client

Esther Fibush

In the summer of 1959, before freedom rides, sit-ins, and James Baldwin had become everyday front page news, E. Franklin Frazier discussed matters of common interest with a small, informed group of caseworkers from various settings in the San Francisco area. "Color blindness" was then the accepted tradition in many social work circles, but throughout the profession there was a beginning awareness that by ignoring color, social workers were ignoring one important aspect of reality. The group was therefore delighted to have the opportunity to talk with such an authority as Frazier about socioeconomic and cultural factors that might have a bearing on casework with Negro clients.

While the intellectual impact of Frazier's remarks was great, it was far outweighed by the emotional impact. He said that, because of their color blindness and their middle-class, "liberal" orientation, social workers were appallingly ill-equipped to understand and work with Negro clients; they imagined that middle-class Negroes necessarily shared their values, and they were oblivious of the strengths inherent in the lower-class Negro "folk culture." In short, according to Frazier, most social workers, Negro and Caucasian alike, were naïve and ignorant about the psychology of Negro clients and the emotional and sociocultural dynamics with which they were trying to deal.

In the years since that meeting, the strength of these dynamics has been made increasingly clear by the civil rights movement. Consequently, social workers have had no choice but to become increasingly cognizant of their operation, one way or another, within all Negro clients—whether the dynamics are expressed in the Negro's participation in the civil rights movement or in the psychosocial attitudes that influence the casework relationship.

Much of Frazier's indictment was leveled at Negro as well as white social workers, but he thought it likely that the gap in understanding was both greater and different when the worker was white and the client was Negro. The shocked reaction of the white workers to the powerful presentation by the Negro sociologist attested to the existence of that gap, and to the part that it must have been playing in the casework relationship between these white workers and their Negro clients.

The emotional dynamics operating within the white caseworker and their effect on his work with the Negro client are not easily pinpointed.

Reprinted from *Social Casework*, XLVI (May, 1965), pp. 271–277, by permission of the author and the Journal.

Differences have been documented between the values and standards of the middle-class therapist and those of the lower-class client, and the resulting problems have also been shown to influence treatment;[1] yet it should be recognized that not all Negroes who are treated at family service agencies are members of a lower socioeconomic class than that of the workers. To date, the psychological and cultural factors operating when the worker is white and the client is Negro have been given far less attention than those of social class. In part, this neglect can be explained by the prevalence of the dominant doctrine of color blindness.

Recently, the effect of race on the attitudes of the Negro worker has been discussed, but little attention has been given to the attitudes of the white worker who deals with Negro clients.[2] Yet the white worker cannot afford to remain unaware of the myriad subtle and covert emotional reactions that can be triggered within himself and the Negro client by their racial difference. This difference can touch off a complex set of social and psychological reactions and interactions affecting the casework relationship and casework treatment.

It may well be true, as Frazier indicated, that no social worker, Negro or white, is well equipped to work with Negro clients. Statistics recently released by the Family Service Association of America show that though Negroes applied to family service agencies in proportionately greater numbers than Caucasians, they remained in treatment only half as long.[3] Usually they did not remain long enough for the worker to alleviate their problems. No data were given on the race of the workers, but, obviously, the problem extends beyond the relationship between the white caseworker and the Negro client.

To explore the larger issues would require research on a scale far beyond the scope of the individual practitioner, and financing on a scale far beyond the means of the average family service agency. Fortunately, no special financing is required to examine one's own practice. If the premise is accepted that the relationship between worker and client is basic to all casework treatment,[4] then the relationship between the white worker and the Negro

---

[1] August B. Hollingshead and Frederick C. Redlich, *Social Class and Mental Illness: A Community Study*, John Wiley & Sons, New York, 1958.

[2] Leonard C. Simmons, " 'Crow Jim': Implications for Social Work," *Social Work*, Vol. VIII, July, 1963, pp. 24–30; Andrew E. Curry, "The Negro Worker and the White Client: A Commentary on the Treatment Relationship," *Social Casework*, Vol. XLV, March, 1964, pp. 131–36. For a discussion from the point of view of color blindness, yet one still applicable in many ways, see Inabel Burns Lindsay, "Race as a Factor in the Caseworker's Role," *Journal of Social Casework*, Vol. XXVIII, March, 1947, pp. 101–107.

[3] "Non-White Families Are Frequent Applicants for Family Service," *Family Service Highlights*, Vol. XXV, May, 1964, pp. 140–44, 157.

[4] Florence Hollis, *Casework: A Psychosocial Therapy*, Random House, New York, 1964, p. 149. The general theoretical orientation in this article is similar to that of Hollis. It should be understood that the focus on casework treatment is not intended to disparage or disregard other forms of therapy, but was chosen for the purposes of this paper because its theory and its practice are more familiar to the author.

client should be worthy of examination. Although factors other than race influence the relationship in cases of this kind, only those will be examined in this article that stem specifically from the difference in race between worker and client. The major focus of this examination is the worker's attitudes and practices, but it must be kept in mind that these are always in some measure a response to the client's attitudes and his approach to the casework relationship.

Intellectual and Emotional Understanding

To put the discussion in perspective, something should be said first for the basic truth underlying the doctrine of color blindness. This doctrine declares the common humanity of all people—regardless of their color or their other physical characteristics; each individual is equally human and each has the same basic potential for good or for ill, whatever his cultural, socioeconomic, ethnic, or racial group may be. Caseworkers have been correct in insisting on the basic truth underlying this doctrine and in viewing each client as an individual in his own right. But the doctrine of color blindness, which was intended to eliminate bias, has created a tendency among workers to deny the existence of differences arising out of membership in different racial groups.

With the recent influx of social science concepts into social work, caseworkers are becoming increasingly knowledgeable about differences among cultural, socioeconomic, ethnic, and racial groups. They now have access to much information that may bear on their casework practice. It must be kept in mind, however, that social science generalizations, which may be, on the whole, true of most members of a group, cannot be assumed to apply to the specific, individual client. A common cause always affects the individual client in an individual way;[5] even when a sociocultural condition applies to all members of a group, its impact will vary according to the individual's unique constitutional endowment, developmental history, and environmental circumstances.

An obvious pitfall for the caseworker to avoid is the wholesale application of sociocultural generalizations to specific clients without adequate regard for the psychological meaning to them of the conditions they are confronting. Caseworkers have long had a dual responsibility: their work must take into account both social pathology and individual psychopathology.[6] If anything differentiates the casework approach from that of other therapies, it is this obligation of the worker to integrate understanding derived from sociological and psychological knowledge. Since there is as yet no definitive integration of sociological and psychological knowledge into

[5] Elizabeth G. Meier, "Social and Cultural Factors in Casework Diagnosis," *Social Work*, Vol. IV, July, 1959, p. 16.
[6] Henry S. Maas, "Use of Behavioral Sciences in Social Work Education," *Social Work*, Vol. III, July, 1958, pp. 62–69.

one theory, the caseworker must take responsibility for integrating, as best he can, the knowledge he has gained from both fields.

If the caseworker assumes that such integration requires only the addition of sociocultural information to his already existing body of knowledge, he will fall far short of the mark. Ernest Jones, in his memoirs, quotes Croce: "A thinker who does not suffer his problem, who does not live his thought, is not a thinker." Without emotional understanding, information remains a sterile collection of isolated pieces of fact; it does not even become knowledge, let alone wisdom. Elizabeth Herzog's warning is a sound one: Sociocultural concepts should not be adopted "with less than the amount of blood, sweat, and tears required" to know how to apply them.[7]

Andrew Curry has pointed out that the social distance between client and worker has been carefully studied by social scientists but that they have not studied the perhaps equally important question of emotional distance.[8] If the relationship between worker and client is basic to casework treatment, then the success of treatment depends in large measure on the kind of relationship that is established—and emotional understanding is crucial to it. This is not to say that diagnostic skill, treatment techniques, and a fund of pertinent knowledge are not essential, for indeed they are. Without a facilitating relationship, however, treatment will fall far short of its therapeutic potential, and may fail entirely, for the rapport between worker and client provides the emotional climate in which these other essentials can become effective.

The appearance and location of the agency setting will have some effect on the establishment of rapport. Perhaps most crucial in this regard for Negro clients is the presence of Negro staff. Whatever the attitude and competence of the individual caseworker, the Negro client is more likely to expect a white caseworker to understand and accept him if he is aware that the agency practices a policy of integration.

To borrow Hollis' happy use of the term "blend," a rapport between worker and client is a blend of many things. For instance, at intake a favorable blend for the client may contain, among other things, a respect for the agency's reputation; a recognition of the worker's nonjudgmental attitude; and a positive, but not significantly regressive transference reaction. The worker thus benefits from the client's realistic and emotional appraisal of the situation. With such an immediate, positive response, the worker has some assurance that he will have a chance to help the client, and the client then benefits from the worker's actual competence and his therapeutic optimism, which is itself a blend of reality and countertransference elements. Thus, treatment proceeds on the basis of the two-way communication of feeling that is set up.

Because of a combination of psychic and sociocultural processes, the white worker may not gain the benefit of the Negro client's optimal positive

[7] Elizabeth Herzog, "Some Assumptions about the Poor," *Social Service Review*, Vol. XXXVII, December, 1963, p. 395.
[8] Curry, *op. cit.*, p. 133.

transference. In this circumstance he will not experience an optimal therapeutic countertransference spontaneously. Without this advantage the worker who is accustomed to operate in the benign climate of the positive transference may feel anxious and inadequate. Since the client's realistic appraisal always plays a large part in the situation, the caseworker's professional competence can be relied upon to establish the basis for a positive object relationship. When the client senses that the worker is able, despite the apparent sociocultural differences between them, to understand his special circumstances and problems and to identify with him in his struggle to meet his emotional and material needs, client and worker can establish positive rapport without the benefit of a positive transference on the part of the client.

If the basic aspects of the client's and the worker's reality coincide, their similar perception of events can become the basis for a rapport that will facilitate treatment, for the ego must perceive reality and deal with it effectively if a person is to meet his needs and attain his goals.[9] Casework treatment depends, however, on the caseworker's ability to make effective contact with the client's sound ego capacity. If the caseworker identifies with the client on the basis of similar sociocultural attitudes, or if he is unable to identify with the client because of a difference in their sociocultural attitudes, he may in either case be failing to identify with the client on a basic ego level. The outcome of treatment depends on whether he can help the client develop enough healthy ego functioning to permit some adaptive modification or shift in defense mechanisms.

To identify with the client's ego is to identify on a common human ground shared by people of all races, regardless of sociocultural manifestations. When the worker identifies with the client on this level, he can view and deal with sociocultural factors as he deals with ego defenses—that is, as being useful or not useful in realizing the client's basic strivings. Treatment goals, too, can then be formulated in psychodynamic terms related to the effective use of the client's capacities rather than in terms of specific sociocultural attitudes or behavior; thus the goals become meaningful to the client in terms of his own reality.

When the worker and client arrive at a mutual understanding of important aspects of the client's reality, the worker has established the basis for developing optimal rapport without encouraging a regressive transference or unnecessary dependence. His identification with the client's effective ego functioning enables the worker to use the relationship "blend" flexibly, in response to the client's verbal and nonverbal communications. The worker, accordingly, is constantly required to use his best professional judgment in determining which components of the relationship blend are

---

[9] Hollis, *op. cit.*, p. 29, describes the client's ego as "his capacity to think, to reflect, to understand." See Heinz Hartmann, *Ego Psychology and the Problem of Adaptation*, David Rapoport (tr.), International Universities Press, New York, 1958, for a discussion of the concepts of a conflict-free ego sphere, autonomous ego-development, and the process of adaptation.

useful for treatment purposes at different times. The degree of emotional support that may be needed, at one point, to engage the ego of the client on a meaningful level may be, at another point, unnecessary or even detrimental. But whatever the optimal relationship blend may be, it must always be determined by the client's needs and should not be subject to the worker's socially conditioned emotional distance.

Responding to the Client's Needs

Undoubtedly, factors making for social distance contribute to the failure of the worker and the client to develop a suitable level of rapport. Hollis suggests, however, that "the great emphasis in casework training over the past thirty years on acceptance of differences and on self-determination for the client" may have provided a fairly adequate counterforce.[10] Now the danger may lie in spelling out sociocultural differences in such a way that a new version of "tender condescension" (Frazier's term)[11] may enter the caseworker's relationship with the Negro client. While the Negro client has inevitably suffered from segregation and discrimination in some measure, and has often suffered comcomitant economic deprivation, the worker would be mistaken to assume that the Negro client is necessarily "culturally deprived." Current clichés can be as handicapping to true understanding as were past stereotypes, for the worker must achieve an emotional understanding of the way in which both social and psychological forces affect the client's internal and external circumstances.

A recent institute sponsored by the San Francisco Psychoanalytic Society on "The Effect of External Reality on Internal Conflict and Symptom Formation" included a good deal of discussion on work with Negro clients. In response to one of the participant's exclamation "Understanding is not enough!" another responded, "Or is it that we don't know how to convey our understanding?" The caseworker may well add a further question: Or is it that we are conveying our understanding of the wrong thing?

With regard to the client's inner and outer reality, the worker must be as flexible in his use of sociological and psychological understanding as in his use of the relationship blend. He must be able to recognize when social or psychological factors must come to the fore, retaining full awareness that both are vital and inseparable in treatment. If the worker conveys to the client that he understands his psychological problems when the client needs, above all, to know that he understands the social pathology that is contributing to his problems, the worker is conveying his understanding of the wrong thing.

[10] Hollis, *op. cit.*, p. 163.

[11] Lois Pettit, "Some Observations on the Negro Culture in the United States," *Social Work*, Vol. V, July, 1960, p. 105, refers to an earlier version of "tender condescension," i.e., the denial or negation of real and existing differences, in favor of an "exaggerated evaluation of the Negro's . . . achievements."

Several years ago a young Negro woman applied at a family service agency for help with her marital problem. She and her husband had many psychological problems, and Mrs. C recognized the need to work on these problems. She had masochistic tendencies; she acted out her feeling of emotional deprivation in her grooming and attire, conveying a picture of the "deprived" and "underprivileged" Negro.

Mrs. C, who had teaching credentials, had been seeking employment without success. Her appearance obviously was not enhancing her prospects, but it was also true that at that time Negro teachers were rarely appointed to secondary schools, the level at which her credentials qualified her to teach. Realistically, she had little chance of obtaining such an appointment. The worker discussed this with Mrs. C, sharing with her his recognition of this injustice. At the same time he attempted to help her consider other job possibilities and to develop some awareness of the handicap she herself created by her masochistic presentation of herself as deprived.

Mrs. C's wish to find employment that would satisfy her ego strivings was realistic, but she was not able to come to terms with the reality barrier. The worker finally allowed himself to identify with her feelings sufficiently to voice in his own mind the question that was troubling her: Why should she adapt herself to an unjust reality? At that point, overcome by his own feelings (and out of his emotional understanding of the client's reality), he suggested that she ask the NAACP to fight against discriminatory practices in the school system.

At the start of her next appointment Mrs. C asked the worker, "Is there something different about me? The receptionist didn't recognize me." She was well dressed and well groomed, and she had the bearing of a capable and confident woman. Mrs. C had not discussed her problem with the NAACP, probably knowing, better than did the worker, that the leadership was not at that time ready or able to take a stand; instead she had applied for a job at a child care center, where she knew Negro applicants were accepted, and she had been employed. From that time both Mrs. C and the worker had a far greater proportion of conflict-free ego available for work on Mrs. C's psychological problems.

Just because Negro clients, whatever their social class, have been, and continue to be, exposed to a virulent form of social pathology, the worker must not assume that they will necessarily need or want help with problems related to this condition. If the worker conveys his understanding of the client's sociocultural problem when the client is seeking understanding of his psychic or familial problem, the worker is conveying his understanding of the wrong thing at the wrong time.

Mrs. R was seeking help with her marital problem. The color of her skin was very light, and she was well dressed and beautifully groomed. Mr. R was a graduate of the local university and the local public schools. By reason of geography, socio-economic status, and familial and personal circumstances, Mrs. R had escaped the grosser forms of prejudice and discrimination. Her capacity for insight into emotional problems was remarkable, and she made an immediate, positive transference to the caseworker.

In one interview, Mrs. R mentioned that she had once attended a (*de facto*) segregated school. When the caseworker attempted to pursue the subject, Mrs. R was silent. After the worker commented on her silence, Mrs. R replied, "I am sitting here wondering what kind of person you really are."

Her reply could not be categorized as resistance, for it was based on a real question about the worker's attitudes and competence in regard to a problem area with which Mrs. R was not consciously seeking help, and one in which she was not sure she could trust him. The question also indicated a breakdown of the client's unrealistic appraisal of the worker, occasioned by the positive transference, and required building into the relationship blend some opportunity for the client to make a realistic appraisal of his attitude and competence in what was obviously a problem area for her. Because her reaction was primarily ego-oriented at that point, he did not pursue an inquiry that might have jeopardized the treatment relationship.

In neither of these case illustrations was the client of low socioeconomic status. Whatever the values, psychological and sociocultural, shared by worker and client, their different vantage points could have been fatal to the outcome of treatment. Clearly, race is a distinctive factor in the casework relationship and treatment process, regardless of social class.

Barriers to Establishing the Basis for Treatment

The social-class status of most Negro clients who seek help at family service agencies is low, and their external circumstances are such that their primary need is likely to be for financial assistance, legal aid, or some other kind of concrete service that is unavailable at the family service agency. The worker offers help by referring such clients to appropriate resources, but he often recognizes that they need help with an internal conflict or with an interpersonal relationship. It is in these situations that the caseworker most often fails to establish a continuing treatment relationship. This failure may be the result of differences in the worker's and client's psychological and sociocultural values and in their behavioral patterns. There seems reason to believe, however, that it may sometimes be the result of a mutual perception of external reality circumstances that must be remedied or alleviated before treatment of internal problems can be undertaken.

Some Negro clients are themselves well aware of the inseparability of psychological and sociocultural factors in the etiology and current dynamics of their problems. Moreover, the impact of the civil rights movement has apparently made it possible for some Negroes to speak more freely about race, and the worker now has more opportunity to explore the subject with them. When these clients are able to enter into an optimal rapport with a white caseworker, the ensuing exploration is as enlightening to the worker as to the client. In order for it to benefit the client as fully as possible, the caseworker may have to re-examine some of his own attitudes, both personal and professional.

Nothing more may be required of the caseworker than his acknowledgment that the mere fact of difference in appearance can be disquieting, especially for a person whose range of experience with people of different races is somewhat narrow. The experience of difference, even on so simple a level, gives rise to feelings. Although caseworkers who are imbued with the tradition of color blindness cannot realistically deny the existence of difference in color, they often feel constrained to deny or suppress any feelings they have as a result of that difference—and it is axiomatic that denied or suppressed feelings (to say nothing of repressed ones) will affect any relationship upon which these feelings impinge.

According to an early formulation by Luna Brown, which appeared fifteen years ago, ". . . a denied 'feeling against' Negro clients may underlie a good deal of the difficulty and lack of success of some white workers. Whether based on uneasiness due to lack of association with Negroes, or a learned but ingrained attitude toward them, or a personal need to find security through a sense of racial superiority, the worker's feelings may interfere with workable relationships."[12] The significance of the white worker's denial of feelings was a small point in Brown's article, and one that was subsequently largely unheeded; however, if the worker is to think effectively about rapport in the casework relationship, he must start with this point. If removal of the mechanism of denial does not in itself reduce the emotional distance between the Negro client and the white worker, it at least open up for consideration the factors that may be blocking the development of rapport.

If it were possible to eliminate the question of prejudice entirely to speak only of professionally acceptable social and psychological reactions to difference in race, caseworkers might find it easier to recognize and deal with their feelings. Unfortunately, by reason of both geography and personal history, the prejudice of some caseworkers may be so deep-seated that professional training and supervision, or even psychoanalysis, may not disperse it. The responsible caseworker must then disqualify himself from working with Negro clients, just as a caseworker may need to disqualify himself from working with the physically handicapped, the aged, or the members of any group with which he knows he is unable to handle his emotions adequately.

For most caseworkers, however, difference in race arouses only minor feelings of uneasiness and discomfort, suggesting that their underlying anxiety or guilt is consciously being denied or suppressed. The anxiety may be as minimal as that arising from the simple fact of difference in the Negro's appearance or the worker's lack of association with Negroes, or its source may be more complex, involving problems related to sexuality or other areas of conflict. In view of "the developmentally inseparable forces of psychic and sociocultural processes,"[13] it is inevitable that individual psychopathology and institutionalized social pathology will reinforce each other, and the worker must be able to sort them out.

Guilt is unlikely to distort the practice of the white caseworker who can recognize this feeling toward his Negro clients, which perhaps arises from a sense of having acquiesced in some degree of practices of discrimination or segregation. Moreover, as a result of segregation, he himself has suffered his own variety of "cultural deprivation," and his own personal adjustment, if

---

[12] Luna Bowdoin Brown, "Race as a Factor in Establishing a Casework Relationship," *Social Casework*, Vol. XXXI, March, 1950, p. 96.

[13] Maas, *op. cit.*, p. 65.

not actually infected by the virus of prejudice, has at least been put in jeopardy by it. Recognizing that he himself is thus also in some degree the victim of segregation and prejudice may alleviate the guilt he may experience, consciously or unconsciously, as a result of his identification with his race.

If special problems of transference and countertransference arise in the relationship of the white caseworker and the Negro client, the caseworker may need to turn for help to persons with special competence in resolving transference problems. The caseworker must take responsibility for being aware of this possibility and for recognizing clues indicating that consultation is required. Examination of the transference and countertransference in such cases might yield further understanding of the ways in which sociocultural and psychological factors operate together.

Conclusion

Casework is a method of inquiry into problems as well as a method of treating problems. In a matter in which no one can claim as yet to be an expert, the caseworker can hope to make a contribution by a study of his work with Negro clients, their developmental histories, and the current state of their inner and outer circumstances. Through such study the interrelationship between sociocultural and psychological factors will be revealed more clearly. It seems likely that an increased understanding of all clients will result from such studies. With this improvement in their understanding, caseworkers will not distort their vision either through being color blind or through focusing on differences or similarities.

The thoughts presented in this article are primarily derived from the casework treatment of individual clients. Such thoughts are necessarily preliminary, and may be modified, expanded, or supplemented by the results of systematic research. Whatever the research design, however, the importance of the casework relationship and the contribution it can make to the understanding of human beings should not be overlooked.

Social Class—General

Casework and Social Class

Florence Hollis

Students of social-class phenomena have observed that many persons follow a life style that is characteristic of the particular socioeconomic class to which they belong. If this observation is valid, caseworkers should attempt to answer two questions. To what extent are differences in life style of major importance for casework among people of different socioeconomic classes? The second question goes further and can be stated more specifically: To what extent is it true that a person who is impoverished needs a kind of casework that is basically different from the kind needed by a person who has an adequate income? Before presenting some of the data available that may help us to find answers to these questions, I should like to call to mind the concern that social workers—family caseworkers, in particular—have traditionally shown for low income and impoverished families and to emphasize the fact that service to these families continues to be a responsibility of family service agencies.

A Long-Held Commitment

The wave of concern now being felt in this country for those who are not sharing in our general prosperity, who are underfed, shabbily clothed, and poorly housed, is reminiscent of the spirit of the early and middle 1930's, when a cure was sought in social reforms that were primarily economic in nature. Social workers viewed the mass unemployment of those years chiefly as the result of failures in the economy. We constantly fought the opinion so often expressed by comfortably employed and employing citizens that "people are too lazy to work"; and we sought to show that, except for a small minority who were socially disturbed, the physically fit unemployed would gladly return to work as soon as work became available. Moreover, we were insistent that, until work was available, adequate financial assistance had to be provided so that families could live in decency. The validity of our point of view was amply sustained by the events of the late thirties and the war years, when public assistance rolls shrank to a small fraction of their former size and thousands of persons, previously classified as completely unemployable, again became wage-earners.

Reprinted from *Social Casework*, XLVI (October, 1965), pp. 463–471, by permission of the author and the Journal.

Today we are again aroused by the problem of poverty, as automation, migration, lack of education, and other factors combine to prevent full employment of our potential labor force. More jobs there must be; but the new jobs will be different from the old ones, and workers must be provided with the skills needed to fill them. The school drop-out is the symbol of the new concern, associated as it is with delinquency and unemployability, rooted as it is in conditions that are derived from the very fact of poverty itself.

Obviously social work is not a complete answer to the problem of unemployment. Overcoming this social ill will require the efforts of many disciplines, but social work does have work to do with the individuals who have been victimized by joblessness. Although personal problems are not a major *cause* of unemployment, they often are the end *result* of the social deprivations and pressures brought about by the poverty created by unemployment. Once these poverty-induced problems have become imbedded in the individual, employment alone can no longer cure them.

Within the social work sphere, casework carries the major responsibility for direct work with individuals and families grappling with the day-by-day realities of life without an adequate income. Dealing as it does with both the individual environment and the individual personality, casework alleviates some of the pressure of poverty, on the one hand; on the other hand, it attempts to undo, or to help the individual overcome, the damage his personality has suffered from years, or even a lifetime, of grinding and humiliating deprivation.

This obligation to the victims of poverty has been recognized by casework ever since its beginnings. But despite the widespread recognition among the casework leaders of the thirties of the need for casework services in public assistance,[1] in most states relatively little emphasis was subsequently placed upon the training of graduate caseworkers for the public assistance field. This was in contrast to the situation in child welfare, where the Children's Bureau had long been able to give leadership to the development of adequately trained personnel. Today the aspirations of the public welfare workers of the early thirties are about to become a reality. The current push for the expansion of income-maintenance programs on an insurance instead of a "needs" basis and for the long-needed simplification of eligibility procedures will increase the opportunities for providing casework service under public auspices and so increase the demand for professional skill in working with low-income families.

Family caseworkers in voluntary agencies are also deeply engaged in serving low-income families. In the past thirty years casework service to middle-income clients has greatly expanded. Its value to persons above the poverty line has been demonstrated, and caseworkers have developed a

[1] Elizabeth H. Dexter, "Has Casework a Place in the Administration of Public Relief?" *The Family*, Vol. XVI, July, 1935, pp. 132–37; Rosemary Reynolds, "Do We Still Believe Case Work Is Needed in a Public Relief Agency?" *The Family*, Vol. XIX, October, 1938, pp. 171–77.

methodology particularly relevant to problems of personal and interpersonal adjustment. But the family agency's extension of its service to middle-income clients by no means signifies that it has abandoned casework with low-income families or work with practical problems. Problems of personal and interpersonal adjustment are not a monopoly of middle- and upper-income clients. The poor have psychological problems too! Although family agencies vary in the socioeconomic make-up of their caseloads, a survey made up by the Family Service Association of America showed that, in 1960, 72 per cent of the clients interviewed and 67 per cent of those who had five or more interviews were in the lower or lower-middle class. The lowest socioeconomic class (the group which approximated the population designated as Class V in the August Hollingshead two-factor index of social position) accounted for 43 per cent of all clients interviewed and 37 per cent of those who had five interviews or more.[2] Clearly, the family agency is deeply involved in serving the economically deprived.

Confusions About Class Differences

Turning now to the question concerning social class differences in life style and their significance for casework, I should like to comment on some of the confusions inherent in this subject. The first confusion is the result of lumping together—as if they were all the same—multiproblem families, hard-to-reach families, and impoverished families. Although there is considerable overlapping of these groups, they are by no means identical. Reports of the St. Paul study of multiproblem families indicate that more than 25 per cent were above the public assistance income level and that 53 per cent functioned above the marginal level in economic practices. Furthermore, 64 per cent functioned above the marginal level in their relationship with the worker.[3] Similarly, many low-income families are not multiproblem families, nor are they all hard to reach. Countless low-income families can use casework service, once it is made available to them, with no more difficulty than can financially secure families. Their problems are augmented by their poverty and consequent pressing, practical problems, but they are not *necessarily* hard to reach.

The second confusion about the matter of class differences arises when low-income families are erroneously viewed as a homogeneous cultural group. It is easy to recognize that within this group are found many older persons and families, reduced to poverty by illness or other misfortune, who really belong to the middle class by virtue of their educational level and their

---

[2] Dorothy Fahs Beck, *Patterns in Use of Family Agency Service*, Family Service Association of America, New York, 1962, p. 26, supplemented by a memorandum, August, 1964.

[3] Ludwig L. Geismar and Beverly Ayres, *Families in Trouble*, Family Centered Project, Greater St. Paul Community Chest and Councils, St. Paul, Minnesota, 1958, p. 48; Ludwig L. Geismar and Beverly Ayres, *Patterns of Change in Problem Families*, Family Centered Project, Greater St. Paul Community Chest and Councils, St. Paul, Minnesota, 1959, p. 39.

previous employment. After these segments are eliminated, however, the term "culture of poverty" is sometimes used to refer to the ways of life of clients whose incomes approximate the level of public assistance or are even less—and many non-public-assistance families fall in this group—who have not finished high school, who are able to do only unskilled work, and who are, often, members of "female-based" families.

It is frequently claimed that persons in this latter type of low-income family tend to lack motivation for self-improvement, to feel that their lives are controlled by fate rather than by their own efforts, to prefer present to future gratification, and, therefore, to be uninterested in long-time planning. They are supposed to be "expressive" in the sense of acting out feelings and emotional needs rather than controlling them, to have a poor time sense, to project the blame for their troubles on external forces, to be unable to express feelings in language or to comprehend abstractions, to have no belief in the value of talking as a way of solving problems or straightening out feelings, and so to be inaccessible to what is called "traditional case-work."

In actual fact, how much homogeneity is there in this low-income, poorly educated, vocationally unskilled group? In it can be found first- and second-generation families from many ethnic backgrounds; old American families—white, Negro, and Puerto Rican—who have recently migrated to the city from rural areas; and families that have lived in the same general area for three or more generations. These families also vary widely in religious affiliation, in family structure, and in education. The educational gap between the illiterate or barely literate individual and the high-school dropout is surely as great as that between the high-school graduate and the holder of a graduate degree.

And to what cultural influences will these different kinds of low-income families be exposed? All will be influenced to some degree by the dominant middle-class culture. They will be influenced by the values and customs of the blue-collar working class of which they are a part. They will be influenced by the values and customs of their parental families if these differ from their own culture and by the values and customs of any subgroup that they themselves may comprise.[4] Robert Merton, Lloyd Ohlin, and Richard Cloward hold very persuasively that a significant portion of juvenile delinquency in low-income families is caused by one aspect of this fact—that is, by the conflict between the high aspirations youngsters have assimilated from middle-class culture and the meager opportunities available to them for realizing these aspirations. There is every reason to believe that many, many low-income, poorly educated individuals do not share a common "culture of poverty." Hylan Lewis and Camille Jeffers stress the diversity

[4] For similar points of view, see William L. Yancey, *The Culture of Poverty: Not So Much Parsimony*, a paper based on research sponsored by the National Institute of Mental Health, Grant No. MH-09189 (unpublished); Jerome Cohen, "Social Work and the Culture of Poverty," *Social Work*, Vol. IX, January, 1964, pp. 3–11.

found among lower-class individuals in the Child Rearing Study in Washington, D.C.[5] In the Stirling County study it was found that there was "more diversity than consensus . . . and . . . a tendency . . . toward isolated behavior and unpredictability."[6] Richard Slobodin says of Upton Square, "individuality and idiosyncrasies of character flourished there as they do not at present in conformist middle-class society."[7] In work with low-income families we must steer clear of any tendency to stereotype. Stereotyping can lead to undue discouragement, unwillingness to persevere, the offering of even less service than the client can use, and even abandonment of the willingness to try to help at all.

The Effects of Persistent Poverty

At the same time that we resist the temptation to stereotype, we should be alert to any data that can add to our understanding of either the personalities of low-income persons or the situations by which they are confronted. Material based upon participant observation is particularly valuable when combined with psychological understanding. Caseworkers are beginning to join sociologists in studies of extremely deprived families. Louise Bandler, in her report of the South End Family Program in Boston, describes work done with thirteen extremely deprived Skid Row families.[8] The mothers in these families were virtually children, competing with their own offspring as if they were siblings; their households were completely disorganized; the parents were so inarticulate that they literally did not have words for their emotions, or knowledge of abstraction, or even such fundamental knowledge as why a baby cries.

The workers in this program found that they could visit these clients without an invitation and that if they returned regularly, chatted in a neighborly fashion, and offered help with practical problems when they could, they would be allowed to stay. They might then have the chance to demonstrate that a baby stops crying more quickly if someone feeds him,

[5] Hylan Lewis, "Culture, Class and the Behavior of Low-Income Families," a paper given at the Conference on Lower Class Culture, New York, N.Y., June 27–29, 1963, sponsored by the Health and Welfare Council of the National Capital Area, Washington, D.C. (unpublished); Hylan Lewis, "Child-Rearing Practices Among Low-Income Families," *Casework Papers, 1961,* Family Service Association of America, New York, 1961, pp. 79–92; Camille Jeffers, "Living Poor," a report for restricted circulation, Child Rearing Study, Health and Welfare Council of the National Capital Area, Washington, D.C. (unpublished).

[6] Charles C. Hughes and others, *People of Cove and Woodlot,* "Stirling County Study of Psychiatric Disorder and Sociocultural Environment," Vol. II, Basic Books, New York, 1960, pp. 394–95, cited by Lewis, "Culture, Class and the Behavior of Low-Income Families," *op. cit.*

[7] Richard Slobodin, " 'Upton Square': A Field Report and Commentary," Child Rearing Study, Health and Welfare Council of the National Capital Area, Washington, D.C., 1960, p. 13, cited by Lewis, "Culture, Class and the Behavior of Low-Income Families," *op. cit.*

[8] Louise S. Bandler, "Casework with Multiproblem Families," *Social Work Practice, 1964,* Columbia University Press, New York, 1964, pp. 158–71.

changes his diaper, turns him over, or picks him up than if he is yelled at or hit. Gradually the workers learned that even these little-girl mothers wanted to do better by their children than they themselves had been done by; that the mother yelled at the baby and hit him partly because she actually did not know why he was crying or what else to do and partly because the crying made her feel so bad—so inadequate in the care she was giving her child.

Both experience and study show that longtime poverty results not only in actual deprivation of food, inadequate and shabby clothing, crowded and run-down housing but also in illness or at least depleted energy, a strong sense of inferiority or lack of self-esteem, and often a great sensitivity to criticism, even though this sensitivity may be overlaid by defensive hostility, denial, and projection. The client who is the victim of persistent poverty is often discouraged to the point of being chronically depressed. He almost surely has underlying resentment, anger, and disbelief that the caseworker— a well-dressed, healthy, well-educated member of the middle class—can respect him or be relied upon to help him. Motivation and aspiration are often not absent; but disappointment after disappointment and frustration after frustration may have forced him to bury his hopes for himself—if not for his children—so that he will no longer be vulnerable to so much pain. Jeffers has observed a cycle in the aspiration level of low-income families: the unrealistically high goals of early life are replaced by discouragement, embitterment, and apathy, except for the hope that the children will succeed where the parents have failed.[9]

Oversimplifications Concerning Poverty

Much has been made in recent years of the failure of the middle-class worker to understand the ways of the lower-class family. The implication has been that caseworkers seek to impose their own middle-class values and goals inappropriately on the lower-class client. Perhaps the sheer size of the problem of helping these families and our frustrations at the slow progress we have made have led us to do some scapegoating of our own. Perhaps we have created an easy victim by accusing the middle-class worker of imposing his values on lower-class clients. If this does, in fact, occur, it is indeed an error. But an even greater error is the more subtle one of failing to see the aspirations and motivations—the craving for liking, respect, and help—that may lie beneath the client's hostile, couldn't-care-less, touch-me-not exterior. (We should remember, too, the months of hard work that sometimes are required to overcome the resistance of the economically secure client.)

Guilt, too, can be underestimated or not perceived because we are accustomed to look for certain behavioral signs more common to the middle class. Deborah Shapiro's preliminary study of illegitimacy among girls of different classes and racial backgrounds indicates that both the parents and the children in low-income Negro families share in the general cultural

[9] Jeffers, *op. cit.*

disapproval of bearing children out of wedlock.[10] The sense of alienation, or anomie, so often cited as prevalent in low-income groups may well be due, in part, to the real lack of group-accepted, internalized norms of conduct that make the individual's behavior predictable to himself so that, in a sense, he knows himself as a stable entity. But it may also be a reflection of his lack of self-esteem—a lack induced partly by the attitudes of others and partly by his own dissatisfaction with his inability to achieve the goals he has set for himself.

It must always be kept firmly in mind that a family's life style is influenced not only by the amount of its income but also by its ethnic background and religious affiliation, the educational level of its members, its place of residence (urban or rural), and—perhaps more than any other factor—family structure. The fatherless, or "female-based," family—or, to put it another way, the family in which the father's relationship is tenuous— is found so frequently in the low-income group that our observations of the behavior that appears to be characteristic of this type of family structure often color our conclusions in regard to the total group. (It is estimated that this type of family makes up about 40 per cent of the lowest income group.) Much of the behavior of adolescent boys in these families seems traceable to the effort of the growing boy to escape the domination of his mother by identifying with an exaggeratedly aggressive and tough ideal of masculinity. The significance of this factor of family structure and behavior, as contrasted with economic differences, was high-lighted in a recent study of twenty adolescent boys who were making a poor adjustment to school despite their having superior intelligence. Richmond Holder and Edliff Schwaab found that these boys had been cared for in early life by parent substitutes; their mothers were dominant in the home but preoccupied with affairs outside the home; they had too little contact with their fathers; they had a negative feeling toward education, a sense of futility and indifference toward their own future work, a lack of motivation, a desire for success by magical means, a poor self-image, an orientation to pleasure-seeking, and a lack of impulse control.[11] Without doubt these boys would have been school dropouts had they not been the children of *wealthy* parents suffering from an overdose of *affluence*.

The Old and the New

Having answered the first question by citing a number of characteristics commonly found in persons who have been subjected to poverty over a long period of time—but which are by no means absent in other strata of society—

---

[10] Deborah Shapiro, *Social Distance and Illegitimacy: A Report of a Pilot Study*, Columbia University School of Social Work, New York, 1965.

[11] Richmond Holder and Edliff H. Schwaab, "The Impact of Affluence on the Personality Functioning of Adolescent Boys in Treatment," a paper delivered at the Annual Meeting of the American Orthopsychiatric Association, New York, March, 17–20, 1965 (unpublished).

we can now turn to the second question. To what extent do such differences as do exist point to the need for a different kind of casework for people from different classes? Those who feel strongly that casework with low-income families is different often speak of "traditional casework" and characterize it as a form of psychotherapy designed for verbal, well-motivated, middle-class neurotics. To anyone truly knowledgeable about modern casework, this description has a curiously nostalgic but hollow ring. Where, oh where, has the middle-class neurotic gone! It is true that the middle-class client does not find the office interview by appointment the same kind of obstacle to getting help that the low-income client may find it. But is the ceremony of an office interview the essence of casework? As a matter of fact, it is only in the child guidance clinic, the mental hygiene clinic, and the family service agency that private interviewing rooms are the prevailing mode. Even in these agencies, much that proved so disconcerting about the home interview of a few years ago is no longer so troublesome, as the use of joint and family interviews has increased. As one of my students put it, "Why should it be harder for the caseworker to listen to the turned-on television set of the resisting, home-visited client than to the weekly intellectualizing of the resisting, office-appointment client?" Resistance may take different forms in different classes, but it certainly is not unknown in work with economically secure people.

Earlier in this article reference was made to certain characteristics of casework practice with the low-income family—the use of the home visit, the worker's persistence in visiting even when the family seems to be resistive, the need to overcome the client's initial distrust partly by "doing for him" rather than relying wholly on the verbal handling of the resistance. Practical problems certainly play a larger part in work with disadvantaged families than they do in casework with those who are economically secure. There is a greater need for actual demonstration and for giving information. The importance of the worker's maintaining an accepting, noncritical attitude in order to overcome the client's lack of self-esteem and lessen his inner feelings of guilt and unworthiness cannot be overestimated. The worker must refrain from counterattack when the client's hostility bursts through and must avoid challenging the client's defenses except under special circumstances, for example, with certain types of acting-out delinquents. Over and over again the literature stresses the critical importance of these familiar components of casework practice in work with the low-income family.

A few ingenious new techniques and new combinations of familiar procedures have been devised recently. Rachel Levine has reported the worker's use of games, arts, and crafts during the home visit as a means of observing the family members' behavior patterns and of teaching, by demonstration, less destructive and hostile ways in which they can relate to one another, the use of words instead of acting out to settle differences, and so on.[12] Frank Riessman advocates role-playing and other game-like

[12] Rachel A. Levine, "Treatment in the Home," *Social Work*, Vol. IX, January, 1964, 19–28.

devices and suggests the use of "helper therapy" as is now done by Alcoholics Anonymous and similar organizations.[13] Indigenous homemakers and home teachers have been used as an adjunct to the treatment process at Mobilization for Youth in New York City. This organization has also established neighborhood service centers through which emergency help can be given and from which referrals for more sustained service are sometimes made. Riessman also recommends that service be available in the evenings and during week ends.

Another facet of casework with the low-income client, which is frequently mentioned in the literature, is the importance of accepting him for service at the point of crisis. Waiting lists are particularly inappropriate for this group. Moreover, the likelihood that the client will be reached and held in treatment is thought to be significantly greater when he is assigned directly to the worker who will be responsible for the case. A change of workers after the first interview should be avoided. It is widely recognized that what Riessman has called "anticipatory socialization" will usually be necessary: the client will have to be gradually aided to understand how talking can help, that there is something he can do about his own situation, and that the worker has no magic but that by their talking together ways can be found to make life somewhat better. This process is often equally necessary with the middle-class client!

Much has been made of the difficulty of the worker's finding the right words to use with the low-income client, particularly in the discussion of feelings. There are, of course, some clients with whom this is truly a problem. Most workers report, however, that if they use simple, everyday English, they have no difficulty. Intellectualization and the use of technical language is helpful with neither lower-class nor middle-class families.

How Basic Are the Treatment Modifications?

In the foregoing discussion we have been noting certain techniques and styles of working that seem to be particularly useful in the casework treatment of low-income families. Do these techniques and styles constitute a brand of casework that is entirely different from the "standard brand"? Or are they only relatively minor variations? In discussing this question of methodology, I should like to refer to my own recently developed classification of casework procedures.[14] In this classification distinction is first made between direct work with the client himself and work in the environment on the client's behalf. Direct work with the client is then subdivided into six major sets of procedures, the first four of which also apply to environmental work:

[13] Frank Riessman, *New Models for a Treatment Approach to Low Income Clients*, Mobilization for Youth, New York, March, 1963 (unpublished).
[14] Florence Hollis, *Casework: A Psychosocial Therapy*, Random House, New York, 1964, Chapters IV, V, VI, and VII.

1.   Sustaining procedures in which the worker shows interest in the client and acceptance of him, and, by making reassuring comments, tries to increase his self-confidence or decrease his anxiety.

2.   Procedures of direct influence in which suggestions, advice, and sometimes admonition are given in an effort to guide the client's behavior.

3.   Exploration and ventilation.

The next three types of procedure deal with communications involving three types of reflective consideration:

4.   That pertaining to current person-situation interaction

5.   That pertaining to the dynamics of response patterns and tendencies, and

6.   That pertaining to early life factors of developmental significance to present ways of functioning.

Indirect work—that is, casework with others on the client's behalf—makes use of the first four of these sets of procedures and an additional one, the mobilizing of resources.

Practically everything the worker does in the traditional casework treatment process can be classified under one of these headings. Different client problems and different personality diagnoses call for various blendings of these procedures and various emphases. If this classification is applied to casework with low-income families, what do we find?

First, we certainly find that environmental treatment—indirect work—is of very great importance. Here the worker must exercise resourcefulness, persistence, and ingenuity; he must be skillful in working with other social agencies and knowledgeable about both agency and nonagency resources. He must often work with other persons on the client's behalf; and though the contact may be of short duration, an interview with such a person calls for skill in all the procedures used in direct work with the client, with the exception of dynamic and developmental understanding. Furthermore, legwork as well as telephone work is essential. Over and over again it has been demonstrated that the initial building of the relationship with the client in the economically hard-pressed group is greatly facilitated by skillful environmental work. Be it noted, however, that environmental work is also of great importance with children and older people and with many seriously disturbed clients with or without a good income.

In direct work with the client, it seems quite clear that the client of low income with little education usually needs a large measure of *sustainment*—comparable, in fact, to the amount needed by the depressed or extremely anxious or guilty client in the better educated, economically comfortable group. The need for sustainment has been stressed over and over again in the material produced by workers who have been concentrating on casework with the low-income client. He is often highly distrustful of the caseworker, and if his self-esteem is low and his fear of criticism pronounced, he will need a very large measure of the expression of interest and concern, of respect for him and his abilities, and of the worker's desire to help him.

Much of the literature also emphasizes that this client more often needs *suggestions and advice* than do others. To a degree this may be true, but the worker must carefully assess whether or not a particular client really does need this approach. The low-income client is often quite capable of thinking about himself and his situation if the worker sticks close to the realities of life and to the client's true concerns, and if he uses words that are simple and expressive. If the client does, indeed, need suggestions and advice, the worker must be sure that his standing with the client is on firm enough ground to make his advice acceptable—to say nothing of the fact that it must be advice well attuned to the client's values and circumstances.

Exploration may sometimes proceed at a slower pace than with the more verbal, better-educated client. But once the low-income client's confidence has been established, he is likely to speak freely, particularly of feelings of anger and frustration, sometimes directed against the worker himself. The worker's acceptance and understanding of these feelings, combined with his continued interest in the client and his nonretaliation, will go a long way toward establishing a firm relationship.

As with the middle-class client, when the low-income client is able to think things through for himself, it is preferable that he do so. Simplicity of language and slowness of thought should not be mistaken for incapacity. As with most clients, whatever their income, in reflective discussion the emphasis will often be on understanding practical problems, understanding other members of the family, and foreseeing the outcome or effect of the client's own ways of acting and handling things rather than on intrapsychic understanding. The client's learning to see reality clearly, and thinking of what to do about it, often occupy the major part of his interview time. In this process, the worker may have to take more initiative in giving information, explaining, and demonstrating than would be necessary with the better-educated client.

In the worker's use of demonstration his clarity about what is to be conveyed and his careful judgment about the right time for transmitting it effectively to the client are based on the same knowledge that underlies his use of the verbal procedures through which the client is led to greater understanding in other forms of reflective consideration. Moreover, it should by no means be assumed that the low-income client does not need to, and is unable to, understand his own feelings; the way in which he responds to the environment; and those happenings in his daily life that touch off his feelings. Poor education is not synonymous with low intelligence, and simple ways can be found to express fairly complicated ideas if the worker has enough ingenuity to devise them.

It is probable that the caseworker makes less use of procedures designed to encourage reflective consideration of dynamic factors in the personality and factors of developmental significance when the client has had little education, but these procedures are not entirely ruled out. As a matter of fact, contrary to popular impressions, caseworkers make relatively little use of these procedures, even with the middle-class client. Some of the doubts expressed about the appropriateness of "traditional casework" for low-income families reflect a gross misunderstanding of the nature of present-day case-work treatment; it should not be confused with psychoanalytic psycho-therapy, which is practiced by psychiatrists. Casework is noted as much for its emphasis on environmental and supportive work as for its techniques of clarification and experiential treatment. In all its various procedures special emphasis is given to the value of a warm, accepting relationship as both a supportive and a corrective experience for the client. The case-worker's attempts to effect personality change are limited to specific modifi-cations of the client's ego or superego that can be brought about through an understanding of conscious and preconscious content, through a corrective relationship, and, under certain circumstances, through environmental changes. Casework does not attempt to effect a basic reorganization of the client's personality through his gaining insight into deeply buried experiences. The emphasis of present-day casework is on helping people to deal with their immediate problems, to understand others better, and, when appropriate, to bring about limited but highly important changes in their ways of func-tioning and, therefore, in their personalities. For many low-income people these are by no means impossible goals.

Summary

There are, indeed, differences between casework with the average low-income, poorly-educated client and casework with the average middle-income, well-educated client. But these are differences in specific techniques and in emphases rather than in basic casework *method*. Work with im-poverished families involves the use of all the procedures valued in work with more advantaged groups. In addition, it requires the use of certain innovations or modifications of traditional techniques—for example, demon-stration and role-playing, which have heretofore been used chiefly in work with children and with borderline or recovering schizophrenics.

In trying to understand clients of low income, we must beware of the stereotype. They differ from one another fully as much as do clients in the middle class. At the same time, we must be sensitive to the effects of grinding deprivation, of poor education, of being devalued in a status-minded society, and often of growing up in a fatherless family in a neighborhood where opportunities for crime abound and opportunities for reaching the goals to which their membership in American society leads them to aspire are very, very scarce.

We must also guard against depriving these clients of the opportunity of receiving adequate casework help by our holding stereotyped and erroneous preconceptions about their limitations. The caseworker trying to help impoverished families needs not only all the skill in both diagnosis and treatment that he needs in work with other types of families but also great ingenuity, resourcefulness, flexibility, and patience. Above everything else— as the work of Overton, Henry, Wiltse, Fantl, Cloward, Riessman, Bandler, and many others has amply demonstrated—he needs to have faith in the possibility that the client is capable of change and a deep desire to help him do so.

Acknowledgments

I should like to acknowledge the contributions of three students— Rosalyn Lowenstein, Alice Schmacher, and Mary E. Woods—to the content of this paper. Their term papers were of distinct value for both information and ideas.

The Lower Class

Casework in Lower Class Districts

Berta Fantl

This is not more than an attempt to describe our initial impressions, changing attitudes and approaches following our move from a downtown school child guidance center into neighborhoods where poverty, crowded housing, lack of community facilities and delinquency are as high as services of trained social workers are rare. Without benefit of a research team or even a limited caseload our impressions are open to revisions and, hopefully, they eventually will be subjected to systematic investigation.

Ethnic Composition, Social Class, and Family Structure

The majority of our clients are Negroes, many of them from the South. Among other ethnic groups are American Caucasians, a considerable number of Latin American families, a sprinkling of Chinese and Filipinos, European immigrants, re-located American Indians and a few Samoans. Economically, occupationally and socially our clients belong to the lower, lower classes. If there is a recession they are the ones who are hit first and hardest. Many are one-parent families who are receiving Aid to Needy Children. Even if there is a father in the home, his wages as an unskilled laborer may not be sufficient to support a family without supplementation from public aid. The size of families is large; six to nine children are more the rule than the exception, and 11 to 16 children in one family is not uncommon. Whether natives of the United States or foreign-born, many families came from rural—frequently impoverished—backgrounds. They are living in low-rent public housing built during World War II to accommodate the influx of war workers and now gradually being replaced by permanent housing projects.

During this unforseen expansion little attention was paid to such other needs of tenants as neighborhood centers, schools, proper sidewalks or streetlights, adequate bus services. Many of the organized churches are located in adjoining districts. Most of our clients attend church regularly; some walk a far distance, while others belong to informal religious groups

Reprinted with permission from *Mental Hygiene*, XLV (July, 1961), pp. 425–438.

right in the projects. Several of our clients are ministers or assistant ministers. Their positions seem to give them status within their group and provide them and their families with a few socially approved outlets. We are told that people who are upward mobile leave the more isolated districts as soon as they are able to do so. This coincides with the wishes expressed by clients.

Perception of Clients by Others and Clients' Low Self-Concept

Members of various service professions who work hard and conscientiously frequently feel isolated. There is little status or challenge[1] to work in our area and many ask for a transfer to a "better" district as soon as they get here. They have trouble understanding and communicating with the various ethnic groups and they feel that their efforts to help people are not appreciated. Some are inclined to consider our clients "lazy," "dumb," "people on relief," "bad" and "indifferent."

This perception of our clients is reflected in the low concept the clients have of themselves, especially in relation to the helping "outsider." Depending on the strength or weakness of their core identification with their own cultural group, clients may feel worthless, hopeless and helpless in dealing with the endless cycle of daily stresses and deprivations. They are highly conflicted and confused about when to call for help from one of the many authority figures—the police, housing authority, school, public welfare, court—or when to reject them. They feel self-conscious about their speech and clothing and uncertain about how to act in initial contacts. They may have nothing to say or they may flood us with material which seems of little relevance to the question of why the school referred Johnny. It is up to the worker to size up the situation sensitively, to put the parents at greater ease and—through listening, questions and restatements—to engage the parents in meaningful discussions. We may have to listen to many other problems pressing on the parent's mind before we get to talk about Johnny, as well as obtain adequate information about Johnny's developmental history and other background information which frequently has little meaning to the client.

Even young children seem keenly aware of their lack in social skills. A nine-year-old, proud of the knowledge he gained in school about the Revolutionary War, asked his worker to show him "which is right and which is left." Another boy, supposedly retarded and in a special class, expressed his liking for his new teacher "because he does not just tell kids to do things; he shows them how they are done."

Early last school year we engaged in some heated discussions on whether some of the things we responded to in clients, or even occasionally

---

[1] Caseworkers are not exempted from this status dilemma. Occasionally "professionalization" of services is equated with an increase of referrals from professional sources, with a decrease of services to unskilled laborers and the appearance of a clientele which is less economically deprived—despite an economic recession—and with scheduled versus unscheduled appointments.

initiated, were "therapeutic" or "educational" and if the latter, were they within our function? As the school year wore on, those doubts must have become dissipated, since whenever we were able to enhance a client's concept of himself as emotionally or socially more adequate, we realized that we had accomplished a step toward helping him to see others differently and to relate to them in new ways.

Lower, Lower Class and Working Class District

Casework in a lower, lower class district poses somewhat different problems from a more regular working class district. In a working class district there is a higher degree of family cohesiveness, more permanent male figures with whom to identify, membership in labor unions and a greater pride in achievements in spite of recurring obstacles, including unemployment. The lower, lower class district has an aura of being caught with no way out, daily drudgeries with few rewards and an almost greater hanging together and understanding for each other in times of trouble than a common purpose and mutual joy in the rare moments of calm.

On the other hand, people in our districts show a great need for contact with the "outside world" and a genuine appreciation for any little thing accomplished or gesture extended to them. A call to a mother who is ill or a card as a reminder of Mother's Day to the members of our Mothers' Group was responded to warmly and elaborately and mentioned for several weeks. Among the 150 referrals made to us from one of the most deprived districts, we do not remember one family whom we were unable "to reach" as long as we met the clients in a way which made sense to them and as we did not expect them to respond in some stereotyped "therapeutic" fashion.

Function of the School Child Guidance Services

The major functions of the School Child Guidance Services are direct services to clients, consultation to school personnel and participation on community committees. Because of the high number of referrals to us and our desire to give quick services to the school, *our direct services to clients* consist mainly of one or two intake interviews or a brief series of interviews accompanied by psychological tests. Such intakes or short-term evaluations are followed up whenever indicated by referrals to appropriate community resources, mostly family agencies and psychiatric clinics. Each worker also carries a small continued treatment load, but the major function of direct service is in the area of intake and evaluations with referrals elsewhere.

Consultation services to school personnel, as a complex and rapidly expanding function of the Child Guidance Services, grew out of the realization that as professional workers we have a commitment to develop—gradually and thoughtfully—techniques to effect the health and welfare of larger groups of people. We also realized that knowledge and skills need to be used cautiously and imaginatively and in more ways than one. The goal of consultation is to enable school personnel to deal more effectively— in their professional roles as administrators, counselors, teachers—with the many disturbing school situations they encounter. Consultation is not focused on the teacher as a person, but on the problem situation and the professional role the teacher is asked to perform. With increased interest in giving equal services to "tough" as well as middle-class districts, *participation of caseworkers in community committees* and neighborhood councils became a small yet integral part of their daily activities.

When we moved into very deprived neighborhoods we were ready for some surprises, but we did not realize how poorly our former way of referring cases elsewhere would work for all but a handful of "non-typical" clients. As our communication with clients increased, just the reverse seemed to happen between us and our usual referral sources, all of which are located downtown.

We found ourselves conversing in different languages. Even when we knew that clients needed and wanted help we could not be sure that the client would keep appointments at a certain hour and day in a district strange to him and far from his home. Even when we were convinced of the client's good intelligence and ego strength in the face of insurmountable difficulties, we found ourselves at a loss to know whether his "ego capacity" to "use treatment" would be exactly what the worker on the other end of the line had in mind. We soon could see that our limited time was better spent with clients or on community committees than by trying to explain the need for flexible services to individual workers who were caught in those structures of the agencies which were geared to another echelon of clients.

Acute Stresses and Ego Defense

Families with "social crises" are referred to us—a suspension of a child from school for stealing, continued misbehaving, using "foul language," "breaking into" a school with a group of other young children.[2]

Acute stress situations, even with *clients with whom we continue to work,* are much more common than internalized conflicts, guilt and self-blame. Anxiety is expressed by blaming others, by apparent indifference, passivity and depression-like behavior. We have much to learn about how clients cope not only with inner conflicts but also with stresses[3] which are largely

---

[2] Our referrals come from elementary and junior high schools. However, because of the size of the families we are aware of the problems of older teen-agers.

[3] In Myers, Jerome K. and Bertram H. Roberts, *Family and Class Dynamics* (New York: John Wiley & Sons, Inc., 1958), 15 and 16, Dr. Myers makes the useful distinction between *external presses* and *internal stresses*. A press is a potential pressure on the individual from the environment; it may be either *stressful* or *supportive*. Emotional stress, on the other hand, may add to the individual's negative presses.

produced by outside circumstances—irregular employment, no food in a society of plenty, repeatedly experienced social barriers and cultural strains. We have become cautious about the terms we are using to diagnose and describe clients' difficulties. Not only norms for behavior or style of impulse expression may be influenced by ethnic group identification and class structure; we also will need to examine carefully what additional factors to consider when we describe the ego's mode of dealing with inner and outer conflicts.

Denial of difficulties, projection-like behavior and the sometimes long-winded "rationalizations" by clients are not necessarily the neurotics' rigid distortions of reality. Often it is an anticipation based on repeated reality experiences during which the client experienced attacks and injuries to his self-image.[4] As soon as the client senses that the worker understands his underlying anxiety of being "attacked," the "denials" and "projections" seem to diminish quickly—although often only temporarily and, first, in relation to the worker. It seems to us that the neurotic client experiences some level of emotional and social enrichment before he resorts to his symptoms as a compromise. We doubt that our clients experienced the same type of emotional and social enrichment since their biological drives and resources were nourished in a different social environment and exposed to a chronicity of stressful situations.

Toward an Understanding of Deviant Group Behavior

Current casework practice cannot, without adaptation of methods and techniques, be applied to large families, who frequently come from rural areas and whose needs and wants for love, affection and security are the same as everyone else's but whose value system as to time, property rights, manner of speech and clothing, expression of feeling and sex behavior are different from the conventional norm. In attempting to emphasize the social side of human behavior, there is perhaps a tendency to overstress the "differences" in human beings or to lose oneself in generalizations. It is well to remember that people differ only in degree and that they are much more alike than they are different. The differences might be small, yet subtle enough to obscure communication between different groups of people, and after all *communication—verbal and nonverbal*—with an *adequate understanding for the subtle aspects of the situation under which communication takes place* is the vehicle for all treatment.

To know the way the client *is likely* to view his problem, the agency and the worker, from his ethnic point of view or class position, are of utmost importance in the design of new services. Therefore it is not merely a matter of "reaching out" or decentralizing offices before services with certain client

---

[4] Although the author takes full responsibility for any opinion expressed in this article, she is indebted to Erika Chance, Ph.D., research associate, Department of Psychiatry at Mount Zion Hospital in San Francisco, for her helpful criticism and discussions.

groups will become more effective. This must not be misunderstood to mean that just because a client is a member of a certain milieu, he will respond a priori in an expected manner. People and milieux are much more complex, and in the last analysis *each client's problem is inevitably unique and personal*; it is the product of the individual's biological equipment and his life experiences. However *certain types of problems* occur more commonly under certain *subcultural pressures* which are operating in the client's life experience.

When working in certain neighborhoods one cannot help being impressed by the high number of deviant behavior patterns. Of course what defines "normal" or "deviant" behavior is relative to each society. Therefore what may seem an "antisocial" act to the school may be normal—if not expected—behavior for clients. This does not necessarily mean that parents or children are without conflict about conventional values and expectations. Our commitment to democracy—with the ideal of an equal success goal for all, supported by our social institutions and mass media—instills a desire for a better life, i.e., a middle-class life style which hardly anyone can escape. Who the ones actually are who achieve these goals, to what stratum of society they are more likely to belong, what price in strain they or society may have to pay for the pursuit of such aspirations is another story.

Deviant behavior as a *group response* can be understood only by a thorough knowledge of environmental pressures. It is a form of adaptation to strain when conformity to societal expectations is positively motivated, yet at the same time frustrated and unacceptable.[5]

To the individual—regardless of society's prescription of what is "normal," "deviant," "good" or "bad"—only those groups to which he has actual and not fictitious access make sense—where he can learn skills necessary for group membership, where he is recognized as "someone" and is able to relate without losing face. The cultural milieu as an intermediary between the larger social norms and the individual chooses certain behavior forms to give greatest tension relief from particular strains and stresses. It is important for social work to pay increased attention to those societal strains induced by inconsistent demands and promises which lead to the formation, changes and disbandments of subcultural groups[6] and which influence the various behavior adaptions of groups[7] to which the individual belongs. Although we are far from having arrived, we gradually are becoming equipped to see the environment take on new and systematic dimensions; until now we were not able to give it—as an uncharted plot—more than

---

[5] See Cohen, Albert K.. *Delinquent Boys* (Glencoe, Ill.: The Free Press, 1955), 179.

[6] As an example of the development of a subcultural ideology see Cloward, Richard A., *New Perspectives for Research on Juvenile Delinquency* (Washington, D.C.: U.S. Department of Health, Education and Welfare, May, 1955), 80–92.

[7] See Dubin, Robert, "Deviant Behavior and Social Structure;" Cloward, Richard A., "Illegitimate Means, Anomie, and Deviant Behavior;" and Merton, Robert K., "Social Conformity, Deviation and Opportunity Structures," *American Sociological Review*, 24 (April, 1959), 149, 164–76, 177–89.

vague recognition. This is not an irresponsible take-off into interdisciplinary skies but a challenge for the social work profession.

A Look into the Future

There is presently a great need among caseworkers to clarify to what degree a "presenting symptom" is due to psychopathology and to what extent is a cultural adaptation to the client's group memberships. Although we can expect the dichotomy of what is "personal" and what is "sociocultural" to disappear eventually, at present it exists perceptually.[8]

With increased knowledge about the client's dynamic environment, we shall be able to differentiate systematically between *various types* of deviant group adaptations, their formation, persistency and operations.[9] This will lead to a differential diagnostic and treatment approach, much-needed to make treatment fit the client. Erikson's concepts of ego identity, social role and perception by others, his repeated emphasis on mastery, pride in workmanship, the need for individualized opportunities offer the most perfect synthesis of biological drives, childhood identifications and added societal expectations presented thus far.[10]

Our present diagnostic and treatment skills, sensitively tuned and refined to deal with situations of intrapsychic conflicts, will need broadening to include those environmental aspects which influence the client's psychodynamics. Our colleagues in group work are developing treatment approaches of which we in clinics and in public and private agencies are taking notice.[11]

In no way minimizing the major importance of intrafamilial experiences on the personality structure, we began to realize that other meaningful individuals and groups may have a profound impact on clients' behavior and on the developing personality. For many lower class children, the peer group provides emotional if not physical security; it is a place to be recognized, an orientation to what is right and wrong, what to say and to whom and under what circumstances.

[8] We might eventually conceive of a continuum with more or less "pure" psychogenic disturbances on one pole. For instance, as a school agency in a lower, lower class district we did not receive a single referral of school phobia in a two-year period. Although there will be exceptions to this, on the whole mothers do not have *this tyoe* of emotional investment in their children, and fathers are shadowy figures. On the other end of the continuum we may place "strictly" sociocultural reasons for deviant behavior like the delinquent gang in a well-integrated criminal adult subculture. Most cases will fall somewhere in between the two poles.

[9] See Cloward, Richard A. and Lloyd E. Ohlin, *New Perspectives on Juvenile Delinquency* (New York: New York School of Social Work, Columbia University, 1959), 169, Mimeographed.

[10] Erikson, Erik H., "Identity and Life Cycle," from *Selected Papers: Psychological Issues* (New York: International University Press, 1959), 171, Vol. 1, No. 1.

[11] Lerman, Paul, "Group Work with Youth in Conflict," *Social Work*, 3 (October, 1958), 71–77; and "Hard to Reach Youth Project" in *Befriending Troubled Youth* (Chicago: National Federation of Settlements and Neighborhood Centers, 1958).

People have many links between their inner selves and their environments and many different perceptions of what roles to take. They see themselves as persons they think they are; they have other concepts of what they want to be or should be; they have a desire as to how they want others to see them, and they are afraid of how others see them. A person takes one role with respect to some people and another role with respect to others. As the person grows up and as he works, marries and has a family, roles may change with time and in different settings.[12] A certain amount of role experimentation and "sameness" or continuity in self-perception and role-taking are necessary for the development of a wholesome identity. From a group point of view (and every individual belongs to some groups) minority adaptations to majority norms may be complicated by double identities which may result in ambivalent identities or even self-hatred and negative group identity. This means that certain individuals already psychologically prone to develop a negative identity are more likely to develop it under certain subcultural pressures.

Viewing our client from this broader perspective, we may want to learn more about his actual and imaginary group associations, in other words about "significant others" who influence his values and aspiration level. Who are the ones he admires or hates? Whom does he want as his friends? What are their values and goals? To what group does he actually relate and have access? In other words, what are his "social" frustrations, his actual social barriers which are so important to us in our work with clients of various ethnic groups and lower social classes? In what way can we help to strengthen his inner self and widen his social opportunities for a more productive life for himself and others?

Practice Approach

Incomplete as our knowledge about human behavior may be, we felt secure enough to make our services as easily accessible, available and uncomplicated for the clients as we were able to do within our limitations of time, being greatly understaffed and dealing with overwhelming problems. We reconsidered such things as the 50-minute hour and careful selection as to whom we see and whom we do not—which in our district means no services whatsoever. To be sure, our approach is very family-centered; if anything, we are *more family- and community-oriented* than we ever were, but this does not mean that parents have to make a formal application for services or keep their weekly appointment six times in a row before we dare to see a child. We feel that our clients are neither that delicate nor our techniques that precarious.

We do not make home visits without some evaluation of what is best, realistic and most integrative to the total situation of each family. We are

[12] Erikson, Erik H., *op. cit. See also:* Merton, Robert K., *op. cit.*, Chap. VIII, pp. 255–386.

surprised how few home visits we actually make, yet a firm belief has evolved that a "reaching out" visit in the client's home or in his yard or wherever we find him right then—for 30 minutes to two hours—might be more therapeutic than an office visit three weeks hence. Remember, we are dealing with acutely felt stress and "social crisis," i.e., an immediate situation as far as the client is concerned and as chronic as the situation may be from our point of view. Postponement of even concrete gratifications, let alone "therapy" or "talking out a problem," is not the usual neighborhood pattern.

If someone has trouble in our neighborhood, he is more likely to get into a fight right then, to swear, to tell his neighbors how wrong the other guy was. Therefore, we do not expect clients to be "motivated" for help in the way we used to perceive motivation, and we do not expect verbalization of "inner conflict." We listen to "projection-like" behavior and "rationalizations" in the same way we used to listen to "insight" and "self-blame," and we accept withdrawal and passivity as if the client would express an urgent desire "to bring about a change within himself," great as his resistance to such change may have been.

If one deals with these types of ego defense, the immediate interaction between the client and the worker becomes extremely important. The client is apprehensive about the worker, because, up to that point, to come to an agency to "talk out one's problems," had not been the accepted thing to do within his social setting. The worker has to demonstrate through his attitude and behavior that he can be of help; this is more of a personal task, "an achieved status"[13] than when he works in a clinic or agency which is highly esteemed by the client population. The worker is also exposed to the community's pressure to do something about the "antisocial" actions of the clients, and he must know what the clients' behavior means to his own defenses.

The mutual focus on the immediate situation makes it possible for the client to identify with the worker; this is more important than an emphasis on insight, although a certain amount of increased self-understanding frequently will result. The worker is a participant/observer in each interview situation; he has to know when to intervene, when to deal with some distortions, when to be supportive and when to listen questioningly. In order to do that, the worker has to understand the client's situation truly in its social context. He has to evaluate realistically the client's social handicaps, along with his emotional difficulties, to clarify and show him possible avenues out of his dilemma, offer concrete help if necessary or state that such help is not available. Clear, forthright and correct statements are ego-supportive. Mere passive listening on the part of the worker may be felt as hostility and may increase anxiety of "acting out" behavior. However, if the worker intervenes insensitively, the client is likely to withdraw.

[13] Lerman, Paul, "Group Work with Youth in Conflict," *Social Work*, 3 (October, 1958), 76.

In clients who are judged derogatorily by the community, the desire to relate, together with their fearful anticipation needs special consideration.

By successfully helping clients around "immediate" crisis situation, the following may be accomplished: *1]* Some relief is experienced in his ability to control his behavior, and   *2]* There is a growing feeling of confidence in the worker because he understood the client's feeling of extreme anger, fear of losing control or isolation from others, without becoming frightened, "hopeless" and discouraged about the client or deserting him as other helping professions might have done in the past. We know of examples of complete silences and passivity in the initial interviews, followed by *"reaching out" on the part of the client* when the worker continued to drop in on the client. One of those clients is now among the most active participants in our Mothers' Group; this does not mean that she attends every session or that she is always on time. She has six children under eight years of age; there is a different orientation toward time in her culture, and we do not minimize her resistance against involving herself in a close relationship.

Other Methods of Support

The emphasis in treatment is on the integrative capacity of the clients, on strengthening the healthy part of their defense structure and on an emotional relearning of interpersonal experiences as well as on neurotic conflicts. Since it is easier to project blame onto external circumstances, it is important for the worker not to overidentify with the client's difficulties and to distinguish when discrimination and other cultural material is used defensively to obscure intrapsychic conflict. With clients whose egos are rather impoverished and who have relatively low internalized tension build-up, the need in treatment is less on abreaction than for strengthening their controls and for the enhancement of their self-concept so that they feel less overwhelmed and helpless. For this we have to look not only for anxiety, anger and conflict (of which they have plenty) but also for such positive experiences and opportunities accessible to them as joy and mutual satisfaction.

We found it gratifying to come across an article by Jerome D. Frank,[14] which stresses this, among other important points. Anyone working with "hard to reach" families knows about the endless crises and often clinically defined traumatic experiences which haunt them. In our Mothers' Group, which is composed of clients we never thought we would "reach" let alone see join a group, emotions and content become so heavily loaded with stories of violences, jails and brutalities that one of the coleaders spontaneously responded (to what we are starting to call "flood release") by asking whether there was anything enjoyable in their daily lives. Since cruelty and other abuses could not fill their entire day, how did they get started in the morning, and what was a "typical" day like? This openly

¹⁴ Frank, Jerome D., "The Dynamics of the Psychotherapeutic Relationship," *Psychiatry*, 22 (February, 1959), 17–39.

guided expectation of what can be discussed and looked at in addition to "problems" had amazing repercussions for the following group sessions and resulted in a number of beneficial changes in the family lives of these mothers.

Joint Interviewing

We began to see jointly both parents or whole family groups on a continued basis. Our impressions here are tentative and we are aware of the much more systematic efforts in family interviewing taking place in our field. So far we have found continued joint interviews useful and supporting the *strength* in a family situation (although differences are aired) when, to begin with, there are evidences of some family cohesiveness. In families who are psychologically pulled apart we do not find this to be the case. Our major focus is on the family as a unit—its collective strength, stresses within the unit, problems and strains in relation to the community and possibilities and limitations of growth potentials. We focus on the individual to assess his roles and the possible strains on these roles which lead to his inadequate functioning as a member of his family. We found individual interviews for a severely disturbed family member an important adjunct to the joint sessions. To work gradually toward a more conceptualized frame of "family identity"—as expressed by Kermit Wiltse[15]—with families who are socially and culturally handicapped seems an important task. We are neither so naive nor foolish to think that the road ahead of us is an easy one.

Unimportant and "superficial" as it may sound to those who are more interested in the hidden aspects of behavior, the mere act of pulling up chairs, getting and talking together in the presence of a person who is interested, ready to observe, restate and clarify what is said and observed, and who is not hesitant to make occasional appropriate suggestions, may have great meaning for the internal aspects of the family structure. It also may be the beginning of a more gratifying experience between the family and the community. The worker then becomes truly a specialist in human relations. "Interaction" and "communication" per se have little meaning unless the worker as a participant/observer is sharply tuned to the psychological and environmental forces operating in clients and between himself and his clients. He has to understand his clients' and his own verbal and nonverbal behavior and expression as well as his own attitudes, which are based on his background and experiences; these are likely to color his perception and feeling for the situation which is confronting him.

Our experience in joint interviewing has been short and limited so it is perhaps a little presumptuous to present a brief and partial example of what happened in a family we had known for six months. Only because similar trends were noticed in working with other families do we believe

---

[15] Wiltse, T. Kermit, "The Hopeless Family," *Social Work*, 3 (October, 1958), 20.

that our preliminary report warrants mention here and that it may be of interest to others:

> The family is large—16 children ranging in age from a new baby to a twenty-three-year-old. Fourteen are living at home. Without exception, all of the school age children are reported to have had *serious* behavior difficulties in both school and community, although these difficulties are too numerous to list here. The parents are Negroes, born in the South where they began hard work on farms at an early age, with a minimum of educational or other opportunities to prepare them for the more competitive life they would seem to like for themselves and for their children.

> This family may be somewhat different from their neighbors—or at least different from those with whom we come in contact—because the father not only has a steady job but one which also ranks high among unskilled laborers, considering his ethnic background and limited early opportunities. Also, the parents stayed together over the years despite severe marital discord. Like other clients, they easily perceive their children as "bad" and "headed for jail," especially when they misbehave in the community. Yet, despite their anger and expressed disappointment, they seem to have real concern and warmth for each other and for the children. There is real babying and enjoyment of the tiny ones, but this turns into harsh treatment, hollering and punishment as soon as the children are no longer babies. There is endless pride in the older children who succeeded in the army, in white-collar jobs or in college.

> We contacted the family by phone regarding what was an *immediate* and *major* crisis in school. The parents, feeling haunted by the police, the court and the school, did not want anything to do with us. The mother was sure that we, like everyone else, were against her, after her and sure to drive her children into jail. The worker was primarily a listener throughout the entire 30-minute telephone conversation but she did ask a few relevant questions, admitting that the situation was an awful mess and spelling out, tentatively, some alternatives to think about.

> The mother's tirade subsided, and when the worker suggested that it might be a good idea to get together sometimes to meet the father and whichever children were around, the mother asked, "Right now?" For the next few weeks the worker met with this family every week for two hours or more. The parents were always present; of the older children, those participated who wanted to come or those who presently had problems at home or in school.

> The little ones stormed in and out of the room, sometimes trying busily to make friends with the worker. It should be noted that most of the joint interviews were conducted in our offices upon mutual agreement between parents and worker; that we went back to home visiting when it became too difficult for the mother to pack up her family because of her advanced pregnancy; and that at no time was a meeting canceled or broken.

> We found that in the beginning, as was our experience with other families, complaints were raised against school, police, court and neighbors and then shifted to bitter accusations against each other. The worker listened, restated some of the problems, asked questions and finally picked out *one* area—among the many expounded on lengthily or repeatedly ("flood release") or touched upon briefly—about which something could perhaps be done. After the customary initial "no," substantiated by reasons frequently based on realities, the worker succeeded—by further questions, listening to feelings expressed and by realistic appraisal of the situation in her own mind—in pointing out a number of ways the situation could be handled more satisfactorily.

> As we carefully tapped the ego strength of the clients (in our case it is

the strength of the family) by empathizing with some of the clients' difficulties for which there are no ready answers[16] and as we realistically attempted to clarify and sift out possibilities within the clients' reach, we found the family became less hopeless and less helpless about the many real and imaginary odds stacked against them. They began to look actively for resources in the family and community which could handle a few things differently. The court, the police, the many injustices and social barriers experienced became less the cause and object of attack for "all problems," although in time of renewed crisis they are likely to respond with their old pattern, not infrequently with some justification.

In the fourth session, one of the adolescents who rarely talked at home, even without a stranger around, grudgingly expressed his anger—if not his rage—that his parents would call on the police to beat him up, take him away for a day[17] when he was "bad" or he would take off from home to get away from the noise and quarrels. Both parents seemed truly surprised that all of this would bother the boy to this extent, and father and son finally talked to each other after months of silence.

Space does not permit us to report on the worker's contacts with the school, the nurse and court, all of which we find to be an equally important part of our work.

After seven joint interviews several shifts had taken place. After eight years of employment the father got up the courage to explain to his white foreman that he was needed at home in the evenings; within days he was working on a different shift. He and his older boys started to talk to each other; the mother began to reconsider whether "all that was wrong" with her daughters was that they were "rotten and spoiled." The father said if it had not been for his wife he would have left a long time ago since she is the one who holds the family together; this remark led his wife to bake him a cake for his birthday.

The following sentiment about the worker was expressed by the mother: "That's the first time anyone talked to us like that; usually I am treated like an animal." The father remarked: "The 'right' kind of people never speak to us; we have to pick our friends where we can find them."

Open House Afternoon

Our original plan was to set aside three hours each week during which two workers would be available to see school-referred clients either in a group or in individual interviews. We called our group "Mothers' Group" because of the small numbers of fathers in our caseload. At this writing we had held 25 sessions and we were as excited as we were "tentative."

As a start we thought of our open house afternoon as a social affair— to acquaint clients with our services and with each other. We reasoned that the group meetings gradually might become more problem-centered and that a core of clients might emerge who could go into a regular group therapy session. We gave a good deal of consideration to whom we would

[16] Sometimes a brief statement by the worker—such as "that's surely tough"— may convey to the client that the worker is fully aware of the impact of his experience, and the client may be able to move on to an area of more productive discussion or activity.

[17] The "authorities" are frequently called in to settle personal disputes among our clients which a middle-class family would handle by themselves, or perhaps through a friend or lawyer.

want to select for the more "therapeutic" group, through what methods, and to which clients might be better suited for individual interviews.

We had a slow start, especially with our "Mothers' Group," since unintentionally we became too selective and too slow about inviting mothers to the group. With clients who avoid tension build-up and who respond best to help when internal and external pressures are great, a "waiting list" of even two or three weeks becomes meaningless. Things changed as soon as we made the group the starting contact with a new client, with perhaps a 15 to 30 minute interview preceding the first group session. Our most responsive clients come from very deprived neighborhoods. We never could claim perfect attendance, but from the beginning the meetings seemed meaningful to the mothers. The sessions are not only problem-centered; they are more family- and self-focused with "less projecting out" than are some of our individual interviews. In many ways we expected this, since discussing problems in a group may be less threatening than discussing them in individual interviews. The refreshments and babysitting arrangement we tried to work out are incidental to the meetings. We are surprised about the leadership quality and initiative our mothers show in the group, considering that the neighborhood is said to have no potentials for any kind of leadership. Some of the clients have been coming from the beginning while some others who came once or twice keep in touch with us by phone or by unexpected office visits. At times a father might show up or an older daughter and not infrequently clients arrive a day earlier or at 10:00 A.M., instead of 1:00 P.M., and we talk to them,—pointing out the correct time of the meeting but listening to their problems anyway.

Although the group attendance of mothers might be irregular, we can be sure of a prompt knock on the door from a group of six- and eight-year-olds who started to drop in on us on the afternoons following the mothers' meeting. Some are the sons of clients, and we usually notice them roaming the streets, since they are too disruptive and restless to take part in the organized after-school activities. We recently contacted a neighborhood center in another district and our inquiry about the possibility of obtaining a group worker for these boys met with a favorable response. Unfortunately we have neither staff nor time to respond to the many groups of youngsters who come by, first to look us over, next to return to "sit around the big table and talk" or use the playroom, or report some important news or who just come and say nothing.

Putting Back the "Social"

In our diagnosis and tentative treatment plans we try to deal with the "social" in the client's environment in more than a descriptive way. To say that a client or his family lives in a slum area, that there are 15 siblings, that the family is Negro or Filipino, that the father is an unskilled laborer, presently unemployed and therefore unable to pay for casework services or "not ready to use casework services," is not sufficient for our purpose. The client's exposure in the social structure brings about different stresses and strains which impinge on his "psychological" make-up from without. This is true whether he belongs to the upper, upper classes or to the lower, lower classes, as our clients do. The strain and stress systems differ, depending on where the client and his family is located in the social structure, and to what ethnic, occupational or religious group he belongs. Although greatly pressured with requests for services, we do not feel that our time is ill spent because clients are not "motivated" for help, have little "insight" and do not readily phone for an office appointment. We consider every cultural improvement we are able to bring about to be a psychosocial improvement— in the true sense—for the client.

Johnny or any of his siblings may steal because they are just plain hungry and the swiping of food, money and toys is not such an exceptional misdeed in Johnny's neighborhood. More often than not, he steals continously because there exists an emotional conflict of one kind or another in addition to all the other social handicaps within his family—disturbed or changing parent figures, older siblings in trouble with the law or unemployment with all its emotional, physical and social implications. Johnny may or may not have experienced emotional and physical traumata at an early age; he is living *presently* in a situation which does not prepare him for a socially useful life. Some of the children may be less "emotionally sick" than we think they are and our chance to treat them and their families with our present psychological techniques remain slim unless we gain a deeper understanding of their environmental stresses.

In addition to Johnny's or his family's psychopathology (*which needs to be treated* whenever it is present) where are the *strengths* in Johnny's situation? What is left of his family unit, including older siblings, grandparents, etc., and what are his positive resources for growth and social integration? Who are his peers; what kind of behavior pattern do they show as a group and what is Johnny's attachment, relation and role to them? Who are the "significant others" outside his family—teachers, nurses, ministers, policemen —whom we could enable to have a more satisfactory relationship with Johnny and his family? Family caseworkers and clinicians will need to expand their horizons—if they are not doing so already—to collaborate more freely, more effectively, less preciously and confidentially with other agencies around so-called "multiple problems families" and to *develop techniques*[18] *to further communication and understanding between various key figures and the clients*. The best planned casework job with a family might falter as long as the children's teachers and others who come in contact with the family perceive the family as "no good" and "hopeless." We deal not just with child-parents relationships; we also need to *deal with the community perception of the clients*. For example, to enable a teacher, through case-centered conferences, to have Johnny—who is a poor learner in addition to being a disturbing nuisance—accomplish a small task which he was never

---

[18] Caplan, Gerald, *Mental Health and Consultation* (Washington, D.C.: U.S. Department of Health, Education and Welfare, 1959), 269.

able to accomplish before will give both teacher and child a sense of mutual satisfaction. This might not seem much but if repeated, Johnny and children with similar problems might develop friendlier relationships with their teachers.

Johnny might not go to school for another seven years being perceived as lazy and a nuisance, the only consistent self-image he ever was able to form—until he becomes convinced of it, too—that this is his place in society. Many misunderstandings between people and misconceptions about people are caused by cultural differences, distorted expectations and a breakdown in communication. This leads to increased anxiety and stereotyped perceptions of each other. Once we become clear as to what these differences are we may be able—by helping others in the community—to deal more satisfactorily with our clients.

By its mere existence a service like ours—small and incomplete as it is—demonstrates to the neighborhood and to the other key figures (probation officers, police, nurses, etc.) that they are no longer alone to tackle problems which are overwhelming, that someone thinks, spends money and time to work with "those" families that we too fail at times, no matter how hard we try. Let us remember that it is tought to live or work in certain districts. We try to become part of the neighborhood and this seems the easiest part of the job. The schools, the police and the merchants welcome the opportunity to talk to someone about the way they see the problems; we need them just as urgently, for as caseworkers we can no longer work in a professional vacuum. We have to understand the place we occupy in the community along with all the other helping professions; we have to be clear about our professional value system and goals which may be slightly different from the other helping professions; we have to be more accepting and more understanding and less punitive, just as we need to be clear about how the clients are viewed by the community and how they may perceive us.

Putting back the "social" into social work, therefore, does not just mean making more home visits and doing otherwise "exactly what we have done before." Nor does it mean returning to "old-fashioned" social work, although this would be better on many occasions than doing nothing.

It means seeing the environment in a new, dynamic way and becoming cognizant of the social processes which impinge on the individual from without.[19]

Our perception, in the light of new knowledge of what is important, is changing as new formulations of diagnosis and treatment are developed.

---

[19] Stein, Herman D., "The Concept of the Social Environment in Social Work Practice," *Smith College Studies in Social Work*, (June, 1960), 188–210.

Multiproblem Families

Individualizing the Multiproblem Family

Carol H. Meyer

During the last ten years, ever since the publication of the study of social problems undertaken in St. Paul, Minnesota, by Community Research Associates,[1] the professional literature has abounded with material on the multiproblem family. The term "multiproblem family"—literally, "a family with many problems"—has come into general use not as a description but as a pseudodiagnostic classification. It is not derived from an explicated theory, and it does not have the same meaning to everyone who uses it. Yet it has taken on a kind of magical significance as a convenient device by means of which the social worker is presumed to be able to identify a particular group of clients—those families in a low socioeconomic class whose members act out, are umotivated to get help, suffer from character disorders, and fail to function adequately in their social roles. In this article, I shall examine some of the most important characteristics of the families to which we have assigned the label "multiproblem" and suggest the means by which social workers can bring them the help they need.

First, I should like to make a few additional comments about the term "multiproblem." Although it is not a diagnostic term, it is preferable to certain other terms, such as "hard-to-reach," "hard-core," "self-defeating," or "acting-out," which are laden with value judgments or have a pseudo-clinical implication.[2] "Multiproblem" at least does not convey the idea that the family so labeled is judged to be lacking in inner resources, unmotivated, overly dependent, or hopeless. In the absence of a better term, it can be used to identify a group of clients who carry a particularly heavy burden of

[1] Bradley Buell and Associates, *Community Planning for Human Services*, Columbia University Press, New York, 1952.

[2] *Multi-Problem Families and Casework Practice*, New York City Chapter, National Association of Social Workers, New York, 1960 (mimeographed).

Reprinted from *Social Casework*, XLIV (May, 1963), pp. 267–272, by permission of the the author and the Journal.

social problems and to whom the social work profession bears a special responsibility.

Characteristics of Multiproblem Families

Multiproblem families have been the subject of many community studies.[3] From these studies, one is led to conclude that such families exhibit the following characteristics. They are families that have been overwhelmed by the cumulative effects of chronic economic dependency, which are manifested in some of the following difficulties: periodic unemployment, indebtedness, inadequate housing, poor standards of housekeeping, conspicuous marital discord, school failure, delinquency and other major misconduct, chronic illness, alcoholism, narcotics addiction, and prostitution. Also characteristic of these families are the repetition of their difficulties in succeeding generations, their long contact with social agencies, the pervasiveness of their personal and social breakdown, and the fact that they have become troublesome to the communities in which they live. Certain characteristics of the families vary with the particular community, for they are often members of racial minorities, newcomers, or marginal workers. Moreover, the studies emphasize that multiproblem families are resistant to offers of help from social workers and disinclined to ask for service.

This listing of the gross characteristics of multiproblem families offers a composite picture of the client group I am considering here. I would submit, however, that there is only *one* characteristic universal to this group— poverty. The fact that these families are *poor* is the fundamental issue in understanding them and in planning appropriate treatment. No proof has ever been offered that their difficulties are related to particular racial or ethnic backgrounds or to specific psychiatric typologies or to their behavorial patterns. Furthermore, I should like to point out that even the fact of their poverty does not provide an adequate basis for determining what a social worker must do in order to help them. Professional help can be given only if each multiproblem family is individualized in relation to its own unique characteristics and the particular constellation of factors that have created

---

[3] See, for example, L. L. Geismar and Beverly Ayres, *Families in Trouble*, Family Centered Project, Greater St. Paul Community Chest and Councils, St. Paul, Minnesota, 1958; L. L. Geismar and Beverly Ayres, *Patterns of Change in Problem Families*, Family Centered Project, Greater St. Paul Community Chest and Councils, St. Paul, Minnesota, 1959; *Reaching the Unreached Family*, Youth Board Monograph No. 5, New York City Youth Board, New York, 1958; *A Study of Some of the Characteristics of 150 Multiproblem Families*, New York City Youth Board, New York, 1957 (mimeographed); Kenneth Dick and Lydia J. Strnad, "The Multi-problem Family and Problems of Service," *Social Casework*, Vol. XXXIX, June, 1958, pp. 349–55; Elizabeth Wood, *The Small Hard Core*, Citizens' Housing and Planning Council of New York, New York, 1957; Kermit T. Wiltse, "The 'Hopeless' Family," *Social Work*, Vol. III, October, 1958, pp. 12–22.

its special internal and external difficulties. In other words, the treatment of multiproblem families must take place within the frame of reference of social work.

The Pressures of Poverty

From a socioeconomic point of view these are poverty-stricken families who have suffered for generations from unemployment and underemployment. As members of cultural minority groups, they have been the victims of discrimination and of countless forms of exploitation in their jobs as unskilled workers. The lack of steady work inevitably leads to chronic financial insecurity, with all its attendant problems: poor nutrition and lack of regular medical and dental care, hence poor health and often illness; housing that is inadequate in size, comfort, and cleanliness, hence extreme crowding or indifference toward housekeeping and homemaking; children deprived of sufficient clothing, recreational outlets, room and time for homework, and attention from parents preoccupied with making ends meet, hence maladjustment at school, dropout, delinquency, and behavior problems; the exhausting pressures of poverty that lead husband and wife to become disappointed in each other when there seems to be no way out, hence all forms of marital conflict. For many of these families there is the ever-present fact of public assistance and marginal living. In the AFDC program, for example, men have been driven out of their homes through legal statute.[4] Thus the AFDC family has often become a maternal household with a working mother or adolescent and latchkey children who must assume a host of extra responsibilities because the family is fatherless.

Viewed from a socioeconomic standpoint, therefore, "treatment" of the multiproblem family and of the cyclical problems that pervade its life must reside in broad social reform: the promise of full employment throughout the year, legal provisions such as family allowances and health insurance, a higher minimum wage that will at least purchase the necessities of life, more readily available and better co-ordinated neighborhood services, better schools, renovation of slum areas, and more suitable public housing. A better world must be created for the seventy-seven million Americans who now live in poverty and deprivation.[5] The answer to the multiproblem family is to be found, in large part, in eliminating economic insecurity.

Until drastic social and economic reform effects the changes and improvements demanded by the complexities of our largely urban society, we cannot hope to build a social order in which there is no multiproblem family. In the meantime, social workers will have to assume their rightful responsibility for meeting the needs of such families—a responsibility they have traditionally been assigned by society.

[4] Elizabeth G. Meier, "Casework Services to ADC Families," *Public Welfare*, Vol. XIX, January, 1961, pp. 19–22.

[5] *Poverty and Deprivation In the United States: The Plight Of Two-Fifths Of A Nation*, Conference on Economic Progress, Washington, D.C., 1962, p. 2.

Psychosocial Problems

It is not sufficient, however, to consider the multiproblem family only from a socioeconomic point of view. Poverty exacerbates a variety of problems that may have their origin in psychological or emotional malfunctioning. Although behavior disorders in children, parental breakdown, marital conflict, out-of-wedlock pregnancies, school failure, mental illness, neuroses, and character disturbances are not solely problems of the poor, the lack of resources accompanying the state of poverty makes it more difficult for the poor to cope with them. Morevoer, each social class expresses its problems in a particular manner. The way in which the lower-class family expresses its problems gives it greater visibility in a society saturated with middle-class values. For example, in a middle-class family, the husband who is in conflict with his wife may take his highball into another room, where he can be alone. But in the lower-class home, where there is no spare room and no chance for solitude, the husband may lose his temper out loud in front of his wife and children, or he may go to the corner bar for solace. Whichever he does, his marital conflict will be apparent to the community.

Another example can be cited. Children in all economic classes are subject to behavior disorders. The poor family trying to cope with such a problem, however, cannot rely on a change of neighborhood, a better school, a camp in the summer, or cultural and recreational outlets that might alleviate the child's difficulty. Neither can the family utilize psychiatric or clinical services that require the payment of a fee. Frequently it cannot even articulate its concerns well enough to communicate with a social agency—if indeed the child's disorder is at all as bothersome to the family as it is to the community.

In summary, working with multiproblem families does not involve dealing with new clinical entities, hereditary problems, or "lower-classisms." It requires dealing with psychosocial problems that have long been familiar to social workers but have been made worse by poverty, lack of resources, and rejection in practically every aspect of life.

As social workers search for means of helping multiproblem families, they must be alert both to their own and to the community's attitudes toward them. Much has been written about "lower-class cultures" and "deviant behavior in lower-class groups," "street-gang culture" and "the maternal family in the lower classes." One may wonder whether a poor person any longer has an individual identity! In my opinion, it is indefensible to write off as "culturally acceptable" to a certain group poverty and its terrible hardships, personality disturbances and their painful results, or the pervasive effect of impaired relationships. How often we have heard that in a particular cultural group it is acceptable for a teen-age girl to have a baby out of wedlock! Whether or not this is a valid generalization is for the sociologist to study. The social worker, on the other hand, must be concerned about the loneliness a teen-age girl feels when she has no husband with whom to share her parenthood, when she cannot return to school, when her friends go out on dates while she stays at home to care for the baby, or when her friends get their first jobs and she must apply for public assistance.

The same kind of generalizations on the cultural acceptability of deviant behavior have been made about adolescent delinquency and about a family's failure to meet socially approved standards in homemaking or in the education of the children. Even if the adolescent who is behaving in a deviant manner—truanting from school, hanging around the streets, participating in delinquent acts or gang warfare, or using narcotics—*is* reflecting what is normal for his primary reference group or his economic class, this generalization cannot form the basis of a plan of treatment. To understand this boy and help him, the social worker must know the nature of his particular family relationships, the kind of upbringing he has had, and how he expresses his personal values and his troubles through behavior that is meaningful to him.

The family that is failing to meet standards may indeed be reflecting the attitudes of its particular cultural or economic group. On the other hand, its lack of interest in household cleanliness and order or in having the children finish high school may be the natural outcome of grinding poverty and discrimination in the midst of a striving and affluent community. The social worker's help, however, must be based on an understanding of why the family is hopeless or hostile. It must be directed toward removing the obstacles that stand in the way of the family's own efforts to meet the expectations of the community.

Treatment of the multiproblem family must be based on an understanding of the manifold sources of its pathology. Walter Miller has stated that this understanding can be facilitated "by clarifying the cultural sources of the pathology and indicating more directly the nature of feasible treatment goals."[6] I agree with this statement, but I should like to add that physiological and psychogenic sources are of equal importance. There is no evidence that a single causative factor produces the multiproblem family. The search for a primary cause is futile; there are many possible sources of pathology—psychological, social, and cultural—which must be analyzed not for multiproblem families as a distinct group in society but for *each* family we attempt to treat.

Amelioration

I should like now to examine some aspects of the problem of ameliorating this client group's serious condition. It is somewhat startling that after almost a century of professional development, social workers are still "discovering"

---

[6] Walter B. Miller, "Implications of Urban Lower-Class Culture for Social Work," *Social Service Review*, Vol. XXXIII, September 1959, p. 234.

multiproblem families; relating themselves to "the poor"; using such so-called new techniques as reaching out, beginning where the client is, making home visits, offering services in terms that the client can understand, accepting cultural differences, raising a cry for community action, and working with indigenous groups. Not one of these techniques is based on a new theoretical formulation; all are as old as social work itself. Yet they are not being employed in precisely the same way as in earlier years. Today our use of these techniques has taken on greater precision and greater depth, because it is based on our expanded knowledge of ego psychology and on the new insights provided by the social sciences.

In the early settlement-house and COS movements, social work practice was based chiefly on the recognition by a few outstanding leaders that an industralized society would inevitably victimize some of its members. What these early-twentieth-century leaders did was to take an aggressively charitable stand in behalf of those who were poor, maladjusted, uprooted, sick, and lonely. A few persons, such as Jane Addams and Lillian Wald, became the embodiment of social work practice. Today, the expression of the humanistic and ethical values of our profession cannot take the same form. We have experienced marked changes in social philosophy, in the organization of social work, and in the availability of knowledge and skills. Although many of our social problems and the goals of social work are similar to those of Jane Addams' day, we have come to recognize that the force for change does not lie in the outstanding abilities of one leader but rather in the capacity of social workers generally to enable clients to participate in bringing about the social changes necessary to productive living.

The content and methods of practice, having become communicable, are shared nowadays by all social workers and are embedded in innumerable community agencies. No longer should social workers rely primarily on exhortation or conviction; because we have a body of accumulated knowledge and tested skills, we have an obligation to demonstrate the validity of our professional practice and to utilize a scientific method of investigation and treatment. That we have not produced a leader of the stature of Jane Addams in the past fifty years does not show a lack of conviction on the part of the profession; it shows, rather, that the profession is now beyond the need to rely on any one person for its humanitarian spirit.

Even though it no longer suffices to "do good for others" and to romanti-cize our function, the fact remains that we cannot divorce methodology from values. As social workers we cannot operate a social service for the motivated client and deny help to those who, for a multitude of reasons, are uninitiated into our social work system, different from ourselves, over-burdened by problems, difficult to help, and perhaps most in need of the help we can and should give. A set of values must be the basis of all our practice. We have no alternative but to help the multiproblem family as best we can, notwithstanding our own differing attitudes, prejudices, and identifications.

Techniques of Helping

From my earlier discussion, it is obvious that I believe that help to the multiproblem family must be based on the social worker's precise knowledge of the sociocultural and economic forces that shape its way of life, its intimate family relationships, and the behavior and ideals of each family member. The appropriateness of a family's behavior in its daily functioning and the significance of a particular problem to an individual and his family can be understood only if the worker has this knowledge. Understanding of the psychosocial aspects of the multiproblem family's breakdown in functioning or adjustment is now available to the social worker as a result of recent advances in ego psychology. The use of ego psychology in casework practice has been described thus:

> The client who needs help with various problems describes these in terms of everyday behavior and attitudes. Everyday behavior is a complex psychosocial phenomenon. We must analyze it in various ways—as a social role and as family interaction, as an expression of ideals and values, as physical processes, as an expression of psychological processes, such as instintual drives and defensive operations. Casework practice requires that we use all these frames of reference.[7]

Within this broad scope of concern for the client's external and internal problems, the techniques of working with multiproblem families become self-evident. On the assumption that multiproblem families are living under adverse conditions and are acting in ways alien to the expectations of the community—the same community that has contributed to their problems— social workers can be certain that these families would not willingly come to social agencies for help. Thus, we must reach out to them if we are to demonstrate our concern. It has been aptly stated that "reaching out is neither a physical act nor a technique. It is rather a frame of mind, a psychological readiness, a determination of the social worker to find a way to help the client whether the means is physical, psychological, social, or some combination."[8]

What does reaching out involve for the social agency that wants to help? It may require that the agency locate its office in the same neighborhood as the people it wants to serve; it may mean that the agency maintain an open-door policy for those in need of help, even if the help they need will take a great deal of staff time and will show little immediate result. All the community's resources for prevention and treatment must be mobilized. The agency's staff must be available at night and on week ends, when crises are most likely to occur. Service programs must be of a kind that makes sense to people who do not value talk in a one-to-one interview as a way

[7] Isabel L. Stamm, "Ego Psychology in the Emerging Theoretical Base of Casework," in *Issues in American Social Work*, Alfred J. Kahn (ed.), Columbia University Press, New York, 1959, p. 87.

[8] Walter Haas, "Reaching Out—A Dynamic Concept in Casework," *Social Work*, Vol. IV, July, 1959, p. 44.

of solving their problems. Concrete forms of help are likely to have more significance for the multiproblem family than verbal communication. The programs should include group activities (recreational, educational, or cultural), services within the family's home (homemaker, home economist, or caseworker to help with shopping, meal-planning, housework, child care), and neighborhood services (provisions for day care of preschool and school-age children, interpretation of the family's needs to the schools, work with hospitals toward less waiting on clinic days, help to the managers of housing projects in understanding their tenants).

What does reaching out involve for the caseworker and the group worker? It means that they must discover creative ways of making the help they offer tangible, concrete, and meaningful to clients. As workers *demonstrate* their concern in tangible ways, rather than in words alone, they will have less need to *promise* help. Obviously, however, there are families for whom the traditional interview is a valuable therapeutic technique. No matter what the worker's technique, he must select it on the basis of sound diagnostic understanding of why it is appropriate, not on the basis of whim alone. The technique of reaching out, then, should take its place as one of a range of professional techniques that may improve the effectiveness of social work practice with multiproblem families.

Conclusion

In conclusion, it does not seem inappropriate to quote what Jane Addams said in an article in the *Atlantic Monthly* in 1899:

> We sometimes say that our charity is too scientific, but we should doubtless be much more correct in our estimate if we say that it is not scientific enough. ...A man who would hesitate to pronounce an opinion upon the stones lying by the wayside ... will, without a moment's hesitation, dogmatize about the delicate problems of human conduct, and will assert that one man is a scoundrel and another an honorable gentleman, without in the least considering the ethical epochs to which the two belong. ... In our charitable efforts, we think much more of what a man ought to be than of what he is or of what he may become; and we ruthlessly force our conventions and standards upon him.

About the social worker's role with his clients, Miss Addams said:

> Recently, ... there has come to my mind the suggestion of a principle, that while the painful condition of administering charity is the inevitable discomfort of a transition into a more democratic relation, the perplexing experiences of the actual administration have a genuine value of their own ... The social reformers who avoid the charitable relationship with any of their fellow men take a certain outside attitude toward this movement. They may analyze it and formulate it; they may be most valuable and necessary, but they are not essentially within it. The mass of men seldom move together without an emotional incentive, and the doctrinaire, in his effort to keep his mind free from the emotional quality, inevitably stands aside. He avoids the perplexity, and at the same time loses the vitality.[9]

[9] Jane Addams, "The Subtle Problems of Charity," *Atlantic Monthly*, Vol. LXXXIII, February, 1899, pp. 163–78.

Since 1899 social work has experienced the backing and filling of all professions that have moved from a largely intuitive response to social need to a reliance on scientific thinking. At last we have learned that the development of new content and the refinement of professional methods do not require us to deny the validity of the tested knowledge and skills that have served as the building blocks of present practice. It may be that through our work with multiproblem families and through our continuing recognition of multiple causation and the psychosocial determinants of behavior, we shall achieve the genuine integration of many theories that have significance for social work practice. The social work profession is committed to helping those who need its services. When we discover that our skills are faulty, we must search for new techniques through which our historic values and convictions can be put to work in behalf of our clients. Doing this will not be difficult if we but use the rich scientific and humanistic knowledge now available to us.

The Middle Class

The Challenge of the Middle Class— Casework Off the Beaten Path

Ruth Fizdale

The Arthur Lehman Counseling Service began some six years ago as a pilot project for the field of social work. Its mission was to offer family counseling services to the middle and upper income groups exclusively, and to determine from its experience what was important for other social agencies to know should they wish to extend or expand their services to these groups. A pilot project has the obligation to make its experience known for others to use and to present its experience for the critical appraisal of colleagues.

Casework agencies have always had the policy of an "open door." Anyone desiring the help of a social agency could and would be certain of a willingness on the part of the caseworker and the agency to serve him insofar as possible. Certainly in the area of family counseling, a client from any walk of life can be sure of assistance from any family-oriented setting. Therefore, most casework counseling agencies have served some persons from the middle and upper income groups.

With these clients, nothing is so different in the problems they present, and understandably so. The same basic causes of emotional problems, mental illness, family disruption exist, regardless of economic strata of a family. A child suffers from the absence of a father, whether it is caused by economic failure and desertion, or by great personal ambition for financial success. A mother who neglects her children because she has no capacity to love creates similar effects on the children whether she lets them roam the streets, sends them off to a boarding school, or leaves them in the care of a governess. Illness, physical or emotional, creates shifts in family patterns and often carries with it strains in the intra-familial relationships. Similarly, the treatment needs of these clients are identical with those of our former clients, despite the often greater articulateness of this group and its greater *seeming* sophistication with psychological terms and concepts.

One of the theses of this paper, however, is that an "open door" policy is not enough to attract or offer service to the majority of potential clients

---

Reprinted from the *Journal of Jewish Communal Service*, XXXVII (Fall, 1960), pp. 103–111, by permission of the author and the Journal.

of the middle and upper income groups. The fact remains that the number of clients from these economic groups who do use the services of social agencies does not reflect their proportion in the community. Although all agencies are aware of this fact, they seem to believe that a good public relations program will be the remedy. The experience that we have had in ALCS, however, indicates to us that more than a clever campaign of interpretation of services is involved. Some shifts in how the service is offered to these upper income groups is essential. If the agencies wish to serve everyone in the community, certain changes in their procedure must occur. These changes will affect the character of the social agency. They will affect its place in the field of social work and may affect the nature of staff-board relationships that we have known in the past.

By way of background, I will briefly describe the ALCS structure and some of its experience. I will then discuss what I believe our observations imply for the social agency of the future. I would like to ask your indulgence in seeing my comments as being primarily related, at this point, to agencies offering counseling services unrelated to specific, concrete services. Although I know the ALCS experience will also have pertinence to other social agencies, such as hospitals and child care organizations, I have not had the opportunity to consider what meaning our observations will have for agencies offering concrete services to upper income client groups.

ALCS Structure

The ALCS was conceived, originally, by six lay leaders. Their experience as members of boards of directors in social agencies had made them conscious of the development of casework into a profession with unique skills and knowledge in helping persons with problems they broadly defined as "those of daily living." They were impressed with the value of casework and were concerned that persons in the middle and upper income groups were not using this assistance. They were convinced that if casework services were offered to these groups as other professional services are, not only would such clients pay for the help but they would develop a clearer understanding of the profession of social work as a whole. These groups would become more knowledgeable in their role as contributors to social agencies and would be more likely to desire high standards in social agencies, public and voluntary. They would also support research in the field. The status and stature of the social work profession, as well as services given to all clients, would thus be strengthened. These six lay leaders checked their thinking with professional leaders in social work and were encouraged to try out their premises in a pilot project. This pilot project was established in July, 1954, as a non-profit, non-sectarian, foundation-supported organization. Its purpose was to reach the middle and upper income groups and to make its experience known to the field of social work. It has a Board of Directors who share an interest in extending casework counseling to persons in all walks of life and who have in common long years of experience as members of boards of directors of other health and welfare agencies. The Board has no fund-raising responsibility and serves primarily in an advisory capacity. We have a Technical Advisory Committee, consisting of the executive directors of five of the major family agencies in New York City, and the executive director of the Family Service Association of America. The Technical Advisory Committee serves in an advisory capacity to me as executive, and to the Board of Directors, in determining what the ALCS might undertake experimentally. They are also the eyes of the profession on our experience, helping us to evaluate it.

Since we were set up to offer services to the person who desired and could pay for a "private" service, it was natural that we had to determine what he sought in "private" help. Our "hunches" were that the client sought a qualified, competent practitioner who charged a fee that reflected the "going rate" for this kind of help. On this basis, we decided to have only experienced staff. We would not carry the usual responsibility of other social agencies for training students and beginners in the field. We also decided to have a single fee which would reflect the cost of running a sound casework service. On this basis of estimates, this fee is currently $12.50 an interview.

Experience and Observations in ALCS

In the past year, we have reviewed our original objectives of reaching the middle and upper income groups. On the basis of facts related to education, income and vocation of our clients, and in comparison with clients served by the other family agencies in the city, our Technical Advisory Committee concluded this year that we have indeed reached a group that the family agencies in New York City have not served, that our clientele is primarily an upper-middle and upper income group. (Facts concerning our clientele are available. However, to give you some brief idea of whom we served, most of our clients fall in an income group of $10,000 and over. The range in the upper areas goes to beyond $300,000 a year annual income. Educationally, our clients have had the advantages to be anticipated for these economic groups. About 74 per cent of our clients hold bachelors degrees or postgraduate degrees; about one-third of our clients are in the professions—doctors, lawyers, social workers, architects, editors, etc.—one-third of our clients hold executive positions in large firms or own their own businesses. Only 3 per cent of our clients are in unskilled vocations.)

Our income from fees has steadily increased. In the first year of our experience, 30 per cent of our total budget was covered by fees, and in the fiscal year ending July, 1959, 81 per cent of our total budget was covered. Some of the expenditures that we incur are related to our second purpose, that of being a pilot project in the field. Also, some of our publicity is related to publicizing the field of social work rather than the ALCS. If these expenditures (that have no relation to the running of a service-giving agency) were deducted, in the first year we were 33 per cent self-supporting, and in the last year's experience, we were 90 per cent. In considering these figures, another fact needs to be borne in mind. The primary objective of the ALCS is to offer a high calibre counseling service. Thus we have not filled positions, despite waiting lists, until we have found persons who met the qualifications that we have set. In the past year, we have had only five of our seven posisions filled.

On the basis of the above facts, we feel comfortable in telling the field of social work that a service set up on principles like those underpining the ALCS can offer sound professional service on a self-maintaining basis. *There is no need for the community to support services for the middle and upper income groups.*

We believe that an important factor in our successfully having reached the group we had set out to serve is that of our experienced staff. Most clients ask what the qualifications of staff are. The fact that no one on staff has had less than ten years of experience is obviously an important one to clients in deciding to come. Often, clients or referring persons indicate that they prefer the ALCS because they have heard that we have only experienced staff. Although they know that they might get equally experienced people in another agency, they prefer not to run the risk of getting someone who might be inexperienced. We are aware that some research will need to be done on why we did reach a group who did not use the social agency, and are planning on this. We are reasonably sure of the validation of our original "hunch" that the middle and upper income group person seeking counseling services desires a qualified, experienced professional counselor.

One consequence that we had not anticipated is that the client who desires and seeks a "private" service expects to form a continuing relationship with his casework counselor just as he does with other sources of professional help, such as his doctor or lawyer. He expects that if he finds his caseworker helpful, and someone he can trust, he will be able to continue with him for as long as he may need help, or be able to return to him if problems recur or new ones arise. Although we had noted early in our experience that our clients would not accept transfer from one caseworker in intake to another one for continuing contact, the occasions for this procedure were so few that we really did not evaluate the observation. Since our staff was entirely experienced, there was no need to use the strength of the more experienced person for the diagnostic process in intake. Neither was there any other administrative reason for this. Hence we began with the idea of continuity with the same worker unless the treatment objectives required a shift in counselors.

In the third year of our experience, however, one of our staff members left the staff to move out of the state. In the six weeks that she was preparing for leaving, she naturally concluded with a number of her clients who were ready for termination of service. However, a number of her clients still needed help, and here she encountered an unexpected problem. Despite her skill and previous experience in other agencies in helping clients accept transfers, and despite consultation that she had from the rest of staff, one-third of her case load terminated contact prematurely rather than accept transfer to another person. These clients in many instances accepted that they were not quite ready to deal with their problems on their own. However, they preferred trying rather than to begin with someone new. This experience gave us serious pause. We saw a possible disservice to some clients in staff turnover. We watched subsequent experience, and further confirmation of this fact was gained. We, therefore, agreed to adopt a new policy related to hiring. Workers who come on staff are now informed that one of the conditions of hiring is an agreement that when they desire to leave the agency, they will terminate their responsibility only as this is consistent with the client's ability to conclude contact or to accept transfer (excluding, of course, where life situations make such an agreement impossible to follow).

This year a staff member accepted a position in another agency. Some of her cases were transferred to other workers, some concluded naturally. However, in the group review of her case load, it was agreed that in eight cases, transfer at that point would create a disservice to the clients involved. She continued to work with us three evenings a week, seeing these clients. None terminated prematurely, although some have concluded contact. A few are still being seen by her.

I believe that continuity of service is equally sought by the client who cannot afford to pay full cost for services. He may, however, feel he is not in a position to voice his demand because he has no alternative. He must stay where service is given him at a fee he can afford. The client who pays what he considers to be full fee feels himself to be in a different position. He believes his money can buy him other services and, therefore, is less inclined to accept shifts in caseworkers when these are unrelated to his treatment needs. This is an area that, of course, would require research and is merely offered here as a deduction from experience we have had to date.

Implications of ALCS Experience—Costs of Service and Fees

If our observations are borne out by future experience and research, what are some of the implications then for the field of social work as casework services are extended to all economic groups in the community?

If the ALCS experience that the person who pays for service desires the help of an experienced caseworker is correct, then social agencies will need to review whether their "open door" policy is really sufficient to enable clients from all walks of life to use their services. I believe that social agencies will need to face the fact that despite their willingness to see all comers, they have been operating as clinics in the community. Procedures and practices appropriate to clinical services create obstacles for the use of agency services by those who can pay full costs. By clinic I means a community-supported or subsidized organization that gives needed professional services to patients or clients according to their ability to pay. A clinic is the recognition on the part of the community that some people cannot afford private care and that the community must provide a free or subsidized service. A clinic is also a place where training and development of future professional personnel and research are carried out. One of the hidden costs clients pay in return for services is possible involvement in these programs. I believe our clients have always known agencies were clinics, but that we in the profession have been somewhat reluctant to face this.

Historically, this is understandable since in the beginning we did not anticipate the development of our profession into one that would serve all economic groups. Originally, we were set up only to serve those who were financially disadvantaged. We never considered whether agencies were clinics. As our profession developed knowledge and skills and matured, others began to ask us for service. This took us somewhat by surprise. We have never really faced the fact that with the influx of this new client group, we may be in need of re-examining some of the bases on which our services are offered.

When the field's first fee structures were set up, the principle of a sliding scale was used. This concept in itself reflected our anticipation that the social agencies would serve clients who required free or subsidized services. The field did not anticipate serving the economically advantaged. Had they done so, I think they would have probably come to the conclusion that we in the ALCS did, namely that a fixed fee, meeting cost of service, at least, should be set for upper income groups. In New York City, some agencies cannot charge more that $3.00 or $10.00 an interview. This is established by charter. Yet to my knowledge, they have never refused service to anyone, even though the client's income may well be above that of the group the founding fathers had in mind when they set these limits on fees.

One of the opportunities we have had in ALCS is discussing our program with members of boards of other agencies. We have been impressed with the fact that they are not sure they wish their agency to serve the upper income groups. They respect the special knowledge and professionals skills of the social work profession and see their value for persons in need of help, regardless of their economic status. Yet they are not sure that they wish to or should be serving those in economically advantaged positions. Traditionally, they have conceived of their agency as offering service to the economically disadvantaged and are not sure they wish to depart from this role. It is the resolution of this question, in my opinion, that will affect, the eventual role of the social agency. The person who desires a private service will seek it, and if he cannot secure it through the social agencies, he will secure it through private practitioners. More of the experienced casework staff may leave agencies to meet these new demands for service. The agency may then find itself in the position of being primarily a training or teaching institution. This may not necessarily be bad, if this conclusion stems from advance planning. In our field, too often we permit changes that can be clearly forseen to occur without any attempt to plan ahead for the soundest way the change might be made. We then become concerned with the detrimental aspects of what grew like "topsy." Facing the issue that the profession must now provide for private services as well as clinic services can only result in a sound approach to services given to both groups, and to the provision of training for future professional personnel.

In the planning ahead, some of the ALCS experience may be of value. I would like to re-state that a service to the middle and upper income groups should be self-supporting and should not become a financial burden to the community. To some extent, the current "open door" policy does make the community carry responsibility for subsidy of service to the middle and upper income groups. Lest there be any misunderstanding, I do not intend that the social agency not continue to offer a free or subsidized service to those in need of help on such a basis. Fund-raising problems cannot be solved by fees. The community must continue to raise and provide funds for free and subsidized services. Nothing in the ALCS experience alters this fact. On the contrary, the ALCS could not offer as sound a service as it does were it not for the existence of the agencies who provide service on a sliding scale basis. Our profession has come to the point where it must provide two types of resources: one for those who cannot pay full cost, and one for those who can.

The service for the middle and upper income groups will probably have to be based on a fixed fee. At ALCS the fee is $12.50 per interview, regardless of the client's income. The client knows the fee is expected and does not have to go through a process of establishing his eligibility for it. It is our impression that one of the obstacles for upper income clients in the use of social agencies is the necessity of discussing income before a fee is set. The applicant is uncertain as to what he is paying for when fees must be established through this process. He does not know whether he is a recipient of charity or the unwilling donor to services for others. The person who can afford to pay does not see the need for him to accept charity. Neither does he wish to be made an unwilling donor at a time when he is involved with a personal problem. If we read our experience correctly then this may be an important fact for agencies to consider.

Arriving at what the cost of an interview is, is by no means an easy process, even in an organization like the ALCS. Our staff is experienced, salaries are identical, purpose of records can be defined more easily because we do not carry training responsibilities, and so forth. In the social agency, this problem is doubly compounded by the dual purposes of training and services. It may be necessary to consider separate divisions for private services in agencies undertaking both programs.

The Need for "Experienced" Staff

If our observation is correct, that the client who pays full cost desires an experienced, qualified practitioner, then it may be necessary to staff the private service with experienced personnel. When I have made this comment in the past, I have been asked whether I believe it is right to give better service to the client who pays full cost than to the one who pays nothing or only a fraction of cost. There is nothing in my statement that would mean that the agency would not use experienced people also to serve those receiving free or subsidized services. Any good clinic has to have experienced persons to carry responsibility for treatment and for training. Currently in agencies, assignment of a case is always made with one eye on the needs of the client and the other eye on the student's or worker's ability to meet these needs, alone or under supervision. What I am suggesting would in no way shift what is currently being done. I am merely saying that for the private services that agencies may wish to open, they may find that they cannot attract or hold this client group unless experienced counselors are available. By "experienced," I do not necessarily mean that one would have to seek for the level of competence that we in the ALCS have tried to maintain. We were an experimental project and it was natural that we would seek the most qualified persons we could find in the field. Thus we picked only persons from the group who had achieved the status of independent practitioners, who had successfully carried supervision but preferred direct treatment. I believe that persons of less experience will be acceptable to the middle and upper income client group.

Who is experienced or qualified to practice is a question that has become increasingly troublesome to our profession. Historically, training and service have been so intertwined in our profession that we have never definitively answered the question as to when an agency ceases to train a person for the field, and when development and growth are entirely the responsibility of the professional individual who has available to him various resources for help either in serving a particular client or in increasing his general professional competence. Many organizations are at work on this problem. The National Association of Social Workers also has undertaken responsibility for determining when a social worker is qualified to practice. Setting up private services may give new impetus to the resolution of this problem. Another result may be a clearer allocation of costs of training of students and inexperienced personnel. At present, such costs, I believe, are always included in cost of the interview. While cogent arguments for this may be given, in my opinion, training of future professional personnel should not be charged to the person currently needing service but should be charged to the community.

Continuity of Relationship—With Agency or Worker?

Perhaps the most intriguing change that I forsee is one that I believe will affect the concept that the client is "the agency's." Historically, casework was related to the giving of a specific service to a client such as financial assistance, foster placement, and so on. The skills we developed in helping people came as a result of administering such services, provided by the community through the agency. Thus the client was the client of the agency. The services he desired were the agency's to give. He might find the caseworker more or less helpful but as long as he was eligible, regardless of the worker's skill, he would at least receive the specific service he needed. In counseling, this distinction is less clear. The service the client seeks and is given is the skill of the caseworker. The factor of the agency is less apparent to him unless he cannot afford private care and needs the subsidy of the agency to receive any help at all. The ALCS observation is that the client who pays fully for service expects to form a continuing relationship to his caseworker as he does with his other professional sources of help. If this observation is correct, there may have to be some shift in the concept that the client is "the agency's."

Last year one of our staff members entered into private practice.[1] The question of what would happen to her case load then came up for staff's consideration. We reviewed her case load jointly and arrived at a decision that a disservice would occur to some of her clients were transfer to another worker made mandatory. This question was taken up with our Technical Advisory Committee and serious thought was given to our recommended policy that these clients should be allowed to decide whether they wished to terminate with the ALCS and continue with this worker in her private practice. The conclusion that the Technical Advisory Committee came to was that this policy made the client's welfare the primary consideration and offered the only ethical means for a caseworker to continue with a client whose interest required such continuity. Further to safeguard the client's welfare, a procedure was instituted by which the professional group reviews with the departing staff member which of his clients should be offered a choice of continuing with him. When this worker left staff, some of her clients were given the choice indicated. All elected to go with her and none discontinued their help prematurely. We have since been asked whether a person leaving our staff and going to an agency that offered casework counseling would be able to take his case load with her into another agency's practice. In our opinion, the same policy would hold, but, of course, we have not yet had the opportunity to test the reactions of other agencies.

Again, if we have correctly observed that the client who pays full cost of service expects a continuity of relationship with his caseworker, what are some of the implications for us as caseworkers? As caseworkers, we have been a very mobile group. We move to other agencies to get better supervision, to deepen or strengthen skills by experience in another setting or function of casework, to get better pay, to improve our professional status, or to follow a field of greater personal interest. We, too, feel that the client is the client of the agency. I do not wish to imply that we are irresponsible. Far from this. We work hard to help our clients. We care deeply about their welfare. We have skillfully devised ways of helping them deal with problems created for them by our mobility or by agency needs. However, we cannot deny that our attitude toward the client is colored by our acceptance of the tradition that he is the client of the agency. Let us look at the practice of a "month's notice." This is never questioned by any of us. Yet I am certain many caseworkers have been concerned at some point of changing jobs about the effect of a month's notice upon a particular client. At times we

[1] Ruth Fizdale, "Formalizing the Relationship between Private Practitioners and Social Agencies," *Social Casework*, Vol. XL, No. 10, December, 1959, p. 539–544.

have felt that a serious disservice was done to the client, but we did not feel that we could go against the tradition of the client being "the agency's."

What is the basis of this policy now? Is it still necessary because of observed client needs, or is it related to employer-employee relationships? The question which we caseworkers may have to face is whether there is some point where those of us who choose counseling as the area of vocational choice must give up our mobility. When one is beginning in the field and trying to decide which of its many areas will be one's vocational choice, mobility can be justified. However, if one finally elects casework counseling (instead of supervision, administration, and public assistance, to name a few), can mobility be as justified?

This is a two-sided question and is not only for the caseworker to answer. This problem is equally the responsibility of administrators and boards of directors. Although as administrators we have been concerned with the effect of mobility on clients, we have reacted often as if this were a problem staff created. I am suggesting that this problem requires responsible review of current attitudes and policies on the part of caseworkers, boards, and administrators to see how stability can be maintained *in the interest of the client*. Staff stability is important to self-support, but it is important also for client welfare and for client confidence in our profession. Continuity of service is important, but must be achieved without penalty to the caseworkers.

Two factors are important in staff stability: income and professional satisfaction. I do not know how agencies will provide for the experienced person an income consistent with his experience and skill and yet not increase the burden to the community. The experienced and truly independent practitioner likes to have some sense of control over his income, and rightly so. Whether these problems can be solved in agency settings is a question for the future. At ALCS we are currently involved in one possible solution. At this moment, I am far from certain how our idea will work. We have been experimenting with an idea which may be a precursor to a form of group practice. Perhaps at some future date, I will be able to report on this. At this point, I can tell you that we have been astonished, irritated, and often frankly amused by the tenacity of the "employee attitude" in caseworkers. Caseworkers have a problem conceiving of themselves as *building a practice*, with all that this involves in financial as well as in professional responsibility. I do not know what problem social agencies will encounter as they try to encompass both clinic and private services under one roof. I know of one agency that is trying to do this, using some of the ALCS experience in how its private services are set up. I look forward to the results of this and other agency experiments.

In Summation

I aver that the profession has arrived at a point where its skills are recognized and can be sought after by persons who can pay for service. These persons bring certain attitudes and expectations of their professional services. Social work's current agency structures were built during a period when the profession was young, when training and service were inextricable from one another, and when our expectation was to serve only those in economic need. The challenge of the middle and upper income groups lies in their unwillingness to tolerate some of the procedures appropriate to an earlier time in our profession and reflecting unresolved problems within the profession. Their challenge lies in forcing us to recognize the lag between our profession's growth and our recognition of it. They provide new impetus for the resolution of some problems and a new view of old traditions. If we accept their challenge, as indeed we will need to, our service for all clients—those we have always served and those who now come seeking our help—will be strengthened. The status of our profession will similarly be advanced.

Values

Client Value Orientations: Implications for Diagnosis and Treatment

Shirley C. Hellenbrand

The imprint of value orientations is to be found in all aspects of casework practice. Values are reflected in client, caseworker, and agency. They affect behavior, personality, the nature of client problems, and methods of solving them. This paper will present a theroretical framework within which the cultural determinants of value orientations can be viewed and will examine some of the implications of value orientations for diagnosis and treatment in casework.

The following three propositions are suggested as guideposts for this discussion.

1. An individual's way of life and his orientation to life problems are determined by a number of factors. His salient environment, as well as his biologic and psychic constitutional endowment, his particular family situation, and other idosyncratic features fashion and color the life experiences he will have. A major agent in the individual's approach to these experiences, in his role commitments and role performances, is his culturally conditioned value orientations.

2. These value orientations and their far-reaching effects on the individual's functioning need to be part of the data of diagnosis. Treatment concepts and techniques need to be broadened to include a greater variety of approaches that can respond effectively to particular value orientations.

3. Recognition of differences in cultural value orientations, respect accorded to these differences, and a more intensive attempt to understand them should not constitute a deification of cultural relativism.

Present knowledge about human behavior, incomplete as it is, offers

Reprinted from *Social Casework*, XLII (April, 1961), pp. 163–169, by permission of the author and the Journal.

conclusive evidence that answers to many of the problems of clinical diagnosis are intricately linked with the delicate but steely strong threads of cultural patterning. The connections are evident if we look at typical problem "themes," such as a particular type of parent-child relationships, of management or housekeeping practices, of attitudes toward scholastic or vocational achievement and choices, or of reaction toward revealing or discussing intimate problems and anxieties. The diagnostic question is: To what extent are these and other types of behavior reflections of the individual's character structure which evolved from his idiosyncratic responses to his personal life history, and to what extent are they the reflections of his cultural conditioning?

Regardless of origins, the individual's attitudes and behavior may be equally internalized, unconscious, disguised, and defended. Nevertheless, it is of great importance diagnostically to know which set of influences—the personal idiosyncratic or those that are culturally patterned—had priority in fashioning certain attitudes or behavior traits. If problematic attitudes, behavior, and role definitions represent cultural norms, the individual is likely to have less question or conflict about his behavior than if his feelings and his functioning are at variance with his "reference group." A crucial issue in diagnosis and treatment is whether the individual's environment sustains and supports his role interpretations and responds to them in a complementary fashion, or whether the environment implicitly or explicitly questions or condemns them. In order to understand the particular behavior patterns an individual has "chosen," we need to know the nature and variety of the norms of his group and the ranking of these norms on the group's value scale. An understanding of the norms and of their hierarchal order should play a significant part in the caseworker's evaluation of the the possibilities for favorable changes in the client.

As is implied in the preceding statements, treatment should also be closely related to the client's cultural patterning and value orientations. A glance at a few of the key elements in treatment will serve to illustrate the point. For example, motivation is generally considered a major item in treatment prognostication. The nature and degree of motivation, however, depend on a number of factors, one of which is whether or not the client, as a result of his cultural conditioning, believes that personal efforts *can* effect changes in his behavior and in his situation. Another important element in treatment is verbal communication. Ability to communicate verbally is not only related to intelligence and personality but also to the role assigned to language and verbal exchange by a particular culture. The capacity of an individual to use a professional helping relationship, as well as the nature of his ensuing transference reactions, are conditioned not only by his personal life history and character but also by his culturally defined orientations to people. Another element in treatment is the goal of helping the client to achieve greater skill at reality testing and to improve his reality perception. His distortion of reality or his limited perception may not be idiosyncratic but may be colored by cultural definitions and norms.

These examples clearly suggest that the cultural determinants of value orientations have major importance for diagnosis and treatment. The problem of how to use cultural data is complicated by the richness and intricacies of ethnic and class cultures and subcultures in our society. Two questions arise. What kinds of cultural data should we try to obtain and understand? How can we use this knowledge for more effective helping?

Theoretical Schemes

Florence Kluckhohn has proposed a scheme for the "systematic ordering of cultural value orientations within the framework of common—universal problems" which, it seems to me, offers rich possibilities to caseworkers. The basic assumptions of this scheme, which have been described in a number of articles by Kluckhohn[1] and Spiegel,[2] are being used by them in a research project at the Laboratory of Social Relations at Harvard University.

In brief, Kluckhohn's postulates may be recapitulated as follows: *1]* There is a limited number of common human problems for which all people at all times must find some solution; *2]* there is variability in the solutions to these problems but the variability is neither limitless nor random, it is variability within a range of possible solutions; *3]* all variants of all solutions are present in all societies at all times in varying degrees. Kluckhohn also identifies five problems that appear to be crucial to all human groups at all times: *1]* human-nature orientation, *2]* man-nature orientation, *3]* time orientation, *4]* activity orientation, *5]* relational orientation. For each of these problems she suggests three styles of solution, noting that one will be the "preferred" style and that the others will also be present, ranking lower in the hierarchy of values.

In my opinion, there is an equally crucial question for casework which does not seem to be explicitly formulated in the Kluckhohn scheme: In a particular group, what is the emotional coloring of interpersonal responses? In other words, what is the basic orientation to other people? I can envisage a threefold value classification covering such emotional responses: *1]* moving toward, away from, or against others; *2]* relating to others trustfully, or with caution, or with suspicion; *3]* in terms of affection for others, seeking power over them, or seeking to exploit them. As we know from psychoanalytic theory, responses to people are rarely fortuitous. We also know that certain attitudes are characteristic of certain cultures.[3]

---

[1] Florence Rockwood Kluckholm, "Variations in the Basic Values of Family Systems," *Social Casework*, Vol. XXXIX, Nos. 2–3 (1958), pp. 63–72.

[2] John P. Spiegel, "Some Cultural Aspects of Transference and Counter-Transference," in *Science and Psychoanalysis*, Vol. II, Jules H. Masserman (ed.), Grune & Stratton, New York, 1959.

[3] For example, in *Les Carnets du Major Thompson*, by Pierre Daninos, the Major comments on the typical Frenchman's response, "Je me defends," to the question, "How are things going?" The response is suggestive of the wary attitude of French people toward government, politics, and so on.

Social Class and Value Orientations

For some time, caseworkers and psychiatrists have been increasingly aware that the success or failure of treatment is dependent on more variables than the apparent motivation of the client or patient, the apparent degree of his pathology, and the skill of the therapist. Schaffer and Myers state that "what happens therapeutically to a person who becomes a psychiatric patient is, to a senificant degree, a function of his social class position in the community." They continue, "If it is justified to assume the existence of a culture of classes, then one may assume that persons from different classes undergo different kinds of experiences, integrating these experiences in different terms. Thus they have more or less different frames of reference for human relations, or different kinds of orientations for acting with others."[4]

This point is further clarified by Spiegel. He states that these integrations, these frames of reference and orientations, become "behavior without awareness . . . the making of an unconscious discrimination between two or more choices of behavior when the act of discrimination cannot be brought to the status of conscious report because it has never at any time existed in consciousness. Since the value orientations of a culture are outside of awareness to begin with and are learned in childhood only through their indirect impact on conscious behavior, they can be expected to have a powerful effect on the therapeutic relationship."[5]

It seems to me that casework must proceed on the proposition that certain of the "differences" alluded to by Schaffer and Myers stem from *value* orientations that are culturally transmitted, are internalized in the process of development, and are supported in various ways by the milieu and the larger environment. I have already suggested that Kluckhohn's formulation throws significant light on the kind of data needed to deal effectively with problems of diagnosis and treatment. I should like to illustrate the proposition through an analysis, tentative as yet, of several crucial questions of value orientation and their implications for casework with clients from lower-class subcultures. I have chosen this group for two reasons: first, because the members constitute a large proportion of social agencies' clientele and we should, therefore, rightfully be concerned about our effectiveness with them; and, second, because the differences in value orientations are more gross than the subtle differences in the subcultures of the middle class and are, therefore, more visible to our still poorly trained eyes.

At this point, it may be helpful to restate some of the characteristics of lower-class subcultures which seem to have particular pertinence to this.

[4] Leslie Schaffer and Jerome K. Myers, "Psychotherapy and Social Stratification," in *Advances in Psychiatry*, Mabel B. Cohen (ed.), W. W. Norton & Co., New York, 1959, p. 87.
[5] John P. Spiegel, *op. cit.*, p. 161.

discussion.[6] The characteristics include: *1]* involvement in unskilled or semi-skilled occupations, often seasonal and cyclical and often characterized by long hours of monotonous work; *2]* a median of school years per adult much lower than in other classes; *3]* housing often inadequate from the point of view of sanitation, privacy, and esthetic appeal; *4]* many families of the three- or four-stem type, as a result of frequent separation, desertion, or divorce; *5]* a large number of female-based households, frequent serial mating; *6]* the peer group's superseding the family as the primary reference group; *7]* *carpe diem* as the prevalent philosphy—"Live today, let tomorrow take care of itself"; *8]* deep-seated distrust of authority figures transmitted by attitudes, deeds, and words from adults to children; *9]* a tendency toward self-centeredness, suspicion of and hostility toward institutional controls, and suspicion among members of the group.

In an analysis of gang delinquency, Miller defines a number of attributes of persons in lower-class subcultures.[7]

Toughness: the emphasis on masculinity is almost compulsive and reaction-formational in nature.

Smartness: to outsmart, to "con," even ingenious aggressive repartee carries status value.

Excitement: alternation between relatively routine activity and danger or risk; "trouble" (any form of illegal activity) is one source of excitement while gambling, use of dope, and sexual activity are others.

Fate: "Everything rides on the dice"; man is a pawn.

Autonomy: the mask of independence and toughness covering strong dependency yearnings; there is a discrepancy between what is overtly expressed and what is covertly desired. Authority and nurturing seem to be connected, and the person often searches for a highly restrictive environment.

It must be emphasized that much careful research is needed to determine the frequency of these attributes and their nature in various subtypes of lower-class culture.

Crucial Questions for Diagnosis and Treatment

Crucial questions for diagnosis and treatment pertain to client conceptions about innate human nature and man's relation to natural or supernatural forces. Although such questions may appear at first glance to be

---

[6] The characteristics listed are drawn from formulations by: August B. Hollingshead and Frederick C. Redlich, *Social Class and Mental Illness: A Community Study*, John Wiley & Sons, New York, 1958; Henry S. Maas, *et al.*, "Socio-Cultural Factors in Psychiatric Clinic Services for Children," *Smith College Studies in Social Work*, Vol. XXV, No. 2 (1955); Walter B. Miller, "Lower Class Culture as a Generating Milieu of Gang Delinquency," *Journal of Social Issues*, Vol. XIV, No. 3 (1958), also "Implications of Urban Lower-Class Culture for Social Work," *Social Service Review*, Vol. XXXIII, No. 3 (1959).

[7] Walter B. Miller, "Lower Class Culture as a Generating Milieu of Gang Delinquency," *op. cit.*

highly philosophical, almost metaphysical or theological, and to have little relation to the problems of helping people, there is evidence that such conceptions influence attitudes and behavior.

One set of questions may be shown graphically, as follows:

WHAT IS THE CHARACTER OF INNATE HUMAN NATURE?

Evil
Neutral (mixture of good and evil) } Mutable
Good } Immutable

Spiegel has pointed out that a person's conception of the nature of man has an effect on his personality development, on both his problem formation and his defense formation.[8] The struggle involved in changing a way of behaving and of feeling and reacting is never lightly undertaken. It is necessary to ask if it can be undertaken at all by an individual who believes that man's nature is evil and not likely to be changeable. We might also ask what people in certain segments of lower-class society feel about their essential nature, if we keep in mind Miller's discussion of their characteristics. He points out that in the female-based household the children, from their earliest days, are exposed to the value that men are no good and are not to be relied upon. When the boy first steps outside the home for some affirmation of his masculinity, he is warned, "Don't be like your father," and when he disappoints his mother he is told that he is "just like his father after all." Is it not likely that children in such a culture carry into adulthood a deep-seated feeling about the inevitable and unchanging evil nature of men? They absorb this idea from family "teaching" and it is supported by the larger culture in which they grow up and have their experiences.

Does not treatment need to take into account the imprint of the cultural value system on personality, as well as the more familiar effects of familial jealousies, hostilities, and sexual identifications? A treatment orientation that includes cultural factors might lead to new approaches, perhaps along the lines of re-education and resocialization.

A second crucial question pertains to man's relation to natural and supernatural forces. His orientation may be: (1) subjugation to nature, (2) harmony with nature, or (3) mastery over nature.

The general orientation in America, as is well known, is mastery over nature except, as Spiegel points out, when people are faced with the invincible tragedies of fatal illness and death. Social work, itself, is "all-American" in its adherence to the creed of fight and mastery. It has retained a close philosophical tie to pragmatism, holding to the belief that man can create his own environment and to the principle that the individual has a right to self-determination. These value orientations form the foundation of our treatment approach.

[8] John P. Spiegel, *op. cit.*

In many lower-class subcultures, however, as was noted earlier, man is viewed as a powerless pawn of destiny—"It all rides on the dice." The "family teaching" about powerlessness and inevitability is reaffirmed by the adverse social and economic conditions under which many of these people live. A natural response under such imprisoning circumstances is, "Live today, let tomorrow take care of itself."

It is not possible to suggest treatment techniques for problems of this scope, that is, where outer and inner forces combine to imprison the individual in a destiny which seems so bleak that he can see no purpose in struggling. As a first step to new approaches, we must develop an awareness that the impulse to struggle, to endeavour to intervene actively and purposively in one's destiny, is *not* a dominant trait in all subcultures. We must learn to scrutinize and evaluate clients' value orientations in regard to their relation to nature. If subjugation to nature is the dominant pattern, we may need to intervene energetically by suggesting choices, and by initiating, stimulating, and teaching various forms of social activity. I am not proposing that we return to earlier periods of social work practice and become manipulators. I am merely suggesting that, on the basis of a cultural differential diagnosis, we adapt our treatment "styles" to the needs of the situation. If changes take place in the institutional arrangements in the larger society, which would provide wider choices for individuals and greater chances for achieving goals, the "right to self-determination" would be more realistically based. We might then find fewer clients with the subjugation-to-nature orientation.

Social work orientation is also different from the orientation of certain lower-class subcultures in relation to temporal focus and the modality of human activity. The social work culture is future-oriented while most lower-class subcultures are present-oriented. This time-gulf creates significant differences in the ways the caseworker and the client approach problems of planning, management, and so forth. Similarly, difficulties arise because of differences in their concepts of modalities of activity. The wild alternation between monotonous routines and frequent excursions into excitement, and even danger, by persons in lower-class subcultures is in great contrast to the rational, orderly organization of living that social work holds as a treatment goal. These differences in orientation also have important implications for treatment.

I should like to refer now to the question I raised earlier about the interpersonal or emotional orientation of persons in various cultural groups. The basic emotional orientation of a client to other people will determine to a large extent the nature of his problems as well as the character and fate of the client-worker relationship. In designing a treatment approach, the caseworker must take into account, with certain clients, the status value they place on "toughness," and "conning," their suspicion of authority figures, as well as the discrepancy between their mask of independence and their convert longing for dependence and nurture.

The data we would secure from clients, in response to inquiry about these "crucial questions," should provide us with a rough sketch of the modal personality in a variety of subcultures. Analysis of the typical ways a group operates in relation to life problems would help us become familiar with the variant value orientations of particular groups. At the same time, we need to enlarge our understanding of the multiple ways in which the "salient environment" shapes, reinforces, or weakens cultural value orientations and patterns. Certain kinds of economic and social institutions, such as those that affect occupational opportunities, income distribution, housing, and education are particularly salient. If these institutions circumscribe the human potentialities of certain groups of individuals, the end result can only be an increase in their feelings of defeatism. Study may reveal that certain clinical entities, or at least certain constellations of symptoms and defenses, have a correlation with value orientations of the family and the larger cultural environment. With greater knowledge about the interaction of clinical and cultural variables, we would be in a better position to develop differential treatment methods and procedures and to chart social action programs.

Philosophical and Theoretical Considerations

For obvious reasons, we in this country have a philosophical and intellectual commitment to cultural pluralism. Social workers, in keeping with the ethics of the profession, also have a deep respect for the principle of cultural relativism. The worship of this principle, however, placing it above all others, is naive. There are at least two kinds of conditions that indicate the need for modification of cultural patterns. When these conditions exist, the goal of social work and of the larger society should be directed toward cultural change. One such condition is the existence of a source of danger to the society. For example, a society may have worked out social and economic structures and a set of values that permit its survival at the cost of the well-being of its members. The people may be diseased and physically weak, or continually frightened and anxious. Graham Greene in *Journey into Night*, published about twenty years ago, gives an account of his travels in West Africa, describing villages where the inhabitants are diseased, poorly nourished, apathetic, and in constant terror of the witch doctors who hold top power positions. We need not go so far afield to find cultures in which the physical, emotional, and intellectual development of people is stunted, in which deprivation corrodes their potentialities for growth, and in which such conditions become sources of disease and danger for the whole society. In our country, certain subcultures in lower-class society represent such a danger. It also is possible that some middle- and upper-class subcultures constitute similar, although less visible, sources of pathology and danger. The role of the social worker is not to "respect" such cultures and leave them untouched.

A second condition that calls for modification of cultural patterns is the imbalance between the requirements of a society and the living patterns of its members. A society may change more rapidly than the life patterns and the behavioral characteristics of the people. In general, certain cultural influences and institutional pressures operate to produce personality patterns that are adaptive to the particular society at a particular time. In discussing this concept, Inkeles points out that "integration between personality patterns developed . . . and the requirements of the roles provided and required by the *ongoing* social system may be highly imperfect, and since personality resides in individuals and not in social systems, that personality once developed, becomes a more or less independent entity which is in interaction with the social system."[9]

The current social and economic conditions, and the current demands on members of our society, often make a "poor fit," particularly for persons in some subcultures. Our society doubtless will have need to work out new patterns of living for many people, in order to cope with automation, increase in leisure time, and geographic mobility with its resulting "stranded" nuclear family. The extension of terrestrial boundaries may some day create other new problems. Cultural patterns and value orientations are continually changing and evolving for all groups in our society. Social work should consciously assume responsibility for helping to accelerate the rate of change, either in society or in the living patterns of people, and to give direction to such change.

Operational Problems

I should like to conclude by calling attention to some of the operational problems involved in applying the theory discussed in this paper. One thorny problem is how to secure from clients the data needed to understand the value orientations of different subcultures. How can the differences in frames of reference and the difficulties in communication be sufficiently overcome so that we know what to look for and what and how to understand our interlocutors? A second problem pertains to means of organizing the data. How can these new data be related to existing knowledge about personality development, pathology, and treatment techniques? Social workers sometimes have had a tendency, on the discovery of exciting new concepts, to "redecorate" the house completely, throwing out all the old furniture. For example, there is risk that our present interest in role theory may make us lose sight of psychological theory. We have also tended to add new concepts to old ones, even though they may contradict, rather than complement, each other. The theoretical problem, which has not yet been solved, is how to integrate new and old concepts so that they form a unitary framework of knowledge about personality development and social functioning.

A third problem is how to find a system for classifying various kinds of

[9] Alex Inkeles, "Sociological Observations on Culture and Personality Studies," in *Personality in Nature, Society and Culture*, Clyde Kluckhohn, Henry A. Murray and David M. Schneider (eds.), Alfred Knopf, New York, 1953.

problem entities in the person-in-the-situation configuration. Such a classification, it seems to me, must take into account three types of data: *1]* personal, iodiosyncratic; *2]* cultural, value orientation; and *3]* the complex role of the salient environment.

A system of classification of problem entities would lay the groundwork for the construction of a network of treatment approaches, each of which might be related in a broad way to a specific problem classification. Any such classification scheme and its correlated treatment techniques, in my opinion, can be only a general guide. I do not believe that the rich variety of human experience can be compressed into neat, tight, diagnostic categories or that a treatment plan, like a blueprint for a house, can be drawn to precise scale. However, there are broad ways of looking at data systematically and of ordering crucial human problems, as is evidenced in Kluckhohn's scheme. I believe caseworkers need to develop a conceptual scheme from their own practice and research which will have usefulness for understanding the person in his total situation and for treatment.

A Comparison of Procedures in the Treatment of Clients with Two Different Value Orientations

Francis J. Turner

Caseworkers have been concerned for some time about the paucity of research on the casework treatment process. Recently Ann Shyne wrote: "Historically, the client and the outcome have received greater attention [in research] than the casework process . . . little attention has been given to the process—what we do, how we do it, and how our actions are related to the client's needs and responses."[1] The project described here—an effort to help remedy this lack in casework research—was an empirical study of the relationship between client and worker activities in casework interviews and the value orientation of the client.

The importance of client values for the practice of social work has long been acknowledged and has been frequently stressed by the social work profession, but the precise influence of values on the treatment situation has

[1] Ann W. Shyne, "Casework Research: Past and Present," *Social Casework*, Vol. XLIII, November, 1962, p. 468.

Reprinted from *Social Casework*, XLV (May, 1964), pp. 273–277, by permission of the Journal.

been insufficiently highlighted and examined because suitable methods have not been available for eliciting, assessing, and quantifying them. As interest in values has grown, however, so have efforts to classify and measure them.

For several years social workers have been cognizant of Florence Kluckhohn's work in this area[2] and have acknowledged that her definition, description, and classification of values and value orientations offer an important aid to practitioners. Recently some attempts have been made to apply her classification system to specific treatment situations, but these efforts were of necessity descriptive and impressionistic rather than experimental.[3]

Two methodological instruments of potential importance to social work have now been developed. The first, designed by Kluckhohn and her associates, is a precise method of eliciting and classifying values.[4] The second, formulated by Florence Hollis, provides a means of making an intensive assessment of interview content.[5] (The Hollis classification scheme was made available to the author before it was published.)

Both the Kluckhohn and the Hollis instruments were employed in the project described, in part, in this article.[6] By means of the first instrument, the value orientations of selected clients were identified; by means of the second, the recorded content of interviews with these clients was analyzed and assessed.

The rationale of the study was as follows: A person's values affect his attitudes toward life and determine his ways of solving problems. It is safe to assume that the persons who apply to social agencies for treatment have different value orientations. It should follow that these variations in value will affect the content and form of the treatment process. Two questions were posed: Does the Kluckhohn instrument elicit differences in client values? If so, is there a relationship between these differences and the content of casework interviews?

The Sample and Method

A sample of forty clients meeting the following specifications was selected for the study. First, the clients were being treated in one of three family agencies in Ontario, Canada, by workers with at least three years'

[2] Florence Rockwood Kluckhohn, "Family Diagnosis. 1. Variations in the Basic Values of Family Systems," *Social Casework*, Vol. XXXIX, February–March, 1958, pp. 63–72.

[3] Shirley C. Hellenbrand, "Client Value Orientations: Implications for Diagnosis and Treatment," *Social Casework*, Vol. XLII, April, 1961, pp. 163–69; John P. Spiegel, "Some Cultural Aspects of Transference and Countertransference," in *Individual and Familial Dynamics*, Jules M. Masserman (ed.), Grune & Stratton, New York, 1959, pp. 160–82.

[4] Florence R. Kluckhohn and Fred S. Strodtbeck, *Variations in Value Orientations*, Row Peterson & Co., Evanston, Ill., 1961.

[5] Florence Hollis, *Casework, A Psychosocial Therapy*, Random House, New York, 1964.

[6] Francis J. Turner, *Social Work Treatment and Value Differences*, Columbia University, 1963 (doctoral dissertation).

experience.* Second, they were either Anglo-Saxon Protestants, French-Canadian Catholics, on first- or second-generation Polish-Ukrainians. The ethnic background of the client was specified on the presupposition that it would produce three distinct value profiles. (Different value profiles were indeed found, but these were not related to ethnic origin.) Third, the clients were receiving treatment for a marital problem in which the giving of financial assistance was not part of the treatment plan. Fourth, they were members of the lower-middle socioeconomic class. Socioeconomic class was determined by the occupation of the head of the household and his education, the neighborhood in which the family lived, and the worker's judgment.

The Kluckhohn value orientation instrument was designed primarily for use with rural persons.[7] Therefore, it was modified slightly to make it suitable for use with the urban clients in the sample.†

Kluckhohn postulated five value orientations as making up the value profile of any individual: the human-nature orientation, the man-nature orientation, the time orientation, the activity orientation, and the relational orientation. This article deals with only the relational orientation—man in his relationship to other men. Kluckhohn postulates that man relates to his fellow men in one of three ways—individualistically, collaterally, or lineally.

When the individualistic orientation is dominant, the person's own goals or ambitions have primacy over those of either his family or his peers. Such a person tends to seek his own goals even if he must separate himself from his peer group or family in order to do so. When the collateral orientation is dominant, the person identifies himself with a social group and its goals rather than with individualistic goals. The goals of the extended peer group are of first importance to him, and he accepts the "one for all and all for one" theme. In this instance, the group is a present-oriented group that does not necessarily continue over a long period of time. When the lineal orientation is dominant, the person also stresses group, rather than individualistic, goals. However, the group is one that remains in existence and is seen as continuing through time as in kinship situations, family lines, and a succession of positions.

In seven of the twenty-two items in the Kluckhohn instrument the respondent is asked to rank the three relational alternatives, thus permitting the computation of the over-all preference for this particular orientation.

When the data were assessed after the instrument had been used with the forty clients in the sample, it was found that the preferred relational orientation of most of the clients was either the individualistic or the collateral. Therefore the sample was divided into two groups according to the primary relational orientation of the client—twenty-three individual-

---

[7] Kluckhohn, *op. cit.*

*The Family Service Association of Metropolitan Toronto; Catholic Family Center, London; and Catholic Family Service Bureau, Windsor.
†These modifications are available on request from the author.

istically oriented clients in one group and seventeen collaterally oriented clients in the other.

Assessment of Interview Content

In the planning stages of the project it was decided that the clients selected for the sample would be limited to those who had continued beyond the intake process. This decision was made to avoid possible standardization in the exploratory phase, in view of the fact that differences in interview content were being studied. It was thought that by the sixth interview both the worker and the client should have had time to "size up" each other and that by then the process of selectivity or patterning in the interview should have begun.

It was decided that three consecutive interviews were enough for discerning patterns in most cases. At the same time, this number of interviews decreased the likelihood of obtaining interviews that were atypical either in the content introduced by the client or in the level and method of interviewing selected by the worker. The earliest interviews that were used in the study were the sixth, seventh, and eighth. If a case had been open for a considerable period of time, the interviews used were the three that took place immediately after the selection of the case for the sample. It would have been preferable, of course, if all the cases selected had been at the same point in treatment. It was not possible, however, to follow this procedure because it would have taken too much time to find forty clients beyond the intake stage who possessed all the requirements for inclusion in the sample.

The instrument for assessing interview content required written case records. The workers were asked for process recording that would approximate as closely as possible the interchange between the clients and themselves; they were asked to record nonverbal activity when it seemed important. They were encouraged to incorporate in the record not only the client's activity but also their own and to include all their sustaining activities, so often taken for granted and not recorded even though they are such an important part of the treatment process. The workers were also asked to dictate the records within two days of the interviews; this was, however, not always possible.

The activities in the interview were rated according to the Hollis classification outline of treatment procedures, which postulates that six basic, or root, interviewing procedures are used in current casework practice: *1]* sustaining procedures by which the worker shows his interest in the client and his desire to help, and offers the client acceptance, reassurance, and encouragement; *2]* procedures of direct influence by which the worker expresses his own opinion to influence the client to accept an approved course of behavior; *3]* procedures that include those activities of the client or worker in which there is exploration, description, or ventilation of the client's life situation; *4]* procedures that encompass those activities of the client or worker in which there is reflective consideration of the current person-situation configuration; *5]* procedures that involve the reflective consideration of the dynamics of response patterns or tendencies; *6]* procedures that include those activities of client and worker in which there is reflective consideration of developmental factors in response patterns or tendencies. The first two of these procedures are activities performed only by the worker; the remaining four are activities performed by both the worker and the client. The formulation used in this article was drawn from an earlier draft of Hollis' classification than the one that appears in her recently published book.[8]

The Hollis classification scheme was selected because it is more precise than other similar ones. It is particularly valuable as a research instrument because, unlike other systems, it enables the rater to make a line-by-line analysis of the interview. By making a judgment about each activity of the worker and of the client and then classifying it in terms of the six procedures, it is possible to make a quantitative analysis of the interview. Each study interview was coded in this way, and the frequency of each procedure was computed. The totals for the three client interviews were then combined into one score for each procedure.

Since the assessment of the records was based on the judgment of one person, two samples of randomly selected interviews were rescored to test the reliability of his judgments. A reliability coefficient of ·90 was obtained.

Findings

The scores of clients whose orientation was predominantly individualistic were compared with the scores of clients whose orientation was predominantly collateral. Separate comparisons were made between the scores of workers and clients.

Two statistical tests were used to assess the significance of the resulting relationships. When a particular procedure was used in all or almost all the cases, the relationship was assessed by the Mann-Whitney *U* Test.[9] When some of the treatment procedures were used infrequently—for example, the fifth and sixth—the relationship was assessed by the chi-square test of two independent samples.[10]

When the groups were compared, it was found that there were six statistically reliable relationships between the value orientation of the client and the interview content.

It was found that the workers used sustaining procedures more often with individualistically oriented than with collaterally oriented clients ($p<.05$). The former are presumed to be more likely to stand on their own, to face challenges without help, and to be free of dependency situations. Since they are the less prone to receive help from others, they can be.

[8] Hollis, *op. cit.*, pp. 71–75.
[9] See Sidney Siegel, *Nonparametric Statistics for the Behavioral Sciences*, McGraw-Hill Book Co., New York, 1956, *passim*.
[10] Siegel, *op. cit.*

expected to require more encouragement and reaching-out from the worker to help them remain in treatment.

Workers relied more on procedures of a ventilative nature when treating clients having an individualistic orientation ($p<.05$). These clients themselves also made use of this procedure more often than did those with a collateral orientation ($p<.05$). These findings were surprising: it had been expected that the collaterally oriented clients would require this type of treatment activity more often than the clients in the other group. It is possible that, since the clients with an individualistic orientation are not accustomed to sharing problems, they find fewer acceptable opportunities for ventilating their feelings in their day-to-day lives and so utilize this procedure more often in the treatment situation.

The workers used procedures of direct influence more frequently in working with the clients with a collateral orientation ($.05<p<.10$), as had been expected. These persons are less self-oriented and more accustomed to receiving directives from others, especially, as in the treatment situation, when they view the directives as being in their own interests. Although it has been said frequently that workers do not engage in advice-giving, it was observed that they often do express their opinions to clients, more or less overtly, in attempting to influence them.

It was further observed that collaterally oriented clients displayed more activity focused on the consideration of developmental patterns than the clients in the other group ($p<.05$). They also showed more reflective consideration of the dynamics of behavior ($.05<p<.10$). These two procedures, in general terms, lead to the development of intrapsychic understanding. The collaterally oriented clients were more aware of and more identified with other persons than the clients with an individualistic orientation; they were more sensitive to their interaction with others in their social milieu. Thus workers moving into these areas as a part of the treatment program could expect a greater response from these clients than from the others.

Summary and Conclusions

In contrasting clients with different value preferences, six statistically reliable differences in interview content were found. The explanations given above are postdicta rather than predictions; the effort has been to explain observed phenomena rather than to validate preformulated hypotheses. Possible interpretations of the findings are offered, but caution should be exercised in applying them to treatment situations except in an experimental manner.

That a relationship was found between the value orientations of the clients and the content of the interviews is not of itself necessarily either good or bad. There has been no evaluation of the relationship in terms of its effect on, or usefulness in, treatment. It is believed, of course, that the treatment procedures selected for each case should be related to the value orientations of the client as well as to his problems and his personality. It is not known, however, whether the treatment procedures should be aimed at challenging his value orientations or working within them. To work only within the client's framework of values may not be the most beneficial approach; at times, in fact, it may hold him back from actively working on his problems. Further research may provide the solution to this problem.

Two conclusions of importance to the profession emerged from this study; one concerns methodology and the other direct practice. The first conclusion is that the Kluckhohn and Hollis instruments are sufficiently sensitive at their present state of development to detect differences in the value orientations of clients and in the recorded activities of clients and caseworkers in the interview situation, respectively. The second conclusion is that clients with different value orientations behave differently in the interview situation. As yet it is not known whether the differences arise from the client's control of the interview content or from the response by the worker, either conscious or preconscious, to the client's value orientation. The fact remains that differences have been proved to exist.

Persons with either an individualistic or a collateral value orientation are frequently encountered in casework practice; therefore future research should be directed toward specifying further how particular constellations of treatment techniques relate to each. The goal is twofold: to improve the quality and objectivity of service to clients and to aid in the economical use of available treatment time.

This project has demonstrated the possibility of isolating and identifying some of the variables operating in the interview situation. It thus moves us one small step closer than we were to communicable precision and objectivity in social work treatment and to the attainment of the proper balance in our profession between art and science—a balance so long weighted in favor of the former.

Index

A

Abraham, Karl, 161, 179, 294
Acceptance, and cultural differences, 519
  of the homosexual, 264
  and nonjudgmental attitude toward
    Eskimos, 523
  of the retarded child by the family,
    399-402
Ackerman, Nathan, 225, 273
Acting out, in character disordered
    persons, 191
  in patients with tuberculosis, 509-10
Addams, Jane, 598, 600
Addicted clients, use of institutions in
    treatment, 156-57
Addictions, alcohol, treatment of, 215-21
  narcotics, treatment of, 229-38
Adjusting to the onset of blindness, 435-41
Adolescence, nature of, 49, 50
  role of relationship in treatment of, 57
  role of self-image in treatment, 51
Adolescent, casework treatment with
    learning inhibitions, 58
  control of acting out in therapy, 94
  counseling with emotionally disturbed,
    49-57
  and the decision for surgery, 460-63
  group therapeutic techniques with, 92-94
  group work treatment of, 81-82, 87-89
  homosexual acting out, 253-64
  identifications in, 253-54

  involvement in therapy, 89-90
  libidinal energy in, 253
  manipulation of therapist, 91
  obstacles to group therapy with, 90-91
  therapeutic techniques with, 90
  transference in treatment, 94-95
  treatment of, 3
  use of anxiety in treatment, 94
  use of authority in treatment, 93
Adolescent girls, group psychotherapy
    with, 89-96
Adult and the decision for surgery, 463-65
Adult children, of aged client, 143-45
Advice giving, in the treatment of
    sado-masochistic clients, 211
Aged, organic psychiatric disorders of,
    411-17
  society's attitudes towards, 412-13
Aged client, and adult children, 143-45
  individuality of, 145
  medical diagnosis for, 142
  role of grief in, 140
  treatment of, 129-45
  and treatment relationship, 140-41
Alcohol addiction, treatment of, 215-21
Alcoholic; see also Alcoholism
  need for facts in diagnosis, 217
  joint treatment of, 227-28
  motivation for help with spouse who is,
    226-27
  reaction to community's attitudes, 216
  resistance to treatment, 216-21

DATE DUE

APR 3 '75			
MAR 8 '76			
DEC 6 '77			
JAN 2 '78			
24 1979			
GAYLORD			PRINTED IN U.S.A